LAWYER'S DESK BOOK

SIXTH EDITION

1980

by

The IBP Research and Editorial Staff

Institute for Business Planning, Inc.

IBP Plaza, Englewood Cliffs, New Jersey 07632

Sixth Edition
© Copyright MCMLXXIX
Institute for Business Planning, Inc.
IBP Plaza, Englewood Cliffs, New Jersey 07632

Fourth Printing......August, 1980

Library of Congress Cataloging in Publication Data

Institute for Business Planning, inc.
    Lawyer's desk book.

    Includes bibliographies and index.
    1. Law--United States. 2. Practice of law--United
States. I. Title.
KF386.C3 1980   340'.0973   79-13813
ISBN 0-87624-323-5

HOW TO USE THIS BOOK

This Sixth Edition of the Lawyer's Desk Book has been updated to reflect the impact of the Revenue Act of 1978, the Energy Act of 1978, and the technical corrections to the Estate and Gift Tax Provisions. The Desk Book is designed to give you quick reference and a practical overview of those areas of the law that will cross your desk most frequently. While it does not include all areas of the law, it does provide you with a source from which you can obtain fundamental information pertaining to a particular client problem. It is ideally geared for use in preparation for and in conjunction with client interviews to help you elicit valuable and necessary information.

Among the exciting features in this volume are: Checklists covering compensation and pension planning; the latest developments in estate planning techniques; truth-in-lending law (including consumer loans, consumer leases, and consumer related advertising); antitrust problems; the requirements of the Real Estate Settlement Procedures Act (RESPA); checklists for corporate formation; and how to handle tax disputes.

Of particular interest to the practitioner are the comprehensive tables and reference charts contained in the Appendix. Included are state-by-state guides for such topics as state incorporation fees, annual corporate taxes and fees, corporate indemnification statutes, attachments, interest rates, competency of minors to contract, death taxes, and a garnishment guide. In addition, you will find tables already worked out for self-liquidating mortgages at various interest rates, expected returns on joint and survivor annuities, present worth of periodic future payments, and a compound discount table, to name just a few.

We've already done the work—now all you have to do is put it to use. Once you have taken a preliminary look at your client's problem, more extensive research will be necessary. To facilitate your work, we have included sources for further reference.

Note: The Research and Editorial Staff of IBP is composed of both females and males. However, for the purposes of clarity, we all agreed that the constant use of he/she and him/her, would, after a short reading, become more tedious for the user of this volume than a demonstration of our attempt to eliminate sexism in the law. Therefore, any time a reference is made to ''he'' or ''him'' please read this term as a generic abbreviation for he/she and him/her.

ACKNOWLEDGEMENT AND DEDICATION

This edition of the Lawyer's Desk Book was made possible through the cooperative effort of the research, editorial, and support staff of the Institute for Business Planning.

We dedicate this book to the fond memory of Laura Mark and Babette Schneider.

Burton J. DeFren
Editor-in-Chief

iv

TABLE OF CONTENTS

Paragraph [¶]

Paragraph [¶]

APPENDIX

Page

Page

AGENTS AND INDEPENDENT CONTRACTORS

[¶101] The distinctions between an agent and an independent contractor can influence the liabilities of the principal, powers of the parties, tax withholding consequences, workmen's compensation, and ability to seek relief under national labor relations laws. Parties will not necessarily be able to establish the nature of their relationship merely by a recital of their agreement. While this recital may be binding as between principal and agent/independent contractor, it may not bind third parties. The table at ¶102 indicates some factors used by courts in determining the type of relationship that exists.

Who can act as an agent? Any person may act as an agent provided he is not incompetent. A principal may not cite the infancy of its agent as a reason for avoiding a contract made by that agent. However, an infant principal can avoid a contract made by his agent unless the contract was for necessities or some other contract the infant could not avoid if he were the principal and contracted for himself.

[¶102]   **COMPARISON OF AGENT AND
INDEPENDENT CONTRACTOR**

	Independent Contractor	Agent (Employer-Employee)
Basis of Compensation	The person employed agrees to do particular work for a specific sum.	Remuneration will be determined in accordance with the length of the employment.
	The compensation will be based on the amount of work done by the person doing the work.	In some jurisdictions, when there is a cost plus arrangement, it will lean in favor of principal agent rather than an independent contractor relationship.
	The remuneration is to be based on the amount of money the agent is to disburse.	
Control	The contractor exercises complete control over the work and his only obligation is to get the work done, e.g., one who is engaged in the trucking business, uses his own truck, loads it himself, and comes and goes as he pleases.	The employer has the absolute control over the work—however, the employee may exercise some control over the work without effecting a change.
	When employed to exterminate an apartment house.	
	Contracts to paint smokestacks for a fee—and furnish his own tools.	A tractor owner who spent his entire time in the employ of one trucker operating his own tractor was held to be an employee since the trucking company designated routes, times, etc.
	Contracts to drill the holes and place the dynamite at a specific sum per foot, when he furnishes his own assistants.	

1

	Independent Contractor	Agent (Employer-Employee)
	The contractor has the complete control over and pays the other workmen on the job.	
	The person has the right to discharge workmen on the job.	
Materials and Tools	When the contractor furnishes the materials and tools, this will be an indication of his independence.	Merely furnishing the tools in a trade as carpenters, machinists, etc., will not mean that there is no employee relationship.
Nature of the Calling	Persons operating certain vessels, architects, painters, physicians, nurses, plumbers, window washers, etc., are generally considered independent contractors if they are in business for themselves.	Domestic servants, chauffeurs, gardeners are generally not considered independent contractors although they have their own callings.

[¶103]

LACK OF EMPLOYER-EMPLOYEE RELATIONSHIP

In the following instances, it has been held that an employer-employee relationship did not exist:

☐ *Life Insurance Agent:* The relationship between a life insurance company and its agent is not that of employee-employer within the meaning of the unemployment insurance law.

☐ *Motor Truck Operator:* A motor truck owner-operator who furnishes his own truck, fuel, and maintenance and is paid by the mile or ton is not an employee within the meaning of the unemployment insurance law.

☐ *Subscription Solicitor:* For purposes of workmen's compensation, a person who solicited newspaper circulation was not an employee but an independent contractor even though the newspapers supplied him with papers, etc., and he was required to turn in subscription lists and money at the end of each day (less, of course, his percentage commission).

A book subscription solicitor was held to be an independent contractor—the publisher was not liable for the independent contractor's torts. In this case, it appeared that the solicitor sold books for several publishers, was paid on a commission basis, had no limited territory, and was furnished with samples and order books by the publisher.

☐ *Garageman:* A garageman called to repair a car is not an employee of the owner for the purpose of holding the owner liable for the garageman's torts. The garageman may be a bailee. However, some states have statutes that hold a bailor liable for the torts of his bailee while operating the bailor's motor vehicle.

☐ *Auto Race Mechanics:* The owners, drivers, and mechanics involved in a commercial auto race are not the employees of the promoter of the series of races for labor law purposes.

☐ *Repairman:* When the contract was to repair the water tower and the city had no control over how the repairman was to make the repairs, the court held that no employee-employer relationship existed in that case.

The hotel hired a man engaged in the roofing and cornice business to repair the roof so that pigeons would not nest in the cornice; the court held that the repairman was an independent contractor rather than an employee of the hotel.

For forms relating to sales agency agreements, see *IBP Forms of Business Agreements and Resolutions.*

[¶104] ESTABLISHING THE AGENT-PRINCIPAL RELATIONSHIP

There are four ways in which an agent-principal relationship may be created:

(1) Principal may appoint an agent to act for him.

(2) Principal may tell a third party that an agent has authority to act.

(3) Principal may authorize an agent to act, and may subsequently become liable for additional actions by the agent. This apparent agency power protects third parties who come in contact with principal's agent.

(4) Principal may subsequently ratify the actions of someone who is not previously authorized to act on principal's behalf.

In addition, some statutes may presumptively create an agency relationship; e.g., someone driving a car within the state is said to designate the Secretary of State as his agent for purposes of accepting service of process in the event he is involved in an auto accident while driving in the state.

[¶105] ABILITY TO BIND PRINCIPAL

Agents may bind a principal when the agency relationship is disclosed. However, the ability to bind the principal will be governed by the nature of the agency and the authority that has been expressly vested in the agent. If an agent has been expressly denied particular authority, but the principal has made it appear that the agent has the authority, or has placed the agent in a position when it would be customary for the agent to have such authority, the principal will be estopped from denying the agent's authority. However, if the agent acts beyond his authority and the doctrine of apparent authority is not applicable, the third party dealing with the agent generally will not have a cause of action against the principal. In some jurisdictions, the third party will have a cause of action against the agent for breach of the agent's implied warranty of authority.

☐ *Undisclosed Principal:* When an authorized agent acts for an undisclosed principal (identity and existence unknown to the contracting third party), usually both agent and principal are liable. Under UCC §3-403, an undisclosed principal is not liable on a negotiable instrument executed by an authorized agent. (See also ¶110.)

[¶106] IMPLIED AUTHORITY OF AGENT

An agent generally has whatever authority is necessary to carry out the purpose of the agency—subject to extension or limitation of the agreement between the parties.

Implied authority refers to power that an agent *reasonably* believes he has. An agent may also assume implied authority if he knows that agents in a similar position usually have such authority, or if the principal has previously sanctioned though not expressly authorized similar conduct.

[¶107] AGENT'S ABILITY TO DELEGATE

A principal may authorize an agent to delegate some or all of the agent's authority. But, no sub-agent can have greater authority than that originally delegated from principal to agent. Absent express or implied authority from the principal, an agent cannot delegate. If the agent is the principal's employee, his right to delegate to or employ sub-agents may be implied due to the nature of the employment. For example, if an employee is hired to manage a business, he will generally be deemed to have broad authority to bind his principal and will be authorized to hire sub-agents or employees for the principal.

When the agent is hired for "personal or confidential" reasons, delegation may not be allowed unless specifically authorized by the principal.

In the case of an authorized delegation, the principal will be bound by the sub-agent's acts and will be liable for the sub-agent's torts to the same extent as he would be for actions by the agent, provided they are conducted within the scope of employment. If the delegation is authorized, and the agent has used due diligence and care in selecting a sub-agent, then the sub-agent is considered an agent of the principal, and the principal must recover directly from the sub-agent for negligence or misconduct.

If the delegation is unauthorized, the agent is liable for any actions of the sub-agent.

[¶108] AUTHORITY TO MAKE PURCHASES

The agent's authority to make purchases of personal property will depend on the nature of the position in which the principal has placed the agent. If the agent is a manager of a retail shop, it will appear that he has the authority to purchase goods so long as it is customary for an agent in his position to have the authority to make such purchases. If an agent has the authority to make purchases, he will generally have the implied authority to set the price. However, if the price that he sets is so unreasonable as to put a prudent man on his guard, the price set by the agent will not be binding on the principal. When a principal authorizes his agent to make purchases for cash and supplies him with the necessary cash, the agent will have no implied authority to make purchases for credit in an ordinary case.

An agent may also have discretion in deciding the amount (quantity) of an item to be bought.

As a corollary, an agent authorized by principal to effect a sale may have certain implied powers, but usually not the authority to give an option to buy. He may fix price, terms, and conditions of sale so long as they are reasonable, unless his authority is limited to a set of particular terms. Unless otherwise instructed, the sale is for cash, not credit. An agent may usually make general warranties regarding the items sold, provided such warranties are usual and customary for the particular type of transaction.

[¶109]   AGENT'S DUTY OF LOYALTY

An agent has an absolute duty of loyalty to his principal unless this absolute duty has been altered by the agreement between the agent and principal. Generally, absent a specific agreement to the contrary, an employee will be required to devote his full time to the principal's business—and not compete with the principal. When the contract calls for full-time employment, the employee will be permitted to use some time for the conduct of his personal affairs without breaching the employment contract.

An agent must obey the principal's directions unless they are unreasonable, or be liable for losses resulting from disobedience.

An agent paid by a principal must conform to a standard of care reflecting local community expectations and the skills for which the agent was hired. The standard of care for the gratuitous agent is far more lenient and less exacting.

If the agent breaches his duty to the principal, the principal may pursue the following course of action:

(1) Sue the agent for contract breach or for tortious conduct.

(2) Sue to recover ''secret profits'' made by the agent due to his relationship with principal.

(3) Sue for an accounting to have dollars returned to principal.

[¶110]   UNDISCLOSED PRINCIPAL

Often an agent will have the authority to enter into a transaction but will not disclose the identity of his principal. If the agent indicates that he is representing a principal and fails to identify the principal, or if he conceals the fact that he is representing a principal, the agent remains liable on the contract. However, once the principal's existence has been disclosed, the principal will also become liable on the contract.

[¶111]   **PRINCIPAL'S RATIFICATION**

When an agent acts without authority, his principal may ratify the act and the result will be the same as if the agent was acting with full authority. For a principal to ratify, he must have full knowledge of the material facts, the act must have been done for the principal initially, and the principal must have the intention to ratify. The principal must also ratify the entire transaction, and must have the capacity to ratify. A principal may ratify any act that he could have done legally; an undisclosed principal may not ratify.

Ratification may be done expressly or may be indicated by the principal's conduct, e.g., by accepting benefits of agent's acts, by failing to disaffirm, or possibly by suing on the underlying transaction.

[¶112]   **CONTROL: THE EMPLOYER-EMPLOYEE
                         RELATIONSHIP**

When the principal wants to exercise absolute control over the agent, he will want to make the agent an employee. However, if the employer really wants to have the agent accomplish a particular goal, and does not care how the goal is accomplished, he may appoint the employee an independent contractor. The degree of control will be extremely important in determining whether the representative is an agent, an independent contractor, or an employee.

[¶113]   **LIABILITY PROBLEMS**

If the representative is an employee, the principal will have a vicarious liability for the employee's torts—and other wrongs arising out of the employment. A principal may be relieved of liability for his employee's torts when the torts occur outside of the scope of the employment. The employer is generally not liable for the torts of an independent contractor or the employees of the independent contractor. If the employer maintains control of the work or interferes with the contractor's performance of the work, the employer will be responsible for any tortious injuries that occur as a result of his interference or control over the work. An exception may also be made to the rule if the work performed is inherently dangerous.

The employee's liability will generally be concurrent with that of his employer. In many situations the employer will be entitled to indemnification from the employee, if the employer was required to answer for the employee's torts.

When the employer *knows* he has selected an incompetent to perform the task, the employer may be liable for contractor's negligence.

An employer is usually not liable for *intentional* torts committed by an employee, since an intentional tort is, by definition, outside the scope of employment. But in some circumstances, an employer could be liable, such as when an intentional tort is committed incidentally within the scope of employment. A common example is that of a bouncer inflicting injury on a rowdy bar patron, since it is the bouncer's job to remove rowdy persons from the premises.

[¶114]   **SPECIAL PROBLEMS REGARDING SALES AGENTS**

Special rules are applicable to sales agents. The greatest flexibility in setting up a transaction in advance generally surrounds how to handle sales agents or other sales people. A sales agent will generally have the authority to do whatever is necessary to make the sale. This is true without regard to what specific category he may fit into (agent, independent contractor, employee, etc.). A commercial traveler who has been given a catalog, and possibly samples, will generally be authorized only to solicit orders for acceptance by his home office. A salesman who has been entrusted with the goods will generally have the apparent authority to accept the money and deliver the goods. When the sales agent is a merchant dealing in the type of goods involved, he will have the authority to sell any goods that have been entrusted to his possession. Section 2-403 of the Uniform Commercial Code provides that any entrusted possession of goods to a merchant who deals in goods of that kind gives him power to transfer all rights of the person entrusting him with possession to a buyer in the ordinary course of business.

As a general rule, an agent who is authorized to sell is authorized to sell only for cash unless he is specifically authorized to sell on credit.

An agent may have the express authority to give a warranty. Absent express authority, the agent will have implied authority to warrant the goods if it would be normal for an agent in his position to have such authority. The agent will also have the authority to bind his principal to a warranty that would, in the absence of an express warranty, be implied. Thus the agent would have the authority under the Uniform Commercial Code to bind his principal to the warranty of merchantability and the warranty of fitness for purpose. Similarly, when a sales agent makes a sale by sample, there is a warranty that the bulk of the goods will conform to the sample.

In some states an agent will require express authority of his principal to sell real property. In some states, this express authority must be in a writing sufficient to satisfy the requirements of the statute of frauds.

[¶115]   **WITHHOLDING PROBLEMS**

Wages paid to an "employee" are subject to income tax withholding. The Treasury Regulations provide that the employer-employee relationship generally exists when the person for whom services are performed has the right to control and direct the individual who performs the services, not only as to the result to be accomplished by the work but also as to the details and means by which that result is accomplished. It is not necessary that the employer actually direct or control the manner in which the services are performed to bring the employee within the definition for withholding tax purposes. As is the case in state law, the right to discharge is also an important factor indicating that the person possessing that right is an employer (see Reg. §31.3401(c)-1).

The following table indicates situations when withholding tax has been required to be paid.

Employee	Nonemployee
Accountant keeping the books of a concern under the direction of the person engaging him.	Accountant offering his services to the public.
Attorney engaged by a law firm as an associate.	Attorney retained by a person or firm, paid a retainer on a yearly basis (S.S.T. 86; CB 1937-1, 462).
Auctioneer whose employer controls and directs his professional services (S.S.T. 149, CB 1937-1, 380).	Auctioneer.
Nurses aids, nurses on the staff of a hospital.	Corporate director (unless also an employee of the corporation).
Physician who works under the supervision of the head physician for a company, is required to be present for a set number of hours each day, and receives all the benefits of an employee.	Registered Nurse and licensed practical nurses engaged in private duty nursing.
	Physician engaged in private practice who also treats the employees of a company on a part-time basis.
	Real estate salesmen who do not receive a guaranteed amount of compensation.
Persons engaged in performing services for a trust or estate are employees of the trust or estate.	Fiduciary or trustee for a trust, a bankrupt, etc., within the scope of his official duties.
Bakery goods "dealers" who were required to furnish their own trucks when it was determined that they were employees.	Cab drivers who rent the cabs and are not accountable for the fees collected.
Newspaper correspondents compensated on a monthly basis, although not required to furnish a minimum amount of work.	Individual who operates a laundry business on a commission basis when the operator pays rent, heat, etc., of the store out of the commission (*Rev. Rul. 56-15*, CB 1956-1, 451).
A professor engaged by a university to carry out a research contract.	Owner-driver of a truck who is not given any rules to follow, his route cannot be changed without his consent, and he is responsible for seeing that his route is covered at all times.

Generally, similar rules will be applicable in determining whether unemployment compensation, workmen's compensation, and disability taxes must be paid. These rules will vary from state to state.

8

NOTE: Under the Revenue Act of 1978, IRS is prevented from issuing new Regulations or Revenue Rulings to define "employee" or "independent contractor," until 1980, for purposes of requiring the payment of employment taxes.

In addition, IRS cannot impose employment tax liability for pre-1979 years in cases when an employer made a "reasonable decision" that a particular worker was an independent contractor, provided that the employer filed the required federal tax returns. A reasonable decision is one based on factors such as industry practice, court cases, published rulings, or letter rulings issued to the particular employer.

ANTITRUST PROBLEMS: PRICES AND UNFAIR COMPETITION

[¶201] Businesses cannot operate effectively without a knowledge of the restrictions placed on them by the federal antitrust laws, particularly in the area of pricing arrangements and market agreements. The following paragraphs highlight some of the areas of common concern to most business operations.

[¶202]   MONOPOLIZATION

Monopoly power is the power to control prices or exclude competition in the relevant market. Section 2 of the Sherman Act reads:

"Every person who shall monopolize, or attempt to monopolize, or combine or conspire with any other person or persons, to monopolize any part of the trade or commerce among the several States, or with foreign nations, shall be deemed guilty of a misdemeanor, and, on conviction thereof, shall be punished by fine not exceeding fifty thousand dollars, or by imprisonment not exceeding one year, or by both said punishments, in the discretion of the court."

To come within the §2 prohibition of monopolization, a single firm must (1) possess monopoly power in the relevant market, and (2) have acted purposefully or deliberately.

[¶203]   THE RELEVANT MARKET

The share of the product and geographical markets that any company has presently captured is the principal determinant of monopoly power. When looking to the product market, those items that consumers can reasonably use interchangeably must be taken into account.

[¶204]   PURPOSEFUL ACT

Conduct that is used to attain or maintain a monopolistic position (e.g., predatory or coercive conduct) is in violation of the law. The fact that a company did not have a specific intent to monopolize is not relevant.

An "innocently acquired monopoly"—i.e., one gained through superior skill, a lawfully obtained patent, or thrust upon a company by other factors—does not violate §2. However, the later predatory use of such innocently acquired power will violate §2.

[¶205]   ATTEMPT TO MONOPOLIZE

The attempt to monopolize is also prohibited by §2 of the Sherman Act. Even

10

if the monopolization attempt fails, a company's conduct that creates a dangerous probability of success is proscribed.

[¶206]   HORIZONTAL RESTRAINTS

Section 1 of the Sherman Act provides that "every contract, combination in the form of trust or otherwise, or conspiracy, in restraint of trade or commerce among the several States, or with foreign nations, is hereby declared to be illegal. Every person who shall make any contract or engage in any combination or conspiracy hereby declared ... to be illegal shall be deemed guilty of a felony, and, on conviction thereof, shall be punished by fine not exceeding 1,000,000 dollars, if a corporation, or if any other person, 100,000 dollars or by imprisonment not exceeding three years, or both said punishments, in the discretion of the court."

Price-fixing, division of markets among competitors, tying arrangements, and group boycotts are all examples of per se violations of §1. The following paragraphs discuss this proscribed conduct.

[¶207]   PRICE-FIXING

Setting a minimum price is illegal, as is fixing maximum resale prices. Even if competitors are free to sell below the maximum, the fact that a maximum price exists is sufficient to artificially stabilize prices. Agreements to limit production are illegal and agreements among buyers setting the price they will offer is also a per se violation.

[¶208]   INTERSELLER PRICE
                    VERIFICATION PROHIBITED

If a price is quoted to a customer, and that customer replies that a competitor gave him a lower price quote, the business person cannot call the competitor to confirm that statement *(United States v. U.S. Gypsum Company,* 98 S. Ct. 2864, 1978). Such interseller price verification is a violation of §1 of the Sherman Act. However, this does not mean that the price cannot be lowered to meet the competition. If there is a *good faith belief* that a price concession is being offered by a competitor, the price may be lowered as per §2(a) of the Robinson-Patman Act. Good faith belief can be established by showing that:

☐ Evidence was received of a competitor's lower price from other complaining customers;

☐ Threats of cancellation of sales were made, if the discount price was not met; or

☐ The competitor's discount price could be corroborated from available market data.

In other words, if the need to match the competition's price is shown to be within the business's interest, and that a diligent attempt has been made to independently verify the existence of a price discount (without contacting the competition), no violation of §1 of the Sherman Act will be found.

[¶209]   **DIVISION OF MARKETS**

An agreement among businesses that perform similar services or that deal in similar products to divide the available product market among them is illegal per se, and there is no justification or defense, since the agreement operates to give each participant a monopoly with respect to his market share.

[¶210]   **REFUSALS TO DEAL**

When a group of competitors agrees not to deal with a certain party, or to deal only on certain terms, that amounts to a §1 combination in restraint of trade. To the extent that an industry attempts self-regulation in this area, courts have found a §1 violation to exist.

However, if several companies all feel that it is in their best economic interests not to deal with a particular party, and each can show that its decision was *independently* arrived at, this probably will not constitute a concerted refusal to deal *(Coughlin v. Capitol Cement Co.,* CA-5, 571 F. 2d 290, 1978). But remember, it must be verifiable that the refusal to deal was *unilateral* as opposed to conspiratorial conduct. The best safeguard is to make certain that there is sufficient evidence to document the position taken. The following checklist offers some helpful suggestions:

☐ Retain all correspondence and memoranda concerning customer accounts, particularly where bills are outstanding.

☐ If a customer's order is refused, state the reasons in a letter to the customer, and/or in an interoffice memorandum for the files.

☐ If contemplating a change in the terms of a contract with a customer, in response to rumors circulating in the industry, confer with corporate counsel to make certain that the business is not engaging in conscious parallelism or a group boycott.

[¶211]   **CONSCIOUS PARALLELISM**

Even in the absence of an actual agreement among companies, substantially identical conduct among competitors may violate §1 of the Sherman Act. The proof of parallel behavior does not in itself establish a §1 conspiracy—it would depend upon whether the businessperson can show his independent decision to act. Such "independence" might be evidenced by minutes of corporate meetings, economic factors, and lack of discussion with other competitors.

[¶212]   DATA DISSEMINATION

Frequently, competitors will exchange information through their trade association regarding prices, costs, production, and inventories. The exchange of price information is inherently suspect as a §1 violation. Such discussion should be avoided, particularly where:

(a) There is an exchange of information on current or future prices;

(b) The business is part of a concentrated or oligopolistic market structure, since such disclosure might discourage price variation to the point of stabilizing and preserving each company's market share;

(c) The members of the trade association deal with the same parties.

If the businessperson and his competitors do participate in a trade organization, advise him that all participants should limit such discussions to past performance, and that this information should be distributed to all members of the industry—regardless of membership in the trade association. If the trade association meetings should begin to stray into "forbidden" conversations, it may be necessary to resign as a member to avoid antitrust problems.

[¶213]   LOBBYING ACTIVITIES

Lobbying activities are not illegal, even if undertaken for anticompetitive purposes. However, the attempt to monopolize a market by instituting state and federal proceedings to the point of harassing competitors or interfering with their right to access would violate §1.

[¶214]   VERTICAL RESTRAINT AGREEMENTS
BETWEEN SELLER AND BUYER

An indirect attempt to achieve price maintenance by contractually setting the price (minimum *or* maximum) at which customers can resell products is a per se violation of §1 of the Sherman Act. Furthermore, if there are attempts to induce customers to adhere to suggested retail prices by the use of any system of suspensions and reinstatements of retailers who have not adhered to the suggested price, this too constitutes unlawful resale price maintenance. Once goods are sold to the buyer, price restrictions can no longer be imposed.

Although vertical price restrictions are a per se violation of §1 of the Sherman Act, this is not the case with *nonprice vertical restrictions*, (i.e., a location restriction). In *Continental TV v. GTE Sylvania, Inc.* (433 US 36, 1977), the Supreme Court held that the imposition of nonprice vertical restrictions would be governed by the "rule of reason." In order to withstand an allegation that a nonprice vertical restraint violates §1 of the Sherman Act, the manufacturer imposing the restraint must be able to show that:

(1) Sufficient *interbrand* competition exists to provide a significant check on

the exploitation of the manufacturer's intrabrand market power; or

(2) The potential benefits of vertical restraints in promoting interbrand competition are particularly strong where the manufacturer imposing the restraints is seeking to enter a new market or to expand a small market share; or

(3) The manufacturer has used the least restrictive means to enhance its ability to compete.

[¶215]   **TYING ARRANGEMENTS**

Section 3 of the Clayton Act prohibits "tying arrangements" that "may substantially lessen competition or tend to create a monopoly in any line of commerce."

Note that §3 applies only to goods or commodities and not to intangible services (e.g., loan of copyright license) or real property. Tying arrangements with these are dealt with by §1 of the Sherman Act.

A tying arrangement is usually illegal per se if its effect is to substantially lessen competition or to tend to create a monopoly in any line of commerce. For example, if your client enjoys a monopolistic position with respect to the "tying product," or if there is simply great demand for the "tying product," the tacking on of a "tied product" would tend to create a monopoly in the tied product as well, or would substantially lessen competition.

[¶216]   **PATENTS AND THE ANTITRUST LAWS**

A patent is a legal monopoly granted pursuant to statutory authority. Therefore, a valid patent can be a defense to a §2 Sherman Act Monopolization Change. A patent is granted only for the discovery of any new and useful process, provided such invention is not obvious to a person having only ordinary skills in the particular art (see ¶2201 et seq.). The granting of a patent gives the inventor the right to exclude others from making, selling, or using the invention for a period of time (see ¶2201).

A patent holder may assign or license his patent rights.

A patentee cannot extend his lawful patent monopoly by engaging in an unlawful tying arrangement. A royalty agreement or contract extending beyond the expiration date of a patent is unlawful per se.

[¶217]   **PATENT ACCUMULATION**

It is not illegal per se to include in a patent license a covenant requiring the licensee to assign to the licensor any improvement patents developed by the licensee.

[¶218]   **PRICE-RESTRICTED LICENSES**

Abusive licensing and cross-licensing can operate as restraints of trade, with anticompetitive effects. Owners of two patents may not cross-license and fix prices to be charged by themselves and their licensees for their respective products, nor may they divide up territories or agree to boycott others.

[¶219]   **USE-RESTRICTED LICENSES**

A patentee can properly limit a licensee to one or more uses, and grant such rights exclusively or nonexclusively. A patentee may restrict his licensee to any territory he wishes.

[¶220]   **FOR FURTHER REFERENCE . . .**

American Jurisprudence, Monopolies.
"Antitrust Symposium," 10 Southwestern University Law Review 35-131 (1978).
Bureau of National Affairs, Antitrust and Trade Regulation Report.
Hoffmann, Malcolm A., and Arthur I. Winard, "Hoffmann's Antitrust Law and Techniques."
Kuhlman, J.M., "Price Fixing, Nonprice Competition, and 'Focal Point' Pricing: a Rose by Any Other Name?," 10 Antitrust Law and Economics Review 75-86 (1978).
"Legal and Economic Status of Vertical Restrictions," 23 Villanova Law Review 547-79 (March 1978).
Von Kalinowski, *Business Organizations*, Vol. 16E, "Antitrust Laws and Trade Regulation."

ARBITRATION

[¶301] Commercial arbitration is often an attractive alternative to litigation—it's more economical, speedier, offers more privacy, and is more effective. Naturally, these benefits are qualified by the individual situation—in some cases the parties may end up in court litigating the right to arbitrate the underlying dispute.

Arbitration has a preferred status in the law. If parties have agreed in advance to arbitrate, courts are loath to involve the judicial process. Ordinarily, except for the factors mentioned in ¶314 (vacating arbitration award), unless the arbitrator has exceeded the specific authority granted by the parties, the award will not be upset or overturned or even modified by the courts, no matter how outrageous it may appear on its face.

Since most states have statutes governing arbitration, check local law.

For forms of agreements to arbitrate contained in various form contracts, see *IBP Forms of Business Agreements and Resolutions.*

[¶302]   APPRAISEMENT

Arbitration must be distinguished from appraisement. Although these two terms are frequently used interchangeably, they are separate concepts. An arbitration agreement will involve the resolution of an entire dispute, an award will be made, and judgment will be entered. An appraisal will involve only a determination of actual value and/or the amount of loss, with the court retaining jurisdiction over the remaining issues.

[¶303]   COURT-APPOINTED REFEREE

Arbitration must also be distinguished from the use of a court-appointed referee. Whereas arbitration is extra-judicial in the sense that the parties will agree among themselves to submit a dispute to arbitration and be bound by the arbitrator's decision, a referee has no final authority—his findings are turned over to the court, which may follow his advice or disregard it.

[¶304]   HOW TO PROVIDE FOR ARBITRATION

An agreement to arbitrate future disputes does not constitute a submission, but only a basis for a motion to compel arbitration. The American Arbitration Association (AAA) recommends that a standard arbitration clause be inserted in all commercial contracts:

"Any controversy or claim arising out of or relating to this contract, or the breach thereof, shall be settled by arbitration in accordance with the Rules of the

American Arbitration Association, and judgment upon the award rendered by the Arbitrator(s) may be entered in any Court having jurisdiction thereof.''

The AAA also recommends a form that may be used for submitting *existing* disputes to arbitration:

''We, the undersigned parties hereby agree to submit to arbitration under the Commercial Arbitration Rules of the American Arbitration Association the following controversy: (cite briefly). We further agree that the above controversy be submitted to (one) (three) Arbitrators selected from the panels of Arbitrators of the American Arbitration Association. We further agree that we will faithfully observe this agreement and the Rules and that we will abide by and perform any award rendered by the Arbitrator(s) and that a judgment of the Court having jurisdiction may be entered upon the award.''

Parties to an agreement to arbitrate may amend the agreement, as they would amend any other part of a contract. An invalid arbitration agreement is usually severable from the main body of the contract.

It is within the courts' jurisdiction to decide whether a specific issue is included in an agreement to arbitrate. An intent to arbitrate all issues stemming from the principal agreement is usually given full effect by the courts.

The agreement to arbitrate is a contractual obligation. Therefore, the parties must have capacity to contract and consideration must be furnished (the consideration requirement is usually satisfied by the parties' agreement to abide by the arbitrator's award).

[¶305]   ARBITRABLE ISSUES

Parties may provide for arbitration even if there is no corresponding cause of action for court suit available.

In order to arbitrate, there must be a controversy—a question of fact—between or among the parties. Arbitration is usually unavailable when a party clearly violates the unambiguous terms of the contract.

Arbitration is generally available for the following (however, check local law for variations):

(1) Property rights in real property or personalty;

(2) Probate matters and decedents' estates (however, since probate proceedings are *in rem*, some states may not allow arbitration);

(3) Tort nuisances.

Claims based on underlying *illegal* contracts are *not* arbitrable. Alleged violations of the antitrust laws are not subject to arbitration.

[¶306]   WHO MAY ARBITRATE

Since arbitration is part of the underlying contractual obligation, contract law also governs the capacity of the parties to enter into an arbitration agreement.

General contract law usually regulates the ability of an infant to make an

17

arbitration agreement. Fiduciaries may also submit the dispute to arbitration, if allowed under state statute. Usually, court approval is required for executors and trustees to engage in arbitration in their representative capacity.

In general, an agent cannot bind his principal to submit to arbitration unless such authority is express or implicit in their agency relationship. The fact that an agent is authorized to accept payment or settle an account may not be taken to imply an ability to submit the dispute to arbitration.

An attorney generally has the implied authority to submit his client's case for arbitration, but law may vary, so check the applicable state statute first.

Partners may not usually bind their partnership by a submission, although an individual partner may bind himself. However, if all the partners agree to arbitrate a future issue, then one partner may, at a later date, submit an issue to arbitration.

Corporations may submit disputes to arbitration, and such submission is made by the appropriate officer or board member.

[¶307]   ENFORCEMENT OF ARBITRATION
                      AGREEMENTS

Many state statutes provide machinery for the enforcement of arbitration agreements on a summary basis.

The Uniform Arbitration Act and the Federal Arbitration Act provide for summary remedy in case one of the parties refuses to arbitrate or denies the existence of a valid arbitration agreement.

If the agreement is revocable, the courts will generally refuse to specifically decree performance of agreements to arbitrate because the parties have a right to revoke (see *Red Cross Line v. Atlantic Fruit Co.,* 264 US 109, 1924).

If the arbitration agreement is irrevocable, the statutes in many states provide for a proceeding to enforce the arbitration clause, in which case it will be treated as an action for specific performance. Under the Federal Arbitration Act a proceeding for enforcement of an arbitration agreement is treated as an action for specific performance.

Usually, a party to an arbitration agreement may not revoke it, but certain events may constitute revocation: e.g., bankruptcy, lunacy, or the destruction of the subject matter. Check local law.

Although the death of a party will revoke an agreement to arbitrate, the parties may expressly state that death prior to the rendering of an award will not revoke the agreement. After a party's death, his legal representatives may ratify the submission by continuation of arbitration and acceptance of the award. Revocability by death may be dealt with by state statute, therefore, consult local law.

Assignees of a contract containing an arbitration clause that is irrevocable and enforceable may have the agreement to arbitrate enforced against them as if they were the original party to the agreement. Similarly, an assignee may also enforce the arbitration agreement as against the other original party to the contract.

[¶308] ## RATIFICATION OF ARBITRATION
AGREEMENT

If a party appears at an arbitration hearing without objecting to any terms of the agreement, he or she is deemed to have ratified the agreement in its entirety and may not object to particularities later on.

[¶309] ## WAIVER OF ARBITRATION RIGHTS

If a party to an arbitration agreement sues in court, that party may be deemed to have waived his right to arbitration. If the other party in his court pleadings fails to raise his right to enforce the arbitration agreement, then he, too, is deemed to have waived that right. However, a defendant may assert his right to arbitration as a defense and move for a stay of the court proceedings.

[¶310] ## QUALIFICATIONS OF THE ARBITRATOR

Any competent, disinterested person can be an arbitrator irrespective of legal status. However, in some cases, the parties will want to designate an attorney or someone familiar with the applicable legal principles. If the arbitrator is biased or interested in the transaction or dispute, he may be removed. An arbitrator will not necessarily be disqualified although he has previously served as counsel to one of the parties in different litigation, is friendly with one of the parties, or has previously served as an arbitrator in similar cases. Trade associations frequently employ a panel of arbitrators to settle disputes between their members.

[¶311] ## SELECTING THE ARBITRATOR

When a contract calls for settlement of disputes by arbitration, the arbitrator will be determined either prior to the dispute or subsequent to the dispute. When a particular arbitrator is appointed prior to the time the dispute arises, the parties should appoint an alternate in the event the original arbitrator is unable to serve. The parties may also provide that the arbitrator is to be determined in accordance with the rules prescribed by the American Arbitration Association. Under those rules the American Arbitration Association will send each party a copy of a list of proposed arbitrators, technically qualified to resolve the controversies involved. In preparing this list, the Association is guided by the nature of the dispute.

Each party has seven (7) days from the time of mailing to cross off any objectionable arbitrators from the list and to number the remaining arbitrators according to preference.

The Association will appoint an arbitrator who is acceptable to both parties. If no arbitrator is acceptable to both parties, a new list will be provided. If the parties are unable to select an arbitrator mutually acceptable, the Association will administratively appoint an arbitrator, but the appointed arbitrator will not be one of those crossed off previously by the parties.

An alternative method for selecting arbitrators is to provide that each party to the controversy will appoint an arbitrator and the arbitrators will appoint a third arbitrator. If the arbitrators are unable to agree upon a third arbitrator, the court may be called upon to do so.

[¶312]   **ARBITRATION PROCEDURE**

The Commercial Arbitration Rules of the American Arbitration Association, as amended may be obtained by request to 140 West 51st Street, New York, N.Y. 10020, or from any regional AAA office.

[¶313]   **ENFORCEMENT OF THE
ARBITRATION AWARD**

An arbitration award is not self-executing. However, either party is entitled to bring an action on the award and have it enforced as a contract. The Federal Arbitration Act provides for confirmation of an arbitration award within one year. However, the parties will not be precluded from maintaining an action on the award after the one-year statute of limitations for the summary remedy of confirmation has elapsed.

The Uniform Arbitration Act (§11) also provides for the confirmation of an award unless grounds are urged for vacating, or modifying, or correcting the award. In addition, the Uniform Act provides for the entry of the award as a judgment enforceable as any other judgment (see Uniform Arbitration Act §14 and 15).

Once an award is reduced to judgment in one state, it is entitled to full faith and credit in other states. Other states cannot question the judgment unless it could be questioned in the state rendering it.

[¶314]   **VACATING ARBITRATION AWARD**

The Uniform Arbitration Act provides that a court may vacate an arbitration award under the following circumstances:

(1) There was evidence of corruption, fraud, or other unlawful behavior in the procurement of the award;

(2) A party's rights were prejudiced in that the arbitrator was partial to the other side, although the arbitrator was agreed on as a neutral party;

(3) The arbitrator exceeded his powers;

(4) The arbitrator refused to hear all relevant evidence, or to accord a party a reasonable delay or postponement based upon compelling reasons;

(5) A party objected to the arbitration proceeding on the ground that no arbitration agreement existed, and the hearing was conducted over the party's objections.

In addition, the Uniform Act provides that a party seeking to have an award vacated must make such a request to the court within 90 days of the award, except that a party may request vacation of the award under (1) above within 90 days after discovery of the fraud, or 90 days after such corruption should have been known.

ATTORNEY-CLIENT RELATIONSHIPS

[¶401]   An attorney is responsible for more than just advising clients on how to handle business and personal affairs. The lawyer must also conform to the legal ethics of the profession vis-à-vis present clients, potential clients, and the judicial system. The American Bar Association's *Code of Professional Responsibility* is designed to outline basic ''standards of professional conduct expected of lawyers in their relationships with the public, with the legal system, and with the legal profession.'' The ABA Code is comprised of the general Canons, the Ethical Considerations, and Disciplinary Rules. While the Canons and Ethical Considerations express ''aspirational'' objectives, the Disciplinary Rules ''are mandatory in character . . . [and] state the minimum level of conduct below which no lawyer can fall without being subject to disciplinary action.'' The following paragraphs discuss various aspects of professional responsibility and areas of particular concern and conflict for the attorney. This discussion is not intended to be conclusive, and any attorney confronted with an ethics problem should seek help from the local or state bar association.

[¶402]   ESTABLISHING THE PROFESSIONAL
                         RELATIONSHIP

Canon 2 states that ''a lawyer should assist the legal profession in fulfilling its duty to make legal counsel available.'' However, an attorney should never consent to represent a client if the sole purpose is to harass another, if the claim is without merit, or if the complaint does not state a cause of action for which relief can be granted.

An attorney may properly advise a layman that the particular case warrants professional legal advice if that person may not otherwise understand the nature of the legal problem or the need to secure an attorney. It is usual in such cases for an attorney giving such advice not to personally take on the case. This does *not* prohibit an attorney from advising a relative or steady client and then accepting the case.

An attorney is not obligated to represent every person seeking to employ his services, but this should not be taken to mean that an attorney may refuse a client simply because the client or the cause of action is ''unpopular.'' However, a lawyer may refuse to accept additional clients if competent representation of that person would not be possible due to a heavy caseload, a conflict of interest, or other factors.

Frequently, the court will appoint an attorney to represent a client unable to obtain counsel. In such a case, the attorney should not attempt to refuse service merely because of the circumstances of the case or because he doubts the client's innocence.

Withdrawal from a case is a serious matter and must not be taken lightly. Frequently, the mere act of withdrawal, even for the most compelling reasons, may prejudice the client's case. If withdrawal is necessary, the attorney should aid the client in securing new representation and provide the new counsel with all papers related to the claim. Court approval may also be necessary if the case is already pending before a tribunal.

The Disciplinary Rules (DR-2-110) provide that an attorney, upon discovering that a client has undertaken a suit maliciously or for harassment, should withdraw from the action. An attorney should also withdraw if physical or mental health impairs his or her ability to competently represent the client.

[¶403] THE ATTORNEY-CLIENT PRIVILEGE

Canon 4 provides that "a lawyer should preserve the confidences and secrets of a client." In order for a client to best aid counsel in preparing the case, communications with the attorney are to be held in strictest confidence. Of course, a *client* (not the lawyer) may consent to the disclosure of those communications.

Attorneys must distinguish between the "preservation of confidences and secrets" and the more limited "attorney-client privilege." As used in the ABA Code, " 'confidence' refers to information protected by the attorney-client privilege under applicable state law, and 'secret' refers to other information gained in the professional relationship" that the client feels would be embarrassing or harmful.

Preservation of confidences and secrets continues past the termination of professional services. There are situations, however, when the attorney can reveal such confidences and secrets absent the consent of a client:

(1) If the client has confided an intent to commit a crime, or

(2) If such information is necessary to establish or collect a fee, or to defend an action against a client's accusation of improper conduct.

[¶404] REPRESENTING YOUR CLIENT

Canons 5, 6, and 7 indicate the expected behavior of an attorney in the course of representing a client:

☐ A lawyer should exercise independent professional judgment on behalf of a client.

☐ A lawyer should represent a client competently.

☐ A lawyer should represent a client zealously within the bounds of the law.

An attorney should refuse employment if there are financial, personal, or property interests that could possibly cause a conflict of interest in his or her representation of a particular client. Similarly, after accepting a case, an attorney should not acquire any property interest in a client's case, except to secure a fee or in the case of a contingent fee arrangement.

Sometimes an attorney will be requested to represent two or more clients, even though their interests are not identical. If *all* clients consent, and multiple representation would not be detrimental to their interests, an attorney may represent them. An attorney should never represent both clients in a domestic relations problem between spouses.

An attorney for a corporation should bear in mind that he or she represents the *corporation* and not any individual or group of shareholders, officers, or directors.

When accepting employment, an attorney should consider his or her own qualifications, in order to be sure that he or she will be able to offer competent preparation and representation. Frequently, a case may require an attorney to call on an attorney with more experience in the law pertaining to a client's case.

[¶405]   THE RIGHT TO ADVERTISE LEGAL SERVICES

Attorneys have a First Amendment right to truthfully advertise the "availability and terms of routine legal services" *(Bates v. State Bar of Arizona,* Dkt. No. 76-316, 1977). However, the Court opinion clearly indicates that this First Amendment right is not absolute but is subject to proper restraints when such advertising is "false, deceptive, or misleading" and indicates that it will expect the states and the bar to formulate guidelines for attorney advertisements that do not overstep constitutional bounds.

[¶406]   FINANCIAL ABILITY TO PAY COUNSEL'S FEE
AND THE CONTINGENT FEE ARRANGEMENT

The Ethical Considerations of Canon 2 indicate that attorneys' fees should be reasonable so as not to deter the layman from seeking professional help. Disciplinary Rule (DR) 2-106(B) indicates that "a fee is clearly excessive when, after a review of the facts, a lawyer of ordinary prudence would be left with a definite and firm conviction that the fee is in excess of a reasonable fee." Factors to be considered as guides in determining the reasonableness of a fee include:

(1) The time and labor required, the novelty and difficulty of the questions involved, and the skill requisite to perform the legal service properly.

(2) The likelihood, if apparent to the client, that the acceptance of the particular employment will preclude other employment by the lawyer.

(3) The fee customarily charged in the locality for similar legal services.

(4) The amount involved and the results obtained.

(5) The time limitations imposed by the client or by the circumstances.

(6) The nature and length of the professional relationship with the client.

(7) The experience, reputation, and ability of the lawyer or lawyers performing the services.

(8) Whether the fee is fixed or contingent.

Contingent Fees: Frequently, an attorney will accept a civil case on a contingent fee basis, as this may be the only way his client can afford to secure legal services. Although the ABA Code indicates that an attorney should avoid a contingent fee arrangement if a client can afford to pay a reasonable fixed fee, an informed client may, nevertheless, opt for a contingent fee.

An attorney may not enter into a contingent fee arrangement for representing a client in a criminal case [DR2-106(C)].

BANKRUPTCY

[¶**501**]   The Bankruptcy Act of 1898 (11 USC §1 et seq.) controls all federal bankruptcy proceedings. The first seven chapters of the Bankruptcy Act (11 USC §1-74) cover ordinary or straight bankruptcies. The remaining chapters are principally intended for the relief of debtors and are designed to permit the bankruptcy process to be successfully invoked without necessitating a liquidation of the bankrupt's assets.

The Bankruptcy Reform Act of 1978 (H.R. 8200) will become effective October 1, 1979, repealing the Bankruptcy Act of 1898. Changes between the old law and the new law are reflected in the italicized material appearing at the end of each paragraph, designated "New Law."

Note that the new law is comprised of Chapters 1, 3, 5, 7, 9, 11, 13, and 15. Chapter 11 replaces Chapters VIII, X, XI, and XII of the old law.

[¶502]   **INVOLUNTARY BANKRUPTCY**

Two distinctive types of involuntary bankruptcy are possible. In cases in which the bankrupt has fewer than 12 creditors, a single petitioning creditor with a claim of more than $500 may initiate proceedings. When there are more than 12 creditors, three creditors with claims aggregating more than $500 are necessary. It will be necessary to show one of the six acts of bankruptcy found in Bankruptcy Act §3. These include fraudulent transfers, preferential payments during insolvency, failure of an insolvent debtor to discharge a judgment within 30 days. Bankruptcy (or insolvency) means an inability of the debtor to meet his obligations as they mature; it is possible for a debtor whose assets exceed its liabilities to be adjudged a bankrupt if it is not possible to pay obligations as they mature.

New Law: An involuntary bankruptcy case is commenced against a debtor if

(1) Three or more persons (or estates, trusts, or governmental units) file a petition with the bankruptcy court, provided that:

(a) each person holds (or represents a holding of) a claim that is not contingent as to liability, and

(b) such claims total at least $5,000 more than the value of any lien on property securing the creditors' claims; or

(2) There are less than 12 creditors; then one or more creditors who hold a total of $5,000 of claims file a petition with the bankruptcy court.

An involuntary petition may only be commenced under Ch. 7 (Liquidation) or Chapter 11 (Reorganization) of the new Act.

Note that the six acts of bankruptcy required by the 1898 Act have been repealed. The new law requires only that a debtor has not generally repaid his debts as they became due. The Bankruptcy Reform Act does provide one other ground for creditors filing an involuntary petition: If a custodian (other than a trustee, receiver, or authorized agent) was appointed or took possession of the

debtor's property within 120 days before the petition was filed, then involuntary
bankruptcy proceedings may be initiated.

[¶503]   **VOLUNTARY BANKRUPTCY**
A voluntary petition constitutes an adjudication of bankruptcy.
New Law: No change.

[¶504]   **PROCEDURAL STEPS IN**
                        BANKRUPTCY PROCEEDINGS
There are six basic steps in any bankruptcy proceeding. These include:
(1) Filing of petition—a voluntary petition constitutes an adjudication, an
involuntary petition may be contested.
(2) To contest a petition, an answer has to be filed. Usually, it will deny the
act of bankruptcy or deny the insolvency, which is necessary for a preferential
payment or permitting a judgment lien to constitute an act of bankruptcy.
(3) The bankrupt must file an inventory of all his property and a list of all his
creditors, secured and unsecured, showing the amount owed each. He must also
file a "statement of affairs" giving information as to his financial history, the
volume of business, his income, and other pertinent information. The schedules
are prepared in triplicate and filed with the clerk of the court and must be sworn to.
The schedule must claim any exemptions the debtor believes he's entitled to,
otherwise the exemptions may be lost.
(4) When adjudication takes place, the referee fixes a date for the first
meeting of creditors not less than 10 days nor more than 30 days after adjudication
and gives the creditors written notice of the meeting. The meeting is presided over
by the referee and the bankrupt is required to attend and to submit to a broad
examination covering every phase of his operations. If it turns out to be a "no
asset" case, the applicant for examination may wind up having to pay the
stenographer's fee. This suggests the wisdom of having an agreement with other
creditors before assuming the initiative. It's worth noting that the creditors don't
have to wait until their first meeting to examine the debtor but can do so even
before adjudication.
(5) The trustee in bankruptcy is elected at the first meeting of creditors by a
majority of the unsecured creditors both as to number and amount of claims.
Claims of secured or priority creditors aren't counted except to the extent they
exceed the value of their security or priority. This, of course, can lead to a contest
and the referee will have to decide which claims he'll allow to vote.
(6) The trustee has the key role in bankruptcy proceedings; he must take over
and gather together all the bankrupt's assets. He has the job of uncovering fraud
and concealment and recovering preferences and fraudulent transfers. In this job
he will be assisted, of course, by the attorney he selects.

[¶505]   **BANKRUPTCY FILING FEES**

Filing fees for voluntary petitions of bankruptcy are: $37 for the referee's salary and expense fund [11 USC §68(c)(1)], $3 for the clerk of the court [11 USC §80(a)], and $10 for the trustee [11 USC §76(c)]. Filing fees in ordinary bankruptcy proceedings generally must be filed with the clerk of the court at the time of the filing of the petition. However, Rule 107 permits bankrupts to file without prepayment of the filing fee if they agree to thereafter pay the fees in not more than four installments over a period of not more than six months after the date of filing [Bankruptcy Rule 107(b)(para.2)]. Petitioners for voluntary bankruptcy have no right to proceed without agreement to pay a filing fee, either at the time the petition is drawn or within the six-month period thereafter—in effect requiring bankrupts to have at least $50 in order to relieve themselves of obligations incurred. *In forma pauperis* proceedings without prepayment of court costs or fees (except to the extent permitted by Rule 107) are not applicable to bankruptcy proceedings.

New Law: The cost of filing a bankruptcy petition is now $60, thus increasing the minimum fee for a trustee in a no-asset case from $10 to $20.

[¶506]   **UNIFORM FRAUDULENT CONVEYANCE ACT**

Certain transfers are voidable as to any creditor. Fraudulent transfers of assets or fraudulently underlying debts are valid grounds for attack against the bankrupt. If a trustee in bankruptcy is not able to prevail under other provisions of the Bankruptcy Act, it is still possible to void a security transfer under Article IX of the Uniform Commercial Code as a "fraudulent conveyance" according to either §67(d) or 70(e) of the Bankruptcy Act. There are no post-UCC cases in which a trustee has been able to successfully invoke fraudulent conveyance law against a secured creditor, although there is an Illinois case of a successful attack just prior to the adoption of the UCC *(In re Process-Manz Press Inc*., 236 F. Supp. 333, N.D. Illinois, 1964, reversed on other grounds, CA-7, 369 F. 2d 513, 1966, *cert. denied* 386 US 957, 1967). A similar circumstance occurred in North Carolina *(In re Farmers Federation Cooperative Inc*., 242 F. Supp. 400, W.D. North Carolina, 1965).

Section 70(e) of the Bankruptcy Law provides that if any transfer is made or an obligation incurred by a debtor or person adjudged to be a bankrupt that is fraudulent as against, or voidable for any other reason by, any creditor of the debtor, the transfer is null and void as against the trustee. The trustee then succeeds to the right of the creditor who has been wronged under the applicable "fraudulent conveyance" law of the pertinent state. The essential ingredient is for the trustee to establish that, but for the debtor's bankruptcy, the creditor could have shown that the security transfer was a fraudulent conveyance.

There are 25 states in which the Uniform Fraudulent Conveyance Act is in force. In those states, a trustee may establish that a transfer is fraudulent by showing any of the following factors: A conveyance or obligation incurred by a person who is (or will be rendered thereby) insolvent even if the actual intent is not to make the individual insolvent (if consideration is lacking); a conveyance of partnership property if the partnership is or will be thereby rendered insolvent and if the conveyance is made to any partner, or to a person not a partner without fair consideration (fraudulent as to partnership creditors); a conveyance or any obligation incurred without any fair consideration when the person undertaking the action believes he will incur debts beyond his ability to pay as they mature (fraudulent as to present and future creditors); a conveyance designed to hinder, delay, or defraud either present or future creditors; and a conveyance made by an individual about to engage in a business transaction when the property remaining in the hands of the individual thereafter is unreasonably small capital (applies without regard to actual intent). If a fraudulent conveyee is guilty of actual fraud, the trustee may void his security interest *in toto* — not just *pro tonto* — provided that a conveyance is made with actual intent to defraud (§7 of the Uniform Fraudulent Conveyance Act).

[¶507]   STRONGARM PROVISIONS OF BANKRUPTCY

Here is the heart of the bankruptcy proceeding. First, §70(a) spells out the property of the debtor that passes to the trustee. Section 70(c) puts the trustee in the position of a lien creditor whose interest vests in all the bankrupt's property at the moment of adjudication, regardless of whether or not such a lien creditor actually exists. This puts title in the trustee ahead of all unsecured creditors and all secured creditors who have failed to perfect their liens. The Bankruptcy Act of 1898 provides three exceptions to the trustee's powers to avoid transfers: (1) Payments to a fully secured creditor with a perfected lien; (2) transfers of exempt property (determined by case law); and (3) rights of set-off under §68.

New Law: The new Act's exceptions are more numerous. The trustee cannot nullify the following transfers:

(1) A transfer of property that is intended to be, and substantially is, contemporaneous with an extension of new credit;

(2) The payment of a debt that is within the ordinary course of business affairs (or financial affairs if the debtor is a consumer) between the debtor and creditor, and made according to ordinary business terms, provided the payment is made 45 days after the debt was incurred. (Note, however, that the language of the item is vague and allows ample room for litigation on the meaning of "ordinary course" and "ordinary business terms");

(3) A transfer that secures a loan to enable the debtor to acquire collateral, if it is perfected within 10 days after the security interest attaches (i.e., a purchase-money security interest under UCC §9-107);

(4) A preferential transfer to a creditor who thereafter extends new unsecured credit (i.e., the amount of the new credit reduces the amount of the

preferential transfer that the trustee can avoid);

(5) A transfer of inventory or receivables in which the creditor has a perfected security interest, unless it improves that creditor's position (at the expense of unsecured creditors) at the time the petition of bankruptcy is filed over his position as of 90 days (one year for insiders) before bankruptcy; and

(6) A transfer that fixes or satisfies a valid statutory lien.

[¶508] AVOIDANCE OF PREFERENCES

A bankruptcy trustee may avoid preferences for creditors through the use of §60 of the Bankruptcy Act. There are six essential elements to any preference. These are: (1) A transfer of the debtor's property (voluntary or involuntary with the latter taking in liens by legal proceedings); (2) while insolvent; (3) for or on account of an antecedent debt; (4) within four months of the filing of the petition in bankruptcy; (5) enabling the creditor to get a greater percentage of his debt than other creditors of the same class; and (6) the creditor must know or have reasonable cause to believe that the debtor was insolvent at the time of the transfer.

New Law: The Bankruptcy Reform Act's equivalent preferences provision (§547) preserves the perfection requirement of §60(a)(2), but reduces the grace period to 10 days. However, the new law makes two major changes in the elements a trustee must establish in order to avoid a preferential transfer: (1) The time period is reduced from 4 months to 90 days, and (2) the trustee no longer has to prove that the creditor had reason to believe that the debtor was insolvent when the property was transferred.

If the creditor is an "insider," the crucial time is extended to the period within one year of bankruptcy, and the trustee must still prove that the creditor should have known of the debtor's insolvency. If the debtor is an individual, an "insider" is defined as a partner, relative, relative of a partner, or a corporation in which the debtor is a director, officer, or "person in control." If the debtor is a corporation or partnership, an "insider" includes a director, officer, person in control, partner, or a relative of any persons who fall into these categories.

[¶509] MAKING CLAIMS AGAINST A BANKRUPT

Proof of claim against a bankrupt is dealt with under §57 and §63 of the Bankruptcy Act. Proof of claim forms have been fixed by the United States Supreme Court. For practical purposes nearly every claim is provable with two important exceptions: Negligence action (if litigation has not been instituted prior to the bankruptcy filing), and landlord claims, which, if provable, are limited under §63A(9) of the Act. Trustees should be notified by the claimant as soon as he learns of the bankruptcy. Proof of a secured debt (under Article 9 of the UCC) must also be furnished.

[¶510] HOW CLAIMS ARE PROVED

All claims provable under the Act must be filed within six months of the first meeting of creditors. If a claim is timely filed, it can usually be amended after the six-month period so long as the amendment doesn't amount to an entirely new claim.

Claims should be submitted on the official forms. While the claim itself need not be verified, if a power of attorney is filed with it, the power should be acknowledged before a notary. If the claim is based on a written instrument, the instrument should be attached to the proof.

New Law: The Reform Act (§501) merely states that all proofs of claims must be timely filed. A creditor or indenture trustee may file a proof of claim. If a creditor does not timely file a proof of claim: (1) An entity that is liable to such creditor with the debtor, or that has secured such creditor, may file a proof of such claim; or (2) the debtor or trustee may file a proof of such claim.

[¶511] ALLOWANCE OF CLAIMS

At the first meeting of creditors, a provisional allowance of claims will be made for voting purposes but this isn't an allowance for purposes of dividend participation. However, as a general rule, claims filed at or before the first meeting will be allowed at that time if no objection is raised. If an objection is raised, either by the trustee or one or more creditors, the referee will fix a date to hear and determine the points raised. There's no time limit on filing objections, but the referee may in his discretion refuse to entertain objections filed too late. Secured and priority claims will be allowed only to the extent they're unsecured. If a creditor has received a transfer, lien, or preference that is voidable, his claim won't be allowed until he surrenders it to the trustee.

New Law: A claim or interest, proof of which is filed pursuant to §501 of the Bankruptcy Reform Act is deemed allowed, unless a party in interest, including a creditor of a partner in a partnership that is a debtor in a case under Chapter 7 of the new law, objects.

If an objection to a claim is made, the court, after notice and a hearing, shall determine the amount of such claim as of the date of the petition.

[¶512] HOW ASSETS OF THE BANKRUPT ARE DISTRIBUTED: PRIORITIES OF CLAIMS

Five distinctive classes of claims entitled to priority are set up under the Bankruptcy Act. The order of payment to the five priority classes requiring satisfaction of each category before the next category may be satisfied is:

☐   Administrative costs (this takes in almost every expense in connection with

31

the proceeding including fees for the attorney of the bankrupt, the trustee, the petitioning creditors, and the receiver, and commissions for the trustee and receiver);

☐ Wage claims up to the amount of $600 earned within three months (vacation and severance pay may present problems);

☐ Costs and expenses incurred by *creditors* in successfully opposing a discharge or getting it set aside or in getting evidence resulting in conviction of a bankruptcy offense;

☐ Tax claims—federal, state, and local—all stand on an equal footing within the class (taxes accruing during bankruptcy will normally be within the first class);

☐ Debts having priority under federal law and rent claims entitled to priority under state law.

New Law: The Reform Act creates six classes of claims entitled to priority, in the following order:

(1) Administrative Costs. Note—fees for referees' salaries are no longer included in this category.

(2) Unsecured claims arising in the ordinary course of the debtor's business or financial affairs after the commencement of the case, but before the appointment of a trustee or the order of relief (whichever is earlier).

(3) Unsecured claims for wages, salaries, or commissions earned within 90 days before the date of filing the petition or cessation of the debtor's business (whichever is earlier), with a maximum claim of $2,000 per individual.

(4) Unsecured claims for contributions to employee benefit plans arising from services rendered within 180 days before the filing of the petition or cessation of business (whichever is earlier). The claim cannot exceed the number of employees, multiplied by $2,000, minus any monies paid for wage claims (see (3) above).

(5) Unsecured claims of $900 per individual for monies deposited in connection with the purchase, lease, or rental of property, or the purchase of services for the personal, family, or household use of such individuals, that were not delivered or provided.

(6) Tax claims.

[¶513]   **DISCHARGING A
                                BANKRUPT'S DEBT**

Discharge of a bankrupt's debts are the single most important feature of any bankruptcy proceeding. A bankrupt is entitled to discharge as a matter of right, unless proper objections are sustained by the court. In a case of a corporation, adjudication requires an application made within six months or right to discharge is forfeited. (As a matter of practice, corporations rarely apply for the discharge because of the lack of individual liability.)

[¶514] **GROUNDS FOR OBJECTING TO OR DENYING DISCHARGE**

Bankruptcy law provides that there are seven basic grounds for objecting to and denying discharge. These are:

☐ Commission of criminal bankruptcy offense at any time in any bankruptcy proceeding;

☐ Failure to keep or preserve books or records showing financial condition and business transactions;

☐ Obtaining money or property on credit by false financial statement (applies only to those in business as sole proprietor, partner, or corporate executive);

☐ Fraudulent conveyance or concealment of property in year before filing of petition;

☐ Discharge in bankruptcy or confirmation of an arrangement or wage earner plan during six-year period before filing petition;

☐ Refusal to obey a lawful order of the court or to answer a material question approved by the court; or

☐ Failure to satisfactorily explain any loss or deficiency of assets.

[¶515] **ATTACK ON UNDERLYING DEBT**

If a trustee can show that a debt of a bankrupt is a sham, the fraud may be sufficient to defeat the secured creditor—no matter what the validity of his security interest. Actual debts may not necessarily be legally enforceable even though there is a security interest that is otherwise valid and enforceable. If a debt, for example, is barred by the statute of limitations, it may be unenforceable though the security interest remains valid. Under §70(c) of the Bankruptcy Act, the trustee in bankruptcy succeeds "to all defenses available to the bankrupt as against third persons." It is also useful to consider that a debt may be unenforceable because of interest rates that prove to be usurious. Some recent cases have held that a usurious debt is a fraudulent conveyance, though it has been held that a lender can evade usury laws by using a corporation (see *Wergerhaines Corp.,* 302 N.Y. 930, 1951). For a comprehensive review of the pertinent interest rate and usury limitations, see the Appendix.

[¶516] **BULK TRANSFERS**

Article VI of the Uniform Commercial Code governs certain types of bulk transfers. A bulk transfer is defined as any transfer in bulk that is not in the ordinary course of business that consists of the major part of the materials, supplies, merchandise, or other inventory of the business, or the transfer of a substantial portion of the equipment of a business if the equipment comes from inventory. Businesses that are subject to the bulk transfer provision of the UCC are "all those whose principal business is the sale of merchandise from stock, including those who manufacture what they sell."

33

Several types of transactions that might otherwise fall within the scope of Article VI are specifically exempted. First, security interests are exempt (UCC §6-103(1)). Second, general assignments for the benefit of all creditors, as well as subsequent transfers of the assignees of the transferor, are also exempt (UCC §6-103(3)). Next, judicial and other sales by court officers or public officials are exempt (UCC §6-103(4),(5),(8)). When public notice is given of a proposed bulk transfer, an individual who becomes bound to pay the debts of the transferor in full is exempt (UCC §6-103(6)). Finally, certain transfers that merely reflect changes in the formal structure of a business enterprise (without any significant change in substance) are also exempt (UCC §6-103(7)).

Some parties to a bulk transfer may fail to comply with Article VI because they believe it is inapplicable to their transaction. Nonetheless they are liable to the trustee in bankruptcy for failure to comply in the event that the transferor becomes insolvent. Responsibility for the completeness and accuracy of the listing of creditors in a bulk transfer transaction rests on the transferor—transfer is not rendered ineffective by errors and omissions unless a transferee is shown to have had actual knowledge. Assuming that the transferor goes into bankruptcy, it is possible that his trustee in bankruptcy still might not be able to reach bulk assets that have been transferred. To the extent that the transferee gave fair consideration, the bulk transfer would not constitute a fraudulent conveyance—absent a showing of actual fraudulent intent. Bulk transfers are not a voidable lien under §67 of the Bankruptcy Act (11 USC §107(a)), which applies only to liens against the property of a person obtained by attachment, judgment, levy, or other legal or equitable process or proceeding. A showing of fraud, however, changes the picture considerably.

[¶517]   WHAT DEBTS AND LIABILITIES CONTINUE AFTER DISCHARGE?

Here is a checklist of what a bankruptcy discharge does not relieve by way of obligation:

☐ Claims not provable, such as certain tort claims, fines, and penalties;

☐ Taxes—generally, federal, state, or local, owing within three years preceding bankruptcy;

☐ Liability for obtaining money or property by false pretenses or representations;

☐ Liability for willful and malicious injuries to the person or property of another;

☐ Alimony and child support payments;

☐ Liability for seduction;

☐ Debts not scheduled;

☐ Fraud or embezzlement by the bankrupt while acting as a fiduciary;

☐ Wages earned within three months prior to bankruptcy;

☐ Sums due employee by bankrupt employer under contract authorizing retention of sums to secure faithful performance of employment contract.

New Law: Nondischargeable debts are essentially the same as under the *Bankruptcy Act of 1898. The only addition to the list of nondischargeable debts is:*

☐ *Government educational loans, unless such loans first become due more than five years before the date of the filing of the petition, or if nondischarge of the loan would impose an undue hardship on the debtor or the debtor's dependents.*

[¶518]   **FOR FURTHER REFERENCE . . .**

Alderman, R.M., "Selected Bankruptcy Law Bibliography," 83 Commercial Law Journal 411-417 (August-September 1978).

American Jurisprudence, Bankruptcy.

Balch, B.L., "Does Bankruptcy Discharge the Personal Liability for Unpaid Corporate Taxes?" 55 Taxes 355 (1977).

Collier, *Bankruptcy* (9 vol.).

"Current Developments in Bankruptcy 1977," Practising Law Institute, New York, N.Y.

Goldstein, A.S., *Commercial Transactions Desk Book,* Institute for Business Planning, Inc., Englewood Cliffs, N.J. (1977).

Herzog, *Bankruptcy,* Matthew Bender, New York, N.Y.

Hirsch and Krause, *Bankruptcy and Arrangements Under Chapter XI of the Bankruptcy Act,* Practising Law Institute, New York, N.Y.

Modern Bankruptcy Manual: Law and Practice with Forms, Lawyer's Co-op Editorial Staff.

Newton, G.W., "Salvaging the Financially Troubled Business: Tax Planning Factors to Consider," 18 Taxation for Accountants 282 (1977).

"Postdischarge Coercion of Bankrupts by Private Creditors," 91 Harvard Law Review 1336-46 (April 1978).

BROKERAGE

[¶601] A broker's right to his commission will depend on the contract with his principal, for whom he is acting as agent. The arrangement can vary from an open listing (in which the principal is free to hire other brokers) to an exclusive agency (no other broker can bring about the sale) or an exclusive right to sell (broker earns his commission when the property is sold even if the principal sells it himself).

[¶602]   WHEN IS THE COMMISSION EARNED?

Unless some additional condition is provided in the contract between the parties, a broker is entitled to his commission when he can show the following:

(1) His services were performed during the time of the agency as specified in the contract.

(2) The broker produced a buyer who was ready, willing, and able to buy. "Ready" means that the buyer will execute a contract of sale. "Willingness" is the voluntary act of the purchaser without any compulsion or coercion. If the broker has brought the parties together and they make a different contract than the one that the broker was employed to make, the broker will nevertheless be entitled to his commission. "Able" means that the buyer will be able to get up the necessary funds to close the deal within the time required. He must have the money to meet the cash payment and be able financially to meet later installments.

(3) There was a meeting of the minds between the parties. This basic tenet of the contract doctrine provides that a binding contract exists between parties when all the material terms of the agreement between them exist.

(4) The broker was the procuring cause. The broker must be able to show that his efforts were the primary and direct cause of the consummation of the transaction. If the broker had an exclusive right to sell, procuring cause would not enter into the brokerage situation and he would be entitled to his commission regardless of how the sale took place. Or in the case of an exclusive agency, the broker gets his commission even if the principal hired another broker who actually sold the property, since here the owner broke a contract he made to sell only through this broker. To establish that he was the procuring cause the broker can show that: he advertised the property; he introduced the parties; he was the first to call the purchaser's attention to the property; he was continuously engaged in the transaction by correspondence or conversations.

If several brokers were involved, if there was a disagreement between the parties after the first broker brought them together, and later a second broker came in and got the parties to agree, the second broker is the procuring cause. However, the first broker is a procuring cause if he brought about a substantial agreement and the second broker worked out details.

(5) The deal was consummated. This will be important if the broker's right to a commission has been conditioned upon the consummation of the transaction.

Here, again, if the deal goes through the broker is entitled to his commission even if the parties have changed the terms from those that were originally given to the broker. Or, if the deal does not go through because of default (in bad faith) on the part of the owner, the broker is entitled to his commission. In an exclusive agency or an open listing, when the broker's right to a commission has not been conditioned on the final conclusion of the transaction, the broker will get his commission even if the purchaser fails to carry out the deal after having made a valid contract.

BUSINESS ORGANIZATION

[¶701] Tax costs, liability exposure, and the practical convenience of various forms of business are the points that most clients raise when they consider setting up a business organization. Different types of ventures require different organizational means: The sole proprietorship, the partnership, the limited partnership, and the corporate form are all possibilities. Even within the corporate structure, many different kinds of operating procedures are possible. The following paragraphs offer summaries of various aspects of business organization.

[¶702] ## SIMPLICITY OF OPERATION

If the venture is likely to be a stable one with little prospect of growth, there is a lot to be said for the sole proprietorship or, if there are several working together, the partnership form. Orders are easy to give; formalities are easy to forget. Dissolution is available at the will of any partner at any time, so that he may freely make a new start in a new direction if he wishes, in the absence of any contract to the contrary. The very large number of firms that remain as partnerships is a sufficient demonstration of the workability and practicality of this simple method of doing business.

[¶703] ## FLEXIBILITY OF ORGANIZATION

The corporate form permits great variation in operation and development. Greater or lesser powers may be conferred, for example, on a governing board of directors, with a larger or smaller number of members. Smaller working committees, with specified powers, may be established for particular purposes, whether overall management on an interim basis, like an executive committee, or special fields on a continuing basis, like a finance committee or a retirement committee. Departments may be created and branches established and offices created at various levels with supervisory personnel below them in any number of levels that the needs of the business may require. The modern corporate form has, in short, developed an almost unlimited flexibility of managerial organization. Its advantages increase in direct proportion to the size of the business involved.

[¶704] ## FINANCING

In the early stages, financing will probably depend on the personal credit of the principals. They will have to endorse corporate paper. But if the business accumulates assets and shows earning power, it should be able to get credit without involving the principals. Further on in this development, the availability of corporate shares will be important in providing additional capacity to attract financing and liquidity for the interest of the owner.

[¶705]   CONTINUITY

Continuity is assured through the corporate form better than through any other. An individual dies and a partnership terminates upon the death of a member. In each case a final accounting must be had with a determination of the current value of assets. As the size and complexity of the business increase, the burden of these steps becomes all the more oppressive. But a corporation continues no matter how many of its directors or officers or stockholders die. Its title to property remains unaffected and likewise its contracts. Stock transfers can be accomplished speedily and new elections can be held as needed. The corporation is the vehicle ideally suited for continuing a business beyond a single generation and this advantage grows in importance with the size of the business.

[¶706]   TRANSFERABILITY OF SHARES

If a business prospers, its owners will normally desire to distribute interests in it to their children over a period of years. This cannot be done directly in a sole proprietorship and only with difficulty in a partnership. It is, however, readily feasible through the corporate form by transfers of stock.

[¶707]   GOODWILL

If goodwill is likely to develop into an asset of substantial value, the corporate form is likely to be advantageous in accumulating goodwill and maintaining public identification.

[¶708]   COMPENSATION ARRANGEMENTS

The corporate form makes it possible to attract and reward talent with stock options, stock purchases, deferred compensation arrangements, participation of the owners in pension and profit-sharing plans, etc.

[¶709]   LIQUIDITY OF ESTATES OF
                    DECEASED SHAREHOLDERS

The possible future sale of corporate shares and the possible creation of a public market hold the promise of easing estate liquidity problems. Even when this is not likely to occur, the corporate form may make the way easier to accumulate earnings and pay for insurance to facilitate the redemption of shares owned by a deceased stockholder.

[¶710]   **PARTICIPATION OF INACTIVE**
                        (PASSIVE) INVESTORS

The corporate form is the best medium for capital appreciation. On the other hand, a limited partnership may offer an investor a better route to participation in earnings because his share in earnings would not be burdened by a tax at the corporate level, as is the case of dividends on common and preferred stock.

[¶711]   **SPLITTING INCOME**

A family partnership may be the best way of splitting both income and capital values to children and other members of the family.

[¶712]   **TAX FACTORS**

The choice of the form of doing business will play an important and continuing role in determining the tax cost of doing business. Different forms will be indicated at different times. The basic strategic considerations are these:

(a) A new and risky business or one in which losses are sustained to build capital value should be operated in unincorporated form or in a going corporation so that any losses may be applied against income and offset with tax savings;

(b) A very small business may best be operated in unincorporated form to avoid double tax on corporate and dividend income:

(c) After reaching the 17%, 20%, 30%, 40%, or 46% corporate rates in the individual brackets, the corporation is at least a temporary tax shelter;

(d) But unless earnings can continue to be used to expand the business, the point of double taxation is reached as it becomes necessary to distribute dividends;

(e) In the corporate form there is a latent capital gain tax to pay when accumulated earnings from liquidation or sale of stock are cashed in. If stock is held until death and then sold by the family, capital gain tax is avoided on the accumulation of earnings;

(f) Income can be brought into lower tax brackets by splitting it through a family partnership or by dividing operations between several entities, corporations, or a combination of corporate and unincorporated entities;

(g) If the business is closely held (fewer than five stockholders at the last half of the taxable year) and close to 60% of the income will come from investment sources, care must be exercised to avoid the personal holding company penalty tax.

(h) In the case of certain professionals, such as doctors, lawyers, architects, and others, professional corporations formed under the pertinent laws of each jurisdiction are a cross between the partnership and the corporation. Attendant benefits and problems are discussed elsewhere.

40

[¶713] PARTNERSHIP VS. CORPORATION

The choice isn't limited to either incorporating or remaining a proprietorship. For instance, there is the alternative of operating as a partnership. Following is a comparison between the two forms—corporation and partnership—with respect to the factors that will be most important. The checklist covers first general considerations, then tax considerations.

[¶713.1]   General Considerations

Partnership	Corporation
Life	
For the term specified in the partnership agreement; death of a partner may dissolve it earlier.	Continues until dissolved by law (unless statute limits the time).
Entity	
Has no separate entity from the partners.	Has entity separate from its stockholders. Can sue and be sued, hold and deal in property.
Liability	
General partners are individually liable for all partnership obligations; limited partners usually liable only up to the amount of their capital contributions.	Stockholder has no individual liability; only his capital contribution is involved (exception: some state laws subject bank stockholders to double liability).
Changing Ownership	
Change in interests creates a new partnership. Other partners must consent. Arrangements necessary to end liability of ex-members.	Stock can ordinarily be sold or otherwise transferred at will.
Raising Capital	
Only by loan, by new membership, or contributions of present members, or by remaking the firm.	By sale of new stock or bonds or other securities.
Making Policy	
Unanimous agreement of partners usually required; involves problems of personality.	Authority centered in board of directors, acting by majority agreement.
Credit	
Depends on standing of individual partners; partnership interests usually can't be pledged.	As separate entity, has credit possibility apart from stockholders; in close corporation, stock is available as collateral.

Partnership	Corporation

Management

By partners; they are responsible (except silent partners).	Stockholders not responsible; managers are employed.

Flexibility

Partners have leeway in their actions except to the extent limited by the partnership agreement (occasionally by law).	Limited to the powers (express and implied) in its charter from the state; may be subjected to judicial construction.

[¶713.2] Tax Considerations

Income Tax

Partners taxed on proportionate shares of partnership income whether or not distributed. Partnership return is merely an information return.	Income taxed to corporation; stockholders taxed only on dividends distributed to them, reduced by dividend credit.

Accumulation

Partners taxed on accumulated as well as distributed earnings.	Stockholders not taxed on accumulations. However, penalty tax applies if purpose is to avoid tax and accumulation exceeds certain amount.

Capital Gains and Losses

Partners taxed on their proportionate shares of gain and loss. They apply the limitations just as if they had only individual gains and losses.	Uses the alternative computation, but, unlike individuals, there is no deduction of 60% of the excess of long-term gain over short-term loss.

Exempt Interest

Partners not taxed on exempt interest received from the firm; however, credit for partially exempt interest received cannot exceed proportionate shares of partnership income.	Exempt interest distributed by a corporation would be fully taxable income to the stockholders.

Charitable Contributions

The partners add their proportionate shares of the partnership's contributions to their own personal contributions in computing their incomes.	Corporations take their own deduction for charitable contributions; but the limitation is only 5% as against the individual limitation of 50% (20% for private charities).

Pension Planning

Partners can be beneficiaries of a Keogh plan.	Officer and employee stockholders can be beneficiaries of a pension plan. Corporation can deduct its payments to the extent allowed by law.

42

Partnership	Corporation

Social Security

Partners don't pay Social Security tax on compensation from the firm, but must pay self-employment tax.	Compensation to officer and employee stockholders is subject to Social Security tax.

Assignment of Income

Partner's interest can't be assigned except with the consent of all partners; new partnership may result.	Stockholder has freedom to assign his stock without consulting anyone; but earnings can't be assigned apart from the stock.

Death Benefits

No exemption for payments to partner's beneficiares.	Benefits up to $5,000 can be received tax free by stockholder-employee's beneficiaries (IRC§101).

State Taxes

In most states, partnerships not subject to state income and purchase taxes.	Corporations subject to these taxes, although deductibility on federal return lessens cost.

[¶714] OTHER ORGANIZATIONAL POSSIBILITIES

In addition to corporate or partnership entities, several other combinations of these business choices are ordinarily available. These are explored in the paragraphs below.

[¶715] LIMITED PARTNERSHIPS

These have all the legal and tax features of partnerships except that the liability of limited partners can be limited to the capital that they commit to the venture.

[¶716] COMBINATION OF PARTNERSHIP AND CORPORATION

The corporation can be set up to manufacture or perform some other function, for which limitation of liability or some other objective makes the corporation particularly suitable, and the partnership can sell or perform some other associated function. Here it is necessary to keep the price or commission rates charged on transactions between the corporation and the partnership on arm's-length terms, supported by comparisons with the terms of similar transactions between unrelated entities.

[¶717]   MULTIPLE CORPORATIONS

It might be possible to divide a business into several corporations and realize substantial tax savings, if it were not for IRC Sections 1561-1564. The potential tax breaks are prevented by the special rules that apply to corporations that are members of a "controlled group." For tax years prior to 1979, corporations falling into the "controlled group" category were entitled to one surtax exemption. Since the surtax was removed by the Revenue Act of 1978, IRC §1561 has been amended to limit members of controlled groups to an aggregate amount of $25,000 in each of the new corporate tax brackets which range from 17% to 46%. Members of a controlled group are still limited to one accumulated earnings credit divided among all the corporations of the controlled group. It doesn't matter if there is a bona fide business purpose for operating an enterprise as two or more corporations. Likewise, it doesn't matter if the multiple corporations are used to operate multiple businesses. If common ownership of the multiple corporations makes them component members of a controlled group, they are subject to the rules.

Of course, there may be valid nontax reasons for using multiple corporations.

[¶718]   INCORPORATE BUT KEEP CERTAIN ASSETS OUT OF THE CORPORATION

Frequently it is desirable to keep a patent or piece of real estate out of the corporation and have the corporation make rental or royalty payments to the individual owner for that property. Here again caution is necessary to justify the rates of rent and royalty, particularly to stockholders. This arrangement offers an opportunity to take income out of the corporation on a deductible basis.

[¶719]   CORPORATION ELECTING NOT TO PAY CORPORATE TAX

A small corporation might choose to qualify under Subchapter S of the Internal Revenue Code in order to avoid income tax at the corporate level while retaining all the legal advantages of a corporation, particularly, limited legal liability. For a detailed discussion of the tax consequences of Subchapter S incorporation, see ¶3908 et seq.

[¶720]   FOR FURTHER REFERENCE . . .

Berger, "Limited Partnership Agreement," 22 Practical Lawyer 35-52 (Sept., 1976).

DeFren, B.J., *Partnership Desk Book,* Institute for Business Planning, Inc., Englewood Cliffs, N.J. (1978).

Fink, P.R., "Selecting a Form of Business Predicated on Characterization of Income Flows," 56 Taxes 587 (October 1978).

Hess, R.P., *Desk Book for Setting Up a Closely Held Corporation,* Institute for Business Planning, Inc., Englewood Cliffs, N.J. (1979).

Horwood, R.M., "Tax Considerations Involved in Deciding Whether a New Business Should be Incorporated," 19 Taxation for Accountants 324 (1977).

Israels, *Corporate Practice,* Practising Law Institute, New York, N.Y.

Knapp and Semmel, *Forms of Business Organization and the Federal Tax Laws,* Practising Law Institute, New York, N.Y.

Lehrman, A., *Tax Desk Book for the Closely Held Corporation,* Institute for Business Planning, Inc., Englewood Cliffs, N.J. (1978).

Parkinson, J.L., "Choosing the Investment Vehicle: Corporations, Subchapter S Corporations, and Partnerships," 27 Tulane Tax Institute 20 (1977).

Rohrlich, C., *Organizing Corporate and Other Business Enterprises,* 3rd Ed., Matthew Bender, New York, N.Y.

Sarner, Leonard, and Shinehouse, George F., Jr., *Organizational Problems of Small Businesses,* Joint Committee on Legal Education.

Tax Planning, Institute for Business Planning, Inc., Englewood Cliffs, N.J.

CHECKLIST FOR DRAFTING A CONTRACT

[¶801] The following checklist should be consulted whenever a contract is contemplated or drafted.

☐ What restrictions are necessary to keep the other party from adding an unwanted term or condition?

☐ Will all prior communications be merged into the written agreement?

☐ Will the possibility of future oral modifications be excluded?

☐ What future acts may be deemed to constitute a waiver of a contractual right?

☐ If the other party's representations are being relied on, they should be stated as an express warranty, rather than a mere "whereas" recital. If it is merely a recital, fraud must be proved in order to get relief if the facts are different; if the misrepresentation is innocent, the contract may be voided if it's set up as a warranty.

☐ Does the party who signs the agreement have the necessary authority?

☐ If one side's obligation is dependent on the other party doing something, make the condition express and explicit. Otherwise there may be a claim for damages in the event the other party fails to perform.

☐ Stipulate whether or not representations are to survive the transaction.

☐ If something is sold "as is," expressly exclude any implied representations. State that the assignment is without recourse if there are to be no warranties of title.

☐ Provide for duration and right to terminate. If it appears that the parties are likely to continue on in a business relationship beyond the express term, consider providing for automatic renewals for a year or some other appropriate period of time, always preserving the right to terminate on appropriate notice.

☐ Spell out exactly what constitutes performance (use quantities, descriptions, time, drawings, specifications, acceptance tests, etc.). Specify who is responsible for taking all steps necessary for getting permits and meeting all other necessary requirements of performance.

☐ Insert a time-of-the-essence clause, with a provision for cancellation of the contract, if the other party fails in timely performance.

☐ Guard against liability from unforeseeable contingencies by inserting a force majeure clause.

☐ In the absence of a contrary provision, delivery and payment are concurrent provisions. If the intention is otherwise, express provision is needed. If payment is to be made in installments, consider acceleration and prepayment provisions.

☐ If collateral security is to be furnished, see ¶3401 et seq.

☐ If the other party's performance is to be guaranteed or a party is to be indemnified or held harmless, see ¶3401 and 3601.

☐ If the sale or use of an item might infringe on a third party's patent, have a patent indemnity clause.

☐ If a deposit is made, consider getting that accepted as liquidated damages. If liquidated damages are provided for, make sure they are not so heavy as to be held to be a penalty.

☐ Protect against inadvertent default by providing for notice and a subsequent time period within which any default may be cured. Provide whether notice becomes effective upon mailing or upon receipt and whether it has to be given by registered or certified mail.

☐ If the governing law can be specified, this will avoid perplexing conflict of laws problems.

☐ Provide explicitly whether the contract is to be assignable or not, and whether or not the original party is released from liability upon assignment. Consider providing that the assignment is not effective until the assignee assumes the assignor's obligations in writing.

☐ Use special care in drafting conditions. If one party is excused from performance on the happening of a condition, say so clearly. If the condition is concurrent, as, for example, delivery of merchandise on payment of the price, make this clear. If the condition is subsequent, as where the agreement is continued until either party exercises his option to cancel it, make it clear that only on compliance with the termination procedure may the agreement be canceled. If the condition is precedent, as where one party must complete his part of the agreement before the other party is obligated to render his performance, make it clear that substantial or full completion is necessary before the other party is obligated to act. The use of conditions will also determine whether the parties intend the agreement to be entire or severable. Provide for concurrent or conditional performance, if it is not desirable to have the agreement divided into separate, self-contained units each independent of the next unit and standing alone as a separately enforceable agreement.

☐ Whenever money or goods have to be advanced before completion of the other party's performance, find out whether protection against insolvency is needed. If it is, have money placed in escrow and see that either title to or a lien on property is retained.

☐ Is a provision to be included stating that each party has made his own investigation and has not relied on any statement or preliminary representation made by the other?

☐ If arbitration is to be used, see ¶301 et. seq.

☐ It is always safest to specify the consideration that makes the contract binding, even though in some states the law makes a written instrument of agreement binding without consideration. If consideration is necessary it will make later proof easier if it is specified.

☐ In preliminary negotiations, avoid the risk that oral and letter negotiations may create an agreement, make it clear that there is no agreement until a final document is signed.

☐ If a party is to have the right to cancel the agreement if it is breached by the other party it is advisable to include a clause to that effect. Otherwise, it may be necessary to establish that the breach is serious enough to defeat the purpose of the contract in order to be relieved of its obligations.

☐ Exclude the authority of any salesman or agent of one of the parties to change the conditions of sale and shipment specified in the agreement.

☐ Are the parties to have any right to inspect the books and records of another party?

☐ Specify who is to carry risk of property loss during contract period. What insurance is to be carried? By whom?

☐ If concurrent performance is a condition say so. If complete and exact performance is a condition say so. If a party is to be relieved of a performance upon the happening of some event, say so. If exact performance is required, expressly exclude the doctrine of substantial performance.

☐ Should a provision be included requiring any change and modification of the contract to be in writing and signed by both parties?

☐ Is the illegality of any provision to invalidate the contract as a whole?

☐ An all-purpose modification clause should spell out the "how" of changing the agreement, especially when there is maximum daily contact on all levels between both parties. This will protect against unauthorized amendments agreed upon by subordinates without the party's approval. Limit modifications to formal contacts between the highest levels, or name the authorized personnel.

☐ If the agreement leaves certain items (price, delivery dates, etc.) to be revised later, as conditions change, make sure an "escape," an arbitration, liquidated damage, or cancellation clause is included.

☐ Is an escape clause necessary? Usually, escape clauses are two-way streets—each party has the same option to end the agreement. But the one-way escape clause is not uncommon and serves usefully to end an agreement when the other party has defaulted or has breached or when some basic consideration (obtaining favorable tax rulings, zoning clearance, export license, steel quota, franchise renewal, etc.) has backfired. A good escape clause should fix a period and method of notice, leaving no doubt about items that have accrued prior to the termination date.

For forms illustrating the various points made above, including price terms, risk of loss, storage of goods, passage of title, manner of shipping, default provisions, and warranties, see *IBP Forms of Business Agreements and Resolutions.*

[¶802]   **FOR FURTHER REFERENCE . . .**

American Jurisprudence, Contracts.
Corbin on Contracts, West Publishing Co., St. Paul, Minn.
Mandel, *Preparation of Commercial Agreements,* Practising Law Institute, New York, N.Y.
Restatement of Contracts, American Law Institute (state annotations are available for some states), Philadelphia, Pa.

COMMERCIAL PAPER

[¶**901**]   Checks, certificates of deposit, notes, drafts, and all forms of negotiable instruments except money, documents of title, or investment securities are governed by Article 3 of the Uniform Commercial Code (Commercial Paper). Provisions of Article 3 of the UCC are also subject to the provisions of the Articles on bank deposits and collections (Article 4) and secure transactions (Article 9). Both Articles 3 and 4 are in effect in each of the 50 states and the District of Columbia. Louisiana was the last state to adopt Article 3, in 1975.

[¶902]   THE IMPORTANCE OF NEGOTIABILITY

"Substitutes for currency" is the best definition of negotiable instruments. Essentially, negotiable instruments are contracts to pay money—though, unlike nonnegotiable contracts, once they are passed to a third party they are no longer subject to the defenses of nonpayment that may be used in an ordinary contract.

[¶903]   TYPES OF COMMERCIAL PAPER

The following are the types of promises that, if in writing, will form negotiable instruments (UCC §3-104(2)):

(a) A draft (bill of exchange), if it is an order;

(b) A check, if it is a draft drawn on a bank and made payable on demand;

(c) A certificate of deposit, if it is an acknowledgment by a bank of receipt of money with the requirement that it be repaid;

(d) A note, if it is a promise other than a certificate of deposit.

It is important to recognize that the terms draft, check, certificate of deposit, and note may also refer to instruments that are not negotiable—the qualification following each of those terms is what makes them a negotiable instrument.

[¶904]   PROMISSORY NOTES AND BILLS OF EXCHANGE

A promissory note is a written promise to pay a certain sum at a future time or on demand. Installment notes, mortgage notes, and collateral notes are some examples of promissory notes. Even if a note is not for a definite sum (e.g., for a specified amount plus interest), it may nonetheless be a promissory note because a certain sum is defined as either being a stated or determinable amount. Bills of exchange—a check or draft instrument—differ from promissory notes because the maker or drawer orders a drawee (bank) or acceptor to pay. In a promissory note, the issuer promises to pay.

Simple time and demand notes with interest, judgment notes, secured notes, installment notes, and other varied forms of notes are found in *IBP Forms of Business Agreements and Resolutions.*

[¶905]   **HOW TO MAKE A NOTE NEGOTIABLE**

In order to make a promissory note negotiable, UCC §3-104(1) sets forth the following requirements. The note must be:
☐ A writing,
☐ Signed by the maker or drawer,
☐ Containing an unconditional promise (or order) to pay a sum certain in money,
☐ Containing no other promise (order, obligation, or power),
☐ Payable on demand or at a definite time,
☐ Payable to order or to bearer.

[¶906]   **MAKING A PROMISE UNCONDITIONAL**

Conditional promises are sufficient to defeat negotiability of an instrument. UCC §3-105 provides a number of instances when certain qualifications that may appear to make a promise conditional do not do so. In the chart below, several different types of provisions, commonly found in commercial paper, are listed. Each relates to certain "qualifications" that might effect conditionality; the UCC has legislatively stated that in the examples below, there is no effect directly or indirectly on negotiability.

Type of Provision in Note	Rule under UCC
Statement in note that it was given in exchange for an executory promise (i.e., one still to be carried out).	Not conditional; note is negotiable.
Promise to pay is expressly conditioned on carrying out executory promise.	Conditional; not negotiable.
Informational references—e.g., nature of the consideration given for the note; the transaction that gave rise to the note; promise to pay matures in *accordance with* or *as per* some transaction.	Not conditional; references to a separate agreement or that note arises out of the agreement, and references to letter of credit under which the notes are drawn do not create conditions or affect negotiability.
Statement that the note is *subject to* or *governed by* another instrument.	Conditional; not negotiable.
Recital of the security given in so-called title security notes.	Not conditional; negotiable.
Statement that note is to be paid from a particular fund.	Conditional; not negotiable.

Type of Provision in Note	Rule under UCC
Same as above, but note is issued by a government, government agency, or government unit; or note is issued by a partnership, unincorporated association, trust, or estate payable out of the entire assets of the issuer.	Not conditional; negotiable.

[¶907] PROMISE TO PAY A SUM CERTAIN IN MONEY

In order for the amount of the note to qualify as a sum certain, the holder must be able to determine from the instrument itself the amount that is payable. Computations are permissible—such as a requirement for interest at a specified percentage rate. However, wording such as "current interest rates" render the instrument nonnegotiable because the computation cannot be made from the instrument itself.

Where the language of the contract provides that the holder *may* pay taxes, assessments, and insurance if the obligor fails to do so, and then recover what is paid from the obligor, the instrument is nonnegotiable because of the uncertainty as to the sum actually owed (Opinion Attorney General Iowa, No. 65-7-5, 1965).

If a note provides for interest at a particular percentage, the phrase "or at maximum legal rates" has been held to be an expressed provision to pay a definitely ascertainable maximum legal rate and no more, therefore making it negotiable *(Woodhouse, Drake, and Carey, Ltd. v. Anderson,* 307 N.Y.S. 2d 113, Supreme Ct. N.Y., 1970).

[¶908] ADDITIONS TO A SUM CERTAIN

Following is a checklist of what may be included in addition to a fixed monetary sum that will not render an instrument nonnegotiable.

☐ Payments to be made with stated interest and stated installments.

☐ Payments to be made with stated different rates of interest before or after default of a specific date.

☐ Payment to be reduced by a stated discount for early payment.

☐ Additional payment required if paid after maturity.

☐ Payment to be with exchange or less exchange, whether at a fixed rate or at current rate.

☐ Provision for acceleration of payment (UCC §3-106).

☐ Provision for payment with costs of collection or attorneys' fees or both upon default (UCC §3-106). But consult local law as to validity and enforceability of this type of provision. Even in states where these provisions are unenforceable, the note's negotiability isn't otherwise affected, whether the provision is for a percentage or a fixed amount. In any event, only reasonable fees will be allowed (UCC §3-106(e)).

☐　Provision for payment in foreign currency (UCC §3-107). The UCC provides that *unless otherwise agreed*, an instrument payable in foreign currency "may be satisfied by payment of that number of dollars which the stated foreign currency will purchase at the buying sight rate for that currency on the day on which the instrument is payable, if payable on demand, on the day of demand."

[¶909]　　　　　## ADDITIONS TO SUM CERTAIN
AFFECTING NEGOTIABILITY

Provisions permitting interest to be computed at the "current rate" render an instrument nonnegotiable since the sum payable is not certain. Provision to pay taxes levied on commercial paper would also render the instrument nonnegotiable according to judicial decisions (the UCC itself is silent).

[¶910]　　　　　## WHEN THE NOTE IS PAYABLE

In order for an instrument to be negotiable it must either be payable at a specified time or on demand. To the extent that a note provides for payment at or before a specified date, it is considered payable at a definite time *(Mecham v. United States Bank of Arizona,* 489 P. 2d 247, Arizona, 1971).

[¶911]　　　　　## DEMAND INSTRUMENTS

Demand instruments are payable at sight or on presentation (UCC §3-108). Use of the phrase "payable on demand" or "on demand promises to pay" removes any ambiguity. The holder of the note has the option to call for payment at any time and the maker has the option of paying at any time.

[¶912]　　　　　## PAYABLE AT A FIXED TIME

The time of payment is definite only if it can be determined from the face of the instrument (UCC §3-109). Promissory notes payable at a fixed period of time after the death of the maker are not considered negotiable. However, a postdated check payable at the death of the drawer or at the stated date is an enforceable negotiable instrument *(Smith v. Gentilotti,* 20 UCC Reg. Serv. 1222, Mass., 1977).

[¶913]　　　　　## ACCELERATION CLAUSES

An acceleration clause does not alter the effect of payment at a definite time. If the holder of a note feels insecure about payment, and an acceleration clause permits a calling in for payment at whim, the note is nonetheless negotiable (UCC §3-109(1)(c)). Under the prior negotiable instruments law, this would have rendered the note nonnegotiable.

[¶914]   **WORDS OF NEGOTIABILITY**

In order to render an instrument negotiable, words of negotiability (payable to order or bearer) must be used. A note payable to order is payable to (1) either the order, or (2) assigns of a named person, or (3) to him, or (4) to his order. Both order and bearer instruments are negotiable—although there is a significant difference between the two that dictates the use of order instruments in most situations. If a bearer instrument is either lost or stolen and winds up in the hands of a bona fide purchaser for value, the instrument is good and cannot be defeated in an action for payment. Order paper, on the other hand, is protected against theft even through fraudulent endorsement by the payee.

If a note meets the basic requirement of order paper, it may be payable to the maker, a payee not the maker, or two or more payees together or in the alternative. If payable to two or more payees, give thought to whether they're to be joint tenants with a right of survivorship or simply tenants in common, and use clear enough language to accomplish the intention of the client.

The UCC provides that an order instrument may be payable to an estate, trust, or fund (§3-110), in which case it is payable to the representative or to his successor. The UCC also provides that an order instrument may be payable (1) to an office or an officer by his title, in which case it is payable to the principal, but the incumbent or his successors may act as the holder, or (2) to a partnership or unincorporated association, in which case it is payable to the partnership or association and may be transferred by any person authorized by it. UCC §3-117 further provides that an instrument made payable to a named person with the addition of words describing him as an agent, officer, or fiduciary is payable to the principal.

It's clear that a note will be considered bearer paper if it's payable to: (1) bearer; (2) a named person or bearer; or (3) cash or the order of cash. Occasionally a note will be issued payable to ''order of bearer.'' This usually happens when a printed form of order note is used and the word ''bearer'' is filled in where the name of the payee is intended to go. In such case some authorities had taken the view that this is an order note. The UCC, however, rejects this view and makes it a bearer instrument (UCC §3-111).

In the case of a note payable ''to the order of,'' the UCC makes clear that it is to be treated as an incomplete instrument.

Where checks bore a restrictive notation stating that the instrument would be dishonored unless a particular contract was awarded, the instrument made as a bid deposit could not be considered as either a draft, check, or demand note within the meaning of the requirement that a bid deposit be made payable on demand (Opinion of the Comptroller General of the United States #B-162984, 1968). This and any other limitation upon payability to order or bearer should be sufficient to negate negotiability.

[¶915]   ADDITIONAL AND OMITTED TERMS THAT DO NOT AFFECT NEGOTIABILITY

Following is a checklist of terms that may be added or omitted without affecting an instrument's negotiability (UCC §3-112).

☐ Statement of consideration is omitted.

☐ Place where the instrument is drawn or payable is omitted.

☐ Statement that collateral has been given to secure obligations either under the instrument or otherwise is included.

☐ Statement that, in case of default, the holder may realize on or otherwise dispose of collateral is included.

☐ Promise or power to maintain or protect collateral, or to give additional collateral, is included.

☐ Term authorizing confession of judgment, if the instrument is not paid when due, is included.

☐ Term purporting to waive the benefit of any law intended to protect the obligor is included.

☐ Term in a draft providing that the payee's indorsing or cashing the draft acknowledges full satisfaction of an obligation of the drawer is included.

☐ Statement in a draft drawn in a set of parts (to the effect that the order is effective only if one part is honored) is included.

See ¶917 for ways to use some of these provisions.

[¶916]   PROVISIONS TO INCLUDE OR AVOID IN A NEGOTIABLE INSTRUMENT

Interest Rates—Usury: It is permissible to include a provision for interest at a particular rate, or at maximum legal rates. Use of this type of provision does not render the note usurious: The note remains negotiable, even though it contains an express provision to pay a definitely ascertainable maximum legal rate, and not more *(Woodhouse, Drake and Carey Ltd. v. Anderson,* 307 N.Y.S. 2d 113, N.Y. Sup. Ct., 1970)

Also see: "State Guide to Interest Rates" in the Appendix.

Sale of Collateral: A provision can be incorporated in a note that will authorize sale of collateral by the holder of the note, without destroying negotiability of the note. Such a provision might be desirable if the maker of the note doesn't have an especially good credit rating—and so is required to give collateral that may be sold pursuant to the authority in the provision. Under the UCC it may be made operative upon any default, including default in the payment of interest (§3-112(b)). The UCC also permits a clause containing a promise or a power to maintain or protect collateral, or to give additional collateral, whether on demand or on some other condition, which will not affect negotiability. See also UCC §9-504.

For forms of collateral notes, see *IBP Forms of Business Agreements and Resolutions.*

Confession of Judgment: A confession of judgment is authorized by the UCC only if the instrument is not paid when due (§3-112). If the clause allows judgment to be confessed prior to the default, the instrument is nonnegotiable *(Cheltam National Bank v. Snelling*, 326 A. 2d 557, Penn. Superior Ct. 1974).

Notes Payable at a Bank: A draft drawn on a bank payable when it falls due out of any funds of the maker or acceptor available for payment may be considered either an order or an authorization for the bank to pay it. UCC §3-121 permits the various jurisdictions to elect either of these choices. Alternative A states that a note payable at a bank is equivalent to a draft drawn on the bank; Alternative B says that the note or acceptance is not an order.

Alternative "A" has been adopted in Alaska, Connecticut, Delaware, District of Columbia, Hawaii, Kentucky, Maine, Massachusetts, Missouri, Nevada, New Hampshire, New Jersey, New York, North Dakota, Ohio, Pennsylvania, Rhode Island, Texas, Vermont, Virgin Islands, West Virginia, and Wyoming.

Alternative "B" has been adopted in Alabama, Arizona, Arkansas, California, Colorado, Florida, Georgia, Idaho, Illinois, Indiana, Iowa, Kansas, Louisiana, Maryland, Michigan, Minnesota, Mississippi, Montana, Nebraska, New Mexico, North Carolina, Oklahoma, Oregon, South Carolina, South Dakota, Tennessee, Utah, Virginia, Washington, and Wisconsin. Both California and Virginia have adopted additional modifications to Alternative "B."

Waiver of Benefit of Any Law: A provision under which the obligor waives the benefit of any law intended for his benefit will not destroy negotiability under the UCC, although it might be invalid under local law. A waiver of the benefits of the statute of limitations, for example, is invalid under the law of many states. On the other hand, a waiver of presentment and notice of dishonor is universally recognized as valid, and is included in most notes as a matter of course.

[¶917]   **TRADE ACCEPTANCES AND**
                          BANK ACCEPTANCES

Trade acceptances have already been defined as drafts drawn on the purchaser of goods and accepted by him. If, instead of the draft being drawn on the purchaser, it is drawn on the purchaser's bank, which has agreed with the purchaser to accept on his behalf, then on acceptance by the bank there is a bank acceptance.

Here's how a bank acceptance might be used in foreign commerce: Let's say a person in San Francisco wants to sell $5,000 worth of widgets to a merchant in Yokohama, Japan, with whom he's never done business and whom he doesn't know. He might make arrangements with his bank in Yokohama to accept drafts drawn on it up to the amount of $5,000 on presentation of specified documents (bill of lading, insurance papers, etc.) The bank on presentation of the draft and documents will accept as agreed on and the seller will have a piece of paper, assuming that the Yokohama bank is sound and well-known, that will be readily convertible into cash. A trade acceptance in that situation would obviously not be so readily convertible.

[¶918]   DISCOUNTING TRADE ACCEPTANCES

Under Federal Reserve Board rules, trade acceptances may be rediscounted provided maturity is not more than 90 days from the date (nine months may be permissible for agricultural or livestock acceptances). If a draft is payable at sight or on demand, any Federal Reserve Bank may purchase or discount the draft if it arose in connection with a domestic shipment or foreign shipment of nonperishable, readily marketable goods. There are four basic requirements for this:

☐ The acceptance must bear on its face the statement that it arises out of the purchase and sale of goods.

☐ The acceptance must be a clear, definite order to pay without any qualifying conditions.

☐ The acceptance must be written across the face of the draft.

☐ The draft must be conspicuously labeled "Trade Acceptance."

The Code provides that an otherwise unconditional promise or order does not become unconditional merely because the nature of the underlying transaction is stated on the face of the instrument (UCC §3-105(b)). Therefore, this phrase should be included on an acceptance:

"The transaction which gives rise to this instrument is the purchase of goods by the acceptor from the drawer."

Any variance from this form may involve the risk of having the instrument declared nonnegotiable. For example, the addition of words such as "per invoice of" or "as per contract" has been held to affect negotiability. A title retention clause has also been held to render it nonnegotiable. However, the UCC contains provisions in §3-105 that may alter the result of these decisions and permit references such as those quoted above and to retention of title.

In any case, the following clauses may be inserted without affecting negotiability:

☐ Waiver of exemption and attorneys' fees.

☐ Provision for costs of collection.

☐ Provision for payment of interest after maturity.

[¶919]   CHECKLIST FOR TRADE ACCEPTANCES

Here are the major additional points that must be kept in mind in dealing with trade acceptances. Because these rules aren't limited only to trade and bank acceptances but apply to all drafts, they are discussed below under a separate heading at ¶920.

☐ A trade acceptance should never be used if you wouldn't grant an open account credit.

☐ A trade acceptance shouldn't be used to cover a past due account.

☐ If the seller indorses an acceptance, he guarantees that it will be met at maturity. The seller must, therefore, be sure that the paper is good.

☐ An acceptance form authorizing a discount if paid before a certain date may render the instrument nonnegotiable according to some authorities. Make this arrangement outside the draft; e.g., 2%, 10 days, net 30, would give the purchaser the option of discounting in 10 days.

☐ Make sure that the acceptance form matches the terms of the sale.

☐ If a trade acceptance is made payable at a bank, as a general rule, it will be treated as a check drawn on a bank.

☐ The acceptor of a trade acceptance has the same right to stop payment as the maker of a check would have.

☐ If the drawer of a trade acceptance would otherwise have a mechanic's lien for the goods, he won't as a general rule lose his lien merely by taking the trade acceptance. However, watch out if the time of payment of the trade acceptance runs beyond the time for enforcing the mechanic's lien. Some courts have held that this amounts to waiver of the lien.

[¶920]   **UCC RULES AS TO TRADE ACCEPTANCE**

A drawee isn't liable on a draft or check until he assents in writing to the order of the drawer. This assent is called acceptance in the case of a draft and certification in the case of a check.

Under the UCC, acceptance may be simply by signature. It is perfectly clear that the acceptance must be written on the draft (§3-410). The drawee's failure to accept before the close of business the day after presentment does not operate as a constructive acceptance (UCC §3-506). It should be noted that the UCC's rejection of the doctrine of constructive acceptance in case of refusal of the drawee to accept or return the draft doesn't mean that the drawee can't be held liable for conversion or breach of a contractual obligation. On the contrary, UCC §3-419 recognizes the possibility of liability for conversion and UCC §3-409 recognizes the possibility of contractual liability.

The UCC provides that if the holder of an instrument assents to an acceptance varying the terms of the draft, each drawer and indorser who does not affirmatively assent to the variance is discharged (§3-412(3)).

The UCC contemplates that the drawee named in the bill is the person to be looked to in the first instance for acceptance, but states that you may designate another person to whom resort may be had in case of dishonor by the named drawee. This secondary party is known as a "referee in case of need." The usual form followed is to write below the drawee's name: "In case of need apply to John Doe." This will give the holder the option to resort to the person secondarily named. He may, however, ignore this and treat the instrument as dishonored if the drawee refuses to accept (UCC §4-503).

[¶921]   **CERTIFICATION OF CHECKS**

Certification of checks is acceptance (UCC §3-411(1)). Usually, a certification discharges the drawer and all prior endorsers, but a certification requested by the drawer continues liability for that party. Unless otherwise agreed, a bank is not required to certify a check (UCC §3-411(2)).

The statutory effect of a certification is to render the bank directly liable on the instrument when it is properly endorsed. A drawer has no power to stop payment on a check following certification whether the certification was made at the request of the holder or the drawer *(Maintenance Service Inc. v. Royal National Bank of New York,* New York Sup. Ct., 1967). However, if a bank voluntarily chooses to dishonor a certified check—which it might do for a good customer—the holder will have a valid cause of action against the bank. There have been some lower court rumblings with respect to a stop-payment order on a bank check; however, the consensus is that even though businessmen treat bank checks like cash, it is not proper for a bank check to discharge a buyer from the underlying obligation under UCC §3-802.

Under the UCC, a certification must be in writing and signed by the drawee (§3-410 and §3-411).

The UCC says certification must be on the check itself. The UCC rejects all forms of extrinsic acceptances or certifications.

Even if the drawer's signature is forged, the certifying bank will be liable to a holder in due course—on the theory that it knows the drawer's signature and by certifying, warrants its genuineness.

Under UCC §3-413, the certification relates to the check as it is at the time of certification and not as it was originally. So even though the amount of the check has been increased or the name of the payee changed, the bank will be fully liable—provided that the bank's form of certification doesn't undertake to pay the check only as originally drawn. In the past, many banks have adopted this form of limited certification.

[¶922]   POSTDATING AND ANTEDATING CHECKS

Negotiability of a check is not necessarily affected by the fact that it is postdated, provided the bank handling the check acts in good faith and in accordance with the obligations to use ordinary care in handling customer funds. However, the purchaser of a postdated instrument who knows at the time of the purchase that the instrument is postdated may be precluded from asserting a holder-in-due-course defense. If a check is antedated or postdated, and it is payable either on demand or after a fixed time, the stated date controls.

[¶923]   STOPPING PAYMENTS ON CHECKS

The UCC permits orders for stop payment on a check that has been issued. Payments made in violation of an effective stop order are improper and the bank is liable for damages suffered (though the customer has the burden of proving the amount of loss) (§4-403(3)). Payment may be stopped any time before acceptance, certification, or actual payment. Both oral and written stop payment orders are recognized. An oral order is good for only two weeks (14 days), while a written one is valid for six months unless renewed in writing (UCC §4-403(2)). It is useful to remember that checks are considered stale after 30 days, and thus a written stop payment order rarely must be renewed. This Section of the UCC is in effect in 50 states, the District of Columbia, and the Virgin Islands. Louisiana adopted Article 4 of the UCC effective January 1, 1975. Minor variations of this Section apply in Arizona, California, District of Columbia, Florida, New Mexico, Nevada, Texas, and Utah. Consult local law in these states.

[¶924] BAD CHECK LAWS

An individual who makes or issues or negotiates a check knowing that it will bounce violates the "bad check laws," which are individual to each state. Generally, the offense is a misdemeanor (although it may be a felony, depending upon the amount involved). At common law, a bank was permitted to recover the amount of an overdraft that it paid against a customer's account. This is given full credence in UCC §4-401(1), which permits a bank to charge the customer whenever the customer writes a check that is in other respects properly payable from his account, even if payment creates an overdraft. In this instance, the customer remains liable and the check is good. The bank usually imposes a service charge or treats it as a loan. The basic requirement is that the bank act in good faith in making payment to a holder.

Intent to defraud may generally be proved by the mere issuance of the check and its subsequent dishonor for lack of funds. The presumption is, of course, rebuttable.

[¶925] HOW AN INSTRUMENT IS NEGOTIATED

You can negotiate an instrument either by delivery or by indorsement and delivery. If it's "bearer" paper, delivery will be enough. For "order" paper, it will take indorsement plus delivery.

Set forth below in checklist form are the matters to be considered in making or dealing with indorsements:

☐ *Who Must Make:* An indorsement must be made by the holder or someone authorized by him.

☐ *Where Made:* Usually on the instrument and on the back side. The use of an allonge (a writing attached to the instrument) is acceptable only when necesary, for example, if the instrument is covered with indorsements and there's no more room.

☐ *Ambiguous Signature:* Unless the instrument clearly indicates a signature is made in some other capacity, it will be considered an indorsement (UCC §3-402).

☐ *Two or More Indorsees:* Indorsement in favor of two or more indorsees, e.g., "Pay A and B," will be effective negotiation. Indorsees will normally take as tenants in common, rather than joint tenants. Spell out the desired result in order to make sure.

☐ *Partial Assignments:* An indorsement that purports to transfer less than the entire instrument or the unpaid balance under it is a partial assignment and will be ineffective as a negotiation. Examples of partial assignments: "Pay A one-half"; "Pay A two-thirds and B one-third."

☐ *Words Accompanying Indorsement:* Words of assignment, condition, waiver, limitation or disclaimer of liability, or guaranty will not, under UCC §3-202(4), prevent an indorsement from being effective as a transfer of the indorser's interest, but they may affect the rights and liabilities of the indorser, the indorsee, or subsequent holders.

☐ *Misspelling or Wrong Name:* Under the UCC, if an instrument is payable to someone under a misspelled name or a name other than his own, he may indorse in either name or both and a person paying value for the instrument can require indorsement in both (§3-203). As a transferee, you would insist on both names.

☐ *Maiden Name of Married Woman:* If the paper uses the maiden name of a woman and she tries to negotiate by her married name, have her use both names in her indorsement.

☐ *Rights if Order Paper Transferred Without Indorsement:* In such case the transferee gets whatever rights his transferor had, and if the transferee paid value, he can insist on indorsement, but he gets status of holder in due course only from the time of indorsement and not from the time of transfer (UCC §3-201).

☐ *Blank, Special, Qualified, Restrictive, or Conditional Indorsements:* These are the various types of indorsements that may be used. Set out at ¶926 is a table listing these various types of indorsements giving specimen forms of each type, and showing their meanings and effect.

☐ *Effect of Indorsement:* An unrestricted, unqualified, and unconditional indorsement passes title to the paper and makes the indorser secondarily liable to subsequent holders—that is, the indorser impliedly contracts to pay if the party primarily liable, the maker, drawer, or acceptor, fails to. The effect of various types of indorsement under the UCC is shown in the following table.

[¶926] **TABLE OF INDORSEMENTS—
THEIR MEANING AND EFFECT**

Type and Wording	*Meaning and Effect Under the UCC*
Blank:	
(1) Kay Johnson	Specifies no indorsee of person to whom paper payable; payable to bearer and negotiable by delivery until specially indorsed (§3-204(2)).
(2) Pay to bearer Kay Johnson	Blank indorsement may be converted into special indorsement by holder (§3-204(3)).
Special:	
(1) Pay to John Jones or order Kay Johnson	Specifies person to whom or to whose order instrument is payable and may be negotiated only by special indorsee's indorsement (§3-204(1)).
(2) Pay to order of John Jones Kay Johnson	

Type and Wording	*Meaning and Effect Under the UCC*
Qualified:	
(1) Without recourse Kay Johnson	Code doesn't use term but §3-414 makes clear that ordinary contract of indorser can be disclaimed or qualified.
Restrictive:	
(1) Pay to order of First National Bank for Deposit Kay Johnson	Makes bank agent of depositor for collection and credit to depositor's account. Any transferee other than intermediary bank must act consistently with purpose of collection. Does not prevent further negotiation. See §3-205, 3-206.
(2) For collection Jane Silver	Makes indorsee agent of indorser for collection. Comments in re paragraph (1) above apply. Relatively rare.
(3) Pay any bank all prior indorsements guaranteed Second National Bank	Indicates purpose of deposit or collection. Except for intermediary bank must act consistently with purpose. Does not prevent further negotiation. See §4-205, 4-206. "Prior indorsements guaranteed" is implied (§4-207(3)).
(4) Pay any bank, banker, or trust company Third National Bank	Common form used by banks but not expressly mentioned in UCC. See comments re paragraph (3) above.
(5) Pay to John Jones only Jane Silver	Same as unrestricted indorsement. Further transfer or negotiation not prevented. See §3-205, 3-206. Same is true of any other indorsements purporting to bar further transfer.
(6) Pay to John Jones as trustee for Jack Smith Kay Johnson	Rule is the same as for restrictive indorsements for deposit or collection except here the duty to act consistently with indorsement is limited to first taker. See §3-206(4).
(7) Pay John Jones as agent for Jack Smith Joe Rose	See comments re (6).
(8) Pay John Jones for Jack Smith Jim Kelly	See comments re (6).
Conditional:	
(1) Pay the within sum if and only if the SS Roe arrives in N.Y. by Sept. 30, 1981. John Doe.	Rarely used. Treated as restrictive indorsement. Payor *must* disregard condition. Collecting bank not affected by. Other indorsees must see to application of proceeds and to extent they do become holders in due course and further negotiation not prevented (§3-205, 3-206).

[¶927] **CHANGING BEARER PAPER TO ORDER PAPER (AND VICE VERSA)**

The last indorsement on order paper controls the next negotiation. If the last indorsement is in blank, the order paper is bearer paper negotiable by mere delivery. If, however, the indorsement is special, it is order paper that may be negotiated only pursuant to the special indorsement. Bearer paper that is specially indorsed becomes payable to the order of the special indorsee and may be further negotiated only by that individual's indorsement (UCC §3-204). A blank indorsement may be converted into a special indorsement by writing over the indorsee's signature the words "payable to the order of (specified person)." This protects against the possibility of loss or theft of paper and acquisition by a bona fide purchaser.

[¶928] **PRESENTMENT, NOTICE OF DISHONOR, AND PROTEST**

In order to charge parties who are secondarily liable with liability if the primary party fails to pay an instrument, presentment is required. Presentment is a demand for payment or acceptance on the part of the maker, drawee, acceptor, or other payor by or on behalf of the holder.

Notice of dishonor is an indication of an item that a primarily liable party has refused to pay or accept.

In order to make an indorser liable, presentment and notice of dishonor are both necessary (UCC §3-501).

[¶929] **RIGHTS OF A HOLDER IN DUE COURSE**

The single most important feature of any negotiable instrument is that a holder in due course takes the instrument free of any claims or defenses that would be available against another holder—for example, an assignment of a claim. In order to qualify as a holder in due course, a holder must have:

☐ taken the instrument for value,
☐ taken the instrument in good faith,
☐ taken the instrument without notice that it is overdue,
☐ taken the instrument without notice that it has been dishonored,
☐ taken the instrument without any knowledge of any defense or claim against it
(UCC §3-302).

Purchases of limited interests in a negotiable instrument may qualify for holder-in-due-course treatment to the extent of the interest purchased (UCC §3-302(4)).

The Federal Trade Commission has acted to preserve certain consumer claims and defenses against negotiable instruments that they have executed that are subsequently sold or assigned to an individual who would otherwise be able to raise a holder-in-due-course defense against the consumer. On May 14, 1976, the FTC Trade Regulation Rule concerning preservation of consumer claims and defenses became effective (16 CFR Part 433). In adopting the rule, the FTC determined that it was an unfair and deceptive practice in trade for the seller in the course of financing or arranging the financing of a purchase of consumer goods or services to employ any procedure that rendered the consumer's duty to pay independent of the seller's duty to fulfill his obligations. The rule specifically requires the insertion of a clause in the consumer credit contract to permit the consumer to raise against the creditor any claim or defense that he could raise against the seller under applicable law.

The clause must be in 10-point boldface type, and must contain the following: "Notice: Any holder of this consumer credit contract is subject to all claims and defenses which the debtor could assert against the seller of goods or services obtained pursuant hereto or with the proceeds hereof. Recovery hereunder shall not exceed amounts paid by the debtor hereunder." The same provision must be included in purchase-money loan agreements; the FTC rule defines a purchase-money loan as a cash advance, on which a finance charge is imposed, made to facilitate the purchase of goods or services from a seller who arranges credit or is affiliated with the lender. (See ¶933-935 for further discussion of seller-lender affiliation.) A consumer does not have the right to withhold payment unilaterally under the rule. Both the manner and procedure by which any buyer may assert a claim or defense are governed by the terms of applicable state law and contractual obligations.

[¶930] **REAL DEFENSES AGAINST A HOLDER
IN DUE COURSE**

Although personal defenses may not be asserted against a holder in due course, "real" defenses may be successfully asserted against him. Failure of consideration, mistake, and breach of warranty are considered personal defenses and, consequently, not assertable against a holder in due course. Forgery and fraud in the execution, however, are real defenses that may be raised. Infancy is a real defense to the extent that it would be a defense against a simple contract (an infant may assert the defense against a holder in due course, even though the effect of infancy would be to make the instrument voidable, not void) (UCC §3-305(2)(a)). Misrepresentation to induce a party to sign an instrument (fraud in the inducement) is also a real defense (UCC §3-305(2)(c)). Discharge and bankruptcy or insolvency proceedings are also good against a holder in due course.

[¶931] **RIGHTS AND LIABILITIES OF A HOLDER
NOT IN DUE COURSE**

Holders of a negotiable instrument who have not taken in due course take subject to the following:
☐ All valid claims against it on the part of any person;
☐ All defenses of any party available in a simple contract action;
☐ The defense of no consideration;
☐ The defense of nonperformance of any conditioned precedent;

☐   The defense of improper delivery or improper payment inconsistent with the terms of a restrictive indorsement.

[¶932]   DISCHARGE OF UNDERLYING OBLIGATION

If a bank is either the drawor, maker, or acceptor of an instrument that is taken for the settlement of an underlying obligation, the obligation is discharged and there is no recourse against the underlying obligor (UCC §3-802(1)(a)). In the case of any other obligation taken for an instrument, the instrument is discharged, and action may be maintained on either the instrument or the obligation. Taking in good faith a check that is not postdated does not in and of itself extend the time on the original obligation so as to discharge a surety.

[¶933]   AFFILIATED COMPANIES AND THE HOLDER IN DUE COURSE

If a seller is affiliated with the creditor by common control, contract, or business arrangement, the FTC rules require that the seller use the notice found in ¶929 in a consumer loan contract. Common control is defined as when a creditor and seller are ''functionally part of the same business entity,'' or if the affiliation has been created by contract or business arrangement. The arrangement may be oral or in writing. Commercial checking accounts are not affiliations between banks and customers within the meaning of the rule, nor is a commercial credit agreement between a seller and credit institution that has no relationship to the consumer sales activities or the financing. The FTC has further stated that the mere fact that a creditor issues a joint proceeds check to the seller and the buyer (which is common in a purchase of an automobile, for example) does not necessarily constitute a business arrangement or contract if the seller and lender must confer in order to perfect the security agreement under applicable law.

[¶934]   REFERRALS AND THE HOLDER-IN-DUE-COURSE RULE

Sellers are prohibited from accepting proceeds of purchase-money loans under any credit contract unless the required notice is given when the seller ''refers consumers to the creditor.'' The FTC has stated this provision is intended to deal with those situations in which a seller cooperates with a lender to steer consumers towards that credit source on a continuing basis. This differs from affiliation, and requires that seller and creditor be engaged in a cooperative or concerted conduct to channel or direct a consumer to a particular lender. The fact that a seller may suggest credit sources to his customers does not invoke the rule.

When a seller and lender work together to arrange financing for the customers of a seller, the notice must be incorporated into the loan contract. The FTC states that the conduct must occur on a continuing basis—that occasional referrals not a part of the ordinary business routine of the seller are insufficient to trigger the rule. The FTC emphasizes that the fact that no money changes hands between the seller and the lender for these services is not important. That the seller and the lender are cooperatively engaged in an effort that is mutually beneficial to their separate business interests is considered sufficient.

[¶935]   EXAMPLES OF THE HOLDER-
              IN-DUE-COURSE RULE

(1) The creditor makes an agreement with a seller to maintain loan application forms in the seller's office. When a buyer requests financing, the seller assists the buyer in filling out the forms. This relationship constitutes an *affiliation*, and notice must be included in the consumer credit contract.

(2) Seller regularly sends customers to a particular creditor, who in turn agrees to provide favorable financing arrangements for the seller's inventory, or directly or indirectly provides some other consideration. Seller and lender are *affiliated,* and notice must be included in the consumer credit contract.

(3) Seller routinely suggests that customers in need of credit go to a particular source of financing. Although the creditor is aware that seller is referring some of his customers, creditor provides no tacit or explicit *quid pro quo.* Notice is not required.

(4) Buyer asks seller for credit sources and the seller provides a list of lenders in the area and information on the general availability of credit merely as an accommodation to his customers. Seller does not contact the creditor to arrange credit nor is there any affiliation with the creditors. Notice is not required.

(5) Seller has an existing referral or affiliation contractual relationship with the creditor. A buyer, on his own, goes to that very creditor to obtain a loan to purchase an item from the seller. The notice must be included.

[¶936]   FOR FURTHER REFERENCE . . .

"Assault II - Attack on the Holder in Due Course Doctrine, Waiver of Defense Clauses and Direct Loan Immunity," 83 Commercial Law Journal 319-34 (August/September 1978).

Bailey, *Brady on Bank Checks*, Banking Law Journal.

Clark, John J.; Bailey, Henry J., III; and Young, Robert, Jr., *Bank Deposits and Collections.*

Edmonds, J.W. III, "Commercial Paper, Bank Deposits and Collection, Letters of Credit," 33 Business Lawyer 1893-915 (April 1978).

Fox, F.H., "Stopping Payment on a Cashier's Check," 19 Boston College Law Review 683-97 (May 1978).

"FTC's Holder in Due Course Rule: an Ineffective Means of Achieving Optimality in the Consumer Credit Market," 25 UCLA Law Review 821-61 (April 1978).

Littlefield, N.O., "Corporate Signatures on Negotiable Instruments," 55 Denver Law Journal 61-95 (1978).

"Overview of Promissory Notes Under the Federal Securities Laws," 6 Fordham Urban Law Journal 529-52 (Spring 1978).

Penney, Norman, "Uniform Commercial Code—A Summary of Articles 3 & 4," The Banking Law Journal, American Law Institute, Philadelphia, Pa.

Willier and Hart, *Forms and Procedures Under the U.C.C.*, Matthew Bender, New York, N.Y.

COMPENSATION AND FRINGE BENEFITS

[¶1001]   Compensation includes salary and bonuses and so-called "fringe benefits" which are an essential ingredient in attracting key personnel. Fringe benefits include such arrangements as pension and profit-sharing plans, deferred compensation arrangements, stock options, insurance, death benefits, low-interest loans, and employee stock purchase plans.

[¶1002]   **REASONABLE COMPENSATION**

All payments to compensate an employee for services rendered are tax deductible—provided they are "reasonable." The question of reasonableness frequently arises concerning payments to stockholder-employees of closely held corporations. If the payment to a stockholder-employee is compensation, the company gets a tax deduction; if the payment is a dividend, the company gets no deduction.

The question of reasonable compensation is one of fact. Generally, it is the amount that would "ordinarily be paid for like services by like enterprises under like circumstances" (Reg. §1.162-7).

Items most frequently referred to by the courts in determining whether compensation paid to an employee is in fact reasonable include:

☐ Size and complexity of business.
☐ Comparison of salary payments to dividends (particularly in a small corporation).
☐ Payments for past services and compensation in prior years.
☐ Comparison of salary and the ownership of stock by the employee.
☐ Special qualifications of the employee.
☐ Scope and extent of the employee's work.
☐ General economic conditions.
☐ Rate of compensation for similar positions in other firms.
☐ The "arm's-length" salary that would ordinarily be paid.

[¶1003]   **BONUSES**

Bonuses, like salaries, may be deducted by the company in the year in which they are either paid or accrued—depending on the accounting method. It is possible for an employer to deduct a bonus in one taxable year even though it is paid in another, so long as the events that fix the amount of the liability have occurred. This general rule is not applicable when stockholders in a closely held corporation are involved. There, the company may deduct the accrued bonus provided that it is either paid or constructively received within two-and-a-half months after the close of the employer's taxable year. If later payment is made, §267 of the Code denies the deduction.

67

An employee on a cash basis is normally not taxed until he actually or "constructively" receives the bonus. An employee "contructively" receives a bonus when it is unconditionally made available to him. There must be an unrestricted right to the payment in order for constructive receipt to attach. If, within two-and-a-half months after the corporation's taxable year, the employee is in constructive receipt of the bonus the corporation qualifies for the compensation deduction (Reg. §1.267(a)-1(b)).

[¶1004]　　　**PENSION AND PROFIT-SHARING PLANS**

Pension and profit-sharing plans are two of the most attractive methods of compensation. In a typical arrangement, the company makes a contribution (or current payment) for the employee's services—but the money is not ordinarily available for the recipient's use until his or her retirement or termination of employment.

When a pension or profit-sharing plan qualifies under IRS rules, the company gets a tax deduction for its contributions. What's more, the contributions earn a tax-free return. The employee is not taxed until monies are withdrawn from the fund. Further, in the case of a profit-sharing plan, the worker's account may increase as a result of the reallocation of the "non-vested" units forfeited by employees who have left the job.

These are some of the tax advantages of pension and profit-sharing plans that qualify under IRC §401:

☐　The corporation can deduct contributions to the plan.

☐　Earnings on funds held by the plan are allowed to appreciate tax free.

☐　Lump-sum distributions on retirement, death, or other termination are taxed under a favorable income-averaging formula. Distributions attributable to pre-1974 contributions may be taxed at capital gain rates.

☐　Distributions paid out over a long period get special annuity tax treatment.

☐　Distributions are exempt from gift tax if the employee made no contributions to the plan.

☐　Death benefits attributable to the corporation's contributions are exempt from estate tax provided they are payable to a named beneficiary (not to the employee's estate) and payments are made in installments (or, if payment is in a lump sum, the recipient elects irrevocably to have the entire amount taxed as ordinary income without any 10-year averaging). Death benefits attributable to contributions made by an employee are subject to estate taxes.

☐　Up to $5,000 of death benefits provided by an employer can be received income tax free by the employee's beneficiary.

☐　Distributions are usually taxed at a lower rate because the employee receives them at a time (retirement) when he is in a lower tax bracket.

☐　Employees can also use the plan as a tax-sheltered savings account if the plan permits voluntary contributions.

[¶1005]   **PENSION OR PROFIT SHARING?**

Both pension and profit-sharing plans offer features that fill various corporate needs. Depending upon the objectives of the company, as well as potential profits, one type of plan may be better than the other. In choosing between a pension or a profit-sharing plan, a corporation must carefully analyze not only the needs of its employees, but also its own requirements. The cost of administration of the plan may also be a significant factor in making the determintion.

Comparison Between Profit-Sharing and Pension Plans

Profit-Sharing

(1) Generally, favors younger employees.
(2) Need not provide retirement benefits.
(3) Contributions can be made only from profits (includes accumulated earnings).
(4) Definite contribution formula not necessary; contributions need only be "recurring and substantial."
(5) No benefit formula.

(6) Annual contributions for any single participant (plus forfeitures and employee contributions exceeding 6% of his compensation) cannot exceed the lesser of $25,000* or 25% of his compensation. Tax-deductible contributions cannot exceed 15% of total compensation of all participants (carryovers may raise limit to 25% in some years).
(7) Forfeiture may be allocated under a nondiscriminatory formula in favor of remaining participants or may be used to reduce future employer contributions.
(8) No more than 49.9% of a participant's account may be invested in ordinary life insurance with the balance invested in stocks, bonds, or other investments. Entire account may be fully funded by retirement income endowment policies.
(9) If account is split funded with life insurance and other investments, death benefit

Pension

(1) Generally, favors older employees.
(2) Must provide retirement benefits.
(3) Contributions must be made for loss as well as for profitable years.
(4) Must have a definite contribution formula that will provide for definitely determinable benefits.
(5) In defined-benefit plans, annual benefits for any participant cannot exceed the lesser of $75,000* or 100%** of the three highest-paid consecutive years.

(6) Tax-deductible contributions at least to the extent of minimum funding requirements.

(7) Forfeitures must be used to decrease future contributions by employer.

(8) Same rule.

(9) Same rule.

---

*$25,000 and $75,000 limits to be adjusted by IRS annually for increases in cost of living. Last quarter of 1974 is the base. In 1978, the figures were $30,050 and $90,150.
**In a negotiated pension plan, benefits may exceed 100% of final average pay, up to $37,500 (adjusted for cost-of-living increases).

Profit-Sharing	Pension
may equal face value of policy plus value of other investments. If account is fully funded with retirement income endowment contracts, death benefits may equal face value of policy or cash value at death, whichever is larger.	
(10) May provide incidental health and accident benefits, disability benefits, and layoff benefits.	(10) May provide disability benefits, and only incidental post-retirement health and accident benefits. May not provide layoff benefits.
(11) Distributions may be made after a fixed number of years (e.g., at least two years of accumulation) sufficient to indicate that it is a deferred compensation plan.	(11) Distributions may be made upon retirement, disability, death, or other termination of employment; generally not during employment.

[¶1006]   CASH OR DEFERRED PROFIT-SHARING PLAN?

A qualified profit-sharing plan that allows participants to elect to take cash or defer receipt of benefits runs the risk of being disqualified if only highly paid employees elect to defer (since, in that case, the deferred compensation plan would be discriminatory in favor of the highly paid). The Revenue Act of 1978 amended IRC §401 to provide that a plan will not lose its qualified status merely because its participants are permitted to elect either deferred benefits or immediate cash.

To qualify, the plan must meet the §401(a) rules for qualification, must provide full immediate vesting of benefits, and must not discriminate. To meet the nondiscrimination test, the actual deferral percentage of the highest paid one-third of the employees must be either:

☐ Less than or equal to one-and-a-half times the deferral percentage of all other employees, OR

☐ Be within three percentage points of the deferral percentage of all other employees, and not more than two-and-a-half times the other employees' deferral percentage.

[¶1007]   SIMPLIFIED EMPLOYEE PENSIONS

The Revenue Act of 1978 amended §408 of the Internal Revenue Code, adding provisions for the use of Individual Retirement Accounts (IRAs) in a "simplified employee pension." An employer may contribute up to $7,500 a year, or 15% of an employee's compensation (whichever is smaller) to an Individual Retirement Account or Annuity for the employee. The plan may not be discriminatory. The employer must make contributions on behalf of every employee over 25 years of age who has worked for the employer in three out of the past five years. Contributions must be made in a uniform ratio for all employees (e.g., 7½%

of compensation) with only the first $100,000 of compensation taken into account for this test.

Amounts contributed to a simplified pension must vest immediately. The employer is not permitted to place any restrictions on an employee's right to withdraw from the Individual Retirement Account or Annuity. If the employer's contribution is less than the ordinary maximum IRA contribution ($1,500), the employee is allowed to supplement the employer's contribution by making his own contribution.

A simplified employee pension must be written, and must contain an allocation formula giving the requirements for qualification and the method of computing the employer's contribution.

[¶1008]   **DEFERRED PAY CONTRACTS**

When a company wants to defer the compensation of a key employee but does not wish to adopt a qualified plan, a deferred pay contract is the normal course of action. The company can accumulate funds to be paid out at a later period (usually in the post-retirement years), which minimizes the individual's income tax liability. An employee who takes a deferred compensation arrangement is not taxed on the amounts until they're actually or constructively received. The company is not entitled to any deduction for monies owed until payment is actually made (*Rev. Rul. 60-31,* CB 1960-1, 174).

When a trust or annuity contract is used to fund a nonqualified plan, the employee reports the company's contributions as income at the time all rights become transferable or are not subject to a substantial risk of forfeiture (IRC §83).

A substantial forfeiture provision exists when the condition imposes "upon the employee a significant limitation or duty which will require a meaningful effort on the part of the employee to fulfill and there is a definite possibility that the event which will cause the forfeiture could occur." (See *Rev. Proc. 71-19,* CB 1971-1, 698.)

Maximum Tax: The 1976 Tax Reform Act amended IRC §1348 to provide that the maximum tax of 50% formerly applicable to earned income now applies to "personal service" income—including periodic payments from deferred compensation arrangements and pensions.

[¶1009]   **CASH BONUS PLANS**

Cash bonus plans give employees an immediate share of company profits over and above regular compensation. If the bonus plan is not contractually provided for, the amount of the bonus and the recipients are usually determined on an annual basis.

[¶1010]   **STOCK BONUS PLANS**

Stock bonuses to employees made under a stock bonus plan are assessed for income tax purposes at their fair market value.

Qualified stock bonus plans are similar in structure to pension and profit-sharing plans that qualify under the Internal Revenue Code. The difference, essentially, is that contributions as well as distributions are made in company stock. When an employee receives the corporate stock as a distribution, tax on the appreciated portion is not payable until the stock is actually sold.

[¶1011]   **EMPLOYEE STOCK OWNERSHIP PLANS**

The Employee Stock Ownership Plan (ESOP) is a variation of a qualified stock bonus plan. Such plans are not recent innovations. However, relatively few such plans were established until the past few years. With the added impetus of the Employee Retirement Income Security Act of 1974 (ERISA) and the need to find more favorable financing in a tight money market, ESOPs have become popular. Further incentives to set up an ESOP have been provided employers in the Tax Reduction Act of 1975 and the Revenue Act of 1978, granting special tax credits to companies when stock ownership plans are established.

The term "Employee Stock Ownership Plan" has been statutorily defined for the first time in ERISA (§407(d)(6)) as an individual account plan "which is a stock bonus plan which is qualified, or a stock bonus plan and money-purchase pension plan both of which are qualified, under section 401 of the Internal Revenue Code of 1954, and which is designed to invest primarily in qualifying employer securities . . . ." The term "qualifying employer security" is defined as "an employer security which is stock; or a marketable obligation."

Qualification requirements for ESOPs are set forth in §409A of the Internal Revenue Code as amended by the Revenue Act of 1978. In addition to meeting IRC §401(a) requirements, an ESOP must provide:

☐   Allocation to participants' accounts in proportion to compensation.

☐   Nonforfeitable rights to participants.

☐   Allocated securities may not be distributed to an active participant before the end of 84 months after allocation.

☐   Passthrough of voting rights.

☐   Participant may demand distribution in the form of securities or cash determined under a fair valuation formula.

☐   Contributions must stay in the plan, even if investment credit is recaptured or redetermined.

☐   Plan must be established before the due date for filing the employer's tax return for the taxable year in which the plan year ends.

An employer is entitled to an investment credit against income tax of 11% (or 11½% if there are matching employee contributions) for amounts contributed to an ESOP (IRC §46(a)(2)).

72

[¶1012] **STOCK OPTION PLANS**

No qualified stock option plans may be set up after May 20, 1976. Qualified stock option plans adopted before May 21, 1976, can continue to grant options, but the employee must exercise the option before May 21, 1981, to receive qualified stock option treatment. Amendments to existing plans that increase the number of shares to be granted under the plan will be treated as a new plan. A narrow exception applies to new options substituted for existing qualified stock options in the event of a corporate merger, consolidation, or other reorganization. For instance, the surviving corporation in a corporate merger could substitute options on its stock for options on the stock of the merged corporation, if the options are of equivalent value and the new option does not provide for any additional benefits for the employee.

The tax rules for nonqualified stock options are found in Reg. §1.421-6 and under IRC §83—Property Transferred in Connection with Performance of Services. The employee reports income at one of the following appropriate times—grant, exercise, or when restrictions are removed—and the employer takes a corresponding tax deduction at the same time.

[¶1013] **EMPLOYEE STOCK PURCHASE PLANS**

In qualified plans that permit eligible employees to purchase stock at between 85% and 100% of value, participants do not have to report taxable income at either the time of grant or on the date of exercise.

If shares purchased under the plan are disposed of more than 2 years after the grant date or 12 months after the exercise date, whichever is later, the employee will realize ordinary income equal to the lesser of (a) the spread between the option price and the fair market value of the share on the grant date, or (b) the excess of the sale price of the shares (or the fair market value if disposed of by gift or at death) over the purchase price. In the event the shares are sold, long-term capital gain or loss is realized equal to the difference between the selling price and the purchase price of the shares increased by the amount reported as ordinary income.

If the shares are disposed of prior to 2 years after the grant date or 12 months after the exercise date, whichever is later, the employee is considered to have made a "disqualifying disposition." The employee must report as compensation the difference between the price paid for the shares and their fair market value on the exercise date. The company takes a tax deduction for a corresponding amount.

[¶1014] **KEY-MAN INSURANCE**

In this type of arrangement, the employer takes out an insurance policy on the life of a valuable employee. The employer pays the premiums and collects the proceeds of the policy. He can use the proceeds, for example, to pay death benefits to the employee's family for a period of time as a continuation of the employee's salary after death; or he can buy the deceased employee's stock in the company at his death.

The employer gets a tax deduction when benefits are paid—not when the premiums are paid on the insurance. When the premiums are paid all the employer is doing is building up an asset—the life insurance policy. But when he pays the benefits of the policy over to the beneficiary of the deceased employee, he is paying compensation and is therefore entitled to a deduction.

[¶1015]   **DEATH BENEFITS**

Up to $5,000 can be paid to the family of a deceased employee income tax free (IRC § 101(b)). If an employee's family receives benefits from two or more employers, the excludable amount is still limited to only $5,000. The rule applies to distributions under a qualified plan, but does not apply to amounts to which the employee had a nonforfeitable right.

[¶1016]   **SPLIT-DOLLAR INSURANCE PLANS**

Under a typical arrangement, the employee pays that part of the premium on an ordinary life insurance policy that is attributable to life insurance protection; the employer pays the balance that is attributable to the annual increase in cash surrender value. The cash surrender value is owned by the employer. At the employee's death, the employer receives an amount equal to the cash surrender value; the employee's beneficiary receives what's left of the proceeds. The advantage of such an arrangement is that after the first few years, the employee is able to obtain high insurance protection at a very low cost, since the employer is, in effect, paying for part of this protection through earnings on funds that belong to the employer. The ''economic benefit'' received by the employee under this plan is taxable *(Rev. Rul. 64-238,* CB 1964-2, 11; *Rev. Rul. 66-110,* CB 1966-1, 12, amplified by *Rev. Rul. 67-154,* CB 1967-1, 11.

[¶1017]   **GROUP TERM LIFE INSURANCE**

This provides pure insurance protection for the insured for a specified period of time, usually on a year-to-year basis. It has no paid up or cash surrender value. An employer can provide an employee with up to $50,000 of this type of insurance tax free, provided it is ''group term'' as defined in IRS Regulations under IRC §79. This is the only type of life insurance coverage that an employer can provide for an employee tax free. All other forms of life insurance protection are taxable to the employee.

[¶1018]   **GROUP PAID-UP LIFE INSURANCE**

This offers permanent protection by purchasing with a single premium a stated unit of life insurance for a specific employee. The insurance remains in force during the lifetime of the employee, without payment of further premium.

[¶1019]   **GROUP LEVEL PREMIUM INSURANCE**

This is a "group permanent contract." The premium on each employee's life is the same every year based upon his age when issued. This type of coverage offers paid-up insurance at retirement age and also makes cash or annuity values available either at retirement or on termination.

[¶1020]   **GROUP HEALTH INSURANCE**

This is another very valuable fringe benefit. It provides for the reimbursement of medical and hospitalization expenses incurred by an employee and his family. Premiums are tax deductible by the employer and not taxable to the employee—even if the plan provides for the protection of the employee's family. Some employers extend their plan to include reimbursement of major medical expenses. This coverage supplements the basic plan and provides some shelter to the employee in the event of a serious or prolonged illness.

[¶1021]   **MEDICAL EXPENSE REIMBURSEMENT PLANS**

Corporations may provide reimbursement for medical expenses incurred by selected employees under a medical expense reimbursement plan (see IRC §105(b) and 106). However, the Revenue Act of 1978 requires that after December 31, 1979, such plans must be nondiscriminatory if benefits are to be excluded from participants' gross income (IRC §105(h)).

A medical expense reimbursement plan will be considered discriminatory unless at least 70% of all employees, or 80% of all eligible employees (if at least 70% of all employees are eligible) can receive medical expense reimbursements from the plan. Class plans are considered nondiscriminatory if IRS approves the class designation. Participation must be extended to all employees except (1) part-time or seasonal employees, (2) employees with less than 3 years of service, and (3) employees under 25 years of age. If health benefits were negotiated in good faith, employees covered by collective bargaining agreements can be excluded from the plan.

Highly compensated individuals (i.e., the company's 5 highest paid officers, 10% shareholders, and eligible employees in the top 25% of the company's salary scale) who receive "excess reimbursement" will realize an equivalent amount of taxable income. If a highly paid person is reimbursed for medical expenses that would not be paid for a wide cross-section of all employees, the entire amount paid is excess reimbursement. If reimbursement for that particular medical benefit is available to other employees, the excess reimbursement is measured by multiplying total reimbursements to the highly paid individual by the fraction: Total Reimbursements to Highly Compensated Individuals ÷ Total Reimbursements to All Employees.

[¶1022]   **CAFETERIA PLANS**

A "cafeteria plan" is a written plan in which all participants are employees (though all employees need not be participants) and in which participants can choose among various taxable and nontaxable benefits. Cafeteria plans are *not* permitted to offer deferred compensation as a benefit. (See IRC § 125, added by the Revenue Act of 1978.)

If a cafeteria plan does *not* discriminate in favor of highly compensated individuals, employees will recognize taxable income only to the extent that they actually select taxable fringe benefits (e.g., group life insurance in excess of $50,000). However, if a cafeteria plan *is* discriminatory, highly compensated individuals must recognize income to the extent that they *could have* selected taxable benefits.

A plan is considered discriminatory if it favors highly compensated individuals with respect to participation, contributions, or benefits. For this purpose, the term "highly compensated individuals" is defined to mean those who are "officers, 5% shareholders, highly compensated employees," or spouses of persons in those three classes.

Whatever their actual terms, collectively bargained plans are deemed nondiscriminatory. Class plans are treated as nondiscriminatory if:

☐ IRS approves the plan's classification requirements;

☐ No more than three years of service is required for eligibility to participate; and

☐ An employee can participate at the beginning of the first plan year after he or she meets the participation requirements.

[¶1023]   **SALARY CONTINUATION PLANS**

The 1976 Tax Reform Act wiped out the sick pay exclusion for most employees. Now a disability benefit exclusion is available only to employees who are:

(1) Under 65,

(2) Retired on disability, and

(3) Totally and permanently disabled when they retire.

In addition, the amount of the exclusion has effectively been reduced—the $100/week ($5,200/year) exclusion still stands, but it is reduced dollar-for-dollar by adjusted gross income (including disability income) over $15,000.

[¶1024]   **FOR FURTHER REFERENCE . . .**

Carey, J.F., "Successors to the Qualified Stock Option," 56 Harvard Business Review No. 1, 140 (1978).

Helm, R.E., "Comparing the Choices Available for a Small Corporation's Deferred Compensation Plan," 6 Taxation for Lawyers 214 (1978).

Hess, R.P., *Desk Book for Setting Up a Closely Held Corporation,* Institute for Business Planning, Inc., Englewood Cliffs, N.J. (1979).

Konz, G.K., "Phantom Stock Compensation Plans," 56 Taxes 320-5 (June 1978).

Ludwig, R.L., "Analysis of Final ESOP Regulations," 30 Southern California Tax Institute 381-431 (1978).

Pay Planning (2 vol. looseleaf service), Institute for Business Planning, Inc., Englewood Cliffs, N.J.

Stoeber, E.A., "Current Planning for Life Insurance," 1978.

Estates, Gifts and Trusts Journal No. 1, 4 (1978).

Also see 36 N.Y. University Institute on Federal Taxation (1978) (ERISA Supp.).

COPYRIGHT LAW

[¶**1101**]   The current copyright law, effective January 1, 1978, completely replaced Title 17 of the United States Code, which had been law since 1909. One important result of the change in the copyright law, which is a comprehensive revision of all aspects of artistic and literary property, is that the United States will now be eligible for full membership in the Berne Copyright Union, an international copyright agreement that 65 different nations have adhered to since 1886. The official citation is Public Law 94-553, 90 Stat. 2541-2602.

[¶1102]   SCOPE OF COPYRIGHT LAW

The copyright legislation, is divided into 8 different chapters beginning with a discussion of the subject matter and scope of copyright. Chapter 2 covers copyright ownership and transfer. Chapter 3 extends copyright duration from the present 28 years plus another 28 years renewable term. Chapter 4 deals with copyright notice, deposit, and registration requirements; Chapter 5, with infringement of copyright and remedial action; Chapter 6 with manufacturing requirements as well as limitations on the importation of certain copyrighted materials, and noncopyrighted materials. Chapter 7 is essentially administrative and deals with the general responsibilities and organization of the copyright offices. The final chapter creates a copyright royalty tribunal that has four essential purposes: (1) to maximize the availability of creative works to the public, (2) to afford copyright creators a fair return for their creative works and to give copyright users a fair income under existing economic conditions, (3) to help balance the interest of copyright owners and copyright users, and (4) to minimize any disruptive impact on industries effectively regulated by changes in the copyright law.

[¶1103]   NEW COPYRIGHT DURATION

Works created after January 1, 1978, are given statutory copyright protection for the life of the author plus 50 additional years. (This corresponds to the time frame utilized in the Berne Convention.) On works that are done ''for hire'' as well as for anonymous and pseudonymous works, the new copyright term will be 75 years from the time of publication, or 100 years from creation, whichever is shorter. For those works already accorded copyright protection, the new law will retain the present term of 28 years for the date of first publication, but in the case of renewal the holding period for the second term is increased to 47 years. Copyrights in their first term must be renewed in order to receive the full 75-year maximum term permitted them by law. Copyrights in their second term between December 31, 1976, and December 31, 1977, are automatically extended up to the 75-year maximum period. Unpublished works that were in existence on the day the new copyright law went into effect are also covered. If they are not yet in the public domain, they generally will have the life plus 50 years protection. If a work has gone into public domain, there is no restoration of copyright protection available under the new law.

[¶1104] EXTENDED RENEWAL TERMS—TRANSFER OF RIGHTS

Under the original copyright legislation, when the first 28-year term of a copyright was completed, the renewal copyright reverted to the author or a specified beneficiary. Except for works that were in their first term of copyright protection on January 1, 1978, this renewal feature was dropped. Instead, the law provides that the author or certain specified heirs may terminate rights that they have transferred after a 35-year period has elapsed. The exact language permits termination "at any time during a period of 5 years beginning at the end of 56 years from the date copyright was originally secured," or January 1, 1978, whichever is later.

[¶1105] NOTICE OF COPYRIGHT

The innocent omissions or errors in the placement of the notice of copyright on the published work will not immediately result in forfeiture of copyright, and can be corrected within certain time limits. However, in such cases, innocent infringement resulting from omission or error will be shielded from liability.

[¶1106] EXCLUSIVE USE OF COPYRIGHT

Generally, a copyright holder is entitled to the exclusive use of all material copyrighted. This includes permission for the owner to reproduce copyrighted works in any manner; prepare derivative works; lend, lease, rent, or transfer ownership; and perform or display them publicly—subject, however, to a number of exceptions set forth in the paragraphs below.

[¶1107] FAIR USE

One of the most important exceptions to the exclusivity of the copyright is the principle of "fair use." Reproduction of materials for criticism, comment, news reporting, teaching (including multiple copies for classroom use), scholarship, or research is *not* infringement of copyright. In determining whether or not "fair use" is being abused, the Office of Copyright indicates that the following factors are to be considered: Purpose and character of the use, the portion used in relation to the copyrighted work as a whole, and the effect of the use on the potential market for the product read.

[¶1108]   **LIBRARY REPRODUCTION**

Single photocopies of certain items may be reproduced by libraries and archives for noncommercial purposes without violating the copyright law or infringing on the exclusivity otherwise mandated by law. In order to be innocent of infringement, however, the libraries or archives must open their collections to the public or to all persons doing research in a particular field. Notice of copyright on the reproduction by the library or archive is essential. Wholesale photocopying of periodicals is not permitted, however, though reproductions of individual articles may be.

[¶1109]   **MUSIC RECORDING RIGHTS**

Phonograph record royalties are now 2¾¢ or ½¢ per minute of playing time, whichever is greater. In addition, unauthorized duplication of sound recordings is prohibited, though no "performance right" is created under the law. Juke box operators, presently exempt from royalty payments, will be subject to an annual royalty fee of $8 payable to the Register of Copyrights for distribution by the copyright royalty tribunal to the copyright owners.

[¶1110]   **GOVERNMENT PUBLICATIONS**

Government publications may not be copyrighted. The government may, however, hold and receive copyrights transferred to it by assignment. For those wishing to compete with the government imprinting operations, note that the public printer of the United States is required to sell "to persons who may apply" additional or duplicate stereotype or electrotype plates from which government publications are printed, at a price not to exceed the cost of composition plus 10%. Because of congressional administrative action requiring all documents from the Government Printing Office to be sold at a price that is more than 10% above actual cost, it is possible to compete with the government for the sale of their documents.

[¶1111]   **CABLE TELEVISION**

CATV is subject to a provision in the copyright law that provides for compulsory licensing, as well as for payment of certain royalties for secondary transmission of copyrighted works. Royalties are paid to the Register of Copyrights for distribution to the copyright owners by the copyright royalty tribunal. (The copyright royalty tribunal was created for the basic purpose of determining the reasonableness of royalty rates and the distribution of statutory royalty fees.) Periodically, the holder of a copyright may be able to petition the tribunal for an adjustment in the royalty rate. Under the law, the tribunal is able to determine whether or not the applicant has a significant interest in the royalty rate in which an adjustment is requested, and if so, it is possible for an adjustment to be ordered. Presumably, this would be of immense help to authors who contract for minimal royalties on a work that ultimately matures into a "best seller."

[¶1112]   **FEES**

The following is a list of the charges made by the Register of Copyrights:

Registration	$10
Renewals	$ 6
Assignments	$10 for first 6 pp. (and only one title); $0.50 for each additional pp. or title
Searches	$10/hr.

Annual Subscription, Catalogs of Copyright Entries $75.00

Pay all fees by check, money order, bank draft, or postal note, payable to Register of Copyrights.

[¶1113]   **TAX ASPECTS OF COPYRIGHTS**

Capital gain treatment in the sale of copyrights or other artistic works is denied if the seller is the author or the artist (IRC §1221(3)). If the person is neither a dealer nor the creator, the copyright may be a capital asset—meaning that it is subject to a 12-month holding period in order to qualify for capital gain treatment.

[¶1114]   **COPYRIGHTS OWNED BY A DECEDENT**

Copyrights, artistic compositions, and literary and musical properties owned by their creator are noncapital assets (IRC §1221(3)(C)). Following the death of the copyright holder who is also the creator, gains realized from the sale of the appreciated asset—formerly taxed as a capital gain—are now taxed as ordinary income. At the artist's death, the basis of the property is stepped-up to its estate tax value (IRC §1014(a)).

CORPORATE FORMATION AND OPERATION

[¶1201]   Once the decision has been made to incorporate, it is important that orderly procedures be followed. Some of the main considerations when forming a corporation appear below.

(1) Determine the basic business objectives of the principals.

(2) Develop the concept of a corporate form, capital structure, financing arrangements, and supplementary agreements that fit these objectives.

(3) Check the organizational plan in light of tax considerations and make the necessary modifications.

(4) Make the fundamental decisions prerequisite to drafting corporate papers, where to incorporate, how many shares and what kind (par or no-par, preferences or not), preemptive rights, any organizational controls, and put them in the charter or separate agreement, etc.

(5) Draft the corporation charter, bylaws, stock certificates, and organizational minutes.

(6) Make the filings, pay the taxes, and take the other procedural steps necessary to bring the corporation into being.

(7) Hold the organizational meeting, have directors accept subscriptions, accept transfers of property, etc.

(8) Determine how corporate control will be established and maintained.

[¶1202]   CHECKLIST OF PROCEDURAL STEPS IN CORPORATE FORMATION

Listed below is a comprehensive checklist of steps for corporate organization. Note that not all of them are required in every jurisdiction.

- [ ] Select *state of incorporation*.
- [ ] Select *corporate name*; check availability and reserve.
- [ ] Complete and execute *pre-incorporation agreement*.
- [ ] Draft and file *articles of incorporation*.
- [ ] Determine whether corporation is going to elect Subchapter S.
- [ ] Pay filing fees and organization tax.
- [ ] File with federal government for *employer identification number*.
- [ ] File for *workmen's compensation and unemployment compensation* insurance in appropriate jurisdictions.
- [ ] Hold organizational meeting.
- [ ] Select corporation's *accounting system* and select calendar or fiscal year.
- [ ] Obtain *corporate seal*, stock register, minute book, and issue securities.
- [ ] Get subscriptions for stock.
- [ ] *Designate agent* for service of process and file any other required papers.
- [ ] *File* in local county or city, as required by law.
- [ ] *Draft bylaws*.
- [ ] Elect first *permanent board of directors* to handle other organizational steps.

☐ *Hold organizational meeting* of permanent board; establish officers' salaries, and prepare Form W-4 for withholding.

☐ *Establish corporate bank account(s)* and designate those persons authorized to transact corporation's business.

☐ Obtain *insurance* on property and key employees.

☐ Obtain any *special licenses* needed for corporate operation.

☐ Pay applicable federal and state taxes for stock issuance.

☐ Look into *employee benefit plans;* determine desirability of pension and/or profit-sharing plan.

[¶1203]   SELECTING THE STATE OF INCORPORATION

While the state of principal business activity is usually the state of incorporation there are other factors that may influence the choice of a particular state. Prior to selecting a state for incorporation, review its corporation laws, keeping these factors in mind:

☐ *Corporate Name:* Some states place restrictions on the use of a corporate name.

☐ *Corporate Purpose:* In some states, certain professions may not be incorporated, such as medicine, engineering, law, and architecture. However, most modern corporation laws permit broad purposes.

☐ *Capitalization Requirements:* Some states require a minimum amount of paid-in capital prior to commencement of business. Some states will not allow the issuance of no-par shares; other states do not permit par value shares of less than $1.

☐ *Shareholders' Meetings:* Some states permit shareholders to meet outside the state of incorporation; this option may be an important factor in choosing a state of incorporation.

☐ *Cumulative Voting:* Some states require cumulative voting.

☐ *Voting Rights and Control:* The percentage of the vote required for certain corporate acts varies from state to state. While many states require only a majority vote for corporate action, some states have supermajority or two-thirds requirements. In addition, some states prohibit the issuance of nonvoting stock. If such restrictions exist, it is not possible to create nonvoting preferred or nonvoting class A stock, and other methods of corporate control must be devised.

☐ *Restrictions on Corporate Indebtedness:* Some states may place restrictions on the corporate power to borrow money or pledge corporate assets. In many instances, such limitations can be overcome by a shareholder vote.

☐ *Restrictions on Stock Redemptions:* Most states prohibit redemption if it causes corporate insolvency. Other states impose limitations preventing redemption if capital stock would be diminished to an amount less than the corporate indebtedness.

☐ *Incorporators:* Some states require as many as three incorporators, while others have reduced their requirement to one.

☐ *Preemptive Rights:* Most states provide that a corporation's shareholders shall have preemptive rights unless specifically denied them by the certificate of incorporation.

□ *Appraisal Rights:* In the event of a merger or consolidation, how are the shares of minority shareholders to be appraised?

□ *Shareholder Liability:* What liability do shareholders have for corporate acts? Some states hold shareholders liable for back wages due to employees in the event of corporate insolvency.

□ *Directors' Liability:* There may be differences among states as to liability of directors for improper declaration of dividends, or for acts or omissions that result in loss to the corporation. These differences may involve the scope of liability or the measure of damages.

□ *Provisions for Indemnity:* Some state corporation laws set forth comprehensive guidelines regarding corporate indemnification of directors, officers, agents, etc., for alleged misconduct.

□ *Dividends:* Are there restrictions as to the sources from which dividends may be paid?

□ *Tender Offers:* Does the state of incorporation regulate tender offers for corporations incorporated there or doing business within the state?

[¶1204]   TAX FACTORS IN SELECTING
            STATE OF INCORPORATION

The difference in costs of incorporating and operating in the various states may be important in determining the state of incorporation. The tables provided in the Appendix may aid in this decision.

□ *Property Tax:* Because property tax is generally levied by the state in which the property is physically located, the property tax is generally not a factor in choosing a state of incorporation, although it may be relevant in determining whether or not a corporation wants to locate its business in a particular state.

□ *Intangibles:* When it appears that there may be an attempt by both jurisdictions to tax intangibles, it may be to your client's advantage to incorporate initially in the state where the principal business office is to be maintained.

□ *Income Taxes:* The income tax may include income from in-state property, in-state or out-of-state business or resources.

□ *Capital Stock Tax:* Some states impose a tax on the market value of the capital stock.

□ *Franchise Taxes:* Some states impose an annual franchise tax on domestic (in-state) corporations and qualified foreign (out-of-state) corporations. The base is the proportion of issued capital or capital and surplus represented by property located and business transacted within the state.

[¶1205]   SELECTION OF THE CORPORATE NAME

The selection, clearance, reservation, or registration of the corporate name in the state of incorporation and in states where business is to be carried on involves not merely legal but also advertising and public relations considerations. While it is easy enough to legally change a name to meet changing needs and styles, the initial selection should be made with a view to permanence so that goodwill attached to the name will not be lost later on, and also to avoid the future expenses of reprinting stationery, packaging, and advertising materials.

The following factors should affect the decision:

(1) In some states, a name can be selected that is similar to one used by an existing corporation, provided the existing corporation consents. Some states permit the use of similar names by related corporations. In any event, before picking a name, check to see whether it is available, usually with the Secretary of State. Another way is to go through telephone directories, trade directories, trademark records, and county clerks' files.

(2) Check local law when deciding to use a name that does not include the words, "Corporation," "Inc.," or "Ltd."

(3) Some states also bar or regulate the use of words denoting fraternal, benevolent, or other nonprofit organizations, or labor or union, official or professional connections.

(4) In addition, a corporation cannot be given a name that suggests the corporation will be engaged in a business that it cannot lawfully follow, or that it is to be a form of public agency, or that it will be affiliated with an organization with which it is, in fact, not affiliated.

(5) The use of a living person's name without his consent may amount to a violation of his right to privacy and is expressly forbidden by some statutes.

(6) While in most states there is no requirement that a corporation's name be in the English language, check local law to make sure a particular jurisdiction does not expressly require the use of English letters or characters.

(7) Statutes in some states regulate the use by corporations of fictitious names or trade names, so check local law.

(8) The Securities and Exchange Commission is apprehensive regarding the inclination of corporate issuers to include "glamour" terms such as "nuclear," "space," "missile," or "electronics" as part of their corporate names when they are not actually engaged in a business normally associated with those words, or engaged in such a business to a very limited extent. In view of this practice, the SEC Division of Corporate Finance has released a guide relating to the misleading character of corporate names.

(9) Finally, in selecting a name, bear in mind the cost of reproducing the name on signs, corporate property, etc.

[¶1206]

TAX CONSIDERATIONS IN CORPORATE FORMATION

The checklist below indicates the major tax considerations in the formation of a corporation.

(1) Tax-Free Incorporation: No gain or loss is recognized when property is transferred to a corporation solely in exchange for stock or securities if the

transferors are in "control" of the corporation immediately after the transfer (IRC §351). "Control" is defined as ownership of at least 80% of the voting power of all voting stock and at least 80% of all other classes of stock (IRC §368(c)).

If money or other property (boot) is received by the transferors in addition to stock and securities, gain (but not loss) is recognized, but only to the extent of the money or other property (IRC §351(b)). In most incorporations, the assumption of a liability by the corporation is not treated as money received by the transferor (IRC §357). However, in two situations liabilities assumed by the corporation are treated as money received by the transferor:

(a) When the transferor's principal purpose in having the corporation assume his liability or acquire his property subject to a liability is to avoid tax on the exchange or is not a bona fide business purpose (IRC §357(b)).

(b) When the liabilities assumed by the new corporation exceed the bases of the assets transferred to it (IRC §357(c)). Note that liabilities of a cash-basis transferor are not counted in determining if liabilities exceed basis, if payment of the liability would be deductible or constitute a payment to a retiring partner or deceased partner's successor in interest of his distributive share or guaranteed payment.

(2) Disproportionate Stock Interests: Giving an edge to a promoter or a member of the family may result in taxable compensation to the promoter. There may be a taxable gift by a party who contributes more to the corporation than he receives in order to benefit a member of his family.

(3) Step-Up in Basis of Transferred Property: If the property being transferred to the corporation has increased in value and if it is desirable to pay a capital gain tax to step up its basis in order to get higher depreciation allowances or for other purposes, it may be desirable to make the incorporation a taxable transaction. Unfortunately, a tax-free incorporation under §351 is not elective. If the requirements discussed above are met, IRC §351 applies automatically. Outside a bona fide sale of assets or the receipt of boot, avoiding §351 usually amounts to avoiding the 80% control requirement.

Keep in mind that various recapture provisions may apply to a taxable transaction to convert capital gain into ordinary income. These same provisions operate when the receipt of boot in an otherwise tax-free incorporation causes recognition of gain. The recapture provisions normally encountered are:

(a) If the transferred asset is depreciable, all gain is ordinary income if the transferor, his spouse, and minor children or grandchildren together own 80% of the corporation (IRC §1239).

(b) Prior depreciation deductions for personalty are recaptured as ordinary income (IRC §1245).

(c) Prior depreciation deductions in excess of straight line for realty are recaptured as ordinary income (IRC §1250).

(d) Prior investment credit may also be recaptured unless the property is retained in the business (IRC §47(a)).

(4) Transfer of Liabilities: If encumbered property is transferred to the corporation and it assumes the debt, the excess of the liabilities assumed, plus

liabilities to which the property is subject, will be taxed to the transferors to the extent that the liabilities exceed the cost or other tax basis of the property (IRC §357(c); see (1) above).

(5) Leasing Instead of Transferring Property: There may be tax savings in leasing property to the corporation and having it pay deductible rent, while the lessor deducts depreciation, rather than transferring the property to the corporation.

(6) Avoiding Tax to Promoters: Consider saving the promoters from having stock received by them taxed as compensation by having them buy cheap stock prior to the full financing of the corporation or by having them transfer patents, plans, or models in exchange for stock in the incorporation transaction. The earlier the promoters acquire their stock the safer they are.

(7) Use of Debt Plus Equity: Ideally, insiders would prefer to have outside investors merely lend the corporation money on an unsecured basis. Practically, though, the cost of such loans would be prohibitive. However, a corporation may still be able to issue unsecured debt instruments (debentures or promissory notes) to outside investors. A commonly used method enables the investor to purchase both common stock (equity) and unsecured debt instruments. In this way, insiders are giving up some of their control in exchange for unsecured loans to the corporation at reasonable rates. The outside investors have some degree of say in the management by which they can protect their unsecured investment.

(8) Thin Capitalization: There are also significant tax advantages to be realized from the issuance of debt instruments to insiders in addition to stock (''thin capitalization''):

(a) It permits tax-free withdrawal of cash from the successful corporation in order to repay the shareholder loans, and shareholders have no tax liabilities on the loan repayments;

(b) It provides the corporation with additional deductions, thus lowering its tax liabilities, since interest paid on the debt instruments is deductible;

(c) It avoids the accumulated earnings penalty tax;

(d) If the corporation fails, then, in an insolvency proceeding, the insiders are creditors of the corporation as well as shareholders, and as creditors may receive a partial repayment on their loan, whereas as shareholders they would receive nothing.

There are some risks involved in thin capitalization, namely that the debt instrument will be deemed an equity investment (stock). If that occurs, the ''interest'' paid on the instrument will be deemed a nondeductible dividend. In addition, the repayments of principal will be treated as a dividend to the investor rather than a tax-free return of capital. In order to avoid this problem, here are steps to insure that the loans will be treated as debt instruments:

(a) Debt-to-equity ratio should be between 2:1 and 3:1;

(b) Debt instrument should on its face bear interest and unconditionally obligate the corporation to pay both interest and principal at designated times;

(c) Debt must be treated as such on the corporate books;

(d) No subordination of shareholders' debts to those of the corporation's general creditors;

(e) A stated maturity date, not too far off in the future. A happy medium of about 10 years should be set with provisions for repayment.

(9) Making Debt Obligations Stand Up: Make sure the debt obligations obtained from the corporation constitute genuine debt—i.e., have a real and definite maturity date, call for interest payments at a fixed rate, give the holders a security status over stockholders. Making stockholder debts subordinate to regular corporate creditors is frequently necessary but it increases the risk that the debt will be considered equity. (See *Wetterau Grocer Co.,* CA-8, 179 F. 2d 158, 1950; *Gooding Amusement Co.,* CA-6, 236 F. 2d 159, 1956. See IRC §385 and regulations thereunder.)

(10) Using Preferred Stock: Consider creating preferred stock as part of the original capitalization. Subsequent creation of preferred stock after the corporation has earnings and profits may result in the preferred stock becoming IRC §306 stock so that gain on its sale is taxed as ordinary income.

(11) Assuring Ordinary Loss Deductions if Business Goes Bad: Qualifying stock under IRC §1244 assures that any loss on the investment will be deductible against ordinary income to the extent of $50,000 a year or $100,000 on a joint return. This rule applies whether the loss was incurred on sale of the stock or on its becoming worthless. It can only be used by the original purchaser of the stock. The following requirements must be met:

☐ The stock must be common stock of a domestic corporation. It does not have to be voting common stock.

☐ The corporation must be a small business corporation, that is, only the first $1,000,000 of stock issued qualifies under §1244.

☐ Section 1244 stock must be issued in exchange for money or other property. Stock issued for service does not qualify. Also, stock of any corporation does not qualify as property for purposes of §1244.

☐ If, during the five-year period prior to the shareholder's loss, or the period of corporate existence, if less, the corporation derived 50% or more of its gross receipts from royalties, rent, dividends, interest, annuities, and sales or exchanges of stock or securities, the stock will not qualify as §1244 stock.

(12) Avoid the Collapsible Corporation Trap: Don't overlook the collapsible corporation rules. These provisions convert the capital gains available on liquidations and the sale of corporate stock into ordinary income. If part of the gain is attributable to appreciated corporate property that has been held for less than three years, these rules may apply (IRC §341).

There are some steps that can be taken to avoid "collapsibility" in order to get capital gain treatment:

☐ *Stock Ownership Not High Enough:* The rules do not apply if after commencement of construction by the corporation of the collapsible property you do not own more than 5% of the value of the corporation's stock. This defense by itself should exempt most shareholders of widely held corporations.

☐ *Gain Attributable to Noncollapsible Property:* If at least 30% of the recognized gain is attributable to noncollapsible property, collapsible status may be avoided (IRC §341(d)(2)). This rule is most useful because collapsibility may be avoided when the corporation has more than one property and a substantial amount of income is realized from one of them.

☐ *Right Timing:* The rules do not apply if gain is realized by the shareholder after the expiration of three years following the completion of construction of the property.

Note: While routine repairs would not constitute "construction" for purposes of IRC §341, substantial improvements would prolong completion of the activity and thus the running of the three-year waiting period.

☐ *Sale of Assets:* If the corporation is thought to be collapsible, it may be best to have the corporation sell its assets and then liquidate. If the corporation is in fact collapsible, the corporation will presumably pay a capital gain tax on the sale, and the stockholders will have to pay a capital gain tax on the liquidation of the amount that's left.

☐ *Tax-Free Reorganization:* The adverse results of a collapsible situation can also be avoided by a tax-free reorganization, since the collapsible rules do not extend to transactions in which there is no recognized gain.

☐ *Multiple Entities:* When the intention is to develop more than one property, it may be advantageous to incorporate each property separately. In this way, the favorable three-year rule can be applied on an individual basis. What's more, if an unfavorable determination is made with regard to one property, it will not affect other properties. However, a single corporation may be preferable to keep the gain above the 30% limit so as to come within this exception.

☐ *Subchapter S Election:* If a potentially collapsible corporation has an office building or other IRC §1231 asset as its principal asset, electing Subchapter S treatment may avoid IRC §341 consequences. If the corporation sells the assets and distributes the proceeds to the shareholders in liquidation, the gain on the sale passes through to the shareholders as a long-term capital gain.

(13) Deducting Organization Expenses: IRC §248 permits a corporation to treat organization expenditures as "deferred expenses," and to write them off as tax deductions. The length of the "writeoff" period may be selected by the corporation provided it is not less than sixty months; and it starts when the corporation begins business.

(14) Employee-Stockholder Benefits: Employee-stockholders of the corporation may secure the benefits of a pension or profit-sharing trust. And the corporation's contributions (within certain limitations) are deductible by the corporation. See IRC §401-404, 1379. In addition other fringe benefits, such as group term insurance (up to $50,000 coverage), reimbursement of medical expenses, etc., are also available. See IRC §79, 104-106.

(15) Avoiding Personal Holding Company Penalties: A corporation in which five or fewer individuals own more than half the stock during the last half of the taxable year may be a personal holding company if 60% or more of its income comes from dividends, royalties, interest, and rents. Rents equal to at least 50% of

adjusted ordinary gross income are not personal holding company income if other personal holding company income does not exceed 10% of ordinary gross income. A personal holding company is subject to a 70% penalty tax (IRC §541-543).

(16) Accumulation of Surplus: A corporation may accumulate up to $150,000 before it becomes liable for the accumulated earnings penalty tax. After that, there is an additional tax liability (27½% on the first $100,000 of accumulated taxable income and 38½% on the balance of that income) if there are unreasonable surplus accumulations. However, a corporation may retain earnings for such business purposes as the redemption of stock to pay death taxes (IRC §537). If the accumulation exceeds $150,000, the penalty tax can be avoided by showing "reasonably anticipated needs of the business" as the purpose of the accumulation (IRC §537). It is not necessary to show that earnings and profits must be reinvested in the business immediately; it is enough to show that future needs (not vague or uncertain) of the business will require that these earnings and profits be plowed back.

[¶1206.1]　Tax Considerations: The Subchapter S Corporation

Subchapter S (IRC §1371-1378) permits certain qualifying corporations to elect not to be taxed as corporations. The major advantage of the Subchapter S election is the avoidance of double taxation—the corporation's taxable income is picked up by its shareholders and each pays an individual tax on that portion of the corporation's total income allocable to him. While the corporate double tax is avoided, the main advantage of incorporation—limited liability—is retained by the Subchapter S shareholders.

The requirements for Subchapter S qualification are:

☐　The corporation must be a domestic corporation.

☐　The corporation must not be a member of an affiliated group of corporations (IRC §1504).

☐　The corporation must have no more than 15 shareholders.

☐　Shareholders must be either individuals, estates, or certain trusts that are treated as owned by the grantor under the grantor trust rules (IRC §671); created primarily to vote the stock transferred to them; and those that receive stock under a will, but only for 60 days after the stock is transferred to the trust. Corporations or partnerships cannot be shareholders. Note that a grantor trust may continue as a shareholder for two years after the death of the grantor, *if* the entire trust corpus is included in the grantor's estate. If the entire corpus is not included, the trust may continue as a shareholder for 60 days, the same period that applies to testamentary trusts.

☐　The corporation must have only one class of stock, with the same voting rights.

☐　No shareholder can be a nonresident alien.

☐　The corporation must not derive more than 80% of its gross receipts from sources outside the United States.

☐   The corporation may not derive more than 20% of its gross receipts from passive investment income.

☐   The corporation, or its predecessor, has not had an election revoked or terminated within the previous five taxable years. This qualification may be waived by IRS.

[¶1207]   **THE CAPITAL STRUCTURE**

The basic elements that may be used to build a capital structure that will reflect the economic interests of the various business participants are earnings, assets, and voting or management power. These various elements are considered separately in the following paragraphs.

[¶1208]   **EARNINGS**

One investor or class of investors may be given a preference in or dispropor-tionate share of earnings by using preferred stock or by using two classes of stock. The use of preferred stock is perhaps the most common way of giving one class of investors a priority in earnings. If the investors are in a position to demand a share in earnings in addition to their preferred dividend, this may be done either (1) by making the preferred participating as to further dividends or (2) by giving them common in addition to their preferred. The first route presents problems, however, if the preferred is to be callable as it normally should be, because then it should also be made convertible if the holders are to share in the growth of the company (as they bargained for), and if it's convertible for an extended period there will be serious problems in working out fair conversion rates. Hence, the second route is apt to be favored.

When the situation calls for one class of investor to receive a disproportionate share of earnings, as distinguished from priority in the earnings, a two-class stock set-up will usually be called for. For example, a two-class stock arrangement might be used if investor A is willing to put in $55,000 and is willing to settle for 45% of the earnings provided he is given 55% of the voting control of the business and B is willing to put in $45,000 provided he gets 55% of the earnings and is willing to wield only 45% of the vote.

If two classes of stock are used, care must be exercised to make sure they are properly labeled. When the two classes share dividends on a percentage basis, for example, it might be incorrect to designate the class getting the larger percentage as "common." Differentiate by calling it Class A. The other class could be designated common.

[¶1209]   **ASSETS**

Some investors may demand priority or preferential participation in the distribution of assets on premature liquidation. For example, suppose one group of

91

investors makes two-thirds of the cash or tangible investment for one-third of the shares, and the so-called talent gets two-thirds of the shares for only one-third of the tangible investment, and let's say the respective investments are $100,000 and $50,000. If the corporation were to liquidate at a time when the assets were worth $150,000, the "talent" would come out with $50,000 more than they invested, this at the expense of the "money" investors. The "money" investors would come out even only if liquidation occurred at a time when the asset value had doubled. Two classes of shares bearing different participation rights in the distribution of assets, as distinguished from a preference in distribution, might be used to assure an equitable result. Thus, Class A might be given $2 for every $1 to be distributed to Class B until the original investments were repaid, with provision for equal distribution of assets thereafter.

[¶1210]   VOTING

The use of securities with different voting rights also affects the distribution of voting power.

Minority investors may want representation on the board of directors. One way of assuring such representation is by establishing two or more classes of shares and providing for the election of a certain number of directors or a certain percentage of the total number of directors by each class. The latter will, of course, prevent changes in representation by changes in the number of directors, and will, therefore, normally, be preferred.

Participation in voting for directors may be made absolute or it may be contingent, or conditional, as on passing preferred dividends for a fixed time. When both common and preferred stock are used, the voting rights of the preferred stock are usually made contingent or conditional on preferred dividends being in arrears (normally for a year or more). When that occurs the preferred shareholders become entitled to elect board members (usually a majority) until the default is cured.

So far the discussion has been limited to voting for directors and on this level it is quite clear that securities may be created without the right to vote for directors. But voting may, of course, concern other matters, and it is equally clear that a class of securities should not be created if it is barred from voting on all matters including those affecting the interests of the class. The statutes of the state of incorporation must be checked to determine the issues on which class voting is required. The issues may include certain types of charter amendments, and mergers and consolidations adversely affecting the class.

On the other hand, the voting rights of particular securities may go beyond those matters as to which shareholder votes or consents are required by law. Voting rights may be conferred as to specific matters when required by the terms of the business agreement. The participation may be on the basis of class voting (requiring a certain percentage of the class) or pooling all the classes and requiring a certain percentage of the votes of all those entitled to vote on the particular issue.

[¶1211]
PROVISIONS FOR REDEMPTION
AND CONVERSION

Debt securities and preferred stock are used to give the investors some protection for their capital investment and some assurance of income. When the corporation has established itself, these senior securities may no longer be necessary or the capital that they represent may be had on better terms. This is what makes it desirable to make the senior securities redeemable or callable at the option of the corporation, or provision may be made for compulsory retirement. When the latter is the case, the security should provide for a sinking fund.

The law of incorporation must be checked as to permissible provisions for redemption, and their application to particular securities, i.e., debt, preferred, common.

Making senior securities convertible may be tied in with the idea of redemption. As the corporation grows and prospers, the holder of a convertible senior security may be induced to give up whatever priorities he may have as to earnings or assets, or both, in favor of a full share in the equity.

[¶1212]
RIGHTS, OPTIONS, AND WARRANTS

Many corporate statutes permit rights and options to purchase shares, sometimes called "warrants." Their use may be considered but normally will be limited to later stages in the development of the business.

[¶1213]
USE OF DEBT SECURITIES

Debt securities are usually issued to represent borrowed money and may take various forms, the most common being bonds, debentures, and notes. Bonds are usually secured and when secured by a mortgage may be referred to as "mortgage bonds." Those secured by a pledge of personal property may be called "collateral trust bonds." "Debentures" or "notes" are generally unsecured. Local law must be checked for provisions authorizing the holders of debt securities to vote for directors or other matters, as well as for requirements as to the consideration for their issuance. The use of debt securities in the capital structure must be with an eye to the tax consequences of "thin incorporation," discussed at ¶1206(8), and with due regard to possible nontax consequences. In case of insolvency, for example, the debt to shareholders may be subordinated to other claims, and shareholders may be held personally liable for the debts. Attention must also be focused on the effect of debt on the balance sheet. It may lead to an investigation by persons transacting business with the corporation of the relationship between the holders of the debt securities and the shareholders of the corporation. If such a relationship is discovered, the next step may be to ask for a contractual subordination of the debt. This will, of course, result in the debt holder being placed in essentially the position of a shareholder.

[¶1214]   **PAR OR NO-PAR STOCK?**

If par or stated value shares are provided for, it will be necessary to see that the consideration for which shares may be issued under the state corporation law—usually money, property (tangible or intangible), and services—has value equal to the stated value of the shares. Otherwise, the shares are not "fully paid and nonassessable," and their issuance will be fraudulent as against the corporation, existing stockholders and creditors, and directors approving their issuance, and purchasers of the shares may be personally liable at least to the extent of the "watering." There will usually be no dollar floor on the consideration that may be accepted for no-par shares, but there is the general requirement that the directors fix a fair value for the shares and make a determination that the corporation has received suitable consideration of that value for shares issued. Statute and case law determine for each state whether speculative patents and secrets, promoters' services, promissory notes, and obligations to render future services or to make future payments constitute suitable consideration for the issuance of shares.

To protect organizers from liability, see that the terms of the bargain between those forming the corporation do not overvalue services and assets contributed by the organizers as against third parties. The tax collector has an interest in this, too, because the value of the shares given to organizers not supported by the value of assets contributed by them may be treated as taxable compensation for services. This "watering" tax and balance sheet problem can usually be handled by getting supporting appraisals for assets or creating a debt or preferred stock leverage in the capital structure. Stamp tax considerations may also play a role in the decision to use par or no-par stock.

[¶1215]   **THE ARTICLES OF INCORPORATION**

A corporation operates under a charter from the state, prepared by counsel for the corporation and filed and approved by the appropriate state official. Following is a checklist of points to be covered in the articles of incorporation:

☐ Corporate name.
☐ Corporate purpose—broad enough to cover all aspects of present and projected operations.
☐ Location of corporate office.
☐ Duration of corporate existence—perpetual or stated.
☐ Powers:
(a) To sue and be sued;
(b) To have a corporate seal;
(c) To purchase, take, receive, lease, acquire, own, hold, improve, use, and otherwise deal in real and personal property;
(d) To sell, convey, mortgage, pledge, lease, exchange, transfer, and dispose of property. The power to deal in property may be restricted in some jurisdictions in which property is not required to further the corporate purposes, e.g., real estate held by realty corporations, agricultural land, and the like. Local law should be checked;

(e) To sell, convey, mortgage, pledge, lease, exchange, transfer, and otherwise dispose of any part of the corporate property and assets. In some states corporate conveyances will be limited to corporate purposes;

(f) To lend money. The power to lend money may be restricted, however. In some states loans may not be made to shareholders. In other states loans may not be made to officers and directors. The authority for a corporation to lend money to its employees, officers, etc., may be important if the corporation wants to initiate a program aiding relocated employees in acquisition of homes, etc.;

(g) To deal in securities of other corporations, partnerships, and associations. Corporations may be prohibited from holding more than a certain percentage of certain types of corporations, like utilities companies or banks. In some states a corporation will be prohibited from becoming a partner or a joint venturer;

(h) To make contracts and guarantees and incur liabilities; borrow money and issue notes, bonds, and other obligations; and secure obligations by mortgage or pledge. In Pennsylvania, a corporation may pledge corporate income as well as property. The power to guarantee obligations may vary from state to state;

(i) To lend money, invest, and reinvest funds; take and hold real and personal property as security for the payment of funds;

(j) To conduct its business and carry on its operations in or out of the state of incorporation. Similarly, the corporate offices may be located in or out of the state of incorporation. In some states, however, the corporation must maintain some form of an office within the state of incorporation;

(k) To elect or appoint officers and agents and fix their compensation;

(l) To make and alter bylaws;

(m) To make charitable contributions. In most states there is specific statutory authorization for charitable contributions. Prior to widespread statutory enactments, there was often a question as to the corporate purpose of charitable contributions;

(n) To indemnify directors, officers, or agents. Often the power of indemnification will be coupled with a procedure spelled out in the statute, dealing with bylaw provisions in regard to indemnification;

(o) To pay pensions and establish pension plans;

(p) To cease its corporate activities and surrender its corporate franchise. Generally, state statutes provide specific machinery for the dissolution and winding up of the affairs of a corporation;

(q) To deal in its own shares. Often this power will be restricted to purchases out of earned surplus. Transactions that would render the corporation insolvent are generally prohibited. In some jurisdictions shareholders' approval will be required.

☐ Designation of Secretary of State as agent for service of process.

☐ Number of shares; how many classes of shares; par or no-par value; voting rights of shares; priority preferences of shares.

95

Optional items for inclusion in the articles of incorporation are:

☐ Minimum capital for commencement of business.
☐ Extension or elimination of preemptive rights.
☐ Liability of shareholders for corporate debts.
☐ Name and address of each incorporator.
☐ Number of directors on initial board.
☐ Restriction on transfer of shares.
☐ Provisions for repeal, amendment, or adoption of bylaws.
☐ Shareholders' right to fix consideration for no-par shares.
☐ Quorum requirements for shareholders' and directors' meetings.
☐ Cumulative voting requirements.
☐ Restrictions on board's powers.
☐ Classification of directors for voting control.
☐ Voting requirements for directors' meetings.
☐ Provision for executive or other (e.g., audit) committees of board.
☐ Reservations for shareholder power to elect officers.
☐ Removal of directors by shareholders.
☐ Provision for special meetings.

[¶1216]   THE BYLAWS

The regulation of business methods is an appropriate matter for the bylaws. Whereas the certificate of incorporation is a matter of public record, the bylaws are private and therefore not open for examination by the general public. Some look upon the bylaws as an administrative checklist for the use of officers and directors and thus include in the bylaws those matters specifically covered by state corporation law. Others follow the practice of excluding from the bylaws provisions already covered by statute and rely upon a separate memo to guide officers and directors.

Usually, bylaws are adopted by the incorporators or the shareholders at the initial meeting. Sometimes, if the certificate of incorporation or the state corporate statute so provides, the bylaws can be adopted by the directors.

Bylaws may be amended by the shareholders. In many states, bylaws can also be amended by the directors of the corporation if the bylaws adopted by the shareholders or the certificate of incorporation authorizes them to do so. In some cases, a greater than majority vote will be prescribed for amendment of the bylaws. If bylaws themselves prescribe a greater than majority vote for certain corporate actions, there should be a provision requiring an equivalent vote to remove the bylaw provision. If a bylaw provision requiring greater than majority voting can be removed or amended by simple majority vote, the control restriction would be rendered useless.

What should be included in the bylaws:

(a) Corporate office location.
(b) Time (date and hour) of shareholders' annual meeting, or procedure for determining the same.

(c) Location of the shareholders' meeting.

(d) Voting requirements—make certain to avoid conflicts between the voting requirements spelled out in the bylaws, articles of incorporation, and the corporate statute of the state of incorporation.

(e) Voting procedure.

(f) Notice requirements for shareholders' meetings.

(g) Proxy requirements. Several states also regulate the length of time for which a proxy may be valid. Proxies must also comply with the rules prescribed by the SEC if the corporation is subject to those rules.

(h) Establishment of the record date for the shareholders' meeting. The record date determines which shareholders are eligible to vote at the meeting.

(i) Authorization for the calling of special meetings of shareholders, and who will have this authority.

(j) Provision for shareholder action by shareholder consent.

(k) Quorum requirements for shareholders' meetings.

(l) The number of directors.

(m)Qualification of directors and their term of office.

(n) Cumulative voting in the election of directors. Although some states deal with this on a mandatory basis in either the articles or corporate statute, a majority of states leave this issue for inclusion in the bylaws.

(o) Procedure for filing board of director vacancies.

(p) Procedure for director removal.

(q) Time and place of directors' meetings.

(r) Notice of directors' meetings.

(s) Quorum at directors' meetings and voting requirements for director action. Provision should also be made for the approval of transactions between the corporation and a director.

(t) Compensation of directors.

(u) Authorization to delegate some board action to an executive committee. However, most states specifically proscribe certain conduct by an executive committee, so take care to check local corporation law.

(v) Indemnification of officers, directors, and other corporate employees.

(w) Identification of the corporate officers: qualifications, selection, duties, and removal. In some states the secretary and treasurer will be required to give a surety bond in an amount to be specified by the bylaws.

(x) Forms of stock to be issued, although details are usually left to the articles of incorporation, as well as provision for the transfer of stock.

(y) Determination of fiscal year and accounting practices.

[¶1217]   CORPORATE BUY-SELL AGREEMENTS

Participants in a new corporate venture will usually want an agreement that will require that on the death or departure of one of them, the survivors will have the opportunity to buy out the decedents' interest. There are several kinds of buy-sell agreements:

(1) The corporation (if it cannot, then the surviving shareholders) must buy and the estate of the deceased shareholder is obligated to sell.

(2) First the corporation, then the surviving shareholders have an option to buy the stock of a deceased stockholder and, if this option is exercised, the estate is obligated to sell.

(3) The estate of a deceased stockholder has the right to offer the stock to the survivors or to the corporation and if it does, either the survivors or the corporation is obligated to buy.

(4) There is no obligation either to buy or sell, but if a stockholder or his estate wants to sell, the stock must first be offered to the other stockholders or to the corporation before it can be sold to an outside party.

Forms of buy-sell agreements can be found in *IBP Forms of Business Agreements and Resolutions*.

[¶1218]　　　　　　　　HOW TO SET THE PRICE IN A
　　　　　　　　　　　　　　BUY-SELL AGREEMENT

There are several methods of valuing stock, a particularly controversial factor when drafting any buy-sell agreement for a closely held corporation:

(1) Fixed Price Method: This is the most common method. The stockholders set a fixed price per share in the buy-sell agreement, and leave room for revising this price, with the controlling price to be the last price stated prior to the death of the first stockholder. For example, the agreement may provide for a new price to be set annually at the close of the year. However, experience has shown that often the annual revaluation is never made. This raises the danger of an unfair depressed or inflated price being used. A possible solution is to use this method in conjunction with the appraisal method, and to provide in the contract that if no revaluation was made within 14 or more months prior to the death of a stockholder, the price of the stock will be determined by appraisal. Another way is to provide that the last agreed price is to be automatically adjusted by increases or decreases in earned surplus.

(2) Appraisal Method: Price is left open for future appraisal. The buy-sell agreement provides that value will be determined at the death of the first stockholder by a disinterested appraiser.

(3) Net Worth or Book Value Method: Valuation is based on the corporation's last balance sheet prepared prior to the death of the first stockholder, and the net worth is adjusted to the date of death. Or the company's accountants may be required to determine book value as of the date of death. Neither way is adequate, since neither reflects the true value of the business as a going concern, including the earning power of intangible assets like goodwill. The use of a stated formula, based on net worth, usually corrects this shortcoming. When this method is used the following items should be considered:

(a) Inventory. Will it be figured at cost or its real worth?

(b) Accounts Receivable. Will there be uncollectible accounts and what percentage of these does not show up in the book figures?

(c) Machinery and Equipment. Does the present book figure fairly reflect the present worth? Has it become obsolete?

(d) Buildings. Does book figure reflect current market value? Real estate is sometimes carried on books at cost and then depreciated substantially.

(e) Insurance Proceeds. If the company is to buy up the interest of the deceased associate and if there is insurance payable to the company, are the proceeds to be considered in determining book value?

(4) Straight Capitalization Method: The corporation's average net profits are capitalized at a specific rate, say 10%, and the result reflects the total value of the business including goodwill. The buy-sell agreement usually calls for averaging the net profits for the last five years immediately preceding the death of the first stockholder, after which they are capitalized at the 10% rate. The resulting total value is then divided by the number of outstanding shares to determine the value per share. Adjustment must be made to reflect the absorption of profits in the form of stockholders' salaries, or the average net profits will be distorted. The multiple at which the profits are capitalized will depend upon the nature of the business and the history of the particular corporation involved.

(5) Years' Purchase Method: This also relies on average net profits. The book value is averaged over a stated number of years, usually allowing a fair return of 6%. This is then subtracted from the average net profits, and the remainder, which represents excess earnings, is multiplied by the stated number of years' purchase to arrive at the value of goodwill. This goodwill is then added to the book value to determine the total value of the business, and the corresponding value per share of stock.

(6) Combination of Methods: A combination of different valuation methods is sometimes used to overcome the shortcomings of one or the other method.

[¶1219] PAYMENT OF PURCHASE PRICE

The agreement must specify how and when the price is to be paid. The plan must provide for the source of the funds. Life insurance on the stockholders will produce the necessary funds when they are needed. The excess of the total price over the insurance proceeds and other free cash available can be made payable on an installment basis. This obligation should be evidenced by notes and secured by the interest being purchased. Additional security can be provided in the form of mortgages on assets or additional insurance policies. Provide the right to prepay the obligations and for acceleration of the full obligation in the event of default of payment, bankruptcy, or sale of the business and other specified contingencies.

[¶1220] STOCK RETIREMENT OR CROSS PURCHASE?

Whether the corporation or the surviving shareholders should purchase the stock of a deceased stockholder may depend upon the following factors:

(1) Source of Funds: The stock retirement plan (i.e., purchase by the corporation) permits the use of corporate funds. The cross-purchase plan (i.e., purchase by shareholders) requires the use of funds that the stockholders have presumably taken out of the business and on which an individual income tax is payable.

(2) Enforceability: A cross-purchase agreement is clearly valid and enforceable while a stock retirement plan may not be enforceable if the corporation has or may have insufficient surplus to make the purchase and state law requires that stock may be redeemed only out of surplus. This potential deficiency in the stock retirement plan can be met by having the agreement provide that the survivors will either purchase or contribute sufficient surplus to the corporation, in the event that the corporation is prevented from retiring the stock of a deceased stockholder by state laws requiring that such purchases be made only out of surplus. In drafting the stock retirement agreement, the corporation should first be required to increase its available surplus by reducing its required capital or by increasing its capital to reflect a value for unrealized appreciation in assets. If this is insufficient and the survivors cannot either purchase or contribute additional funds to permit the corporation to meet the surplus requirement, the decedent's legal representative can be given the right to demand that the corporation be liquidated. These supplementary steps will make the stock retirement plan sufficiently valid and enforceable.

(3) Complication in Ownership of Insurance Policies: If the plan is to be funded by insurance, the stock retirement plan requires only one policy on each stockholder and permits the corporation to have continuous ownership of that policy. In the cross-purchase plan each stockholder has to carry insurance on the lives of the others.

(4) Cost Basis of Stock: In the stock retirement plan, the value of the stock of the survivors is generally increased when the corporation retires the stock of a deceased shareholder. However, the cost basis of the stock of the survivors remains the same. Thus a latent capital gain tax liability is built up. On the other hand, in the cross-purchase plan, when the survivors purchase the stock of a deceased shareholder they step up the basis of the stock to the price at which they buy.

(5) Shift of Control: In the stock retirement plan, the proportionate interest of the survivors automatically remains the same when the corporation buys in the stock of a deceased shareholder.

[¶1221]   HOW TO MAKE THE PURCHASE PRICE
BINDING FOR ESTATE TAX PURPOSES

The price set in a mandatory buy-sell agreement is the value of the business for federal estate tax purposes if:

(1) The price is fair and reflects a normal business intent;

(2) The purchase price is fixed in the agreement; and

(3) The parties to the agreement (as well as their survivors or estates) are required to sell at the fixed price.

[¶1222] DISABILITY BUY-SELL AGREEMENTS

Perhaps even more important than the need to prepare for a shareholder's death is the need to provide for continuation of the business in the event of disability, particularly in the smaller corporation. Business owners may need two-way protection in the event of disability. First, they have to consider providing for adequate income to meet routine personal expenses, including the increased medical expenses. Second, they must protect the value of their ownership interests, which can most easily be accomplished by expanding a buy-sell agreement to cover the risk of total disability.

[¶1223] USING SPECIALIZED INSURANCE TO FUND THE BUY-SELL AGREEMENT

Three basic types of insurance policies are available to fund a buy-sell agreement:

(1) Standard Disability Income Contract: The individuals, corporation, or partnership purchases a disability income policy to protect an individual's income. If the individual is disabled beyond the elimination period, he receives monthly benefit payments as a wage continuation. If the individual is still disabled at the time designated in the buy-sell agreement (e.g., after 18, 24, or 30 months), the wage continuation payments are transformed into monthly payments under the buy-sell agreement until the individual is paid the agreed purchase price of his ownership interest.

(2) A "Specialty Disability Income Contract": Evolved to meet the particular needs of buy-sell arrangements, these policies tend to be optionally renewable and tied in with the regular issue limit. Because of the higher risk of "elective disability" (a form of early retirement) than of "elective death" (suicide), most policies include a co-insurance element and will fund only from 60 to 80% of the purchase price. These policies have nonguaranteed premiums, varying definitions of disability, varying elimination periods, and varying lengths of pay-out periods (including an occasional lump-sum payment). Some companies require a trusteed agreement to assure that benefits are used only to fund the buy-sell agreement.

(3) Lump-Sum Contract: Some insurance companies have developed an even more specialized product—a "lump-sum" policy. These policies clearly set out that the intent is to purchase the ownership interest of the disabled individual once the buy-sell agreement is triggered. At the triggering point, the individual

101

either receives a lump-sum payment for his business interest or opts for an installment purchase if the buy-sell agreement provides for it.

These policies contain the co-insurance element and look at disability in the context of whether the individual can still provide a valuable service to the organization. The insurance companies require the buy-sell agreement to define disability consistent with the policy definition, which is usually some variation of ''completely unable to engage in his regular occupation or any other occupation in the firm he might reasonably be expected to engage in with due regard to his education, training, and experience.''

Other features of lump-sum contracts include guaranteed premiums, conditional renewal, benefit reduction after age 60, conversion privilege to a noncancellable disability income policy, waiver of premium, and option to increase benefit levels.

CORPORATE DIRECTORS' AND OFFICERS' DUTIES AND LIABILITIES

[¶**1301**]   Directors, officers, and even controlling shareholders of a corporation stand in a fiduciary relationship to the corporation. Each must carry out his management responsibilities in good faith. Their powers, whether derived from charter or statute or both, may be exercised only for the benefit of the corporation.

[¶1302]   **DIRECTORS' DUTIES**

Directors of a corporation have many duties beyond merely sitting on a board and occasionally approving decisions of management. These are explored below.

[¶1303]   **DUTY TO ATTEND DIRECTORS' MEETINGS**

If poor health or other factors require that a director regularly miss meetings, he should resign rather than incur the risk of liability for board decisions to which he was not a party. If a director must miss an occasional meeting, there are ways in which he can familiarize himself with what transpired by conferring with fellow directors and examining the minutes and corporate records. If specific issues will be on the agenda, the director can make his views known via a written instrument, particularly if he knows his is the minority view.

[¶1304]   **EXAMINATION OF FINANCIAL STATEMENTS**

A director is supposed to spot the chief executive who may be treating the business as his own, e.g., misapplying funds in good or bad faith for his personal benefit. It's the director's job to supervise the acts of officers. He should get financial reports directly from the responsibile financial officer, not secondhand. He should know the terms of underlying corporate obligations, as well as the provisions of the company's charter and bylaws. If management is pursuing improper policies and practices, a director cannot avoid responsibility on grounds of ignorance.

[¶1305]   **INSPECTION OF BOOKS AND RECORDS**

As a corollary to his obligations as a corporate fiduciary and as part of his management duties, a director enjoys the right and has an obligation to inspect the corporate books and records. The right of inspection exists only for as long as the director remains in office. However, some courts have allowed former directors the right of inspection of records relating to the years during which they served, in order to protect their own liability interests. A few states consider the right of inspection a "qualified" right in that it ceases if it can be shown that the director seeks inspection for reasons adverse to the corporate interest.

[¶1306]   **DUTY OF CARE**

Because directors are responsible for the management of the corporation, they must ultimately be called to account for any corporate losses. While it is clear that a director who perpetrates a fraud, derives a personal benefit at the expense of the corporation, or is found to have engaged in wanton acts of omission or commission is liable for the resultant losses, a more important issue is the standard of care to which a director is to be held for acts that may later appear to have been imprudent, wasteful, or negligent.

The Supreme Court of the United States has noted that directors of banks and other financial institutions are legally bound to use that degree of care "which ordinarily prudent and diligent men would exercise under similar circumstances." This standard has been adopted for directors of business corporations as well. Pennsylvania's Business Corporation Law §408 requires that "directors act in good faith and exercise such care as the 'ordinarily prudent man' would exercise under similar circumstances."

New York imposes a similar standard of care upon its directors. Section 717 of the New York Business Corporation Law states that "directors and officers shall discharge the duties of their respective positions in good faith and with that degree of diligence, care and skill which ordinarily prudent men would exercise under similar circumstances in like positions." The general rule, in force in Delaware, requires directors to exercise "diligence and reasonable judgment honestly and in good faith."

[¶1307]   **DUTY OF LOYALTY**

A director's duty of loyalty to the corporation encompasses many types of activities. The duty of loyalty is frequently used to invalidate a contract between the corporation and the director, to recover profits made by a director from transactions with the corporation, to prevent directors from competing with the corporation, and to prevent a director from taking personal advantage of a transaction based upon his position in the corporation—usually referred to as the doctrine of corporate opportunity.

A director who makes a profit by taking advantage of a business opportunity for which the corporation should have had "first call" is liable to the corporation for those profits. However, not every business opportunity need first be offered to the company. If the opportunity is not essential to the corporation, nor one in which it has an interest or the expectancy of an interest, the director may then treat such an opportunity as his own. A director may also take advantage of a corporate opportunity if his corporation is legally and financially unable to do so, or if the corporation has turned down the opportunity in a good faith exercise of its business judgment. However, a director may not, after resigning as a director, take advantage of a corporate opportunity that came to him while he was a director.

With the increase in the number of corporations having common directors, a frequent issue is the validity of transactions between corporations with interlocking directorates. The liberal trend in this area is to uphold the validity of such contracts, unless the contract is unfair, unreasonable, or fraudulent. Usually, directors seeking to uphold the contract have the burden of overcoming the presumption against the contract's validity. In many states, it makes no difference if the number of common directors constitutes a majority of the board, so long as the contract is fair. For jurisdictions with a more conservative approach, the contract may be voidable at the option of either corporation, without regard to the fairness or reasonableness of the transaction.

Section 8 of the Clayton Act (15 USC §19) prohibits interlocking directorates on the boards of competitor corporations if either company has capital and surplus in excess of $1,000,000. This is to prevent the possibility of agreements not to compete, which would be in violation of the federal antitrust laws. Section 8 does not apply to banks or railroads.

Directors can't play favorites among the stockholders. They can't favor one group of stockholders within the same general class, nor can they favor one class of stockholders over another, except as the stock itself calls for higher preferences or rights of one class of stock over another.

It's expected that an outside director will have other business interests—these may even be competitive. There's no harm so long as information gained from the relationship with the corporation is not used to its disadvantage. If an outside director goes too far, he must expect, if a stockholder prevails in his derivative suit, to account to the corporation for profits derived from the competing business.

Chances are that the employment contract specifically prohibits competition—unless certain exceptions are expressly enumerated. An officer or other employee is required to use his full working time and best efforts on behalf of the corporation. Failure to do so is a breach, even if the other activity is not competition. He is then accountable to the corporation for profits from the other venture.

[¶1308]   OUTSIDE DIRECTORS

An invitation to join a board of directors as an outside director may prompt visions of power, prestige, and influence. Prior to acceptance of this responsibility, a nominee should consult the following checklist:

☐ *Articles of Incorporation and Bylaws:* A careful reading should give some insight as to the purpose of the corporation and its day-to-day operation. These documents also spell out the duties of a director and indicate what provisions the corporation has made with regard to director liability.

☐ *Present Financial and Legal Status of the Corporation:* Review past filings with the Securities and Exchange Commission, inquire as to how the directors are kept apprised of all current financial information, and check as to whether the corporation is facing any pending litigation. Remember, whatever a director doesn't know about the corporation *can* hurt him.

☐ *Any Conflicts of Interest?* Carefully review the position in the business community to determine if there is even the slightest appearance of a conflict, regardless of whether one actually exists. (*Note*: No matter how neutral a director knows he can be, the shareholders, other directors, and general public will not give him the benefit of the doubt.)

☐ *Time Commitment:* Will there be enough time to attend all board meetings, as well as to investigate matters that will be discussed? Frequent absence and lack of preparation can come back to haunt one should future problems develop. Remember, a director is answerable for the actions of the board as a whole if he did not attend the meeting or put himself on record as opposing the contested action.

☐ *Compensation:* Since monetary compensation is usually low, find out whether there will be some additional expenses to assume in order to carry out the duties as a director. Even if there are, the challenge, prestige, and opportunity associated with the position may make it worthwhile anyway.

☐ *Insurance Liability:* Even though an individual may ultimately be adjudged innocent, the costs involved in defending a legal suit can be prohibitive. Find out whether the corporation will absorb legal costs, as well as indemnification for any damages or settlements that might have to be paid.

☐ *Composition and Operation of the Board:* Finally, how is the board divided between inside and outside directors? Do any of the other directors have real or potential conflicts of interest? Are the actions of the whole board merely a reflection of the opinions of the inside directors or control group, or do board meetings provided the basis for thorough discussion prior to a vote? What is the relationship between the board and the officers of the corporation?

[¶1309] CONSEQUENCES OF NEGLECT—SHAREHOLDER DERIVATIVE SUIT

In a shareholder's derivative suit, a shareholder "steps into the shoes" of the corporation to seek relief for wrongs committed against the corporate entity. Since it is unlikely that a corporation would sue its own directors for violations of the duties of loyalty and care, or that a majority shareholder would want to change the status quo, the derivative suit enables a minority shareholder to advance the corporation's claims against its directors or third parties. Following is a list of improper actions that could give rise to a derivative suit:

(1) Improper loans to shareholders.

(2) Continual absence from directors' meetings permitting improper acts to be done by others.

(3) Improper expenditures of corporate funds in proxy contests.

(4) Improvident investment of corporate funds.

(5) Improvident expansion of corporate activities into new fields resulting in losses.

(6) Failure to discover and prevent antitrust violations.

(7) To recover treble damages for damages caused to the corporation by violation of antitrust laws.

(8) Failure to take action against directors who make short-term profits in violation of §16(b) of the Securities Exchange Act.

(9) Use of corporate funds to purchase shares of corporation to combat takeover bid by outside interests.

(10) Improperly paying a dividend.

(11) Issuing stock without obtaining valid consideration.

(12) Failure to obtain competitive bids where required by prudent business practice.

(13) Wasting corporate assets by causing a plant to be dismantled solely to defeat a labor union.

(14) Forgiving an improper loan made by a prior board to an officer.

(15) Diverting the proceeds of a public offering to pay debts other than those authorized to be paid for such proceeds.

(16) Embezzlement by an employee that could have been prevented by careful supervision.

[¶1310] DIRECTORS' DEFENSES TO DERIVATIVE SUIT

Since a plaintiff-shareholder is required to make a demand upon the directors prior to the commencement of the derivative suit, defendants may raise the "business judgment" rule as a defense. Such a defense is predicated on the theory that upon review of plaintiff's allegations, the directors may conclude that the complaint lacks merit. However, in those instances when a court determines that directors could not have exercised their business judgment, it may allow the suit to proceed *(Lasker v. Burks,* CA-2, 567 F. 2d 1208, 1978 *cert. granted,* USSC Dkt. No. 77-1724, 10/2/78).

[¶1311] DUTIES AND LIABILITIES UNDER THE
FEDERAL SECURITIES LAWS

Liabilities under the Securities Act of 1933 and the Exchange Act of 1934 mandate care on the part of corporate officers, directors, and other insiders. Heavy judgments as a result of derivative suits, criminal penalties, and large fines await those who do not diligently meet the laws' requirements. Listed below are some of the areas in which caution is required.

[¶1312] LIABILITY UNDER THE SECURITIES ACT
OF 1933

Most commonly used in the prosecution of a securities law violation is the 1933 Act. Corporate insiders should avoid conduct that might be construed as:

☐ Fraud in connection with the offer or sale of a security [15 USC §77q(a)].
☐ Sale of unregistered stock [15 USC §77(e)].
☐ Promotion or "touting" of a security without disclosing that a promoter has a financial interest [15 USC §77q(b)].
☐ Filing a false or misleading registration statement [15 USC §77x].
☐ Manipulation of the over-the-counter market [15 USC §77q(a)].

[¶1313] LIABILITY UNDER THE SECURITIES EXCHANGE ACT OF 1934

☐ Filing a false annual report or false periodic reports [15 USC §78l].
☐ Filing false proxy materials [15 USC §78n, ff(a)].
☐ Unlawful short sales of listed securities [15 USC §78j(a)].
☐ Manipulation of securities listed on over-the-counter or national exchanges [15 USC §78l].
☐ Failure to file insider ownership reports [15 USC §78p(a)].

The major areas of concern for directors and officers are discussed in detail in the following paragraphs.

[¶1314]   RULE 10b-5

Section 10(b) of the 1934 Act and Rule 10b-5 prohibit the use of any manipulative or deceptive devices in connection with the purchase or sale of securities. The Rule protects both defrauded buyers and sellers. Rule 10b-5 imposes a liability for the use of "inside" information or the disclosure of such information in the trading of securities. Not only are corporate officers, directors, and majority security holders potentially liable under this Rule, but any person having access to or receiving information also is liable for any trading based on nonpublic information. Those persons to whom the material information is transmitted are known as "tippees."

[¶1315]   DISCLOSURE UNDER RULE 10b-5

Rule 10b-5 makes it unlawful to mislead a buyer or seller by omitting a material fact in connection with the purchase or sale of a security. Any information known to an insider that would tend to influence the investment decision of a buyer or seller is probably a "material" fact necessitating disclosure. Here are some illustrations of material facts calling for disclosure under the Rule:

(1) The improved or worsening financial condition of the firm.
(2) A dividend cut.
(3) A contract for the sale of corporate assets.

(4) A contemplated liquidation of a subsidiary for the purpose of capturing inventory appreciation of the subsidiary.
(5) A new ore discovery.
(6) The fraudulent trading in company's stock by a third party (broker-dealer).
(7) Promissory notes in a financial statement used in connection with an exchange offer.
(8) Dividend increase.
(9) Possible corporate merger.
(10) New discoveries relating to products or processes.

[¶1316]   **WHEN MUST DISCLOSURE UNDER RULE 10b-5 BE MADE?**

Basically, Rule 10b-5 is aimed at insiders taking advantage of their position to make a profit on the purchase or sale of securities. Thus, when "inside" information becomes public knowledge, insiders should be able to trade without disclosing, since the public will already have access to the same information.

Courts have struggled with the problem of determining when information becomes public knowledge. There is dictum in the *Texas Gulf Sulphur* (CA-2, 401 F. 2d 833, 1968) case to suggest that insiders should refrain from trading for a "reasonable waiting period" when the news is of the sort that is not readily translatable into investment action, thus giving it an opportunity to filter down and be evaluated by the investing public.

[¶1317]   **WHEN DOES RULE 10b-5 APPLY?**

Rule 10b-5 applies whether or not the firm has securities registered under the 1933 or 1934 Acts. It applies whether the purchase or sale takes place on a securities exchange, in the over-the-counter market, or privately.

Securities Covered: Rule 10b-5 covers transactions in any form of securities, encompassing (but not limited to) any note, bond, certificate of interest or participation in any profit-sharing agreement, preorganization certificate or subscription contract, agreement to form a corporation, or joint venture agreement expressly providing for the distribution of shares of stock in a corporation thereafter to be formed.

Interstate Transactions: The Rule applies only when the requisites of federal jurisdiction are present—use of the mails, any means or instrumentality of interstate commerce, or stock exchange facilities. Even for wholly intrastate transactions, at least one-half the states have adopted the Uniform Securities Act §101, which has the same provisions as the Rule.

[¶1318]   **RELEASE OF INFORMATION**
                   DURING REGISTRATION

Insiders must also be acquainted with the special rules affecting the release of information when a company is involved in the process of registration. It is well-established that during such period neither the company nor its representatives should instigate publicity for the purpose of facilitating the sale of securities in a proposed offering. In addition, any publication of information by a company that is in registration other than by means of a statutory prospectus should be limited to factual information and should not include such things as predictions, projections, forecasts, or opinions with respect to value.

If information should be released, the SEC has indicated how to handle the problem (SEC Act of 1933, Release No. 5180): "In the event a company publicly releases material information concerning new corporate developments during the period that a registration statement is pending, the registration statement should be amended at or prior to the time the information is released. If this is not done and such information is publicly released through inadvertency, the pending registration statement should be promptly amended to reflect such information."

[¶1319]   **SECTION 16(b)—SHORT-SWING**
                 PROFITS RECAPTURE

Section 16(b) applies only to profits made in the trading of equity securities that are basically stocks, as distinguished from debt securities such as bonds or debentures. But it takes in more than stocks. It includes any security that is convertible, with or without additional payment or other consideration, into stock or any security that carries a warrant or right to subscribe to or purchase stock. It also includes any warrant or right to subscribe to or purchase stock; in other words, the warrant or right itself separated from or apart from any other security. It can also include any security that the SEC treats as an equity security under its rules and regulations, but so far the SEC hasn't acted under this authorization.

If any of the equity securities of a firm are registered under the Securities Exchange Act, it will be subject to the short-swing profits recapture provision, §16(b), even though the profits are made in unregistered securities.

[¶1320]   **BENEFICIAL OWNERSHIP**

There are at least a couple of gray areas on the matter of 10% stockholders. Section 16(b) itself says it is not "to be construed to cover any transaction where such beneficial owner was not such both at the time of purchase and sale, or the sale and purchase, of the security involved."

Prior to 1976, there was considerable debate over the language of part of §16(b), particularly the "at the time of" sale provision. A federal Court of Appeals decision indicated that the shareholder who became a 10% stock owner just after or just before a sale was liable. A District Court disagreed. In the landmark case of *Foremost-McKesson, Inc. v. Provident Securities Co.* (423 US 232, 1976), this part of the controversy was put to rest. Writing for a unanimous (8-0) Court, Justice Powell stated that the question presented was whether a person purchasing securities that put his holdings above the 10% level is a beneficial owner "at the time of the purchase" so that he must account for profits realized on a sale of the securities within six months. The Ninth Circuit Court of Appeals indicated in *Foremost-McKesson* that the answer was no (CA-9, 506 F. 2d 601, 1974), and the Supreme Court affirmed. The point is now settled as to the meaning of that particular phrase in §16(b).

There is no authoritative decision on the question of whether to count the transaction by which the stockholder ceases to be a ten percenter; however, one of the outstanding authorities in the field, Professor Louis Loss, has expressed the opinion that such a transaction must be counted. Again, to play it safe, it will be best to count the unloading transaction. In certain situations, a shareholder might want to consider a gift of a portion of the stock as a means of divesting himself of 10% status. There might be situations in which such a technique could be valuable even on a dollar-and-cents basis. Of course, a gift won't help unless it's completely bona fide and with no strings attached. In any case, great care and advice of counsel are called for before trying this.

Problems arise when a ten percenter sells his holdings in two transactions taking place within six months of purchase, the first reducing holdings below 10% and the second liquidating the remainder. For example, an insider by sale number one reduced his holdings to 9.96% and by a second sale to nothing. The Court of Appeals, Eighth Circuit, held that there was no short-swing liability for the second sale and was upheld by the U.S. Supreme Court.

The SEC would have linked the separate transactions and had asked the United States Supreme Court to approve an objective test for short-swing profit liabilities, i.e., a rule that if a person was a more-than-10% beneficial owner at any time during a period in which separate sale transactions occurred within six months of a purchase of the stock, then he has the status "at the time of the sale" as contemplated by §16(b).

The duties and liabilities of §16 cannot be escaped by an insider's having securities registered in someone else's name. Section 16 is aimed at direct or indirect beneficial ownership, not so-called legal ownership.

[¶1321]   **PURCHASE OR SALE**

The short-swing profits recapture section applies to the following types of securities transactions:

(1) Contracts to buy or sell;

(2) Stock options, warrants, or subscription rights granted to an officer or director as compensation for services (although may be exempt if granted under an option plan);

(3) Acquisitions of stock pursuant to the exercise of an option, warrant, or subscription right.

[¶1322]   EXEMPTIONS UNDER §16(b)

(1) Transactions exempt from the reporting requirements are exempt from §16(b) (Rule 16a-10). An acquisition of securities is exempt from the reporting requirements if the acquirer doesn't participate in acquisitions or dispositions of securities of the same class having a total market value of more than $3,000 for any six-month period during which the acquisition occurs (Rule 16a-9).

(2) Acquisitions of stock pursuant to a stock bonus or similar plan and stock options acquired pursuant to a qualified or restricted stock option plan are exempt under Rule 16b-3, provided the plan meets the detailed requirements of the Rule that include approval of the plan by shareholders at a meeting for which proxies were solicited in accordance with SEC rules or the stockholders are given the information called for, if a solicitation was made. The stock acquired on the exercise of an option, warrant, or right is not, however, exempt under the Rule.

(3) Rule 16b-6 exempts the long-term profits from sales within six months of the exercise of a stock option and this Rule has been upheld.

(4) Purchases and sales by underwriters in a distribution of securities and stabilizing transactions in connection with a distribution are exempt (Rule 16b-2).

(5) Transactions by registered investment companies and public utility holding companies that have been passed on by the SEC are exempt (Rules 16b-1 and 4).

(6) When an equity security is acquired in good faith in connection with a debt previously contracted, §16(b) expressly excepts the acquisition. A convertible debenture isn't within the rule.

(7) Transactions by so-called market-makers, other than on a national securities exchange or an exchange exempt from registration, when incident to maintaining a market and not in the ordinary course of their business as securities dealers, are exempt under §16(d). This exemption deals with the situation in which the market-maker, whether it's a partnership or a corporation, has a partner or other representative who sits on the board of directors of the firm whose securities are involved in trading and there is an attempt to impose §16(b) liability on the market-maker as was attempted in *Blau v. Lehman* (368 US 403, 1962). In *Blau*, deputization of the director as the agent or representative of the market-maker was made the test of the market-maker's inability under §16(b), and the Court found such deputization to be lacking in the particular case. The precise nature of the deputization required to satisfy the test is not clear. But it is clear that if the transaction occurs on a national securities exchange, §16(d) is inapplicable; and the *Blau* case remains in effect until overruled.

In addition to these exemptions, there are a number of exemptions of limited and specialized application: certain transactions in which securities are received by redeeming other securities (Rule 16b-5); certain acquisitions and dispositions of securities pursuant to mergers or consolidations (Rule 16b-7); certain securities received under transactions involving deposit or withdrawal under a voting trust or deposit agreement (Rule 16b-8); certain transactions involving an exchange of similar securities (Rule 16b-9); certain transactions involving railroad mergers and acquisitions (Rule 16b-10); and certain transactions involving the sale of subscription rights (Rule 16b-11).

Exempt Securities: Section 16(b) doesn't apply to transactions in "exempt securities." These are generally securities that are issued or guaranteed by governmental agencies. The exemption, therefore, isn't apt to have any interest for the insiders of ordinary corporations.

[¶1323]   **TIMING OF SHORT SWINGS**

Section 16(b) defines the short-swing period as "any period of less than six months." It's been decided that this means that the last day of the period is the second day before the date in the sixth month that corresponds numerically with the day of the month in which the first transaction took place. For example, if you buy or sell on February 1, 1979, the last day of the period would be July 30, 1979. This means you could sell or buy on July 31, 1979, or any time later and be home free as far as §16(b) is concerned. In the case of an ordinary purchase or sale, the transaction takes place when there is a firm commitment to buy or sell. In other cases, the transaction takes place when the right of the parties is fixed. An option, for example, dates from the time it is irrevocably granted. The fact that a sale agreement gives the buyer a right to rescind within a fixed period of time doesn't mean that the sale isn't counted until the time for rescission has run.

[¶1324]   **MEASUREMENT AND RECOVERY OF**
                  SHORT-SWING PROFITS

The measure of damages in an action brought under §16(b) is the profit realized on any purchase or sale or any sale and purchase within six months without any right of set-off, or the adoption of any rule of "first-in-first-out" or other minimizing of recovery. "The only rule," it has been said on good authority, "whereby all possible profits can be surely recovered is that of the lowest price in, highest price out—within six months."

Exchanges: If a purchase and sale involve an exchange of stock for assets and not a direct payment in money, the determination of profit realized will turn on the value of the assets exchanged for the stock.

Commissions and Transfer Taxes: The purchase or sale prices for the purpose of computing profit are determined after the deduction of commissions and transfer taxes.

Dividends: Dividends received are added to the profits; dividends not received are deducted.

A suit to recover short-swing profits can be brought by the corporation or any security holder if the corporation fails or refuses to do so within 60 days of request. The federal district courts have exclusive jurisdiction of these suits.

Statute of Limitations: The suit must be brought within two years from the time the profits are realized, but failure to file a Form 4 reporting the transaction prevents the time period from running. The period will run from the time Form 4 is filed.

Counsel Fees: Counsel is entitled to a generous percentage of the profits recovered as a fee. A fee may also be earned by serving a request on the corporation to institute suit where the corporation does so and recovers.

[¶1325]   **SUMMARY AND COMPARISON OF**
§16(b) AND RULE 10b-5

The following chart summarizes the different coverage, application, and liabilities under the Rules:

Risks and Pitfalls Under §16(b) and Rule 10b-5

	§16(b)	Rule 10b-5
Transactions covered	Short-swing purchase *and* sale or sale *and* purchase	Purchase *or* sale
Subject matter of transaction	Equity security, registered or not	Any security, registered or not
Must firm have other registered securities?	Yes, equity securities	No
Who is subject to liability?	Officers, directors, and 10% stockholders	Officers, directors, and controlling stockholders, plus corporation, and persons with "inside" information
Is misrepresentation, omission, or scheme necessary to impose liability?	No	Yes
Exempt transactions?	Yes, a variety of exemptions exist	No
Is direct dealing with party necessary?	No	No
Who has right of action?	Corporation; shareholder derivative action is also available	Person buying from or selling to insider or SEC

	§16(b)	Rule 10b-5
Remedies available?	Action for damages	Action for damages, rescission, disciplinary proceedings, criminal proceedings
Measure of damages?	Lowest price in, highest out, or vice versa, during short-swing period	Compensatory

[¶1326] INDEMNIFICATION AND INSURANCE PROTECTION FOR CORPORATE OFFICERS AND DIRECTORS

Generally speaking, legal liabilities incurred by corporate directors, officers, and employees as a result of their on-the-job conduct that results in a lawsuit may, under certain circumstances, be subject to indemnification by the corporation. Usually, an initial distinction must be made between a civil or criminal action instituted against a corporate director, officer, or employee by reason of conduct within the scope of employment that has injured another party, and those actions undertaken that are alleged to have injured the corporation itself. Standards for indemnification in each of these cases will vary.

Roots for all indemnification are either statute, portions of the corporate articles of incorporation, bylaw provisions, private agreement (such as an employment contract), a resolution of the board of directors, a vote of the shareholders, or, in some states for a successful defendant only, in a common law (nonstatutory) right to reimbursement.

An unsuccessful defendant to an action, absent corporate provisions or statutory requirements to the contrary, usually has no right to indemnification.

A list of the corporate indemnification statutes may be found in the Appendix at the back of this volume.

[¶1327]   CORPORATE INDEMNIFICATION PURSUANT TO STATUTE

To give a better idea of the factors and exacting requirements of sample indemnification statutes, those of two of the most popular states, New York and Delaware, are examined briefly below.

(1) State Law: State law is the decisive factor in determining whether there's a right or privilege of indemnification ("right" when indemnification is mandatory; "privilege" when it's discretionary). The Delaware Corporation Laws make indemnification permissible except when the corporate official is "successful on the merits or otherwise." If wholly successful, indemnification becomes mandatory. (See (4) below.) The statutory provision is nonexclusive, which means that the corporation can by proper corporate action provide indemnification in cases when not permitted or required by statute.

The New York indemnification provision, on the other hand, is exclusive, meaning the statutory perimeters cannot be exceeded in providing indemnification.

If the statutory scheme is nonexclusive or there is no applicable statute, then, of course, theoretically, the officer or director can look to common law principles to secure indemnification. But the common law is rather a slender reed to lean on, being based on an agency theory and generally requiring a showing of some benefit to the corporation to support indemnification.

(2) Who's Covered? The Delaware law covers past and present officers, directors, employees, or agents, or any person serving in such capacity for another corporation at the request of the corporation. The New York statute limits coverage to officers and directors. However, others may be indemnified on an agency theory.

(3) Type of Case: The right to or extent of indemnification permitted or required may vary, depending on whether the litigation, threatened or brought, is a derivative action, that is, one brought on behalf of the corporation by a stockholder, or is an action, civil or criminal, brought against the corporate officials by third parties, i.e., nonshareholders.

In the Delaware law, for example, any threatened, pending, or completed derivative action or suit is covered; but the New York statute doesn't cover threatened derivative actions. As to third-party matters, the Delaware law covers not only threatened, pending, or completed actions, suits, or proceedings, civil or criminal, but specifically covers administrative or investigative proceedings.

The New York law, on the other hand, is narrower in its terms in that it omits specific mention of administrative and investigative proceedings.

(4) Success: If the defense is successful on the merits or otherwise (for example, failure to bring suit within the time permitted), both the Delaware and New York statutes require indemnification. Nevertheless, the courts have taken the view that they may still disallow indemnification when they think it inequitable.

(5) Settlement: Delaware permits indemnification for the amount paid in settlement if ordered by the court or if, within the corporation, there's a proper determination that the official or executive acted in accordance with the applicable standard (see below). In New York, the rule is the same in third-party suits; but in suits brought on behalf of the corporation, there can be indemnity for a settlement as such, although expenses may be allowed if approved by the court.

(6) No-Contest Plea: Both Delaware and New York provide that a no-contest plea or nolo contendere plea does not give rise to a presumption of a breach of standards.

(7) Failure: Delaware permits indemnity even though there's a finding of a breach of duty in a derivative action for such "expenses" as the court deems proper. In both Delaware and New York in third-party actions, indemnification is possible, despite finding of breach of duty, if the individual charged acted in accordance with a certain standard set up in the indemnification law.

116

(8) Standard of Conduct: In Delaware, the corporation may generally indemnify if the official or executive "acted in good faith and in a manner he reasonably believed to be in or not opposed to the best interest of the corporation," with the added proviso that if in a derivative action he is "adjudged to be liable for negligence or misconduct in the performance of his duty," he can only be indemnified for such "expenses" as the court deems proper. In criminal actions, it must also be shown that he "had no reasonable cause to believe his conduct was unlawful." In New York, in a derivative action, there can be no indemnification if a person is adjudged to have breached his statutory duty as an officer or director. In third-party actions, New York follows the Delaware provision except that it omits reference to cases in which the defendant believed that his actions were "not opposed" to the best interests of the corporation. In criminal actions, New York follows Delaware.

(9) How Satisfaction of Standard Is Determined: The court has power to determine whether or not the required standard has been met and, if so, to award indemnification. But beyond this, the determination may be made by a majority vote of a quorum of disinterested directors, independent legal counsel, or the shareholders.

(10) Advancement of Expenses: In Delaware, the board of directors may make advance payment of expenses on receipt of an undertaking to repay. In New York, the board may do the same but it must first find that the applicable standard has been met.

(11) Reimbursement for Costs in Suit: The successful defendant can usually recover "costs," but costs don't normally include attorney's fees in the absence of a statute so providing. Security-for-expenses statutes may give successful individual defendants some protection in derivative suits.

[¶1328]   **USE OF INSURANCE POLICIES FOR
                  CORPORATE OFFICERS AND DIRECTORS**

The only real alternative to or way of filling in the gaps left by indemnification is insurance. There are two basic types of insurance to cover the risks involved:

(1) Insurance that reimburses the company for the payments it makes on behalf of directors, officers, and others; and

(2) Insurance protecting the individuals involved by reason of their corporate associations.

Basic Legal Limitations of Insurance: At the outset, there is the policy of the common law against permitting a man to insure himself against the consequences of his own intentional wrongdoing. The same consideration would likely apply to acts of extreme negligence.

Also, with insurance, as with indemnification, while state law and policy considerations generally determine what liabilities may be insured against, the policy considerations reflected in federal securities laws may override state law.

The Power of the Company to Buy Insurance: Look to state law and the corporate charter and bylaws to determine the power of the company to buy insurance.

The Delaware statute, which follows the Model Business Corporation Law in force in a number of states, gives the corporation broad power to purchase insurance against any liability asserted against a director, officer, employee, or agent in such capacity, "whether or not the corporation would have the power to indemnify him against such liability" under a particular section of the Delaware law.

What Policies Cover and What They Exclude: Policies generally cover any amount the corporation is required to pay to a director, officer, or any other covered person, as indemnity for claim(s) made against such person during the policy period. Amounts may be paid for damages, judgments, settlements, costs, charges, or expenses incurred in connection with the defense of any action, suit, or proceeding alleging a "wrongful act," to which the covered person is a party.

"Wrongful act" is defined as "any breach of duty, neglect, error, misstatement, misleading statement, omission or other act done or wrongfully attempted" by individual insureds alleged by any claimant or any matter claimed against them solely by reason of their being officers or directors.

The policy excludes fines or penalties imposed by law and any matter that may be deemed legally uninsurable under judicial precedents, administrative determinations, or unilateral determinations by the underwriters.

Amount Payable: Generally, and subject to possible variations among companies, the company policy will pay 95% of the indemnity paid or payable over $20,000, subject, of course, to the overall policy limit.

Ten million dollars is usually adequate. It's hard to get more than $15,000,000.

The deductible amount applies only once to interrelated acts by more than one insured. The policy limit is for each policy year.

[¶1329]   **STATE REGULATION OF SECURITIES:
BLUE SKY LAWS**

The state's right to regulate securities is specifically referred to in §18 of the Securities Act of 1933.

Although several states have adopted the Uniform Securities Act, it is still necessary for the attorney of a corporation planning a public offering to check the "Blue Sky" laws for the jurisdictions in which its securities are going to be sold and to comply with each state's registration requirements.

Most people tend to associate federal regulation with securities transactions. That is a mistake if a corporation is contemplating an offering, since compliance with the federal laws does not automatically give the issuer a right to sell its shares in a particular state. In addition, the fact that a particular offering is exempted from registration under federal law does not necessarily mean that it will be exempt from registration under state law. A classic example is the intrastate offering—even though exempt from federal registration, securities offered within the state where the issuer is located will have to be registered with that state.

Despite the variance among the states, there are certain features common to almost all state Blue Sky statutes:

(1) Prevention of fraud;

(2) Registration of securities;

(3) Registration and/or licensing of securities dealers and salesmen;

(4) Under most Blue Sky laws, the issuer will be required to make periodic reports to the Blue Sky law administrator;

(5) Civil liability provision enabling anyone who purchased a security that was sold in violation of the law, or by means of an untrue or omitted material fact in registration or prospectus, the right to recover the purchase price paid, plus interest and costs (usually including attorney's fees);

(6) Criminal liability provision, subjecting an issuer who willfully violates the state law to a fine and/or imprisonment;

(7) A nonresident issuer is usually required to appoint the Blue Sky law administrator (or Secretary of State) as agent to receive process in connection with civil suits arising out of issuer's efforts within that state.

Most Blue Sky laws also exempt certain types of securities from registration, such as:

(1) Securities that are listed on a national or regional stock exchange (needless to say, this will be the most important exemption for a lot of companies);

(2) Securities of nonprofit organizations;

(3) Obligations of federal, state, or local governments;

(4) Securities of national and state banks or savings and loan associations; and

(5) Short-term commercial paper (less than a nine-month maturity period).

[¶1330]   **FOR FURTHER REFERENCE . . .**

Corporate Planning (Volumes 1 and 2), Institute for Business Planning, Inc., Englewood Cliffs, N.J.

Hess, R.P., *Desk Book for Setting Up a Closely Held Corporation,* Institute for Business Planning, Inc., Englewood Cliffs, N.J. (1979).

Hinsey, J., ''New Lloyd's Policy Form for Directors and Officers Liability Insurance—an Analysis,'' 33 Business Lawyer 1961-92 (April 1978).

Johnston, J.F., Jr., ''Corporate Indemnification and Liability Insurance for Directors and Officers,'' 33 Business Lawyer 1993 (April 1978).

''Recent Developments in Securities Law: Causes of Action under Rule 10b-5,'' 26 Buffalo Law Review 503-87 (Summer 1977).

''Registration Process: The Role of the Lawyer in Disclosure: Symposium,'' 33 Business Lawyer 1329 (March 1978).

''Section 17(a) of the 1933 Securities Act: An Alternative to the Recently Restricted Rule 10b-5,'' 9 Rutgers Camden Law Journal 340 Winter 1978.

CORPORATE LEGAL EXPOSURE AND LIABILITY

[¶**1401**] Most executives tend to minimize or entirely overlook the need to protect themselves and their business from loss and liability. The importance of such protection cannot be overemphasized—what good is it to operate a profitable business if the money it generates is lost through a set of unexpected circumstances for which its owners are ill-prepared? The following checklist indicates those areas that pose the greatest danger to both businesses and individual owners and should be used to review the legal posture of your business. (If the business is incorporated, an individual may be liable in his role as a corporate director or officer; this liability is discussed at ¶1301 et seq.)

☐ *Accident, Liability, and Property Damage:* What types and amounts of risk exposure exist, and what sort of insurance protection is adequate?

☐ *Antitrust Problems:* Do the corporate pricing policy, distribution and licensing agreements, sales procedures and competitive practices in general violate federal law?

☐ *Inventions and Trade Secrets:* Are they adequately protected?

☐ *Discrimination:* Guard against discrimination in employment hiring, promotion, and firing.

☐ *Libel and Slander:* These must be guarded against, whether in the course of labor disputes, proxy contests, employee discharges, collection letters, sales letters, ordinary business letters, or disparaging a competitor's product. Be aware that statements by agents or employees may impute liability to the corporation.

☐ *Breach of Contract:* Do not induce lawsuits in hiring an employee or taking business away from a competitor.

☐ *Product Liability:* Minimize exposure by taking the following steps:
  (a) Get products pretested by an independent laboratory.
  (b) Set up a quality control program.
  (c) Make instructions crystal clear and display them prominently on labels.
  (d) Make warranty definite—stating exactly what is being warranted and what is not. If the component parts or accessories are being warranted by others, see that these warranties are passed on.
  (e) Check product advertising and promotion to see that the claims being made do not unnecessarily attract product liability lawsuits.
  (f) Carry product liability insurance. A policy with proper coverage can protect against claims against defective products, mislabeled ones, products sold for improper use or under improper circumstances, negligence, and breach of implied warranty.

CORPORATE MERGERS, ACQUISITIONS, AND REORGANIZATIONS

[¶1501] The decision to acquire, merge, or sell a business should not be reached without careful consideration of several factors: (1) The business objectives of such a move should be evaluated; (2) The projected future state of the industry should be analyzed; and (3) A long-range (at least five-year) plan for growth should be formulated. After careful review of all the above, if the decision to acquire, merge, or sell is made, the next step is to select the company to be acquired, negotiate, and finalize the deal. In order to do this, it will be necessary to examine the tax considerations, the method of acquisition (stock or cash), existing corporate liabilities, SEC and antitrust problems, as well as any other labor or Blue Sky pitfalls.

Once the terms of the contract are agreed upon, the contract can be prepared, the necessary approvals obtained, the proper filings made, and the transaction closed. The following paragraphs highlight these important areas, and include checklists of items to be covered in any business deal. For forms of contract, see *IBP Forms of Business Agreements and Resolutions*.

[¶1502]   **MERGERS**

An *acquisition* (or merger) usually involves both a willing buyer and willing seller. In this respect, it is different from a takeover or tender offer, which is usually considered an unfriendly acquisition (see ¶1536). Acquisition is an umbrella term and includes more specific terms such as merger, consolidation, asset acquisition, and stock acquisition.

[¶1503]   **STATUTORY MERGER**

A *statutory merger* is usually regulated by the corporation laws of the states of the buyer and the seller corporations. Generally, board of director approval of both corporations is required as well as a stockholder vote to approve the merger. One corporation is merged into the other and the remaining corporation is known as the surviving corporation. The surviving corporation will own all the assets and property of both corporations and will retain the liabilities of both corporations by operation of law.

[¶1504]   **STATUTORY CONSOLIDATION**

The *statutory consolidation* differs from the statutory merger in that there is no ''surviving corporation.'' Instead, both merged corporations disappear and a new corporation is created. Once again, this new corporation obtains all the assets as well as the liabilities of the two now-defunct corporations.

[¶1505]   **ASSET ACQUISITION**

In an *asset acquisition* the buyer acquires all or most of the assets and business of the seller as per a contract entered into between the buyer and the seller. This differs from the stock acquisition which is discussed below.

[¶1506]   **STOCK ACQUISITION**

In a *stock acquisition* the buyer acquires the shares of stock from the stockholders of the seller. It differs from an asset acquisition in that the directors of the selling corporation are not consulted. Rather, the buyer goes directly to the shareholders of the corporation and offers to buy their stock. If management is opposed to the buyer's offer to purchase, you generally have a takeover bid or tender offer, which is regulated by the 1934 Exchange Act. Although the terms "takeover bid" and "tender offer" are used interchangeably, tender offer usually refers to an acquisition of stock or cash.

[¶1507]   **TARGET**

A *target company* is the corporation sought to be acquired by the buyer in an unfriendly takeover offer.

[¶1508]   **INITIAL CONSIDERATIONS FOR THE BUYER**

The decision to acquire a merger business is not one that a buyer can enter into lightly. A great deal of planning should occur prior to the search for a company to acquire. A buyer should first undertake a self-evaluation of its own business and the development of a long-range growth policy, taking into account the following factors:

(1) Value of own business;

(2) Long-range goal;

(3) Industry market development and competition;

(4) Value of business to be acquired.

Once this self-evaluation is completed, it will be easier to identify the type of corporation that should be acquired. In fact, the buyer may even conclude that acquisition is not the best way to remedy its own business defects and that, in fact, it may be preferable to build its company from within rather than acquire from without.

However, once the decision to acquire has been made, the next step is to determine the basic qualifications a potential target should have in order to be considered a likely candidate for acquisition. The following factors should be considered:

(1) Minimum acceptable amount of return on invested capital or earnings per share.

(2) Minimum acceptable potential growth rate for the acquired company.

(3) The sort of management that would be required; would existing management be kept on or would the acquiring company have to provide support personnel?

(4) Geographic location of the acquired company.

[¶1509]   **WHAT KIND OF ACQUISITION
                             SHOULD BE CONSIDERED?**

Once a company has been selected for acquisition, the process of purchasing the company begins. While a seller will normally prefer to sell stock in order to avoid the trouble, cost, and risk of liquidation and depreciation recapture, the buyer will usually want assets in order to get a high basis and to avoid the seller's liabilities, including recapture potential. In addition, if considerable goodwill may be involved, a buyer may prefer to purchase specific assets and thus avoid putting any value on goodwill (which is not recoverable by depreciation or amortization). If the buyer acquires stock, it can liquidate the purchased company tax free within two years and step up the basis to the purchase price under IRC §334(b)(2). But in that case, if there is any depreciation subject to recapture under IRC §1245 or §1250, the liquidating company will have a tax to pay.

There are three kinds of tax-free acquisitions:

(1) The statutory merger or Type "A" reorganization;

(2) The stock-for-stock or Type "B" reorganization; and

(3) The stock-for-assets or Type "C" reorganization.

[¶1510]   **STATUTORY MERGER
                             (TYPE "A" REORGANIZATION)**

This is a merger or consolidation effected in accordance with the corporation laws of the United States, a state or territory, or the District of Columbia. Although a statutory merger has an advantage over other types of reorganizations allowed by IRC §368 (in the sense that specific restrictions aren't placed on the exchanges necessary to carry out the merger) this advantage is not as valuable as it might first appear, since the state itself will impose its own restrictions, and these state law requirements may be difficult to meet. As already noted, another serious drawback lies in the fact that the surviving corporation assumes all of the obligations of the transferor corporation by operation of law.

[¶1511]   **STOCK FOR STOCK
                             (TYPE "B" REORGANIZATION)**

This is described as the acquisition by one corporation, in exchange solely for all or a part of its voting stock (or part or all of the voting stock of a corporation that controls the acquiring corporation), of stock of another corporation if, immediately after the acquisition, the acquiring corporation has control of the other corporation ("regardless of whether or not it had control before.") The acquiring corporation can transfer all or part of the stock acquired to its subsidiary. "Control" means ownership of stock possessing at least 80% of the total combined voting power of all classes of stock entitled to vote and at least 80% of the total number of shares of all other classes of outstanding stock.

A unique feature of the Type "B" reorganization is that it is either fully taxable or fully nontaxable. Note that in the stock-for-stock transaction the agreement is between the *buyer* and the *shareholders* of the seller.

[¶1512] STOCK FOR ASSETS (TYPE "C" REORGANIZATION)

This is described as the acquisition by one corporation, in exchange solely for all or a part of its voting stock (or of voting stock of a corporation that controls the acquiring corporation), of substantially all the properties of another corporation (but assumption of liabilities in connection with such acquisition or the fact that property acquired is subject to a liability is disregarded in determining whether an acquisition was solely for stock). However, if the acquiring corporation issues anything other than its own voting stock in the exchange, the assumed liabilities are treated as cash paid by that corporation. If the assumed liabilities plus the property or securities issued in addition to voting stock exceed 20% of the value of the assets acquired, the transaction is disqualified as a C-type reorganization.

In a C-type reorganization, as long as voting stock is given for property with a market value of at least 80% of the market value of all the property of the acquired corporation, the remaining consideration may be paid in money or other property (80%-20% rule).

The difficulty in successfully bringing about a C-type reorganization under the 80%-20% rule may arise in determining the amount of assumed liabilities.

[¶1513] PURCHASE OF SOME STOCK AND REDEMPTION OF BALANCE

Another way to finance an acquisition is to use some of the corporation's own funds for part of the purchase price. The seller will get his money as capital gain, and there will be no unfavorable tax results to the buyer if in acquiring the initial shares he did not personally obligate himself to redeem the balance of the stock and then have the corporation take over the obligation (*Zenz v. Quinlivan,* CA-6, 213 F. 2d 914, 1954). If the buyer obligates himself to buy all the shares and has the purchased corporation provide some of the money, he will be charged with a taxable dividend *(Woodworth v. Comm.,* CA-6, 218 F. 2d 719, 1955; *Wall v. U.S.,* CA-4, 164 F. 2d 462, 1947).

Three other ways to finance the purchase of a new company are described in the paragraphs below.

[¶1514]   TWELVE-MONTH LIQUIDATION METHOD

Another approach to obtain the part-purchase, part-redemption effect is to have the sellers use a 12-month (IRC § 337) liquidation. If the selling corporation adopts a plan of complete liquidation under §337 and liquidates within that time, it won't be taxed on the sale of all its assets during that 12-month period. The selling stockholders would get one capital gain on the liquidation when they receive the proceeds of the sale and the cash left in the corporation. So the net effect is the same to the sellers as the sale of part of the stock and redemption of the rest. The buyer benefits because he would get a stepped-up basis for the assets he buys. There is no carryover of the old company's earnings and profits, and no accumulated surplus problem.

There is a drawback: A seller will not want to use §337 if the sale is to be reported as an installment sale.

The buyer's planning will often include an attempt to use the acquired company's own funds for future earnings to help pay for the acquisition. Several different techniques are available.

[¶1515]   NEW COMPANY ORGANIZED TO
BUY THE ASSETS

When the buyer wants to use the company's *future earnings* as well as its assets to help swing the deal instead of purchasing the stock personally, he can organize a new corporation, have that corporation buy the stock, and execute notes for the purchase price. The new corporation then completely liquidates the old corporation, and takes over all its assets. The new corporation will then owe the purchase price and will have all the assets of the old corporation, including its future earnings, to apply on the indebtedness for the purchase price. The new corporation will realize no taxable gain or loss on the receipt of the assets in complete liquidation, and the basis of the assets will be stepped up to market value (IRC §334(b)(2)). The old corporation also realizes no taxable gain on tl e liquidation of the transfer of its assets to the new corporation—except to the extent of any depreciation recapture under IRC §1245 or §1250.

In addition, since the debt is an obligation of the new corporation that will own and operate the business, the interest on the debt will be deductible against the income of the business.

[¶1516]   BUYING SOME OF THE ASSETS AND
LEASING OTHERS

By buying only some of the assets and leasing the rest, the future earnings of the company are used to pay the rent. One way to do this is to have a third party buy the assets, sell some to the ultimate buyers, and rent the rest to the buyers. When the stock must be bought in the first place, partial liquidation of the corporation may be required. To avoid any tax on a partial liquidation, the third party can be a tax-exempt organization.

[¶1517]   BROKER'S OR FINDER'S FEE

Be sure to resolve the broker issue prior to price negotiations, since a fee or commission can influence the ultimate amount paid or received. The law varies from state to state and should be consulted if brokerage problems arise.

Lawyers for both parties should determine whether a broker or finder may have been employed by buyer or seller, which party may become legally responsible to pay him, the extent of the liability, and how it is to be divided. If the claim is not explicit, it is desirable to reduce it to a definite understanding before the contract to close the deal is signed, and the contract should represent either that there were no obligations to brokers or finders, or provide who is to pay any admitted obligations.

Many state statutes of fraud require that the broker's or finder's contract be in writing in order to be enforceable. Some states also require licensing of brokers for them to be able to receive their commissions or fees. Remember that an implied contract may exist if the broker acts with the consent of the principal, whether given in writing, orally, or by implication from the conduct of the parties. A conversation about a possible sale, and an introduction furnished by the broker to the ultimate buyer, may be enough to entitle the broker to a commission on the theory that an implied contract of employment existed between the seller and the broker. If this kind of a cloud hangs over the negotiations, try to eliminate it by a written understanding.

[¶1518]   THE PURCHASE PRICE

Having decided upon the type of acquisition and the particular company, the next major task is to establish the purchase price. Buying a business is really no different from buying any other asset. The buyer wants as low a price as possible and the seller wants to maximize his gain. The only real difference in the purchase of an ongoing corporation is that there are more factors to be taken into account, for example, working capital, market conditions, price trends in the industry, patents, and goodwill. The buyer must undertake an independent investigation in order to determine the price that he is willing to pay for the comany. There are several ways for a buyer to get a quick idea as to the value of a corporation under consideration.

One approach is to look at the book value of the business. Usually, however, book value is grossly understated and most sellers will not part with their corporation based on that figure. Another approach is to have an appraisal done for the value of the plant, inventories, equipment, property, and intangibles of the corporation. A third approach, when possible, is to take a look at the seller's corporation and compare it to other corporations in the same industry. The situation can be somewhat easier when you're talking about publicly held companies since their stock is traded on stock exchanges. In that case, it should be fairly simple to establish the price of a share of stock based upon an average of the trading prices. This is frequently the method used when a buyer is interested in making a tender offer or a takeover bid.

Most authorities, however, will agree that the best approach for determining the price to pay for a corporation is by working out its projected earnings over the next five years. Then other factors can be taken into account, such as debts, capital requirements, liabilities, existing contracts, etc.

These methods are not exclusive: Each business is a separate entity, and ultimately the buyer and seller will have to work out a formula that most nearly corresponds to their own needs.

[¶1519]   **ALLOCATION OF PURCHASE PRICE**
AMONG ASSETS

Once the purchase price has been agreed on, the next step is to allocate the sales proceeds among the individual assets of the business and then compute gain or loss accordingly.

Just as the seller and buyer have conflicting views on the purchase and sale of stock vs. assets, so do their interests conflict when it comes to allocating the purchase price among the assets acquired (when there is a sale of assets rather than stock). The seller wants the bulk of the price, within the framework of reasonable allocations, allotted to those assets on which he can realize capital gain. The buyer wants the major portion of the price allocated (1) to the assets on which he will realize ordinary income on resale (i.e., inventory), thereby cutting his taxable income on the resale, and (2) to assets whose cost he can recover via depreciation (e.g., building and equipment) rather than nondepreciable assets (e.g., land).

Depreciation recapture also enters into the picture on allocation of costs. If the seller has a large ordinary income potential in equipment and other personal property (due to the depreciation recapture rules), he may not want too large an allocation to those assets. When it comes to land and building, the seller wants a larger allocation to land, thereby avoiding some depreciation recapture on the building. The buyer wants more allocation to the building so he can recover its cost via depreciation.

Allocations between the parties in their contract are the best evidence of the market value of each of the assets involved. But they must be prepared to show that the allocations were made at arm's-length and that they are reasonable in the circumstances. Fortifying allocations with independent appraisals will help sustain them against IRS attack. Except in cases of mistake or fraud, the parties will not be allowed to challenge the validity of the allocations they made if undesirable tax consequences follow (*Danielson,* CA-3, 378 F. 2d 771, 1967).

The following chart summarizes the conflicting desires of buyer and seller:

Asset	Price Benefiting Buyer	Price Benefiting Seller
(1) *Capital:*		
(Goodwill, trade name, covenant not to compete ancillary to sale of goodwill)	Low (not depreciable)	High (capital gain)
(2) *Property used in the trade or business:*		
(a) Machinery, fixtures, etc.	Medium (recoup cost via depreciation); high (up to $100,000 for investment credit)	High (capital gain or ordinary loss under IRC §1231)
(b) Land	Low (not depreciable)	High (capital gain or ordinary loss under §1231)
(c) Copyrights (for use in business)	Medium (recoup cost via amortization)	High (capital gain or ordinary loss under §1231)
(d) Patents	Medium (amortization)	High (capital gain under §1235)
(3) *Noncapital:*		
(a) Inventory and stock in trade	High (recoup via cost of goods sold)	Low (ordinary income)
(b) Accounts receivable	High (recoverable as collected)	Low (ordinary income)
(c) Copyrights and intellectual property sold by the creator	Medium (recoup cost via amortization)	Low (ordinary income)
(d) Covenant not to compete	Medium (usually recoup cost via amortization)	Low (ordinary income)
(e) Interest on deferred payment of purchase price	Medium (deduct as ordinary business expense)	Low (ordinary income)

[¶1520]   BUYER'S INDEPENDENT INVESTIGATION OF SELLER

Even after the purchase price is agreed on, and the price allocated among the assets, the buyer should undertake a financial and legal investigation of the seller's business. Below are two checklists to guide the buyer during negotiations.

☐ Check into corporate background:
    (a) corporate charter,
    (b) classes of stocks,
    (c) minority and majority ownership,
    (d) subsidiary companies,
    (e) legal location and principal place of business of all divisions.
☐ Evaluate the shares of the corporation.
☐ Check the financial status of the corporation:
    (a) assets,

(b) inventories,
(c) receivables,
(d) bank loans,
(e) accounts payable.

☐ Check out products in which the corporation deals. (This includes the names of competitors and their ranking within the industry. Any business dealings with federal, state, or local government?)

☐ Analyze the corporation's sales, sales organizations, sales policies, advertising, and commercial techniques.

☐ Draw up a detailed chart of management and labor relations, e.g., number of employees by department, directors and officers of the corporation and their duties, employment contracts and benefit programs, union participation by employees.

☐ Examine property and equipment of the corporation.

[¶1521]   BUYER'S LEGAL CONSIDERATIONS

The buyer has four major legal concerns:
(1) Is he assuming the seller's liabilities and obligations to its creditors?
(2) Are there any antitrust law violations?
(3) Must any special stock exchange requirements be met prior to culmination of the transaction?
(4) Are there any state Blue Sky law requirements to be met?

[¶1522]   BUYER'S ASSUMPTION OF
SELLER'S LIABILITIES

If a business is acquired by the acquisition of its stock, the liabilities automatically follow the business into the hands of the buyer. In this situation, the only way to protect the buyer is to require the seller to warrant that the liabilities of the corporation do not exceed those reflected in its latest financial statement and the contractual obligations specified in the purchase contract. Unfortunately, a buyer will discover that the seller is not always willing to make this representation. Therefore, this will be a matter of negotiation, and sometimes the trading power of the buyer is strong enough to get selling stockholders to agree that part of the purchase price be set aside in escrow to meet corporate liabilities or to assume such liabilities to a limited and specified extent.

When assets are purchased for cash in an arm's-length transaction, only those liabilities that are explicitly assumed should follow the buyer, unless:

(a) The buyer makes the mistake of paying the cash directly to the stockholders of the selling corporation rather than to the corporation itself. This may result in the buyer finding himself liable to undisclosed creditors of the seller.

(b) If the requirements of the state bulk sales law are not complied with, undisclosed creditors may be able to enforce their claims against the assets purchased by the buyer. This risk can be handled by requiring strict compliance or, in the event of waiver, getting a warranty and providing for deposit or escrowing of the purchase price.

A buyer of assets for stock may find himself liable to satisfy undisclosed liabilities of the seller, even though the purchase contract specifically provides that the buyer is not assuming any of the seller's liabilities. Sometimes this result is achieved on the grounds that the assets acquired constitute a trust fund for the creditors, sometimes on the grounds that in effect the acquisition constituted a merger in which the acquirer is the continuing company and thus remains liable for all the obligations of both parties to the merger. If the state law can result in this kind of unintended assumption of liabilities, the only way the buyer can protect himself is to get an indemnification from the seller and require that enough of the purchase price be held in escrow to protect the buyer against any such unassumed liabilities.

[¶1523]   **ANTITRUST PROBLEMS**

The seller's contracts and pricing arrangements should be studied to see whether the buyer will be inheriting any antitrust problems. Distribution contracts, the pricing of goods to large customers, and other arrangements that may be basic to the profitability of the business being acquired and to the value being placed upon it should be studied from the antitrust standpoint to determine whether there is a possibility that the value of the business may be undermined if any of these arrangements are found to be in violation of the antitrust laws. Then it is necessary to appraise the chances that the acquisition itself may be blocked as a violation of §7 of the Clayton Act. This can happen in any line of commerce or in any section of the country, if the effect of the acquisition may be substantially to lessen competition or to tend to create a monopoly.

To make an initial determination of whether there is a possible §7 violation, check the share of the market enjoyed by the buyer and seller and see whether the acquisition results in a substantial increase in the share of the market held by the buyer or makes the buyer significantly more dominant in the market. Then evaluate the impact of the acquisition in terms of whether it seeks to substantially lessen competition. Make a judgment as to whether there is likely to be any complaint from competitors, suppliers, customers, or any companies who fear the acquisition would result in the loss of an important market for their products or that it will result in their loss of a source of supplies. There is an advance clearance procedure in the Justice Department under which, on submission of full information about the economic impact of the proposed acquisition, an informal but not necessarily binding opinion can be obtained as to whether or not the acquisition would violate §7 of the Clayton Act.

There are three other federal statutes that heavily influence the determination of whether or not corporate action is in violation of the antitrust laws.

The Sherman Act states that ''every contract, combination in the form of trust or otherwise, or conspiracy, in restraint of trade or commerce . . . is declared to be illegal,'' and that ''every person who shall monopolize, or attempt to monopolize, or . . . conspire . . . to monopolize any part of . . . commerce'' is in violation of the Sherman Act. The Sherman Act has been used to prohibit price fixing, territorial distributions among competitors, and boycotts.

The Federal Trade Commission Act prohibits ''unfair methods of competition in commerce, and unfair or deceptive acts or practices in commerce.''

The Robinson-Patman Act (an amendment to the Clayton Act) ''prohibits discriminations in prices where the probable consequences of such discriminations would be either a substantial lessening of competition or a tendency to create a monopoly or to injure competition between third parties and the person granting or receiving a discrimination.''

[¶1524]   PREMERGER NOTIFICATION

The Hart-Scott-Rodino Antitrust Improvements Act of 1976 added §7A to the Clayton Act. This Section requires companies that are merging to provide the government with certain information regarding the merger and to wait a prescribed amount of time prior to consummating the transaction. This time lapse enables the FTC to evaluate the possible anticompetitive effects of the merger.

Compliance with the premerger notification rules requires full understanding of this complex legislation. It is advisable to consult with counsel regarding the need to file notification with the Justice Department and the FTC.

Who Must File: Both the acquiring and the acquired companies must file notification if:

(A) Either one is engaged in interstate commerce or in any activity affecting interstate commerce; and

(B) (1) The acquiring company has $100 million in total assets or annual net sales and the acquired company has $10 million in total assets or total net sales, or (2) the acquiring company has $10 million in total assets or net sales, and the acquired company has $100 million in total assets or net sales; and

(C) The acquiring company would have 15% or more of the acquired company's stock, *or* the acquiring company would own more than $15 million worth of the acquired company's stock and assets, combined.

Waiting Period: Following the filing of the notification form, the acquiring and acquired companies must wait 30 days prior to consummating the transaction; 15 days if it is a cash tender offer.

Report Form: A copy of the premerger notification report form may be found in *IBP Forms of Business Agreements and Resolutions.*

[¶1525]   STOCK EXCHANGE REQUIREMENTS

If the buyer or seller is listed on the stock exchange, the buyer must take care to make sure that all stock exchange requirements are met.

[¶1526]   SEC REQUIREMENTS

Even though the buyer may not have to register its securities pursuant to federal law, it is not automatically exempted from state registration requirements. State law should be consulted on this point.

[¶1527]   SELLER'S LEGAL CONSIDERATIONS

The seller also has several legal factors to consider when his corporation is sold or acquired:
(1) Obligation to minority shareholders,
(2) Use of inside information prior to public announcement of impending sale or merger,
(3) Demands for appraisal by minority shareholders.

[¶1528]   SALE OF CONTROL AND SELLER'S
          OBLIGATION TO MINORITY SHAREHOLDERS

Courts have generally held that a sale of a controlling block of stock at a price above the market will not by itself subject the sellers to any liability to minority stockholders. However, where the buyers intend to loot the company and the sellers should have anticipated this possibility on the basis of the past performance of the buyers, the sellers may have incurred a liability to minority stockholders. Also, if the selling stockholders participate in a change of control, giving up their offices, resigning from the board of directors, and designating representatives of the buyers to succeed them, the courts may hold that any premium received by the sellers over and above the prevailing market price of the shares constitutes a trust fund in which minority shareholders may participate. The safest way to avoid this risk is to insist that a similar offer be made to all shareholders. If this is not practicable, then it is incumbent upon the selling shareholders to investigate carefully the reputation and the purpose of the buyers and to accept no obligation that might be deemed to constitute a sale of control and an active participation in a change of control over and above the simple sale of their shares.

What obligation do the officers and directors who are selling their stock have to disclose the price and the transaction to minority stockholders? In some states the courts have held that insiders had an obligation to disclose all information to minority shareholders. Other states restricted the directors' fiduciary duty to the corporation and required no disclosure to other shareholders. Today, it is generally considered that Rule 10b-5 under the Securities Exchange Act of 1934 requires full disclosure to minority stockholders. In one important case under the common law, the president of a company who had a deal to sell his stock at a high figure and went out and bought up shares from other shareholders at a lower figure, so that he could profit on the difference, was obligated to turn the difference over to the shareholders whose stock he had bought up.

[¶1529]   **INSIDER TRADING PROBLEMS**

Another problem of which the seller should be aware is the use of inside information by officers, directors, employees, or anyone else who becomes aware of the pending merger or acquisition before it is public knowledge. Of particular importance here is the application of Rule 10b-5 of the Securities Exchange Act of 1934.

[¶1530]   **SHAREHOLDERS' RIGHT OF APPRAISAL**

Shareholders who dissent from a merger transaction may be entitled to have a court place a value on their stock interest, rather than agree to accept the cash value offered in the merger. However, too many demands for appraisal and payment of cash instead of stock to dissenting stockholders may put too great a financial strain on the surviving corporation. These demands can usually be presented right up to the time of the stockholders' vote on the measure, and it may be possible that appraisal demands delivered through the mail can still be effective even though received a few days subsequent to the date of stockholder approval. When the number of stockholders is limited, and state law permits, uncertainty in this respect can be eliminated by obtaining written consent from all stockholders, so that it will be unnecessary to hold a stockholders' meeting to approve a merger. If this uncertainty cannot be avoided, the merger agreement should include a clause giving both companies the right to abandon the merger if stockholders' demands for appraisal are excessive (that is, if they exceed a specified percentage).

[¶1531]   **OTHER ITEMS TO BE CONSIDERED**

In addition to the items previously mentioned, there are many other areas for both buyer and seller to investigate prior to binding the deal.

☐ ***Transferability of Seller's Contracts:*** If any contract contains a prohibition of assignment, or a requirement that the other party's consent is necessary in order to make the assignment effective, counsel for seller must make certain that the selling corporation undertakes to obtain any necessary consent.

☐ ***Labor Problems:*** Check to see whether union contracts contain a provision that they are binding on the buyer or whether there is a nonassignability clause. The seller should be particularly interested in this question if the plant of the acquired company is going to be consolidated or moved. Another important question is whether the surviving corporation must bargain with the union certified as a collective bargaining agent. Courts have held that the successor employer must deal with the union during the period following the merger, usually the balance of the existing year since certification. A problem arises when the successor corporation already has a contract with another union. If the employees of the acquired corporation fall into a minority status in relationship to the employees of the combined or the survivor corporation, they may automatically be absorbed into the

133

existing contract of the buyer's corporation. Another problem involves the consolidation of the work force and the displacement of some employees. If a union is involved the matter will probably have to be negotiated and, in some cases, seniority will control.

☐ *Employee Benefit Plans:* How will the employee benefit plan of the seller's corporation be incorporated into the surviving corporation? Unfortunately, employee benefit plans rarely mesh satisfactorily between the surviving corporation and the absorbed corporation. The choice then is between terminating the old plan and paying out all vested amounts or freezing the old plan and holding the amounts accumulated in trust for the benefit of the employees of the absorbed company until they retire or their service is terminated.

☐ *Executive Arrangements:* The buyer will probably have to assure the management of the absorbed corporation that their services will be needed and that their rights under current executive compensation plans will be respected. This is probably an appropriate topic for inclusion in the acquisition contract. In addition, if there are stock option rights involved, these may have to be converted into stock options of the surviving corporation. If necessary, it may be advisable to have the executives of the absorbed corporation exercise their options prior to the merger.

☐ *Unemployment Insurance:* Make sure the appropriate state agency is notified of the impending merger.

☐ *Bank Loan Agreements:* Check the seller's bank loan agreements to make certain that they do not prohibit an acquisition. If such a clause is included in any loan, it may be necessary to obtain the bank's consent or a refinancing of the bank debt in order to go ahead with the merger. Forms of financing agreements can be found in *IBP Forms of Business Agreements and Resolutions.*

☐ *Inventory Problems:* The seller should be willing to warrant that the inventory is of "merchantable" quality and adequate for the conduct of the business as previously conducted. This is usually not obtainable.

☐ *Accounts Receivable Problems:* Here the buyer may not wish to assume the risk that the seller's reserve for bad debts is adequate. The contract may provide for an adjustment in price to reflect any difference between the accounts receivable shown on the seller's books and the amount actually collected at the end of a specified period of time. If this is the arrangement, the seller is usually given an opportunity to take the uncollected accounts and see what he can do with them. There are usually advantages in having the accounts receivable collected by the continuing business.

☐ *Title Searches:* A real estate title search should be made early, and if there are any clouds on the title that would hurt the operation of the business, they should be brought to the buyer's attention promptly and before the purchase agreement is signed, if possible. The buyer could agree to bear the cost of such a search if the deal did not go through.

☐ *Tax Liabilities:* It's a good idea to have the seller represent the status of the company with respect to tax audits and important to have the seller assume responsibility for tax liabilities other than those represented on the balance sheet submitted.

☐ *Covenant Not to Compete:* It may be critically important to get assurance that the sellers will not compete with the business that they are selling. If there is any payment for this covenant, it will be deductible by the buyer and have the effect of converting that portion of the proceeds received by the sellers from capital gain to ordinary income. To accomplish this, it is important to specify the amount being paid for the covenant not to compete. If this result is not desired and there is a covenant not to compete in the agreement of sale, to protect the sellers from possible ordinary income it is well to provide that the covenant is incidental to the sale of the stock and has not been separately bargained or paid for.

Forms of covenants not to compete will be found in *IBP Forms of Business Agreements and Resolutions*.

A covenant not to compete may not be advisable if the buyer could be charged with a violation of the antitrust laws.

Courts are frequently hesitant to enforce overreaching covenants not to compete, so make certain that the geographical limits and time restraints are necessary to safeguard the buyer's business.

[¶1532]   **THE ACQUISITION CONTRACT**

Once the contract is signed, thereby fixing the rights and obligations of both buyer and seller, neither one can unilaterally change its terms. Therefore, it is imperative that any questions about the deal be raised prior to drawing up the contract. If a change of circumstances comes to light after the contract is signed, it could be costly for either side.

The acquisition contract not only sets forth rights and obligations of both buyer and seller but also provides buyer with a detailed account of the seller's business. In the contract, the seller will make representations regarding the conditions of his business on a given date. It will include information regarding the finances, physical plant, and intangible properties of the seller. The contract will also set forth the transaction itself, as well as the following items: Representation and warranties of buyer; assets to be acquired by buyer; purchase price; assumption of liabilities by buyer; seller's indemnification of buyer; seller's conduct of the business pending closing; conditions precedent to closing; any problems with brokerage; and other general provisions.

Once the buyer and seller have worked out the basic terms of the agreement, it is advisable to reduce this to writing, thereby binding the agreement. There are several methods available to bind the deal: Option, restrictive letter, or letter of intent.

[¶1533]   **OPTION**

Buyers usually prefer an option contract, since it gives them a specified time in which to investigate the business with the knowledge that seller can't sell prior to the expiration of the agreed-upon period. Sellers will generally favor an option if they are interested in selling the business to a particular buyer. An option contract needs consideration, which may be cash paid by the buyer for the option. An option contract usually has an acquisition contract attached.

[¶1534]   **RESTRICTIVE LETTER**

This is similar to an option binding both seller and buyer for a fixed period of time, but it usually does not contain specific language or terms regarding the underlying acquisition.

[¶1535]   **LETTER OF INTENT**

Usually, this is a memorandum of understanding, the acquisition being subject to the approval of the respective boards of directors; thus the letter is not legally binding.

[¶1536]   **USE OF A TENDER OFFER**

Frequently a buyer who wants to acquire a company will find that its board of directors is unwilling to have it acquired or merged. When that occurs, a buyer might resort to the use of a tender offer made directly to the target company's shareholders. In order to make a tender offer, buyer and target must both follow the requirements set forth by the Williams Act.

The Williams Act (§13 and 14 of the 1934 Exchange Act) was designed to protect the shareholders of target corporations from some of the practices of corporate raiders by requiring more disclosure by an offeror. To some extent, §14(e) of the Williams Act parallels the disclosure requirements of §10(b) and Rule 10b-5, in that both prohibit false and misleading statements. Set forth below are the basic provisions of the Williams Act:

(A) Section 13(d)(1) requires any person who becomes the beneficial owner of 5% equity security of:

(1) a class that is registered pursuant to §12, or

(2) any equity security of an insurance company that would have been required to be so registered except for the exemption in §12(g)(2)(G), or

(3) any equity security issued by a closed-end investment company registered under the Investment Company Act of 1940, within 10 days after such acquisition, to send to (a) the issuer at its principal place of business by registered or certified mail (b) each exchange where the security is traded, and (c) the SEC, a Schedule 13D-G containing the following information:

(a) Identity of persons for whom the sales have been made;

(b) Amount and source of funds used by the offeror for the purchases;

(c) Purpose of the purchase;

(d) The number of shares that are beneficially owned and the number concerning which there is a right of acquisition;

(e) Information as to any contracts, arrangements, or understandings with any person with respect to any securities of the issuer.

(B) Section 14(d)(1) states that it shall be unlawful for any person to make a tender offer that would result in the beneficial ownership of more than 5% of the issuer's equity securities unless such offeror has already filed with the SEC a statement containing the information required by Schedule 13D-G.

(C) Section 14(d)(4) requires that any solicitation or recommendation to the holders of a security to accept or reject a tender offer cannot be made unless the person making such solicitation/recommendation has already filed a Schedule 14D with the SEC pursuant to Rule 14d-4.

(D) Section 14(e) makes it unlawful to make an untrue statement of material fact or to omit to state a material fact in connection with a tender offer or solicitation in favor of or in opposition to a tender offer.

[¶1537]   STATE TAKEOVER STATUTES

More than one-half of the states have enacted some form of legislation to regulate tender offers. However, the constitutionality of these statutes is in doubt. In *Great Western United Corporation v. Kidwell* (CA-5, 577 F. 2d 1256, 1978, *cert. granted*, USSC, Dkt. No. 78-759, 1/8/79), the Fifth Circuit Court of Appeals held that the Idaho takeover statute was unconstitutional in that it (1) was preempted by the Williams Act, and (2) imposed an undue burden on interstate commerce.

Until the Supreme Court resolves this issue, tender offerors should check local laws. Some offerors may discover that several state statutes apply, thus creating additional compliance problems.

[¶1538]   WHAT TO DO WHEN A TENDER OFFER
                          IS MADE

In the event an unfriendly tender offer is made, the ability to respond quickly and decisively is paramount. Morris M. Lee, Jr., a public relations consultant frequently called upon to aid target management, has suggested certain steps that should be part of a company's defensive plan:

☐ Analyze the company's true worth—the company will need this in order to argue that the offeror's price does not reflect the true worth of the stock.

☐ Guard against improper use of stockholder lists.

☐ Watch for any sudden surge in the trading of the stock.

☐ Break down the shareholder list by geographic distribution, institutional investors, etc.

☐ Establish a rapport with the largest shareholders and institutional investors.

☐ Prepare a telephone solicitation team, but remember that SEC rules prevent certain communications in telephone contacts.

☐ Set up a plan for an emergency directors' meeting.

☐ Keep up-to-date records on stock transactions by officers and directors.

☐ Prepare and address in advance shareholder mailing envelopes; know how long it will take to print a shareholders' letter.

☐ Know how long it will take to file all necessary documents with the SEC.

☐ Have skeleton 14D forms on hand.

[¶1539]   CLOSING AND POST-CLOSING STEPS

Once all the details of the merger or acquisition are agreed upon, the only steps that remain will be the closing and post-closing steps.

In order to facilitate the closing, lawyers for both buyer and seller should prepare a checklist of the items that will be exchanged upon completion of the transaction.

The buyer may also want to have some publicity regarding the acquisition. It may be especially important to inform the seller's customers and suppliers that there has been a change in ownership of the acquired corporation. Whether or not the acquisition should be emphasized depends upon the individual circumstances and, of course, the nature of the reorganization.

Finally, here is a checklist of some steps that should be taken following the closing of the acquisition:

☐ **Publicity:** Comply with the requirements of public announcement, if any, contained in the agreement. Furnish wire services with immediate accurate release. Place advertisements if required.

☐ **SEC Reports:** File Form 8-K.

☐ **Tax Returns:** Prepare tax returns for the acquired corporation for part of the fiscal year before closing.

☐ **Changeovers:** Change bank accounts, insurance policies, unemployment compensation filings, workmen's compensation filings, and similar items.

☐ **Corporate Name:** Protect the corporate name of the acquired corporation. (One way is to form a dummy corporation.)

☐ **Pending Litigation:** Effect substitutions of parties.

☐ **Registration Statements:** Check to make sure of compliance with SEC requirements including filing of past-effective amendments to registration statements and prospectuses.

☐ **Withdrawal of Acquired Corporation:** See that the acquired corporation is withdrawn from states where it may be registered.

[¶1540]   FOR FURTHER REFERENCE . . .

Corporate Planning, Institute for Business Planning, Inc., Englewood Cliffs, N.J.

Davis, F.T., Jr., *Business Acquisitions Desk Book: With Checklists and Forms,* Institute for Business Planning, Inc., Englewood Cliffs, N.J. (1977).

Freling, R.A., and Martin, R.J. Jr., "Current Reorganization Techniques," 55 Taxes 852 (1977).

Horvitz, J.S., "Strategies for Incorporating a Business that Secures Maximum Tax Benefits for Incorporators," 18 Taxation for Accountants 344 (1977).

Kessler, R.A., and Hancock, J.H., "Planning a Corporate Power—Financial Structure," 24 Practical Lawyer 13 (April 1978).

McLendon, R.G., "Accounting Treatment of Acquisitions—Taxable vs. Nontaxable," 36 New York University Institute on Federal Taxation 519 (1978).

Sturm, M., "Fresh Start Basis and Stock Buy-Sell Agreements," 24 Practical Lawyer 89 (March 1978).

Tax Planning, Institute for Business Planning, Inc., Englewood Cliffs, N.J.

"Tender Offer: Symposium," 23 New York Law School Law Review 375 (1978).

CREDIT AND COLLECTIONS

[**¶1601**] This chapter covers the validity of creditors' claims against debtors, as well as against those who may be jointly or severally liable. Legal and practical considerations to lay the groundwork for both the extension of credit and payment thereof are included—as well as the most recent trends in consumer credit.

[¶1602]   TRUTH-IN-LENDING APPLICABILITY

The Fair Debt Collection Practices Act (amending the Truth-In-Lending Act) went into effect on March 20, 1978. It regulates collection activities when debts of consumers are involved. Beginning at ¶1622 is a discussion of the Act. To the extent that any individual extends credit and permits repayment in four or more installments, other provisions of Truth-In-Lending apply. A detailed explanation of the comprehensive and superseding role of Truth-In-Lending over state law is found beginning at ¶4101.

[¶1603]   FORMS FOR EXTENSION OF CREDIT

Long forms that spell out the rights and duties of parties under most conceivable contingencies are generally preferred to short ones. To the extent that a particular provision expressly states what might otherwise be implied, it will tend to eliminate ambiguity and confusion.

[¶1604]   EXECUTION OF FORMS

Ordinary contract principles of execution generally apply to most credit transactions. Normally, the party to be charged with liability should sign the instrument.

[¶1605]   BINDING A CORPORATION

Major transactions with a corporation may, under some circumstances, require sanction by corporate resolution or bylaw. To the extent that a corporation exceeds its authority (known as ultra vires), it is possible to void a transaction. In the case of a small corporation, it is sometimes wise to attempt to bind a major stockholder, requiring the individual to sign individually as well as in a corporate capacity. This is in the role of a surety (see ¶3601).

[¶1606]   **BINDING A PARTNERSHIP**

Partners are generally assumed to have authority to undertake a transaction—and as to all transactions, even if the partner lacked authority, all partners are personally liable.

[¶1607]   **LIABILITIES OF FAMILIES AND**
                          INDIVIDUAL MEMBERS

Parents are generally liable for the "necessaries" (consisting of food, clothing, housing, and medical care) of their children. In some states, a spouse may be held liable for the other spouse's necessaries as well. Emancipation of a minor will remove the necessaries liability; emancipation similarly will alter the voidability of contract of a minor.

[¶1607.1]   **Liability of Parents for Child's Education**

This area of the law is in a state of flux. Courts in some states have held that the parent may be liable for a child's college expenses (including tuition) based upon the "necessaries" doctrine. However, in most instances, courts are reluctant to use the necessaries doctrine for educational purposes.

[¶1608]   **HOW TO HANDLE COLLECTION CLAIMS**

As soon as a claim is received, a numbered file should be opened for it and the client furnished with an acknowledgment of receipt showing the file number. The acknowledgment should also refer to any special fee arrangement that applies and should call for additional details that may be necessary to process the claim.

[¶1609]   **INFORMATION TO BE OBTAINED**

Following is a checklist of questions for your client to answer before you proceed with the collection process:
☐   Name of the debtor.
☐   Address of the debtor (if a post office box, a street address also, if available).
☐   Age of the debtor, if relevant (a minor, for example).
☐   Marital status (where material).
☐   Type of debtor (partnership or corporation).
☐   Had debtor been known by any other name?
☐   Nature of claim (alimony, installment contract, goods sold and delivered, money lent, or services not received).
☐   Evidence of the claim.

☐　Other persons liable.
☐　Security involved.
☐　Nature of the liability of others (joint or several, as a guarantor or surety).
☐　Evidence of other individuals' liability.
☐　Number of bills sent by the client to the debtor and accepted without protest.
☐　Defenses, if any, to the claim.
☐　Client's evaluation of the claim.
☐　Client's estimate of the largest amount that can actually be realized (to what level will a client go to settle?).
☐　Names of witnesses and expected testimony.
☐　Valuation of business relationship and continuation.
☐　Solvency of the debtor.
☐　Did the debtor furnish any financial statement?
☐　Current credit report.
☐　Assets including real estate, bank accounts, cars, and securities of the debtor.

[¶1610]　　　LEGAL PITFALLS OF DEBT COLLECTION

It has been reliably estimated that there are approximately 5,000 professional debt collection services in the United States, and more than 2.5 million credit grantors who constitute about 99% of debt collection activity. Professional debt collection services are currently licensed and regulated in 33 states, though collection practices of retail credit grantors are presently regulated in only 8 states. The Fair Debt Collections Practices Act regulates collection activities if the debt is a consumer debt (see ¶1622).

Aside from statutory standards, debt collectors may also be exposed to legal action, such as libel or slander, invasion of privacy, mental anguish, and civil and criminal liability.

[¶1611]　　　CONTACT AND SETTLEMENT

When examining the problems involved—including the amount of the claim, the relationship between the debtor and the creditor, and past efforts at collection—it is necessary to make a determination as to whether initial contact should be by personal visit, phone, or mail. Often a letter is the best approach. It should point out that the debtor will not only be liable for the amount owed, but also for the costs of legal action (including reasonable attorney's fees).

Settlement rather than suit is ordinarily the best approach: It is both less costly and much faster for the creditor. Once settlement has been reached, an agreement should be signed in which the following factors are included:
☐　The amount initially claimed.
☐　The amount proposed for the settlement.
☐　Terms of payment.
☐　Place of payment.

☐ Grace periods (if any).
☐ Interest charges (if any; compliance with Truth-In-Lending legislation and state usury ceilings may be required).
☐ Statement of any defenses, counterclaims, or setoffs.
☐ Default clauses (in the event of nonpayment, entire amount owing becomes payable immediately).
☐ Judgment by confession (where permissible by state law).
☐ Specifics on notes or post-dated checks.
☐ Collateral (if any) for payment.
☐ Use of general release (if demanded).
☐ Means of payment (cash or certified check suggested).

[¶1612]   COLLECTION BY LAWSUIT

When all other means have failed, it is necessary to proceed by lawsuit. Even this, however, may not be an ideal solution—for if there is a dispute over the debt, or the amount is very small in relation to the costs of proceeding by suit, it may be better to write off the amount.

To the extent that a choice of courts is available (generally dependent upon the jurisdictional minimums), it is often wise to choose an inferior court because of greater speed and economy of effort. Local procedural laws should be complied with, and the use of verified complaints where verified answers are required should increase the chance of settlement.

[¶1613]   REMEDIES AFTER OBTAINING JUDGMENT

Once judgment has been obtained against a debtor, the number of remedies that are available to the creditor to obtain the funds vary widely from state to state. Nonetheless, there are some general rules that should be used as an operating guide. First, it is necessary to take out a judgment lien. Next, execution of the lien is necessary to enforce the judgment by reaching real or tangible personal property in a debtor's possession. Examination of the debtor is another practical tool to discover the assets that may be available for satisfaction of the judgment. A number of forms concerning residence, occupation, employment, salary, history, Social Security numbers, bank accounts, insurance policies, and other items are widely available.

It is sometimes also useful to examine unrelated parties who might have a knowledge of the debtor's assets. Garnishment of wages and salaries of the debtor is another possibility. For a table covering garnishment, see the Appendix.

[¶1614]   SETTING ASIDE TRANSFERS

To the extent that the debtor is a business entity, the bulk sales provision of the Uniform Commercial Code (Article 6) ordinarily prevents sales that could be regarded as fraudulent. Those that are made in violation of the UCC provisions may be set aside. Under the Uniform Fraudulent Conveyance Act, it is possible to set aside a transfer made by any debtor that is either void or voidable as against the creditor, because of fraud or other reasons. In this instance, property may be levied against and sold under an execution order.

[¶1615]   WHAT IS A FRAUDULENT TRANSFER?

Fraudulent conveyances involve the transfer of property that the debtor had title to when the creditor acquired the right to have the claim satisfied, and transfer was made with the aim of putting the property of the debtor beyond the creditor's reach.

[¶1616]   EVIDENCE OF FRAUD

In order to prove fraudulent intent, a number of statutory presumptions are made. Transfers presumed to be fraudulent include the following:
☐   Transfers that render the transferor insolvent.
☐   Transfers made without fair consideration by a person in business leaving the transferor with unreasonably small capital.
☐   Transfers made without fair consideration if the transferor intends or believes he'll incur debts beyond his ability to pay.
☐   Transfers by a partnership when insolvent if to a partner or if to a nonpartner without fair consideration.
☐   Transfers made in anticipation of or pending litigation.
☐   Transfers with secret reservations of beneficial interest.
☐   Transfers that leave the transferor in possession on some fictitious ground.
The Bankruptcy Act invalidates conveyances that are invalid under state law and at the same time has its own provisions governing fraudulent conveyances in violation of the terms of the Bankruptcy Act (see ¶501 et seq.).

[¶1617]   HANDLING REMITTANCES

Upon receipt of payment of an item on which collection was sought, the client may be sent the full amount together with a bill, or the net amount after deducting the attorney's fee. Deciding which approach to use depends on the preferences of the individuals involved.

[¶1618]   CHECKS MARKED "PAYMENT IN FULL"

Checks made out for less than the full amount owed that are marked "payment in full" have been termed an exquisite form of commercial torture. In general, the payee must usually regard a check drawn for less than the amount owed as an offer for accord and satisfaction. If the check is cashed, the offer is accepted. Prior to the adoption of the UCC, disclaimer of payment in full over the indorsement was ineffective—the act of cashing the check was held to have accepted the offer on the debtor's terms. UCC §1-207, however, appears to have altered the rule. Through the use of words such as "without prejudice" and "under protest," it is possible for the payee not to forfeit legal right to demand the balance of payment through the mere act of cashing the check. At least two courts have held that a "deposited under protest" reservation was valid. See, for example, *Baillie Lumber Co. v. Kincaid Carolina Corp.,* 167 S.E. 2d 85, N.C., 1969.

[¶1619]   FORWARDING OF COLLECTION ITEMS

It is clear, of course, that an attorney can have a hand in collecting items all over the country and in other countries, and is not limited to his own particular bailiwick, and this fact should be brought home to the client.

The normal way of handling out-of-town collections is by forwarding them to another attorney. Barring an established contact or a solid reference, the attorney to whom the matter is to be forwarded should be selected from one of the established law lists certified as complying with the American Bar Association standards. The publisher of the list will also have certain standards for listing that he will disclose on inquiry.

The forwarding letter to a new contact should indicate the basis of selection—law list or reference—and should discuss the fee. If, for example, you should decide to use the Commercial Law League schedule of fees, the letter should make this clear. These fees will not, of course, include the fees of the forwarding attorney who must add his own fee when he bills his client.

A number of law lists use bonded attorneys, and where this is the case you should notify the publisher of the list as soon as you forward a matter to an attorney on his list. If you fail to do so, the bond may not be available to you if and when you need it.

The forwarding attorney can't just forget about a matter once it has been forwarded. He must check periodically with the out-of-town attorney and keep the client informed as to the status of the collection process.

[¶1620]   FEES

There is, of course, no precise formula for determining fees for handling items for collection. The fee must vary with the amount collected, the nature of the item, and the nature of the services called for. Nevertheless, the schedule of rates charged by mercantile agencies may offer a worthwhile guide to the attorney in working out a fee arrangement. The schedule of the Commercial Collection Division of Dun & Bradstreet may be considered fairly representative, and as such, useful for illustrative purposes.

Their arrangement calls for a one-year subscription contract for $60 as a minimum annual service charge, plus charges based on the rates set forth below, as well as disbursements and any other extraordinary expense that may be incurred at the request of the subscriber:

(1) Reminder Service. Two courteous and effective reminders for claimant's use on letters and statements before accounts are placed for collection. No additional charge for results.

(2) Free Direct Demand Service. A demand written on the stationery of Dun and Bradstreet, Inc., and mailed direct by it for payment of undisputed commercial accounts. No additional charge for any payments received during Free Direct Demand period, the number of days for which is designated by claimant but not to exceed 10 days from date of demand. No accounts accepted for Free Direct Demand Service only.

(3) Supplementary Service. Additional efforts consisting of various types of demands for payments appropriate to the individual account. Customary charges, contingent upon collection, on commercial accounts are: 24% of amounts from $208 to $2,000 collected; 20% of the next $8,000 collected; 15% of sums collected in excess of $10,000.

(4) Personal Collection Service. Tactful presentations of accounts by trained representatives throughout the United States and Canada. Customary charges, contingent upon collection, on commercial accounts are the same as stated in paragraph 3.

(5) Forwarding Service. Forwarding accounts to attorneys or others, in claimant's behalf, and conducting, as a convenience to claimant, the necessary correspondence with those to whom accounts are forwarded, in accordance with instructions from claimant. The charges, contingent on collection, of most attorneys on commercial accounts are the recommended minimum charges of The Commercial Law League of America, as follows: 20% on collections of $125 to $300; 18% of next $1,700 collected, and 13% in excess of $2,000; minimum charges: $25 on collections of $75 to $125 and 33⅓% of collections less than $75. *There are additional charges by attorneys when suits or other legal proceedings are authorized by claimant, consisting of a suit fee, advance costs, and, in some instances, a retainer.*

In addition to the charges of attorneys or others to whom commercial accounts are forwarded in claimant's behalf, customary charges for the separate services rendered by Dun & Bradstreet, Inc. in Forwarding Service are: 7% on collections of $210 to $2,000 and 6% of collections in excess of $2,000. *The charges of* Dun & Bradstreet, Inc., *are not dependent upon any services rendered by attorneys or others in claimant's behalf but are for services rendered and expenses incurred by it.*

Bear in mind that these are rates for commercial accounts, that is, claims against corporations, partnerships, or individuals engaged in business; that agencies usually reserve the right to accept or reject accounts offered for collection, including commercial accounts, and may accept them only if higher rates are agreed to; and that additional charges may be imposed if installment payments are involved.

The League's schedule spells out details as to suit fees.

(6) Suit Fees. Minimum suit fees to the receiving attorney $7.50. A suit fee is not contingent. It is payable in addition to commissions. It belongs exclusively to the receiving attorney unless there is a division of service or responsibility between the attorney forwarder and the receiving attorney. Where a division is recognized between the attorney forwarder and the receiving attorney, each shall receive such portion of the suit fee as is commensurate with his service or responsibility, but in no event shall the suit fee to the receiving attorney be less than $7.50. Before starting suit, the attorney should always endeavor to arrange for a suit fee commensurate with the services to be rendered, the amount involved, and the results to be accomplished.

[¶1621]   RECENT TRENDS IN CONSUMER CREDIT

Emerging trends in consumer credit today are governed by five basic sources of law: The Uniform Commercial Code (in effect in all states except Louisiana); The Consumer Credit Protection Act (Truth-In-Lending, 15 USC §1601 et seq.); state consumer protection legislation (the Uniform Consumer Credit Code and other legislation); substantive rule-making power of the Federal Trade Commission (utilizing 15 USC §57); and the due process clause of the 14th Amendment.

Among the pitfalls facing a secured creditor attempting to use Article 9 of the Uniform Commercial Code is the UCC's failure to define "default." Section 9-501(1) permits that term to be defined by the creditor in the security agreement itself. Default frequently can cause waiver, or estoppel under UCC §1-103 to take effect. The use of "insecurity" clauses or acceleration clauses are an added problem.

Repossession, replevin, and self-help have been subject to new requirements in the light of *Fuentes v. Shevin* (407 US 67, 1972). Basically, *Fuentes* held that the state has the power to seize the goods of a consumer prior to final judgment in order to protect the security interests of creditors, so long as those creditors test their claim to the goods through the process of a fair prior hearing. "Due process is afforded only by the kinds of 'notice' and 'hearing' which are aimed at establishing the validity, or at least the power of the validity of the underlying claim against the alleged debtor before he can be deprived of his property . . ." *(Sniadach v. Family Finance Corp.,* 395 US 337, 1969).

The impact of *Fuentes* and *Sniadach* may have been lessened by a 1978 Supreme Court decision *(Flagg Brothers, Inc. v. Brooks,* May 15, 1978), which upheld a warehouseman's right to sell a consumer's goods in its possession to satisfy unpaid storage charges, pursuant to UCC §7-210. The Supreme Court held that no prior-to-sale hearing was required, because a state's enactment of the UCC (or any law) is not sufficient state action to trigger the application of the 14th Amendment. However, unlike the situations in *Fuentes* and *Sniadach*, the creditor in *Flagg Brothers* already had possession of the disputed goods. When the creditor is not in possession of the goods, there are three situations in which outright seizure (without an opportunity for a prior hearing) is permitted. First, when the seizure is directly necessary to secure an important governmental or general public interest (such as an attachment of property necessary to secure jurisdiction in a state court); second, when there is a special need for very prompt action; and third, when the person initiating the seizure is a government official responsible for determining, under the standards of a narrowly drawn statute, whether it was necessary and justified in the particular instance to undertake the seizure.

[¶1622]   WHO IS COVERED BY THE FAIR DEBT
                 COLLECTION PRACTICES ACT

Effective March 20, 1978, the Fair Debt Collection Practices Act (Truth-In-Lending §801-817) regulates creditors' collection tactics when the debtor is a consumer. Not every consumer debt is covered by the Act: The obligation to pay must arise out of a transaction in which the money, property, or services financed is primarily for personal, family, or household purposes. Therefore, a business loan would be excluded from the law's coverage.

Nor is every creditor attempting to collect a debt covered: Basically, you must be in the business of collecting debts to fall within the Act's definition of "debt collector." The Act also lists the following specific exemptions from that definition:

☐ Officers, employees, or agents of a creditor who act within the scope of employment while trying to collect a debt.

☐ Individuals acting as debt collectors for another person, if that person's business is not primarily the collection of debt.

☐ Officers or employees of the United States or any state, to the extent that the collection or attempted collection is within the scope of the performance of official duties.

☐ Individuals serving (or attempting to serve) legal process in connection with the judicial enforcement of a debt.

☐ Nonprofit organizations acting at the request of a consumer that counsels consumers, and assists them in debt liquidation.

☐ Any attorney-at-law collecting a debt as an attorney on behalf of, and in the name of, a client.

☐ Any person attempting to collect a debt that is incidental to a fiduciary obligation or escrow arrangement.

☐ Any person attempting to collect a debt that originated with him. (However, the Extortionate Credit Legislation Section of the Truth-In-Lending Act may apply.)

☐ A lender who feels "insecure," and attempts to collect the full amount payable (as provided in UCC §1-208).

[¶1623] PROHIBITED CONDUCT UNDER THE FAIR DEBT COLLECTION PRACTICES ACT

The Fair Debt Collection Practices Act regulates the manner in which a debt collector may communicate with a debtor, and prohibits harassment, making misleading statements, and engaging in unfair collection practices, as defined by the Act. These subjects are treated in detail in the material that follows.

Communication With a Consumer-Debtor: A debt collector who is covered by the Fair Debt Collection Practices Act is restricted in communicating with a consumer-debtor. Absent the consumer's prior consent or express judicial permission, a debt collector may not communicate with a consumer in connection with the collection of any debt:

☐ At any unusual time or place.

☐ At any time or place that is ''inconvenient'' to the consumer.

☐ Other than between 8 a.m. and 9 p.m. (unless specific circumstances indicate that other times are neither unusual nor inconvenient).

☐ If the debt collector knows that the consumer is represented by an attorney and the name and address of the attorney is either available or readily ascertainable.

☐ At the debtor's place of employment (unless permitted by the employer).

☐ If the consumer gives the debt collector written notice that he refuses to pay the debt or wishes the debt collector to stop all communications, except to:

(1) Inform the consumer that debt collection efforts are being terminated;

(2) Notify the consumer that the debt collector or creditor may seek certain judicial remedies.

Harassment and Abuse: Debt collectors may not resort to harassment or abusive tactics while trying to collect a debt. In addition the Act lists conduct that is absolutely prohibited:

☐ Use or threat of violence that could harm the person, property, or reputation of any individual (as opposed to the debtor alone).

☐ Use of obscene, profane, or abusive language to the debtor.

☐ Publication of a list of consumers who allegedly don't pay their debts (except for consumer reporting agencies covered by other sections of Truth-In-Lending).

☐ Advertising for sale any debt to coerce its payment.

☐ Making anonymous telephone calls to the debtor.

☐ Making continuous or repeated telephone calls to the debtor.

False or Misleading Statements: A debt collector may not make false or misleading representations concerning:

☐ Character, amount, or legal status of a debt.

☐ Compensation the debt collector receives.

☐ Professional status of the debt collector (such as claiming to be a lawyer).

☐ Taking legal action that is actually illegal.

☐ Crimes resulting from failure to pay a debt.

☐ Status of documents, including those purporting to be of a court or an agency of the United States, or any state.

☐   Turning accounts over to an innocent purchaser for value.

☐   Name of the debt collection agency or business.

☐   Status of legal documents received by the consumer (so as to deceive him into thinking he doesn't have to answer in court).

☐   Relations between the debt collector and a consumer reporting agency.

☐   Communicating credit information that is known to be false.

Unfair Practices: The following conduct violates the Unfair Practices Section of the Act:

☐   Collecting any money that is neither expressly authorized by the credit agreement nor otherwise permitted by law.

☐   Accepting a postdated check, unless the debt collector gives written notice that he intends to deposit it (at least 10 days or 3 business days before deposit).

☐   Soliciting a postdated check with the intention of using bad check laws or creating a possibility of criminal fraud prosecution.

☐   Causing the accrual of charges to the consumer without disclosing their nature in advance (such as collect telephone calls).

☐   Threatening nonjudicial action against property in which there is no security interest, or if there is actually no intention to repossess the property, or if repossession would be illegal.

☐   Communicating about the debt by means of postcards.

☐   Using a symbol other than the debt collector's address on an envelope used to communicate with the debtor, except that the debt collector's name may be used if it doesn't reveal the nature of its business.

[¶1624]   **FOR FURTHER REFERENCE . . .**

"Consumer Credit: Proceedings of the ABA National Institute, June 16-17, 1977," 33 Business Lawyer (February 1978).

"Consumer Protection: Judicial Approaches to Rescission and Restoration under the Truth-In-Lending Act," 53 Washington Law Review 301-17 (February 1978).

Forms of Business Agreements, (Vol. 3), Institute for Business Planning, Inc., Englewood Cliffs, N.J.

Mortimer, H.E., *Consumer Credit 1977,* Practising Law Institute, New York, New York.

"Supplement VI to Regulation Z Truth-In-Lending," 64 Federal Reserve Bulletin 481-6 (June 1978).

ESTATE ADMINISTRATION

[¶1701] Administering an estate can be a lengthy and complicated process, particularly as the size of the estate increases and more sophisticated planning techniques such as pourover trusts or stock redemptions are employed. Although the services of attorneys, accountants, brokers, securities analysts, and other experts may be employed, the primary responsibility for administering the estate lies with its personal representative (usually an executor or administrator). The representative must exercise reasonable care during his tenure; failure to do so can result in personal liability to him as fiduciary, as well as financial loss to the estate.

The important aspects of estate administration are highlighted in the paragraphs that follow. While many of these activities must be carried on simultaneously, some, of course, must precede others.

[¶1702]   INITIAL STEPS

One of the first steps is to locate the decedent's will, if any exists. Even if there is reason to believe that the decedent died intestate, a diligent search is required in order to petition for letters of administration. Once the will is located, the executor named in the will (or another person qualified to do so under local law) should present the will for probate and request authorization to serve as executor or administrator. If the decedent died intestate, his or her estate is administered by a court-appointed administrator. Once letters have been issued, the personal representative will proceed to collect the decedent's assets and provide for their protection. (If it is expected to take more than a few months to procure letters, the appointment of a temporary personal representative may be necessary.)

The steps that must be taken during this phase of the administration are listed below in their approximate order of occurrence. In all cases, of course, it will be necessary to check local law and practice.

(1) Notify banks where decedent had accounts; obtain information as to date of death balance, form of ownership, etc.

(2) Arrange for the collection and custody of decedent's personal property.

(3) Check insurance coverage on all of decedent's property.

(4) Investigate all of decedent's brokerage accounts.

(5) Make a preliminary estimate of the decedent's estate to determine the form of the probate and/or administration. Obtain values as of acquisition date, date of death, and December 31, 1976 for all estate assets as soon as possible.

(6) Have additional copies of the will made for beneficiaries, taxing authorities, personal representatives, etc.

(7) List contents of decedent's safe deposit box, if any, in the presence of a member of decedent's family and taxing authorities.

(8) Hold preliminary conference with family members and others named in the will for the purpose of reading the will and determining whether there will be any objections or renunciations.

(9) Hold conference with the decedent's personal representative(s) to obtain all the facts needed for the preparation of the petition for probate.

(10) Make arrangements with the post office for custody of the decedent's mail.

(11) File the will and petition for testamentary letters (or petition for administration) with probate court.

(12) Make copies of the petition available to the executor and taxing authorities, accompanied by an affidavit as to the value of the property affected by the will, and the amounts going to the beneficiaries, together with their relationships to the decedent.

(13) Obtain copies of the death certificate (as many as possible).

(14) Assist beneficiaries in the collection of life insurance proceeds, obtaining necessary IRS forms from insurance companies.

(15) Collect unpaid wages, salary, or commissions owed to the decedent.

(16) Inquire as to the exact benefits due from company pension and/or profit-sharing plans and other company programs, and from union or association benefit programs.

(17) Change automobile registration, if in the decedent's name.

(18) If decedent was a business person, check for business continuation agreements, etc.

(19) Arrange for continued collection of loans, rents, interest, dividends, royalties, etc., and attempt to collect delinquent obligations.

(20) Mail notice of hearing on petition together with order limiting time to file claims (all in accordance with local law requirements).

(21) Arrange for publication of order for hearing (in accordance with local law).

(22) File affidavit of mailing of notice of hearing (in accordance with local law requirements).

(23) Send copies of the will and preliminary estimate of estate to the appropriate heirs.

(24) Arrange for ancillary administration, if necessary.

(25) Collect all pertinent information for income tax returns.

(26) If the decedent was the sole proprietor of a business, determine if there is an outstanding obligation for employers' tax.

(27) Collect all amounts due from retirement plans, etc.

(28) File Social Security claims.

(29) File VA claims, if any.

(30) Arrange for witnesses to appear at hearing, obtaining written depositions, if necessary.

(31) Send copy of the will to surviving spouse and minor children, if not already done, and notify them as to their rights (and advise them as to tax considerations).

(32) File affidavit of mailing of notice of surviving spouse's and children's rights (as required by local law).

(33) Assemble data on all nonprobate property (joint tenancy property, life insurance, living trusts, property subject to a power in the decedent, etc.).

(34) Inquire into all substantial gifts made by the decedent within three years of his death or after 1976, and all transfers made in trust at any time.

(35) Make inquiry as to requirements for fiduciary bond, discussing same with the named executor, and prepare application therefor, if necessary.

(36) Prepare executor's form of acceptance.

(37) Attend formal court hearing on petition for probate with witnesses and any required written testimony.

(38) File acceptance by executor.

(39) File fiduciary bond, if required.

(40) Obtain certified copies of letters testamentary.

(41) To limit appeal time, serve copy of order on petition to interested parties.

(42) Have appraisers appointed, if necessary.

(43) Executor should notify post office, banks, creditors, IRS, and others of his appointment.

(44) Documentation of all the items listed above should be obtained (originals or photocopies when appropriate). Particularly important are copies of federal gift tax returns (Form 709) for transfers made after 1976.

[¶1703]   FIDUCIARY RESPONSIBILITY (AN OVERVIEW)

In general, the executor's duties include:

(1) The collection and conservation of the personal property of the estate. Since real property usually vests immediately in the devisees, the executor is able to sell such property only in the event that personal property is inadequate to meet claims.

(2) The payment of all valid debts, including funeral costs, fees and expenses incurred in administration, death taxes, income and other taxes owed by the decedent, etc.

(3) The distribution of remaining property in accordance with the testator's wishes.

If a testamentary trustee is named, most of his duties are prescribed by the will; however, certain duties and restrictions may also be imposed by state law. The trustee's duties include:

(1) Taking possession and control of the trust property.

(2) Investing and reinvesting such property prudently for the production of income.

(3) Paying all necessary taxes and other reasonable expenses of trust administration.

(4) Exercising all mandatory directions recited in the governing instrument, except those that are impossible to fulfill.

(5) Exercising any discretionary duties in good faith and within the bounds of reasonable judgment.

(6) Keeping records and rendering accounts when required to do so.

(7) Paying over income (and principal, depending on the terms of the

governing instrument) to those entitled to receive it.

(8) Refraining from dealing with the trust property to his own advantage and from commingling such property with his own.

(9) Dealing impartially with the beneficiaries.

(10) Defending the trust against the claims of third parties.

(11) Refraining from delegating any of the above duties to others except to the extent permitted by the governing instrument or by local law.

[¶1704]   TAX DUTIES OF FIDUCIARIES

An estate or trust is a taxable entity. The responsibility for filing returns, paying taxes, and performing other tax duties lies with the executor or trustee, as the case may be. In the case of an estate, the federal and local returns that must be prepared by the executor include the estate tax return, the estate income tax return, the decedent's final income tax return, unfiled gift tax returns, and other delinquent returns. The trustee must file the appropriate federal and local income tax returns.

[¶1705]   FEDERAL ESTATE TAX RETURN

The federal estate tax return (Form 706) must be filed by the executor or administrator within nine months after the date of death, unless an extension has been granted. The deadline for paying the tax is the same. Returns for U.S. citizens or residents dying in 1977 or thereafter must be filed if:

Decedent Dies In	*With a Gross Estate of More Than****
1977	$120,000
1978	134,000
1979	147,000
1980	161,000
1981 and after	175,000

A return must be filed for a nonresident alien if the value of his gross estate situated in the United States exceeds $60,000 (again, reduced by the value of any post-1976 taxable gifts and the applicable exemption). Form 706NA is to be used in this instance.

The return must be filed with the service center for the state or district in which the decedent had his domicile at the time of his death. For a nonresident citizen the return must be filed with the Internal Revenue Service Center, 11601 Roosevelt Boulevard, Philadelphia, Pennsylvania 19155.

---

*These threshold amounts must be reduced by the sum of post-1976 taxable gifts and any specific exemption (for gift tax) used for gifts made between September 8, 1976 and January 1, 1977.

[¶1706]   **ESTATE INCOME TAX RETURN**

If the estate has $600 or more of gross income, it must file Form 1041. If there is a nonresident beneficiary, the return is required regardless of the amount of gross income. For purposes of filing, a taxable year for the estate must be selected. It need not be a calendar year and need not coincide with the date of death. It may be advantageous to use a short taxable year for the estate's initial return. Bearing in mind the tax interests of the beneficiaries, the choice of a fiscal year may help split the income and thus reduce the aggregate tax burden.

The return must be filed by the 15th day of the fourth month following the end of the tax year; estates and trusts can pay the tax quarterly. It may be advisable to complete the return early in order to be able to give advance notification to the distributees of the amounts they must include in their own returns.

[¶1707]   **DECEDENT'S INCOME TAX RETURNS**

The executor must also file the decedent's final income tax return on Form 1040 and, if necessary, delinquent returns for prior years. If death occurred between January 1 and April 15, there will generally be two returns to file, assuming the decedent was on a calendar-year basis.

The decedent's return is more difficult for the executor to compute than the estate's return. He has the information for the latter, but unless the decedent was the unusual taxpayer who kept detailed records of such things as deductions, the executor may have to make an estimate under the *Cohan* (CA-2, 39 F. 2d 540, 1930) rule.

A joint return may be filed for a married decedent for the year of death, unless the surviving spouse should remarry before the close of the tax year, or the decedent or the surviving spouse had a short tax year caused by a change of accounting period. The liability for the full tax in such cases is joint and several. If the decedent's income was less than that of the surviving spouse and the latter isn't the sole beneficiary, the executor's consent to a joint return, without limiting the estate's liability, may expose him to surcharge.

The surviving spouse may file a joint return if the decedent filed no return for the year and if no executor has been appointed by the time the joint or surviving spouse's return is due. If the executor qualifies within a year after the due date (including any extensions for filing), he may disaffirm the joint return by filing a separate return within the one-year period. This rule protects the estate in the event the surviving spouse files a return that is detrimental to the estate. It will be up to the executor to disaffirm unless the estate is fully indemnified.

Note: A surviving spouse may take advantage of the joint income tax rates for the two taxable years following the year of the decedent's death if he or she maintains a household that is the principal place of residence of his or her dependent child (son, stepson, daughter, or stepdaughter). The surviving spouse must furnish over half of the cost of maintaining the household and be entitled to take a personal exemption deduction under IRC §151. (See IRC §2(a)(1)).

[¶1708]   **GIFT TAX RETURN FILED BY EXECUTOR**

The executor should review the decedent's entire lifetime giving; a gift tax return may have been required (Form 709), even though no gift tax was payable. If there is doubt about the necessity to file, the executor probably should file anyway in order to start the statute of limitations running. The executor should always seek the surviving spouse's consent to have half the decedent's gifts attributed to him or her, so as to reduce any gift tax payable by the estate. If the spouse made the gifts during the decedent's lifetime, the personal representative must carefully weigh the consequences of attributing half to the decedent.

[¶1709]   **TRUST INCOME TAX RETURN**

The trustee (whether the trust is testamentary or inter vivos) must file an income tax return (Form 1041) for any year in which the trust has any taxable income or has gross income of $600 or more. Gross income of the trust or estate is determined in the same manner as an individual's. The trust or estate reports its income and is allowed an offsetting deduction for the income distributed or required to be distributed to the beneficiary. The beneficiary, in turn, is taxable on the income required to be distributed to him or her. As with estates, the choice of fiscal year and method of accounting may be significant in determining the total tax impact on the ultimate beneficiaries.

[¶1710]   **TAX RETURN CHART**

The chart provided in the appendix summarizes the tax duties of fiduciaries. It also briefly describes the requirements for obtaining extensions of time to file returns and to pay the tax.

[¶1711]   **TAX LIABILITIES OF FIDUCIARIES**

The duty to discharge the tax liability may be particularly onerous. Although normally the fiduciary is responsible for paying out only the funds entrusted to him as a fiduciary, in some cases he can become personally liable for the taxes.

An executor or administrator who pays a debt due by the person or estate for whom he acts before he pays debts due to the United States becomes personally liable for these debts, to the extent they remain unpaid.

Debts due to the United States include federal taxes. Thus, whenever a personal representative makes distributions or pays other obligations, he or she runs a personal risk if the estate is unable to pay federal taxes. However, debts to the United States have no priority over prior specific and perfected liens (*Union Guardian Trust Co.* 41 BTA 1306, *acq.* CB 1940-2), or debts given priority by state law (such as funeral expenses, administration expenses, and, in some cases, allowances for surviving spouses). Thus, the personal representative should be able to make such payments safely.

There are two tests to determine whether a personal representative who makes payments before paying debts to the United States is personally liable:

(1) The Insolvency Test: The priority given to United States debts must be established by proving that the estate is "insolvent" or showing that it has "insufficient funds to pay all the debts due from the deceased"; and,

(2) The "Knowledge" Test: The representative must have been aware of the unpaid debt to the United States. According to *Rev. Rul. 66-43*, (CB 1966-1, 291), the executor or administrator of an estate cannot be held personally liable unless he or she either has or should have had personal knowledge of the debt. As a general rule, the government should have no difficulty in satisfying this requirement in the case of estate taxes, since one of the executor's first duties is to estimate the amount of taxes.

In addition to his representative and personal responsibilities, the fiduciary is also subject to transferee liability like any other taxpayer (IRC §6901(h); 7701(b)).

[¶1712]   PROTECTION FROM PERSONAL LIABILITY

Although the possibility of personal liability is a serious problem for the fiduciary, he is not without protection. For example, unpaid gift taxes are not likely to be charged against him, since the tax follows the gift and can be satisfied out of the gift property. Even if the donee has parted with the property, the fiduciary is still safe, since the gift tax then becomes a lien against the donee's other property. The fiduciary may be in some danger when the gift is in trust; because of the difficulty in reaching the beneficiaries, the Treasury may contend the trustee is to be treated as the donee.

With respect to the estate tax, the executor can ascertain the amount of estate tax due by making a written request to IRS. The latter must notify the executor of the amount within nine months of the executor's request or the filing of the Form 706 (whichever is later—but not after the end of the assessment period). If the executor pays this amount, he is entitled to a written discharge from personal liability (IRC §2204). Discharge from personal liability for decedent's gift and income taxes is also available (IRC §6905).

IRS may require the executor to furnish a bond prior to releasing him from personal liability for any amount for which an extension of time to pay has been granted.

There is also a time limit on the personal tax liability threat to the fiduciary. Any assessment against the fiduciary personally must be made not later than one year after the liability arises or not later than the expiration of the period for collection of the tax in respect of which the liability arises, whichever is later (IRC §6901(c)(3)). This is in addition to the six-year period within which IRS is permitted to collect a validly assessed tax.

157

Enforcement of personal liability against the fiduciary is made by the same processes (jeopardy assessment, distraint, etc.) and is subject to the same restrictions (90-day letter, etc.) as any other tax collection.

[¶1713] POST-MORTEM TAX PLANNING

Although the drafter of the will, the executor, and the beneficiaries can collaborate to achieve important tax savings after the testator's death, the time to think of these matters is prior to or at the time of drafting the will. However, some opportunities will remain open to the executors or present themselves for the first time after the testator's death. The tax savings available here fall into these categories:

    (a) Estate tax savings by altering the testamentary dispositions;
    (b) Income tax savings for the estate in administration;
    (c) Income tax savings for the beneficiaries.

[¶1714] CHECKLIST OF POST-MORTEM
TAX PLANNING STEPS

Here is a checklist of some post-mortem maneuvers that can be employed by executors or estate beneficiaries to achieve certain tax advantages.

☐ **Election Against the Will:** A failure to qualify for the marital deduction can be remedied by a spouse who (pursuant to local law) exercises his or her right to take against the will.

☐ **Will Contests and Family Settlements:** If a will contest or settlement results in property passing to the surviving spouse, the property qualifies for the marital deduction provided the surrender or assignment is a bona fide recognition of enforceable rights in the decedent's estate.

☐ **Renunciation or Disclaimer:** Property that passes to a surviving spouse by disclaimer increases the marital deduction provided the interest itself qualifies for the deduction (IRC §2056(d)(2)). For federal tax purposes, a qualified disclaimer must meet the following requirements: (1) It is a written, irrevocable, and unqualified refusal by a person to accept an interest in property; (2) It is received by the transferor of the interest, his legal representative, or the holder of legal title to the property within nine months of (a) the day on which the transfer is made to the disclaimant or (b) the day on which the disclaimant attains age 21; (3) The disclaimant has not accepted the interest or any of its benefits, and (4) As a result of the refusal, the interest passes to a person other than the disclaimant (IRC §2518). Disclaimer by the spouse as to property in excess of the marital deduction can avoid an estate tax on the spouse's death.

☐ **Picking a Fiscal Year for the Estate:** By selecting a fiscal year that will produce a short year at the beginning of the estate administration and a short year at the end, income that will be taxed to the estate can be spread out to maximum advantage. Since an estate beneficiary must report the income during his taxable year within which the tax year of the estate ends, the selection of a taxable year for the estate also has a direct bearing on the beneficiary's tax picture.

☐ *Timing of Distributions:* If the executor has discretionary powers with respect to the distribution of estate assets, he is in a position to make substantial savings in taxes by proper timing of the distributions from the estate. In years when the estate is in a lower bracket than the beneficiaries of the estate, the executor might want to accumulate the income of the estate in order to have it taxed in its lower bracket. If the beneficiaries are in lower brackets than the estate, the executor might want to accelerate the distribution of the income of the estate in order to have it taxed as the income of the beneficiaries.

☐ *Valuation of Estate:* The valuation placed on estate assets for estate tax purposes will affect (a) the amount of the estate tax; (b) the amount of the marital deduction and the size of the shares of the surviving spouse and other beneficiaries, and (c) the taxable gain or loss on a subsequent sale of the assets by the estate or by the beneficiaries. The relationship of the applicable estate tax rates and the future income tax rates will point up possible tax savings here.

☐ *Deduction of Administration Expenses:* The executor must elect whether to deduct administration expenses on the estate tax return or on the estate's income tax return. They can also be split between the two returns. It is not enough to look at the respective rate tables. The executor must think in terms of effective rates—i.e., if the full marital deduction is claimed, the effective rate of tax saving from an estate tax deduction of an administration expense is roughly one-half of the nominal estate tax rate. The executor must also look at the effect of his election on the interests of the beneficiaries. An election based strictly on effective tax rates may warp the interest of competing beneficiaries—for example, if the income and residuary interests are not the same.

☐ *Termination of Administration:* The termination of the estate closes its taxable year. While the termination cannot be unduly delayed, wherever possible the executor should avoid having more than 12 months' distributions taxed to the beneficiaries in one year. Ideally, the estate should be closed at such time as will bring the final distribution of income into another tax year of the beneficiary. On the other hand, if the final year of the estate includes excess deductions that can be claimed by the beneficiaries, it might be preferable to close the estate at a time when the beneficiaries can realize the maximum benefit from the excess deductions.

☐ *Income in Respect of a Decedent (IRD):* Income that has been earned by the decedent during his lifetime that is received by his estate will not be taxed in the last income tax return of the decedent. Instead, it will be taxed when it is received (actually or constructively) to: (1) The decedent's estate, if it is entitled to receive the IRD, or (2) The person who, due to the decedent's death, is entitled to the IRD, or (3) The person to whom IRD has been properly distributed by the estate.

Income in respect of a decedent is also included in the decedent's estate tax return, but the estate tax paid on this income can be taken by the recipient as an income tax deduction (IRC §691(c)). While most of the planning for income in respect of a decedent should be taken care of before death (via contractual provisions or will provisions), there is still much that can be done by the executor—especially if the will gives him discretionary powers in this regard. If he has the power to distribute these income rights before they are collected, he can spread them over a number of beneficiaries rather than have them come into the estate, which is taxed as a single taxpayer.

☐ *Decedent's Final Income Tax Return:* If the decedent was married at the time of his death, the executor and the surviving spouse can file a joint return. This will, as a rule, bring about a lower tax than would the use of separate returns. However, local law will have to be checked if the will itself does not contain explicit authorization to the executor to join in a joint return, since the joint return may subject the estate to liability for the income tax on the surviving spouse's income.

☐ *Deferring Tax Attributable to Business Interest:* An executor can pay the estate tax in 10 equal installments rather than within nine months after the decedent's death provided a major estate asset is a closely held business (IRC §6166A). The value of the business interest must exceed 35% of the gross estate or 50% of the taxable estate. Making the election does not prohibit the executor from obtaining early discharge from personal liability for any future estate tax deficiency. As a result of the election, the estate, in effect, receives a loan of the amount of the installments at a low interest rate. Thus, the executor can meet the estate tax liability without affecting the business interest, which otherwise might have to be sold or liquidated to meet the tax obligation.

An alternative way to avoid forced sales of business interests to pay estate taxes is the 15-year installment payment method provided by Code §6166. If the value of the business interest exceeds 65% of the adjusted gross estate, the executor can elect to defer tax payments (except the interest thereon) for five years and then pay the tax owed in 10 annual installments.

☐ *Moratorium on Carryover Basis Rules:* The Revenue Act of 1978 imposed a three-year moratorium on the effective date of the carryover basis rules introduced by the Tax Reform Act of 1976. Thus, the recipient's basis for property acquired from a decedent dying before January 1, 1980 will be stepped up to its fair market value at the date of death or alternate valuation date. The basis of carryover basis property (basically, property that would be taxed at capital gain rates with certain specific exclusions) acquired from a decedent dying after December 31, 1979, is equal to the decedent's adjusted basis for the property immediately before his or her death, but increased by certain adjustments.

[¶1715] ACCOUNTING FORMATS

There are no generally accepted forms for estate accountings. Some courts merely require statements of receipts and disbursements, especially if the estate is small. More substantial estates should have detailed statements. Although the fiduciary should check local law before submitting an accounting, a statement that separates the estate's operating and income expenses from receipts and disbursements pertaining to estate principal represents the most prudent approach. The statement should, of course, also show what assets have come into the fiduciary's hands (e.g., inventoried assets, gains on sales, income, etc.), what disbursements (expenses, payments for debts, bequests satisfied, taxes paid, etc.) have been made, and what balance remains for distribution. Each item in the statement may be supplemented by detailed schedules.

[¶1716]   ESTATE ACCOUNTING

Estate accountings, whether judicially mandated or informally completed, serve several purposes. First, they provide the local court having jurisdiction over the administration of the estate with a means of overseeing and reviewing a fiduciary's activities. The court may require periodic (usually annual) accountings from the representative. When the estate is settled, a final accounting is nearly always made. However, informal accountings (not submitted to a court) are acceptable if all parties with an interest in the estate agree to such a method. A well-organized accounting and bookkeeping system also helps the fiduciary keep track of the progress of the estate. Interim accountings can alert the executor or administrator to possible cash shortages and difficulties in satisfying bequests. When a final accounting has been accepted by the local court and the estate beneficiaries, the fiduciary can be released from further liability and obligation in connection with his administration of the estate.

Finally, accountings give the beneficiaries a detailed picture of the fiduciary's activities. Thus, if they are displeased with the performance of his duties as reported in the accounting, they can raise objections in court.

[¶1717]   FOR FURTHER REFERENCE . . .

Denhardt, *Complete Guide to Estate Accounting and Taxes,* Prentice-Hall, Inc. Englewood Cliffs, N.J.

Estate and Trust Practice and Fiduciary Responsibility, Institute for Business Planning, Inc., Englewood Cliffs, N.J.

Estate Planning (2 vols.), Institute for Business Planning, Inc., Englewood Cliffs, N.J.

Huffaker, Stutsman, Angvire, Wiener, *Tax Problems of Fiduciaries,* 2nd ed., American Law Institute—American Bar Association, Philadelphia, Pa.

Michaelson and Blattmachr, *Income Taxation of Estates and Trusts,* 10th ed., Practising Law Institute, New York, N.Y.

Newman and Kalter, *Postmortem Estate Planning,* American Law Institute, American Bar Association, Philadelphia, Pa.

Nossaman, *Trust Administration and Taxation,* Matthew Bender, New York, N.Y.

ESTATE PLANNING

[¶**1801**]   When preparing an estate plan, it is useful to take a multi-discipline approach. The planner should have a working knowledge of many fields, though he or she should not hesitate to obtain expert advice where it is needed. Thus, the financial implications of every available planning technique should be examined, the legality of a particular device must be ascertained, the impact of economic factors such as inflation should be considered, and, of course, the tax consequences of each transaction must be analyzed. Finally, as the mass of tax laws and reporting requirements grows and as the complexity of the plan increases, accurate and detailed accounting systems must be employed.

[¶1802]   **THE PLANNING PROCESS**

The estate planning process is often thought of as solely directed at saving estate taxes at an individual's death. Ideally, however, it is a financial plan that helps attain the client's lifetime objectives and executes his dispositive scheme at death, both at minimal income and transfer tax costs. For information on wills see ¶4201 et seq.; for information on trusts see ¶4001 et seq.

Step 1: To prepare an effective estate plan, the planner must obtain a comprehensive breakdown of the client's assets and liabilities, and secure vital personal data about the client and his family. This information, together with a thorough knowledge of the client's personal and financial objectives, will help the planner to identify problem areas and suggest planning techniques. For example, if the client's principal asset is an interest in a closely held business, his eventual estate may experience a cash shortage when federal and state death taxes are imposed. A common solution to this problem is to prepare a buy-sell agreement funded with life insurance. (The inventory form provided in *IBP Estate Planning, Vol. II—Checklists/Forms* is an effective way of gathering the required data.)

Step 2: Estimate the amount of debts and claims that will have to be paid. This estimate should include current income tax liabilities, debts, funeral and last illness expenses, and administration costs.

Step 3: After deducting from the total value of assets at death the estimate of all debts and claims, calculate the estate tax liability that will probably be due. If the individual is married, the total tax liability that will fall due at the death of both spouses should be determined. By this calculation, it can be estimated what will be left for the children if both parents should die within a relatively short period of time. If estate tax liability is to be minimized by use of the marital deduction, it is necessary to determine how much greater the liability will be if the spouse with the smaller share of the assets dies first. By adding the total estate taxes, expenses, and debts in both estates, the estate owner can be shown a close approximation of the total transfer cost to his children or other ultimate beneficiaries under the current estate plan.

Step 4: Schedule the liquidation of estate liabilities. Apply cash amounts from the list of cash assets and assets convertible into cash against the schedules of debts, claims, administration costs, and estate tax liability. Then decide whether there is enough cash to meet the cash needs of the family during the administration of the estate. This comparison of cash available and liabilities will point up whether there is a surplus or deficit of liquid assets. The estate owner and the estate planner can then determine whether it is necessary to arrange for the conversion of additional assets into cash or to secure additional liquid resources such as life insurance.

Step 5: Assign the remaining assets to individuals or trusts according to the estate owner's will. This will indicate how much is available to satisfy the testamentary wishes of the estate owner and will provide a basis for his reevaluation of the disposition.

Step 6: Prepare a schedule showing the assets that will be in the hands of each beneficiary after distribution and how much annual income these assets will produce. If it is a capital asset, factor in the capital gain tax due upon the beneficiary's disposition of it. Include the separately owned property of each beneficiary. The annual income available from these sources should be compared with the amount of annual income that the estate owner thinks should be available for the beneficiary.

Step 7: Suggest methods of reducing liabilities and administrative expenses.

Step 8: Show how assets can be increased. For example, inadequacy of liquid assets to meet cash liabilities or of net assets to produce family income may call for additional insurance or additional annual savings to complete an investment program.

Step 9: Show how income can be reorganized to increase liquidity or add to family assets. For example, the shifting of income-producing properties to other members of the family will save income tax as well as estate tax.

Step 10: Make final projection of assets, liabilities, liquid assets available to meet liabilities, net assets available for distribution, and annual income produced by these assets—after considering the steps that have been recommended to increase assets, improve liquidity, and reduce estate liabilities.

Step 11: Project the increase and accumulation of estate assets until the owner's retirement age. Take annual savings, assume a conservative rate of investment return, apply a compound interest table to determine what should be accumulated at the age that the owner specifies for his own retirement. Take the cash value of insurance policies at that time and convert that into annual income. Add to this any Social Security and any retirement income or profit-sharing assets that may become available at that age. Tabulate total assets and anticipated income for the owner at retirement age. Determine whether or not additional saving or other steps are indicated to provide for the owner's retirement security.

Step 12: Review the plan whenever there are changes in the individual's financial or personal status, or in the tax law or applicable local law.

CHECKLIST OF DOCUMENTS NEEDED FOR ESTATE PLANNING

☐ *Birth Certificates:*
Husband
Wife
Children

☐ *Documents of Title:*
Deeds
Leases
Purchase and sale contracts

☐ *Appraisals*

☐ *Business Interests:*
Partnership agreement
Redemption agreement
Buy-Sell agreement
Disability agreement
Close corporation charters, bylaws, minute books
Balance sheets for previous five years
Profit and loss statements for previous five years
Federal and state income tax returns for previous five years

☐ *Employment Records:*
Employment contracts
Pension benefits
Profit-sharing plan benefits

☐ *Matrimonial:*
Separation agreement
Property settlement
Divorce decree

☐ *Trust Instruments*

☐ *Wills:*
Husband
Wife
Other family members

☐ *Instruments Creating Powers of Appointment:*
Donor
Donee

164

☐ *Insurance Policies:*
Life insurance
General
Health

☐ *Income Tax Returns (past five years):*
Federal
State

☐ *Gift Tax Returns*

☐ *Personal Financial Statements*

[¶1804]   THE UNIFIED FEDERAL ESTATE
                            AND GIFT TAX

The estates of decedents dying after December 31, 1976, are subject to a unified estate and gift tax rate schedule introduced by the Tax Reform Act of 1976. The first step in calculating the federal estate tax is the determination of the gross estate. All property the decedent possesses at death plus all transfers made within three years of the decedent's death for which a gift tax return was required to be filed are includible in the gross estate. Also included is the amount of gift tax paid on the transfers within three years of death. Deductions such as administrative expenses, debts, and funeral expenses are subtracted from the gross estate to arrive at the adjusted gross estate.

The next step is to compute the marital deduction in order to determine the taxable estate. The greater of $250,000 or 50% of the adjusted gross estate may be deducted provided that the amount passed to the surviving spouse constituted "qualified property." (The maximum estate tax marital deduction is reduced by the amount of the marital deduction allowed for lifetime transfers in excess of 50% of the value of such transfers.)

A tentative tax is computed under the new rate schedule on the total amount of the taxable estate and the adjusted taxable gifts made by the decedent after 1976 (other than gifts includible in the decedent's gross estate). This tentative tax is reduced by the amount of gift tax paid on the decedent's post-1976 gifts to obtain the estate tax before credits.

Once the estate tax has been calculated, the unified credit is applied as follows:

Year of Gift or Death	*Amount of Credit*
1977*	$30,000
1978	34,000
1979	38,000
1980	42,500
1981 (and thereafter)	47,000

*For 1977 gifts, a credit of only $6,000 is allowed for transfers between January 1 and June 30, 1977. Beginning July 1, 1977, the full $30,000 credit is available.

Other available credits include: State death taxes paid in respect of property included in the gross estate, foreign death taxes paid, and estate tax paid by the transferee on prior transfers.

Carryover Basis: The 1978 Revenue Act imposed a three-year moratorium on the application of the carryover basis rules. Thus, property received from decedents who die before 1980 has a basis that is stepped-up to its estate tax value.

[¶1805]   **VALUATION**

The value of an asset for estate tax purposes is its fair market value at the date of the owner's death or the alternate valuation date. Fair market value is "that price at which the property would change hands between a willing buyer and a willing seller, neither being under any compulsion to buy or to sell and both having reasonable knowledge of all relevant facts." Property such as stock or cash usually has a readily ascertainable value, but an interest in a closely held business poses a complex and vexing valuation problem. As noted in the IRS valuation training manual, the question of value is one of fact, subject to solution only in the light of all circumstances having a bearing on the issue. When a unique asset (e.g., real property, business interest, etc.) is to be valued, there is no mathematically "right" answer based on a formula or otherwise; there is only a range of possible right answers that can be supported by logical and convincing reasoning.

☐ *Listed Stocks and Bonds:* If there is a market for stocks or bonds on a stock exchange, in an over-the-counter market, or otherwise, the fair market value per share or bond is the mean between the highest and lowest quoted selling prices on the valuation date. IRS permits valuation by reference to the records of combined exchanges as reported in composite listings or publications of general circulation. A discount from the market price is appropriate if there are substantial indications that marketing a large block of stock would have a depressing effect on the price and/or involve considerable administrative expenses (e.g., attorneys' or accountants' fees, registration expenses, transfer taxes, etc.).

☐ *Real Estate:* Each parcel of real property must be valued individually, taking into account the facts and circumstances of the particular situation. The expert testimony of well-informed and experienced real estate brokers, operators, and investors is desirable, in order to relate the local market situation to the specific parcel of land. In general, these experts base their opinions on the assessed valuation of the property, keeping in mind the percentage of assessed value that the average sales in the area have realized in the period immediately preceding the appraisal, as well as the earning power, replacement cost, and sales of similar property.

☐ *Life Estate, Annuity, and Remainder Interests:* Although intangible property interests can be difficult to value, certain types of intangible assets can be valued with reasonable certainty by the use of actuarial tables published in the Regulations.

☐ *Cash and Bank Accounts:* Cash belonging to the decedent at the date of death is includible in the gross estate whether it is on hand or on deposit with a bank. The amount of any check written by the decedent for bona fide obligations is not includible if the checks are subsequently honored by the bank. Interest on a savings account accrued to the valuation date is includible, unless the decedent died during an interest period and under bank policy interest does not accrue until the end of the period.

☐ *Household and Personal Effects:* If the estate is relatively small, personal effects of a decedent who lived in an apartment can be assigned a minimal value. For larger estates, or if valuable items (e.g., jewelry, paintings, antique furniture, etc.) are involved, the estate practitioner has two options: (1) He may present a room-by-room itemization of the effects, describing each item and assigning a value thereto (however, items in the same room, none of which exceed $100 in value, can be grouped), or (2) The estate's personal representative may submit a sworn statement setting forth the value of the decedent's effects as determined by a competent appraiser (one of recognized standing and ability).

When the estate includes items of marked artistic value or intrinsic worth valued in excess of $3,000, the practitioner *must* submit an expert appraisal made under oath. The appraisal should be accompanied by a sworn statement made by the estate's personal representative as to the competency of the expert and thoroughness of the expert's appraisal.

☐ *Insurance:* The value of the proceeds of insurance on the decedent's life receivable by or for the benefit of the estate is taxable. If the proceeds are receivable by beneficiaries other than the decedent or his estate, they are includible if the decedent possessed incidents of ownership in the policy. If the insurance is on the life of an individual other than the decedent and the decedent owned the policy at the date of his death, the estate tax value is the interpolated terminal reserve of the policy combined with the proportionate part of the last premium paid before the date of death that covers the period between the premium due date and the date of death.

☐ *Business Interests:* Partners or stockholders in a closely held business often enter into agreements that set forth the price and terms under which the interest of a retiring or deceased individual is to be purchased by the remaining partners or stockholders. Whether a restrictive stock agreement (in the case of an incorporated business) or a partnership buy-sell agreement is involved, the price agreed upon will normally be accepted for estate tax purposes.

If no valid purchase agreement exists, alternative approaches must be taken to determine the estate tax value of a business interest. It is important to remember that not every approach is appropriate for every kind of business interest, and in some cases a combination of methods is advisable. The appraiser must thoroughly investigate each valuation issue, and then apply his experience, common sense, and judgment to arrive at a fair value. Particular emphasis should be placed on the income-producing ability, book value, and dividend-paying capacity of the business.

☐ *Special Use Valuation:* As a general rule, real property must be included in a decedent's gross estate at its fair market value. This value is normally based on the land's "highest and best" use. However, if the property is used for farming purposes or in some other closely held business, the fair market value of the land may greatly exceed its value to the owner's heirs, who may wish to maintain the farm or business. If the income produced by the land is insufficient to pay the additional estate tax, or no steps to increase the estate's liquidity are taken, a sale of some or all of the property may be necessary. Recognizing this hardship, Congress has given the personal representative of an estate the option to value real property that is used in a farm or other closely held business at its actual, rather than optimum, use.

[¶1806]   **PLANNING TECHNIQUES**

The following planning techniques can be used to (1) reduce the client's income tax burden, either through the creation of deductions or through the shifting of income to a low-bracket taxpayer; (2) "freeze" the estate so that it does not increase in value; (3) minimize the estate tax through utilization of various estate tax deductions; and (4) provide liquid assets to help meet the tax burden and other expenses incurred by the client's estate. Keep in mind that these devices can be useful for several purposes, and that none of them should be proposed unless they conform to the client's objectives.

☐ *Lifetime Trusts:* A lifetime trust can be an extremely flexible and relatively straightforward method of splitting the client's income tax bill. The various types of trusts and their functions are examined in greater detail at ¶4001 et seq.

☐ *Gift-Leasebacks:* A gift of business assets to an independent trustee, in conjunction with a leaseback of the property to the transferor can result in considerable tax savings. The transferor can deduct his rent payments, while the trustee or trust beneficiaries pay tax on the rent income at their lower rates. However, these transactions are almost certain to end up being litigated by IRS, which has been upheld with some frequency in the courts.

☐ *Family Partnerships:* A partnership interest can be acquired by another member of the family either by gift or by purchase so that future income and increments of value will accrue to his benefit.

☐ *Charitable Transfers:* These can take many forms, depending on the individual donor's motives. If the charity qualifies under the IRC, the individual will be entitled to federal income, gift, and estate tax deductions.

The simplest type of charitable gift is an outright cash contribution or bequest. If the donor wishes to retain the enjoyment of the property for his life and for specified members of his family, a charitable remainder trust is a good vehicle. At the end of the designated payout period, the entire corpus of the trust must be irrevocably transferred to or for the use of a qualified charity. In order to deduct the present value of the charity's remainder interest for tax purposes, the trust must meet the Code's strict definition of a charitable remainder unitrust or annuity trust.

☐ *Installment Sales:* Selling property to members of the family for a small down payment plus installment obligations shifts income and future appreciation to the buyer. In order to defer taxation on the gain, the installment sale rules of IRC §453 must be followed. The terms of the transaction must be set realistically to avoid possible imposition of gift tax on any bargain element of the sale.

☐ ***Salary Continuation Agreements:*** An employer is committed to make continued payments to the surviving spouse of the employee. These payments, if kept in reasonable line with the value of the employee's services during his life, can shift substantial value to his spouse or children; these values will be supported by payments that the employer can deduct and the estate tax will be based on the actuarially reduced value of the future payments at the time of the employee's death.

☐ ***Interest-Free Loans:*** The right to use property without having to pay anything for its use can be a valuable planning technique. This situation frequently occurs among family members when one relative permits another to use or share items of real or personal property for little or no consideration in return. If the amounts of money or property involved are relatively modest, IRS is not likely to claim tax avoidance; however, if one family member lends a significant sum of money to another, the possibilities of confrontation with IRS are great.

☐ ***Forgiving Debts:*** A client can transfer the property to the beneficiary, taking back a purchase-money mortgage secured by that asset. If the purchase of a home is contemplated, a parent can lend cash to his child, securing the loan with a mortgage on the house. In both cases the face amount of the notes, which are non-interest bearing, is made equivalent to the property's fair market value. As the notes become due, the mortgagee forgives an amount that is within the available annual exclusion limits; thus, the beneficiary is given immediate use and possession of the property, while the client's gift taxes are kept to a minimum. The client also realizes estate tax savings, again because lifetime transfers not exceeding $3,000 annually per donee are not normally added back to the gross estate.

☐ ***Lifetime Gift Program:*** The 1976 Tax Reform Act severely reduced the efficacy of making lifetime gifts in order to minimize estate taxes. However, the gift tax annual exclusion (IRC §2503) emerged from the hands of the "reformers" unscathed and remains, particularly for modest estates, the most convenient and useful way to reduce one's taxable estate. The unification provisions of the 1976 Tax Reform Act require the addition of a donor's lifetime gifts to the taxable estate. However, since IRC §2503 excludes $3,000 from each inter vivos taxable transfer, none of these amounts is subject to estate tax. Thus, if an individual is planning to bequeath property to various beneficiaries anyway, some of the transfers should be made during life. Over a number of years a substantial amount of property can be given away tax free (if split gifts are made, the exclusion covers $6,000 annually per donee).

☐ ***Private Annuities:*** Property is transferred in exchange for the promise of the transferee to make annual payments over the balance of the transferor's life. Because the property is not included in the transferor's gross estate, he pays no estate tax. Neither will the exchange of property for a private annuity give rise to a gift tax, as long as the annual income promised is set at a figure that has the same actuarial value as the present value of the transferred property.

☐ ***Gifts of Life Insurance:*** Although the 1976 Tax Reform Act severely reduced the tax benefits of making lifetime gifts, inter vivos transfers of life insurance policies remain a valuable planning technique. In general, if the owner of a policy relinquishes complete dominion and control over the policy more than three years before death, and the proceeds are not payable to the estate, the proceeds will not be subject to the unified estate tax. The estate tax saving is accomplished at the relatively minor cost of a gift tax on the value of the policy. If the gift of the policy is made when its value does not exceed the available annual exclusions, the gift tax may also be avoided.

☐ **Flower Bonds:** Certain Treasury bonds that were issued before March 31, 1971, may be purchased at a substantial discount by an individual before death, and redeemed by the estate's personal representative at par value to pay the federal estate tax. Because of the great disparity between the purchase price and redemption price, these bonds are useful in lessening the impact of the estate tax.

☐ **Bequests to Surviving Spouses and Orphans:** Bequests to an individual's surviving spouse or orphaned children are deductible for estate tax purposes. See the discussion at ¶4201.

☐ **Marital Agreements:** Antenuptial agreements (between prospective spouses) and marital contracts (for married couples) define the property rights of a husband and wife in assets acquired before and/or during marriage. These contracts are particularly useful for individuals entering into a second marriage, and for domiciliaries of community property jurisdictions.

☐ **Buy-Sell Agreements:** Buy-sell agreements are contracts that provide for the orderly transfer of an individual's business interest after death. The agreement usually binds the decedent's estate to sell and the surviving partners or shareholders to buy the business interest at a stated price. Insurance purchased on the life of the individual is normally used to fund this arrangement. If a fair price has been set for the decedent's interest, the price will be accepted by IRS as the estate tax value of the interest.

☐ **Guardianships, Conservatorships, etc.:** Incompetency, whether due to illness, accident, or degeneration, must be anticipated by the estate planner. Depending on state law, some of the tools available to the planner are guardianships, conservatorships, durable powers of attorney, and the "living will." Lifetime trusts are another useful planning alternative.

[¶1807]   **JOINT OWNERSHIP**

Although numerous estate tax problems are associated with jointly owned property, this form of ownership is still very popular. In general, if an asset is owned as a joint tenancy with a right of survivorship, the surviving tenants automatically receive the ownership interest of a deceased tenant. For estate tax purposes, the full value of the tenancy is includible in the gross estate of the tenant who dies first, unless one of the following exceptions applies:

(1) If the decedent received the interest in the property as a gift from another co-owner, that interest is not subject to the estate tax, unless the tenants elected to treat the tenancy as a qualified joint interest;

(2) If the decedent and the other co-owners acquired their interests through gift or inheritance, the decedent's estate should only include his ratable share of the property;

(3) If the decedent and co-owners each made contributions toward the acquisition of the tenancy, only the portion of the property that is attributable to the decedent's contribution is taxable;

(4) If the tenancy is a "qualified joint interest" (owned by a husband and wife), only half its value is includible in the estate of the first spouse to die;

(5) If the jointly owned property is an "eligible joint interest" (a business owned by a married couple), the portion of the value of the property that is attributable to a noncontributing spouse's material participation is excludable from the decedent's estate.

[¶1807.1] Qualified Joint Interests

If a married individual dies owning a qualified joint interest, only one-half the value of the property is includible in the gross estate, regardless of who furnished the consideration. This rule applies only if the joint tenants were married, and elected to treat the creation of the tenancy as a completed gift.

[¶1807.2] Eligible Joint Interests

The entire value of a business interest is includible in its owner's gross estate, even if the spouse contributed capital and/or services to the business. However, this rule does not apply if the surviving spouse can prove the value and extent of his or her contribution, or if the business is an "eligible joint interest." Eligible joint interests are assets used in a trade or business that are held by a married couple as joint tenants. The value of each spouse's material participation in the business is not subject to estate tax when the other spouse dies. The regular performance of services or participation in management decisions are examples of material participation.

[¶1808] COMMUNITY PROPERTY

Community property is generally defined as property that is acquired by a husband or wife during their marriage, while they are domiciled in one of the eight community property jurisdictions (Arizona, California, Idaho, Louisiana, Nevada, New Mexico, Texas, and Washington). Under the laws of these states, each spouse has an equal "vested" interest in the community property that may be given away during the spouse's life or bequeathed at death. Thus, for estate tax purposes, only one-half the value of the community is includible in the gross estate of the spouse who dies first. Each spouse's other assets (separate property) are also taxable.

☐ *Rights During Life:* During life, each spouse has exclusive management and control over the separate property. In most community property jurisdictions, community assets are subject to the spouse's joint management and control. Similarly, each spouse may freely give away separate assets, but gifts of the community require mutual consent. If the couple divorces, community assets are divided equally.

☐ **Rights at Death:** Each spouse has the right to make a testamentary disposition of separate property and one-half interest in the community.

☐ **Quasi-Community Property:** In California and, to a lesser extent, in Arizona, quasi-community property principles apply to certain assets of married individuals who were previously domiciled in a common-law state. In general, property acquired while the spouses were domiciled in a common-law state is quasi-community property, if the property would have been community property if acquired in California (or Arizona). The quasi-community property rules come into play only if the couple divorces or one spouse dies. Thus, upon divorce or death, one-half of the quasi-community property passes to the other spouse. For federal estate tax purposes, the quasi-community property is treated as separate property.

☐ **Conversions of Community Property:** A husband and wife may enter into an agreement converting community property interests into separate property and vice versa. Such agreements are recognized in all the community property jurisdictions and usually apply to property presently owned or acquired after execution of the agreement. However, local law should be checked to determine the validity of the contract (e.g., the agreement cannot foster divorce, may have to be written or recorded, etc.).

[¶1809]   **SELECTING THE FIDUCIARY**

Unless a fiduciary is carefully selected, the most well-conceived estate plan may go awry, resulting in frustration of the client's wishes and financial loss to the client's beneficiaries. Moreover, fraud, dishonesty, or even mere mismanagement can expose the fiduciary to personal liability. Ideally, the fiduciary should be an individual or institution with a high degree of integrity, well-versed in business matters, and familiar with the client's personal and financial background. Keep in mind, however, that the fiduciary is normally allowed to seek assistance from qualified experts (e.g., attorneys, accountants, investment advisors, etc.).

Occasionally, the fiduciary nominated in the will or trust instrument is unwilling or unable to accept the position. In other cases, a fiduciary who has already been appointed may die, become disabled, or be disqualified to continue functioning. The beneficiaries may also decide that the fiduciary is simply not managing the trust or estate competently. If the will or trust instrument is silent in this respect, the parties will have to petition the appropriate court for the appointment of a successor fiduciary. This procedure can be cumbersome, time-consuming, and expensive, and can easily result in intrafamily conflict. These problems can be avoided by providing for successor fiduciaries in the governing instrument or by giving a third party (e.g., a committee or even some of the beneficiaries) the power to remove a fiduciary and appoint a new one.

If the value of the trust or estate is relatively modest, the tendency is to name an individual as the fiduciary. However, as in any other area of estate planning, this rule should not be rigidly applied. Most individuals do not have the experience or time to carry out the complex, technical duties that are required of an executor or trustee, even if modest amounts are involved. On the other hand, the client may not feel comfortable with a corporate fiduciary with whom he or she has had little personal contact. Much of the uncertainty over whether to name an individual or corporate fiduciary can be resolved by selecting one of each; however, the advisability of this arrangement should be carefully examined. While the appointment of a relative, friend, or business associate can add a personal touch to the fiduciary-beneficiary relationship, a corporate fiduciary may be reluctant to share authority with another individual. Thus, this decision, too, depends on the particular case and the estate planner's judgment. Finally, remember that if an individual names his spouse as a fiduciary, adverse estate or income tax consequences may result.

[¶1810]   **FOR FURTHER REFERENCE . . .**

Behrenfeld, W., *"Estate Planning Desk Book,"* 4th edition, Institute for Business Planning, Inc., Englewood Cliffs, N.J. (1977).

Cantor, G., and Franklin, R., *The Ten Best Ways to Save Estate Taxes,* Institute for Business Planning, Inc., Englewood Cliffs, N.J. (1978).

Casner, *Estate Planning* (2 Vol.), Little Brown & Co., Boston, Mass.

Cowley, J.M., and Jones, S.L., "Estate and Gift Tax Unification: the Concepts and Selected Giving Problems," 36 New York University Institute on Federal Taxation 273 (1978).

Douglass, P., *Guide to Planning the Farm Estate: With Checklists and Forms,* Institute for Business Planning, Inc., Englewood Cliffs, N.J. (1978).

Englebrecht, T., and Moore, M., *Income Taxation of Estates, Trusts and Beneficiaries,* Institute for Business Planning, Inc., Englewood Cliffs, N.J. (1978).

Erdman, J., *Complete Guide to the Marital Deduction in Estate Planning,* Institute for Business Planning, Inc., Englewood Cliffs, N.J. (1978).

Estate Planning (2 Vol.), Institute for Business Planning, Inc., Englewood Cliffs, N.J.

Kirby, J., *Estate Planner's Kit,* Institute for Business Planning, Inc., Englewood Cliffs, N.J. (1978).

Lazara, "Approaches to Reviewing Estate Plans and Related Documents in Light of TRA 1976," 4 Estate Planning 242 (1977).

Lehrman, A., *Complete Book of Wills and Trusts,* Institute for Business Planning, Inc., Englewood Cliffs, N.J. (1978).

Stephens, Maxfield, and Lind, *Federal Estate and Gift Taxation,* Warren, Gorham & Lamont, Boston, Mass.

Wilkins, "Drafting for the Small Estate: Techniques to Maximize New Marital and Orphan's Deductions," 4 Estate Planning 194 (1977).

FAIR CREDIT REPORTING

[¶**1901**] Federal regulation of the consumer reporting industry has been effective since April 25, 1971, exactly six months after passage of the Fair Credit Reporting Act (15 USC § 1581-1681T), which is Title VII of the Truth-In-Lending Act. Aimed at insuring that consumer reporting agencies exercise their responsibilities with fairness, impartiality, and respect for the consumer's right to privacy, the law specifically requires that consumer reporting agencies adopt reasonable procedures to provide information to credit grantors, insurers, employers, and others in a manner that is both fair and equitable to the consumer with regard to the confidentiality, accuracy, and proper use of such information.

Regulation of consumer reporting agencies by placing obligatory disclosure requirements on users of consumer reports is the primary purpose of fair credit reporting. Under the law, users of consumer reports must inform consumers when an adverse action (defined as a denial of credit, insurance, or employment) is made on the basis of any such report, and the user must identify the reporting agency that undertook the initial examination of the consumer.

Businesses that collect their own information are not affected by the statutory code of conduct for the consmer reporting industry, which is generally defined as credit bureaus, investigative reporting companies, and other organizations whose primary business is the gathering and reporting of information about consumers for the use of others. Additionally, information that is reported by one business to another is not considered to be a consumer report when that information relates to the company's own experience with the consumer. For example, a company could state "my records reflect that Mr. Smith was late on 8 of 12 payments," and the report would not be covered by the legislation. However, a businessman who regularly reports information that is not based on his personal knowledge has made a consumer report within the meaning of the Fair Credit Reporting Act. The Federal Trade Commission cites as an example a statement by a businessman, "I have no file on Mr. Smith, but I know that he has a poor record of payment at the bank."

Consumer reports do not necessarily have to contain derogatory information. Any information—whether good or bad, oral or in writing—that bears on a consumer's creditworthiness, credit standing, credit capacity, character, personal characteristics, mode of living, or reputation is considered a consumer report if it is either (a) used or expected to be used or (b) collected in whole or in part for the purpose of considering the consumer's eligibility for consumer credit, insurance, employment, or other related business purpose.

[¶1902] SUMMARY OF CONSUMER RIGHTS CREATED BY THE FAIR CREDIT REPORTING ACT

The Fair Credit Reporting Act provides that when a consumer is rejected for credit, insurance, or employment, he must be given the name and address of the appropriate consumer reporting agency at the time of the denial. This is designed to make a consumer aware of any adverse information so that misinformation in the consumer's file may be corrected. If credit is denied based on information from a source other than the consumer reporting agency, the Fair Credit Reporting Act gives the consumer the right to learn the nature and substance of information in files of the prospective creditor—but not to see the actual file itself.

[¶1903]   ACCESS TO INFORMATION AND CREDIT FILE

Whether or not an adverse action has been taken, a consumer does have the right of access to learn the nature and substance of information in the file of a consumer reporting agency. With the exception of medical information and sources of investigative information that can only be obtained through discovery procedures of a court, all information in the file is available to the consumer. The Federal Trade Commission states that "nature and substance of all information" means only that an individual need not be permitted to physically handle his file or receive a copy of the file, though the Act does not prohibit this.

[¶1904]   SOURCES AND RECIPIENTS OF INFORMATION

Other than investigative sources, the consumer has the right to be told the sources of information for data in the file of a consumer reporting agency.

[¶1905]   REINVESTIGATION OF DISPUTED ENTRIES

Consumer reporting agencies are required to reinvestigate disputed items of information and correct those found to be inaccurate. Unverified or inaccurate information must be deleted from the report of a consumer. If the dispute is not resolved, the existence of the dispute must be noted in the consumer's file and a brief concise statement of the consumer's version of the dispute must also be included if the consumer desires.

[¶1906]   CREDIT REPORT OF CONSUMER
REPORTING AGENCY

General requirements under the Fair Credit Reporting Act are that agencies provide only those reports requested that bear a reasonable and legitimate business purpose, and that they maintain "reasonable procedures" to assure that report recipients are authorized to receive them. Moreover, the reporting agencies must make sure that the reports do not contain obsolete information.

[¶1907]   **OBSOLETE DATA—ELIMINATION**

If adverse information of public record (such as law suits, tax liens, arrests, indictments, convictions, bankruptcies, or judgments) is reported, the agency must follow one of two procedures: It must indicate to the consumer that the information is being reported to a potential employer, or it must maintain strict procedures to verify the current status of information of public record. The general rule under the law is that information may not be reported if older than 7 years—though bankruptcy going back 14 years may be reported; suits and judgments are governed by the 7-year rule or the statute of limitations, whichever is the longer period.

[¶1908]   **OBTAINING INFORMATION UNDER
                        FALSE PRETENSES**

An individual who obtains information from a consumer reporting agency under false pretenses is liable for criminal penalties, and a consumer reporting agency may be liable for providing information to someone unauthorized to receive it.

[¶1909] **ENFORCEMENT OF CONSUMER REPORTING ACT**

Consumers are permitted to bring civil suit for willful noncompliance with the Act; there is no ceiling on the amount of punitive damages they may receive. The consumer is also permitted to sue for negligent noncompliance in the amount of the actual damages sustained. A two-year statute of limitations applies in civil suits under the Fair Credit Reporting Act; however, if the consumer reporting agency has willfully misrepresented information that must be disclosed under the law (and the information is material to the establishment of the liability of the consumer reporting agency), the statute of limitations does not begin to run until the discovery of the misrepresentation. Suits may be brought in any United States District Court without regard to the amount in controversy (instead of the usual $10,000 minimum) or in any other court of competent jurisdiction.

In addition to consumer enforcement, the following federal agencies have jurisdiction over Fair Credit Reporting violations, and may also issue regulations:
- [ ] Department of Agriculture;
- [ ] Civil Aeronautics Board;
- [ ] Comptroller of the Currency;
- [ ] Federal Deposit Insurance Corporation;
- [ ] Federal Home Loan Bank Board;
- [ ] Federal Reserve Board;
- [ ] Federal Trade Commission;
- [ ] Interstate Commerce Commission;
- [ ] National Credit Union Administration.

[¶1910] **DEFAMATION**

Suppliers of information, users of information, and consumer reporting agencies are not subject to civil action for defamation or invasion of privacy based on information disclosed to a consumer pursuant to the Act unless the information is false or furnished with malice or willful intent to injure the consumer, or there is negligent noncompliance with the Act. If the consumer learns that the information is in the files independently of disclosure by the agency, the defamation action may be brought.

[¶1911] **FORMAL FTC INTERPRETATIONS UNDER FAIR CREDIT REPORTING**

Following are some FTC interpretations of specific areas under the Fair Credit Reporting Act from the Code of Federal Regulations.

[¶1912] **CREDIT GUIDES**

Guides published by credit bureaus and leased on an annual basis to credit grantors that rate how a consumer pays various bills are viewed by the Federal Trade Commission as ''a series of consumer reports, since they contain information which is used for the purpose of serving as a factor in establishing the consumer's eligibility for credit'' (16 CFR §600.1). The FTC believes that publication or distribution of these credit guides violates the Fair Credit Reporting Act. Its interpretation clearly proscribes credit guides in their present form—though it does not preclude a consumer reporting agency's furnishing information that is coded so that the consumer's identity is not disclosed, since the information is not a consumer report until decoded. The FTC suggests that using unique identification devices such as Social Security numbers, driver's license numbers, or bank account numbers would provide adequate coding.

[¶1913] **PROTECTIVE BULLETINS**

Lists of consumers who have issued worthless checks or who for other reasons appear not to be creditworthy are frequently distributed by trade associations and other organizations. Distributions of certain types of lists and bulletins discussing the creditworthiness of particular individuals are restricted under the Fair Credit Reporting Act.

The FTC states that restrictions against distribution of protective bulletins do not apply to those limited to a series of descriptions (usually accompanied by photographs) of individuals who are being sought by law enforcement authorities. The FTC notes that these descriptions are usually accompanied by statements such as: ''Information as to further activities, location or arrest of any of the following persons should be communicated to police authorities named in the warnings.'' While the FTC holds that bulletins are not consumer reports, it does state that information of this type can only be distributed ''to credit grantors and others who have specific legitimate business need for information'' about individuals in connection with an application for credit, insurance, employment, or similar business transactions (16 CFR §600.2).

[¶1914]   LOAN EXCHANGES

Local consumer finance companies may own and operate loan exchanges; members may be required to furnish to the exchange the full identity and loan amount of each borrower. This is covered under the Fair Credit Reporting Act (16 CFR §600.3).

[¶1915]   REPORTS RELATING TO MOTOR VEHICLES

Reports of various state Departments of Motor Vehicles that generally reveal a consumer's entire driving record (including arrests for speeding, drunk driving, and involuntary manslaughter) are commonly used by insurance companies and others desiring information that bears on the personal characteristics of the consumer. Under Fair Credit Reporting, the users (i.e., insurance companies) are required to identify the Motor Vehicle Department as the source of the report if it is used as a factor in denying, cancelling, or increasing the cost of insurance. In turn, the Motor Vehicle Department is required to disclose the ''nature and substance'' of the consumer's motor vehicle record when requested to do so by the consumer. Moreover, reinvestigation is required if the consumer so requests. (16 CFR §600.4).

[¶1916]   GOVERNMENTAL NEWS OF
                   CONSUMER REPORTS

Governmental agencies are entitled to receive consumer reports on credit; for insurance to be used primarily for personal, family, or household purposes; or for employment purposes—or if the government is required by law to consider a consumer's financial responsibility or status before granting a license or other particular benefit. However, if the governmental agency is not able to demonstrate the need for the consumer reports, the consumer reporting agency is not permitted to release the reports to the government (Hoke v. Retail Credit, CA-4, 521 F. 2d 1079, 1975, cert. den. 423 US 1087, 1976).

[¶1917]   STATE AND LOCAL LAW

Except to the extent that they are inconsistent with or less stringent than federal law, state laws on credit reporting are valid. Such laws exist in the following states:

Arizona, California, Connecticut, Florida, Kansas, Kentucky, Maine, Maryland, Massachusetts, Montana, New Hampshire, New Mexico, New York, Oklahoma, Pennsylvania, and Texas.

[¶1918]   **FOR FURTHER REFERENCE . . .**

"Consumer Credit: Proceedings of the ABA National Institute, June 16-17, 1977, New York City," 33 Business Lawyer 226 (February 1978).

Geltzer, R.L., "Current Practice under the Fair Credit Reporting Act," 65 Illinois Bar Journal 702-13 (July 1977).

Goldstein, A., *Commercial Transactions Desk Book,* Institute for Business Planning, Inc., Englewood Cliffs, N.J. (1977).

FORECLOSURE OF REAL ESTATE AND OTHER COLLATERAL FOR DEFAULTED LOANS

[¶2001]   The foreclosure of real estate and chattel mortgages and similar security interests in personal property is largely statutory and subject to local variances. Hence, it will always be necessary to check specific statutory provisions. Nevertheless, the Uniform Commercial Code marks out a common pattern for the foreclosure of security interests in personal property, and a common pattern is also discernible in the case of real estate mortgages, although there is no "uniform" law as such in this area.

[¶2002] **FORECLOSING AND REDEEMING A REAL ESTATE MORTGAGE**

The attorney in general practice will on occasion be faced with the problem of representing either the mortgagor or the mortgagee in a foreclosure proceeding. Financial institutions in many cases are reluctant to foreclose because legal expenses, loss of interest, and commissions often exceed 20% of the value of the property. This frequently will exceed the property owner's equity and thus result in loss to the lending institution. So the attorney representing a client faced with foreclosure should always first attempt to obtain a period of forbearance by the lender or an extension agreement that will reduce monthly payments without scaling down the total debt. To make an extension stick, it must normally be supported by consideration. If no satisfactory agreement can be reached, however, the following points should be borne in mind:

[¶2003] **NOTICE REQUIREMENTS**

Many mortgage instruments prevent the lender from commencing foreclosure proceedings until notice of the default has been given to the property owner and he has had a chance to cure the default within a specified period. Usually this will be 30 days, although in certain circumstances it may be more.

[¶2004] **THE FORECLOSURE PROCESS**

A mortgage is often in form an absolute conveyance of property that will become void upon the mortgagor's compliance with stated conditions (payment of the debt and compliance with other conditions such as payment of taxes, etc.). Some authorities say a breach of any condition by the mortgagor immediately vests absolute title in the mortgagee. Others minimize or deny that a mortgage operates as a conveyance and regard it as a security or lien for the performance of an obligation. In fact, all jurisdictions require the mortgagee *either* to initiate a

180

judicial proceeding *or* to make a public sale of the property. The purpose of these requirements is to give the mortgagor an opportunity to redeem his interest or to insure that if the value of the property exceeds the mortgage debt, the excess will be returned to the mortgagor. There are four variations of the foreclosure process followed in the various American jurisdictions.

[¶2005]   **STRICT FORECLOSURE**

This method requires the mortgagee to maintain an action for foreclosure. Once a decree of foreclosure is issued by the court, the mortgagor has a relatively short period of time (up to six months) during which he may regain or redeem the property by payment of the mortgage debt plus litigation expenses incurred by the mortgagee. If the mortgagor fails to pay within the redemption period, the court will then confirm title in the mortgagee, without any requirement of a public sale. This type of foreclosure is used extensively in Connecticut and Vermont, although it is permissible in other states that allow judicial foreclosures.

[¶2006]   **JUDICIAL FORECLOSURE FOLLOWED
BY SALE**

This is the most commonly used method of foreclosure. It varies from strict foreclosure in that after the redemption period has expired, a public sale of the property is required. In theory, this will result in the mortgagor receiving the difference between the value of the property and the mortgage debt. However, since these sales often take place during depressed markets or because the property has undesirable features, the mortgagee is often the only bidder. In some states, a redemption period also follows the sale. This further reduces the probability that the property's true value will be realized. To insure an adequate price, the court, which has the power not to confirm a sale, may set an *upset price*, i.e., the lowest acceptable bid. Once the sale is made, the title so acquired relates back to the original recording of title and wipes out all claims of the mortgagor and all those obtaining interests under him.

[¶2007]   **NONJUDICIAL FORECLOSURE FOLLOWED
BY SALE**

Although barred in some states, a frequently used method of foreclosing is by the exercise of a power of sale that is given to the mortgagee in the mortgage instrument (usually a deed of trust). The power of sale clause authorizing this method will spell out what constitutes defaults that permit the power to sell as well as the manner in which the sale will be advertised, where it is to be held, and when the deed is to be given. This eliminates any need for a judicial proceeding, which, in addition to being time-consuming, is expensive. The sale must be a public one, preceded by proper public notice and advertisement. There may or may not be a period of redemption following the sale.

[¶2008] JUDICIAL FORECLOSURE BY ENTRY AND POSSESSION

In several of the New England states, the mortgagee obtains a decree of foreclosure after a judicial proceeding, and after the redemption period he may enter and take possession of the property. A period of redemption also follows the repossession. This method may be used without a judicial proceeding provided repossession can be made without force. In effect, this type of proceeding is similar to strict foreclosure.

[¶2009] REDEMPTION

Even after he defaults in the payment of his mortgage obligation, the mortgagor is given a chance to pay his debt and cure his default. This is known as equitable redemption, and this right continues until the property is sold under a foreclosure judgment or decree. Some states provide a statutory right of redemption whereby the mortgagor may redeem the property after the sale (the statutory redemption period will vary from state to state but it's usually one year). This gives the mortgagor a last chance to redeem his property, and if he fails to redeem the property it is deeded to the purchaser who receives such title as the mortgagor had at the time the mortgage was made.

[¶2010] DEEDS IN LIEU OF FORECLOSURE

If foreclosure seems imminent and the mortgagor has no hopes of redeeming the property or realizing an excess on foreclosure, the parties should consider a voluntary conveyance to the mortgagee to avoid the expense and delay of a judicial proceeding. The consideration for the transfer of the property is the cancellation of the mortgage debt.

[¶2011] PERSONAL JUDGMENT FOR DEFICIENCY

If the proceeds from the sale of the property following the foreclosure are insufficient to satisfy the mortgage debt, the mortgagee in most states may obtain a personal judgment against the mortgagor for the deficiency. As a practical matter, this is not often done since the mortgagor presumably is without assets. However, if the mortgagor is a business concern that remains in operation, a deficiency judgment may well be sought. As a result of the experience of the 1930s, when foreclosed properties were often bid in far below their value, many states now give the mortgagor a defense of "fair market value" in a proceeding for a deficiency judgment. The effect of this is to limit the judgment to the difference between the unpaid mortgage debt and the fair market value of the property. The bid price at the foreclosure sale is irrelevant. Since these laws have never been tested in a period of severe recession, it is impossible to say how well they would protect mortgagors under such circumstances.

[¶2012]   ADDITIONS TO MORTGAGE INDEBTEDNESS

The mortgagee is entitled to add to the unpaid debt the expenses of foreclosure as well as taxes and other obligations of the property that are paid by the mortgagee. Generally, the mortgage instrument will provide for interest to be paid even after default and this will usually be allowed by the court. Attorneys' fees will be allowed if provided for in the instrument; otherwise they may not. However, any specified amount must be reasonable. Similarly, insurance premiums on the property may be added to the unpaid debt in some jurisdictions provided the mortgage instrument so provides.

INSURANCE AGAINST LOSS AND LIABILITY

[¶2101] Two factors that are critical in business operations and in many transactions are risk of loss and potential liabilities. Often, a lawyer will be called upon to determine a client's potential loss exposure (what events could cause loss?) and loss potential (what is the maximum amount that might be lost in any single event?). Insurance coverage is the inevitable hedge against possible liabilities.

[¶2102]   **LOSS EXPOSURE**

This requires the identification of all possible risks that are involved in the particular business or activity in question. One way to approach the problem of loss to the insured is to study any available financial statements. The balance sheet will indicate all the assets subject to loss or damage. The profit and loss statement will reveal sources of income that may be shut off or interrupted. Another approach, for uncovering possible liability is to analyze the property and operations of the client to determine what can happen to whom.

[¶2103]   **LOSS POTENTIAL**

This involves an estimate of the maximum loss that may be incurred. The fact that a loss is unlikely is not usually the relevant consideration, since the purpose of insurance is to guard against the unlikely. In addition, the more likely the loss, the less is the economic justification for insurance, since the premium must be large enough to compensate for the loss and permit payment of the insurer's expenses and profit. Small losses, even though unlikely (and hence subject only to a small premium for insurance), may call for self-insurance by the client, since his own resources may be sufficient for this purpose. In brief, it is the *maximum* and *unlikely* loss that must be guarded against.

[¶2104]   **TYPES OF RISKS AND INSURANCE**

Generally speaking, risks fall into two classes:
(1) Liability risks (the insured may be liable to others because of his own actions or those of his employees and agents).
(2) Property loss, including credit and income loss (the insured may suffer personal loss or injury due to his own actions or the actions of others).
The tables at ¶2118 list the most common types of risks for business transactions generally, for particular types of business transactions, and for the owners or lessees of real estate. The usual insurance policy to cover each risk is also indicated in the tables.

184

[¶2105] **LIABILITY INSURANCE**

Those engaged in commercial transactions are exposed to the hazard of lawsuits not only for their own negligence, but also the negligence of their employees, agents, and other representatives. Particularly exposed are sole proprietors and partners who do not have the limited liability provided by the corporate umbrella.

The liability policy generally provides coverage only for sums which the insured becomes *legally obligated to pay resulting from accident*. The basic policy provides no coverage against liabilities for which the insured is not obligated under negligence law, or liabilities assumed by the insured voluntarily. Nor does it provide coverage for occurrences that are not considered accidents, i.e., illnesses caused by repeated exposure to unhealthy or unsanitary conditions over long periods of time. Broader coverage on policies can often be obtained for an additional premium, such as deleting the words "caused by accident" and substituting "occurrence." Some policies, such as Comprehensive General Liability, offer broader coverage in the basic policy.

Most liability policies are divided into two separate sections—Coverage A for bodily injury liability, and Coverage B for property damage liability. Different limits of liability may be provided for each coverage, or the policy may be written under Coverage A only.

[¶2106] **BASIC LIABILITY COVERAGE**

In the paragraphs below, four basic types of liability coverage are explained.

☐ *Owners', Landlords', and Tenants' Liability Policy:* The basic policy insures against claims resulting from the ownership (or lease) and operation of the covered premises. Office buildings, retail stores, wholesale stores, hotels, theatres, etc., are insured under this form of policy. The policy is usually a scheduled policy, that is, it names the particular properties and risks insured against. Another type of policy, the Comprehensive General Liability Policy offers similar coverage on a nonscheduled basis. A manufacturer or contractor can obtain parallel coverage under a Manufacturers' and Contractors' Liability Policy (M & C).

☐ *Product Liability Policy:* This covers liability arising out of the handling or use of goods or products that are manufactured, sold, handled, or distributed by the insured. The liability depends upon the existence of a defect or unsafe condition in the goods. Product liability also covers a service business or a contractor who installs equipment against claims arising from a defect in the installation or the equipment.

☐ *Contract Liability Policy:* This policy covers liability arising out of a contract or agreement. Manufacturers, distributors, retailers, and servicemen sometimes assume liability under easement agreements, railroad sidetrack agreements, purchase orders, or sales and service contracts. The contractor may enter into an agreement with his principal in which he undertakes to hold the principal harmless

185

and indemnify him for any accidents arising out of the work being done. A lessee frequently agrees to protect his lessor from any consequences arising out of the leased property.

☐ *Owners' and Contractors' Protective Liability Policy:* This covers an owner or contractor against any liability arising out of work done by another, such as an independent contractor or a subcontractor. Both tort and contractual (including warranty) claims are covered.

[¶2107]   **SUPPLEMENTARY BENEFITS UNDER LIABILITY INSURANCE**

In addition to satisfying money claims, liability insurance provides a number of valuable services and additional benefits.

(1) Defense of Suits: The insurance company will defend, in the insured's name, all suits brought against him even if false and groundless (but the suit must be one that if successful would constitute a claim under the policy). The policy pays all costs including investigating the claim, procuring witnesses, and legal defense.

(2) Court Costs and Interest on Judgment: These are paid by the insurer.

(3) Premiums for Bonds: The policy also pays for bonds required in the appeal of any suit and bonds to release attachments.

(4) Reimbursement of Insured's Expenses: Reasonable expenses incurred by the insured at the company's request, other than his loss of earnings, are reimbursed. Examples of such expenses are travel, obtaining witnesses, getting affidavits, etc.

(5) Immediate Medical and Surgical First Aid: If furnished by the insured at the time of an accident, this will be paid for by the policy.

(6) Inspection Service: It is standard practice for insurance companies to inspect risks to minimize hazards.

The above benefits are payable, regardless of their amounts, *over and above* the limits of the policy.

(7) Medical Payment Coverage: This can be added to a liability policy for an additional premium. It covers all reasonable medical, surgical, funeral, etc., expenses, incurred within one year of an accident, to each person who sustains bodily injury, sickness, or disease caused by an accident regardless of whether the insured is legally liable or not. Medical payments do not usually cover the insured, any partner, tenant, or any person regularly residing on premises, or any employee of the insured or tenant.

Medical payment coverage is generally written with two limits. The first limit is the limit per person; the second is the limit payable to all persons injured in a single accident.

[¶2108] **PROPERTY INSURANCE**

Property insurance covers direct loss to tangible property, and usually also covers loss of use of the property actually damaged. Consequential loss, such as loss of use or lessening in value of property that is not itself physically damaged, can sometimes be added for an additional premium.

There is a certain amount of overlapping among various property coverages, and it is often possible to provide coverage in several different ways. There has been a trend to combine separate coverages into one package, loosely termed "multiple-peril coverages," or to provide all-risk coverage under a "floater" policy.

In the following paragraphs, the more important types of property coverage are explained.

[¶2109] **FIRE INSURANCE**

This covers the perils of direct loss by fire and lightning. It also covers certain types of damage by smoke—for example, smoke damage caused by hostile fire whether involving the insured property or uninsured property, such as a neighboring building. Other types of smoke damage, caused, for instance, by a defective heating apparatus on the premises, are not covered by the basic fire policy.

☐ **Extended Coverage:** Coverage for other perils can be added by endorsement to the fire policy. The *extended coverage* endorsement insures against windstorm, hail, explosion, riot, civil commotion, aircraft, smoke, explosion, and vehicles. The *additional extended coverage* endorsement insures against collapse, explosion of steam or hot water systems, fallen trees, glass breakage, vandalism and malicious mischief, vehicles owned or operated by insured or tenant, water damage, and ice, snow, and freezing.

Some of these types of coverage may be written separately, such as the vandalism and malicious mischief endorsement. The extended coverage must be written for the same amount as the fire policy itself, and the face amount of the policy is not increased—the coverage is extended to include the added perils.

☐ **Allied Lines:** This generally is placed as an endorsement on fire insurance or may be undertaken as a separate insurance contract to cover destruction from natural disasters such as earthquakes or hail damage to growing crops, or such events as fire sprinkler leakage.

[¶2110] **PHYSICAL DAMAGE TO MOTOR VEHICLES**

Physical damage to autos, trucks, tractors, etc., can be insured under collision, comprehensive, fire and theft, and other policies. Type of coverage and rates will vary with the construction and use of the vehicle, the principal city in which the vehicle is garaged, and radius of miles in which the vehicle is used. Larger risks can get reductions through fleet rates and experience rating.

Similar physical damage coverage is available for company-owned airplanes, yachts, etc.

[¶2111]   **BURGLARY AND THEFT**

The open *stock burglary* policy insures against loss by burglary of merchandise, furniture, fixtures, and equipment (not money, securities, records, and accounts) and damage to the premises.

The *mercantile safe burglary* policy covers loss of money, securities, and other property and other damage resulting from burglary of a safe.

The *mercantile robbery* policy covers various robbery hazards both inside and outside.

The *paymaster robbery* policy is designed for businesses where the principal danger would be robbery of payroll funds.

The *storekeeper's burglary and robbery* policy is a package policy for smaller mercantile risks.

The *office burglary and robbery* policy is a package policy for professional offices and service businesses.

The *money and securities broad form* policy is comprehensive coverage for most mercantile risks, providing coverage against virtually all risk of loss of money and securities.

[¶2112]   **FIDELITY BONDS**

This type of bond covers an employer against the loss of any kind of property—money, securities, raw materials, merchandise, equipment, real property—resulting from dishonest actions of employees. Some bonds insure only named individuals, others cover all occupants of named positions, and others cover all employees of a firm. If the insured is a partnership, the fidelity bond will not cover actions of partners, since they are not employees. In a corporation, all officers are covered since they are employees. Directors of a corporation are excluded unless they are also officers or employees.

[¶2113]   **MULTIPLE PERIL COVERAGE**

Multiple peril, or package, policies combine in one policy many different types of coverage. The advantage to the insured is broader coverage, elimination of overlapping coverage and claims, and lower cost. Some policies provide all-risk coverage while others insure specified perils.

Manufacturers' output policy insures merchandise and other personal property of manufacturers while the property is away from the premises of the manufacturer. It is intended for large stocks of goods in dispersed locations.

Industrial property policy covers all the personal property held by a manufacturing concern, including property of others, on its own premises, usually in diversified locations. It may also insure buildings.

Commercial property policy insures all kinds of personal property of retailers and wholesalers, including limited off-premises coverage. It is not available to businesses that can buy the ''block'' policy, such as jewelers or furriers.

Office contents policy covers all forms of personal property located in an office. It may be purchased by someone who occupies an office and also owns the building, as well as by tenants. An *office package policy* is designed for the owner of an office building.

Jeweler's block policy insures a jeweler for loss or damage to goods in his possession—his own property and property of others. Other lines of business have similar types of coverage, for example, the furrier's block policy.

[¶2114]   **CREDIT INSURANCE**

Credit insurance indemnifies a wholesaler, manufacturer, or jobber for unusual losses incurred by him through the failure of his customers to pay what is owed. This coverage is generally not available to retailers, since credit rating and information are usually lacking on their customers. Most prudent firms have a reserve for bad debts, usually the amount ascertained by experience to be the average annual loss. This may be satisfactory in a normal year, but unexpected losses, such as the bankruptcy of one large customer, might wipe out profits. This is where credit insurance comes in.

Coverage is provided under *specific* and *general policies*. Specific policies are used by businesses that have occasional, high-class accounts to whom considerable credit is extended for short terms. Coverage of these accounts is usually afforded after investigation of each specific risk by the insurance company. General policies cover the accounts of the insured described in the policy. These usually are all customers who have the credit rating required by the policy, and there is no need for investigation and approval of individual transactions.

One valuable benefit of credit insurance is the collection service offered to policyholders. Specific policies usually provide for compulsory collection of accounts due—the insured must file a claim for collection within two months after an account is due. Other types of policies provide severe penalties if claims for collection are not filed within 90 days. A few policies make filing for collection optional with the insured.

[¶2115]   **SURETY BONDS**

Many commercial transactions are guaranteed by suretyship—an individual, corporation, or partnership lends its name or credit to obligations of another. A typical example is a stockholder in a close corporation being co-signer of a loan to the corporation. In many types of business transactions, corporate suretyship provided by bonding companies or insurance companies is required.

☐ **Contract Bonds:** Contract bonds are required in many cases to guarantee the satisfactory completion or performance of a contract. These bonds are written for the *term of the contract* and cannot be canceled during this term. The initial premium usually covers a period of two years, and the renewal premium charged after that is based on an estimate of time needed to complete work still remaining.

☐ **Bid Bonds:** These bonds are generally required to accompany bids of contractors for public work jobs. They are sometimes required by private builders, too. The bond guarantees that the bidder, if awarded the contract, will enter into the contract and furnish the prescribed performance bond (and payment bond if required). If the bidding contractor defaults, the surety becomes liable for the difference between the bid of its principal and the next lowest bid. The bid bond may be written with a *fixed penalty* or an *open penalty*.

☐ **Performance Bonds:** The various types of performance bonds include the following:

Construction contract bond—guarantees faithful performance by the contractor for construction of a building. It may run to the lender of construction monies and may be called a *completion bond.*

Labor and material payment bond—guarantees that the contractor will pay all bills for labor and materials. This is written either as a separate policy or as part of the construction contract bond.

Maintenance bond—guarantees that work done by the contractor will be free of defective workmanship or materials. This is written either as a separate policy or as part of the construction contract bond.

Supply contract bond—guarantees a contract to supply goods or materials.

[¶2116]   CONSEQUENTIAL LOSS COVERAGE

A fire or other peril may cause a financial loss other than that resulting from the direct destruction of the property. Such losses are called "consequential losses" and include those resulting from the loss of use of the property destroyed (such as interruption of business), and property loss from indirect connection with the hazard rather than from direct destruction. The main types of insurance against consequential losses are:

(1) Business interruption insurance.

(2) Contingent business interruption insurance, which covers losses resulting from the interruption not of the insured's business, but of a supplier or some other activity on which the continued conduct of the business is dependent.

(3) Extra expense insurance, which covers the cost of emergency operation.

(4) Rent insurance, which covers the loss of rents during the time when a building has become unusable because of fire or other insured peril.

(5) Delayed profits insurance, which covers loss of profits that might result from a delay in the completion of a project.

(6) Profits and commission insurance, which covers profits on finished

goods when sales will be lost as a result of the destruction of goods. This is appropriate for seasonal goods, specially built machinery, etc.

(7) Leasehold insurance, which covers a tenant's financial loss if his lease is canceled.

[¶2117]   **HOW MUCH INSURANCE?**

Probably the most difficult question that any individual considering insurance must answer from the outset is how much coverage to carry. Co-insurance and contribution clauses added to policies make the choice an important one. Owners of insurance policies that have a contribution clause and who carry insurance for less than 80% of the value of the items insured (this is the usual level) may suffer a penalty in the event of only partial loss. A co-insurance clause means that the owner is entitled to only a pro rata share of the loss based upon the ratio of the actual amount of coverage to the required amount of coverage.

For example, a building having an insurable value of $100,000 is insured against fire under a policy bearing the 80% contribution clause. The owner should carry at least $80,000 of insurance. If he does carry $80,000, he meets the requirement of the contribution clause and any fire loss he sustains will be paid in full up to the limit of the policy.

On the other hand, if the same owner carries only $40,000 of insurance, he is carrying only half of the required amount. Under these circumstances, if he sustains a loss, he will be paid only half of the loss, up to the limit of the policy. In this example, if he sustains a loss of $1,000, he will collect only $500 and will have to contribute or absorb the other $500.

Since the contribution clause can inflict severe penalties for underinsurance, many prudent owners carry more insurance than is required by the contribution clause. For example, their policies may contain the 80% clause, yet they may carry 85% of the insurance to insurable value. This is relatively inexpensive and leaves a margin for error or for a future increase in value.

What Amount of Liability Insurance? The limits or amounts of liability insurance to be carried are determined by the judgment of the owner. The size of a building or business is not necessarily the determining factor. Serious accidents can occur in small buildings as well as large. The extent of injuries bear no relationship whatever to the size or value of the building or to the financial responsibility of the owner. In all cases, the owner has to decide on limits that he feels will adequately cover him.

Limits are generally expressed as "$100/300" or "$100,000/300,000," each meaning the same, namely, up to $100,000 available for the payment of a claim for injuries to one person hurt in one accident and if more than one person is injured, up to $300,000 total liability, limited to $100,000 for any one person. A series of accidents is fully covered with the limits applying separately to each, and no reduction in the amount of coverage occurs by reason of payment of claims.

    TABLES OF RISKS AND COVERAGE

The following tables summarize the various risks arising in business, the potential losses, and the available insurance coverage to protect against those risks. Unless a specific value is listed in the tables, the maximum loss would be determined by the facts in each case.

General Business Risks

Risk	Liability to Others	Loss to Insured	Maximum Loss	Policy
Boiler or machinery explosion	Yes	Property damage (P.D.) and personal injury (P.I.)		Boiler and machinery
		Consequential damage through loss of use		Consequential damage endorsement
Tort (false arrest, libel, etc.)	Yes			Personal injury liability coverage
Tort by advertisement (defamation, etc.)	Yes			Advertiser's liability
Employee accident or disease	Yes (Workmen's compensation—or common-law liability)			Workmen's compensation and employer's liability
Liability assumed by contract	Yes			Comprehensive general liability
Accident on premises	Yes			Comprehensive general liability
Accident on elevators	Yes			Comprehensive general liability
Accident due to operation of independent contractors	Yes			Comprehensive general liability
Defective or unsafe product	Yes			Product liability

General Business Risks *(continued)*

Risk	Liability to Others	Loss to Insured	Maximum Loss	Policy
Patent infringement	Yes			Patent infringement
Airplane accidents	No	P.I.		Aviation accident
Broken glass	No	P.D.	Replacement cost	Comprehensive glass
Burglary	No	Loss of inventory or equipment	Replacement cost	Mercantile open stock
Robbery (on and off premises)	No	Loss of property		Mercantile robbery
Employee fraud or dishonesty	No	Loss of property		Blanket position bond or individual fidelity bond
Damage to suppliers or purchasers	No	Loss of earnings		Contingent business interruption
Damage to business	No	Loss of earnings		Business interruption
Fire or lightning	No	P.D.		Fire
Windstorm and hail	No	P.D.		Windstorm and hail
Earthquake	No	P.D.		Earthquake
Water leakage or overflow	No	P.D.		Water damage
Loss of cargo at sea	No	Property loss	Value of cargo	Ocean marine cargo
Loss of books and records	No	Noncollection of accounts receivable	Value of accounts receivable	Accounts receivable
Loss or damage to personal property	No	P.D. or property loss		Inland transit floater
Nonpayment by customers	No	Loss of income	Loss experience	Commercial credit

General Business Risks *(continued)*

Risk	Liability to Others	Loss to Insured	Maximum Loss	Policy
Automobile accident (insured's automobile)	Yes	P.D. and P.I.		Automobile comprehensive
Aircraft accident (insured's aircraft)	Yes			Aircraft liability
Decrease in corporate net worth due to its liability	No	Value of stock		Stockholder's protective insurance
Loss of securities or other instruments	No	Property loss		Lost securities bond

Some Specific Business Risks

Risk	Liability to Others	Loss to Insured	Maximum Loss	Policy
Banking— criminal acts and disappearance	No	Property loss	Depends on deposits	Bankers' blanket bond
Garages— accidents to person and property	Yes			Garage liability
Druggists— error in prescription	Yes			Druggists' liability
Innkeeper— loss or damage to guests' property	Yes			Innkeepers' liability
Manufacturers and contractors —accidents from operations	Yes			Manufacturers' and contractors' liability
Stockbrokers— criminal acts and disappearance	Yes			Brokers' blanket bond

Some Specific Business Risks *(continued)*

Risk	Liability to Others	Loss to Insured	Maximum Loss	Policy
Vending machines— damage or loss	No	P.D. and loss of income		Vending machine floater
Warehousemen— loss or damage to customer's property	Yes			Warehouse-men's lia-bility
Malpractice by professionals	Yes			Professional liability

Risks Involving Real Estate

Risk	Liability to Others	Loss to Insured	Maximum Loss	Policy
Damage dur-ing construction	No	P.D.	Cost of completed building	Builders' risk
Losses due to delay in construction	No	Loss of rent or use		Rent insurance
Damage to completed building	No	P.D.	Replacement cost	Fire and extended coverage
		Loss of rent or use		Rent insurance
Injuries to persons or property on premises	Yes			Landlords' protective liability
Injuries to lessees or their property	Yes			General liability
Loss of lease-hold due to damage to building	No	Leasehold interest	Market value of lease minus rent	Leasehold interest

195

[¶2119]   **PROTECTING CREDITORS' INTERESTS**
                        THROUGH INSURANCE

There are a number of methods of providing insurance protection to creditors:

(1) Separate Policy for a Creditor: The creditor takes out, or is furnished with, a separate policy covering his interest. The owner may have a separate policy covering his ownership interest.

(2) Assignment of Owner's Policy: The owner assigns his policy to the creditor. Whether the consent of the insurance company is required and what the rights of the respective parties are may depend upon the type of insurance and the jurisdiction.

(3) Loss Payable Clause: This is an endorsement on the owner's policy of a "loss payable clause" that stipulates "loss, if any, payable to _____, as his interest may appear." The effect of this varies in different jurisdictions—some put the creditor in the same position as the owner, while others give him broader rights. The creditor normally is given possession of the policy and the owner gets a certificate or memorandum of insurance.

(4) As Interest May Appear Clause: This may be found in a policy such as one covering a bailee, which covers "for the benefit of whom it may concern" or "for others as their interests may appear."

The procurement of insurance and the payment of the premiums is covered by the agreement between the debtor and creditor. The agreement should spell out the kind and amount of coverage, who is to get the coverage and keep the policy, who is to pay the premium, what happens if one party or the other fails in his duties with respect to insurance or payment, and any other matters that are important in the transaction.

[¶2120]   **FOR FURTHER REFERENCE . . .**

"Executive Summary for the Final Report of the Federal Interagency Task Force on Product Liability," 1977 Insurance Law Journal 686-99 (November 1977).

Fish, W.R., "Overview of the 1973 Comprehensive General Liability Insurance Policy and Products Liability Coverage," 34 Journal of the Missouri Bar 257-63 (June 1978).

Hershbarger, R.A., and Miller, R.K., "Impact of Economic Conditions on the Incidence of Arson," 45 Journal of Risk and Insurance 275-90 (June 1978).

Tierney, G., "National Flood Insurance Program: Explanation and Legal Implications," 8 Urban Lawyer 279-306 (1976).

INVENTIONS, TRADEMARKS, IDEAS, AND SECRETS

[¶**2201**] The need for protection of ideas, secrets, or technological property may arise in any area of commercial practice—corporate, entertainment, or advertising—and may be associated with any number of particular transactions—employment, sale of business, manufacturing, research and distribution contracts, licensing arrangements, and international investments. Sometimes the protection is easy to achieve, especially if the idea, trade secret, or invention is patentable. Forms of expression—literary, musical, artistic, and even photographic—can be protected by copyright (see ¶1101 et seq.). Trademarks are often registered. The most difficult problem arises in connection with the protection of the "pure idea,"—the concept that cannot be reduced to practice and that can have any number of modes of expression. In this section the various methods of protection afforded by federal, state, and common law are examined.

[¶2202]   **PATENTS**

Patent law is a sophisticated field and requires the expertise of an experienced patent agent or attorney. In order to work effectively with the patent attorney, it is necessary to understand the broad procedures associated with securing a patent, as well as the related problems regarding licensing, cross-licensing, and assignments. The material provided in the following paragraphs is designed to give a broad explanation of the general law.

[¶2203]   **AVAILABILITY OF PATENT PROTECTION**

A patent grants the inventor a "statutory monopoly," the right of exclusive use for 17 years (see ¶2214). A patent can be obtained for any "new and useful process, machine, manufacture, or composition of matter, or any new and useful improvement thereof." New methods, new combinations, and new designs may be patented. However, no one can obtain a patent for a new or better idea for doing business. The advice of a patent lawyer is essential on the prospective patentability of a new development.

No patent may be granted for an invention if it was "patented or described in a printed publication in this or a foreign country, before the invention thereof by the applicant for patent" (35 USC §102(a)).

[¶2204]   **THE DECISION TO APPLY FOR A PATENT**

A patented invention is subject to public disclosure. A new development may conceivably receive more protection if it is kept a trade secret—the probable

197

patent protection may be so meager that it is not worth the expense, or it is considered better to rely on trade name, nondisclosure of techniques, accumulation of know-how, etc. Further, the business prospect may be worthwhile but not sufficient to justify the cost of patenting. As a general rule, if the invention is to be commercialized, patenting is advisable.

[¶2205]   WHO SHOULD APPLY FOR THE PATENT?

Only the inventor should apply; he is the one who takes the inventive step. If there is more than one inventor, they should apply as co-owners of the patent, and each one, upon the granting of the patent, obtains an "undivided interest in the entire patent." However, the usual rules of co-ownership do not apply in the patent situation. Therefore, when one co-owner seeks to license or assign his rights under the patent, it is best to consult a patent attorney.

Patents issued in the name of anyone other than the true inventor or inventors are invalid if the facts are proven, except where it can be shown that a wrong party was included through error and without any deceptive intent. The employer has no right to designate an applicant who is not the true inventor. An inventor may not have multiple patents for the same invention (no "double patenting"). An inventor who later improves on his invention may apply for additional patents to cover the improvements.

Once an inventor has a patent for his invention he cannot obtain a patent for the means of producing his already-patented invention.

[¶2206]   PATENTING EMPLOYEE INVENTIONS

Frequently, an employee will develop an invention during the course of his employment. If there is no agreement with an employee, the employer may be entitled to a "shop-right" in the employee's invention, thus claiming ownership under an implied agreement to assign. If the employee has been hired to invent or in a capacity that gave rise to the expectation that he would assign his invention to the employer, the courts will usually recognize an obligation to assign the invention to the employer. It does not matter in what capacity an employee works, if he patents an invention he conceived and developed on the job, the employer has a "shop-right" to use the invention in his own business, but only if the invention was developed during working hours, on the company's time, and with its materials.

To avoid the uncertainty of proof of an implied obligation to assign and the nonexclusivity and other limitations of the shop-right, it is important to get a written agreement with an employee who is likely to contribute to an invention, obligating him to assign it to the employer. Moreover, full protection for the employer requires more than creating an obligation to assign patent rights. It may be just as important to place the employee under obligation not to disclose secret or confidential information or knowledge obtained during his employment for a period of time after he leaves that employment. It may be desirable to restrict him from engaging in any activity in a specified field of industry or research and development for a period of time after termination. An employee can be obligated to assign improvements to an invention made after employment, provided they relate to an invention made during employment. See *IBP Forms of Business Agreements and Resolutions*.

[¶2207]   **WHEN TO APPLY FOR A PATENT**

Several circumstances may trigger the need for a patent application:

(1) If the invention is described in a publication, used publicly, or placed on sale by the inventor, it is necessary for the inventor to apply for the patent within one year from the time of publication, use, or sale.

(2) If an application for a foreign patent has been filed abroad, application for a U.S. patent should be made within one year of the foreign filing.

(3) Where two or more parties are competing for a patent on the same invention, the first to file prevails in the great majority of cases. The other party has the very heavy burden of proof that he is the first inventor.

[¶2208]   **GUARDING AGAINST COMPETING**
                              PATENT CLAIMS

It is not uncommon for two or more applicants to lay claim to the same invention, or to challenge an existing patent on the grounds that the invention was known prior to the date of the applicant's discovery. In order to guard against this problem, one practice often used by inventors is to: (1) Write a description of the invention; (2) Execute it before a notary public; (3) Mail it to the inventor's address by registered mail, and (4) Lock it up to provide proof of date of invention, should that ever become necessary. However, this approach is of doubtful value since at best it shows only conception. An early date of conception is of little value unless it can be shown that it was followed by diligence in adapting and perfecting the invention.

The acts that help in establishing the priority of invention are the following:

☐ Reduction to practice;

☐ Diligence in adapting and perfecting the invention;

☐ Disclosure to others;

☐ Making the first written description and the first drawing, and then only, early conception.

The date of reduction to practice is the most decisive factor bearing on the date of invention. Filing an application is constructive reduction to practice, and early filing avoids expensive proof that otherwise would be required. But if an adverse claim is based on invention before filing, it requires corroboration to establish date of invention, and disclosure of all essential details of the invention to others is important in proving not only conception but also diligence and reduction to practice. Diaries and laboratory notes are recommended as a means of recording the progress of an invention, its conception, due diligence in reducing it to practice, etc.

[¶2209]   THE PATENT APPLICATION—PRELIMINARY SEARCH

In a preliminary patent search, sometimes called a patentability search, the object is to see whether there are any patents outstanding that would indicate that the proposed development is not novel and that it would therefore be a waste of money to file an application. It is also designed to turn up matters that are related and that may be of help to the patent attorney in preparing the patent application. There are other types of patent searches:

(1) Validity Search: designed to find earlier patents that would throw doubt upon the validity of a patent that has been interfering or threatens to interfere with the client's business. This is an extensive search that is usually made as a basis for a patent lawsuit contesting the validity of a patent.

(2) Infringement Search: to determine if a proposed product or improvement will infringe on the claims of an unexpired patent.

(3) Assignment Search: to determine who is the present recorded owner of a particular patent.

(4) Index Search: to determine what patents have been issued to a particular inventor or patent holder.

[¶2210]   ABANDONMENT OF AN INVENTION

An inventor may not obtain a patent if "he has abandoned the invention" (35 USC §102(c)).

Abandonment may either be shown by express conduct or implied by the inventor's conduct.

An inventor who conceals his invention by not patenting it cannot claim a prior right as against a subsequent inventor who in "good faith and without knowledge" invents and applies for a patent on the same invention. The issue as to what constitutes unreasonable time so as to indicate concealment, abandonment, or delay is a question of fact to be determined on a case-by-case basis.

[¶2211]   ASSIGNMENT VS. LICENSING OF PATENTS

A patent is *assigned* when all the rights ("to make, sell and use the invention") are granted exclusively to another party. A *license* is granted when something less than the full rights are conveyed. When the full rights under a patent are confined to a particular geographic area (territorial grant), the patent has been assigned.

In deciding whether to make an assignment or merely grant a license, the following considerations should be kept in mind:

(1) Assignments should be recorded; licenses need not be.

(2) All owners of title must join in suit against an infringer but a licensee need not be joined (except in limited cases).

(3) Receipts from an assignment, although a percentage royalty, may be treated as capital gains, whereas receipts from a license are fully taxable as ordinary income. License payments may be deducted; the price paid for an assignment may be depreciated. Even when the price is on a percentage basis, under the *Associated Patentee* case (4 TC 979, 1945) these percentage payments may be deducted as depreciation of the patent.

For forms of assignment and licensing agreements, see *IBP Forms of Business Agreements and Resolutions*.

Drafting the instrument for the assignment or license of the patent is an intricate art, best left to an experienced patent attorney.

[¶2212]   MISUSE OF PATENT PRIVILEGES

The owner of a patent has the exclusive right to make, use, and sell the patented item. However, when the owner seeks to control unpatented items, sales, or otherwise unlawfully restricts his licensee by contract, he is misusing his patent. Such misuse can render a patent unenforceable, and misuse is frequently a defense to an owner's infringement suit.

Although a patentee may fix the price at which a licensed manufacturer may sell a patented article, he may *not* fix the resale price of a patented product once it is sold. The owner of a license may not combine with another patentee under a cross-license to fix prices under their respective patents. A patent owner may not compel a prospective licensee to take a license on patents he does not want in order to obtain a license under the patent that he does want.

[¶2213]   SUING FOR PATENT INFRINGEMENT

Preliminary injunctions are seldom obtained in patent suits because, among other reasons, if the suit fails, the party enjoined would have a case for heavy damages against the party claiming infringement. To get a preliminary injunction, it must be shown that irreparable harm would be done if the infringement continued, that the validity of the patent is clear, and that the infringement is beyond any reasonable doubt. Injunctions are almost always granted when infringement has been adjudicated, but there have been cases when an injunction was denied the victor in an infringement suit on the basis that the injury to the infringer would be greater than the benefit of the owner of the patent. Of course, the owner of the patent is entitled to an accounting of profits. In patent infringement suits, agreements with others executed in good faith before the beginning of the suit have been held to set a standard for reasonable royalty.

[¶2214]   **DURATION OF PATENT**

Patents have a 17-year life (35 USC §154). Design patents can be granted for 3½, 7, or 14 years, depending upon the inventor's request (35 USC §173). When the patent expires the item or process becomes public property.

[¶2215]   **TRADEMARKS AND TRADE NAMES**

A trademark is usually associated with a specific product, while a trade name is representative of the business itself, its established reputation, and goodwill.

Trademarks (unlike patents and copyrights) are not exclusively within the federal domain. Federal power to regulate trademarks is based on the commerce clause and in the past a narrower view of "interstate commerce" has been adopted than in other branches of the law. For example, federal registration of trademarks has been denied hotels, restaurants, service stations, etc., even though their customers may come from across state lines and are solicited by interstate advertising. However, a recent registration of a service mark used in only one state may possibly reflect a new trend.

[¶2216]   **COMMON-LAW PROTECTION**
                            OF TRADEMARKS

Under common law, the true owner of a trademark used for goods and services may prevent the unauthorized use of his mark (or of a similar mark on the same or similar goods or services) by another to the confusion of the public and his own detriment. Thus, while the owner of a trademark operating in a common law, "no-registration" area is not completely without legal protection for his mark, it must be recognized that the absence of registration makes the establishment of ownership difficult and encourages unscrupulous competitors to try to get away with appropriating the mark. At the same time, the absence of registration makes it difficult for even well-intentioned competitors to discover the prior mark. In any case, conflicts that might have been avoided by registration are apt to flourish.

[¶2217]   **STATE TRADEMARK LAWS**

The great diversity of the various state trademark statutes rules out detailed consideration of them in this work. However, some indication of their scope and limitations will be apparent from the following comparison with the federal law:

(1) Federal provisions are broader in terms of marks registrable than any state act;

(2) Federal law gives better relief than state law, except as to penalties;

(3) Federal registration provides notice to the entire country;

(4) Federal, but not state, registration, gives the right of registration in a large number of foreign countries;

(5) Federal, but not state, registration gives the right to prevent importation of goods bearing infringing marks; and

(6) Federal registration by itself gives the right to sue in federal courts—state registration requires other elements of federal jurisdiction.

[¶2218] FEDERAL TRADEMARK ACT

The Trademark Act of 1946 (Lanham Act, 15 USC Chapter 22) defines a trademark as "any work, name, symbol, or device, or any combination thereof adopted and used by a manufacturer or merchant to identify his goods and distinguish them from those manufactured or sold by others." The Act also provides for the registration of service, certification, and collective marks.

"Service marks" are those used in the sale or advertising of services to distinguish those of one person from another.

"Certification marks" are those used on or in connection with the products or services of persons other than the owner of the mark to certify the origin or other characteristics of the goods or services. The Good Housekeeping "Seal of Approval" would be an example.

"Collective marks" are those used by a group to indicate membership in an organization.

[¶2219] FEDERAL REGISTRATION OF A TRADEMARK

The Lanham Act sets up two registers: (1) principal, and (2) supplemental. The principal register is for so-called "true" or "technical" marks—coined, arbitrary, fanciful, or suggestive marks, if otherwise qualified. A mark may not be registered on the principal register if (1) when applied to the goods of the applicant it is merely descriptive of them;(2) when applied to the goods of the applicant, it is primarily geographically descriptive or deceptively misdescriptive of them, except as indications of regional origin; or (3) it is primarily a surname, except when shown that such marks have become distinctive as applied to the applicant's goods in commerce. (Proof of continuous use for five years makes a prima facie case.)

Marks not qualified for registration on the principal register may be registered on the supplemental register, provided they (1) are capable of distinguishing the applicant's goods and (2) have been used in commerce for at least a year.

[¶2219.1]   Registration in the Principal Register

Registration provides the following protection:

(1) Constructive notice of claim of ownership;

(2) Prima facie evidence of the validity of the registration, the registrant's ownership of the mark, and the registrant's exclusive right to the use of the mark, subject to any conditions and limitations that may be stated in the registration; and

(3) The right to prevent importation of goods bearing an infringing mark.

[¶2219.2]   Registration in the Supplemental Register

Although registration here gives none of the above protection, it does give the registrant:

(1) The right to sue in the federal courts and statutory remedies;

(2) Possible right of registration in a foreign country whose laws require prior registration in the home country; and

(3) Protection against registration by another of the same or a confusingly similar mark in either register.

The Lanham Act requires any person opposing the registration of a trademark by the principal register to file a verified opposition (15 USC §1063). Disposition of the dispute is handled by a Trademark Trial and Appeal Board (15 USC §1067).

**[¶2220]   HOW TO PRESERVE EXCLUSIVE RIGHTS
IN A TRADEMARK**

Rights in a trademark are first acquired through *use*—i.e., by selling the product with the mark affixed either to the product or to its container. If the mark is to be registered, it must be used in interstate commerce, so the product should be shipped to a customer in another state.

Keep a record of the first use of the trademark. The following will help substantiate the use:

☐ A copy of the invoice. The invoice must show the trademark followed by the generic description of the product.

☐ The bill of lading signed by the carrier.

☐ A letter from the buyer stating he received the product and mentioning the trademark.

This first use of the mark doesn't mean that exclusive rights have been acquired. Someone else may have been using it before—no search can guarantee that you are the first user. Therefore, don't start extensive selling and advertising campaigns until initial test sales leave you reasonably sure there's no infringement and as a result, the mark won't have to be abandoned.

After the first use, continued and proper use of the mark is necessary to establish your exclusive rights. What constitutes "proper" use? The following checklist may provide some help:

☐ Use the trademark as an adjective only to modify the *generic name* of the product, and at least once on every page. Don't separate the trademark and the generic name with another word or any punctuation.

☐ Use the mark in a distinctive way, that is, different type face, italics, capitals, within quotation marks, or in some way to make it more conspicuous than the other words preceding and following it.

☐ Use of the mark must be consistent. Once adopted, the mark must be continuously used.

[¶2221] **TRADEMARK SEARCHES**

In order to minimize the possibility of opposition or conflict, a trademark search may be made before applying for registration. Most searches are run in the Patent Office. Word marks are classified on an alphabetical basis. Nonword marks are classified according to a system of symbol classification. There are two main locations or collections. The first comprises subsisting and expired registrations and the second published and pending registrations. The search system is not without serious deficiencies: (1) It doesn't cover prior unregistered marks; (2) The classification system is alphabetical and not phonetic and doesn't take into account synonyms and foreign equivalents; (3) It doesn't cover applications abandoned before publication; and (4) It doesn't show current use or status of the mark.

Because of the weaknesses or deficiencies in the classification system, an effective search requires skill and imagination on the part of the searcher, takes time, and is apt to be fairly expensive. Do not be taken in by those advertising "searches" at "low, low" prices.

The Patent Office maintains records of assignments of registered marks and pending applications by which ownership of marks or of applications may be searched.

If an owner is to effectively protect his mark against dilution and be in a position to oppose published applications for marks, he must maintain a continuous search of the Official Gazette, which is published by the Patent Office and lists registered trademarks.

Searches such as those discussed above are best done by trademark specialists. There is one type of search that the general practitioner can make and that is via the trademark section of *Shepard's United States Citations, Patents & Trademarks,* which contains a reference to every trademark litigated or mentioned in any state or federal case.

[¶2222] **APPLICATION FOR TRADEMARK REGISTRATION**

An application for registration must be filed in the name of the owner of the mark. It should give details as to a variety of matters including the date of the applicant's first use of the mark as a trademark on or in connection with goods specified in the application, the date of the first use of the mark in interstate

205

commerce, specifying the nature of the commerce, the manner in which the mark is used in connection with the goods, and the class of merchandise according to the official classification if known to the applicant. It must also contain various averments as to ownership and right to use the mark. Further, it must be signed and verified and must include a drawing of the mark, five specimens or facsimiles, and the required filing fee. There are special rules for foreign applicants. The Patent Office will supply printed forms of applications for (1) individuals, (2) firms, or (3) corporations or associations.

The drawing must be a substantially exact representation of the mark as actually used. If the mark is incapable of representation by drawing then the application must describe it.) Regulations cover such matters as the type of paper and ink, the size of the sheets and margins, the heading, the character of the lines, the use of linings for showing color, and how the drawings are to be shipped. The Patent Office will make drawings when possible, at the applicant's request and expense.

The five specimens should be duplicates of actually used labels, tags, containers, or displays or portions thereof if flat and not larger than the size of the drawing. If specimens can't be furnished (due to the mode of applying the mark or using it or the nature of the mark), then a photograph or other acceptable reproduction not larger than the size of the drawing may be used. If a disc recording is to be registered special regulations apply.

If on examination of the application and the accompanying papers it appears that the applicant is entitled to have his mark registered in the Principal Register, it will be published in the Official Gazette and will be subject to opposition by any person who believes he'll be damaged, a period of 30 days after publication being provided for filing opposition. If the Patent Office finds a conflict between two co-pending applications, it determines which applicant is entitled to register. If there's no notice of opposition and no interference, a certificate of registration will be issued in due course.

Forms of assignment of a trademark registration and of an application for registration are set out in *IBP Forms of Business Agreements and Resolutions*.

[¶2223]   **ASSIGNABILITY OF TRADEMARKS**

Trademarks are not readily assignable, since their existence is dependent upon their connection with the business or product for which they are used. When a business using a trademark is sold or assigned, the continued use of the trademark must be for an item substantially similar to the one for which it was used by the assignor. In addition, if there is a sale of a business having a trademark registered under the Lanham Act, the assignment of such a trademark is regulated by the Act (15 USC § 1060).

Trademarks or trade names representing "personal care and skill of a certain individual" are usually not assignable, for the obvious reason that the assignee cannot claim to possess his assignor's personal care and skill.

[¶2224]   ABANDONMENT OF THE TRADEMARK

Failure to use a trademark or trade name may result in its abandonment under common law. Under the Lanham Act, nonuse of a registered mark for two consecutive years is prima facie abandonment (15 USC §1127).

[¶2225]   SOME PRACTICAL CONSIDERATIONS IN THE
            SELECTION OF A TRADEMARK

Trademark registration may be a matter of law, but trademark selection is a business judgment, best left to specialists in advertising and marketing. Although registration is not obligatory, anticipate future need when making the original trademark selection and avoid adopting a mark that will be refused registration. The following checklist indicates some trademarks that can pose a problem:

☐ Name, portrait, or signature of a living person without his consent.

☐ Name, portrait, or signature of a deceased U.S. President during the life of his widow, without her consent.

☐ Flag or coat of arms of the United States, any state, municipality, or foreign nation.

☐ A mark that is merely descriptive of the goods, or deceptively misdescriptive.

☐ A mark that when applied to the goods is primarily geographically descriptive or deceptively misdescriptive of the goods.

☐ A mark that is primarily merely a surname.

☐ A mark that resembles a trademark previously registered or used by another and not abandoned, if its use is likely to cause confusion or mistake or to deceive purchasers.

☐ A mark that disparages or falsely suggests a connection with persons living or dead, institutions, beliefs, or national symbols, or brings them into disrepute, or contempt.

☐ A mark that is immoral, deceptive, or scandalous.

A mark can be registered even though it is merely descriptive, geographically descriptive, or is primarily a surname, if it has become distinctive of the registrant's goods in commerce. Five years of exclusive and continuous use prior to filing application may be accepted by the Commissioner of Patents and Trademarks as prima facie evidence that the mark has become distinctive. Marks that are unregistrable because of the other prohibitions noted above can never become registrable as distinctive.

[¶2226]   CORPORATE NAME STATUTES

Trade name value may inhere in a corporate name or the name of a product. A corporate name may be protected by the creation of inactive corporations in the states in the market area. The name of a product may be protected by incorporating it in a trademark that is used and registered.

Corporate name statutes grant only limited protection. They merely insure that the name will be protected against subsequent adoption as a corporate name by another entity within the state and against granting of permission to a foreign corporation to do business in that state under that corporate name. The usual corporate name section grants no protection against use of the same name as a trade name or mark; rather, the corporation must seek its relief under the nonstatutory precedents available to it in the state law of unfair competition. Further, such statutes do not purport to protect a corporate trade name against names used by unincorporated businesses. Apart from these procedures, judicial protection of business names has developed as a part of the overall law of unfair competition.

Forms of agreements permitting the use of names and likenesses are found in *IBP Forms of Business Agreements and Resolutions.*

[¶2227]   FICTITIOUS NAME STATUTES

All but a handful of the states have enacted a fictitious name statute in one form or another. Generally, they provide that one doing business under an assumed or fictitious name must file certain information in affidavit form in each county where business is transacted and, in addition, may require other acts on the part of the user calculated to inform the public of the actual ownership of the business. Some of these statutes apply by their terms to corporate trade names; some that do not, have been construed to apply to corporations when transacting business under names other than their corporate names.

The purpose of these statutes is universally recognized to be the prevention of fraud by providing potential customers and more particularly potential creditors with information about those with whom they are dealing. Whether or not sanctions are enforced to a degree sufficient to compel compliance with a particular statute, it is apparent that no substantive protection is sought to be given to a name registered or certified under its terms.

[¶2228]   PROTECTION OF IDEAS AND SECRETS

Protection of ideas and secrets is an integral part of commercial practice. Major problems arise in connection with ideas or accumulations of information that are not patentable but are trade secrets. The protection of an idea or secret involves not only the safeguarding of its commercial value, but also the protection of both the creator of the idea and the person to whom the idea is submitted.

Here are some initial observations regarding protection of ideas and secrets:

(1) A concept cannot be copyrighted.

(2) Copyright—statutory or common law—protects only methods of expression—the word or symbol used.

(3) Pure ideas are free for all—only when the pure idea is converted into a property right is it protected.

[¶2229]   **CONVERTING THE PURE IDEA INTO A**
PROTECTABLE INTEREST

In order for a pure idea to be a protectable property interest, two initial steps must be taken:

(1) The idea must be original or established as such. Although there are not really any truly original ideas, the idea must be established as being *different*.

(2) The idea must be reduced to concrete form. This means putting it down on paper or in some other concrete form like a model or projection. The more detail in the concrete form, the better. If it is an advertising idea, it should be developed into a campaign. If it is an entertainment idea, it should be developed into a script.

[¶2230]   **UNSOLICITED IDEAS FROM OUTSIDERS**

Merely listening to an idea submitted by an outsider may place the listener and his business under an obligation to compensate the outsider if the idea is subsequently used, even though the listener may have been developing the same idea concurrently and independently. In order to avoid possible litigation, certain precautionary measures should be taken when dealing with the ideas of persons outside the business.

In the case of inventions and technical improvements, the most satisfactory way for both the inventor and the corporation to be protected from litigation and misunderstanding is for the inventor to obtain a patent on his invention. This will clearly establish his rights in the invention and will give him a firm basis on which to negotiate with companies that may wish to use or develop his invention. But the inventor may not be able to or may not wish to patent his invention for a variety of reasons: (1) He may be the owner of the trade secret but not the actual inventor of it; (2) He may not be able to show the novelty, utility, and invention that are necessary to obtain a patent; or (3) He may wish to keep the invention secret.

A corporation that has invited an inventor to discuss an idea or development with the intent of purchasing it receives such a disclosure in confidence. Therefore, the corporation cannot use the idea without buying it, and if it does use it without the inventor's permission, it will be liable for the profits made from the invention.

Following are some points for a company to keep in mind when dealing with outside inventors:

☐ Prepare a form letter responding to volunteers. When an offer to disclose an idea or invention is received by the company, a properly worded letter to the suggester will help prevent liability. The courts have held that where the company makes certain stipulations or lays down certain conditions subject to which it will accept the disclosure, the inventor is bound by these conditions if he then submits his idea.

☐ Require the person submitting the idea to sign a statement indicating that he agrees to stipulated conditions along these lines:

(a) In taking any suggestion or idea under consideration we assume no obligation of any kind.

(b) We will not receive any submitted material in confidence, we will not establish a confidential relationship with anyone in respect to such material, and we make no guarantee of secrecy. You agree that in consideration of our examining your idea, we may freely use and communicate it to others without any liability to you. You agree to release us from responsibility or connection with your suggestion or liability because of use of any part thereof except such liability as may arise under valid patents now or hereafter issued to you.

(c) We will not consider ideas submitted from outside the United States unless a United States patent application has been filed.

(d) If the idea you have submitted is found to be of no interest to us, we will so inform you. However, we assume no obligation to inform you of the reasons for our action.

(e) If the idea appears to be of interest to us, we may enter into negotiations to explore the possibility of acquiring rights. No obligation is assumed by the company unless or until a formal written contract has been entered into and the obligation shall be only such as is expressed in the formal written contract.

(f) It is necessary for us to retain a complete record of the matter submitted and, therefore, it must be submitted in writing. Since material may become lost or mislaid in transit between the submitter and the company or between various departments of the company, no obligation can be assumed by us for the safekeeping of submitted matter.

[¶2231]   **LICENSING "KNOW-HOW"**

The following checklist is designed to highlight the important considerations involved in dealing with licensing "know-how."

☐ *Reduce Know-How to Tangible Form:* When know-how is being transferred or licensed, it should be reduced to tangible form. This frequently has to be accomplished by careful and sometimes exhaustive definition. The elements of know-how must be detailed, including such things as plans, calculations, design sheets, design data, manuals, drawings, processes and materials, performance and purchasing specifications, test data, operating instructions, assistance in selecting factory sites, supplying engineers and technicians for installing machinery, assistance in purchase of machinery, technical service bulletins, special assistance by engineers and other technicians, architectural assistance (factory layouts and provisions and training of key personnel).

☐ *Limitations:* If the transferor or licensor cannot or does not wish to supply know-how in a particular area of his knowledge, that fact should be spelled out.

☐ *Reciprocal Rights:* Are licensor and licensee to have reciprocal rights to all improvements during the period of the agreement, or will there be additional or cross royalty arrangements?

☐ *Where and by Whom Will Know-How Be Used?* To what product is know-how to be applied? Is it available to licensee's subsidiaries, sublicensees, and subcontractors? Who has the obligation to insure that royalties are paid?

☐ *Exclusivity:* Is the license exclusive, or does the licensor have the right to license others? It may be desirable to restrict the right to license to organizations, that by the nature of their business or their location, are not in competition with the original licensee.

☐ **Secrecy:** When the know-how involves information that is considered a trade secret, the agreement should spell out the parties' understanding with respect to procedures for maintenance of trade secret status. A procedure for placing the obligation on employees of the licensee to maintain the trade secret should also be included.

☐ **Return of Information:** Provision for termination in the agreement should call for the return of all copies of plans, drawings, and specifications delivered in connection with the license. The licensee should be under an obligation to stop using the know-how acquired under the agreement. In some cases, this may mean that he has to stop his activities in the field.

☐ **Personnel:** If personnel is provided, the agreement should clearly specify the number, the time limits within which personnel is to be made available, and who will pay the personnel during the term of the agreement, including the obligation of travel, living expenses, etc.

☐ **Minimums:** When a license of know-how is based on a sales royalty, the licensor will generally look for some form of minimum, or in the absence of a minimum license fee, it will seek an obligation on the part of the licensee to achieve a minimum level of promotion.

☐ **Duration:** Generally, technological know-how has a life of about five years; after that time it becomes obsolete. When a royalty arrangement is involved, the licensor should avoid an arrangement that can be construed as payment for a patent after the patent has expired.

☐ **Restrictive Covenants:** Know-how and trade secrets that have been licensed should be safeguarded by restrictive covenants whereby the licensee agrees not to divulge trade secrets to others or use them himself after the license expires. This restrictive covenant can also prohibit disclosure to other than indicated personnel in the licensee's organization. Generally, this type of clause is subject to enforcement through injunctions.

☐ **Know-How of Trade Secret Must Have Value:** A license that transfers know-how of little or no value together with the licensor's covenant not to compete, export, or trade in the licensee's territory is, in effect, an agreement by the licensor to keep out of the licensee's market. The licensor will be paid royalties for abiding by these terms, but such a license would probably violate the antitrust laws. For this reason, some price tag should be put on the know-how transferred, or there should at least be records to prove the value of this intangible asset.

☐ **Foreign Licenses:** If foreign manufacture and distribution are licensed to a foreign concern, it is customary to base royalties on a percentage of net sales or gross sales. They can also be based on units produced, units installed, or sale price per item. The royalty clause can further be used to keep the foreign licensee in line. For example, increased production can be stimulated by a royalty clause reducing royalties after a certain maximum production is reached. The royalty clause should be geared so that if the licensee oversteps his market, underproduces, or undersells, he must pay higher royalties. There should be a minimum royalty due per year to check the occasional foreign licensee who takes the license to prevent foreign competition in his own market.

☐ *Foreign Currency:* Difficult to draft, this clause should take account of hard or soft currency in the country involved.

☐ *Default:* Protection against nonpayment and other defaults can be covered by a clause giving the licensor the right to terminate the license, with an immediate cessation of rights as to trademarks, names, and patents when the violation occurs. When know-how has been licensed, return of all trade secrets, processes, records, etc., should be required. As a protection against default, make sure the license agreement has been drafted to satisfy all local requirements as to notarization, recording, translation, etc., so that it will be enforceable in a local court. If trademarks, patents, or copyrights are involved, local registration laws should be complied with at the outset.

[¶2232]   **PROTECTION OF TRADE SECRETS**

''A trade secret may consist of any formula, pattern, device or compilation of information. . . used in one's business, and which gives him an opportunity to obtain an advantage over competitors who do not know or use it'' (Restatement of Torts §757, Comment b, 1939).

[¶2233]   **WHAT QUALIFIES AS A TRADE SECRET?**

Section 757 of the Restatement of Torts says:

''The subject matter of a trade secret must be secret. Matters of public knowledge or of general knowledge in an industry cannot be appropriated by one as his secret. Matters which are completely disclosed by the goods which one markets cannot be his secret. Substantially, a trade secret is known only in the particular business in which it is used. It is not requisite that only the proprietor of the business know it. He may, without losing his protection, communicate it to employees involved in its use. He may likewise communicate it to others pledged to secrecy. Others may also know of it independently, as, for example, when they have discovered the process or formula by independent invention and are keeping it secret. Nevertheless, a substantial element of secrecy must exist, so that, except by the use of improper means, there would be difficulty in acquiring the information. An exact definition of a trade secret is not possible. Some factors to be considered in determining whether given information is one's trade secret are: (1) the extent to which the information is known outside of his business; (2) the extent to which it is known by employees and others involved in his business; (3) the extent of measures taken by him to guard the secrecy of the information; (4) the value of the information to him and to his competitors; (5) the amount of effort or money expended by him in developing the information; (6) the ease or difficulty with which the information could be properly acquired or duplicated by others.''

[¶2234]   **TRADE SECRETS AND COVENANTS**
                              NOT TO COMPETE

As part of the written contract of employment or in a separate agreement, the employer should have his employees sign an agreement not to compete with the company after they leave its employ. Key employees, such as officers, executives, supervisors, engineers, scientists, and salesmen, may be asked to sign an employment contract that incorporates the restrictions against competing after leaving the job, in an agreed area and for a specified time. Restrictions on other possible forms of competition, such as the use of trade secrets and customer lists, should also be included if applicable. Employees having less important positions may agree to such restrictions as part of their employment applications or in a separate agreement. In any case, the clause or separate agreement is usually referred to as a "covenant not to compete."

Here's a checklist for drafting a covenant that will stand up:

☐   Make sure the terms of the agreement are clear and unambiguous.

☐   The restrictions as to area and time should be reasonable and not greater than what is required for protection.

☐   Do not include in the restrictions an area in which the company has no business or in which the employee has never worked.

☐   If applicable, show on the face of the contract that the employee is entrusted with trade secrets, confidential information, or is in a position of close contact with customers.

☐   On the face of the contract show the relationship between the prohibited activities and their necessity for the protection of customers or trade secrets.

☐   Do not phrase the restriction in such a way as to make it an absolute prohibition against working for a competitor in any capacity, or which would force the employee to change his profession or trade in order to keep comparable employment.

[¶2235]   **PROTECTING CUSTOMER LISTS**

Customer contacts are vital to most businesses. A valued employee will generally work directly with the customers. If the employee is hired by a competitor or sets up his own competing business, it may be easy for him to persuade customers to switch companies.

An employee can solicit the customers of his former employer, unless the list itself is considered to be confidential information. The list is confidential if the names of the customers could have been learned by the employee only through his employment. This would include lists that have been assembled on the basis of past selling experience, lists combining information on customers with product purchased and price, and, generally, lists that have been accumulated as the result of much time and effort.

The term "secret list" would not include a list of firms or individuals that could be compiled from a directory or from some other source that anyone could examine. If the employee knew the customers before he went to work for the original employer, he cannot be accused of learning about them only as a result of his job.

[¶2236]   **FOR FURTHER REFERENCE . . .**

Johnson, W.F., Jr., "Remedies in Trade Secret Litigation," 72 Northwestern University Law Review 1004-31 (January-February 1978).

Lane, F.J., Jr., "Primer for the General Practitioner on Trademarks and Unfair Competition," 34 Journal of the Missouri Bar 86-94 (March 1978).

Stein, S.M., "What Every General Lawyer Should Know About Patents," 52 Florida Bar Journal 542-7 (July-August 1978).

Williams, S.P., "Trade Secrets and Perpetual Royalties: How Long Can You Collect?" 60 Journal of the Patent Office Society 442-67 (July 1978).

LANDLORD AND TENANT

[¶2301]   A lease can be defined as a contract between the owner of the land (the landlord or lessor) and a tenant (lessee) in which the lessee agrees to pay a stipulated sum (rent) for the use and enjoyment of the property for a specified period of time. Besides determining the legal rights and duties of the parties, the lease also serves as a basis for assessing the tax treatment of each of the parties.

Each party to a lease will naturally try to shape the various lease provisions to achieve maximum legal as well as tax advantages from the relationship. The wording of the lease is all-important, since it can determine upon whom the tax burden will fall, when the tax will be imposed, whether or not certain deductions will be allowed, which party will be entitled to these deductions, when the deductions may be claimed, and so on. To summarize these points and to provide a quick reference, the table on the following pages will tell at a glance the tax consequences of payments, deposits, improvements, and alterations for all parties to the lease.

[¶2302]   TAX CONSEQUENCES TO LANDLORD AND
                TENANT OF PAYMENTS, DEPOSITS,
                IMPROVEMENTS, AND ALTERATIONS

Item	Effect on Landlord	Effect on Tenant
Tenant's Security Deposit	No immediate tax effect on either landlord or tenant if the deposit is properly restricted. If forfeited, the security deposit is treated for tax purposes the same as a payment of the obligation for which it is forfeited would have been treated.	
Tenant's Payment to Renew	Rental income to landlord.	Cost of renewal amortizable over life of lease.
Payment by Tenant to Modify	Rental income to landlord.	Cost of modifying lease amortizable over life of lease.
Payment of Broker's Commission by Tenant	None	Amount amortizable by tenant over life of lease. In case of premature cancellation of lease, amount not recovered is deductible in year of cancellation.
Payment of Broker's Commission by Landlord	Amount amortizable by landlord over life of lease. If lease prematurely canceled, amount not recovered is deductible in year of cancellation.	None.

Item	Effect on Landlord	Effect on Tenant
Payment of Bonus by Tenant to Landlord for Lease	Taxable when received by landlord as additional rental income.	Amortizable by tenant over life of lease.
Advanced Payment of Rent by Tenant	Rental income to landlord.	Amortizable by tenant over life of lease.
Payment by Landlord to Cancel	Amortizable over life of lease. If made for purpose of selling premises, amount of payment is added to basis of property for purpose of figuring gain on sale.	Amount is treated as capital gain when received.
Payment by Tenant to Cancel	Additional rental income to landlord.	Deductible as rent by tenant in year paid.
Payment of Taxes, Interest; Insurance, and Operating Costs by Tenant	Additional rental income to landlord.	Deductible as rent by tenant.
Payment of Debt Against Property by Tenant	Additional rental income to landlord.	Deductible as rent by tenant. when paid.
Alteration of Premises by Landlord for Tenant	Landlord can take depreciation deductions for improvements. Cost is amortizable by landlord over life of lease if improvements are suitable only for tenant.	None.
Installation of Trade Fixtures by Tenant	None.	Tenant may take depreciation deductions over useful life of trade fixtures if useful life exceeds a year; otherwise currently deductible.
Permanent Improvements by Tenant Not Intended as Rent	Not income to landlord when improvements are made or when lease terminates.	Tenant may take depreciation deductions over useful life of improvements or over life of lease, whichever is shorter.
Restoration of Premises by Tenant at End of Lease	Landlord can deduct depreciation improvements to leasehold unless lessee is required to replace improvement.	Cost is deductible by tenant when restoration is made.

[¶2303]   NEGOTIATING AND DRAFTING LEASES

At the negotiating stages the lessor and the lessee will each normally try to slant the lease so that the various provisions will yield the maximum economic and tax advantages to themselves. The reconciliation of the two possibly conflicting viewpoints shows the necessity for proper planning and drafting at the earliest stages of any lease arrangement.

These problems are less likely to arise in a short-term lease, involving a residence, an apartment, or the average retail store, than a long-term lease involving substantial business properties. In the former case, standard forms are generally used, and the tax effects are usually accepted by the parties without further negotiation. While this may be the common practice, it should not be inferred that the short-term lease does not present various points of contact with the tax laws.

In long-term leases, the tax advantages that are obtainable by either the lessor or the lessee may not only be substantial—they may, in fact, be the motivating force behind the whole transaction. This is especially true when the lessee is required to erect new buildings on the property or to make substantial improvements or alterations to the property. Since the lessor and the lessee usually have equal bargaining power in the long-term situation, the final lease is ordinarily preceded by extensive negotiations at both the economic and the tax levels. The number of detailed provisions in the lease will ordinarily reflect this bargaining process.

[¶2303.1] Construction of Lease

It is the objective of every person who prepares a lease to use language that will convey the intention of the parties as clearly and exactly as possible. The nature of a lease—the complex nature of the property rights and obligations it covers, the many different situations and contingencies it must anticipate—makes it inevitable under certain conditions that outside construction of its provisions will be required. If the courts are called upon to settle disputes between the parties as to the meaning of a lease, the instrument will generally be construed against the person who drew it, usually the lessor. Before executing a lease, both parties should understand not only the terms of the instrument, but also the legal and tax effect of those terms.

Construction of a lease may also be necessary in tax proceedings before IRS and the courts. The intent of the parties may have been clear to them, but for tax purposes intent is evidenced to some degree by the provisions of the written agreement. The written agreement is therefore a most important document. The following paragraphs highlight the significant points to be kept in mind when negotiating and drafting leases.

[¶2303.2] Worksheet for Negotiating and Drafting a Lease

(A) Nature and Duration
    (1) Number of years lease will run.
    (2) Is lease a net lease? (Give details.)
    (3) Give details of duties undertaken by lessor.
    (4) State when the lessee is entitled to take possession of the premises.

(B) Renewal and Purchase Options

    (1) Will there be an option to renew the lease?

    (2) How many options to renew will there be?

    (3) What does it take to exercise the option to renew? (Give details.)

    (4) What is the term of each option to renew in years?

    (5) State the rent for each option term.

    (6) Will the rent decrease on successive options in response to the fact that the lessor has liquidated the mortgage loan over the original lease term?

    (7) Will the lessee get an option to purchase building and land?

    (8) When is the option to purchase to be exercised? (Give date.)

    (9) State method of exercising option to purchase.

   (10) What price does the option to purchase call for?

(C) Holding Over

    (1) If the lessee holds over, will there be a month-to-month tenancy?

(D) Rent

    (1) What is the gross annual rent?

    (2) When and how is the rent payable? (State details.)

    (3) State the gross annual rental per square foot of usable space.

    (4) If a month-to-month tenancy is created by the lessee's holding over, what will the rental be during such tenancy?

(E) Grace Period

    (1) What is the number of days of grace, if any, during which a default may be cured?

    (2) Grace period for default in payment of rent.

    (3) Grace period for other breach of lease.

    (4) Will the lease carry a confession of judgment clause?

(F) Measure of Damages and Counsel Fees

    (1) Will the lease set forth a measure of damages for particular breaches of lease terms?

    (2) On a breach by the lessee, will the measure of lessor's damages be the deficiency in rental that the lessor realizes by renting to another lessee? How about liquidated damages?

    (3) Is the lessee obligated to pay the lessor's attorney's fees incurred in enforcing the lease? Are there any qualifications or limitations on lessor's right to recover attorney's fees, e.g., must fees be reasonable, arise out of court action, be approved by court? Must lessor prevail in court action to recover attorney's fees? Will the lease provide that the party that wins the court action is entitled to attorney's fees?

(G) Subletting and Assignment

    (1) Will the lessee be entitled to sublet the premises?

    (2) Will the lessee be entitled to assign the lease?

(3) Will the lessor's written consent be required for a subletting of the premises or an assignment of the lease by lessee?

(4) Will the lessor agree not to withhold consent unreasonably?

(5) Will the lessee be given the right to sublet without lessor's consent provided the sublessee is responsible and has a specified credit rating?

(6) Will the lessee be given the right to assign to a subsidiary without lessor's consent?

(7) What is the legal effect of the lease on a merger of lessor or lessee?

(H) Lessee's Status Under Existing Lease

(1) How must longer does the lessee's term under his present lease have to run?

(2) Does the lessee have the right to assign or sublet under the terms of his present lease?

(3) If the present lease requires the lessor's consent to an assignment or subletting by lessee, will consent be forthcoming?

(4) Will the prospective lessor assume lessee's liability under his present lease? (Give details.)

(I) Responsibility for Taxes, Charges, and Expenses

(1) Who is responsible for real estate taxes?

(2) If lessee is to pay all the real estate taxes, what were the taxes on the property for the past five years?

(3) Were these taxes on vacant land or on improved property?

(4) What is the trend in real estate taxes in the area?

(5) If the lessee is to pay any increase in taxes over the base year, what is the base tax payable to lessor?

(6) Will there be a maximum annual increase payable by the lessee?

(7) What is the annual increase payable by the lessee stated as a percent of the base tax?

(8) Who is to pay utility charges?

(9) Who is to pay maintenance and service charges (snow removal, painting, cleaning, refuse disposal, janitorial, etc.)? (Give details.)

(10) If lessee is to pay for these items, will he have the right to contract for them directly rather than purchase them from the lessor?

(11) Will the lessor pay the normal utility service connection expenses?

(12) Is the lessee to make all ordinary and necessary repairs to the building, roadways, etc.?

(13) Is the lessee to perform all the usual maintenance?

(14) Who is to be responsible for extraordinary repairs?

(15) Who is to be responsible for structural repairs and alterations?

(J) Title, Zoning, and Other Restrictions on Use of Land

(1) Does the lessor have simple title to the land?

(2) What is the legal description of the land?

(3) Will the lessee receive copies of all covenants and restrictions of record that regulate the use of the property?

    (4) Will lessee have to cross the land of other property owners or use private roadways to get to public streets or highways? Are there recorded easements entitling lessee to use such land or roadway for ingress and egress? Will lessee be furnished with copies of those easements?

    (5) Are there utility easements to serve the property? Will lessee be furnished with copies of those recorded easements?

    (6) What are the zoning regulations applicable to the building?

    (7) Is the contemplated use permissible?

    (8) Is lessee to be provided with a copy of the local zoning ordinance and a plat of survey?

(K) Building and Construction

    (1) If the building is constructed for the lessee, will lessor obtain and deliver to lessee a certificate of occupancy or certificate of compliance showing that the building conforms to all laws, ordinances, building codes, etc.?

    (2) In the case of an existing building, will lessor agree to warrant that he has conformed to all the laws, etc., and that he will fully reimburse lessee for the cost of necessary repairs or alterations after the lease commences to correct code violations that existed before lessee took possession?

    (3) Has lessee considered retaining the services of a local attorney to check these matters if answers to (a) and (b) are "No"?

    (4) Will a building be constructed on vacant land by lessor for lessee?

    (5) Have plans and specifications been prepared?

    (6) Who is the architect retained by the lessor to prepare the plans and specifications?

    (7) Will the plans and specifications be made part of the lease as an exhibit?

    (8) Is the lessor to pay the architect's fees?

    (9) In the event that final plans and specifications are not ready when the lease is signed, will the final plans and specifications be subject to review and approval by lessee?

    (10) If only the preliminary plans will be attached to the lease, what limitations will there be on lessee's right to withhold approval of final plans and specifications?

    (11) What is the cut-off for delivery to lessee of a complete set of final plans and specifications?

    (12) When is construction to begin?

    (13) When is construction to be completed?

    (14) Will there be liquidated damages payable by lessor if construction is not completed by the date specified and lessee is forced to vacate his space in his former building?

    (15) Will lessee be entitled to terminate the lease because of a delay in completing building beyond agreed period? What is effect of act of God, strikes, etc.?

(16) In the case of an existing building, has lessee inspected the building?

(17) What is the condition of existing building?

(18) Will lessee have the right to inspect the building before execution of the lease and before taking actual possession?

(19) What is the actual size of the building and its usable floor area?

(20) Can the building be enlarged? Additional stories? A wing or addition? Is adequate land available? Does zoning ordinance permit expansion or addition? Set-back and side-yard lines preventing additions?

(21) Location of the building?

(22) Type of construction?

(23) Age of building?

(24) Condition of equipment in building?

(25) Will lessor warrant equipment to be in good operating condition at the beginning of the lease term?

(26) Is lessee to have the benefit of equipment warranties?

(27) Will lessor make alterations and improvements to make building suitable for lessee's use? What improvements will be made? At whose expense? Name and address of architect who will prepare plans and specifications? Will these plans be subject to lessee's prior approval? When will the work start? When will the work be completed?

(28) Will dock and loading facilities be available and accessible to large trucks?

(29) Will rail transportation service to the building be available?

(30) Will truck transportation service to building be available and adequate?

(31) Will there be ample room to maneuver, load, and park trucks?

(32) Will there be ample parking for employees who will drive to work?

(33) Is public transportation available for employees who do not drive to work?

(L) Liability, Insurance Coverage, and Subrogation

(1) Will lessee carry public liability insurance for both lessor and lessee?

(2) What are the policy limits to be carried? For personal injury? For property damage? For workmen's compensation?

(3) Will lessor agree to accept lessee's liability insurance company and the policy form it issues?

(4) Will lessee carry fire and extended insurance for both lessor and lessee?

(5) What is the amount of insurance to be carried?

(6) Will lessor agree to accept lessee's fire insurance company and the policy form it issues in the state where the building is located?

(7) Will lessor and lessee waive claims against the other party for damage to property?

(8) Will waiver be only to the extent property is covered by fire insurance policies?

(9) Will each party agree to notify its fire insurance carrier of this provision?

(10) Will each party agree to have the fire insurance policies endorsed to prevent invalidation of coverage because of such mutual waivers?

(11) Will lessor be excused from all liability for injuries to persons or property arising out of the use of the property?

(12) Will lessor be excused from injuries resulting from lessor's own negligence in making structural repairs, alterations, etc.?

(13) Will lessee excuse lessor from injuries caused by latent defects existing in the building when turned over to the lessee?

(M) Destruction or Condemnation of Premises

(1) Will lessor have responsibility to rebuild if building is a total loss by fire or other casualty?

(2) Will parties agree that fire insurance proceeds will be made available for such rebuilding?

(3) Will lessor have a reasonable time after the fire to decide whether to rebuild?

(4) Will lessor have the right to elect not to rebuild only if a year or two is left to the lease term when the fire occurred?

(5) Will lessor agree to notify lessee of his decision on whether or not he elects to rebuild within that time?

(6) Will lessor agree to abatement of rent from date of the fire until the premises are rebuilt and are again ready for occupancy?

(7) Define what constitutes "total destruction."

(8) If the lessor is required or elects to rebuild, will lease continue in effect during rebuilding? Will rent abate during rebuilding? When is rebuilding work to begin? Will lessor agree to undertake the work promptly after taking possession and to prosecute the work with due diligence? When will the rebuilding work be completed? Will lessee have the right to approve lessor's architect who will supervise the rebuilding? If insurance proceeds are insufficient to cover the entire cost of rebuilding, will the lessor put up the difference?

(9) If lessor elects not to rebuild, will the lease terminate as of the date of the fire or other casualty? Will the rent abate as of that date? Will lessee have right then to elect to rebuild, using the fire insurance proceeds to do so? Will the lessee give the lessor notice of his election within a specified time?

(10) Who will be responsible for rebuilding if building is partially destroyed or damaged by fire or other casualty?

(11) Will all parties agree that fire insurance proceeds will be made available for rebuilding?

(12) Will lessor agree to abatement of portion of the rent from the date of fire until the premises are rebuilt and again ready for occupancy?

(13) What is the formula for measuring what portion of the rent is to abate?

(14) Define what constitutes partial destruction.

(15) When is the rebuilding work to begin?

(16) Will the party responsible for rebuilding agree to undertake the work promptly after being able to take possession of the damaged portion and to prosecute the work with due diligence?

(17) When is the rebuilding work to be finished?

(18) If lessor selects the architect who is to supervise the rebuilding, will the lessee have a right to approve the choice?

(19) What is the standard of quality of the rebuilding?

(20) Should insurance proceeds be insufficient to cover the entire cost of the rebuilding, will the lessor or lessee put up the difference? What is the maximum limit on the amount to be put up?

(21) If insurance proceeds go to the lessor's mortgagee to pay off part of the outstanding mortgage debt, will the lessor agree to replace the proceeds thus diverted?

(22) Will lessee surrender his share of a condemnation award if all or part of the land and building are taken for public purposes?

(23) If only part of the property is taken, will lessee be entitled to terminate the lease if remaining portion is insufficient for lessee's needs?

(24) Will rent abate from the date that lessee has to surrender possession, rather than date title to the property passes to the public body?

(25) To what extent will rent be abated on a partial taking?

(26) How will this be determined? Set up a formula?

[¶2304]   **RENTAL PAYMENTS**

Rent is ordinarily treated as income by the lessor and is deductible by the lessee. The most important question about it normally is the amount to be paid. There are a number of ways to fix rent, as described in the following paragraphs.

[¶2304.1]   **Flat Rental**

This calls for a uniform rate throughout the term and is most common in short-term office leases. Its drawback for the landlord is that it fails to protect him against increases in taxes and operating expenses.

[¶2304.2]   **Step-Up Lease**

This arrangement provides for a gradually increasing amount of rent, stepped up at specified intervals. It may be used to compensate the landlord for increased expenses, but it is most commonly used as an inducement for a tenant who is starting in business and initially can only afford a small rental.

[¶2304.3]   Expense-Participating Lease or Escalator Lease

Long-term office leases usually are of this type. Under it, the tenant pays a basic fixed rent plus a specified portion of the real estate taxes, insurance, and repairs other than structural ones. The expense-participating lease requires the tenant to pay an immediate share of these costs, while under an escalator lease the tenant pays only his proportionate share of any increases in costs during the lease term.

[¶2304.4]   Net Lease

Under this type of lease, the tenant agrees to pay, in addition to the fixed rental, *all* other costs, expenses, and obligations connected with the property, including such expenses and charges as real estate taxes and assessments, insurance, maintenance and repairs, heat, water, etc. In short, the idea behind a net lease is that the rent paid to the landlord is a net rent that comes to him free and clear of any offsets or deductions.

[¶2304.5]   Cost-of-Living Lease

Here, the tenant's rental obligation is increased or decreased at specified intervals depending on the fluctuation of the dollar according to price indices or other agreed-upon measures of the economy.

[¶2304.6]   Re-evaluation Lease

This calls for an appraisal of the property and a fixing of the rent as a percentage of the appraised value at specified intervals. The new rental value may be fixed on the basis of the value of the land and building, or on the rental value of the premises occupied by the tenant. The latter method may result in a higher figure because the appraisers may take into consideration the business success of the tenant.

[¶2304.7]   Specifying When Payments Are to Be Made

In addition to the amount of rent, the lease should set forth the method of payment. Many leases state the rental obligation in terms of a yearly figure and in theory the landlord may require it to be paid one year in advance, even though monthly payments are customary. Sometimes, when the tenant's income is seasonal, monthly payments may be of unequal amounts.

The date for the initial rental payment should be set forth specifically. The tenant will want the lease to postpone the payment of rent if occupancy is unavailable at the agreed-on date. If the landlord has granted rent concessions, the lease should indicate the months that are to be rent free. Part of the concession may come at the beginning of the lease and the remainder at the end.

[¶2305]　　　　**PERCENTAGE RENTALS**

In leases of commercial space for terms of three years or more, percentage rental arrangements are commonplace. Figuring the rent on a minimum rental basis plus a percentage of sales above an established minimum permits the owner to cope with inflation and also share in the success of the enterprise. The tenant benefits in that he pays only the minimum rent unless his sales rise above a specified figure, and then he pays the agreed percentage of the excess. The minimum and percentage rental must be acceptable to both sides. A method must be established for measuring the lessee's sales on which the percentage rental will be based so that it is as simple and foolproof as possible and lessens the chance for future disputes.

There are at least four possible types of percentage rentals:

(1) Fixed minimum rent with a percentage of gross sales added to the minimum.

(2) Fixed minimum rent with additional rent based on percentage of gross sales being payable only after the applicable percentage applying to the gross has earned the minimum.

(3) Percentage lease with no minimum.

(4) Minimum rent plus the percentage with a maximum rent that the percentage may produce.

[¶2305.1]　**Some Important Bases to Touch in Providing for a Percentage Rental**

☐ *Definition of Gross Sales:* What is included in "gross sales" should be clearly covered. Generally, gross sales should be defined to include all sales made from or at the demised premises, whether for cash or credit, deductions being allowed for refunds for returned merchandise.

☐ *Methods of Payment:* The lessee may be required to report gross sales, in writing, to the lessor at specified times and to pay sums due within an agreed time thereafter.

Where dealing with a seasonal business, the lessee may insist on a provision whereby percentage rentals are paid monthly, but if the total percentage rentals paid over a 12-month period are greater than the specified percentage of the total volume of business for that period, the lessee is entitled to a refund or a credit for the excess. Another method is to provide for percentage rentals to be paid after the expiration of each lease year or to fix payment periods that include anticipated periods of seasonal variations in business volume, thereby eliminating the need for making adjustments. Of course, if the minimum rental is set at a figure that allows for slack months, the lessor should be entitled to look to the high-volume months to make up the difference.

☐ *Records of Gross Sales:* The lessee should be required to maintain, and the lessor should be entitled to audit, books and records in which all transactions on which percentages may become due are entered. If any deficiency is found, the lessor should be entitled to immediate payment. Provisions for payment of expenses of audits should also be included.

☐ *Diligent Operation of the Business:* The lessor may want to covenant that the lessee will devote his full time to the business. If the tenant has other outlets, he may be required to give assurance that he won't try to divert business to them. A provision under which the lessee agrees that he will not compete with the business opened on the leased premises in any way within a specified radius may be desired. Also, provisions should require the lessee (1) to be open for business during those business hours that are customary for its particular type of business, (2) to maintain a staff of personnel adequate to assure the maximum in gross sales, and (3) to have sufficient stock for sale as compared with similar enterprises.

☐ *Tax Participation:* The lessee may be required to pay, in addition to the stipulated rental, increases in taxes or assessments over and above the taxes and assessments for a specified year. A provision whereby the excess taxes paid by the lessee are credited against the total percentage rentals due may be included.

☐ *Lessor's Option to Terminate:* When the minimum rental fixed in a long-term lease is lower than what is normal for a similar business in a similar location or when the volume of business done is expected to increase substantially, a provision may be included that if gross sales do not reach a specified figure within a specified time, the lessor is entitled to terminate the lease, or the lessee may elect to increase the minimum rent to a sum that the lessor would receive if a stated amount of gross sales had been achieved, thereby keeping the lease in full force and effect.

☐ *No Partnership Created:* Because he's sharing profits, the landlord may be construed to be a partner of the tenant unless a contrary intention is clearly spelled out in the lease.

[¶2306]   SECURITY DEPOSITS AND ADVANCE RENTS

In order to protect himself against a tenant's abandonment, nonpayment of rent, or default, the landlord will use one of the following security devices:

Security Deposits: The tenant is required to deposit security or rents with the landlord. Frequently, a lease will provide that if the tenant abandons the property or is evicted for a default in rent, the landlord may relet the premises and collect damages out of the security deposit. For tax purposes, a security deposit is not the landlord's property. It remains the tenant's property, with the landlord holding it in trust. Of course, the security deposit will become income if and when appropriated by the landlord because of default, abandonment, etc.

If security deposit treatment is desired, the lease should not contain provisions that apply the security deposit to the last month's rent. If the lease contains an option to purchase and the lessee makes a security deposit, the following rules apply: If the deposit is to be applied to the purchase price if the option is exercised, and is otherwise returnable, the payment is considered a security deposit. But if the lessor is not obligated to refund the money if the lessee fails to exercise the purchase option, the money is considered advance rent and is taxable on payment.

Advance Rent: The tenant is required to pay a bonus for obtaining a lease and the landlord is entitled to this money whether or not the tenant fulfills his obligations under the lease. For the landlord, advance rent, whether or not it is to be eventually returned to the tenant, is treated as income when received. The tenant who pays a landlord rent in advance, commissions, or other expenses for acquiring a lease must capitalize such sums and write them off over the term of the lease (Reg. §1.162-1(a)).

[¶2307]   **TERMS OF THE LEASE**

The tenant's willingness to sign a long-term lease will depend in part on his privilege to increase or decrease the amount of space he must pay for. Therefore, the space and time provisions of the lease should be treated as interrelated obligations.

Usually, basic terms of a lease are 5, 10, 15, 21, or more years. New buildings usually require terms of 10 or more years. The landlord normally wants as long a lease as he can get. His ability to obtain financing depends, among other things, on the stability of his rent roll. The tenant may prefer a shorter term, on the theory that as newer buildings are put up, his bargaining position will become stronger. However, if the tenant expects to make expensive alterations, he will want a term that's sufficiently long enough to amortize them.

If the tenant is in a position to demand it, he will want a renewal option at the same or at a slightly higher rental. At the very least, however, the landlord will demand that the renewal rental cover any increase in real estate taxes and operating costs. For this purpose, an escalator clause may be used.

[¶2307.1]   **Cancellation and Additional Space Options**

Two common problems for tenants who sign long-term leases are what happens if expected growth fails to occur, and what happens if growth is far greater than anticipated? Both of these can be solved by options, if the landlord will grant them. Under a cancellation option, the tenant has the right at designated periods and upon adequate notice to drop a specified amount of space. Usually a penalty will be payable to the landlord. The additional space option works in a similar manner: At designated periods, the tenant is given the right to lease additional space at a fixed rental.

The landlord should not overlook the benefits of these types of options. With a cancellation option, he may be able to fill up the building more quickly and with a fewer number of tenants, which simplifies his financing and bookkeeping problems. In many cases, the "normal" 3% growth in white-collar workers will insure that cancellation options are not used. The additional space option is even more beneficial to the landlord. According to some experts, 80% of the tenants who leave well-maintained office buildings do so because they can't obtain additional space in the building. In some cases, a landlord will go so far as to make short-term leases for space adjoining that of his major tenants so that space will be available when and if required by them.

[¶2308]   **SUBLETTING SPACE**

A provision giving the tenant the right to sublease space (or requiring the landlord to have reasonable cause for refusing his consent) will not only protect the tenant against unexpected developments but is one way to solve the problems of changing space requirements. If the tenant believes he will need less space in the future, a sublease clause can be substituted for a cancellation option. If more space will be needed, the tenant can lease it immediately and sublet it during the interval when it isn't required. Sometimes, the landlord himself will agree to be the subtenant; then he has the responsibility of finding someone to occupy the space.

Apart from local variations, there are two basic types of sublease clauses. One is a standard clause contained in the printed form of many commercial leases. This states that the tenant may sublease with the written consent of the landlord. The other modified version of this clause adds that the landlord will not unreasonably withhold his consent.

In leases where the standard form is used, there are few alternatives open to the tenant if the landlord is unwilling to give his consent. Consequently, a tenant signing such a lease should be prepared to remain at the location for the full term; in the event he does wish to move, the landlord is in a position to demand a substantial consideration even though he may already have another tenant ready to move in.

[¶2308.1]   **When Is a Landlord's Refusal Reasonable?**

Even when the modified clause prohibits an unreasonable withholding of consent by the landlord, he may refuse to approve a sublease for a number of reasons that could not be anticipated at the time the original lease was executed.

A landlord refusing consent, of course, risks the possibility that the tenant will begin a court action to determine if the landlord's actions are actually reasonable. Or, as an alternative, the tenant may proceed to make the sublease with the prospective subtenant even without the landlord's consent. The lease should contain a stipulation that no brokerage commission will be payable until the necessary consent has been obtained. The present tenant could then draft a letter to the landlord giving a detailed description of the new tenant's business, reliability, and background, pointing out that the new tenant meets all reasonable requirements relative to leasing space in the building, and requesting the landlord's consent. The tenant could take the position that a refusal under these circumstances would be unjustifiable, capricious, a violation of the original leasing agreement, and would render the original lease null and void.

The next move, in this event, is up to the landlord. Should he decide to continue to withhold consent, the tenant will probably stop paying rent, which leaves the landlord in a position in which he must go to court to collect. Should the landlord resort to legal action, the tenant can file a counter suit against him for failing to approve the sublease. Of course, the tenant also takes the risk that the court will find the refusal reasonable, in which case full back rent must be paid and the tenant has lost any opportunity to negotiate a termination of his lease.

[¶2308.2] The Difference Between Subletting and Assigning

The difference between subletting and assigning depends on how much the tenant is giving away: If the tenant transfers the remainder of the term created by the lease, there is an assignment. On the other hand, the transfer is a sublease if the tenant retains part of his interest in the lease (no matter how small it might be). An assignee becomes liable to the original landlord for rent under the lease. The subtenant is liable only to his sublandlord (the original tenant), who remains liable to his landlord.

[¶2308.3] The Back-to-Back Lease

In some cities, the competition for tenants will force the landlord to offer to take over the unexpired term of an existing lease in order to rent space. If such a concession has been offered, the landlord's obligations should be spelled out in the new lease. If the landlord already has found a subtenant for the old space, the lease should specify any obligation on his part if the subtenant defaults on the sublease.

Parties who enter into such a "back-to-back" lease should be aware of the problems involved. One is that the landlord under the existing lease will very often have no incentive to make alterations when he already has a signed lease for the space. So this will deter a prospective new subtenant. Sometimes the tenant may be persuaded to make a contribution towards alterations of its present space to conform to the requirements of its prospective subtenant. If not, the landlord must make a careful analysis of the space so that he can show a prospective subtenant that a move would require little or no alteration.

Another problem presented by "back-to-back" leasing is the reluctance of prospective subtenants to negotiate for space occupied by a tenant who has not signed a lease for other quarters in another building. It is not uncommon to find both the sublandlord and the subtenant in agreement and ready to execute a sublease only to discover that the new space for the proposed sublandlord has already been leased to someone else during the time that the sublandlord was seeking to obtain a subtenant.

Try to avoid this situation by keeping the owner of the new building informed of what is going on. The full leasing negotiations can be simultaneously planned and executed. There can also be a simultaneous closing arranged, involving the two tenants and the owners of both the new and the old buildings.

[¶2309] ALTERATIONS

The alteration clause is very important and should cover a number of points. If the landlord is to make alterations for the tenant, the nature and extent of such alterations should be spelled out in detail and quality specifications should be included when relevant. The obligation to pay rent should be conditioned on these alterations, so that the tenant need not move in until they are made.

Alterations made by the tenant are usually subject to the landlord's consent.

Potential disputes can be reduced if a list of approved alterations is included in the lease. Denial of consent for future alterations should require reasonable cause for the lessor's objections. In addition, the lessor may agree that certain minor types of alterations can be made at any time without consent.

Finally, the lease should provide for disposition of any fixtures attached or affixed to the premises by the tenant. The standard lease provides that all alterations shall be the property of the lessor unless he elects otherwise, and if he does elect otherwise, the tenant is responsible for removing them (and restoring the space to its original condition). The tenant may seek to modify this clause to provide (a) that the tenant may remove specified fixtures when he vacates or (b) that the tenant need not remove specified alterations when he vacates because of the expense involved.

[¶2310]   IMPROVEMENTS

Leased property is almost always improved property or property that will be improved during the term of the lease. An important factor in measuring the value of the lease and in negotiating rent and other terms is who will make the improvements and who will be entitled to take the depreciation for them. In the following paragraphs the tax and economic consequences of improvements made by either the landlord or tenant will be examined.

[¶2310.1]   Improvements Made by the Landlord

Improvements made by the owner of leased property are capital expenditures and as such are depreciable over the useful lives of the improvements (without regard to the lease terms). Unless it has contributed to the cost of improvements built by the landlord, the tenant is not allowed to depreciate such costs (see *Weiss v. Wiener,* 279 US 333, 1929). When the tenant does contribute to the costs of the improvements, the amounts that he and the landlord may deduct will depend on whether the contributions are rent.

In exchange for the costs incurred to improve the property, the landlord will normally demand a higher rent. In effect, at the expense of laying out the cash for the improvements (or the cost of financing them), the landlord will receive (1) an annual depreciation deduction measured by the useful lives of the improvements and (2) a higher rent, which is taxable to him as ordinary income. Depending on the circumstances, the net additional rent income may or may not offset the net cost of the improvements.

On the other side, the tenant, by paying the additional higher rent, (1) is saving cash that might be better used in his business and (2) has a fixed annual rental deduction instead of an amortization deduction that (if there is a renewal option) may have to be spread over the renewal period as well as the initial term of the lease.

[¶2310.2] Improvements Made by the Tenant

Improvements made by the tenant are not included in the landlord's taxable income if they are not rent (IRC §109), nor is the landlord's basis affected. In other words, the landlord realizes no income either when the improvement is made or at the termination of the lease (§109). In effect, when the tenant makes the improvements, the landlord anticipates an increase in the value of his property at no cost to himself, in lieu of receiving a higher rent and an additional depreciation deduction.

The tenant, on the other hand, may depreciate the improvements over their useful lives or the term of the lease, whichever is shorter (Reg. §1.167(a)-4). In addition, he pays a lower rental than if the landlord did the work. But he must provide the cash or financing for the initial expenditures.

If, in return for the tenant's improvements, the landlord reduces the rent, the fair market value of the improvements will be treated as rental income to the landlord (Reg. §1.109-1(a)). The amount added to the landlord's income then becomes his basis with regard to the improvements, and is recoverable (via depreciation) by him over the improvement's useful life *(Isidore Brown,* CA-7, 220 F. 2d 12, 1955). For the tenant, the cost of the improvements is deductible as rent (as it corresponds to the landlord's income) *(Your Health Club, Inc.,* 4 TC 385, 1944). Whether improvements made by the tenant will be deemed rent depends on the intent of the parties as seen from the terms of the lease and the surrounding circumstances.

[¶2310.3] Summary of Consequences of Improvements

The following table summarizes the advantages and disadvantages—from both the landlord's and tenant's point of view—of improvements made by either of them:

Improvements by Landlord

From landlord's point of view:
(1) Higher rental obtainable.
(2) Landlord bears cost of construction.
(3) Rental taxable at ordinary income rates.
(4) Landlord may deduct for depreciation. Basis may be increased. Possible recapture of excess depreciation.

From tenant's point of view:
(1) Tenant pays more rent.
(2) No cost of construction.

Improvements by Tenant

From landlord's point of view:
(1) Lower rental obtainable.
(2) No cost of construction.
(3) Increase in value recognized only on disposition of property, and usually treated as capital gain taxable at favorable rates.
(4) No deduction for depreciation.

From tenant's point of view:

(1) Tenant pays less rent.

(2) Tenant bears cost of construction, but is entitled to depreciation deductions or amortization. Possible recapture on disposition.

[¶2311]   **REPAIRS**

Repairs are an area in which tenants may take on unexpectedly burdensome obligations. Naturally, the tenant should be responsible for his own neglect, as well as that of his employees, so he should be adequately insured. But the repair clause in most standard leases goes beyond this and makes the tenant responsible for damage from the air-conditioning unit or system (without distinguishing whether the air-conditioning was the landlord's or the tenant's), short circuits, flow or leakage of water, steam, gas, sewer gas, sewerage or odors, frost, bursting or leaking of pipes or plumbing works or gas, or from any other cause of any kind or nature whatsoever due to his carelessness, neglect, etc. This is fine where the tenant is in possession of the entire building, but the tenant may well consider the clause too broad when he merely occupies a part of a building that is under the landlord's control. The tenant may want a clause that provides that he is only obligated to make repairs if damage is the result of his misuse of the property and that all other repairs are the landlord's responsibility.

[¶2312]   **LEASE SUBORDINATION**

Ordinarily, a subordination clause will provide a blanket subordination of the lease to any future underlying mortgage or any future underlying lease. This may be alright if the future mortgage is placed with a lending institution. But a private individual may toss out all of the tenants if he forecloses. Therefore, a tenant might try to have his clause provide that the lease will be subordinated only if the holder of any future lease or mortgage agrees that the lease will not be terminated or otherwise affected by an enforcement of such mortgage or lease as long as the tenant is not in default. If he can't get this type of clause, the tenant might try to limit subordination to mortgages placed with lending institutions. Before signing the lease, the tenant should try to get a nondisturbance agreement from the holder of any existing mortgages or underlying leases.

[¶2313]   **DESTRUCTION OR CONDEMNATION**
                              OF PREMISES

If the premises are completely destroyed, the landlord has the option of rebuilding, but, in the usual standard lease form, he may notify the tenant, within 90 days of the casualty, that he will not rebuild. At this point the lease will come to an end. But the tenant is given no option to cancel his lease even though the remaining period may be short and it would be more practical for him to permanently relocate elsewhere. Nor does the clause usually spell out the tenant's rent obligation adequately during the period between the destruction of the premises and its restoration.

Several things can be done to improve this clause from the tenant's point of view. For one thing, he can provide that the landlord's insurance policies cover all possible causes of destruction and that the landlord will look to his insurer in the event that the premises are destroyed. The tenant will want no distinction to be made no matter whose neglect may have caused the destruction. In the event of a total destruction of the premises, the tenant will want an option to cancel the lease if the destruction occurs during the last few years of the term. The tenant may also try to keep the period during which the landlord has the option to cancel relatively short, about 30 days rather than the usual 90.

As far as condemnation is concerned, the landlord will ordinarily want to include a clause entitling him to the full condemnation award. A tenant who plans to make substantial improvements and who is in a strong bargaining position may be able to modify this in order to obtain some reimbursement for his investment. Otherwise, a tenant can only try to ascertain if there is any risk of condemnation during the term of the lease.

[¶2314] SOME LEGAL ELEMENTS OF THE LANDLORD-TENANT RELATIONSHIP

As defined earlier, a lease is a contract, and the parties to it may insert any provisions they want (with a few exceptions) to govern their relationship. In some instances a tenant will occupy property without entering into a formal agreement with the landlord. Sometimes a comprehensive lease may leave certain matters to be governed by common law or statutory rules. While such rules may differ in detail from one jurisdiction to the next, there is a general similarity in the legal principles involved. Some of the more important points are discussed in the following paragraphs.

[¶2314.1] Types of Tenancies

The landlord-tenant relationship exists by virtue of either a formal written lease or a periodic tenancy. The basic difference between the two is that when a written lease exists it is deemed to be the complete agreement between the parties, and the rights and obligations of the parties are governed by this instrument. If there is no formal lease and a periodic tenancy exists, the rights and obligations of the parties are governed by the jurisdiction's rules of law.

What follows is a brief discussion of the various types of tenancies that exist in the absence of a formal written lease.

Periodic Tenancy: This type of tenancy is created when the tenant occupies the property without any agreement as to term. There is deemed to be a tenancy for a period measured by the rental payments. Therefore, unless an intent to the contrary is expressed, a periodic tenancy or a tenancy from year to year exists if a yearly rent is paid, even if such rent is paid in quarterly or monthly installments. When the rent is not an annual rent but is for a shorter term, such as the common situation where monthly rent is paid, a month-to-month tenancy is said to exist. When a lease is of unspecified duration and rent is payable monthly, the tenancy is from month to month even if the tenant remains in possession of the premises and pays rent for more than a year.

A periodic tenancy continues until the party who wishes to terminate the tenancy serves a proper notice of termination on the other party. In order for such notice to be proper it must be served at the proper time under state law and must state the proper termination date. (A periodic tenancy may not be discontinued nor may the rent be increased at any time except at the end of the term.) Thus, where a month-to-month tenancy commences on, say, January 15, the notice of termination must state that the tenancy is to terminate on the 14th day of the desired month.

Tenancy at Will: This type of tenancy, which is for an indefinite term, may be terminated by either party to the transaction. The courts do not favor this form of tenancy and will, where possible, construe the lease in question as being a periodic tenancy. Unlike a periodic tenancy, which may be terminated only by giving proper notice, a tenancy at will may be terminated by the death of either the landlord or the tenant.

Tenancy at Sufferance: This type of tenancy is created when a tenant who has rightfully possessed the premises continues to possess the property after the expiration or termination of his lease. The tenant at sufferance may be ousted by the landlord at any time without notice. The death of a tenant at sufferance terminates the relationship.

[¶2314.2] **Holding Over**

It is agreed, either expressly or impliedly, in all leases that at the end of his term the tenant will deliver possession of the premises back to the landlord. Therefore, a tenant who continues to remain in possession of leased premises after the lease term, without the landlord's consent, is a wrongdoer. (It should be noted that although the holdover tenant is considered a wrongdoer, he is not immediately treated as a trespasser.) In states that have not changed the common-law rule by statute, a holdover tenant may be held by the landlord for a further term. This is true even if the tenant holds over just for a day. Of course, the landlord, rather than holding the tenant to an additional term, may evict him. Once the landlord elects how he'll treat the tenant (i.e., eviction or holdover), he is bound by that decision. It should be noted that a tenant has no reciprocal right to hold the landlord.

As can be seen, the holdover rule is harsh. Courts will often not apply it if they find that the tenant was unable to move for compelling reasons or if the landlord impliedly consented to the holding over. For example, if the parties are actively negotiating a new lease when the old lease expires, the tenant will usually be considered as a month-to-month tenant. In addition, the parties may agree in the original lease that holding over will not convert the tenancy into a year-to-year one.

[¶2314.3] Eviction

Technically interpreted, an eviction may be defined as the disturbance of a tenant's possession or his explusion so that he is deprived of his enjoyment of the demised premises, in whole or in part, by reason of the landlord's title, entry, or act. An eviction can be either actual or constructive. An *actual* eviction is deemed to occur when the landlord's acts deprive the tenant of some right to the premises to which he is entitled. If the landlord's acts merely interfere with the tenant's beneficial enjoyment of the premises, the eviction is *constructive*. It is not to be inferred from this that all landlord interference with tenants' possession or enjoyment constitute constructive evictions. To qualify as a constructive eviction the landlord's interference must be intentional and so substantial as to deprive the tenant of his enjoyment of the premises and the tenant must in turn, as a result of such interference, abandon his possession of the premises within a reasonable time. Whether a landlord's acts constitute a constructive eviction is usually a question of fact.

[¶2314.4] Possession

Leases are frequently silent about the landlord's duty to deliver actual (as opposed to legal) possession of the property at the commencement of the term. In such cases, the states are divided as to whether the landlord or the new tenant has the duty of evicting a holdover tenant.

[¶2314.5] Implied Covenants in a Lease

Most courts in this country agree that when an agreement to lease real estate employs the terms demise, let, or grant, the landlord impliedly covenants that he has good title to make the lease and enter into the landlord-tenant relationship.

Also, as agreed to by most courts, a covenant of quiet enjoyment is implied in a valid lease. The purpose of this covenant is to protect the tenant from people who claim to have title that is better than the landlord's. Thus, in the usual situation, the covenant of quiet enjoyment protects the tenant's status under his lease when ownership of the property is transferred.

[¶2314.6] Repairs

Frequently, a lease will specify which party has the duty to repair the premises but will not indicate what the other party may do if the duty is breached. In most jurisdictions, if the landlord fails in his duty to repair, the tenant has several alternatives. He may make the repairs himself and deduct the cost from the rent; he may pay the rent and sue the landlord for the decrease in rental value; or he may pay a lesser rental due to the decreased value of the premises. If the tenant is injured by the landlord's failure to repair, there is a split as to whether the landlord is liable for the injuries. The states that hold no liability do so on the theory that the tenant had the duty to make the repairs and then seek to recover the cost from the landlord.

If a defective condition exists in an area over which the landlord does not retain control, the landlord's duty to repair (if it exists) depends on prior notice of the defective condition. Since this is invariably a matter of dispute between the parties, such notice should always be in writing.

[¶2315]   **LEASE-CLOSING CHECKLIST**

In order to avoid any unanticipated problems at the last minute, use the lease-closing checklist that follows. This checklist, which is geared to the landlord's attorney, is not exhaustive but it may serve as a basic guide.

☐ *Lease:* Be sure to bring enough copies of the lease, fully prepared and ready to be signed.

☐ *Signatures:* Be sure all necessary signatories are present.

☐ *Bill of Sale:* If personal property is being sold when the property is leased, the lessee will want a bill of sale for items conveyed.

☐ *Property Data:* It's a good idea to bring appropriate maps, surveys, and diagrams to the closing, as they may contain information that will be useful to the tenant.

☐ *Additional Data:* Just in case any questions might arise at the closing, bring the following items: title abstracts, certificates and guarantees, certificates of occupancy and inspection, and mortgage data.

☐ *Notary*

☐ *Costs:* Tax receipts, assessments, as well as bills for water, fuel, utilities, and other expenses that may be apportioned when the premises are leased, should be brought along.

☐ *Maintenance Contracts*

☐ *Insurance Policies*

☐ *Forms for Consenting to Alterations and Repairs*

☐ *Leasing Material:* Bring subordinate leases as well as necessary information about security deposits.

☐ *Receipts:* To avoid embarrassment or disagreements, be sure to bring receipts for documents and money delivered to you, the attorney, or the tenant.

☐ *Miscellaneous:* Before the closing, it may be desirable to write a letter to the prospective tenant reminding him to bring necessary documents such as power of attorney or other authorizations he'll need. Also remind him to bring cash or a check for rent, security, or adjustments.

[¶2316]   **FOR FURTHER REFERENCE . . .**

Brown, M.L., "Effect of Top Leases: Obstruction of Title and Related Considerations," 30 Baylor Law Review 213-43 (Spring 1978).

Greaney, J.M., "Developing Duties of a Landlord with Regard to Tenant Safety," 63 Massachusetts Law Review 61-7 (March-April 1978).

"Tax Treatment of the Cost of Terminating a Lease," 30 Stanford Law Review 241 (November 1977).

Thompson, E.G., "Some Tax Problems on Midstream Modifications and Termination of Leases," 4 Journal of Real Estate Taxation 214 (1977).

LEGAL FEES AND THEIR DEDUCTIBILITY

[**¶2401**]   As a general rule, legal fees are deductible if they are ordinary and necessary business expenses (IRC §162). In the case of individuals, a deduction is also allowed for those legal expenses paid or incurred for the production, collection, maintenance, or conservation of income, as well as for the management, conservation, or maintenance of property held for the production of income. Also, deductions made in connection with the determination, collection, or refund of any tax (nonbusiness expenses) are permitted (IRC §212). Expenses incurred in defending or perfecting title to property are capital expenditures (Reg. §1.263(a)-2(c)). Thus, expenses that are incident to ownership are deductible while those designed to acquire, defend, or perfect ownership are nondeductible.

[¶2402]   DEDUCTIBILITY OF SPECIFIC TYPES OF LEGAL FEES

Certain specific legal fees may be deductible, as outlined in the paragraphs below.

[¶2403]   LABOR PROBLEMS

Payments for the resolution of National Labor Relations Board problems are considered ordinary and necessary business expenses. Accordingly, legal and accounting fees for this purpose are deductible.

[¶2404]   BANKRUPTCY

Bankruptcy claims, as ordinary and necessary business expenses, are deductible *(International Shoe Company*, 38 BTA 81, 1939).

[¶2405]   ANTITRUST

Except to the extent that legal services relate to the imposition of a fine or penalty under federal antitrust legislation, expenses involved in the defense of federal or state antitrust actions are generally deductible.

[¶2406]   HOUSE COUNSEL

To the extent that a corporation employs an attorney for day-to-day consultation, the cost of his advice is an ordinary and necessary expense of doing business—even if the services performed relate to the acquisition of capital assets. As long as an employer-employee relationship exists, the salary is deductible.

[¶2407]   **ESTATE PLANNING**

Legal fees incurred for tax planning in the overall estate plan are deductible under §212(3) (see *Merians,* 60 TC 187, 1973, *acq.* CB 1973-2, 2). The cost of review of estate plans submitted by another law firm are fully deductible *(Nancy R. Bagley,* 8 TC 130, 1947). To the extent that legal fees are directly connected with the management and conservation of the taxpayer's income-producing properties, a portion of the attorney's fees incurred for preparation of a will is deductible under IRC §212(2), (3).

[¶2408]   **DEFENSE OF PROFESSIONAL LICENSE**

Expenses involved in opposing a suspension of a professional license or disbarment from practicing in a profession may be deductible (compare *Buder,* TC Memo 1963-73; *Tellier,* 383 US 687, 1966).

[¶2409]   **LIBEL AND SLANDER**

If a taxpayer's trade or business is directly affected or involved, the legal expenses of defending a libel or slander action may be deductible. The key question in this area is whether the claim arose out of the taxpayer's business activity or his personal life. If the claim's nature and origin is personal rather than business, the expense is nondeductible (see *McDonald*, CA-2, 8/8/78, *rev'g* TC Memo 1977-202; *Lloyd*, CA-7, 55 F. 2d 842, 1932).

[¶2410]   **LOBBYING**

When a taxpayer appears before specific legislative bodies or committees in connection with specific legislation in which the taxpayer has a direct interest, §162(e) of the Internal Revenue Code authorizes deductibility of his expenses. The same applies if an attorney appears on behalf of the taxpayer *(Johnson,* TC Memo 1962-299).

[¶2411]   **PATENTS**

Prosecution of patent infringement suits are deductible, as are attorney's fees needed to perfect a patent application *(Urquart,* CA-3, 215 F. 2d 17, 1954). Expenses allocated to defend a patent title are not deductible.

[¶2412]   **OBTAINING TAX RULINGS**

If the taxpayer expends money in order to obtain a tax ruling, it's deductible under IRC §212 *(Kaufmann,* DC Mo., 227 F. Supp. 807, 1964).

[¶2413]   **CRIMINAL CHARGES AND STATUTORY VIOLATIONS**

Under certain circumstances, legal fees incurred in the defense of a criminal charge may be deductible. The expense is deductible only if the claim against the taxpayer arises in connection with his business or a profit-seeking activity. Legal fees are not deductible as a business expense merely because a failure to incur the expense might result in the taxpayer losing his trade or business *(Messina,* Ct. Cl., 6/20/73). Similarly, the effect that the litigation may have on the taxpayer's income-producing property is not determinative. If the legal fees are otherwise deductible as a business expense, the outcome of the criminal suit will not affect the taxpayer's deduction. In *Tellier* (383 US 687, 1966), the Supreme Court held that it does not violate public policy to permit a taxpayer to deduct the expense of an unsuccessful defense to a criminal charge when the illegal activity arose in connection with the taxpayer's business.

[¶2414]   **MARITAL MATTERS**

If a spouse's divorce claim stems entirely from the marital relationship and not from any income-producing activity, expenses of another taxpayer to resist the claim may not be deemed ''business'' expenses and therefore are not deductible *(Patrick,* 372 US 39, 1963; *Gilmore,* 372 US 53, 1963).

[¶2415]   **FOR FURTHER REFERENCE . . .**

Fogg, R.E., ''Current Tests Used by the Courts and IRS to Determine When Legal Fees Are Deductible,'' 5 Taxation for Lawyers 334 (1976).
Legal Fees Incurred in Litigation Involving Title to Assets—Allocation Between Deductible Ordinary Expenses and Non-deductible Capital Expenditures,'' 126 University of Pennsylvania Law Review 1100 (May 1978).
Phillips, T., ''Deductibility of Legal Expenses Incurred in Corporate Stock Redemptions, Partial Liquidations and Separations,'' 5 Duke Law Journal 941 (1977).
Wegher, A.C., ''Deductibility of Fees for Professional Services—Accountant or Attorney; Divorce and Separation; Estate Planning; Tax Advice; Title Matters, etc.'' 34 New York University Institute on Federal Taxation 163—187 (1976).

LIFE INSURANCE

[**¶2501**]   The life insurance policy is frequently a vital element in a plan for family security, an estate plan, a program to retire corporate stock or partnership interests, a plan to provide business continuity, an employee pension and profit-sharing plan, and other family and business arrangements. It is important for the lawyer to understand the elements of the life insurance contract, the alternatives available to the insured, the status of life insurance as property, how life insurance is taxed, and other essential elements of insurance.

[¶2502]   **TYPICAL STANDARD PROVISIONS**
                         IN A LIFE INSURANCE POLICY

The following provisions are customarily included in life insurance policies. A number of them are required by state law.

Grace Period: Generally 30 or 31 days following the premium due date, during which period the insurance company will accept payment without penalty. If death occurs during the grace period, the permium due is deducted from the proceeds paid.

Extended Term Insurance: A nonforfeiture option that provides that if premiums are not paid within the grace period, the policy will not expire. The cash surrender value, less indebtedness, is used as a single premium to purchase term insurance at the attained age of the insured for the face amount of the policy for as long a period as possible.

Reinstatement: The policyholder's right to reinstate a lapsed policy within a reasonable time by paying the unpaid premiums with interest. Satisfactory evidence of insurability is required.

Incontestability Clause: Once the policy has been in force for two years (one year in some cases), the beneficiary will receive the death proceeds without contest by the company even if misstatements were made in the original application. However, if the misstatement pertains to the insured's age, then an adjustment in the amount of the death benefit will be made.

Suicide: If death results from suicide within two years after the policy is issued (one year in some policies), the beneficiary will recover only the actual premiums advanced; after two years, the full death benefit will be paid.

Cash Value: The amount available to the owner at any given time if the policy is surrendered to the company.

Loan Values: Permanent-type insurance usually permits the owner to borrow up to 95% of cash value at guaranteed interest rates.

Paid-Up Insurance: The policy contains a table showing the amount of paid-up life insurance that can be taken instead of cash when the policy is surrendered. The paid-up policy also has a cash value.

Payment of Dividend and Dividend Options: Participating policies provide for payment of a dividend and describe the various dividend options, such as cash, reduced premium, paid-up additions, interest, or additional one-year term.

Ownership Clause: A provision that the policy may be owned by someone other than the insured. For example, in order to remove proceeds from the insured's estate, the insured's spouse or a trust may be owner of the policy.

Beneficiary Provisions: The insured can name first, second, third, or further contingent beneficiaries and arrange payment of proceeds through settlement options. Some policies, such as group insurance, may restrict the number of beneficiaries that can be named and the variety of settlement arrangements that can be chosen.

Conversion Privilege: A provision that allows the policy owner to elect to change the policy to a different plan. Policies can generally be converted without medical examinations to higher premium plans or with a medical examination to lower premium plans. Generally, conversion to term insurance is not permitted.

Assignment: The policy outlines the procedure for making an assignment. Usually the company states that it is not bound until written notice of assignment is received, that the assignment is subject to any loan to the company, and that the company accepts no responsibility for the validity of the assignment.

[¶2503]   LEGAL ASPECTS OF LIFE INSURANCE

Although a life insurance policy is a legal contract, applicable contract law has been modified by statutes in many respects. These changes protect the policyholder and cause the contract to be interpreted strictly against the insurance company in the event of a dispute between the company and an insured.

Some of the most important legal aspects of life insurance are the following:

☐ *Offer:* If the application is accompanied by payment of the first premium, an offer is deemed made by the applicant; the company generally accepts the offer by issuing a conditional receipt to insure the applicant if he meets the insurability requirements of the company. If a policy other than that applied for is issued, then the new policy becomes a counteroffer by the company. An application without the premium is merely an invitation for the company to make an offer, which it does by issuing the policy and delivering it.

☐ *Acceptance:* An offer may be accepted if the company delivers the policy or the insured pays the first premium. Unreasonable delay by the company in processing an application accompanied by the first premium is considered in most states to be a rejection of the applicant's offer; in some states, it constitutes an acceptance.

There are various forms of conditional receipts used by companies; the wording of the particular receipt determines whether the issuance of the receipt constitutes an acceptance or whether actual delivery of the policy is required.

☐ **Consideration:** The consideration given by the insurance company is the promises set forth in the contract. The consideration given by the insured is comprised of the statements made in the application and payment of the first premium.

☐ **Legal Capacity:** The insured must be of legal age and of sound mind. The usual legal age has been modified in many states for life insurance contracts.

☐ **Insurable Interest:** The applicant must have an insurable interest in the life of the insured. This has been defined as a reasonable expectation of financial benefit from the continued life of the insured, or financial loss if the insured dies. A general rule is that even though an insurable interest exists, the life of another may not be insured without his consent. Insurable interest need exist only when the policy is purchased; it need not exist when the policy becomes a claim. The insured has the right to name anyone as his beneficiary without regard to insurable interest.

☐ **Utmost Good Faith:** Neither "buyer beware" nor "seller beware" applies to a life insurance contract. Each party has the right to rely on the good faith of the other.

☐ **Representation:** Most states provide that in the absence of fraud, all warranties in life insurance contracts (statements in the application and medical exam) are to be interpreted as representations. The policy is voidable by the company if there is a misrepresentation of a material fact—one that would have led the company to deny the insurance or charge a higher premium. However, a misrepresentation of an immaterial fact is not sufficient to cause rescission of the contract.

☐ **Concealment:** The company may rescind a contract if there has been concealment by the applicant—i.e., silence when he had a duty to speak—provided that the concealment was both material and intentional.

☐ **Creditors' Rights:** The rights of creditors of the insured (and sometimes creditors of the beneficiary) have been modified in most states to give special protection to life insurance.

☐ **Authority of Agents:** There is generally a presumption of agency if the company has supplied a person with forms, rate books, applications, etc., that make it logical for one to assume that he is an agent of the company. The company would be bound by acts of this person as though he had been given express authority to act as its agent.

The insurance agent's authority is outlined in his agency contract. His authority usually includes soliciting and taking applications for new business, arranging medical exams, and collecting the first year's premium or a partial premium. Usually excluded are the rights to make, alter, or discharge any contract; to waive any forfeiture; to waive payment in cash; to extend the time of payment for a premium; to accept payment of a past due premium; to approve evidence of good health.

In addition to the express authority granted in his agency contract, the agent is held in common law to have certain implied authority—any authority that the public may reasonably assume an agent to have. Limitations of the agent's authority are communicated to the public in application forms, conditional receipts, and in the policy. Policies contain a provision that only certain designated officers of the company have the power to make or modify the contract or extend time for paying a premium.

The knowledge of the agent is assumed to be the knowledge of the company. Thus, if the agent knows a material fact about the applicant, it is presumed that the information has been given to the company. Should the company discover the information after the policy is issued, it cannot then rescind the contract because of concealment or misrepresentation.

If an agent interprets a policy provision incorrectly to an insured, and the wording in the policy is ambiguous, the agent's interpretation is held valid.

Most states make a distinction between a broker and an agent—the broker is the agent of the insured, not the company. However, other states consider the broker the agent of the company, and some as the agent of the company only for purposes of delivering the policy and collecting the premium.

[¶2504]   **DIVIDEND OPTIONS**

Typical dividend options available to a policyholder are as follows:

(1) Cash: The policyholder can receive his dividend in cash. The most frequent use of this option is for paid-up policies. Another situation where this option is attractive is if the insured is disabled and premiums on the policy are being waived.

(2) Reduce Premiums: The insured can apply dividends as part payment of premiums. This is used when the insured needs funds to help meet premium obligations, or if a low net expenditure for insurance is desired. It is used in minimum deposit plans when reducing coverage is desired.

(3) Accumulating at Interest: This election permits the insurance company to retain dividends on deposit and have them build up at a guaranteed rate of interest. If the company's earnings are less than the rate it guarantees, the policyholder will still be credited with the specified interest rate; should the earnings be greater he usually will receive the higher interest.

Dividend accumulations are often used when an insured policyholder wants to increase guaranteed retirement income provided under the policy's retirement options.

(4) Paid-Up Additions: Dividends are applied to buy additional paid-up insurance. The increased protection acquired via dividend additions requires no medical examination and serves as a valuable tool when poor health makes additional insurance unavailable.

(5) The "Fifth" Dividend Option: This provides for the purchase of one-year term insurance in an amount usually equal to the increase in cash value. The balance of the dividend may be left on deposit to accumulate future cash value purchases or may be applied under one of the other dividend options. This option increases the face value of the policy by the amount of the cash value. The net result is to eliminate the policy owner from becoming a co-insurer on the policy.

[¶2505] **LIFE INSURANCE RIDERS**

There are many extras you can add to a basic life insurance policy. Some of these "riders" cost from a few cents to a few dollars per year for each $1,000 of death benefit provided in the policy; the cost of others is based on the amount of benefit provided in the rider; other valuable endorsements may be added to the policy free of charge. Whether the insured needs some of these "extras" depends on the purpose of the insurance policy—family protection, business insurance, retirement fund, etc.

[¶2505.1] Waiver of Premium

This rider provides that if the policyholder becomes totally and permanently disabled, his insurance will remain in force without any further premium payments. The waiver does not take effect until the disability has continued for a specified period, usually six months. Disabilities typically excluded from coverage are those resulting from war and those that are intentionally self-inflicted.

In addition to the waiver of premiums, if the policies are of the cash-value type—ordinary life, limited-pay life, endowment—the cash values will grow as if the insured were continuing to pay the premiums. If the need arises during the period of disability, the insured can borrow against the cash values in the policy.

For almost all types of policies and purposes, this rider is usually viewed as a necessity. In a family protection policy, it guarantees maintenance of life insurance when the insured's ability to earn enough to pay the premium is impaired. In a retirement plan, it guarantees the accumulation of the retirement fund. In a partnership agreement, it might provide part of the funds for a pay-out of a disabled partner.

Payor Benefit: This is a waiver of premium benefit in some juvenile policies that covers the risk of death or disability of the person responsible for paying the premiums (i.e., usually the child's father) before the policy on an insured child is fully paid or the child reaches a specified age.

[¶2505.2] Accidental Death Benefits

This rider stipulates that if the policyholder dies by "accidental death," the company will pay the beneficiary a multiple of the face amount of the policy (as much as four times in some cases).

Some typical exclusions are deaths due to war, certain kinds of flying accidents, and accidents that stem from illness or infirmity. Death generally must take place within 90 days of the accident and before the insured reaches a specified age, usually 65.

In some cases this rider can serve a useful purpose. For example, it may be used by a business to protect against the loss of key personnel. For an executive who travels extensively by airplane, it provides less costly, year-round coverage for accidental death than other airplane policies.

[¶2505.3]   Accidental Death and Dismemberment

Some policies, such as group and association plans, provide additional benefits for dismemberment—loss of a limb, blindness, etc.

Some policies provide a *disability payout provision* under which the face amount of the policy is paid out in installments in the event of total disability.

[¶2505.4]   Guaranteed Insurability Rider

This rider guarantees that a specified amount of insurance may be purchased by the insured on certain future "option dates" at standard rates and without evidence of insurability. The guaranteed insurability rider can be a valuable extra for a young person as it guarantees an increasing insurance program. It is also a good addition to children's life insurance policies.

[¶2505.5]   Disability Income Rider

Some life insurance policies offer a disability income rider that provides a monthly income to the insured if he or she becomes totally disabled. A typical rider provides a monthly disability income of 1% of the face amount of the policy—a $50,000 policy could provide $500 per month disability income protection; monthly payments continue until age 65; then the policy endows for its face value and all obligations under the contract cease. Thus, a person who becomes totally disabled at age 45 and who has a $50,000 life insurance policy with a 1% disability rider would receive payment of $500 a month until age 65 and then would receive $50,000 in cash. Most riders require a six-month waiting period before disability payments begin.

[¶2505.6]   Free Riders

There are a number of free riders that can be included in insurance policies:

Automatic Premium Loan Clause: This is a provision that makes a policy "lapse-proof." The company is authorized to borrow from the cash value to pay a premium if the insured fails to do so. This valuable clause may keep protection from lapsing due to an oversight or illness.

Settlement Agreement: Payment of policy proceeds under various options and different beneficiary designations can be combined in one agreement attached to the policy in order to effectuate an estate plan. For example, part of the proceeds can be paid in cash to pay off debts, estate taxes, and final expenses, with the balance being paid in the form of a monthly income to the spouse.

Retirement Options: The insured may plan to use the cash values and accumulated dividends in the policies to provide a monthly annuity when he retires. He can receive a lifetime income, installments for a period of time, or a joint and survivor annuity.

Spendthrift Trust Clause: Some states have laws that automatically exempt proceeds of life insurance from the claims of creditors of the beneficiary. Many states also allow the insured to add a "spendthrift trust" provision to the policy to protect the proceeds. These clauses are usually worded so that proceeds are not assignable and are exempt from claims of creditors.

Common Disaster Clause: In states that did not adopt the Uniform Simultaneous Death Law, a common disaster clause might be added to the policy to achieve the same result. This clause states that if the insured and the beneficiary die in a common accident, the presumption will be that the beneficiary died first. The proceeds would then be paid to the secondary beneficiary or, in the absence of any, to the estate of the insured. This will save the cost and delay of the proceeds passing through the spouse's estate instead of going directly to the children.

Deferment Clause: This clause will defer payment of policy proceeds for a 30- or 60-day period. On the death of the insured, the proceeds are held at interest for a specified period and then paid to the primary beneficiary at the end of that period, if surviving, or else to the secondary beneficiary. This clause, like the common disaster clause, will keep proceeds out of a spouse's estate if the spouse dies shortly after the insured—proceeds will go directly to children.

[¶2506] **SETTLEMENT OPTIONS**

Insurance proceeds payable on the death of the insured or cash value when a policy is surrendered can, of course, be received in a lump sum. But that is not the only way the proceeds can be received. There are four other settlement options:

- [ ] The Interest Only Option.
- [ ] The Fixed Period Option.
- [ ] The Fixed Amount Option.
- [ ] The Life Income Option—which may be further subdivided as follows:
  - (a) Straight Life Income.
  - (b) Life Income with a period certain.
  - (c) Cash Refund Life Income.
  - (d) Refund Life Income.
  - (e) Joint and Survivor Life Income.

[¶2507] **PRINCIPAL OWNERSHIP AND BENEFICIARY ARRANGEMENTS**

(A) Insured purchaser and owner—executor named as beneficiary.

(B) Insured purchaser and owner—designated individual as beneficiary.

(C) Insured purchaser—another individual, corporation, or other entity as owner and beneficiary.

(D) Insured purchaser—trustee as owner and beneficiary.

(E) Person other than the insured as purchaser, owner, and beneficiary.

[¶2508] **LEGAL ASPECTS OF BENEFICIARY DESIGNATIONS**

The selection of a beneficiary and wording of the beneficiary designation often have important legal consequences. For example:

☐ Naming the estate of the insured as beneficiary will make policy proceeds subject to creditors of the insured; naming specific beneficiaries will protect the proceeds under state law.

☐ Naming the estate as beneficiary will make the proceeds subject to estate tax. If there is a named beneficiary, it may escape estate tax (e.g., if the spouse is the owner and beneficiary).

☐ If no beneficiary is named in the policy, or if none survives the insured, the proceeds, unless otherwise provided, are paid to the insured's estate.

☐ Failing to name a sufficient number of contingent beneficiaries may cause the proceeds to pass to unintended parties.

A "revocable" designation is one in which insured reserves the right to change the beneficiary. He may make a change without the beneficiary's permission.

[¶2508.1] **Contingent Beneficiary**

In making beneficiary designations, a contingent beneficiary should be named to receive the policy proceeds in the event the first-named beneficiary is dead when the proceeds are paid. This is especially important when payment is made through long-term settlement options if a balance of installment payments or of principal may remain after the death of the primary beneficiary.

An insured might consider naming a qualified charity as a contingent beneficiary. This type of designation might save taxes, in addition to ensuring that there would be an institution in being which would be a worthy recipient of the benefits.

[¶2509] **LIFE INSURANCE AND ESTATE TAXES**

Life insurance proceeds are taxable as part of the decedent's estate—unless measures are taken during life to put the insurance beyond the reach of the estate tax law or to soften the impact of that law.

[¶2509.1] **How to Transfer Ownership to Escape Estate Tax**

A popular estate planning device is the transfer of ownership of life insurance policies to intended beneficiaries. IRC §2042 says that death benefits paid to persons other than the estate are taxable only if the insured at his death possesses "incidents of ownership" in the policy. This means that if the insured makes a complete transfer of the policy and at the time of his death does not possess any rights of ownership, the proceeds are not included in his estate for estate tax purposes.

To achieve this tax benefit, there must be an absolute assignment together with the surrender of any power over the policy and its benefits. The insured must forfeit his right to surrender, pledge, or cancel the policy; to further assign the policy or revoke the assignment; to borrow on the policy; or to change the beneficiary.

However, the insured can continue to pay premiums.

Gifts of insurance policies made within three years of a decedent's death will be included in the insured's estate (IRC §2035). Additionally, under a "gross-up" rule, any gift tax paid on such gifts will be included in the donor's estate. Under the three-year rule, in situations where an insured has made a gift of the policy more than three years before death but has continued to make the premium payments, the amount of the premium payments made during the three years preceding death will be included in the insured's estate, unless the payments fall within the $3,000 annual exclusion.

[¶2509.2]   How Life Insurance Proceeds Qualify for the Marital Deduction

The estate tax marital deduction permits $250,000 or up to one-half of the adjusted gross estate, whichever is greater, to escape estate tax. In order to take advantage of the deduction, qualified property must pass to the surviving spouse under IRC §2056.

Life insurance proceeds may qualify for the marital deduction. However, the policyholder should make sure that the proceeds become vested in his or her spouse upon the insured's death. Some policies state that the surviving spouse must file proof of the insured's death within his or her lifetime before benefits will vest. This provision would prevent the proceeds from qualifying for the marital deduction *(Rev. Rul. 54-121*, CB 1954-1, 196). It is wise in such situations to endorse the policy so that the surviving spouse has an immediate right to the policy proceeds upon the insured's death regardless of when the proof is actually filed. Sometimes, a common disaster clause, which presumes that the spouse survived the insured, has the same effect (Reg. §20.2056(b)-3).

Generally, there are three ways by which life insurance proceeds will qualify for the marital deduction:

(1) By making the proceeds payable to the surviving spouse in a lump sum.

(2) By making the proceeds payable to a qualifying trust.

(3) By making the proceeds payable under any one of the installment options if:

    (a) The principal or any remaining unpaid installments are payable to the surviving spouse's estate on his or her death or,

    (b) The surviving spouse is given a general power to designate the beneficiary of the principal remaining at his or her death.

If the proceeds of a life insurance policy are payable to the surviving spouse and then to contingent beneficiaries, and the surviving spouse has the power to appoint all the proceeds, the proceeds qualify for the marital deduction if the power of appointment satisfies these requirements:

☐ All proceeds are payable to the surviving spouse solely during his or her lifetime.

☐ Payments must be payable annually or more frequently and must commence within 13 months after the insured's death.

☐ The surviving spouse has the sole power to appoint all the proceeds or a portion of them to himself or herself or his or her estate.

☐ The power is exercisable in all events.

☐ The surviving spouse's power is not subject to a power in any other person to appoint any part of the proceeds or a portion of them to anyone other than the surviving spouse (Reg. §20.2056(b)-(6)(a)).

It is not necessary that the surviving spouse actually exercise his or her power of appointment. Neither is it necessary that the phrase "power of appointment" be used in the policy. The surviving spouse's right to withdraw the principal sum in installments is, in itself, the equivalent of a power of appointment and qualifies for the marital deduction, provided this right exists from the time of the insured's death (Reg. §20.2056(b)-(6)(e)).

[¶2510]   PROTECTION OF LIFE INSURANCE FROM CREDITORS

These are the general rules affecting creditors' claims:

☐ *Creditors of the Insured—Cash Values:* In most states, the wording of laws exempting insurance from creditors' claims is broad enough to exempt cash values of policies from creditors of the insured. Court opinions have been divided where the statute is not clear. In some cases, where the statute uses the term "proceeds" without adding "cash values" or "avails," cases have restricted the protection to death proceeds only.

☐ *Creditors of the Insured—Death Proceeds:* Most state statutes restrict the rights of creditors of the insured in proceeds of life insurance. Some states exempt the entire proceeds; others limit it to a certain amount. Some limit the protection to proceeds payable to the insured's spouse or children; others to any dependent relative; and some to any beneficiary other than one who is himself the insured.

Proceeds paid to a trust for the benefit of a specific beneficiary normally have the same protection from creditors as if paid directly to the beneficiary.

☐ *Creditors of the Beneficiary—Cash Values:* Usually creditors of the beneficiary have no claims against cash values. The beneficiary has no vested right to cash values unless named irrevocably, and even then cannot usually cash in the policy without the insured's consent. Thus the beneficiary's creditors would have no rights without the consent of the insured.

☐ *Creditors of the Beneficiary—Death Proceeds:* Most statutes exempt proceeds from the claims of the insured's creditors only. In a few states the exemption applies to creditors of the beneficiary also.

If law does not exempt the proceeds from the beneficiary's creditors, the insured can extend this protection by adding to the settlement agreement in the policy a *spendthrift trust clause.* This states that proceeds payable to the beneficiary may not be assigned, transferred, commuted, or encumbered by the beneficiary, nor subject to legal process, execution, garnishment, or attachment. Policy proceeds must be made payable to the beneficiary under an installment or life income option. This arrangement usually has to be set up by the insured. The spendthrift trust clause only protects the money held by the company—when the beneficiary receives a payment, the money is available to creditors.

Annuities: Creditors' rights in annuities are not usually limited by exemption laws applying to life insurance—an annuity may be reached by creditors of the annuitant. A few states give a limited exemption to annuity income. One case held that a trustee in bankruptcy could reach the annuity income payable to an insured from the cash values of a life insurance policy *(Schaeffer, 189 Fed. 187).*

[¶2511] **FOR FURTHER REFERENCE . . .**

American Council of Life Insurance, *Life Insurance Fact Book,* American Council of Life Insurance, New York, New York.

Cantor, G., and Franklin, R., *The Ten Best Ways to Save Estate Taxes,* Institute for Business Planning, Inc., Englewood Cliffs, N.J. (1978).

Cuneo, D.C., ''How to Use Life Insurance as an Estate Planning Tool in Light of the New Law,'' 20 Taxation for Accountants 28 (1978).

Erdman, J., *Complete Guide to the Marital Deduction in Estate Planning,* Institute for Business Planning, Inc., Englewood Cliffs, N.J. (1978).

Forms of Business Agreements (2 vol. looseleaf service), Institute for Business Planning, Inc., Englewood Cliffs, N.J.

Life Insurance Planning (looseleaf service), Institute for Business Planning, Inc., Englewood Cliffs, N.J.

Stoeber, E.A., ''Current Planning for Life Insurance,'' 1978 Estates, Gifts and Trusts Journal No. 1, 4 (1978).

MATRIMONIAL MATTERS

[**¶2601**]   Matrimonial matters include premarital planning as well as separation and divorce proceedings. Protection of property rights of individuals prior to marriage, upon separation, and at the time of dissolution are important considerations for any lawyer. Alimony, child support, custody and visitation, and the tax treatment of antenuptial transfers are among the elements that must be carefully examined for each prospective client.

[¶2602]   ANTENUPTIAL AGREEMENTS

Prospective spouses may use an antenuptial agreement to define their property rights in property already existing or to be acquired during the marriage. By such an agreement, which may also be executed with a third party (e.g., parents), the property rights that would otherwise arise upon the marriage by operation of law are often substantially altered. Assuming that the parties have contractual capacity, antenuptial agreements are valid in all states.

[¶2603]   NONTAX CONSIDERATIONS

In order to be enforceable, an antenuptial agreement must comply with local law concerning consideration, disclosure of husband's assets, adequacy of the provision for the wife, undue influence, and other matters. In the majority of states, the Statute of Frauds requires that the agreement be in writing. In some states, the agreements must be executed in accordance with strict statutory requirements or else risk being declared void. The requirements pertaining to disclosure are particularly stringent, in light of the intimate nature of the relationship between the prospective spouses. The duty to disclose encompasses advising the relinquishing spouse of the nature, extent, and value of the released interest. Fraud, deceit, misrepresentation, or concealment by either party, or the exercise of duress or undue influence may void the agreement.

[¶2604]   ESTATE TAX CONSEQUENCES

The typical antenuptial agreement involves a payment by one spouse in exchange for relinquishment by the other of dower, curtesy, or other survivorship rights in the transferor's property. Since an individual's lifetime transfers may be includible in his or her gross estate under IRC §2035-2038 and §2041, except in the case of bona fide sales or an adequate and full consideration in money or money's worth, the following basic principles should be kept in mind:

☐   Under IRC §2035, any transfer within three years of death (for which a gift tax return was required to be filed at the time of the transfer) is automatically includible in the decedent's gross estate;

☐ Inclusion under IRC §2036 can be avoided if the decedent retains no life interest in the transferred property;

☐ In order to escape IRC §2037, the transfer must take effect before death and the transferor must not retain a reversionary interest;

☐ To avoid taxation under IRC §2038, the transfer must not be subject to revocation or amendment;

☐ Section 2041 of the IRC will not apply as long as the transferor has no general power of appointment over the transferred property.

However, if a transfer that would be subject to estate tax under one of these IRC sections is made in consideration of the release of support rights, instead of marital rights, there is no tax liability to the extent of the value of the support rights.

[¶2605]   **GIFT TAX CONSEQUENCES**

A transfer under an antenuptial agreement in exchange for the relinquishment of marital rights is treated as a taxable gift. If the transfer is in consideration of the release of support rights, instead of marital rights, there is no gift to the extent of the value of the support rights (*Rev. Rul. 68-379*, CB 1968-2, 414).

The courts have held that an unconditional promise to make a series of payments constitutes a taxable gift of the entire amount when the promise binding upon the promissor is made and not when the property is actually transferred *(Rosenthal,* CA-2, 205 F. 2d 505, 1953; *Copley,* CA-7, 194 F. 2d 364, 1952; *Harris,* CA-2, 178 F. 2d 861, 1950, *rev'd on other grounds* 340 US 106, 1950). The timing of the antenuptial agreement can give rise to important tax savings. If the agreement is treated as being executed prior to marriage, only the $3,000 annual exclusion is available. But if the "transfer" does not take place until after the marriage, the gift would qualify for the gift tax marital deduction under IRC §2523.

[¶2606]   **CLAIMS AGAINST THE ESTATE**

In order for a claim against the estate to be deductible under IRC §2053, it must be supported by an adequate and full consideration in money or money's worth. If the claim is based on the surrender of marital rights, it does not meet the consideration test and is not deductible. (See, for example *Sutton,* CA-4, 535 F. 2d 254, 1974.) The claim should be deductible if the transfer under the antenuptial agreement was made in consideration of the release of support rights.

[¶2607]   **INCOME TAX CONSEQUENCES**

For purposes of determining the transferee's basis for computing gain or loss on a subsequent resale, the transfer of antenuptial property is treated as a sale rather than a gift (*Farid-es-Sultaneh*, CA-2, 160 F. 2d 812, 1947). The transferee's basis is, therefore, the fair market value of the property at the date of its acquisition.

[¶2608] TERMINATION OF THE MARRIAGE

In most states, the ways of ending or suspending a marriage are: divorce, annulment, judicial separation, separation agreement, absence (presumption of death), and, of course, death.

Just as the state legislatures have power to regulate the creation of marriages, they also have the power to enact statutes prescribing the grounds for ending them. Accordingly, the grounds for termination of the marital relationship vary extensively from state to state.

As a general rule, an annulment differs from a divorce in that an annulment proceeding is brought to have a marriage declared void from its inception whereas a divorce arises from causes after the marriage. A separation agreement, on the other hand, does not dissolve the marriage. In many states, separation for a specified period of time is grounds for divorce.

[¶2609] ADULTERY

In most states, either spouse is given the right to an absolute divorce for the adultery of the other. The two essential elements of adultery are:

(1) Voluntary intercourse, and

(2) Guilty intent.

To prove adultery, both direct and circumstantial evidence, if competent, are generally admissable.

Adultery need not be continuing to constitute sufficient ground for a divorce decree—proof of a single act of adultery will be sufficient. Where adultery is relied upon as grounds for a judicial separation, it may be necessary to prove that the adultery is so open and notorious as to be cruel and inhuman.

Although there are few prosecutions, adultery is a crime in most states.

[¶2610] BIGAMY

When one spouse has a prior spouse living, the second marriage will be void and not merely voidable. In most states, bigamy constitutes grounds for annulment; in a few states, it also constitutes grounds for a divorce. In states where bigamy is the basis of both a divorce and annulment action, the party bringing the action will have the option of bringing the action for annulment or for divorce (*Schwartz v. Schwartz*, 173 N.E. 2d 393).

Before deciding whether or not to bring an action for annulment or divorce, local law should be checked; in some jurisdictions, alimony can only be awarded in a divorce action.

Because a bigamous marriage is void and not merely voidable, the parties may treat the marriage as a nullity without bringing formal proceedings. However, in many jurisdictions, the parties seek an annulment in order to have a decree rendered awarding alimony, child custody, and child support.

[¶2611]   AGE

Each state imposes statutory age requirements for the issuance of marriage licenses. A marriage involving a spouse who has not reached the legal age for marriage, either with or without consent, is voidable rather than void in most jurisdictions. An action to have the marriage annulled may be maintained by the spouse who had reached the legal age for marriage, the guardian of the infant, or the infant's "next best friend." Annulment for non-age will not be available if the spouse who had not reached the legal age at the time of the marriage freely cohabited after reaching the legal age. The non-age of the one spouse will not be available as grounds for an action of annulment to the spouse who was of legal age at the time of marriage.

[¶2612]   CRIME

In many jurisdictions, a criminal conviction and imprisonment may constitute grounds for divorce or the termination of the marital relationship. In some states, if either spouse is sentenced to life imprisonment, the marriage is absolutely and automatically dissolved without the need for legal process. The statutory provisions establishing grounds for divorce often include "infamous crimes," "crimes involving moral turpitude," or a felony.

Some states provide that a divorce may be granted even if the crime was committed before the marriage as long as the sentence was imposed after the marriage.

Although some state laws differ, the subsequent pardon of a convict should not destroy the right to a divorce declared by statute to arise on conviction and sentence.

[¶2613]   CRUELTY

In most states, cruelty constitutes grounds for a divorce or separation. Cruelty is not limited as a rule to physical violence or effects of physical violence but may include mental cruelty. Whether the misconduct constitutes cruelty for divorce purposes is determined by its effect on the person complaining about the acts. The important consideration is the health and safety of the suffering spouse; the motives of the offender are immaterial. What may be cruel behavior toward one person may not be cruel toward another.

The following test was applied in one leading English case: "What merely ruins the mental feelings is in few cases, to be admitted, where not accompanied by bodily injury, either actual or menaced. Mere austerity of temper, petulance of manner, rudeness of language, a want of civil attention and accommodation, even occasional sallies of passion, if they do not threaten bodily harm, do not amount to legal cruelty . . . . Under such misconduct of either of the parties . . . the suffering party must bear in some degree, the consequences of an injudicious connection, must subdue by dissent, resistance or prudent conciliation, and if this cannot be done, both must suffer in silence" *(Evans v. Evans*, 161 English Reprint 466).

The following specific acts of cruelty have been held sufficient grounds for divorce.

☐   Physical violence, even a single act of physical violence if sufficient to endanger life *(Crabtree v. Crabtree,* 154 Ark. 401). However a divorce will not be granted for every slight act of violence that a husband may commit against his wife or a wife against her husband *(Morris v. Morris,* 14 Cal. 76; *Hayes v. Hayes,* 86 Fla. 350).

☐   Habitual intemperance coupled with other acts that make it dangerous for the other spouse to continue in the marital relation (see *Grierson v. Grierson*, 156 Cal. 434). Addiction to narcotic drugs, together with other misconduct, may constitute cruelty *(Youngs v. Youngs,* 130 Ill. 230).

☐   Deliberate use of intemperate language with an intent to injure the other spouse (see *Sneed v. Sneed*, 14 Ariz. 17).

☐   False and unfounded accusations of adultery, especially where made against the wife or a false and unfounded accusation that the wife is a prostitute (see *Cottle v. Cottle*, 40 SE 2d 863).

☐   Refusal of one spouse to speak to the other for an extended period of time *(Hiecke v. Hiecke*, 163 Wisc. 171).

☐   Cruel treatment of a child in the presence of the wife *(Poe v. Poe,* 149 Ark. 62).

☐   Adultery may constitute legal cruelty *(Doolin v. Doolin*, 211 Ky. 207).

☐   Continuation of sexual relations after a spouse knows that he or she is afflicted with venereal disease and communication of the disease to the other *(Holden v. Holden,* 63 Idaho 70).

[¶2614]   **DESERTION AND ABANDONMENT**

In most states, desertion or abandonment for a statutory period of time will be grounds for divorce. The statutory period ranges from six months to five years. To establish desertion or abandonment, the plaintiff must establish an intent on the part of the other spouse to abandon or desert. There must be no justification for the desertion and it must be against the will and without the consent of the plaintiff. Leaving home to serve in the armed forces, to seek employment in a foreign city, to visit a health resort, etc., will not constitute desertion or abandonment. Similarly, separation pursuant to a valid separation agreement will not constitute desertion or abandonment. However, as noted below, where the parties separate pursuant to an agreement, the agreement should be made at or after the time of separation (see ¶2618).

Constructive abandonment will be a defense to an action for desertion or abandonment. If the defendant was justified in abandoning the plaintiff, he or she will have a complete defense to the plaintiff's action for abandonment. The doctrine of constructive abandonment is only applied in extreme circumstances.

Many states have enacted so-called Enoch Arden laws that permit the spouse to apply for a dissolution of the marriage if the other spouse has been absent for a statutorily defined period and he or she is believed to be dead. Generally, it is necessary to show the circumstances under which the missing spouse disappeared and that diligent efforts were made to locate the spouse. If the absent spouse disappeared under circumstances that indicate that it would not be anticipated that he or she would attempt to contact the other spouse and that efforts to locate would be pointless, the rules will not be applied. If the spouse remarries after a dissolution of the earlier marriage because of the absence of the first spouse and the initial spouse reappears, the validity of the second marriage will not be affected.

[¶2615] **DRUNKENNESS**

Habitual intoxication constitutes a statutory ground for divorce in most jurisdictions. A single instance of overindulgence or a tendency to overindulge on occasion will not constitute sufficient intoxication to be grounds for divorce. A statutory cause of action for divorce requires a fixed and almost irresistible habit of drinking alcoholic beverages with considerable frequency so as to produce intoxication. The spouse must have developed the habit after marriage. In some states, the statute requires that the habit must have continued for a period of one to two years.

[¶2616] **FRAUD**

Marriages induced by fraud are not absolutely void but merely voidable at the suit of the injured party during his or her lifetime. In a few jurisdictions, fraud is also recognized as a ground for divorce. To be a ground for divorce, fraud must relate to a matter essential to the validity of the marriage itself.

Marriage is essentially a contract and the rules relating to an ordinary contract will be applicable. Fraud that goes to the essence of the contract will constitute grounds for setting aside the contract. In the following situations, fraud has been sufficient to constitute grounds for annulment:

☐ Misrepresentation as to, or concealment of, prior marital status.

☐ Misrepresentation as to intention to subsequently go through a religious ceremony.

☐ Secret intent not to cohabit or have children.

☐ Concealment of a venereal disease or other serious health impairment.

☐   Concealment of a pregnancy at the time of marriage when the husband is not the father.

☐   False representations as to citizenship.

[¶2617]   INSANITY

The usual remedy for dissolution of a marriage where one of the parties was insane at the time of the ceremony is by a proceeding for annulment. The majority of states permit divorce on the ground of insanity or incurable insanity.

If the insanity existed at the time of the marriage, the sane spouse, in order to maintain an action for annulment, must establish that he or she did not know of the condition at the time of the marriage. If an action for annulment because of insanity at the time of the marriage is maintained by the insane spouse after regaining sanity, it is generally necessary to establish that the parties did not cohabit after the insane spouse regained sanity.

Where a spouse has been incurably insane for a statutory period of time (varying from 2 to 10 years), the statutes of several states specify a procedure whereby the marriage may be annulled. If the plaintiff is the husband, the court may require the husband to make provision for the support of his insane wife (see N.Y. Domestic Relations Law §7).

[¶2618]   SEPARATION AGREEMENT

Generally, a separation agreement will be enforceable where the parties are about to be separated when the agreement is made or the parties have previously separated. If the parties separate without an agreement, one party may be found to have abandoned or deserted the other. The parties must also comply with the statutory requirements as to the manner of execution. For example, most states require that the agreement be in writing.

The separation agreement is an agreement between the parties that they will live separate and apart from one another. It generally will also make provisions for the disposition of joint property and support rights, waiver and release of all future rights as spouse in each other's property; surrender of rights of inheritance, homestead, dower in each other's estate; and the execution of documents needed to implement the agreement.

If it appears that the benefits under the contract are conditioned on one party obtaining a divorce or the terms of the agreement encourage divorce, the agreement may be attacked as violative of the public policy against divorce (see *Pryor v. Pryor*, 88 Ark. 302; *Miller v. Miller*, 284 Pa. 414).

By the marital contract, the husband is obligated to support his wife during their joint lives. Even if the wife agrees to accept a stipulated amount in lieu of his support, the husband remains liable for her support, at least to the extent of keeping her from becoming a public charge.

In some jurisdictions, a valid contract for support of the wife is binding on the divorce court *(Galusha v. Galusha*, 116 N.Y. 635, 22 N.E. 1114). In others, the agreement is merely evidential and the divorce court is not controlled by it *(Williams v. Williams,* 261 N.C. 48, 134 S.E. 2d 227). A divorce court has the power to incorporate the agreement in the divorce decree or base the decree on its provisions.

The most delicate portion of the separation agreement often involves the question of child custody. Numerous factors including the age, health, schooling, and sex of the child will be important in determining which parent is to have custody. Similarly, the ability and the relative willingness of each parent to care for the child will be important. There is an increasing tendency on the part of the courts to award custody to the more qualified parent, regardless of sex.

The separation agreement should also deal with the question of insurance. The agreement will often provide that the husband should keep the insurance in effect and appoint the wife or children as irrevocable beneficiaries.

[¶2619] PROCEDURAL REQUIREMENTS FOR DIVORCE ACTIONS

When bringing an action for divorce, the plaintiff must first select the proper court. A court has no power to grant divorce without state statutory or constitutional authority. A second essential element of the court's divorce power is jurisdiction over the marriage status—that is, one of the spouses must have a domicile in the state.

In personam jurisdiction is generally not a prerequisite to a valid matrimonial decree, although it is necessary for a valid support order, alimony decree or order, or any other decree or order having the effect of an alimony decree.

[¶2620] PROCESS AND APPEARANCE

In many states, there is a special procedure for service of a summons in a matrimonial action. In some states, substituted service may not be available. In other states, notation of the nature of the action must be indicated on the summons if a summons is served without the complaint. Stricter rules concerning the process server's proof of service may be applicable. The process server may be required to prove how he or she identified the defendant.

In divorce actions, as in any other action, the court will not have jurisdiction to grant a divorce unless service of process has been made in accord with both the state and U.S. Constitutional requirements.

[¶2621] RESIDENCE REQUIREMENTS

Courts are generally less liberal in taking jurisdiction in matrimonial cases than in other civil actions. In most states, there is a statutory requirement that a person maintaining a matrimonial action be a resident of the state for a specified period of time prior to commencing the action. The residence requirement will often vary depending on factors such as the state's public policy toward matrimonial actions, whether the cause of action occurred in the state, whether the parties were married in the state, whether the parties are both residents of the state, and the nature of the action.

The residence requirements generally cannot be waived by consent between the parties.

[¶2622] PREPARATION, SETTLEMENT NEGOTIATION, AND TRIAL

Getting full command of the facts, preparing a comprehensive memorandum of law, and obtaining complete information about the financial situation are basic to successful negotiation, settlement, and trial.

This information-gathering process has three primary aims:

(1) Establishment of the acts or the facts that constitute the basis for separation and divorce.

(2) Development of financial factors that are the basis for alimony and settlement of property.

(3) Development of the factors that govern custody and visitation arrangements.

Because of the increasingly liberal divorce statutes, the divorce decree may be a near certainty. The real questions to be resolved will involve the financial and custody arrangements. It is essential to get all the information about family finances, scale of living, insurance policies, real estate, gifts, how living expenses were met, how support was provided, etc. As to children, a case history should be developed as to attitude, responsibility, and interest taken by each parent; medical and psychiatric histories; persons who might testify as to the best interests of the children and the relationship of possible witnesses to the parents; etc.

[¶2623] RECOGNITION OF FOREIGN DECREES

When a court with jurisdiction grants a divorce that is valid within that state, it is regarded as valid in every other jurisdiction.

The full faith and credit clause of the United States Constitution requires that the courts of one state give full faith and credit to the judgments and decrees of the courts in another state. However, full faith and credit are not afforded a decree if the court rendering the decree did not have jurisdiction over the parties to the action, i.e., if neither party had a domicile within the divorce state or the defendant did not receive personal service of process and did not appear in the action.

Similarly, a court need not give any greater credit to a decree of a court rendered in another jurisdiction than the court rendering the decree or another court in that jurisdiction would give the decree. For example, a New York court will look beyond the decree to determine if fraud was committed on an Alabama court in rendering an Alabama divorce if the Alabama court would look beyond the decree for that purpose. However, when a foreign decree has been rendered based on jurisdiction over the parties to the action, the courts in another state, even though it is the domicile of one of the parties to the action, cannot refuse to give the decree full faith and credit.

Foreign divorce decrees are governed by the rules of international comity rather than the stricter rules of full faith and credit dictated by the United States Constitution. However, as a matter of comity, foreign courts will generally recognize a decree of another country, provided it was based on a proper jurisdictional predicate.

[¶2624]   ALIMONY

As an incident to most matrimonial actions, the court will grant alimony. In the case of a separation agreement, the agreement will generally provide for support payments without necessarily using the term "alimony." However, most of the principles applicable to alimony are also applicable to these support payments.

To render a decree including alimony, the court must have in personam jurisdiction of the defendant against whom the decree is to be entered. If the court's jurisdiction is limited to in rem jurisdiction over the marital res because of constructive service on a nonresident defendant, the court will be limited to subjecting the local property of the nonresident defendant to the effect of the alimony decree, provided the property was attached prior to the decree. A majority of states have abolished sex discrimination in awarding alimony, so that husbands are also eligible to receive it.

Alimony may be permanent or temporary. After jurisdiction over the parties has been obtained, temporary alimony may be awarded in the court's sound discretion, to provide support for the needy spouse while the action is pending.

Permanent alimony is generally awarded as part of the divorce decree when all parties are before the court. If the parties entered into a separation agreement prior to the divorce, the agreement may be merged into the decree. Upon being merged into the decree, the agreement will become an integral part of the decree and can be enforced as an alimony decree. The agreement will not be binding on the court—the court may alter, increase, or decrease the provisions of the agreement. If the court has altered a separation agreement, it is the altered amount and not the original amount that is entitled to the special enforcement procedures of the equity court.

[¶2625]   FACTORS INFLUENCING ALIMONY AWARD

In the absence of an agreement to incorporate a prior separation agreement into the divorce decree, the court will set alimony in its sound discretion. Factors used by courts in setting alimony include:

(1) Conduct of the parties (which party is the guilty party).

(2) Financial condition of the parties.

(3) Anticipated earning capacity.

(4) Social standing of the parties.

In most cases, alimony will continue until the death of either spouse or the remarriage of the recipient. When a separation agreement is involved, this rule may be modified by the specific agreement of the parties. The cases are in conflict as to whether the remarriage of the recipient terminates the right to receive alimony when the second marriage is subsequently declared void or voidable.

A decree of permanent alimony may be modified by the court rendering it upon application of either party. Generally, an alimony decree will be modified when there is a showing of need or substantial alteration in financial conditions. The decree will also be modified upon a showing that the husband concealed his assets when the decree was originally entered.

In a few states, the courts have held that they may modify a divorce decree rendered in another state involving a domiciliary where they have jurisdiction over the parties (see *Worthley v. Worthley*, 44 Cal. 2d 465). However, the majority rule is still that a divorce decree must be modified by the court entering it.

[¶2626]   INCOME TAXATION OF ALIMONY PAYMENTS

A thorough understanding of the alimony rules can generate tax savings through incomesplitting. If a divorced or separated spouse makes qualifying payments to his or her spouse, they will be deductible by the payor-spouse under IRC §215 and taxable to the payee under IRC §71. Although the Code Sections presume that the husband will be the payor, IRC §7701(a)(17) makes it clear that the same rules apply if the wife is the payor.

For tax years prior to 1977, the payor could take advantage of the alimony payments deduction only if he or she itemized deductions on his or her income tax return. IRC §62(13) now permits the payor-spouse to subtract the alimony payments deduction allowed by IRC §215 from gross income to arrive at adjusted gross income. As a result, taxpayers with few itemized deductions can take advantage of the zero bracket amount and still deduct alimony payments.

To qualify for this tax treatment, the alimony, separate maintenance, or support payments must fit within one of the following classifications:

(1) Payments made under a decree of divorce or of separate maintenance or under a written instrument incident to such divorce or separation;

(2) Payments made under a written separation agreement; or

(3) Temporary support payments made under a decree pending divorce.

These rules are inapplicable if the spouses continue to file joint income tax returns and the payments do not qualify as periodic payments. Under classification (1) above, these periodic payments must be made in discharge of a legal obligation imposed upon or incurred by the payor because of the marital or family relationship under a court order or decree divorcing or legally separating the husband and wife or a written instrument incident to the divorce or legal separation status (Reg. §1.71-1(b)(1)). Under classification (2), the payments must be made under the terms of the written separation agreement executed after August 16, 1954, because of the marital or family relationship. The same rules apply whether or not the agreement is a legally enforceable instrument (Reg. §1.71-1(b)(2)). As for classification (3), Reg. §1.71-1(b)(3) states that it is not necessary for the husband and wife to be legally separated or divorced.

[¶2627]   **ALIMONY TRUSTS**

The payor's obligations for support and maintenance of the payee may be met by the establishment of a trust in an appropriate situation. When an alimony trust is used, the payee receives the current income and perhaps, ultimately, the principal of the trust.

If the decree or agreement provides for payment to be made through an alimony trust, he or she is taxable on the entire proceeds received, whether paid from income or corpus. The periodic payments are not deductible by the payor, but if the trust is irrevocable and the payor has not retained certain powers over it, the income is not taxable to him or her anyway.

When a payor makes a transfer to his or her spouse or to a trust for his or her benefit, it is in exchange for a valuable consideration if it is in discharge of a claim for support and maintenance. To that extent it is not a gratuitous transfer and is not subject to a gift tax. However, property settlement transfers made when divorce occurs within two years of agreement are treated as made for full and adequate consideration (see IRC §2516).

A typical alimony trust will provide for both the spouse and the children. Often, the remainder interest will be earmarked for the children. Transfers of capital to the children or in trust for them will be subject to the gift tax except to the extent that these transfers are for the support of the children during minority (Reg. §1.2516-2).

[¶2628]   **PAYMENTS FOR SUPPORT TO**
                          MINOR CHILDREN

If the terms of the decree, instrument, or agreement specifically designate that a portion of the periodic payments is payable for the support of the payor's minor children, that portion is neither deductible by the payor nor taxable to the payee (IRC §71(b)). However, according to the United States Supreme Court, ''The agreement must expressly 'fix' a sum certain or percentage of the payment for child support before any of the payment is excluded from the . . . (payee's) income'' *(Lester,* 366 US 299, 1961).

The door is open for attorneys to draft alimony agreements involving the support of a spouse and minor children that can achieve the desired tax effect. If it is most desirable for the payor to get the full deduction and the payee to be fully taxable on the entire amount he or she receives, the agreement should not specify any amount to be paid for the children's support. Provision can still be made for reduced payments to the payee as children marry, come of age, or die. If it is preferable that the payor give up part of the deduction so the payee is not taxed on a part of the income paid to him or her, then the alimony agreement should specify exactly how much is for the payee and how much is for the support of the children.

[¶2629]   ENFORCEMENT OF ALIMONY DECREES

A decree for permanent alimony may be enforced in the same manner as any debt. However, in most states, the equity court can enforce an alimony decree through contempt proceedings. In most states a husband may be committed for contempt of court after notice and a demand for payment (see *Lipton v.Lipton*, 211 Ga. 442). Alimony does not constitute a debt within the meaning of the constitutional prohibition of imprisonment for debt.

Although bankruptcy does not bar the wife's claims for alimony, the husband will not be required to stay in jail if he establishes a bona fide inability to pay (see *Bradshaw v. Bradshaw*, 133 S.W. 2d 617).

Sequestration is a means whereby the wife may obtain security for future payments of alimony or a fund from which defaulted payments of alimony may be collected. When the remedy of sequestration is relied upon, the court may cause the husband's personal property and the rents and profits of his real property to be sequestered and may appoint a receiver for them. In most jurisdictions, enforcement through sequestration will be available for either a domestic or foreign divorce decree.

[¶2630]   CHILD CUSTODY

When confronted with the question of child custody, the welfare of the child is the paramount consideration before the court. Although a divorce decree may fix the custody of the child, the court, at any time, may alter or amend the custodial provisions. Courts may renew the issue of child custody upon a writ of habeas corpus. Although courts often favor the mother when custody is at issue, they will not hesitate to give custody to the spouse who, in the opinion of the court, will be best for the child. If the child is sufficiently mature, the court will generally inquire as to the wish of the child, although the child's wishes will be far from conclusive. When the circumstances of the case require it, the court may grant custody to a grandparent, relative, or other third party to the action. Although they will generally be recognized, unless the welfare of the child dictates otherwise, contracts between spouses as to the custody of children will not be controlling on the court (see *Emrich v. McNeill*, 126 F. 2d 841, 146 ALR 1146).

When custody is awarded to one parent, visitation rights will generally be awarded to the other parent *(Scott v. Scott,* 154 Ga. 659). However, the court may limit the right to visit the child to a particular time and place or make the right conditional upon notice, etc.

Upon the death of the spouse having custody of the child, it is generally held that the right to custody will revert to the surviving spouse. However, the surviving spouse will not be entitled to custody if he or she cannot provide a suitable home.

The court rendering the divorce decree and determining the issue of custody retains jurisdiction to modify or alter the decree as to divorce at any time when it is in the best interests of the child. However, the doctrine of *res judicata* applies to that part of the divorce decree that grants custody, and the court cannot re-examine the facts formerly ajudicated and make a different order upon them. There must be a substantial change of circumstances to justify a substantial change in the custody order (see *Fortson v. Fortson*, 195 Ga. 750). When necessary to achieve the purposes of public policy—the best interests of the infant—the custody order may be modified because of facts existing at the time of the original order, although not brought out in court at that time.

Provision should also be made for visitation rights. If the parties enter into a separation agreement they will generally make some arrangement whereby the children will spend part of their vacations, holidays, and weekends with the other parent. When there is a determination, however, that one parent is not a fit parent, the visitation rights may be highly restricted.

The remarriage of either spouse will not automatically affect the custody of children by the former marriage. However, upon remarriage, the argument is often made that the remarried spouse now has a home for the child to replace the one broken by the divorce.

[¶2631]   THE DEPENDENCY DEDUCTION

Generally, the parent with custody of the children for the whole or greater part of the year gets the dependency deduction for income tax purposes. However, the parent without custody is entitled to the deduction if (1) the divorce or separate maintenance decree or a written agreement between the parents entitles him or her to it and such parent provides at least $600 for the support of the child, or (2) the parent not having custody provides $1,200 or more for the support of each child and the other parent can't prove that he or she provided more support (IRC §152).

[¶2632]   FOR FURTHER REFERENCE . . .

Berall, "Estate and Financial Planning for the Second Marriage: Ante- and Post-Nuptial Agreements," 4 Estate Planning 219 (1977).

Bernstein, "Handling Problems of Divorce and Separation," 34 New York University Institute on Federal Taxation 139 (1976).

Feld, "Divorce, Tax-style," 54 Taxes 608 (1976).

Hauver, Grach, Dickinson, Grande, and Harter, "The Divorce Situation," 10 Real Property, Probate and Trust Journal 633 (Winter 1975).

Thomas, *Tax Consequences of Marriage, Separation, and Divorce,* American Law Institute-American Bar Association, Committee on Continuing Professional Education, Philadelphia,Pennsylvania.

MORTGAGE FINANCING FOR REAL ESTATE

[¶2701]   Mortgages are the most traditional way of financing real estate. Ordinarily the arrangement is as follows: In response to a request or application, a lender advances money to a borrower. This is evidenced by a bond or note. To protect his interest, the lender requires the borrower to put up or mortgage his property. Thus a mortgage is an instrument by which the owner (mortgagor) offers his property as security to his lender (mortgagee). In this country there are two legal theories on how mortgages operate. Under the title theory (the minority view), the mortgagee holds title to the property and permits the mortgagor to possess the property. Once the mortgagor settles his debt with the mortgagee, title revests in him. The *lien theory* is the prevailing view among the states today. It provides that the mortgagee merely has a lien on the property as security for the loan made. In the event of default, the mortgagor can retain possession. Under either theory the premise is the same: The lender's interest is created to protect his interest in the money loaned. In addition to providing the property as security for the loan, the borrower is also personally liable for his obligation. This liability is evidenced by the borrower's note. If, on foreclosure a balance is still owing the lender, he may obtain a deficiency judgment, which is enforceable against any of the borrower's assets.

Mortgages are classified in terms of *time* or *priority*. In time, mortgages are either short-term, (usually one year) or long-term (over five years). By priority, mortgages are either senior or primary (first mortgages) or junior or secondary (second, third, or fourth mortgages). The priority of a mortgage is determined by its date of recordation. Therefore, if one mortgage is senior to another it was recorded first; it takes priority over all mortgages that were recorded after it. Even if a junior mortgage involves more money than a senior mortgage, it is lower in priority which means that if the senior mortgage is foreclosed, the junior mortgagee will receive nothing until the senior mortgage is satisfied.

[¶2702]   **CONSTRUCTION FINANCING**

The most important use of the short-term mortgage is to provide financing for construction of new buildings, or the improvement of existing structures. Some lenders are restricted by law from making these loans, and others do not do so from choice. The furthest these lenders will go is to issue a commitment for a "permanent" mortgage when the building is completed (known as a "take-out" commitment). There are two reasons why construction loans involve extra risk: First, possible delays in construction, or unanticipated costs, can result in failure of the project. Second, changes in the real estate or economic picture can make it impossible to obtain a profitable rent roll.

Short-term construction loans are made by commercial banks, some savings institutions, and private mortgage companies and investors who are attracted by the high return. The loans usually run for 12 to 18 months, although shorter periods can be arranged. The usual procedure for obtaining a construction loan is for the owner to approach the prospective lender with full details about the projected improvements and his own financial position. If the lender agrees to make the loan, it will issue a letter of commitment, which may or may not be legally binding on it, and this will be followed by a formal building loan contract and mortgage. Since it is the intention of both lender and borrower that the building loan will be paid off immediately upon completion of the improvements, there is often an agreement or understanding with the lender who will provide the permanent financing at that time. The result has aptly been termed a financing web in which each party is dependent on the ability and willingness of the others to carry out their commitments. Since the lenders are providing the bulk of the funds for a fixed interest return while the owner keeps the profits, if any, it is understandable that the former impose strict requirements for their loans and subject the property to continuous inspections. In the following paragraphs, which discuss the construction financing procedure in detail, emphasis is on the role of the property owner and his attorney and the extent to which they may be able to vary the relatively fixed requirements of the large institutional lenders that do much of the construction financing in this country.

[¶2703]   OBTAINING THE COMMITMENT

The following steps describe the procedure to obtain a construction loan from a large commercial bank in New York City.

(1) Application to Lender: The prospective borrower submits all information about the property and preliminary plans and specifications for the improvements. He should include the name of the architect, whose experience can be an important factor, and that of the general contractor (assuming the owner will not act as his own contractor) whose credit will be checked along with that of the owner. The borrower should already have ascertained that the particular lender is interested in the type of loan being sought (e.g., fee or leasehold mortgage, specialty loan, assignment of rents) since lenders vary their loans from time to time in order to keep a balanced portfolio and to seek out areas of highest interest return.

(2) Appraisal by Lender: The lender will first obtain a desk opinion (D.O.) from its appraisal division to see if its minimum loan requirements are met. This involves a study of the plans and specifications, a survey or plat plan, zoning requirements, and the economic potential of the proposed building. If this opinion is satisfactory, a physical inspection of the site is made, the title is searched, a formal appraisal (usually using the income capitalization approach) is prepared, and the credit rating of the owner and contractor is checked. The lender will also want to know where the balance of the construction funds will come from and any arrangements that have been made for permanent financing when the building is completed.

(3) Out-of-State Loans: If the borrower and the lender are citizens of different states, the lender will normally want to satisfy itself about several

important legal matters. One is whether the lender will be "doing business" in the foreign state if it makes the loan or if it later resorts to the foreign court to foreclose its loan. If the lender must qualify to do business in the state, it will want to know what is involved. Sometimes, this problem is avoided by having a local lender participate in the loan and carry on the proceedings in its name. The lender will also inquire about the redemption period in the event of foreclosure; this may be several years, during which the lender will be unable to dispose of the property. Mechanic's liens vary from state to state, and the lender will want to know if its loan will be subordinate to them. Finally, the lender will want to know about local property taxes and the likelihood of future increases.

(4) Terms of the Loan: The borrower will normally state in his application the amount of the loan requested and the interest rate he is willing to pay. When the lender comes to fixing the amount of the loan, it will make it a percentage of the value of the improved property. For example, 70% of the value of an apartment or office building may be loaned, or 50% of the value of a motel or other specialized type of business. In addition, the lender may limit the construction loan to 90% of the "take-out" (the commitment for the permanent mortgage loan). The interest rate will be that prevailing for the type of loan involved. In addition, the lender will charge a "processing fee," which in reality is a discount. The discount varies with the term of the loan and the amount of risk. For example, a $1,000,000 loan may be made at 12% interest plus a $10,000 processing fee. Half the processing fee may be due at the time the letter of commitment is issued and will be nonrefundable if the loan does not go through. The other half will be paid at the closing of the loan. The 12% interest will be payable only on funds actually advanced to the owner (although sometimes there is a provision for stand-by interest, payable even though no money is actually loaned). All these factors make the actual interest rate different from the stated rate.

(5) Commitment Letter: If the loan negotiations are concluded satisfactorily, the lender will issue a letter of commitment, which constitutes an approval of the loan application. The letter sets forth the details of the loan as well as the conditions that must be satisfied before the loan closing (final plans and specifications, bonds, etc.). It is unclear whether the commitment letter is legally binding on the lender. Most jurisdictions do not permit the borrower to sue for specific performance of the commitment, but in some states he may recover special damages if they can be shown.

(6) Closing the Loan: The final step in the procedure is the loan closing, at which time the mortgage, bond, if any, and other documents are executed. The lender then will advance funds to the owner in accordance with their agreement.

[¶2704]   **CHECKLIST FOR CONTENTS OF A COMMITMENT LETTER**

The commitment letter for the construction or interim loan will usually cover the following basic points:

☐ Amount and Terms of Loan (details of terms, including interest rate and method of computing it, amount of loan, etc.).

☐ Service Charge or Loan Fee.

☐ Status of Lien (mortgage or trust deed shall be first lien).

☐ Secondary Financing (no secondary financing permitted).

☐ Loan Documents (execution and recording of documents such as promissory note, mortgage, or trust deed, construction loan agreement, assignment of rents, borrower's receipt, tenant's acceptance statement, estoppel certificate, personal guarantees if any, and agreements creating security interests in personal property if appropriate).

☐ Title (title insurance or other evidence of title).

☐ Construction Contract (copy executed by all the parties, submitted before opening the loan, along with copy of building permit).

☐ Survey (obligation of lender conditioned on receipt of survey).

☐ Building and Zoning Requirements (lender's obligation contingent on improvements conforming to zoning and building requirements).

☐ Permanent Mortgage Commitment (borrower to comply with permanent mortgage commitment).

☐ Leases (assignment of leases, if any).

☐ Insurance (fire and extended coverage with standard mortgage clause, liability, business interruption, rent loss, workmen's compensation, completion bonds, with lender named as co-obligee, etc.).

☐ Completion of Improvements (substantial conformity with plans and specifications on which appraisal was based; part of loan balance withheld pending final completion).

☐ Opening of Loan (conditions precedent, such as, for example, that loan balance be deposited with lender in cash or mechanic's lien waivers).

☐ Progress Payments (percentage of completion and number, payment to general contractor on presentation of lien waivers or directly to subcontractors, architect's certificates).

☐ Time for Acceptance (limitation of time for acceptance of commitment and payment of commitment fee).

☐ Accuracy of Application (lender's obligation conditioned on accuracy of information contained in loan application and supplementary documents).

☐ Expiration Date (date when commitment expires).

[¶2705]   **CHECKLIST OF BORROWER'S IMPORTANT CONSIDERATIONS IN REVIEWING A MORTGAGE COMMITMENT**

The following checklist gives a rundown on the important provisions of a commitment for a permanent mortgage, along with suggested accommodations and modifications a borrower might request of the lender under particular circumstances.

☐ *Obligation to Take Loan:* The commitment or acceptance by the borrower will obligate the borrower to take the loan unless it is a standby commitment, in which case provisions obligating the borrower to take the loan and for damages on the borrower's failure to close are not appropriate.

☐ *Evidence of Indebtedness and Security:* The commitment will set forth the amount and terms of the loan and the mortgage note or extension agreement. Since the loan will probably be made on the strength of the security (the property), the borrower might be able to get a provision in the note and mortgage limiting the borrower's liability to its interest in the property.

☐ *Interest Rate:* The rate of interest charged may require a corporate borrower to avoid violating usury laws. There are different approaches to having the corporate entity bypassed for federal tax purposes and having the beneficial owners of the property rather than the corporation, bear the tax consequences of the deal or project.

☐ *Mortgage Lien:* The commitment will provide that the mortgage will be a first lien on a good and marketable title in fee simple. The borrower might want to add language making the coverage subject to covenants, agreements, restrictions, and easements of right-of-way for utilities that are not to be violated by the buildings constructed unless the borrower has a title search, in which case exceptions should be approved in advance.

☐ *Security Interest:* In addition,, the loan may be secured by a security interest duly perfected under the UCC, covering fixtures, equipment, articles of personal property, etc. The borrower should make sure that the security interest covers only property owned by the borrower.

☐ *Prepayment Privilege:* The borrower will want to avoid, if possible, specified prepayment dates and stiff penalties.

☐ *Title and Marketability of Title:* Where the commitment is conditioned on approval by the lender's attorneys as to all matters concerning title and marketability of title, the borrower should make explicit the identity of the title company or companies that will be used and whether the lender, if several are to be used, will accept reinsurance or will insist on coinsurance of title.

☐ *Certificate of Occupancy:* The borrower will try to get approval by the lender's attorneys to close the loan without a certificate of occupancy on a showing that the property has been built in accordance with the building and zoning code and can be legally occupied.

☐ *Appraisal:* The commitment will be conditioned on receipt by the lender of a satisfactory appraisal. The borrower should get a refund of the deposit and a termination of all liability if the appraisal proves unsatisfactory.

☐ *Construction Lender:* The commitment will be conditioned on the execution of a buy-sell agreement with the construction or interim lender. The buyer will want to obtain notification as to whether the interim or construction lender is acceptable to the permanent lender if the permanent lender will take by assignment only.

☐ *Leases and Tenancies:* The commitment will be conditioned on the approval of leases and tenancies. The borrower will want the lender to agree to enter into nondisturbance agreements with tenants whose leases are superior, especially with major tenants who can be expected to insist on nondisturbance agreements.

☐ **Condemnation:** The borrower will want the lender to agree to use condemnation and casualty awards for restoration purposes. Frequently, a lender will want the right to apply the award to the reduction of the balance of the loan still due. The tenant, of course, will want the award to be applied to restoration work.

☐ **Possession of Premises by Tenants:** The borrower should try for a provision that the tenants' acceptance of the premises and commencement of rent payments are sufficient to comply with the lender's requirements in this regard rather than that the tenants must be in possession of the demised premises and open for business (if this type of provision is applicable).

☐ **Substitution of Tenants:** The borrower should try for the right to substitute tenants for any of the tenants that appear in the commitment as long as the substituted tenants are of equal credit standing.

☐ **Modifications, Prepayments, or Termination of Leases:** The commitment may be conditioned on giving the lender control as to modifications, prepayment, or termination of leases, and on the assignment to the lender as additional security of the landlord's interest in the affected lease. The borrower should get a copy of the instrument used by the lender to safeguard the rights covered by this provision of the commitment.

☐ **Deposit:** The commitment may require a deposit of cash by the borrower on acceptance of the commitment. The borrower might try to substitute a letter of credit or a certificate of deposit for a refundable commitment fee in cash. If the borrower's note and mortgage or a letter of credit is substituted for cash, the borrower's costs can be further reduced.

☐ **Real Estate Taxes:** A requirement that the mortgage or extension agreement include a provision for deposits with the mortgagee of estimated real estate taxes should be modified to reflect net leases and the lender's approval of net leases.

☐ **Overages:** Overage provisions should be carefully checked to see whether they include fees collected by the landlord-borrower for services rendered to the tenant. If overages are figured on the rent of each rentable unit, the borrower may be hurt, since he gets no offset for units whose rent was decreased or units that are vacant. Ask for copies of the mortgage instruments.

☐ **Ownership:** Language in the commitment as to the ownership of the property, both legally and beneficially, and that the proceeds of the loan will be used for the borrower's corporate purposes, etc., are inserted in the commitment to avoid the charge of usury. The language may have to be adapted to the particular method chosen to avoid the application of the usury laws.

☐ **Insurance:** The commitment will be conditioned on the delivery to the lender of satisfactory fire insurance policies appropriately endorsed to show the lender's interest as mortgagee. If the borrower has a single major tenant that is a self-insurer, this should be stated in the commitment.

☐ **Fees and Disbursements:** The borrower will be required to pay disbursements and fees. If the lender's attorney gets a title commission, the cost to the borrower may be higher. Disbursements incurred by the lender's attorney to a local attorney should be checked.

☐ **Participations:** If the commitment provides for participations, the borrower should see whether participants will create additional counsel fees.

CHECKLIST FOR BUILDING LOAN AGREEMENT AND MORTGAGE

The building loan agreement (or the letter of commitment when no formal agreement has been made) substantially sets forth the obligation of the lender to make the loan, and of the owner to construct the improvements described therein. The loan is not made at one time, but portions or advances are given when the building reaches each stage of construction specified in the payment schedule. A typical schedule for a large office building might have twelve stages, the final one being full completion of the building, including the issuance of a certificate of occupancy. Other significant provisions of the agreement are as follows:

[¶2707] ## REPRESENTATIONS BY THE BORROWER

(1) Corporate Existence: The lender ordinarily will want the borrower to be a corporation so that any question of usurious interest is avoided. In addition, a "one-shot" corporation eliminates the possibility that outside creditors will be able to proceed against the particular property. The borrower will have to represent that the corporation is in valid existence and that all necessary resolutions of the directors and shareholders have been passed.

(2) Capital Stock of the Corporation: Since the lender will want to know the true identity of the borrower, the names of all shareholders will have to be submitted. In addition, the corporation and its shareholders may be asked to covenant that no stock will be transferred or issued so that the present shareholders will own less than 51%. The construction lender, more than the permanent lender, looks to the experience and integrity of the building owner, since failure to complete the building on time may endanger the loan.

(3) No Violations or Damage: The borrower must represent that no violations exist and that the property has suffered no damage at the time of the loan. This too is important because it might affect the completion date.

(4) Building Leases: The construction lender is vitally interested in leases that the builder makes with tenants because the permanent mortgage, the proceeds of which will pay off the construction loan, is conditioned upon satisfactory leases in terms of both quality and amount of rent. The borrower will have to submit copies of any leases already entered into. Sometimes, a "step-up" loan will be made, i.e., the amount of the loan may be increased as new tenants are signed up.

(5) Construction Plans and Specifications: The lender will want to see completed plans for the improvements and the agreement with the general contractor, unless the borrower intends to act as his own contractor. The lender may want to make a separate agreement with the general contractor and the architect so that, in the event of a default by the borrower, they will work for the lender under the same agreements they have with the borrower. If permitted by state law, the lender may also want the borrower to obtain waivers (in favor of the lender) by the general contractor and major subcontractors of their rights under the lien law.

(6) Performance or Completion Bonds: The borrower-contractor may be required to post a bond for the purpose of insuring completion of the building by a specified date.

(7) Permanent Financing: Representations about permanent financing are discussed at ¶2710.

[¶2708]   **COVENANTS BY THE BORROWER**

(1) Completion of the Improvements: The borrower normally must agree to a definite completion date and agree to proceed with "all reasonable dispatch." Since the failure to comply with either of these stipulations usually constitutes a default and accelerates the entire loan, the borrower should make provision for contingencies, such as weather, labor disputes, fire, etc.

(2) Approval of Lender to Change in Plan: The lender wants the right to approve changes because any substantial modifications may terminate the obligation of the permanent lender.

(3) Inspection of Premises; Financial Statements: The lender will reserve the right to inspect the premises during construction and prior to making any advances. Similarly, it will require the borrower to submit financial statements periodically so that any financial difficulties may be anticipated.

[¶2709]   **RELATIONSHIP BETWEEN THE CONSTRUCTION LOAN AND THE PERMANENT MORTGAGE**

Construction financing is short-term when the source of repayment is clearly understood to be the permanent mortgage that will be placed on the completed building. Construction loans can be classified into four types, depending on their relationship to the permanent financing.

(1) Open-End: In an open-end loan, the borrower has no commitment for permanent financing. The construction lender thus assumes a risk that no mortgage can be obtained when the building is completed. This risk normally is assumed only when the real estate market is very strong or when the borrower has an outstanding reputation.

(2) Take-Out: This is the most common type of construction financing. At the time the construction loan is closed, the borrower already has a commitment for a permanent mortgage. The construction lender thus has an assured source of repayment, *provided* the borrower meets the conditions of the permanent loan commitment. See below.

A variation of the "take-out" commitment is the "standby" commitment. This involves an agreement by a lender to make a permanent mortgage loan in a specified amount within a specified period, when called upon by the borrower. The amount of the mortgage loan is substantially below its face amount (that is, the lender will get the mortgage loan at a discount), and the borrower must pay a standby fee, usually 1% or more. The standby commitment is generally used when mortgage money is tight. At such times, interest rates are high and lenders usually demand a discount to make a permanent mortgage loan. In effect, the builder is gambling that the mortgage money picture will change by the time his project is completed, and that he will then be able to get full financing at a lower rate of interest.

Buy-sell agreements are frequently used in connection with the "take-out" form of construction loan. The agreement essentially provides that the permanent lender will, when the building is completed, buy the construction loan or advance the necessary funds so that the borrower can pay it off. The advantage of the agreement for the construction lender is that he can enforce the agreement against the permanent lender, something he cannot do when there is only a "take-out" commitment in favor of the borrower. The agreement, however, does contain the same conditions as the commitment, e.g., completion by a given date, satisfactory leases, etc.

In a *two-party* buy-sell agreement, the parties are the construction lender and the permanent lender. Since this doesn't bind the borrower, he might conceivably find a lender willing to make a permanent mortgage under more favorable terms and abandon the original commitment. To prevent this, a *three-party* buy-sell agreement is sometimes used, in which the borrower also is a party and is obliged to accept the permanent loan.

(3) Combination Loan: Sometimes the construction lender will also provide the permanent financing, combining the two loans into one. The advantage of this procedure for the builder is that he makes all his financing arrangements at one place and at one time, thus eliminating extra commissions, service charges, and fees. The lender benefits in several possible ways: (1) It assures itself of getting the permanent loan, which is the source of most of its profit. (2) By inspecting the building during construction, it can see that the plans and specifications are properly followed. (3) It can charge a slightly higher overall rate because of the extra risk involved in the construction part of the loan.

The other side of the picture, for the builder, is that by waiting until completion of the building, he may be able to get a 20% larger loan at an interest rate ¼ to ½ point lower. There are several reasons for this. First, more lenders make permanent loans than construction loans. Second, there is considerably less risk in lending on a completed building. Finally, the builder himself is frequently under less pressure in arranging the permanent financing and so he can shop around more.

There is one situation in which the builder may reap a substantial tax benefit by taking out the combined loan. This is when he intends to sell the completed property and wants to defer his taxable gain on the sale. Under the installment reporting rules of IRC §453, he cannot receive more than 30% of the sale price in the year of sale. If he takes out only a construction loan, and the buyer arranges for the permanent financing and pays over the mortgage proceeds to the seller, the 30% limit will normally be exceeded. But since an existing mortgage assumed by the buyer isn't figured in when computing the 30% payment (except to the extent that it exceeds the seller's basis), the combined building and permanent loan may permit use of the installment method, thus permitting a substantial tax benefit.

(4) Guarantee of Payment: The very unusual type of loan is conditioned upon the borrower's guarantee that the loan will be repaid upon completion of the building. Very few builders are in a position to give such a guarantee, and if they were, there would normally be no need for the loan in the first place. Sometimes, the builder may be able to obtain the guarantee of a third party.

[¶2710]   PERMANENT FINANCING

The long-term mortgage loan is the key feature distinguishing real estate from all other forms of investment. In no other area will a lender agree to lend 75% or more of the value of the security for terms of up to 30 years. Real estate will support such loans because of its *stability* and *long-term growth potential*. These features in turn derive from the limited and fixed supply of land that must support a constantly growing population.

Actually, the long-term mortgage reflects the same underlying division of interest in real estate as does the long-term lease. Both divide the long-term investor seeking a fixed return from the short- or medium-term operator who seeks a higher but more speculative return. The lender who extends a 20-year mortgage on a building (and who probably will be willing to refinance it at the end of that period, assuming it has been well maintained) can be compared to the owner who extends a 20-year net lease with renewal options. Looking at it from the other side, the borrower-owner can be compared to the net lessee. Both may have invested approximately the same amount of ''equity'' money (the former to buy the building, and the latter to buy the leasehold) and both anticipate an operating income that will represent a high return on their leveraged investment. If the building loses money, each is prepared to abandon his interest to the long-term investor who has provided the major financing. (This assumes, as is usually the case, nonrecourse loans when neither the operator-owner nor the net lessee is personally liable for his obligations.)

The major sources of long-term mortgage money are insurance companies, pension funds, savings and loan associations, mutual savings banks, and commercial banks.

[¶2711]   CHECKLIST FOR LONG-TERM MORTGAGES

The procedure for obtaining permanent financing is similar to that for construction financing. The borrower applies to the lender, submitting all pertinent data and asking for a loan of a stated amount, term, and interest. If the lender agrees to make the loan, a letter of commitment will be issued. In the case of an existing structure, the closing of the loan will follow shortly thereafter. When new construction is involved, the formal closing will be postponed until the building is completed and only at that time, and provided the conditions set forth in the commitment are met, will the mortgage be signed and the money paid. Many states have statutory forms of mortgages that may be used if the parties wish; their value is that the meaning of many phrases and clauses is spelled out in the statute. Institutional lenders usually have their own forms that they will require to be used; these, naturally, will tend to favor the lender's position.

The following is a brief description of the important provisions of the long-term mortgage:

☐ *Amount:* The amount of the loan is most often determined as a percentage of the value of the property at the time of the loan. Thus many institutional lenders are limited to a ratio of 66⅔% or 75%. The lender will make its own careful appraisal of the property to determine its value. Frequently, however, the value of the completed building is substantially higher than the cost of the vacant land plus construction. This is most often true when value is computed by the income capitalization method (i.e., by capitalizing the rental income provided by the existing leases). On occasion, this value may be so much higher than cost that the borrower is able to obtain 100% of his cost—mortgaging out, as it is called.

☐ *Interest Rate:* This is determined by current money market rates. Normally, a portion of each repayment by the borrower represents interest to date and the remainder is amortization. If the lender is willing, however, the ratio of interest to principal can be set at any proportion the borrower desires.

☐ *Amortization:* Long-term loans may be classified into four groups, depending on the extent that they are repaid prior to maturity:

(1) The Standing Mortgage or Straight Loan: This is a mortgage loan for a definite term of years, payable in full at maturity. Throughout the term of the loan, the borrower pays only the interest on the loan; he makes no payments in reduction of the mortgage principal. When the loan matures, the borrower must either (a) pay the loan in full, (b) ask the lender to extend the loan for another term, (c) refinance the loan for another term with another lender, or (d) have the lender carry the loan as an open or past-due debt.

The straight loan is costly and dangerous to the borrower. No matter how long the term of the loan, the borrower must always pay interest on the original amount and at maturity he still has the full amount of the loan to pay. If he cannot pay the loan in full or refinance it, he may lose his property. For the lender, the straight loan may also be dangerous: The property may depreciate in value, so if the lender has to foreclose, it may not bring enough to pay the loan in full.

(2) The Partially Amortized Mortgage or Balloon Mortgage: Today, most lenders insist that mortgage loans be amortized, that is, the borrower make periodic payments of principal and interest throughout the term. While fully amortized loans are the rule for residential financing, partial amortization is common for income-producing properties. In the latter case, the borrower's periodic payments will not completely liquidate the mortgage loan at maturity. Instead, a substantial amount called the "balloon," will remain unpaid. The lender is willing to agree to the balloon because the loan is based primarily on the

property itself, rather than on the credit of the borrower (as is the case in residential loans). The lender feels reasonably certain that at the maturity of the loan (e.g., 10 or 15 years), the property will be of sufficient value so that the loan can be renewed or extended for the unpaid balance. If extended, there will be further amortization of the mortgage principal during the new term.

(3) The Fully Amortized or Self-Liquidating Mortgage: Here the periodic payments made by the borrower during the term of the loan result in the mortgage being paid in full at maturity. Virtually all home mortgage loans are now self-liquidating. This means that homeowners are constantly increasing the equity in their homes, though not at a constant rate, since most of their payments go for interest in the early years. Similarly, commercial loans on shopping centers, motels, and other specialty properties are ordinarily fully amortized, since the lender is looking to the credit of the borrower as his primary security and is not counting on the property to retain or increase its value. Monthly payment tables are contained in the Appendix.

(4) The Combination Loan and the Variable Amortization Loan: The combination loan combines a period of straight lending with a period of amortization. The smaller the proportion of the loan to the value of the property, the longer the period of straight lending that will be allowed. Sometimes the first few years will be without amortization. This gives the borrower a chance to develop the property and build up income; consequently, it is used mostly for new properties. On the other hand, the lender may want amortization to begin at once so that the amount at risk is reduced; once it reaches a certain proportion of the value of the property, he will permit it to be carried as a straight loan. These same objectives can be achieved by the use of variable amortization as well. If the parties estimate that the income from the property will be highest in the first few years, higher amortization during that period will be borne most easily by the borrower. Alternatively, the amortization can be tied to a varying rate of depreciation.

☐   *Covenant of Repayment:* In most long-term loans on real estate, the lender regards the property as his primary security. With respect to the personal obligation of the borrower, three alternatives exist:

(1) Personal liability—The lender may insist that the borrower assume personal liability, either by a covenant to pay included in the mortgage or by a separate instrument. In the latter event, a corporate borrower should seek to use a note instead of a bond, since this eliminates the cost of revenue stamps. This may not be possible when the lender, by law, is limited to loans on *bonds*.

(2) Use of a nominee or dummy—The lender may be willing to waive personal liability but a statute may require it. In that case, a nominee without assets may act for the borrower and later convey the property to him subject to the mortgage. Local law must be checked, however, to see if the assumption of liability by the nominee (who is the borrower's agent) is imputed to his principal.

(3) No personal liability—When the lender agrees to waive any personal liability and the borrower's cash investment in the property is small, the borrower in effect has a long-term option.

☐ *Security:* The mortgage lien covers all of the real estate described therein, including *fixtures*, i.e., personal property affixed to the realty. The lender may want the mortgage to include a lien on personal property. Since the definition of a fixture varies from jurisdiction to jurisdiction, the lender may list all items of personal property in order to eliminate any question about coverage. Sometimes the security clause will apply to after-acquired property as well. Strictly speaking, this is merely a covenant to give a mortgage at the time the property is acquired. Many lenders will require additional mortgage instruments to be executed at that time. The lender must be sure to record the mortgage both as a *real estate* mortgage and as a *chattel* mortgage in order to preserve his rights.

☐ *Prepayment:* This is a vital clause for the borrower. In its absence, he may not be able to pay off the mortgage even though the property is condemned or destroyed. Or, as is more often the case, he may want to refinance at a time when interest rates have declined. The lender frequently will agree to prepayment after a minimum period (e.g., five years) and at a reasonable penalty.

☐ *Demolition of Improvements:* In the usual printed mortgage, any demolition of existing improvements will constitute a default, since it impairs the lender's security. If the borrower is contemplating demolition, appropriate provision should be made. The lender's agreement will be conditioned on the borrower's obligation to install new improvements.

☐ *Insurance Proceeds:* The lender, of course, will require the borrower to maintain fire and other insurance on the property for the lender's benefit. If the mortgage is silent, the lender may apply the insurance proceeds to payment of part of the mortgage debt instead of for restoration of the property. In that case, the borrower will have to arrange new financing, and if he can't prepay the outstanding mortgage, this may be impossible. The borrower should seek to require the lender to use the proceeds for restoration or, if that is not possible, obtain the right to prepay the remaining loan.

☐ *Condemnation Awards:* In the case of a partial condemnation, the problems are similar to those with insurance proceeds. The lender in this case is much less likely to agree to use the proceeds to restore the property, since its security has been reduced by the condemnation.

☐ *Prohibition Against Junior Liens:* The lender may not want the property encumbered by a second mortgage since this increases the risk of a default followed by a foreclosure by the junior mortgagee, to the possible detriment of the primary mortgagee. A possible compromise is for the borrower to agree that any junior lien will be made subordinate to the existing leases; in this way, a foreclosure cannot terminate the leases, which constitute the real security for the primary lender.

☐ *Encumbrances:* The lender will normally require that there be no encumbrances on the property ahead of the first mortgage—such as mechanic's liens. In addition, this may be a statutory requirement for institutional lenders. In the case of *leases*, however, the situation may be different. Since, as we noted above, the leases are the true security for the loan, the lender wants to be sure that they will not terminate if the first mortgage is foreclosed. The mortgage must make provision for this in light of local law. There are two situations:

(1) Foreclosure terminates all subordinate liens—If the jurisdiction requires the mortgagee to join all subordinate liens (and terminate them) in a foreclosure action, the mortgagee can make existing leases *superior* to the mortgage lien. If the lender is prohibited from doing this by statute, it may execute a nondisturbance agreement, in which it agrees not to terminate the lease as long as the rent is paid. A nondisturbance agreement may be so broad as to be the equivalent of making the first mortgage a subordinate lien.

(2) Foreclosure terminates subordinate liens at lender's option—When the lender may join only such tenants as he wishes in the foreclosure action, it need make no provision in the mortgage. However, certain of the *tenants* may be in a position to demand nondisturbance agreements from the lender in order to protect themselves.

☐ *Assignment of Leases:* The lender may fear that if the borrower is heading toward a default, he may cancel or amend certain leases in favor of the tenants in exchange for cash payments. An "anti-milking" provision may require the borrower to assign all leases to the lender to protect against this contingency. Since this amounts to a future assignment, it may be deemed fraudulent and void in some jurisdictions. As an alternative, the lender may require that no lease be amended or canceled without its consent.

[¶2712]   **LEASEHOLD FINANCING**

Leasehold financing is a special form of secondary financing in which the builder or investor enters into a lease with the property owner and then gets a mortgage on the leasehold. The mortgagee gets a secondary lien, even if the mortgage is a first mortgage, because the lessor's interest takes priority over it. (Note, however, that the lessor can voluntarily subordinate his fee to the leasehold mortgage.) A leasehold mortgage is distinguished from a fee mortgage in that the security for a leasehold mortgage is a defeasible estate (the lease).

Subordination: As indicated above, the owner (lessor) of the property may or may not subordinate his interest in the property to the interest of the leasehold mortgagee. If the lessor's interest is subordinated, the leasehold mortgagee is in almost the same position he'd be in if he were the mortgagee of the fee. Because complications can arise under a subordination agreement, some lenders require a mortgage on the fee along with the leasehold mortgage. Owners, however, are often averse to this arrangement, and some won't consent to a subordination agreement. Besides putting his land in jeopardy, subordination also restricts the owner's power to borrow in the future. To overcome the owner-lessor's hesitation, the following points can be raised:

(1) If the owner subordinates or mortgages his interest, the lessee can get a larger or better loan, which means he can pay a higher rental.

(2) Subordination allows the lessee to put up a more expensive building, which is to the lessor's benefit.

(3) If the owner erected the building himself, he'd have to mortgage the

property anyway, so in terms of risk and credit he'd be no worse off with subordination.

[¶2712.1]   Sources of Leasehold Mortgage Financing

Life insurance companies are the prime lending source for leasehold financing. They are extremely flexible both as to the type of properties and the geographic distribution of their loans. Other lenders include national commercial banks and federal savings and loan associations, and in some states the state counterparts of these institutions, as well as mutual savings banks.

[¶2713]   WHEN LEASEHOLD FINANCING IS USED

When investing in income-producing property, it's important to consider at the outset whether a long-term ground lease (subject to a leasehold mortgage) is better under the circumstances than acquiring outright ownership (subject to a long-term mortgage). With a lease, the existing owner in effect provides part of the financing, since, as a lessor, he retains an interest in the property. The lessee has to raise only the funds necessary to buy the leasehold (or construct the improvements) and then pay the yearly rent. Whether this will work out depends on the prospective seller's evaluation of the property as a good long-term investment for the money he could have obtained from the sale, and on the prospective buyer's willingness to settle for a long-term lease. If the lease is entered into, the buyer gets the tax benefit of deducting his rent payments and, in effect, puts the land on a tax-deductible basis. (If he buys, his payments of mortgage principal would not be deductible—only his interest payments would be deductible.) The seller keeps his depreciation deductions for the property.

Careful analysis is necessary before deciding that a lease (plus a leasehold mortgage) is the best approach under a particular set of circumstances. If minimum capital is available for the investment, maximum financing is available via the lease plus leasehold mortgage rather than via a fee mortgage. However, analysis might reveal that less capital is, in fact, needed or that it is possible to raise the same amount through a fee mortgage plus an unsecured loan for the balance. (Such an unsecured loan would depend on the personal credit of the builder or investor.)

Sometimes property can only be obtained by way of a lease. For example, prime land in cities may be held by owners who never intended to sell. In addition, both the investor and the owner can obtain certain tax benefits by a lease that they could not obtain by a sale. For example, an owner may find it advantageous to lease his property, if his real estate has appreciated to a point that the tax he would have to pay on a sale (even at capital gain rates) would be prohibitive.

[¶2714]   LEASEHOLD MORTGAGE CHECKLIST

☐   *Amount:* The loan will be a percentage of the value of the improved property. Because of the somewhat greater risk in a leasehold mortgage, the ratio is frequently lower than that in a fee mortgage. The value of the property is computed in the same manner as for the fee mortgage, except that the ground rental is an additional item of expense. Put another way, the value of a leasehold is its economic rent (the rent income received from the sublessees) minus the contract rent (the ground rental). This value is the security for the loan.

☐ *Term and Interest:* Because of the higher risk, interest rates are somewhat higher on leasehold mortgages. The term of the loan will not exceed the term of the lease, and normally must be fully amortized within that period. If renewal terms have been included in measuring the term of the lease, the lender may require the borrower to exercise the renewal option at once or within the first few years of the loan. In the case of an institutional lender, the governing statute may prohibit leasehold mortgages for longer than the initial term (regardless of renewal terms). The statute also may require that the initial term be for at least a certain period of years.

☐ *Subordination of the Fee:* The lender, as well as the borrower, will benefit if the landowner agrees to join in the leasehold mortgage and make the land additional security for the loan (however, the landowner will not assume personal liability for the loan). The lender benefits because in the event of foreclosure, it may proceed against both land and improvements. This may justify a higher loan than otherwise, benefiting not only the borrower but also the landowner since this will permit a more extensive improvement, creating more income to the lessee and more security for the rent obligation (and perhaps more rent if the lease relates the ground rent to the lessee's income). On the other hand, subordination prevents the landowner from mortgaging the fee and reduces its value, since there is a risk that it can be foreclosed. If the borrower contemplates refinancing the leasehold mortgage in the future, he should try to get the subordination agreement to apply to such future financing. The landowner is not likely to agree, however, unless he shares in the refinancing proceeds.

☐ *Violation of Lease as Default:* Since the mortgagee must be sure it can act for the lessee if he defaults under the lease, the mortgage will provide that a lease default also constitutes a default under the mortgage.

☐ *Insurance Proceeds:* In a fee mortgage, the lender often refuses to agree to apply insurance proceeds to restoration. In a leasehold situation, however, the lessor will not permit this, since it might mean the property would be left unimproved and no income would be available to pay the ground rent. The lender will want to retain the proceeds and pay them out directly to the contractors working on the property. The application of any excess proceeds is a matter for negotiation. The lender will want to use it to reduce the mortgage while the borrower-lessee will want to keep it.

[¶2715] **CHECKLIST FOR LEASE UNDERLYING
LEASEHOLD MORTGAGE**

The underlying lease ordinarily will have been signed at the time the lessee seeks leasehold financing. However, he should be prepared for requests by the lender to modify the lease as a condition to the loan. Whether or not the landowner will agree depends on the relative bargaining positions of the parties.

☐ *Term of Lease; Renewal Options:* The greater the time ''cushion'' is, the greater the assurance that the mortgagee will be able to recover its loan in the event financial difficulty requires an extension of the loan or foreclosure. In the event of a takeover, the lender will want the right to exercise any renewal options.

☐ *Subordination of Lease:* The lease should not be made subject to any existing or future mortgage on the fee since this would place two claims ahead of the leasehold mortgage (the lessor's rent claim and the rights of the fee mortgagee). The lender will want any fee mortgage to be subordinate not only to the lease, but to the leasehold mortgage as well. The lender will also want to be sure that the lease is not subordinate to any restriction of record on the fee, such as a reverter or possibility of forfeiture.

☐ *Assignment:* Any restriction on the lessee's right to assign or sublet may make the lease unsalable by the mortgagee after a foreclosure. The lessor may be willing to extend this right to the mortgagee in the event it takes over the lease after a default on the mortgage.

☐ *Default:* Here, the leasehold mortgagee is interested in assuring that there is no automatic default provision. He will want the protection for a period of time sufficient for the lessee to cure any default. In addition, the mortgagee will want to make sure there is no provision for default on the filing of a petition in bankruptcy or a reorganization. If the lessor won't agree to this, the lender will want an agreement that the lender can have a new lease on the same terms as the old one. Similarly, if the lessee abandons the lease, or any other noncurable default occurs, the lender will want the right to a new lease. The lender must have control over any contingency, curable or otherwise, that might terminate the lease, which is its only security for the loan.

☐ *Notice of Default:* The mortgagee will want any notices to be served on both the lessee and the mortgagee, with ample time to both to cure the default. The mortgagee will want a longer time for itself, since it will be unable to act until the period for action by the lessee (specified in the mortgage) has expired. The mortgagee will also want a right to enter the premises for the purpose of curing a default of the covenant to repair.

☐ *Covenant to Rebuild or Restore:* If the lease requires the lessee to rebuild the improvements in the event they are damaged or destroyed, the mortgagee will want to insure that the lessee has adequate time to complete the work and that the mortgagee can protect itself if the lessee fails to act.

☐ *Insurance Proceeds:* The lender will want to see that the lease requires the lessee to carry all necessary insurance. In addition, it will object to a provision giving the insurance proceeds to the lessor instead of requiring their use to restore the premises. If this occurred, it would eliminate the lender's security. From the lender's point of view, the best provision is one assigning the insurance proceeds to it for use in restoring the property.

☐ *Condemnation Awards:* The mortgagee's primary concern is to see that the mortgage is reduced to the extent that the leasehold's income-producing capacity is reduced. There are three situations:

(a) Full taking—If the entire property is condemned, the lessee's share should at least be equal to the mortgage debt. Since the lessee will normally want his share to be equal to the cost of the improvements, the lender will be protected. Apportioning the award between the lessee and the lessor on the basis of value may involve a risk to the lender in the event land values rise rapidly.

(b) Partial taking—If the lease provides that a partial taking will terminate the lease, the lessee's share of the award should be sufficient to pay the mortgage debt. If a partial taking will abate the rent, the lessor will probably want as much of the award as represents the capitalization of the lost rent. The remainder should go to restoration of the premises and any excess to reducing the mortgage debt. In the absence of any lease provision, a partial taking at common law did not abate the rent; in this event, the lender would probably have wanted the entire condemnation award to reduce the mortgage.

(c) Damage without taking—This might arise through loss of access, etc. The problem is the same as in the case of a partial taking, except that restoration of the premises is not a factor.

☐ *Mortgagee's Obligations:* The mortgagee will want to make sure that if it takes over the property, neither it nor any subsequent owner will be liable under any covenants of the lease except during periods of actual ownership. Certain "title-theory" states make the mortgagee liable on the lessee's covenants, even though he's not in possession. In addition, the lease sometimes seeks to make subsequent lessees liable for the obligations of their predecessors. This may affect marketability of the lease.

☐ *Option to Purchase:* If the lessee has an option to buy, the lender will want the mortgage debt to be an encumbrance on it as well as on the lease.

☐ *Transfer of Subleases:* The lessor will normally insert a provision in the lease (and in each sublease) that if the lessee defaults and the main lease terminates, the subleases will continue as a direct lease between the owner and the subtenants. The mortgagee, who anticipates taking over the lease if the lessee defaults, will want the owner to agree to assign to it (as the new lessee) its interest in the subleases.

☐ *Modification of Lease:* To protect itself, the mortgagee will want the lease to provide that it may not be amended or modified without its consent.

☐ *Estoppel Certificate:* The lease should require the lessor to provide an estoppel certificate, at the time of the mortgage closing, stating the date to which the rent has been paid, that no default exists under the lease, and that the lease has not been modified.

[¶2716]   **FOR FURTHER REFERENCE . . .**

Bagby, Joseph, *Real Estate Financing Desk Book,* 2nd edition, Institute for Business Planning, Inc., Englewood Cliffs, N.J. (1977).

Bell, R., "Negotiating the Purchase-Money Mortgage," 7 Real Estate Review No. 1, 51 (1977).

Connally, T., "Mortgagor-Mortgagee Problems and the Standard Mortgage Clause," 13 Forum 786 (Spring 1978).

Conway, Lawrence V., *Mortgage Lending*.

Hayes, K., "Refinancing Real Estate: What Is the Real Cost?" 18 Cornell Hotel and Restaurant Administration Quarterly 18 (February 1978).

Hoagland, Stone, & Brueggman, *Real Estate Finance*.

Kratovil, Robert, *Modern Mortgage Law and Practice*.

Murray, J.E., and Judy, H.L., "Federal National Mortgage Association and Federal Home Loan Mortgage Corporation Uniform Multifamily Mortgage Instruments," 33 Business Lawyer 2303-80 (July 1978).

Real Estate Investment Planning (looseleaf service) Institute for Business Planning, Inc., Englewood Cliffs, N.J.

PARTNERSHIPS

[¶2801]   A partnership is an association of two or more individuals who carry on a business for profit as co-owners. Joint tenancies, tenancies by the entirety, joint property, common property, tenancies in common, or part ownership do not of themselves establish a partnership relationship—even if the co-owners share profits made by the use of the property. While the sharing of gross receipts does not of itself establish a partnership, the receipt by any person of a share of profits of a business is prima facie evidence that that individual is a partner in the business—unless the profits were installment payments to a creditor, wages to an employee, annuities to a surviving spouse or representative of a deceased partner, interest to a lender, or consideration to a seller of business goodwill. Properties brought into the partnership or subsequently acquired by purchase for the partnership account are partnership property.

Every partner is an agent of the partnership for the purpose of its business, and the act of every partner when undertaking and carrying on the usual business of the partnership will bind the partnership unless the partner acting has no authority and the person with whom the partner is dealing has knowledge that the partner has no authority. If an act by a partner is apparently not for the purpose of carrying on the business of the partnership in the usual way, the act does not bind the partnership unless all of the other partners authorize it. Under certain circumstances, some actions require approval of all of the partners—it is not possible for a single partner without their consent to dispose of partnership goodwill, to undertake any act that would make it impossible to carry out the order of business of the partnership, to confess a judgment, to submit a partnership claim, to arbitrate, or, under certain circumstances, to pay partnership debts by assigning partnership property in trust for creditors.

When a partner is acting in the ordinary course of business or with the authority of his co-partners, any loss or injury caused to an individual who is not a partner creates a liability to the entire partnership. If the loss results from a partner's tort or breach of trust, all partners are jointly and severally liable. On the other hand, a partner is only jointly liable for the contractual obligations of his firm. Additionally, when an individual represents that a partnership exists and credit is given on the faith of that representation, a partnership by estoppel may be created. Individuals who enter a partnership are liable for all obligations of the partnership—even those arising prior to their admission as partners. Liability, however, may be satisfied only out of partnership property.

[¶2802]   **PARTNERSHIPS VS. CORPORATIONS**

Partnerships and corporations are the two most common methods of more than one individual doing business. Corporations are independent legal entities, partnerships are not. In the paragraphs below, the advantages of the partnership over the corporation, as well as the disadvantages, are explored.

ADVANTAGES OF A PARTNERSHIP
OVER A CORPORATION

Basic advantages of a partnership over a corporation include:

☐ Avoidance of additional income tax (the double taxation on original corporate income and on dividends).

☐ Freedom from certain statutory regulations.

☐ Freedom from miscellaneous taxes including the corporate franchise tax.

☐ Simplicity in organization.

☐ Availability of a ''veto'' power by each partner over partnership decisions.

[¶2804] # DISADVANTAGES OF A PARTNERSHIP

Following are the disadvantages of using a partnership for purposes of doing business:

☐ Each partner is the agent for the other—capable of making decisions binding all other partners.

☐ Personal liability of each partner for all obligations of business (partners do have a right of contribution from other partners to mitigate damages).

☐ Dissolution of partnership upon death.

☐ Unlimited personal liability (avoidable by use of a limited partnership).

[¶2805] # RIGHTS AND DUTIES OF PARTNERS

Every partner, at all times, is permitted to have access to the books of the partnership. Subject to agreement between the partners, books are to be kept at the principal place of business. Partners must account to the partnership for any benefit that they derive and for profits derived without the consent of the other partners. The individual acts as a trustee (thus prohibiting the personal use of the funds and profits). Any partner has the right to a formal accounting of partnership affairs if he is wrongfully excluded from partnership business or under other circumstances where it is deemed necessary.

[¶2806] # DISSOLUTION

Dissolution of a partnership may be accomplished in several ways. Two of these relate to the partnership agreement itself, others to events frequently beyond the control of the partnership.

A partnership for a definite term dissolves at the conclusion of that term. If no definite term is specified, a partnership at will is created, and any partner may express a desire to terminate the partnership—at which time the partnership is dissolved and ''winding up'' begins. Similarly, a partnership may be dissolved without violating the agreement by the express will of all the partners who have not assigned their interests. If the partnership permits expulsion of a partner pursuant to agreement between the other partners, the partnership is also dissolved. Other events that may cause a dissolution are the death of any partner, bankruptcy of any partner or of the partnership itself, or an event that makes it unlawful for the partnership business to be carried on (or for the members to carry it on in a partnership). In all these instances, the partnership is dissolved—but business may continue through the conclusion of the winding-up process. When a partner has been declared mentally incompetent in any judicial proceeding, or becomes incapable of performing part of the partnership contract, or is guilty of prejudicial conduct in the carrying on of business, or is in such consistent breach of the partnership agreement as to make it reasonably impractical to continue the partnership business, a court must decree dissolution on application of any partner. The same holds true if the partnership business can only be carried on at a loss.

[¶2807] RULES FOR DISTRIBUTION OF PARTNERSHIP ASSETS

Once a partnership has been dissolved and the winding-up process concluded, the assets of the partnership are distributed in this order: Partnership property and then the contributions of partners necessary for the payment of liabilities. Partnership liabilities are satisfied in the following order of priority: (1) Creditors other than partners, (2) Loans from partners (other than capital and profits), (3) Capital contributions of partners, (4) Profits of partners.

[¶2808] TAX CONSEQUENCES OF PARTNERSHIP

The following is an analysis of basic partnership tax considerations affected by the Tax Reform Act of 1976 and the Revenue Act of 1978:

(1) Income of a Partner: When a partner determines his income tax, it is necessary for him to distinguish his distributive share of the partnership's gains and losses from sales or exchange of capital assets. For 1977, the holding period for long-term capital gains was nine months; in 1978 and subsequent years it is one year. (Agricultural commodity futures contracts still retain their six-month holding period.)

(2) Oil and Gas Wells: Percentage depletion for oil and gas wells was previously computed by each partner for properties held by the partnership. The partnership basis for oil or gas properties is now allocated to partners proportionately—each partner maintains an individual basis account and computes his own allowance for either percentage depletion or cost depletion on all oil and gas properties.

(3) Partner's Distributive Share: Allocation of a partner's share of income, loss, gain, deduction, or credit is now determined in accordance with the partner's interest in the partnership (determined by taking into account all facts and circum-

288

stances) if the partnership agreement does not provide for a means of calculating the partner's income, or if the allocation to the partner "does not have substantial economic effect."

(4) "At-Risk" Rule: If a partnership engaged in any activity other than real estate suffers a loss, the loss will not be deductible by a partner on his individual tax return to the extent that it exceeds his amount "at risk" in the partnership. In determining his amount "at risk," partnership liabilities on which the partner is not personally liable are not taken into account. If a partnership loss reduces a partner's amount "at risk" to less than zero, it is not deductible until the partner repays the excess to the partnership (IRC §704(d)).

(5) Partnership Returns: The Revenue Act added §6698 to the Internal Revenue Code, which provides that a civil penalty will be imposed on every partnership that fails to file its information return on time or that fails to show the information required by §6031, unless the failure is due to reasonable cause. The penalty is assessed for each month (or fraction thereof) during which the failure continues, up to a maximum of five months. The penalty for each month (or fraction of a month) is $50 multiplied by the number of partners. Partners are liable to the extent they are liable for partnership debts generally.

[¶2809]   CHECKLIST FOR ORGANIZING
A PARTNERSHIP

The following paragraphs comprise a 22-item checklist that should be used in the organization of any partnership. The Uniform Partnership Act (and the Uniform Limited Partnership Act) have been adopted by most states. Rules and limitations differ slightly from state to state, but are for the most part quite similar.

[¶2809.1]   Name

Any name may be used for a partnership unless specifically prohibited by law. Use of a name deceptively similar to that of another business may lead to litigation. Many states have a statutory requirement that partnership names be registered with the Secretary of State, county clerk, or other appropriate filing officer. If individuals' names are used in the partnership name, consideration should be given to whether the name will be continued after the death of a partner and whether this is permitted under local law. The use of the name of itself will not make the individual property of the deceased partner liable for any debts contracted by the partnership.

[¶2809.2]   Business Activity

A careful statement of the nature of the business is necessary to define the scope of the partnership so that no partner becomes involved in a business against his wishes.

[¶2809.3]   Licensing

If the nature of the business is one that might require licensing, etc., state and federal regulatory statutes should be checked. When a license or permit is required, it is wise to provide that the partnership agreement will not become effective until the license or permit is procured.

[¶2809.4]   Term

A definite term of years for the continuation of the partnership business may be agreed upon or the partnership may continue at will. However, any partner may terminate his relations with the partnership even though it be in contravention of the partnership agreement. This may give rise to a suit for damages by the remaining partners, but the partnership nevertheless is dissolved. The partnership agreement may contain a provision for liquidated damages for a partner's premature withdrawal. However, to be enforceable, it must be compensatory in nature rather than punitive. When the agreement specifies a fixed term, the parties may continue the business beyond that term as a partnership at will. However, it is advisable that they either extend the term of the partnership or enter into a new partnership agreement.

[¶2809.5]   Partnership Contributions

Careful distinction should be drawn between contributions to the partnership capital and other types of financial relationships (such as loans) between the partners and the partnership. Contributions to partnership capital may consist of cash, property, or services. When property is contributed, consideration should be given to the statutory right of the partners to reconcile the tax bases and accounting values of the contributed property. These adjustments may be necessary to prevent distortions in the partnership income shares.

[¶2809.6]   Loans and Leases With the Partnership

A partner may, in his individual capacity, lend or rent property to the partnership and receive interest or rent. Since the money loaned or the property leased is not part of the partnership capital, it will not be available in the first instance for the satisfaction of partnership debts.

[¶2809.7]   Interest on Partnership Capital

Generally, the partnership will not pay interest on its capital. If interest is to be paid, the agreement should so state. In businesses that require a large amount of liquid capital to meet regulatory requirements, the parties may feel that payment of interest should be made, particularly when the capital contributions of various partners differ and the distributions of profits do not reflect each partner's capital contributions. Interest paid by the partnership is deductible for income tax purposes.

[¶2809.8] Salary

Ordinarily, a partner is compensated for his services and for his contributions of capital by a share of the profits. Unless provided for in the partnership agreement, a partner will not be entitled to salary or other compensation for his services except in the case of a partner winding up the business of a partnership. However, if a partner does receive a salary, this expense is deductible by the partnership.

[¶2809.9] Sharing Profits and Losses

The essential element in the partnership is the sharing of profits between the partners. While losses are ordinarily shared also, this is not always the case (as when the partner who contributes services only may be relieved from any liability from losses). When both profits and losses are shared, they are usually shared in the same ratio (that is, a partner who is entitled to 10% of the profits is liable for 10% of the losses). However, profits and losses may or may not be shared equally between the partners. (For example, a partner putting up 50% of the capital may be entitled to receive 75% of the profit.) Sometimes, different distribution ratios will apply to different kinds of income (e.g., operating income and capital gains). All of these matters must be spelled out in the partnership agreement. One solution to the problem of unequal financial contributions is to create equal capital accounts and treat additional funds as loans.

[¶2809.10] Tax Treatment of Profits and Losses

The partnership is not a separate entity for income tax purposes. Each partner is taxed on his proportionate share of the profits and is entitled to deduct his proportionate share of the losses. It makes no difference whether or not the partner actually draws or pays any money for the tax period in question. The partnership itself files only an information return.

[¶2809.11] Right to Withdraw Capital

If the right to withdraw funds from the partnership is limited, this should be spelled out in the partnership agreement. If a substantial amount of money is to be accumulated in the partnership, the partners should be permitted to take out sufficient money to meet their income tax obligations.

[¶2809.12] Payments to Retired or Deceased Partner

When payments are made to a partner who retires, or to the estate or heir of a deceased partner, the money paid may represent the withdrawing partner's capital

291

interest, his pro rata interest in unrealized receivables and fees, his share of the potential gain or loss on partnership inventory, or mutual insurance among the partners.

[¶2809.13] Management

In the absence of an agreement to the contrary, all partners have equal rights in the management and conduct of the partnership business. It is, therefore, necessary to have the agreement clearly state each partner's rights and duties. The extent to which the partners are authorized as between themselves to commit and bind the partnership should be clearly spelled out in the agreement. When a partner assigns his interest in the partnership, the assignee during the continuance of the partnership will not have the right to interfere in the management or administration of the partnership business or affairs unless the partnership agreement provides otherwise.

[¶2809.14] Books and Records

Local law frequently requires that books and records must be kept at the principal place of business of the partnership and every partner shall at all times have access to and may inspect and copy them.

[¶2809.15] Death or Withdrawal of a Partner

Provision can be made in the agreement for the continuation of the business after the death or withdrawal of a partner, bearing in mind that such a provision may, along with other corporate attributes, give the partnership the tax status of a corporation. In the absence of such a provision, the partnership will be required to wind up its affairs.

[¶2809.16] Partnership Property

Unless a contrary intention appears, all property acquired with partnership funds will be partnership property.

[¶2809.17] Accounting by Partners

The agreement should require all partners to give to the partnership full information on matters affecting the partnership.

[¶2809.18] Indemnification of Partner

Without any provision in the agreement, the partnership may be required to indemnify each partner for payments made and personal liabilities reasonably incurred in the ordinary and necessary fulfillment of the partnership business.

[¶2809.19] Family Partnerships

Partnership interests can be given to family members and in that way income can be spread over a number of low-bracket taxpayers. But keep in mind that this can be done only when capital is a substantial income-producing factor in the partnership. And the donor-partner must get fair compensation before the balance of the partnership profits is distributed among the remaining partners.

If a trust is a partner, the trustee should have broad powers and be able to act independently as a partner.

[¶2809.20] Collapsible Partnerships

The partners should be alerted to the "collapsible partnership" rule if it is the intention of one or more of their number to invest in the partnership for a limited period of time. Amounts received by a partner for his partnership interest that are attributable to partnership unrealized receivables or substantially appreciated inventory are treated as ordinary income. (Normally, the sale or liquidation of a partnership interest gives capital gain.)

[¶2809.21] Partnership Treated as a Corporation

In some cases, a partnership will be treated as a corporation despite the wishes of the partners. This will come about when the partnership has more corporate characteristics than noncorporate characteristics under the federal tax regulations. The four elements that point to a corporation are continuity, centralized management, limited liability, and transferability of interest. If a partnership has three or more of these elements, it may become subject to a double tax on its income (a corporate tax plus a personal tax on each partner).

[¶2809.22] Limited Partnerships

A limited partnership is one step closer to a corporation than is a general partnership because it includes partners who, like shareholders in a corporation, invest capital, have limited liability, and do not share in the management of partnership affairs. The partnership agreement may provide that the limited partner share in profits or may provide that he be paid a specific amount of income whether or not there are partnership profits. In organizing a limited partnership, it is important that the limited partner be given no rights or powers over partnership affairs that may cause him to be treated as a general partner.

For forms of partnership agreements, see *IBP Forms of Business Agreements and Resolutions*.

[¶2810]   FOR FURTHER REFERENCE . . .

Andelman, D.R., "Reorganizations of Partnerships," 35 New York University Institute on Federal Taxation 151 (1977).

DeFren, B.J., *Partnership Desk Book,* Institute for Business Planning, Inc., Englewood Cliffs, N.J. (1978).

Kalish, A., and Rosow, S.L., "Partnerships, Tax Shelters and the Tax Reform Act of 1976," 31 The Tax Lawyer 755 (Spring 1978).

REAL ESTATE TRANSACTIONS

[¶2901]   The essential elements in the sale and purchase of real estate come together in the contract of sale. To be enforceable, this instrument is required by law to be in writing and signed by the parties to the transaction. Because the contract of sale will control the transaction and will prescribe much of what will follow between the parties, it is vitally important that this instrument be well thought out and explicit with regard to the exact terms of the transaction. The contract must be complete: All the terms of the sale must be settled, with none left to be determined by future negotiations. For example, it was held that failure to specify when a purchase-money mortgage fell due made a contract unenforceable.

The contract will specify the kind of title that the seller is to deliver and will prevent the seller from turning around and selling the property to another party while the purchaser is awaiting the title report. The contract will also prevent the purchaser from changing his mind and backing out as long as the seller can deliver the kind of title he promised.

In the paragraphs that follow, some of the key terms mentioned in a contract of sale are discussed.

[¶2902]   MARKETABLE TITLE

The kind of title that a seller must deliver will depend on the terms and provisions of the contract of sale. If the contract is silent, the seller must deliver marketable title, free from encumbrances. If the contract requires the seller to deliver title ''free from all defects or encumbrances,'' the buyer may be able to reject title if there is even a trivial encroachment or a beneficial easement. Usually the seller lists in his contract the encumbrances that exist and the buyer agrees to take title subject to these encumbrances, (e.g., building restrictions, existing mortgages, etc). If the contract is subject to general language such as ''conditions and restrictions of records, easements, existing tenancies, any state of facts which an accurate survey may show,'' etc., the seller can probably succeed in delivering what he has.

One practical way for the seller and buyer to make definite the kind of title they are talking about is to check the examination of title made at the time the seller acquired the property, and if the restrictions that then existed are satisfactory to the buyer, the seller should commit to deliver a title subject only to the limitations existing when the property was acquired. Another way is for the contract to require the seller to deliver a marketable title and a policy of title insurance. This permits the buyer to walk out on a contract if the title is not marketable or if the title insurance is not forthcoming. If the contract merely requires the seller to furnish title insurance, then the buyer is required to take a title even if it is technically unmarketable as long as a title company will issue insurance, which it will sometimes do on the basis that there is little business risk in a technical defect that may render the title less than fully marketable.

In order to avoid delay caused by clearing a defective title, the buyer may want to fix a time for delivery of the deed and have the contract provide that time is of the essence. If the seller does not have good title at the time fixed for delivering the deed, the buyer can relieve himself of the obligations of the contract.

The buyer should insist that the contract specify the kind of evidence of good title that the seller will be required to produce—e.g., title insurance, abstracts, certificate of title, etc. Evidence of title should show the condition of the title as of the date on which the deed is delivered rather than the date of contract. The contract should give the seller a reasonable time to furnish the buyer with evidence of title, the buyer a reasonable time to examine such evidence and point out any defects, then a further reasonable time for the seller to eliminate or cure any such defects, and a further time within which the buyer can decide to accept or reject a title still carrying a defect that the seller has been unable to cure.

[¶2903]   DEPOSITS

When the buyer makes a deposit or a down payment on the contract, that money applies as part payment of the purchase price if he conforms; if he defaults it can be retained by the seller. This should be specifically covered by the contract. The seller, to protect himself, should require a large enough deposit to cover the broker's commission, expense of title search, and compensation for his loss of time and loss of opportunity to sell elsewhere if the buyer should default. If the seller can't deliver clear title, then the buyer is entitled to take back his deposit.

[¶2904]   MORTGAGES

If the buyer is to take the property subject to an existing mortgage, the contract should so state. It should specify whether the buyer is assuming an existing mortgage or merely taking subject to the mortgage. If the buyer is giving a purchase-money mortgage as part of the payment, the contract should spell out the interest rates, maturity, amortization payments, form of the mortgage, and other details.

[¶2905]   CONTINGENCIES AND LOSS

The buyer's obligation may be made subject to contingencies such as his ability to obtain a mortgage, his ability to get a zoning variance, etc. It is important that the contract spell out the kind of mortgage, the kind of variance, who has the responsibility for getting the mortgage or variance, the time within which the contingency is to be satisfied, when the deal is to be terminated if the contingency has not been satisfied by that time, etc. Specify who is to carry the risk of loss for damage to the property, and the right of the buyer to cancel the deal if there is a substantial loss or to receive insurance money if the deal is not canceled.

[¶2906] **SURVEY**

If the buyer wants the seller to provide a survey at the seller's cost, this should be stated in the contract. The time for delivery of the survey should also be specified. The contract should require the survey to be satisfactory to the buyer's lawyer and a time should be fixed for the buyer to raise objections based on the survey.

The survey should be verified with local ordinances, private covenants and restrictions, party wall agreements, and setback requirements.

Protecting the Buyer When Survey Not Available: The risk of violations, encumbrances, and restrictions can be put on the seller by inserting these provisions in the contract:

(1) Subject to local zoning and setback ordinances that are not violated by the present structure.

(2) Subject to the state of facts an accurate survey will show, provided they do not render the title unmarketable.

(3) Subject to covenants and restrictions of record not rendering title unmarketable or revertible.

A seller will normally refuse to warrant that the property may be used in ways other than that presently used. A buyer in a strong bargaining position, however, may be able to obtain such a warranty with respect to a use specified in the contract.

[¶2907] **OUTSTANDING LEASES AND
LEASE PROVISIONS**

If the purchaser is buying income-producing property as an investment, his attorney will want to examine the leases and check the rentals in those leases against the rental information that has been furnished by the seller. The attorney will also want to look for provisions of leases that include any unusual clauses, particularly those that concern the landlord's obligations to make repairs and the tenants' rights to cancel or renew. Clauses that concern damage or destruction to the premises, either by casualty or fire or taking through eminent domain, will require intensive scrutiny.

[¶2908] **LIMITATIONS AS TO USE**

The purchaser's attorney will examine the types of restrictions, area restrictions, and use restrictions imposed on the property either by government regulation or by private covenant. In order to protect his client, the buyer's attorney may require a provision that the purchaser will not have to buy the property if its intended use is prohibited by such restrictions. The seller of the property usually will not object to this type of a provision unless market conditions are in his favor and he feels that tying up the property during the contract period will unfavorably affect the value of the property. A possible compromise for both parties might be the requirement that the purchaser must acquire the necessary knowledge about existing regulations and covenants within a certain period of time after the contract of sale has been entered into. Typically, this type of provision will give the purchaser an option to terminate the contract during the specified period of time, if there is any prohibition on the particular use to which he intends to put the property.

[¶2909]   **ZONING**

The seller will ordinarily provide a warranty that existing structures on the property are not in violation of any zoning regulations and ordinances. If the purchaser plans to change the existing use of the property, this warranty is not enough. The same considerations will also apply to a purchaser who is acquiring vacant land on which a building devoted to a particular use is to be erected. Here the purchaser will insist on a repetition by the seller that the purchaser's contemplated use of the land will not violate zoning regulations and ordinances. The seller, of course, may not be willing to go that far in his assurances. The ultimate disposition of this problem depends on the parties' bargaining positions.

[¶2910]   **PERFORMANCE TIME**

The seller may want to receive the proceeds of the sale of the property on a particular day since he may intend to either enter into a new venture or to discharge an obligation. Therefore, he may want to make time for performance under the contract *of the essence*. Under a "time of the essence" arrangement, the seller's obligation to convey the property to the purchaser will be relieved by the purchaser's failure to meet the payments on the specific day. In addition, the seller may have a suit for damages against the purchaser. The purchaser's attorney may insist that if time is of the essence it should be so for both parties. The seller will have a good argument against this type of arrangement since the purchaser's only requirement generally is to pay cash on the day of title closing, but the seller has numerous obligations, since he must clear up the property before conveying it to the purchaser. As a possible compromise, the parties may agree that time for performance is of the essence for both parties, but that the purchaser will notify the seller in writing a specified number of days before the date set for the closing of title of all objections to the seller's title. This provision allows the seller to clear up those objections.

[¶2911]   **PURCHASE-MONEY MORTGAGE**

Sellers often take back a purchase-money second mortgage as part of their purchase price for the property. Here, the seller will want to be assured that the purchaser will not milk the property by collecting rents for a certain number of months and then default on the mortgages. The solution is to prepare a timetable that integrates principal and interest payments on the purchase-money mortgage with the purchaser's other obligations (including water charges, taxes, and interest and principal on the first mortgage). Such a timetable assures that the purchaser is obligated to make payments for these different items in different months. This means that the seller can quickly determine whether or not the purchaser has defaulted in his obligations.

Another provision that the seller will want is one protecting against a default in the payment of principal or interest on the purchase-money mortgage, or on the payment of principal or interest on any other mortgage or on the payment of taxes, water rates, or assessments. This provision gives the seller, at his option, the right to accelerate all of the principal amount of the purchase-money mortgage on default of any one of the above-named obligations by the purchaser.

[¶2912]   PERSONAL PROPERTY

When a purchaser acquires a building he ordinarily expects to acquire title to the property within that building (as, for example, gas ranges and refrigerators in an apartment house). But gas ranges and refrigerators are usually considered to be personal property and will not be included in the sale of the real estate unless there is an express provision covering them. It is, therefore, very important for the contract to specify all of the personal property included in the sale. The best practice is to require a bill of sale from the seller covering personal property free of all liens and encumbrances.

[¶2913]   PRE-CONTRACT CHECKLISTS

Prior to executing the contract of sale for a particular property (here, a house), there are a number of matters that the attorneys for the buyer and seller will want to see to.

Seller's Checklist: The following are concerns of the seller that should be taken care of before going to contract:

☐ *Broker:* If a broker is responsible for bringing about the sale, the seller's attorney should prepare a written brokerage agreement. The attorney should contact the broker and confirm the amount of his commission with him. If a binder has been given, the seller or his attorney should obtain a copy of such written binder. Be sure that the broker is present at the execution of the contract and that he signs the brokerage agreement.

☐ *Payment:* The purchase price must be set and the method of payment established. Will the buyer assume the seller's mortgage? Will the seller offer a purchase-money mortgage? If the buyer does not assume the present mortgage on the property it must be satisfied or else the property will be transferred subject to the lien.

☐ **Personal Property:** The seller's attorney should itemize any and all personal property that is to be transferred with title.

☐ **Date:** The seller should have a rough idea of the date on which title is to pass.

☐ **Documents:** The seller should furnish the following documents to his attorney in preparation for the closing:

    (a) Deed;

    (b) Survey;

    (c) Title insurance policy;

    (d) Tax receipts;

    (e) Certificate of occupancy;

    (f) A copy of the present mortgage; and

    (g) Homeowner's insurance policy.

Buyer's Checklist: The following are concerns of the purchaser that should be taken care of before going to contract:

☐ **Price:** The buyer's attorney should check with the seller's attorney to confirm the price, as well as the terms of sale. If the buyer is taking subject to or assumes the seller's mortgage, it should be determined if the mortgage is in fact transferable.

☐ **Binder:** If the buyer has given the seller a binder, he should obtain a copy of the agreement under which the money was given. The buyer should either have the money returned to him or a credit should be awarded to him against the contract price.

☐ **Inspection:** Because most contracts provide that the home is to be transferred "as is," it's a good idea to see to it that the seller makes any necessary repairs prior to contract or that the contract lists any repairs to be made by the seller. Therefore, the purchaser should have the house and the equipment inspected by a qualified engineer before going to contract. The buyer should also arrange to have the property inspected for termite infestation. Copies of all reports should be received before the contract is executed.

☐ **Form of Ownership:** How are the purchasers going to take title? As tenants in common, joint tenants, or tenants by the entirety?

☐ **Moving:** What does the buyer intend to do about his living accommodations? Must he sell his home? When? If the buyer presently has a lease, will it be necessary for him to breach it?

[¶2914] CHECKLIST OF PRACTICAL NEGOTIATING AND DRAFTING CONSIDERATIONS

Although in every jurisdiction there is a standard form of contract of sale incorporating many provisions to which there is rarely any disagreement, there are always areas about which the parties feel free to bargain and when different provisions will be used under different circumstances. In addition, each party will want the contract to contain certain protective clauses that will cover unexpected contingencies. The following checklist points out important considerations to be borne in mind by the attorneys for both parties.

The normal practice is for the seller's attorney to draft the contract, with his client's interests in mind. Included in the following checklist are special considerations of the buyer that his attorney may want to pay particular attention to.

☐ **Form of Contract:** The contract may be a straight bilateral agreement between the buyer and the seller, in offer and acceptance form (in which the seller accepts the offer with all its attendant conditions), or a deposit receipt prepared by a broker containing the conditions of the sale. In some states, the papers and the down payment are held by a third party escrow agent. Regardless of the form of the contract, however, the following considerations should be carefully noted:

Date of Execution of the Contract.

Names and Addresses of the Parties: The full names and addresses of parties to the contract should appear in the appropriate places. It's good practice to have all of the parties present when the contract is executed.

Buyer's Considerations: Be sure the named seller is competent and is the sole owner, or if there are co-owners, that he has the authority to enter into the contract and pass good title.

If the seller is an individual, the buyer should ascertain if his spouse died within the past few years. In some states, any unpaid tax on the decedent's estate becomes a lien on the property in which he has an interest, and this lien will carry over to a later buyer. There is, however, no problem with regard to the federal estate tax, which does not remain a lien on property sold for a fair consideration.

If the seller has a living spouse, determine if there are any dower or other rights in the property. If so, both must sign the contract or it will not be effective.

If the seller is a corporation or a fiduciary, be sure that such representative is acting within the scope of his authority. The buyer should ask for and examine corporate resolutions authorizing the sale or a certificate of letters testamentary or administration.

☐ **Description of the Property:** Usually, the description used in the prior deed is satisfactory, but a later survey or title company report should be used if there have been any changes. If the seller has any rights in the street in front of the property, those rights should be included. The same applies for riparian (water) rights.

Buyer's Consideration: The description of the property should be read and compared with the survey of the property. The description must comply with the survey.

☐ **Purchase Price:** The contract should state the entire purchase price, including any and all mortgages. The price should then be broken down into various components:

Down Payment: Ordinarily, 10% of the purchase price.

Buyer's Consideration: A problem may arise as to whether the down payment should be held in escrow by the seller's attorney between the contract execution and title closing dates. The buyer should insist that the money be held in escrow if the contract is conditional on the purchaser obtaining financing. Even if the contract is not conditional, it's a good idea to have the down payment held in escrow pending the title report showing that the seller has good title and that he can convey marketable title. If the seller doesn't own the property he is selling (e.g., he may have only a contract to buy it), the buyer should insist on an escrow arrangement. Similarly, if the seller is moving to another state before the closing, the buyer may want the protection of an escrow.

Mortgage: Most contracts of sale are conditioned on the purchaser obtaining mortgage financing (included as a "subject to" clause). The conditional contract will recite that the buyer, within a specified period of time, must obtain a commitment from a lender for a first mortgage in a stated amount, for a specified term, and at a specified interest rate. If, after using his best efforts to obtain financing, the buyer is not successful, the contract should provide that he has the right to cancel on written notice to the seller.

If the buyer is to take title subject to or assuming the seller's existing mortgage, the contract should spell out in detail all pertinent information relating to the existing mortgage. It's advisable for the buyer or his attorney to get a copy of the mortgage he is taking subject to or assuming.

If the seller is to take back, as part of the purchase price, a purchase-money mortgage, a copy of the proposed mortgage should be attached to the contract. Otherwise, the contract should indicate such matters as: the amount and how it will be amortized, the due date, the interest rate and how it is payable, the right to prepay in whole or in part, the type of mortgage form to be used, subordination to any existing or future mortgage, and who shall draw the bond and mortgage (ordinarily the seller's attorney is responsible for doing this for an additional fee).

Balance of Purchase Price: The balance of the purchase price should be made due and payable at the time of closing. Seller's attorney should request that payment be made by certified check.

Buyer's Consideration: It's a good idea to have this and any other certified checks made out to the buyer and then have the buyer endorse to the seller. This avoids problems in redepositing the checks should the deal fall through.

☐ **Mortgage Satisfaction:** When the seller's present mortgage is to be satisfied at the closing, the contract should so state. The seller's attorney should write to the mortgagee requesting a statement of the balance due, as well as any additional charges associated with satisfaction of the mortgage. This letter must be presented to the other parties at the closing.

☐ **"Subject to" Clause:** This is one of the most important clauses in the contract and should be considered carefully by the buyer in particular, since a loosely drawn clause may require him to take the property even though it cannot be used in the manner he anticipated. This clause lists the conditions and circumstances to which the property may be subject, without rendering the contract void.

Zoning and Building Ordinances: The buyer will, at the least, want the following to be added to the above clause: "provided the same are not violated by existing structures." In other words, he wants to be sure the property at present doesn't violate the law. He may also ask that this provision be extended to contemplated structures. The seller, however, is likely to say that this is a risk to be assumed by the buyer since it relates to future events.

Private Covenants and Restrictions: These will be contained in prior deeds and possibly in a master declaration recorded at the time the original tract was platted. The first thing the buyer should do is inquire if the seller knows of any restrictions. If possible, the original documents containing the covenants, restrictions, and easements should be examined (a prior title report may have them). If they are not available, add the following: "provided the same are not violated by the existing structure or the present use of the premises, and provided the same may not result in forfeiture." A purchaser in a strong bargaining position may also be able to add the clause "provided the same are not violated by (specified) future structures or uses." In addition, the buyer must modify the exception as stated or else he may find that the property can only be used in a very limited number of ways. One modification is to add "provided they do not make title unmarketable." The seller may object to this since, in some states, almost any minor restriction may make the title unmarketable. A compromise would be to substitute "provided they do not prohibit existing (or contemplated) structures and uses."

The buyer should refuse to take subject to any restrictions that, if violated, would cause him to forfeit the property to a prior owner, since this is an unreasonable risk for him to assume.

State of facts shown by survey: If, at the time the contract is executed, the buyer does not have a current survey, a clause providing that the sale is subject to the state of facts shown by a survey should not be accepted by the buyer. Such a clause is acceptable only if it goes on to say "provided they do not make title unmarketable."

Any violations of municipal ordinances that have been noted against the property: This would require the buyer to take the property regardless of the number or nature of violations noted against it. Unless the buyer is taking dilapidated property "as is," he should insist either that the seller cure any such violations or that the contract be canceled if they are not cured at the date of closing. The seller may be willing to cure the violations provided the expense doesn't exceed a stated figure.

Assessments that may be levied against the property: The problem here is that the purchase price may reflect improvements (e.g., sewers) that have already been installed but not yet paid for. The buyer will thus be paying twice unless this clause is modified.

Termite infestation and damage: Usually a provision is included that gives the seller the option to remedy any such condition or cancel the contract. Some termite clauses permit the buyer the final option of accepting the property with the existing condition.

☐ **Violations of Law:** Violations of law do not ordinarily affect marketability of title. Therefore, the buyer is responsible (civilly, criminally, and financially) for removing any violations unless the contract provides for removal by the seller. The seller will want to limit his liability to violations "noted" of record.

Buyer's Consideration: The purchaser will want the seller's obligation to survive delivery of the deed or provide for escrow of part of the purchase price as security for removal. The buyer will also want the contract to provide that the seller is to present him with the following at the closing: a certificate of occupancy;

plumbing, heating, and electrical inspection certificates; and permits necessary for use and occupancy of the premises.

☐ **Adjustments:** Depending upon the property and the circumstances surrounding the sale, various costs associated with the property will be apportioned between the seller and the buyer at the date of closing:

Rents: If there is a tenant on the premises, rent paid to the date of closing will be apportioned between the parties.

Interest: If the sale is subject to an existing mortgage, interest on the mortgage should be apportioned.

Insurance: Because not all policies can be transferred, the seller's policy should be checked.

Buyer's Consideration: When the buyer is asked to take over a policy, his attorney should insist on examining the policy at the closing.

Taxes: The seller's attorney should bring all tax bills to the closing. The tax calendar should be ascertained and the amounts paid or due should be apportioned.

Buyer's Consideration: The buyer should demand proof that all back taxes have been paid because arrears may become a lien on the property.

Fuel: If oil is used for heating the home, the seller should have his supplier prepare a letter for the closing, stating how much oil is in the tank and the oil cost per gallon. The buyer will be required to pay this amount.

☐ **Deed:** The contract should specify the type and form of deed the seller is to give. Local custom is usually controlling.

☐ **Title Insurance:** In some areas the buyer's attorney or some other attorney will conduct a title search and prepare an abstract of title. However, in the great majority of cases the purchaser or his attorney will engage a title company to search and insure the title. Ordinarily a lender will require the buyer to obtain title insurance.

☐ **Lien:** The down payment creates a vendee's lien in favor of the buyer. The contract should expressly extend this lien to include amounts expended for the title examination and the survey. If the seller is unable to convey title for reasons other than his own acts, his liability will be limited to the down payment, the title examination fee, and the cost of the survey.

Buyer's Consideration: The buyer should try to extend this liability to include his attorney's fees as well.

☐ **Risk of Loss:** In the absence of an express provision on risk of loss, different rules may apply, depending on the jurisdiction: (1) Risk of loss may be on the purchaser as soon as the contract is signed (majority rule); (2) Risk may be on the seller prior to closing (minority rule); or (3) The Uniform Purchaser and Vendor Act, which makes possession decisive, may be controlling. Risks should be spelled out, e.g., fire, windstorm, etc.

☐ **Broker:** If a broker brought about the sale, the contract should state this fact, the broker's name, and that the seller is to pay the commission.

☐ *Personal Property:* The contract should specify all personal property and fixtures that pass with title to the real estate, as well as those items that are to be excluded.

☐ *"As Is" Clause:* The seller's attorney may wish to extend the coverage of the "as is" clause beyond the building to include personal property.

Buyer's Consideration: The buyer will want to limit this by having the seller state in the contract, "Plumbing, heating, electrical utilities, and appliances shall be in good working order at the time title passes." When buying a new home, specify that all warranties will survive delivery of the deed. The seller is to deliver all such warranties to the purchaser at the closing.

☐ *Time and Date of Closing:* The contract will state where the closing is to occur. Closings usually take place at the seller's attorney's office or, if the buyer gets a mortgage, at the lender's office or the office of the lender's attorney. The contract will set a date at which the title will pass. In the absence of a clause making time of the essence, either party is entitled to a reasonable adjournment if one becomes necessary. This may prove embarrassing when, for example, the buyer is selling his old house on the same day he plans to take possession of the new one. A time of the essence clause puts the burden on the seller, in this instance, to complete the transaction on time.

If the problem is that the seller may not be able to move out in time, the buyer may be willing to let him stay on for a designated period. This can be on a daily basis or without charge until a certain date, after which a per diem penalty is payable, backed up by an escrow clause.

[¶2915] CLOSING THE TITLE

Closing of title occurs when the transaction is consummated, the deed and final evidence of good title are delivered, the money is paid, the mortgages are executed, and charges against the property are adjusted between the parties.

The buyer should get the deed; a title report or policy or other evidence of good title; a bill of sale for any personal property passing with the real estate; a receipt for the purchase price he paid; a survey of the property; insurance policies or assignments thereof; a statement from the mortgagee of the amount due on any existing mortgage; release and satisfaction of any mortgage or other lien paid off but not yet recorded; leases and assignments thereof; a letter by the seller notifying tenants to pay future rents to the buyer; a letter by the seller advising the managing agent of the sale and the termination of his authority; a statement by the seller as to rents paid and due; receipts for taxes, water, gas, electricity, special assessments, assessment of any service contracts, and building maintenance guarantees; the seller's affidavit of title security deposits and tenants' consent to transfer if required; Social Security and payroll data on building employees; and keys to the building.

The seller receives the balance of the purchase price including any purchase-money mortgage and notes. He will want evidence of fire insurance protection if he has a continuing mortgage interest.

[¶2916]   **TITLE CLOSING CHECKLISTS**

If the preliminary work has been handled properly, the physical act of closing the title can be accomplished with dispatch. In order for this to occur, however, all the necessary documents (deeds, bills of sale, mortgages, bonds, etc.) must be ready and checked in advance. The actual formal closing then consists of an exchange of documents and checks. The following checklists will help the parties in preparing for a smooth closing.

[¶2917]   **SELLER'S CONSIDERATIONS**

(1) Verifying title—the seller's attorney will want to check title and remove any possible objections. The following considerations should be covered:

(a) Make certain that title evidence has been brought up to date and is in the form agreed upon in the contract. Resolve position as to exceptions and encumbrances (that is, whether or not material; if survey is required by contract, check same). Have building plans and specifications available.

(b) Is title insurance in the agreed amount and form?

(c) Does deed conform to contract requirements? (Marital status of seller, acknowledgment, legal description, tax stamps.) The deed should specify that the conveyance is subject to exceptions, liens, encumbrances, restrictions, and reservations provided for in the contract. Otherwise, seller will be warranting a better title than he has.

(d) Title affidavits to cover period between title evidence and the closing.

(e) Affidavits to clear up objections revealed by abstract and covering mechanics' liens.

(f) Obtain proper waivers, contractor's statements, and architect's certificate for new construction.

(g) Obtain bill of sale covering any personal property included.

(2) Amount of unpaid taxes, liens, assessments, water, sewerage charges, etc., on the property should be ascertained.

(3) Get statement of amount due on existing mortgages, showing unpaid principal and interest, rate of interest, and date of maturity.

(4) Produce the following:

(a) Policies of insurance to be transferred.

(b) Schedule of rents.

(c) Deed from predecessor.

(d) Vault permits.

(e) Power of attorney.

(5) Deed.

(a) Include full names and addresses of seller and purchaser.

(b) Description of property (same as in contract of sale unless there has been a new survey).

(c) Covenants and warrants provided for in contract of sale.

(d) Special clauses in contract of sale.

(e) Recital of exceptions, restrictions, easements, etc., provided in contract of sale.

(f) Description of mortgages, both the mortgages that the purchaser is taking subject to and that the purchaser is assuming. Also include a recital of purchase-money mortgage if there is one.

(6) Additional papers.

    (a) Satisfaction, release, or discharge of liens.

    (b) Purchase-money bond and mortgage.

    (c) Bill of sale of personal property included in the sale.

    (d) Letter of introduction to tenants.

    (e) Satisfaction of judgments.

    (f) Authorization of sale by corporation (if owner is corporation).

(7) Prepare statement showing apportionment of:

    (a) Taxes.

    (b) Electric, gas, and water charges.

    (c) Rents—as adjusted, for prepaid and accrued rent.

    (d) Salaries.

    (e) Services—exterminator, burglary alarm systems.

(8) Have the deed signed, sealed, and executed by the parties necessary to convey good title. Acknowledgments of signatures required. Affix appropriate revenue stamps and prepare proper closing statement and then record purchase-money mortgages.

[¶2918]   PURCHASER'S CONSIDERATIONS

(1) Get affidavit of title.

(2) Obtain letter of introduction to tenants.

(3) Check violations of building regulations, any dwelling laws, health and fire agencies. Determine whether there is a certificate of occupancy outstanding.

(4) Look for chattel mortgages or conditional sales contracts on personal property if the latter is included in the sale.

(5) Examine mortgages and satisfactions of record.

(6) Look at existing leases.

(7) Check town, city, village, and school taxes, water and sewerage rates, and assessments.

(8) If corporations are involved make sure that state franchise taxes have been paid.

(9) Look for assessments and vault permits.

(10) See that the premises comply with zoning rules and restrictive covenants.

(11) Find out who is in possession, and whether they are entitled to be.

(12) Are there licenses and permits for signs on the street?

(13) Have state and federal transfer and estate taxes been paid?

(14) Inspect the premises.

(15) Check the age and competency of the seller.

(16) Look at insurance policies and assignments of service contracts.

(17) Contiguity clause if more than one lot is involved.

(18) Final matters—acknowledgment of seller's signature; title company report; power of attorney recorded, if any; revenue stamps on deed and bond.

(19) Record deed, have endorsements on transfer of ownership on insurance policies, and prepare closing statement.

[¶2919] **AFTER THE CLOSING**

The buyer should record his deed and any releases obtained at the closing. The seller should record any purchase-money mortgage. The seller should notify his managing agent and employees that he is no longer responsible for their compensation. The buyer should arrange for necessary services; get the consent of the insurance company to assignment of policies; get any new insurance necessary; have water, gas, electric, and tax bills changed to his name.

[¶2920] **THE CLOSING STATEMENT**

The contract of sale should provide for the adjustment of costs and income. Rents up to the time of closing are credited to the seller and costs are charged against him. Any costs paid beyond the closing date are credited to the seller.

Customary items to seller's credit are: (1) Unexpired portion of current real estate taxes paid by the seller; (2) Unearned insurance premiums; (3) Unexpired portion of service contracts paid in advance; (4) Unexpired portion of water tax; (5) Fuel on hand; (6) Supplies; (7) Delinquent rents.

Customary items to buyer's credit are: (1) Initial deposit or payment; (2) Current balance on existing mortgages; (3) Unpaid taxes for prior years and pro rata portion of taxes for current year; (4) Special assessments due and unpaid; (5) Amounts due for electricity, gas, and water based on meter readings; (6) Accrued wages; (7) Prepaid rents; (8) Tenant's cash security deposits.

The seller pays for revenue stamps, if any, on the deed and the buyer pays for recording unless the contract provides otherwise.

[¶2921] **ESCROW CLOSING**

In some areas, sales are closed in escrow. An escrow is "the deposit by the vendor of his deed with a third party to be delivered to the purchaser upon payment of the purchase price." That third party is the escrowee. Escrows provide a mechanism to insure safety and convenience in carrying out the provisions of previously executed real estate sales contracts. In some cases, however, there is no written contract, the escrow agreement being the sole contract between the parties.

Most of the matters mentioned in the checklist for real estate closings are applicable when the deal is closed through an escrowee. The mechanical details of the closing, however, are turned over to the escrowee.

Among the many advantages of escrows are the following: The escrowee assumes responsibility for the many ministerial tasks involved in a closing; the danger of title defects arising in the gap between the effective date of title evidence and the date of the deed is avoided; and the possibility that the deal may fail is decreased.

[¶2922]   **CONTENTS OF ESCROW AGREEMENT**

(1) Documents to be deposited by seller, such as deed, insurance policies, separate assignments of insurance policies, leases, assignments of leases, abstract or other evidence of title, tax bills, canceled mortgage notes, notice to tenants to pay rent to buyer, and service contracts.

(2) Deposits to be made by buyer, such as purchase price and purchase-money mortgage, if any.

(3) When deed is to be recorded, whether immediately or after buyer's check clears or after seller furnishes evidence of good title at date of contract.

(4) Objections to which buyer agrees to take subject.

(5) Type of evidence of title to be furnished.

(6) Time allowed seller to clear defects in title.

(7) How and when purchase price is to be disbursed, with directions as to what items are to be prorated or apportioned, if escrow holder is to do the prorating.

(8) Directions to deliver deed, leases, insurance policies, assignments of policy, and service contracts to buyer when title is clear.

(9) Return of deposits to the respective parties if title cannot be cleared.

(10) Reconveyance by buyer to seller if deed to buyer has been recorded immediately on signing of escrow agreement and examination of title thereafter discloses seller's title was defective and incurable.

(11) Payment of escrow, title and recording charges, broker's commission, and attorney's fees.

[¶2923]   **FOR FURTHER REFERENCE . . .**

Anderson, P.E., "Tax Consequences of Selling or Losing a Home," 24 Practical Lawyer 57 (June 1978).

Berman, Ira, *Real Estate Closings,* 6th ed., Practising Law Institute, New York, N.Y.

"Effects of the 1976 Tax Reform Act on Real Estate Transactions: Symposium," 13 Real Property Probate and Trust Journal 365 (Spring 1978).

Friedman, Milton R., *Contracts and Conveyances of Real Property,* Practising Law Institute, New York, N.Y.

Kratovil, Robert, *Real Estate Law*.

Real Estate Desk Book, 5th edition, Institute for Business Planning, Inc., Englewood Cliffs, N.J. (1978).

Real Estate Investment Planning, Institute for Business Planning, Inc., Englewood Cliffs, N.J.

REAL ESTATE TRANSACTIONS: CONSUMER PROTECTION

[¶3001] In addition to Truth-In-Lending provisions that apply to consumer real estate transactions, two other federal laws regulate this area—the Home Mortgage Disclosure Act of 1975 and the Real Estate Settlement Procedures Act of 1974 (amended in 1975). These laws are discussed in the paragraphs below.

[¶3002] HOME MORTGAGE DISCLOSURE ACT

The Home Mortgage Disclosure Act is Congress's answer to the problem of redlining—the practice of restricting the amount of mortgage credit made available in particular districts of metropolitan areas. The Act's purpose is not to encourage the extension of unsound credit, but to gather information to enable consumers and government agencies to determine whether financial institutions are "fulfilling their obligations to serve the housing needs of the communities and neighborhoods in which they are located..." (Act §302).

The Act went into effect on June 28, 1976 for a period of four years.

[¶3003] REGULATED INSTITUTIONS

The Federal Reserve Board issued regulations for compliance with the Act (12 CFR part 203). Disclosure regulations apply to any loan that is a first lien on residential property designed for occupancy by one to four families, if the loan is:

☐ Made in whole or part by an institution that is insured by any governmental agency (such as the Federal Deposit Insurance Corporation), or

☐ Made in whole or part by an institution that is regulated by any government agency (such as the Comptroller of the Currency), or

☐ Insured, guaranteed, or supplemented in whole or part by any government agency (including the Department of Housing and Urban Development (HUD)), or

☐ Intended to be sold to the Federal National Home Mortgage Corporation, Federal National Mortgage Association, or Government National Mortgage Association.

Thus, institutions that are effectively covered by the Act are commercial banks, savings banks, savings and loan associations, building and loan associations, homestead associations (including cooperative banks), and credit unions. An institution may gain exemption from regulation if its assets are less than $10 million.

[¶3004] DISCLOSURE REQUIREMENTS

Each regulated institution that maintains a branch or main office in a standard metropolitan statistical area (SMSA—as defined by the Bureau of the Census)

must compile and make available the following information on its allocation of credit:

☐ The number of mortgage loans by census tract (if readily available) or ZIP Code within the SMSA;

☐ The dollar amount of mortgage loans by census tract (if readily available) or ZIP Code within the SMSA;

☐ The number of mortgage loans located outside the SMSA; and

☐ The dollar amount of mortgage loans located outside the SMSA.

This information must be filed with the Federal Reserve Board, and must also be made available for public inspection at the main office and at least one branch in each SMSA.

Notice of availability of records must be given to depositors and interested persons. The notice must be:

☐ Inserted in a periodic statement or other communication sent to all depositors;

☐ Posted in the lobbies of the main office and branches within the SMSA for at least one month; or

☐ Published in a newspaper of general circulation in the area in which the main and branch offices are located.

[¶3005]   REAL ESTATE SETTLEMENT PROCEDURES ACT

Finding that significant reforms in the real estate settlement process were needed to insure that homeowners are provided with greater and more timely information on the nature and costs of the settlement process, Congress enacted the Real Estate Settlement Procedures Act of 1974. Under this law, which became effective as of June 20, 1975, lenders are required to disclose to buyers and sellers the various costs of settlement.

After less than a year, Congress completely overhauled this new law. On January 2, 1976, the RESPA Amendments of 1975 were signed into law (P.L. 94-205, 24 CFR 3500). Their effect was to repeal or modify the more controversial provisions of the original Act. The Amendments repealed the Act's strict advance disclosure requirements and did away with page 3 of the settlement statement, which dealt with Truth-In-Lending.

[¶3006]   COVERAGE

RESPA, including its Amendments, covers all first mortgages on one- to four-family residential properties made by federally insured or regulated lenders (federally related mortgages).

Specifically exempted from coverage are the following:

☐ A loan to cover the purchase or transfer of more than 25 acres;

☐ A home improvement loan, loan to refinance, or other loan whose proceeds are not used to acquire title to property;

☐ A loan to finance the purchase or transfer of a vacant lot, if no proceeds of the loan are to be used for the construction of a one- to four-family residential structure or for the purchase of a mobile home to be placed on the lot;

☐ An assumption, novation, or sale or transfer subject to a pre-existing loan, except the use of or conversion of a construction loan to a permanent mortgage loan to finance purchase by the first user;

☐ A construction loan, except if the construction loan is intended to be used as or converted to a permanent loan to finance purchase by the first user;

☐ A permanent loan whose proceeds will be used to finance the construction of a one- to four-family structure, when the lot is already owned by the borrower or borrowers; or

☐ A loan to finance the purchase of a property when the primary purpose of the purchase is resale.

☐ Execution of land sale contracts.

[¶3007]   DEFINITION OF FEDERALLY
                           RELATED MORTGAGE

The HUD regulations issued pursuant to the 1975 Amendments define "federally related mortgage" as a loan that is not made to finance an exempt transaction (see above) and that meets all four of the following requirements:

(1) The proceeds of the loan are used in whole or in part to finance the purchase by the borrower, or other transfer of title, of the mortgaged property;

(2) The loan is secured by a first lien or other first security interest covering real estate, including a fee simple, life estate, remainder interest, ground lease, or other long-term leasehold estate

(a) That has a structure designed principally for the occupancy of from one to four families, or

(b) That has a mobile home, or

(c) Upon which a structure designed principally for the occupancy of from one to four families is to be constructed using proceeds of the loan, or

(d) Upon which there will be placed a mobile home to be purchased using proceeds of the loan, or

(e) That has a one- to four-family residential condominium unit (or the first lien covering a cooperative unit);

(3) The mortgaged property is located in a state; and

(4) The loan

(a) Is made by a lender meeting certain specified requirements, or

(b) Is made in whole or in part, or insured, guaranteed, supplemented, or assisted in any way, by the Secretary of HUD or any other officer or agency of the federal government, or

(c) Is made in connection with a housing or urban development program administered by the Secretary or other agency of the federal government, or

(d) Is intended to be sold by the originating lender to the Federal National Mortgage Association (FNMA), the Government National Mortgage Association

(GNMA), or the Federal Home Loan Mortgage Corporation (FHLMC), or to a financial institution that intends to sell the mortgage to FHLMC.

[¶3008]   INFORMATION BOOKLETS

Lenders covered by RESPA are required to mail a copy of *Settlement Costs, a HUD Guide* to every loan applicant within three days after his loan application is received. This booklet provides loan applicants with detailed information about the entire settlement process and includes explanations of the various settlement services and costs.

[¶3009]   GOOD-FAITH ESTIMATES

Within three days after receiving a loan application, the lender must provide the applicant with good-faith estimates of settlement costs.

The HUD regulations state that such estimates "must bear a reasonable relationship to the charge a borrower is likely to be required to pay at settlement, and must be based upon experience in the locality or area in which the mortgaged property is located."

If the lender requires the borrower to use a particular attorney, title company, or insurance company and to pay for all or part of such services, these costs must be included in the estimates and must state whether or not the attorney or company has a business relationship with the lender.

[¶3010]   SETTLEMENT STATEMENT

The only vestige of RESPA remaining after enactment of the Amendments is the Uniform Settlement Statement (HUD Form 1). Under one of the Act's provisions, the person conducting the closing in every qualified "federally related mortgage loan" transaction must complete HUD Form 1 by itemizing all charges to be paid by the borrower and seller, except those charges that the lender does not impose on them or charges that the parties agree to pay "outside of closing." The person conducting the settlement must deliver the completed settlement statement to the borrower and seller at or before the closing. If the borrower requests, the person conducting the settlement must allow the borrower to inspect the completed settlement statement during the business day that immediately precedes the closing date.

If the borrower or his agent doesn't attend the closing or a formal closing meeting is not required, the transaction is exempt from the above requirement; however, the lender must deliver a completed settlement statement to the borrower as soon as practicable after the closing.

The borrower may waive his right to have the completed settlement statement delivered to him no later than at the closing. The waiver must be made in writing at or before settlement. Even if the borrower exercises this right of waiver, the lender must still deliver the completed statement to the seller and borrower as soon as possible after the closing.

The Uniform Settlement Statement is not used in two situations: (1) If there are no settlement fees charged to the buyer (because the seller has assumed all settlement-related expenses), or (2) The total amount the borrower must pay at settlement is determined by a fixed amount and the borrower is informed of this fixed amount at the time of loan application. In the latter case, the lender is required to provide the borrower, within three business days of application, with an itemized list of services rendered.

Although the Truth-In-Lending form, formerly part of the Uniform Settlement Statement, has been deleted (because of the repeal of the section that required it), the lender must still provide the borrower with a Truth-In-Lending statement at the time that the loan is consummated. This statement must disclose the annual percentage rate or effective interest rate that the borrower will have to pay on the mortgage loan. Although the lender is not required to give the Truth-In-Lending statement to the applicant when he gives him the information booklet and good-faith estimates of costs, the borrower may request this information when he makes his application.

The lender or the person who conducts the settlement may not charge either the borrower or the seller a fee for preparing the settlement statement.

[¶3011]   PROHIBITION AGAINST KICKBACKS AND UNEARNED FEES

Section 8 of RESPA prohibits kickbacks and the splitting of unearned fees, stating: "(a) No person shall give and no person shall accept any fee, kickback, or thing of value pursuant to any agreement or understanding, oral or otherwise, that business incident to or part of a real estate settlement service involving a federally related mortgage loan shall be referred to any person.

"(b) No person shall give and no person shall accept any portion, split, or percentage of any charge made or received for the rendering of a real estate settlement service in connection with a transaction involving a federally related mortgage loan other than for services actually performed."

The Amendments specifically exempt from §8 "payments pursuant to cooperative brokerage and referral arrangements or agreements between real estate agents and brokers."

[¶3012]   TITLE INSURANCE

A seller of real estate that will be financed by a federally related mortgage is prohibited from directly or indirectly conditioning a sale on the buyer's purchase of title insurance from a particular company. A seller who violates this provision of the Act is liable to the buyer for a sum of money that is equal to three times all the charges imposed for such title insurance.

[¶3013]   **LIMITATION ON ESCROW ACCOUNTS**

Lenders are restricted in the amount of advance deposits they can require buyers to place in escrow accounts for the purpose of insuring payment of real estate taxes and insurance. Under the Act, lenders may require borrowers to place in escrow no more than the amounts due and payable at the time of settlement, plus one-twelfth of the estimated total amount that will be due during the first year after the closing.

[¶3014]   **ACT'S RELATION TO STATE LAW**

The Act does not exempt lenders from complying with any state law (i.e., does not preempt any state law) on settlement practices. However, if any state law is inconsistent with the Act (as determined by the Secretary of HUD), then the Act overrides the state law, but only to the extent of the state law's inconsistency. If a state law is inconsistent, but offers consumers greater protection than the Act, then the state law takes precedence over the Act.

REAL PROPERTY TAX REDUCTION

[¶3101] When a taxpayer feels that real property has been assessed too high, local law affords him an opportunity to petition for a reduction of the assessment. Such a proceeding is usually initiated by making a formal protest with an application for correction to the taxing authority itself. Only after such an application is denied, either in whole or in part, may a proceeding for judicial review of the assessment be initiated. When tax officials turn down the property owner's protest, this action is usually subject to review by a court in an appeals proceeding. This is a proceeding whereby the tax officials are called upon to produce their records and to certify them to the court so that the court may determine whether the officials have proceeded according to the principles of law that they are required to follow in the performance of their assessing duties.

[¶3102] GROUNDS FOR CHALLENGING ASSESSMENTS

Local tax authorities usually have forms of application to be used in asking for an assessment review. If this application of protest is rejected, the next step is to initiate a proceeding in the appropriate court to review the final assessment. The grounds upon which an assessment may be reduced are usually: (1) overvaluation, (2) inequality, and (3) illegality.

[¶3103] OVERVALUATION

This can be established by showing that the assessment of real property has been set at a sum that is higher than the full and fair market value of the property.

[¶3104] INEQUALITY

This somewhat overlaps with overvaluation and can be established by showing that the assessment was made at a higher proportionate valuation than the assessment of other real estate of a like character in the same area. To obtain relief it is usually necessary to show that the assessment is out of proportion as compared with valuations in the municipality generally. To prove inequality it is necessary to examine a considerable number of parcels of real estate for the purpose of comparing the market values of these properties with their assessed valuation and ascertaining the ratio of assessed value to market value in each instance. A case of inequality exists if such a study shows that the ratio of assessed values to market values generally is substantially lower than the ratio between the assessed value and the market value of the property in question.

[¶3105]   **ILLEGALITY**

This exists when the assessment has been levied in an irregular manner or on a basis erroneous in law or in fact other than an error in the evaluation itself. An example of an illegal assessment is the inclusion on the tax roles of an assessment of a parcel of real estate that is legally exempt from taxation.

[¶3106]   **PREPARING THE CHALLENGE**

Here are some steps that can be taken to prepare a challenge:

(1) Assessor's Report: First, carefully examine the assessor's report for the property. If it is predicated on some factual error such as an incorrect description of the property, an incorrect statement of its actual income or expense, or any other matter that concerns the property itself, submit proof of the correct facts.

(2) Cost: Compare the actual cost of the property with its assessed valuation. If the purchase price is substantially below the assessed valuation that's being challenged, and the date of purchase is not too remote from the assessment date, this information will be relevant, provided it can be proven that the property was purchased in an arm's-length transaction.

(3) Operation: Dig out and study the records of income received from the property and the expenses of operation over several years before the tax date. The earning capacity of income-producing property is the most significant single factor in determining its market value for purposes of seeking a tax assessment reduction.

(4) Similar Properties: Make a comparison of sales prices and assessed valuations and of market value and assessed valuations for other comparable properties in the area. This kind of comparison may have already been made by others, so it may be possible to obtain a great deal of information without having to go to the trouble and expense of getting appraisals on a large number of properties.

(5) Experts: The testimony of expert witnesses is usually the most important part of a court case to reduce taxes. Consider using the testimony of a building expert as well as a real estate expert. While the real estate expert will testify about the market value of the property, the building expert can go beyond this and testify about the building's sound structural value or its reproduction cost.

[¶3107]   **REVIEW PROCEDURE**

The course of a proceeding to review a real property assessment usually runs this way after the attorney is employed: The appraiser is hired to select a number of sample properties anywhere in the assessing jurisdiction whose ratios of assessed valuation he believes to be substantially lower than that of his client. The attorney for the assessing jurisdiction likewise selects his own samples whose assessed valuation ratios will tend to support what he contends to be the prevailing ratio. If the opposing attorneys cannot agree on which of these are to be placed in evidence (and such agreement is hardly likely) they submit both lists to the court, which proceeds to choose from such lists an agreed-upon number of samples. The appraisers for both sides evaluate and analyze these sample properties before the court, and are examined and cross-examined as to their respective appraisals of these samples. The court then makes a finding of the true value of each, compares it with assessed valuation, computes all the ratios, averages them, and accepts the result as the prevailing ratio for this particular proceeding. (This finding does not bind any other litigant in any other proceeding, nor may he use it in his own case over objection.)

Finally, the court listens to both appraisers give their opinions of the full, fair market value of the petitioner's own property, arrives at a decision, applies the "prevailing ratio" just found, and thus determines what the assessed valuation of the subject property should have been.

Of course, this is how the practice works in general. The specific procedure in a particular case will vary depending on whether the state constitution does or does not call for uniformity in real estate taxation, provisions of state real property and tax laws with respect to establishng ratios and providing for equalization rates, and establishing procedural rules for the review of real property tax burdens. For example, in New York, the state establishes equalization rights to be used for the distribution of state aid to localities and for other purposes and by legislative enactment that may be offered in evidence by a party to a certiorari proceeding.

[¶3108]   **FOR FURTHER REFERENCE . . .**

Lee, Harry O., and LeForestier, Wilford A., *Review and Reduction of Real Property Assessments.*

Levine, M.J., *Real Estate Tax Shelter Desk Book,* 2nd ed., Institute for Business Planning, Inc., Englewood Cliffs, N.J. (1978).

Real Estate Desk Book, 5th ed., Institute for Business Planning, Inc., Englewood Cliffs, N.J. (1978).

REMEDIES AND DEFENSES

[¶**3201**] The rights and liabilities of a client are inevitably the most immediate concern of any lawyer. Enforcement, protection, and assertion of those rights and remedies are the nuts and bolts of an everyday law practice. When a party has a claim, it is necessary to determine what remedy or remedies may be available. The other party then must decide what defenses may be asserted. In the paragraphs that follow, a number of different remedies and defenses are examined at length.

[¶3202]   **GENERAL REMEDIES**

Distinctions between actions at law and suits in equity have gone by the wayside. Nonetheless, it is important to distinguish between the two types of relief sought because legal remedies afford a right to a jury trial. Claims for legal relief fall under four main headings:
  (1) Enforcement of money obligations;
  (2) Breach of contract damages;
  (3) Tort damages;
  (4) Recovery of property (real or personal).
Each of these is part of the law of restitution.

[¶3203]   **RESTITUTION**

Perhaps the single most pervasive idea in the law of restitution is to prevent unjust enrichment. A number of different remedies, two of the most important being quasi-contract and constructive trusts, are used to achieve this end. At common law, enforcement of a debt (general assumpsit) was the action utilized to provide for the payment of money. Special assumpsit, on the other hand, was originally developed as an action to enforce a simple contract. The theory behind this is that whenever there is a contractual debt, a promise to pay the debt would be implied as a matter of law (*Slade's case*, 4 Coke 92B, K. B. 1602).
  The most common types of debt are for goods sold and delivered (Quantum Valebant) or for work and labor done (Quantum meruit), a quasi-contract action. The main benefit of a quasi-contract as a remedy is the important privilege of attachment. The most common form of state law provides for attachment "in an action upon a contract, express or implied." In seeking a particular remedy, the attorney should carefully frame his cause of action, anticipating the probable defense. It is useful to consult local statutes of limitations, since under certain circumstances, counterclaim or setoff is available even though a statute of limitations that would support an independent action has expired. This is a means of equity that the law provides—a remedy that usually is not permitted to be used to achieve positive recovery, but can be used to the extent of the amount claimed.

320

[¶3204]   ENFORCEMENT OF MONEY OBLIGATIONS

In an action to enforce a money obligation, the aim is to recover judgment for the plaintiff plus interest, costs, and disbursements. Essentially, there are four basic classes of actions:
(1) Contract debts;
(2) Judgment debts;
(3) Statutory penalties (such as antitrust);
(4) Unjust enrichment.
These are explained in the paragraphs below.

[¶3205]   CONTRACT DEBT

In actions for contract debt, the plaintiff must show: (a) promise to pay money (promise may be implied from conduct, as by retention of goods for which defendant has been billed); (b) consideration for the promise, except when statutory provision eliminates the requirement; (c) performance or happening of conditions, if any, of payment; and (d) nonpayment.

[¶3206]   JUDGMENT DEBT

A new judgment for a money debt may be called for when execution of the prior judgment is in jeopardy by reason of the statute of limitations or when property subject to execution is not within the reach of the prior judgment. The plaintiff must show: (a) judgment, and (b) nonpayment.

[¶3207]   STATUTORY PENALTY

These are actions based on a statutory obligation to pay money. The plaintiff must show: (a) violation of statute by the defendant either by act of commission or omission, (b) resulting injury, and (c) nonpayment.

[¶3208]   UNJUST ENRICHMENT

This is a type of indebtedness not created by contract based on the receipt by the defendant of a benefit he may not in fairness retain. The plaintiff must show: (a) receipt by the defendant from the plaintiff of benefits amounting to unjust enrichment, and (b) nonpayment.

[¶3209]   DAMAGES FOR BREACH OF CONTRACT

Contracts are nothing more than promises that something will or will not happen. In the event that there is a breach of that promise, the plaintiff must show:

(1) an express promise (a writing may be required if the statute of frauds so provides), (2) consideration for the promise, (3) performance or nonperformance of the promise, and (4) the resulting damage.

[¶3210]   **TORT DAMAGES**

Protection of person and property against unauthorized invasion or damage characterizes tort. In most instances, a plaintiff must how actual damages—though nominal damages may be obtained in other instances. In certain instances, there may be an action in either tort or contract.

Under certain circumstances, a plaintiff may seek to waive the tort and sue on the underlying contractual obligation that may be implied as a matter of law. This is phrased in terms of quasi-contract and, while the damages for tort may be quite nominal, those for quasi-contract can often be substantial. The careful attorney will phrase his pleadings in such a manner as to allow for the best possible course of action for affirmative recovery. In any case, under the laws of most states, pleadings today are liberally construed; thus, it may be possible, even after the proof has been entered into the record, to make a motion to modify the pleadings to conform to the proof.

[¶3211]   **RECOVERY OF PROPERTY**

Individuals in possession of real or personal property, whose rights in the property are violated, may seek a judgment for damages. An individual not in possession, but who has an immediate right of possession, may seek one of three common law actions or their statutory equivalents: Ejectment, forcible entry and detainer, and replevin. These are described below.

[¶3212]   **EJECTMENT**

To recover real property, an action in the nature of an ejectment or recovery of real property may be instituted. To succeed, it must be shown (1) that the plaintiff has an interest in the property and a right to immediate possession or control, (2) a withholding or denial of possession by the defendant, and (3) the nature and extent of damages.

In an action for ejectment, it is important to recognize that the operation of law will sometimes be slow—especially in a landlord-tenant situation. Under most circumstances, a tenant will be able to successfully remain in possession for a period of six months following the attempted ejectment. Landlord/tenant courts and other judicial authorities that handle this type of law are increasingly tenant-oriented in remedial action.

In dealing with the purchase of realty in which a tenant is involved, it is the wise attorney who insists on a clause that premises are to be delivered vacant at closing of title. Otherwise, the purchaser may end up with a new home and tenants whom it is impossible to eject for at least several months or longer.

[¶3213] FORCIBLE ENTRY AND DETAINER

When an individual is forcibly removed from land, an action may be brought to restore possession. To recover, the plaintiff must show that (1) there was prior peaceable possession, (2) the defendant forcibly entered the land and dispossessed the plaintiff, and (3) that there was a forcible detention of property by the defendant.

[¶3214] REPLEVIN

Recovery of personal property is most commonly known as replevin, but may also be referred to by the older name of detinue, or as a claim and delivery. To recover, the plaintiff must show (1) an interest in the property and a right to both immediate possession and control, (2) wrongful detention by the defendant, and (3) to the extent suffered, any loss resulting in damages.

In terms of secured transactions, it is useful to note that under §9-503 of the Uniform Commercial Code, a secured party has the right to take possession of the debtor's collateral on default. In taking possession, the UCC states that the secured party may proceed without judicial process, if breach of the peace does not result from that action.

[¶3215] EQUITABLE RELIEF

The main types of equitable relief fall within one of these classes:
(1) Injunctions;
(2) Specific performance of contracts;
(3) Recovery of property by equitable means;
(4) Enforcement of money obligations by equitable means; and
(5) Protection against future and multiple claims.

[¶3216] INJUNCTIONS

Injunctions are an extraordinary remedy used by a court to prevent an occurrence of irreparable harm. The individual seeking the injunction must demonstrate not only that the potential for harm exists, but that other means of judicial process that proceed more slowly are not more appropriate. Courts use injunctions sparingly and cautiously. Under the laws of many states, preliminary injunctions or temporary restraining orders may be granted *without notice, provided it appears that irreparable injury will result in the absence of such an order.*

[¶3217]   **SPECIFIC PERFORMANCE**

A party may be compelled judicially to do what a contract requires (but the individual refuses to do) in an action for specific performance. The plaintiff must prove (1) the making of a promise, (2) performance of all obligations on the part of the plaintiff, including performance of all conditions precedent, (3) breach of a promise or contract by the defendant, (4) facts showing the inadequacy of any legal remedy—for example, money damages not an actual substitute for land or unique items (e.g., works of art).

[¶3218]   **EQUITABLE RECOVERY (RESTITUTION)**

When legal means are inadequate or impractical, the plaintiff may be able to use equity as a way of achieving restitution. This concept covers the principles of equitable accounting, constructive trusts, equitable liens, mistakes as to basic assumption, mistakes as to the existence of a contract, mistakes as to property ownership, mistakes in gift transactions, and mistakes of law.

[¶3219]   **ENFORCEMENT OF MONEY OBLIGATIONS BY
EQUITABLE MEANS**

Money obligations may be enforced by equitable means in these situations: (1) the plaintiff's interest is one that historically was protected only in equity; e.g., right to trust proceeds, right to alimony, or support payments; (2) when the money obligation is secured and enforcement of the security is sought; (3) accounting; (4) as incident to a suit for other relief that is by itself within the jurisdiction of equity; (5) when a person wrongfully takes the money of another individual, places it with his own money in an account, and subsequently makes withdrawals from the mingled funds (equitable lien devolves on the part that remains). When embezzlement occurs, a constructive trust is imposed upon the proceeds—if they advance in value, the beneficiary of this increase is not the embezzler, but the party from whom the funds were embezzled. This basic principle of restitution, called tracing, is to prevent the unjust enrichment of any individual.

[¶3220]   **PROTECTION AGAINST FUTURE
(OR MULTIPLE) CLAIMS**

Equity may be utilized to prevent multiple suits or future actions or to aid in either the prosecution or defense of anticipated suits. The most common types of equitable relief sought are interpretations of a will or other instrument, cancellation or interpretation of a writing, quieting title to land, removing clouds on title, declaratory judgments, and interpleader suits.

[¶3221]   **PARTITION**

An action for partition is a division of property among co-owners and may be undertaken either voluntarily by contract or through judicial division. Jointly held property, as well as property held by tenants in common, are generally subject to an action in partition.

When parties take title to property as tenants by the entirety, there is no basis for an action for partition. The purpose of a tenancy by the entirety is to protect and sustain the family unit—to which partition is inimical. In the event that a judgment debtor is married, the creditor is entitled to control that portion of the tenancy by the entirety that the judgment debtor owns (a one-half undivided interest), but is unable to effect partition. In the event the judgment debtor dies prior to his or her spouse, the creditor's holding of his portion is, of course, extinguished.

[¶3222]   **REFORMATION**

Contracts that do not accurately express the intention of the parties may be subject to reformation (Restatement of Contracts §504 and §505). Reformation may sometimes be ineffective because of the parol evidence rule. It is useful to note, however, that a court of equity may grant reformation based upon mistakes.

[¶3223]   **CANCELLATION OF CONTRACTS
                          OR OBLIGATIONS**

The destruction or cancellation of the document embodying a contract will discharge a contractual duty that arises under a formal unilateral contract where done with the intent to discharge the duty. Surrender of the document to the party subject to the duty or someone on his behalf will have a similar effect (see Restatement §432).

[¶3224]   **DECLARATORY JUDGMENTS**

Declaratory judgments are recognized under both federal and state law. Federal law requires that there be an actual controversy. The Uniform Declaratory Judgment Act covers many different areas, which are explored below.

(1) Scope: Courts have the power to declare rights, status, and other legal relations (even if no further relief is claimed). The declaration may be positive or negative and has the effect of a final judgment or decree.

(2) Power to Construe: Determination of a question of construction or validity of an instrument, ordinance, statute, contract, or other legal relation of an individual interested in any written instrument is permissible under the Uniform Act.

(3) Before Breach: Contracts may be construed either before or after a breach has occurred.

(4) Executors: Declarations of rights or relationships in ascertaining creditors, heirs, or others, or in directing an executor, trustee, or administrator to undertake (or to abstain from undertaking) a particular transaction in his fiduciary capacity, or determination of any facet of will construction is permissible by declaratory judgment.

[¶3225]   **MANDAMUS**

Mandamus is the single most powerful writ available to require performance of a ministerial goverment duty or function. It is always issued in the sound discretion of the court and will not lie in doubtful cases. In many states, mandamus proceedings have been formally abolished by statute, though replaced by other procedural devices.

[¶3226]   **QUO WARRANTO**

Quo warranto is generally invoked to test the right or title to office, remedy the usurpation of franchises, remedy the abuse of franchises, test primary nominations, and test the right to judicial office. In many states the availability of quo warranto is governed by statutes that have spelled out the cases in which the remedy will lie.

[¶3227]   **TAXPAYER'S ACTIONS**

Proceedings against municipal corporations, counties, towns, and villages are often lodged by taxpayers. Generally speaking, the interest of a taxpayer in a federal treasury is insufficient to maintain a taxpayer's action against the federal government.

In *Walz v. Tax Commission* (397 US 664, 1970), the Supreme Court held that the de minima effects on taxpayers do not give them standing to challenge certain tax exemptions given to religious institutions.

[¶3228]   **CIVIL ARREST**

Civil arrest is an action strongly advised against. The key provisos of this extraordinary remedy inevitably permit an *ex parte* application to the court to authorize the civil (as opposed to criminal) arrest of a defendant. Serious doubts as to its constitutionality have been raised in recent years, and scholars in the field tend to believe that due process demands that a defendant be represented in any such action.

[¶3229]   **ATTACHMENT**

Attachment is a proceeding under which the plaintiff acquires control of the defendant's property before determination of any of the issues involved in a lawsuit. If personal jurisdiction over a defendant is not available, attachment may be utilized as a jurisdictional predicate provided service is made prior to, or at the time of, the attachment.

Attachment is another area of the law in which serious constitutional questions have been raised—except when attachment is utilized as a jurisdictional predicate (a means to gain jurisdiction over a defendant who is not present within the state). Normally, any debt or property against which a money judgment may be enforced is subject to attachment, Ordinarily, a sheriff or comparable official is used to levy prior to final judgment.

[¶3230]   **WRIT OF ASSISTANCE**

The writ of assistance is utilized in carrying out equity decrees in much the same manner as the execution is utilized in carrying out an action at law. The writ of assistance is frequently utilized in many jurisdictions to establish the ownership of property or to put a litigant into possession of property.

[¶3231]   **CERTIORARI**

Certiorari is available in many jurisdictions to review the findings of a lower tribunal or an administrative agency. The availability of certiorari varies from state to state. In some states its availability is governed exclusively by statute. Unless otherwise provided by statute, discretion will be important in determining whether certiorari is available. Essentially, certiorari represents the review of a judicial determination. However, the nature of the action rather than the body taking the action will usually determine whether certiorari is available.

[¶3232]   **COMMON DEFENSES**

The paragraphs below provide basic information concerning various legal defenses.

[¶3233]   **ACCORD AND SATISFACTION**

Accord and satisfaction is a means of discharging a contract or settling a contract or tort claim by substituting for the contract or claim an agreement for its satisfaction and then performing in accordance with the agreement. It bars the original claim. Generally, to have this effect, however, the agreement must be fully executed. But the parties themselves may by clear language make the agreement itself and not its performance operate as satisfaction of the original claim.

[¶3234]   ACT OF GOD

This may be used as a defense to action on contract or in tort. The defendant must show that: (a) the act or event complained of was the result of an act of God; (b) the defendant was not responsible and his negligence did not contribute to it in any way.

[¶3235]   ADVERSE POSSESSION

The defendant must show that his possession was actual and not constructive, under a claim of right, hostile, open and notorious, exclusive and continuous for the period required by law.

[¶3236]   ANOTHER ACTION PENDING

The defendant must show that there is pending and undisposed of another action in another court by the same plaintiff against the same defendant based on the same cause of action and involving the same parties.

[¶3237]   ARBITRATION AND AWARD

An award made under a valid arbitration agreement ordinarily operates to discharge the claim submitted to arbitration. The party relying on this defense must show: (a) an agreement on the part of the plaintiff to submit his claim to arbitration; (b) submission of the claim to arbitration as agreed; and (c) making of the award, and notice or publication, if these matters are jurisdictional to proceedings for enforcement.

[¶3238]   ASSUMPTION OF RISK

In negligence cases, it is a recognized principle that one who voluntarily assumes the risk of injury from a known danger can't recover. Under some rules of procedure, assumption of risk is regarded as an affirmative defense that must be specially pleaded, but under others it may be proved under a general denial. While often closely associated with contributory negligence, it is distinguishable. Assumption of risk, for example, may bar recovery even though the plaintiff may have acted with what might be considered due care. Usually this defense is invoked in cases involving a contractual relationship between a plaintiff and a defendant (master and servant, or other relationship), but it can be used in other cases as well. The defendant must show: (a) an unreasonable risk in the situation or thing causing the injury; and (b) knowledge of the risk by the plaintiff at the time.

[¶3239] BREACH OF CONDITION SUBSEQUENT

Breach of a condition subsequent operates to destroy vested estates and contract rights. Because of their effect, they are not favored and will be found to exist only where the language creating them is very clear. In any case, if found to exist, the condition subsequent will be strictly construed.

[¶3240] CAPACITY OR RIGHT OF PARTY TO SUE OR BE SUED

This defense may be raised in the following situations:

(1) The plaintiff is a foreign corporation doing business within the state without having qualified to do so, suing on a business transaction arising within the state;

(2) The plaintiff is not the real party in interest;

(3) The plaintiff is not sui juris;

(4) Other necessary parties are not joined; the plaintiff is not the real party in interest;

(5) The defendant is a foreign corporation, is not qualified to do business within the state, and does not do business within the state, and the cause of action alleged did not arise within the state;

(6) The defendant is without capacity to be sued (as by reason of infancy).

[¶3241] CONTRIBUTORY NEGLIGENCE

There are essentially three forms of contributory negligence with which every plaintiff and defendant should be acquainted. In some jurisdictions, contributory negligence is a complete bar to recovery. In other jurisdictions, contributory negligence is used as an offset to the plaintiff's claim (e.g., 10% negligent plaintiff has his recovery diminished by that amount). Under the third form, which is an amalgam of the other two, a plaintiff must be less than 51% negligent, and his recovery is diminished by a proportional amount (if more than 51% negligent, the plaintiff has no grounds to sue). It is essential not only to consult local law on this subject (where it is currently in a state of flux), but also to frame pleadings in such a manner that if it is required that the plaintiff not be contributorily negligent, this be explicitly stated in the complaint.

[¶3242]   **DISCHARGE IN BANKRUPTCY**

The defendant must show: (a) details as to filing of petition by or against him, adjudication of bankruptcy, and granting of discharge; (b) that the plaintiff's claim was due and owing at the time of the bankruptcy proceedings and was included in the schedules filed or was omitted for specified reasons. Unless it appears from the plaintiff's petition that the claim sued on was provable in bankruptcy and was not excepted from discharge by operation of law, the defendant is sometimes also required to show that the claim was provable and not excepted from discharge.

[¶3243]   **DURESS**

The defendant must show that execution of the instrument relied on by the plaintiff was induced by fear of violence or imprisonment or the result of other wrongful pressure.

[¶3244]   **ELECTION OF REMEDIES**

The defendant must show that the plaintiff had two existing alternative remedial rights, inconsistent and not reconcilable with each other based on the state of facts alleged in the present action, and that the plaintiff prior to the commencement of the present action elected to pursue the alternative remedy.

At the pleading stage, it is possible to plead inconsistency, provided that prior to trial or at trial an election of remedies is made.

[¶3245]   **ESTOPPEL**

The defendant must show conduct or acts, words, or silence on the part of the plaintiff amounting to representation or concealment of material facts, with knowledge or imputed knowledge thereof, and that such representation, silence, or concealment was relied on by the defendant to his damage or detriment.

[¶3246]   **EXTENSION OF TIME FOR PAYMENT**

The defendant must show written agreement based on valuable consideration extending the time of payment until a certain date and that by reason of the extension the amount claimed is not due and payable.

[¶3247]   **FAILURE OR WANT OF CONSIDERATION**

Whenever consideration is required, want or failure of consideration is a defense. If consideration is required but need not be alleged, want or failure is an affirmative defense. Check state statutes making consideration unnecessary for written promises or creating presumption of consideration when a promise is in writing.

[¶3248]   FRAUD

Some courts distinguish between fraud in the making (the person didn't know what he was signing) and fraud in the inducement (he knew what he was signing but was induced to sign by fraudulent misrepresentations) and make the former a negative defense and the latter an affirmative defense requiring a special plea. The defendant must show false representation by the plaintiff, with knowledge of falsity made with intent to defraud the defendant, and that it was relied on by the defendant to his damage.

[¶3249]   LACHES

The defendant must show a claim for equitable relief has been unreasonably delayed, and that hardship or injustice to the defendant will result from its enforcement.

[¶3250]   LICENSE

In actions for damages based on intentional wrong to the plaintiff, a showing that the plaintiff consented to the wrong will usually bar relief. In actions for assault and battery and false imprisonment, the plaintiff must generally show absence of consent, but in actions for intentional damage to property, real or personal, license is an affirmative defense.

[¶3251]   PAYMENT

Payment is normally utilized as an affirmative defense. The most common approach is to utilize it in an answer to a complaint. Ordinarily, a requisite element is that proof of payment be shown.

[¶3252]   PRIVILEGE

Conduct that under ordinary circumstances will subject the actor to liability may under particular circumstances not subject him to liability; that is, the conduct may be privileged. Examples: (a) self-defense; (b) defense of a third person; (c) public necessity, as where property is destroyed to prevent spread of fire; (d) protection or defense of property; (e) parental discipline; (f) seizure under legal process; and (g) privilege to abate nuisance.

[¶3253]   **RELEASE**

A release may take the form of a declaration that a particular claim or cause of action has been discharged or the form of an agreement not to sue. In either form, if it is in writing and supported by consideration, or local law dispenses with requirement of consideration, as it may in the case of instruments under seal, it may be pleaded in bar.

[¶3254]   **RES JUDICATA**

There are three types: (a) merger (claim is merged in judgment recovered by the plaintiff); (b) bar (in prior action on the same claim the plaintiff failed to get judgment); and (c) estoppel (in prior action an issue involved in a second action was settled by judgment of a court and the plaintiff is estopped from relitigating the same issue even though the cause of action is different and the plaintiff cannot recover in the second action unless it's established). If prior judgment is not on the merits, but is based on procedural defect, it will not have the effect of res judicata.

[¶3255]   **STATUTE OF FRAUDS**

Specified transactions are unenforceable unless evidenced by a writing signed by the party to be charged. Transactions within statute: (a) special promise to answer for debt or default of another (contracts of suretyship and guarantee); (b) contracts for sale of interests in real property; (c) contracts for the sale of goods of more than a certain value (under the Uniform Commercial Code, the common sum is $500); (d) contracts not to be performed within a year; (e) contracts to lease real property for more than a year; (f) contracts to bequeath property; (g) contracts to establish a trust; (h) conveyance or assignment of trust in personal property; (i) promise to pay debt discharged in bankruptcy; and (j) contracts made in consideration of marriage.

[¶3256]   **STATUTE OF LIMITATIONS**

Generally, failure of the plaintiff to bring an action within the time limited by statute is an affirmative defense. Sometimes the plaintiff must show, as a condition of relief, that action is brought within the time limit. There are general and special statutes, and the defense must make sure it isn't relying on a general statute when a special statute applies.

[¶3257]   **ULTRA VIRES**

The defendant corporation must show that the transaction on which the action is based was beyond its express or implied powers.

[¶3258]   **USURY**

Local law must be checked as to legal rates of interest, effect of usury (collection of excessive interest barred, collection of all interest, forfeiture of principal), and whether or not a corporation may plead.

[¶3259]   **WAIVER**

The defendant must show that prior to the action the plaintiff voluntarily relinquished interest asserted in action and that the defendant relied on the relinquishment.

[¶3260]   **WANT OF JURISDICTION**

Want of jurisdiction of the person of the defendant must be properly pleaded (almost universally a special appearance is called for) and will be waived by a general appearance. Want of jurisdiction of the subject matter may be raised at any time either by the defendant or by the court on its own motion.

[¶3261]   **FOR FURTHER REFERENCE . . .**

Dobbs on Remedies, West Publishing (Hornbook).
Johnson, W.F., Jr., "Remedies in Trade Secret Litigation," 72 Northwestern University Law Review 1004-31 (January-February 1978).
McDowell, B., "Party Autonomy in Contract Remedies," 57 Boston University Law Review 429-60 (May 1977).
Pillai, K.G.J., "Negative Implication: the Demise of Private Rights of Actions in the Federal Courts," 47 University of Cincinnati Law Review 1-41 (1978).
"Remedies Commodity Options: Implied Civil Remedies for Fraud," 31 Oklahoma Law Review 217-33 (Winter 1978).

SALES AND PURCHASES

[¶3301] Adoption of the Uniform Commercial Code in 49 states, the District of Columbia, and the Virgin Islands (Louisiana has not adopted the entire Code) has served to integrate on a national level buying and selling practices of not only merchants but also consumers. The underlying purpose of the Uniform Commercial Code is to simplify, clarify, and modernize the law governing commercial transactions; to permit a continued expansion of commercial practices through usage, custom, and agreement of the parties; and to make the law uniform among the various states. The effect of any provision in the UCC may be varied by agreement of the parties (unless otherwise provided by the Code). Obligations that are reasonably undertaken in good faith may not be disclaimed by agreement—though the parties may agree by what standards the performance of all obligations may be measured if the standards are not unreasonable (UCC §1-102(3)).

[¶3302] ## HISTORY

Article II of the Uniform Commercial Code, which governs sales, is a complete modernization and revision of what was formerly the Uniform Sales Act, which was written in 1906 and had been adopted by 36 states and the District of Columbia. Coverage in the UCC is far more extensive than the old sales act and was specifically designed to include various bodies of case law that had been developed under the Uniform Sales Act, as well as outside its scope. Article II is arranged in terms of a contract for sale—and the various steps of its performance. Legal consequences are stated in a manner that flows directly from the contract. When property or title passes, or was to pass, is no longer a determining factor. Thus, the written instrument is of paramount importance to a commercial transaction (and, in fact, is required to enforce a contract that is valued at more than $500 or that, by its terms, cannot be performed within one year).

[¶3303] ## OTHER UCC SECTIONS RELATING TO SALES

Sales transactions relating to commercial paper are discussed beginning at ¶901, investment securities at ¶3501, and secured transactions at ¶3401.

[¶3304] ## FORMATION OF A CONTRACT

Contracts for the sale of goods for a price of $500 or more are not enforceable unless some writing between the parties indicates that a contract for sale has been made. The UCC provides that even if a contract omits or incorrectly states a term agreed upon, or material terms are omitted (or imprecisely stated), the contract may be enforced. The price, time, place of payment or delivery, general quantity of goods, or even particular warranties all may be omitted. (To the extent that the quantity of goods is incorrectly stated, a sales contract is only enforceable to the extent of the quantity shown on the writing.) The sole requirement is that the writing afford the fundamental basis for believing that orally offered evidence rests upon a real transaction. Even a pencil writing on a scratch pad may bind the parties to be charged.

[¶3305] **WRITTEN CONFIRMATION
BETWEEN MERCHANTS**

Oral contracts between merchants upon which a written confirmation is subsequently made are binding between parties if the party receiving the written confirmation fails to object to its contents within 10 days after receipt (UCC §2-201(2)).

[¶3306] **THE WRITTEN CONTRACT**

Written contracts under the Uniform Commercial Code have a paramount priority and may not be contradicted by evidence of prior agreement or contemporaneous oral conversations that alter the terms of the written agreement (the parol evidence rule). However, the written contract may either be explained or supplemented by evidence of consistent additional terms, or by any course of usual dealing or usage of trade. Even the inclusion of a ''merger clause'' (stating that this writing contains the entire agreement between the parties) does not bar the use of additional ''usual'' terms (UCC §2-202).

[¶3307] **THE OFFER**

When a merchant offers to buy or sell goods in a signed agreement, and no term for either purchase or sale is provided, it is assumed that there is a three-month period for the sale (UCC §2-205). An offer by a merchant is construed as inviting acceptance in any manner and in any medium reasonable under the circumstances—modifying the older rule that required acceptance to be made in the manner of the offer (e.g., a mailed offer requiring a mailed acceptance). Firm offers no longer require consideration in order to bind the parties. Instead, they must merely be characterized as offers and expressed in signed writing by the party to be charged.

[¶3308] **MODIFICATION TO A CONTRACT**

Acceptance or written confirmation of a contract, even if additional or different terms are agreed to, operates as an acceptance of the contract. Additional terms are construed as proposals to the addition of the contract and, between merchants, all such additions become part of the contract unless a material alteration takes place or the offer expressly prohibits the use of additional terms. This so-called "battle of the forms" found in UCC §2-207 substantively changes prior law, which generally required an acceptance of the offer exactly as it stood.

[¶3309] HOW TO LIMIT ALTERATION OF WRITTEN PURCHASE AND SALES AGREEMENTS

Between merchants, written purchase and sales agreements are necessary in order to prevent the use of unwanted conditions to a transaction, to disclaim warranties, and to control the risk of loss. To the extent that a seller wants no contract formed other than by the terms of sale, a clause in conspicuous type limiting the acceptance to the exact terms of the offer is required (UCC §2-207(2)(a)).

[¶3310] WRITTEN CONTRACT REQUIREMENTS

The statute of frauds requires a contract for the sale of goods to be in writing if the goods are for the *price* of $500 or more. However, part performance would take a contract out of the statute of frauds to the extent of the part performance.

In cases, where goods are to be specially manufactured and are not ordinarily resalable in the normal course of the seller's business, an oral agreement will be binding if the seller has made a substantial beginning on or a commitment to acquire the goods called for in an agreement.

To meet the requirements of the statute of frauds, the agreement generally must be signed by the party against whom it is to be enforced. However, the Uniform Commercial Code provides for the enforcement of a letter of confirmation in transactions between merchants if the person receiving the letter has reason to know of its contents. A person receiving a letter of confirmation may object within 10 days, and avoid its effect.

Contracts for the sale of personal property (not the sale of goods or securities, or pursuant to security agreements) are subject to a different statute of frauds limitation. They're not enforceable by way of action, or defense beyond $500, unless there is some writing to indicate that a contract for sale has been made between the parties at a definite or stated price. The subject matter must be reasonably identified, and the party against whom enforcement is sought must have signed the document (UCC §1-206).

[¶3311] WARRANTIES: THE UCC STANDARD

Under the UCC, warranty by description and warranty by sample are express warranties and they may not be avoided by any disclaimer that is not consistent with the warranty itself. This means that any disclaimer must be explicit and should immediately follow the language of description.

The implied warranty of "merchantability" and "fitness" can be avoided only by a disclaimer that is written conspicuously and expressed in specific language. All implied warranties are excluded by expressions like "as is," "with all faults," or other language that in common understanding calls the buyer's attention to the exclusion and makes plain that there are no implied warranties.

Note that by making claims on a label or container, the seller undertakes that his goods will conform to the claims.

For a table of UCC warranty rules, see ¶3329.

[¶3312]   FEDERAL WARRANTY STANDARDS

Notwithstanding UCC express and implied warranty provisions, the federal government has entered the field with the Magnuson-Moss Act (88 Stat. 2183, 15 USC §2301-2312, Supp. V. 1975). During debate in Congress on this warranty protection bill, it was described as "one of the most important pieces of consumer protection legislation . . . since the Federal Trade Commission Act itself was passed in 1914." The Act creates an entirely new body of federal law with respect to consumer warranties. However, the legislation does not displace pertinent provisions of the Uniform Commercial Code, state requirements that relate to labeling, or disclosure with respect to written warranties or performance not applicable to written warranties complying with the Magnuson-Moss legislation. Magnuson-Moss neither invalidates nor restricts any right or remedy of a consumer under state law or any other federal law, nor does it affect or impose liability on any person for personal injury or supersede any provision of state law regarding consequential damages for injury to the person, or other injury.

Magnuson-Moss does *not* require that a consumer product, or any of its components, be warranted by the manufacturer. While the Act is not at all applicable to products costing less than $5, products costing more than $10 must be designated "Full (statement of duration) Warranty," or "Limited Warranty."

[¶3313]   DISCLOSURE REQUIREMENTS UNDER
MAGNUSON-MOSS

For products costing more than $15, the following information must be included if a written warranty is supplied to the consumer.

☐ Who is entitled to the protection.

☐ Identification of the parts covered by the warranty.

☐ Indication of what will be done to correct defects or failures (including which items or services will be paid for by the warrantor and which expenses must be borne by the consumer).

☐ The date that the warranty becomes effective (unless it is the date of purchase).

☐   Steps the consumer must follow to obtain performance under the warranty (including a statement of the name of the warrantor, the mailing address, name and address of a department responsible for warranty obligations, or a telephone number that the consumer may use without charge to obtain information).

Separate warranty requirements cover the sale of used cars.

[¶3314]   COVERAGE AND DEFINITIONS UNDER MAGNUSON-MOSS

Magnuson-Moss applies only to "consumer products," which means any tangible personal property normally used for personal, family, or household purposes (including any property that is intended to be attached or installed in any real property). Products purchased solely for commercial or industrial use are excluded.

[¶3315]   PRESERVATION OF CONSUMER CLAIMS AND DEFENSES

As a means of giving consumers recourse when the goods that they purchase prove unsatisfactory, the Federal Trade Commission has promulgated rules to preserve certain consumer claims and defenses (16 CFR Part 433). The aim of the Federal Trade Commission's regulations is to insure that a seller fulfills his warranty obligations to the consumer by declaring it an unfair and deceptive practice for a seller in the course of financing a consumer purchase of goods to employ procedures (generally known as a "holder-in-due-course defense") that would make the consumer's duty to pay independent of the seller's duty to fulfill contractual obligations.

In the course of public proceedings, the FTC documented numerous cases in which consumer purchase transactions were financed in such a way that the consumer was legally obligated to make full payment to the creditor despite a breach of warranty, misrepresentation, or even fraud on the part of the seller. Previously, a seller was able to execute a credit contract with a buyer containing a promissory note that was subsequently assigned to a credit company—which took free of any claim or defense that the buyer might have had against the seller (such as breach of warranty). If local statutes prohibited the use of these promissory devices, some sellers inserted a "waiver of defense" in installment sale agreements. The FTC rules are designed to prevent widespread abuses of credit terms and preserve a consumer's legally sufficient claims and defenses so that they may be asserted to either defeat or diminish the right of a creditor to be paid whenever a seller who arranges financing for a buyer fails to keep his side of the bargain. The basic mechanism for accomplishing this is the requirement that a clause be placed in all consumer credit contracts that states, "Any holder of this consumer credit contract is subject to all claims and defenses whch the debtor could assert against the seller of goods or services obtained . . ." (text varies according to circumstances, see 16 CFR Part 433.2, 1976).

[¶3316] WARRANTIES (UCC VS. MAGNUSON-MOSS)

It is important to distinguish between commercial obligations and those involving consumer transactions. The Magnuson-Moss Act, described at ¶3312 is applicable to all consumer goods costing $5 or more for which a written warranty is supplied by the seller. Under the Act, the seller is not required to give a written warranty—but if the seller so elects in a consumer transaction, certain requirements must be met, including a prohibition against disclaimer. For commercial transactions, the UCC governs—not Magnuson-Moss.

[¶3317] DESCRIPTION OF GOODS

Specifications, samples, models, or general descriptive language may be used as a means of describing the subject matter of a sales contract. To the extent that sample and technical specifications conflict, the latter prevails (UCC §2-317(a)). To the extent that a general description differs from a sample, the sample prevails for warranties either expressed or implied (UCC §2-317(b)). If a buyer relies on the seller's skill and judgment in either selecting or furnishing the goods (even if the seller did not know that the buyer did rely—but the seller had reason to know that the buyer might rely on his skill and judgment), a warranty has been created (UCC §2-315). (See table at ¶3329.)

Note that for consumer sales, the Magnuson-Moss Act requires that certain aspects of warranty be designated. The sellers of consumer products with written warranties are required to maintain a binder or series of binders in each department in which a consumer product with a written warranty is offered for sale or for inspection by consumers (16 CFR Part 702.3, 1976). Magnuson-Moss permits the disclaimer of consequential damages under a full warranty only if the exclusion on limitations appears conspicuously on the face of the warranty. It does not permit exclusion of consequential damages if state or other federal law does not so permit.

[¶3318] PRICE

It is possible for a contract of sale to be concluded without a price being specified. If this occurs, the price of the goods purchased will be a reasonable price at the time of the delivery (UCC §2-305(1)).

Below in checklist form are some of the more popular methods for determining price.

☐ *Cost Plus:* The plus factor here is overhead and profit, and any agreement should spell out precisely what is to be included in the cost factor.

☐ *Market Price:* Normally relates to the selling price on some organized mercantile or other exchange that is directly ascertainable.

☐ *Price in a Trade Journal:* If the journal ceases publication, the price is the reasonable price at the time at delivery (UCC §2-305(1)(c)).

☐ *Government-Related Price:* Used in time of price control or other regulatory schemes.

☐ *Price by Leading Suppliers:* Industry leaders' prices are used as a means of pegging the contract price. (It is important to avoid violation of antitrust trade regulations statutes.)

☐ *Price by Appraisal:* An expert in the field sets the price. Unless otherwise agreed, if this method fails, the price will be a reasonable price at the time of delivery.

☐ *Price to Be Agreed Upon:* Ordinarily, this means a fair market price. Should the parties fail to agree, UCC §2-305 requires a reasonable price unless the agreement indicates that the parties did not intend the contract to be made if there was no agreement on price.

☐ *Price Set by Seller:* UCC §2-305(2) requires that the seller use "good faith" in setting prices under this standard.

☐ *Escalator Clauses:* Use of standard price indices published by the U.S. Department of Labor, the Department of Commerce, or other recognized entities reflecting overall economic trends, including price rises, such as the Consumer Price Index or Wholesale Price Index.

☐ *Gold or Foreign Currency Clauses:* An agreement that payment be made in gold, foreign currency, or their dollar equivalents involves some risk that the price of gold or the exchange rate of a "stable" foreign currency is related more to speculation that cannot be anticipated than to actual economic conditions.

[¶3319]   **DELIVERY**

In the absence of a specific agreement between the parties, the place of delivery will be the locale of the goods where they were identified to the agreement at the time the agreement was made. Where the goods were not identified to the agreement at the time the agreement was made, the place of delivery will be the seller's place of business, or if he has no place of business, his home, unless otherwise agreed.

Delivery terms are often spelled out in terms of standard commercial abbreviations. The following checklist of obligations arising from the use of these terms is based upon the definitions contained in the Uniform Commercial Code:

FOB (Place of Shipment): Unless otherwise agreed, the seller must ship the goods and bear the expense of putting the goods in the hands of the shipper. The seller must notify the buyer of the shipment and obtain and deliver necessary documents of title so as to enable the buyer to obtain possession. The buyer must reasonably give the seller proper shipping instructions (UCC §2-504 and 2-319).

FOB (Place of Destination): Unless otherwise agreed, the seller must at his own expense transport the goods to the place of destination, give the buyer reasonable notification to enable him to take delivery, tender delivery at a reasonable time, and keep the goods available for a reasonable time to permit the buyer to take possession (UCC §2-319 and 2-503).

FOB (Car or Other Vehicle): In addition to putting the goods in the possession of the carrier the seller must load them on board the truck, car, or other vehicle used by the carrier (UCC §2-319).

FOB (Vessel): The seller must place the goods on board the vessel designated by the buyer and furnish a proper form bill of lading in an appropriate case (UCC §2-319).

FAS (Vessel): The seller must, at his own expense, deliver the goods alongside the vessel designated by the buyer or on the dock designated in the manner usual in the particular port, and obtain a receipt in exchange for which the carrier is obligated to issue a bill of lading (UCC §2-319).

CIF: The price stated includes the cost of goods, insurance, and freight to the named destination. The seller is obligated to load the goods, obtain a receipt showing that the freight has been paid or provided for, obtain a negotiable bill of lading, insure the goods for the account of the buyer, and forward all necessary documents to the buyer with commercial promptness (UCC §2-320).

If delivery is to be made to the buyer, the buyer must furnish facilities reasonably suited for accepting delivery (UCC §2-503).

When goods are in a warehouse or otherwise in possession of a bailee and the agreement calls for delivery to the buyer without moving the goods, the seller must render a negotiable document of title or procure acknowledgment by the bailee or warehouseman of the buyer's right to possession of the goods. Unless the buyer objects, a nonnegotiable document of title or a written direction to the warehouseman or bailee to deliver is sufficient tender of delivery. When the bailee receives notice of the buyer's rights in the goods, those rights are fixed as to the bailee and all third persons. The risk of loss of the goods will not pass to the buyer until the buyer has had a reasonable time to present the document or direction to the warehouseman or bailee to deliver. If delivery is tendered in the form of a nonnegotiable document of title, the liability for the failure of the warehouseman to honor the document of title remains upon the seller until the buyer has had reasonable opportunity to present the document. Failure of the bailee to honor the document of title defeats the tender.

C & F or CF: These terms are equivalent to CIF, except that the price includes only the cost of goods plus freight to the named destination—insurance is not included. Otherwise, the terms impose the same duties on buyer and seller as under the CIF designation (UCC §2-320).

[¶3320]   **BUYER'S RIGHT OF INSPECTION**

Upon tender of delivery or identification of goods, the UCC provides that a buyer has the right to inspect goods that are being purchased. If the contract requires payment prior to inspection, the nonconformity of the goods does not excuse the buyer unless the nonconformity appears without inspection (UCC §2-512). However, an agreement to pay against documents may be construed as waiving the buyer's right to inspection. When the parties have agreed to a C.O.D. delivery, the buyer is presumed to have waived his right of inspection prior to payment (UCC §2-513).

The right of inspection afforded by the UCC includes the right to inspect goods in any reasonable manner. Inspection may include testing, if the nature of the goods cannot be adequately determined without testing. If the testing by the buyer is unreasonable, such as when the buyer uses an unreasonable quantity of the goods in testing or performs needless tests, his testing may be construed as an acceptance. The cost of testing and inspecting will be borne by the buyer except if the goods fail to conform to the agreement. In that case, the UCC provides that the buyer may recover the reasonable cost of inspection and testing from the seller (UCC §2-513).

[¶3321]   **TIME OF DELIVERY**

Using the standard of commercial reasonableness, the UCC provides that if the agreement is silent as to the time of delivery, it shall take place at a reasonable time. Even contract language calling for immediate delivery is construed as being reasonably thereafter. A "time is of the essence" clause (bargained for in the agreement) means what it says—a delayed delivery may be unacceptable and cause a breach of contract.

Late delivery will be excused if caused by the occurrence of a contingency, the nonoccurrence of which was a basic assumption on which the agreement was made, or the seller's compliance in good faith within the applicable governmental regulations whether or not the regulation later proves invalid (UCC §2-615). The UCC also provides that the seller's delay in delivery will be excused if he suspended performance due to the buyer's repudiation or the buyer's failure to cooperate as required in the agreement (UCC §2-311 and 2-611).

[¶3322]   **OPTIONS AS TO PERFORMANCE**

If one party to an agreement has the right to specify the terms of performance, the UCC provides that if the specifications are made in good faith and within the limits of commercial standards of reasonableness, they will be upheld (UCC §2-311, Official Comment 1; in effect in 49 states, the District of Columbia, and the Virgin Islands). When the agreement calls for the buyer to receive an assortment of goods, the buyer is permitted to determine the assortment, unless otherwise provided by the parties.

[¶3323]   **RIGHT TO RETURN**

The buyer has the right to return goods if they fail to conform to the agreement. However, the agreement may specifically provide for the right to return goods. If the buyer has the right to return goods that he is purchasing for his own use, the contract is considered a sale on approval. If the buyer is purchasing the goods for resale, the contract is characterized as a sale or return (UCC §2-326). In a sale on approval, the obligation of return and the risk of loss are on the seller; in a sale or return, the obligation of return is on the buyer unless otherwise agreed (UCC §2-326 and 2-327). A "consignment" or "on memorandum" sale is characterized by the UCC as a sale or return.

Note: UCC §2-326(3)(a) is not in effect in California.

[¶3324] PASSAGE OF TITLE

The importance of title in commercial transactions has been substantially reduced through promulgation of the Uniform Commercial Code. However, for purposes of delivery and other requirements, it is necessary to understand the applicability of certain rules set forth in the paragraphs below.

[¶3324.1] Seller Controls Performance

Title passes to the buyer when the seller has completed his performance with regard to delivery of the goods to the buyer (UCC §2-401(2)).

For example, if the contract calls for delivery FOB cars at the seller's warehouse, title passes when the goods are placed on the cars at the seller's warehouse.

[¶3324.2] Seller to Ship

When the agreement requires the seller to send the goods to the buyer but does not require delivery at the place of destination, title to the goods passes to the buyer at the time and place of shipment (UCC §2-401(2)(a)).

For example, if the agreement calls for delivery FOB New York and the goods are to be shipped to San Francisco, title passes to the buyer when the goods are shipped from New York.

[¶3324.3] Seller to Deliver

If an agreement requires the seller to deliver the goods to the buyer at the place of destination, title to the goods passes to the buyer on delivery (UCC §2-401(2)(b)).

For example, if the agreement calls for delivery by the seller at the buyer's place of business, title passes when the goods are delivered.

[¶3324.4] Delivery Without Moving Goods—Document of Title

If delivery is to be made without moving the goods and the seller is required to deliver a document of title, title passes at the time and place where the document of title is delivered (UCC §2-401(3)(a)).

For example, if goods in a warehouse are sold with the understanding that delivery will be made by the delivery of a warehouse receipt by which the buyer may take possession of the goods, title passes on the delivery of the warehouse receipt by the seller to the buyer.

[¶3324.5]   Delivery Without Moving Goods

If delivery is to be made without moving the goods and the goods have been identified to the agreement at the time of making the agreement, title to the goods passes to the buyer at the time of making the agreement (UCC §2-401(3)(b)).

For example, if the buyer agrees to purchase an identified machine located in the seller's yard, the title passes at the time of making the agreement, if nothing else remains to be done.

[¶3324.6]   Withdrawal of Acceptance

If the buyer refuses to accept the goods or withdraws his acceptance of the goods, title revests in the seller by operation of law (UCC §2-401(4)).

[¶3324.7]   Sale on Approval

When goods are sold primarily for the use of the buyer rather than for resale, with the understanding that they may be returned, and the agreement is characterized as one of sale on approval, title passes to the buyer upon his approval (UCC §2-326 and 2-327).

For example, if the agreement calls for sale of a machine that the buyer will use in his manufacturing process, he may be given a reasonable time for trial. If after a reasonable trial he approves it, title passes when he approves it or decides to keep it. Similarly, if he has not disapproved or rejected the goods before the end of the prescribed trial period, title passes at the termination of that period.

The parties may not agree that title to the goods are to pass to the buyer before the goods are in existence.

[¶3325]   RISK OF LOSS

Risk of loss is no longer part of the question of title: The UCC's major innovation in this area is the separation of these two principles. As a general rule, the Code's position on risk of loss is that the party that is best equipped to bear the loss (or the party who should be expected to bear it) will bear it. The following paragraphs set forth the rules derived from the UCC for determining risk of loss.

[¶3325.1]   Goods to Be Delivered to Carrier

If the seller is required to deliver the goods to a carrier, the risk of loss shifts to the buyer when the seller duly delivers the goods to the carrier (UCC §2-509).

[¶3325.2]   FOB—Place of Shipment

When goods are sold FOB place of shipment, the risk of loss shifts to the buyer when the goods are placed in the hands of the shipper (UCC §2-319).

[¶3325.3]   FOB—Destination

For goods sold FOB place of destination, the risk of loss shifts to the buyer at the time and place of delivery or the time and place where tender of delivery is made to the buyer (UCC §2-319).

[¶3325.4]   Seller to Deliver

If the seller must deliver the goods to the destination, the risk of loss shifts to the buyer when the delivery is tendered to him so as to enable him to take possession (UCC §2-319).

[¶3325.5]   Sale or Return

If the goods are sold to the buyer for resale, rather than his use, with the understanding that they may be returned, the risk of loss during the return is on the buyer (UCC §2-327).

[¶3325.6]   Sale on Approval

If the goods are sold to a buyer primarily for his own use, rather than resale, and the agreement calls for a "sale on approval," the risk of loss shifts to the buyer when the buyer accepts the goods. If the goods are not accepted, the return is at the seller's risk (UCC §2-327).

[¶3325.7]   Goods Fail to Conform

When goods delivered fail to conform to the requirements of the agreement, the risk of loss remains on the seller until the nonconformity is cured or the nonconforming goods are accepted by the buyer (UCC §2-510).

[¶3325.8]   Buyer Revokes Acceptance

If the buyer initially accepts the goods but subsequently (and justifiably) revokes his acceptance, the buyer may treat the risk of loss as having rested on the seller to the extent of any deficiency in his insurance coverage (UCC §2-510).

[¶3325.9]   Repudiation

If the buyer repudiates the agreement before title to the goods passes to him, the seller may treat the risk of loss as having rested on the buyer for a commercially reasonable time. The seller is limited in holding the buyer for the risk of loss to any deficiency in his effective insurance coverage (UCC §2-510).

[¶3325.10] Delivery of Goods at Buyer's Place of Business—Merchant Seller

If a merchant seller is to deliver the goods at his (the seller's) place of business or the present location of the goods, the risk of loss passes to the buyer on delivery (UCC §2-510).

[¶3325.11] Delivery of Goods at Buyer's Place of Business—Non-Merchant Seller

If a non-merchant seller is to deliver the goods at his (the seller's) place of business or at the present location of the goods to a non-merchant buyer, the risk of loss passes to the buyer on tender of delivery (UCC §2-510).

[¶3325.12] Total Protection

When goods identified to the agreement are destroyed prior to the time the risk of loss would normally have shifted to the buyer without fault of the buyer or seller, the risk of loss is on the seller. However, he may avoid the agreement if the destruction to the goods is total. If the destruction to the goods is partial, the buyer has the option of accepting the goods with a proper price concession or permitting the seller to void the agreement (UCC §2-510(3)).

[¶3325.13] Nonconforming Goods

When the goods or their tender fail to perform to the agreement to an extent that the buyer would be entitled to reject the tender of delivery, the risk of loss remains on the seller until he has cured the defect, or the buyer has accepted (UCC §2-510(1)).

[¶3325.14] Revocation of Acceptance—Insurance Coverage

When the buyer rightly revokes a prior acceptance, he may, to the extent of any deficiency in his effective insurance coverage, run the risk of loss as having been on the seller from the beginning (UCC §2-510(2)).

[¶3325.15] Repudiation—Insurance Coverage

When the buyer repudiates an agreement as to goods that conform to the agreement, the seller may treat the risk of loss as resting on the buyer to the extent of any deficiency in his effective insurance coverage (UCC §2-510(3)).

[¶3325.16] Loss Caused by Third Party—Prior to Identification

If a loss is caused by a third party prior to the identification of the goods to the agreement, the seller may maintain an action against the third party (see UCC §2-501).

[¶3325.17] Loss Caused by Third Party—After Identification

If a loss is caused by a third party after identification of the goods to the agreement, the seller and the buyer both may maintain an action against the third party. Regardless of who sues, any award goes to the one who bore the risk of loss at the time of loss (UCC §2-722(b)).

[¶3325.18] Intention of Parties

Whenever possible, courts will look to the intention of the parties to determine the risk of loss. For example, a manufacturer borrowed a gluing machine under circumstances showing that he intended to buy a larger machine. The court found an agreement to return the machine in the same condition and imposed the risk of loss on the borrower *(Industron Corp. v. Waltham Door and Window Co., Inc.,* 190 N.E. 2d 211).

[¶3325.19] Usage of Trade

If it is the custom or usage of trade for an owner to assume the responsibility for insuring work in progress against risk of loss by fire, in the absence of inconsistent terms in the agreement of the parties, the owner bears the risk of loss *(Mercanti v. Persson*, 280 A. 2d 131, Conn., 1971).

[¶3325.20] Bailee Goods and Possession

Relinquishment of dominion and control so as to constitute delivery to a bailee for storage, as authorized by the buyer, is the ingredient normally required to shift risk of loss from the seller to the buyer *(Ellis v. Bell Aerospace Corp.,* DC Ore., 1970).

[¶3326]   EXCUSED PERFORMANCE

When goods are destroyed prior to the time the risk of loss shifts from the seller to the buyer, the agreement will be voided if they were identified to the agreement prior to their destruction and the destruction was without the fault of either party. If goods identified to the agreement when made are so deteriorated that they no longer conform to the requirements of the agreement or have been partially destroyed without the fault of either party, the buyer has the option of treating the contract as voided or accepting the goods with allowance for the deterioration or destruction (UCC §2-613).

The seller will be excused from performance if performance becomes commercially impracticable due to the occurrence of a contingency, the nonoccurrence of which was a basic assumption on which the agreement was founded (UCC

§2-615). Similarly, the seller's performance will be excused if his performance is rendered impracticable by compliance in good faith with any foreign or domestic governmental regulations.

When the inability to perform applies to only part of the seller's productive capacity, the UCC imposes an obligation on the seller to divide his remaining productive capacity among his customers. He must seasonably notify his customers of their quota of his reduced capacity. Upon receipt of the seller's notification, if the prospective deficiency substantially impairs the value of the contract, the buyer has the option of terminating the agreement or accepting the quantity with which the seller proposes to provide him (UCC §2-615). The seller may include his regular customers in the allocation of production whether or not he has a binding contractual obligation to supply them.

Deposits, Prepayments, and Liquidated Damages: The seller is entitled to keep the buyer's deposit if the buyer refuses to accept the goods or otherwise breaches the agreement provided the deposit does not exceed either 20% of the buyer's obligation or $500, unless the buyer has received a benefit or the seller has incurred damages. If the buyer has benefited or the seller has incurred damages, the amount of the deposit that the seller may keep is increased to reflect the benefit or the damages (UCC §2-317(3)(b)). The UCC recognizes liquidated damages provided they are limited to an amount that is reasonable in light of the anticipated or actual harm caused by the breach. When an agreement calls for liquidated damages, the seller may keep the deposit if it does not exceed the liquidated damages.

[¶3327]   MODIFICATION

The UCC provides that any modification of an agreement must be in writing if the statute of frauds requires that the agreement as modified be in writing. The parties may, however, agree that any modifications of a written agreement must be in writing even though the statute of frauds does not require it (UCC §2-209).

In transactions involving merchants, a provision requiring written modifications must be separately signed by the party receiving the form if that provision appears in a form supplied by the other party.

[¶3328]   ASSIGNMENT

Sellers may delegate their obligation to perform unless the buyer has a substantial interest in having the original seller perform (or control the performance). Assignment, unless specifically prohibited by the terms of agreement, is permissible—though delegation will not relieve the seller of any duty to perform, or prevent liability for breach on failure to perform (UCC §2-210).

All rights of the seller or the buyer arising out of an agreement governed by the UCC may be assigned unless: the assignment would materially change the duty of the other party; materially increase the burden of risk imposed upon him by his contract; or materially impair his chance of obtaining return performance. The right to assign may be restricted by the parties in their agreement. It is essential to note that the Magnuson-Moss Act gives consumers a right of redress against assignees of their consumer credit contracts—thus, the so-called ''holder-in-due-course'' defense is not available to the innocent purchaser for the value of a consumer's debt, which is sometimes repudiated when a consumer is dissatisfied with the merchantability of the product.

[¶3329]   **WARRANTY**

The following table summarizes the UCC warranty rules:

Warranties Under the Uniform Commercial Code

	Warranty	Method of Exclusion
Warranty of Title	Seller warrants that good title is conveyed and that title will be free of any security interest or lien of which the buyer is unaware (UCC §2-312). The warranty of title may be breached by disturbance of quiet possession.	Excluded only by specific language indicating that if the seller does not claim title in himself or that he is selling only the title or rights that he has.
Warranty Against Infringement	A merchant warrants that goods that he sells are free of infringement. A buyer, if he has provided detailed specifications, agrees to hold the seller harmless against infringement (UCC §2-312).	May be excluded by agreement.
Warranty of Merchantability	A merchant warrants that goods will be merchantable. To be merchantable, goods must: (a) Pass without objection in the trade under the contract description. (b) Be fit for the ordinary purposes for which such goods are used. (c) Run with an even kind of quality and quantity. (d) Be adequately packaged and labeled as required by the agreement.	Excluded only by language expressly mentioning merchantability. In a written contract, the exclusion must be conspicuous (UCC §2-316).

Warranties Under the Uniform Commercial Code *(continued)*

	Warranty	Method of Exclusion
	(e) Conform to promises or statements on the label (UCC §2-316).	
Course of Dealing; Usage of Trade	Course of dealing or usage of trade may give rise to an implied warranty based on a particular course of dealing or usage of trade (UCC §2-314).	May be excluded or modified by agreement.
Service of Food	The service of food in a restaurant implies a warranty that goods will be merchantable and fit for consumption.	
Fit for Particular Purpose	If a merchant has reason to know any particular purpose for which goods are required and the buyer is relying on the seller's judgment or skill, he warrants that the goods are fit for that purpose (UCC §2-315).	May be excluded by conspicuous language excluding implied warranties, such as "There are no warranties which extend beyond the description on the face hereof" (UCC §2-316).
Sale by Description	If goods are sold by a description that becomes part of the basis of the transaction, there is an express warranty that they will conform to the description. The description will not be words but may be technical specifications, blueprints, etc. (UCC §2-313).	Language excluding warranties and descriptive language are to be construed as consistent with each other whenever reasonable (UCC §2-316). General language of disclaimer will not disclaim the warranties of description if the disclaimer is inconsistent with the description.
Sale by Sample	A sample or model, if part of the basis of the agreement, will create an express warranty that the goods delivered will conform to the sample. Exact or technical specifications displace a sample if there is a conflict. A sample from existing bulk displaces inconsistent general language of description (UCC §2-317).	General language of disclaimer will not disclaim the warranties that arise from a sale by sample, if the disclaimer is inconsistent with the sample.

Warranties Under the Uniform Commercial Code *(continued)*

Warranty	Method of Exclusion
Express Warranty by Affirmation of Fact or Promise	Any affirmation of fact or promise made by the seller to the buyer that relates to the goods and becomes part of the basis of the bargain becomes an express warranty. Mere statement of opinion as saleman's talk does not (UCC §2-313). It is not necessary that specific language of guarantee or warranty be used to create an express warranty.	Express warranties may be excluded or limited by agreement.
Warranty to Third Parties of Consumer Goods	UCC §2-318 Alternative A extends warranty coverage to a buyer, his family, and reasonably foreseeable users who are household members or guests who sustain personal injuries. Alternative B provides coverage for personal injuries sustained by any reasonably foreseeable user. Alternative C expands Alternative B to include property damage. Refer to state law for the applicable provision.	A seller may not exclude or limit the operation of this section (UCC §2-318).
When There Is No Warranty	If the agreement uses language "as is" or "with all faults" or other language that calls to the buyer's attention the exclusion of warranties, no warranty arises. If the seller examines the goods or is given an opportunity to examine the goods and refuses, no warranty will arise as to defects that the examination revealed or should have revealed (UCC §2-316).	

351

WARRANTY AND PRIVITY

Under certain circumstances, consumer goods purchased by an individual carry a warranty that extends to consumers other than the purchaser—frequently, members of the consumer's household or those who might reasonably be expected to come in contact with the goods, such as a repairman or guest. In some jurisdictions, there is still a requirement of privity of contract. In this situation, a relationship between the injured party claiming under the breach of warranty and the seller must be shown. It is important to consult local law to determine the applicable statutes in this regard, including the most current judicial decisions.

[¶3331]   **SELLER'S REMEDIES**

Just as the buyer has various means of assuring performance, the seller also requires various means of dealing with prospective purchasers under a variety of circumstances. The seller's remedies under the UCC are spelled out in the following paragraphs.

[¶3332]   **BUYER'S INSOLVENCY**

When the seller learns of the buyer's insolvency, the seller may:
(1) Stop delivery unless the goods have been received by the buyer, acknowledgment has been made by a warehouseman to the buyer, the goods have been reshipped by the carrier (which constitutes an acknowledgment to the buyer that the carrier holds the goods for the buyer), or the carrier has notified the buyer, in which case he was holding the goods as a warehouseman for the buyer rather than as a carrier.

The seller must notify the carrier in time to enable him with reasonable diligence to stop the shipment. If a negotiable document of title is involved, it should be presented to the carrier with the order to stop shipment (UCC §2-705).

(2) Withhold delivery if the goods have not been shipped and wait for the buyer to prepay, even though the contract called for shipment on credit.

(3) Reclaim the goods if they were received while the buyer was insolvent, provided notice is given within 10 days. The 10-day limitation does not apply if the buyer has falsely represented his solvency to the seller within three months of delivery (UCC §2-705).

See also the discussion of bankruptcy beginning at ¶501.

[¶3333]   **BUYER'S REPUDIATION OF AGREEMENT**

When the buyer repudiates the agreement, the seller may:
(1) Withhold delivery.

(2) Stop delivery if the goods have not been delivered to the buyer, provided the shipment meets the quantity requirements spelled out in the UCC, i.e., carload, truckload, ship, etc.

(3) Identify and sell conforming goods as well as recover damages for the difference between the resale price and the contract price.

(4) Recover damages for repudiation. When there is an established market price, the damages are the difference between the market price and the contract price at the time and place for the tentative delivery together with incidental damages but less any expenses saved as a result of the buyer's breach (UCC §2-708(1)). Incidental damages include commercially reasonable charges, expenses, or commissions incurred in stopping shipment; commercially reasonable charges, expenses, or commissions incurred in transportation or care of goods after breach; commercially reasonable charges, expenses, or commissions incurred in resale or return of goods; other commercially reasonable charges, expenses, or commissions resulting from the breach. If there is no established market at a place specified for tender, the market price at another locale is substituted, although adjustment is made for transportation differentials. When the damages computed by the difference between contract price and market price are inadequate (i.e., fail to put the seller in as good a position as he would have been had the buyer not repudiated), the UCC permits the seller to recover the profit that he would have made from full performance (§2-710 and 2-708(2)).

Cancellation after the buyer's repudiation does not extinguish the seller's right to proceed against the buyer for damages (UCC §2-106 and 2-703).

If the contract is repudiated after acceptance by the buyer, the seller may maintain an action for the price. An action for the price may also be maintained when the seller has been unable to resell goods identified to the agreement at a reasonable price or the circumstances indicate that efforts to resell would be fruitless. When the seller maintains an action for the price he must remain prepared to deliver the goods. However, if an opportunity arises to sell the goods, he may do so and deduct the resale price from his claim.

A resale must be made in good faith and in a commercially reasonable manner, under the terms outlined in the main text (UCC §2-706; uniform in 49 states, the District of Columbia, and the Virgin Islands).

(5) Suspend performance and await withdrawal of the repudiation for a commercially reasonable time and demand adequate assurance of performance.

The seller must suspend performance if he has not finished the goods and the completion of the goods or the completion of his performance would result in a material increase in damages.

[¶3334]　　　BUYER'S FAILURE TO COOPERATE

When the buyer fails to cooperate as required by the agreement (i.e., specifies assortment, gives needed instruction, etc.), a seller may follow any of these three courses:

(1) Delay his performance without incurring any liability for breach by reason of late delivery.

(2) Proceed to perform in a commercially reasonable manner.

(3) Treat the failure to cooperate as a breach of the agreement.

[¶3335]   **BUYER'S REFUSAL TO ACCEPT**
                        CONFORMING GOODS

If the buyer refuses to accept conforming goods or wrongfully withdraws his acceptance of conforming goods, the seller may resell the goods and recover damages. Damages constitute the difference between the contract price and the resale price less any expenses saved as a result of the breach, but including any costs incurred in reselling.

[¶3336]   **RESALE**

The UCC authorizes, as an element of resale costs, reasonable commission charges and transportation charges plus other incidental damages (UCC §2-701).

When goods are resold, the UCC rules for resale must be followed. However, resale need not be by public sale.

A private sale is justifiable depending on the circumstances, except that the buyer must be notified of the sale. The seller must use reasonable efforts to get the highest possible price for the goods.

For goods resold at auction, the sale must be held at the usual place or market for selling such goods if one is available. The goods must also be available for inspection prior to or at the sale.

[¶3337]   **DAMAGES**

Damages are measured by the difference between market price and the contract price at the time and place specified for delivery when there is an established market price, provided such damages are adequate to put the seller in as good a position as he would have been if the buyer had accepted the goods (instead of wrongfully rejecting conforming goods or wrongfully withdrawing his acceptance of conforming goods). In that case, he is entitled to at least the profits that he would have made if the buyer accepted the goods and fully performed the agreement.

The seller may also bring an action for the price for goods that are not readily resalable or he may cancel the contract.

[¶3338]   **BUYER'S REMEDIES**

Purchasers coping with insolvent sellers, repudiation of contracts, and nonconforming goods also have certain rights under the Uniform Commercial Code. These are explored in the paragraphs below.

SELLER'S INSOLVENCY

When the buyer learns that the seller is insolvent, he may:

(1) Demand adequate assurance of performance if he has reasonable grounds for feeling insecure about the seller's ability to perform.

If the seller fails to give adequate assurance of performance, the buyer may cancel—cancellation will not relieve the seller of the obligations under the contract.

(2) Recover deposits and prepayments by making provision to obtain the goods elsewhere and recover the difference between the cost of covering and the contract price from the seller.

The buyer also is entitled to recover reasonable expenses from the seller.

[¶3340] ## SELLER'S REPUDIATION

If the seller repudiates the agreement, the buyer may:

(1) Cancel and thereby be relieved of his obligation to perform. Cancellation will not relieve the seller of his obligation under the agreement.

The buyer may also recover damages in the amount of the difference between the contract price and the market price. He may cover by making other provision to obtain the goods.

The buyer is entitled to recover from the seller the loss incurred by covering, including reasonable commissions and expenses incurred in covering.

(2) Obtain specific performance if the agreement involves unique goods.

(3) Recover the goods if they were identified to the agreement prior to the seller's repudiation if, after reasonable effort, he is unable to effect cover or the circumstances reasonably indicate that an attempt to effect cover would be useless.

[¶3341] ## GOODS THAT FAIL TO CONFORM

If goods fail to conform to the written terms of the agreement, a buyer has three basic alternatives—rejection of performance, acceptance of performance, or cancellation. These three remedies are explored in the paragraphs below.

[¶3342] ## REJECTION OF PERFORMANCE

In the case of an installment contract, the buyer's right to reject the entire performance is limited to instances where the nonconformity substantially impairs the value of the installment (UCC §2-612).

When the buyer elects to reject the goods, the rejection must be made within a reasonable time after delivery and the buyer must seasonably notify the seller of his rejection. If the goods are in the buyer's physical possession when he rejects them, the buyer has an obligation to hold them with reasonable care at the seller's disposition to permit the seller to recover the goods.

If the buyer is a merchant normally dealing in goods of the kind called for in the contract, he may have a duty to follow reasonable instructions (regarding their care) from a seller who has no agent or place of business in the buyer's locale.

[¶3343] ACCEPTANCE OF PERFORMANCE

Acceptance does not extinguish other available remedies unless the buyer fails to notify the seller of the nonconformity within a reasonable time.

If the buyer accepts nonconforming goods he cannot return them because of the nonconformity if he knows of the nonconformity at the time of acceptance or should have discovered it by reasonable inspection.

[¶3344] CANCELLATION OF PERFORMANCE

After refusing to accept nonconforming goods, without extinguishing his rights to cover or recover damages from the seller (UCC §2-106), a buyer may cancel. He may also cover by making other provision to obtain the goods (see ¶3340).

A buyer who does not cover may be entitled to recover the difference between the market price and the contract price plus incidental and consequential damages.

Incidental damages might include any of the following: Expenses reasonably incurred in inspecting the nonconforming goods; expenses reasonably incurred in the receipt of nonconforming goods; expenses reasonably incurred in transporting the nonconforming goods; loss resulting from general particular requirements and needs of which the seller had reason to know at the time of entering into the agreement and that could not have been prevented by cover (UCC §2-715).

[¶3345] FOR FURTHER REFERENCE . . .

Childres, R., "Buyer's Remedies: the Danger of Section 2-713," 72 Northwestern University Law Review 837-53 (Jan.-Feb. 1978).

"Contracts for Goods and Services and Article 2 of the Uniform Commercial Code," 9 Rutgers Camden Law Journal 303-22 (Winter 1978).

Edwards, C.M., "Contract Formulation under Article 2 of the Uniform Commercial Code," 61 Marquette Law Review 215-43 (Winter 1977).

Forms of Business Agreements (Vol. 3), Institute for Business Planning, Inc., Englewood Cliffs, N.J.

Goldstein, A.S., *Commercial Transactions Desk Book*, Institute for Business Planning, Inc., Englewood Cliffs, N.J. (1977).

"Guide to Federal Warranty Legislation—the Magnuson-Moss Act," 11 University of Richmond Law Review 163-176 (Fall 1976).

Hawkland, William, "Sales and Bulk Sales," American Law Institute.

Lester, P.A., "How to Speak Magnuson-Moss: a Primer on the New Federal Warranty Act," 52 Florida Bar Journal 301-10 (April 1978).

"U.C.C. §2-207: Boiler Plates and Arbitration Clauses," 30 Baylor Law Review 143-52 (Winter 1978).

"U.C.C. §2-713: Anticipatory Repudiation and Measurement of an Aggrieved Buyer's Damages," 19 William & Mary Law Review 253-80 (Winter 1977).

Vold on Sales (2nd ed.,) West Publishing Co., St. Paul, Minn.

"When Does the Statute of Limitations Begin to Run on Breaches of Implied Warranties?," 30 Baylor Law Review 386-92 (Spring 1978).

Williston on Sales, Baker, Voorhis.

Witney, *The Law of Modern Commercial Practices,* Baker, Voorhis.

SECURED TRANSACTIONS

[¶3401] Under the Uniform Commercial Code (Article 9, Secured Transactions), a security interest includes pledges, conditional sales contracts, liens, chattel mortgages, trust receipts, and all other security devices used to secure a monetary obligation with personal property.

In order to be protected against trustees in bankruptcy or other individuals, a seller or lender may not want the debtor to have actual title to the collateral. Throughout secured transactions, the keystone is who will have priority. It is sometimes said that the acid test is whether the secured creditor's claim will stand up against a federal tax lien. (See ¶3801 et seq. for an additional discussion on federal tax liens.)

In addition to these legal risks there are, of course, the following: The possibly insurable risk that the collateral may be destroyed or disappear, the risk that it may decline in value, the risk that the debtor will not be able to make payments when due and the creditor will have the inconvenience and expense of realizing on the collateral and even having to resort to litigation. These nonlegal risks have to be minimized by credit investigation, appraisal, and similar credit techniques.

From a purely legal standpoint, the greatest security is the creditor's actual possession of the collateral, as is the case in a pledge. This eliminates the risk that the debtor will wrongfully deal with the property or that creditors of the debtor will be able to claim an interest by reason of the debtor's apparently unencumbered ownership. But practical business necessities in most instances demand that the security be left in the possession of the debtor and that he be permitted to use it or try to sell it.

[¶3402]   DEFINITIONS (SECURED TRANSACTIONS)

Among the important terms that frequently recur in the area of secured transactions are the following:

☐ *Account:* A right to payment for goods or services rendered.

☐ *Account Debtor:* An individual obligated on a contract right, general intangible, chattel paper, or account.

☐ *Chattel Paper:* Evidence of a monetary obligation and security interest in specific goods.

☐ *Consumer Goods:* Those used or bought primarily for personal, family, or household purposes.

☐ *Contract Right:* A right to payment on an unperformed contract.

☐ *Equipment:* Goods used or bought primarily for use in business (including farming and professions), or if the goods do not fit under the definitions of consumer goods, farm products, or inventory.

☐ *Farm Products:* Crops, livestock, or unmanufactured products of crops or livestock (such as eggs, maple syrup, or wool-clips) that are used or produced in

358

farming operations—if they are in the possession of a farmer-debtor (for example, one who engages in raising, fattening, grazing, or other farming operations).

☐ *General Intangibles:* Personal property other than goods, contract rights, negotiable instruments, or accounts.

☐ *Inventory:* Goods held for the purpose of sale, lease, or to be furnished under service contracts, or for work in progress for eventual use in business (i.e., raw materials).

☐ *Purchase-Money Security Interest:* One in which the seller of collateral personally secures a portion or all of the purchase price.

[¶3403] MAXIMUM PROTECTION UNDER THE UCC

In secured transactions, there are three critical goals that must be achieved to afford maximum protection. The aim is to be sure that the security interest:
(1) Attaches,
(2) Is perfected, and
(3) Has priority over conflicting interests.

[¶3404] HOW A SECURITY INTEREST ATTACHES

A security interest *attaches* automatically when there is an agreement between the parties that it will attach, value (including the satisfaction of a pre-existing debt) has been given, the debtor has acquired rights in the collateral, and the agreement has been put in writing.

[¶3405] PERFECTION

Perfection of a security interest, required under the UCC in order to have a recorded priority, may be accomplished by one of two means. A creditor either takes possession of the collateral or files a public notice in a required place—either at a centrally located office within the state or in an individual county, depending on the jurisdiction. Filing may be either of the security agreement itself or of a separate financing statement.

[¶3406] STEP-BY-STEP PROCEDURE TO OBTAIN MAXIMUM PROTECTION

Following are four basic rules that should be followed in order to protect a seller against improperly filing and perfecting a security interest:
(1) Do not make any advance unless all of the requirements below for creating a perfected and enforceable security interest have previously been met or are thereby met. In addition, before the advance is made, be satisfied that the debtor's rights in the collateral are adequate.

(2) If the security interest is to be perfected by possession, at the time that the advance is made, the creditor or the creditor's bailee should have actual possession of the collateral. There should be no other currently existing security interest in the collateral, including any that had been perfected through filing.

(3) If the security interest is to be perfected by filing, the lender should be satisfied (a) that at the time the advance is made the collateral is not held by or for another secured party; (b) that at the time the advance is made there is no other perfected security interest in existence; and equally important, (c) that at the time of the secured party's filing there is on record no financing statement with an earlier filing date that mentions any "type" of collateral into which the collateral could fit. If, for example, an earlier financing statement on file mentioned "machinery" or "equipment" or the like, a security interest created later (even under an agreement not yet contemplated) could be perfected through the earlier filing, and under the UCC's "first-to-file" rule would take priority over the earlier perfected interest.

(4) Regardless of the method of perfection, the lender must be satisfied that at the time of the advance there is no federal tax lien or other statutory lien (whether for taxes or other purposes), on the debtor's property that might come ahead of his security interest.

[¶3407]   CHECKLIST FOR SECURITY AGREEMENTS

Every security agreement should contain the following basic information:
- [ ] What is the collateral?
- [ ] Does the debtor own the collateral free of any other security interests?
- [ ] Is the collateral in the debtor's possession at the present time?
- [ ] Are there prior liens on other assets of the debtor?
- [ ] Is there notice of a federal tax lien against the debtor?
- [ ] If a corporation is involved, have proper resolutions been passed to make the agreement enforceable and effective?
- [ ] Is after-acquired collateral contemplated?
- [ ] How are the goods characterized under Article 9:
  - (1) Goods—farm products, farm equipment, inventory, or consumer goods.
  - (2) Documents of title, stocks, bonds, notes, chattel paper.
  - (3) Accounts or general intangibles.
  - (4) Are the goods likely to become fixtures (of attached real estate)?
  - (5) Should proceeds be identified at the outset?
  - (6) Is a purchase-money security interest involved?

[¶3408]   IDENTIFICATION OF COLLATERAL

Express identification of collateral that is the subject of a secured transaction is prescribed by UCC §9-110, which merely requires information that could "reasonably identify what is described." Ordinarily, for specific machinery, the manufacturer's name and machine's serial number should be included.

Various forms of security agreements, suitable for use under Article 9, are found in *IBP Forms of Business Agreements and Resolutions. Vol. 3.*

[¶3409] HOW TO MAKE THE SEARCH AND THE ADVANCE

Search the UCC filing records and any applicable pre-UCC chattel security record in order to supplement the debtor's representations. The search, of course, should not be limited to present security interests, but must include present filings under which any future security interests could be perfected. Although filing the financing statement may be done at the same time that a search is conducted, the date that the financing statement is filed does not control all priorities if, between that date and the date value is given, a conflicting lien is obtained by legal proceedings or a federal tax lien is filed. Since the actual date of perfection of each security interest may control priorities between them, the debtor could wrongfully create a possessory lien between the time of filing and the time value is given.

Searching the file is not a perfect check; conceivably a filing could have been made in another district or state where the goods were then located. No legal record would disclose that the equipment was stolen goods, or was subject to a possessory security interest, or was the property of a lessor. Here the secured party must rely on credit investigation, checking the location of the property, a bill of sale or the like, rather than legal records.

A commitment to make an advance constitutes value just as well as the actual making of the advance. Any commitment obviously should be made subject to the condition that the debtor's claims to the collateral are satisfactory at the time the advance is actually made.

[¶3410] EFFECTIVENESS OF SECURITY AGREEMENT

Security interests not given for antecedent debts are given preferential treatment under the law. Prompt filing ordinarily is required. If a debtor wrongfully sells a secured item, proceeds go to the secured party, who may also attack the collateral held by the new purchaser. If a possessory interest of a subsequent individual is later perfected, the earlier security interest prevails (UCC §9-312 (5)(b)).

[¶3411] AFTER-ACQUIRED PROPERTY

Generally, after-acquired property clauses are valid under the UCC, although a purchase-money security interest receives preference over an interest created by an after-acquired property clause. If such a clause requires that the borrower transfer after-acquired property to the creditor within three months of bankruptcy, the transfer is considered to have been taken for new value—rather than for a pre-existing debt. Consequently, the transfer is not a voidable preference under the bankruptcy law.

[¶3412] INAPPLICABILITY OF AFTER-ACQUIRED PROPERTY CLAUSES

In two instances, the after-acquired property rules of the UCC do not apply. Crops that come into existence one year after the agreement are not covered. Neither are consumer goods—unless the debtor gets rights to them within 10 days after the secured party gives value (UCC §9-204(4)).

[¶3413] THE FLOATING LIEN

Floating liens are secured transactions on a shifting stock of goods or inventory. The collateral is in constant flux, undergoing quantitative and qualitative changes, but the lien holder nonetheless retains the security interest. It is no longer necessary to resort to field warehousing in connection with inventory financing, although the lender may still wish to police the collateral as an additional protection device. Even though the UCC permits floating liens, there is no guarantee that the secured creditor will have priority over all liens subsequently attaching or perfected in the same collateral. It may be subordinate to purchase-money interests or federal tax liens.

[¶3414] FUTURE ADVANCES

The UCC makes it clear that you can have a valid security interest in collateral to secure amounts to be advanced in the future, whether or not the advances are to be made pursuant to prior commitment (§9-204(5)).

[¶3415] PURCHASE-MONEY INTERESTS

Purchase-money security interests have important preferential rights under the Uniform Commercial Code. In some instances (farm equipment costing less than a certain amount and consumer goods) a security interest may be perfected without filing (§9-302(1)(c),(d)); when filing is required, a grace period of 10 days is allowed against creditors and transferees in bulk (§9-301(2)); and the purchase-money interest may take priority over conflicting security interests under an after-acquired property clause (§9-312(3), (4)).

To get the preferred status, it is not necessary that the secured party be the seller of the collateral; it is enough that he gives value to enable the debtor to acquire rights in or the use of the collateral if such value is in fact used for either purpose (UCC §9-107(b)). The best way for a lender to protect himself is to pay the seller directly.

PRIORITIES UNDER THE UCC

Special rules under UCC Article 9 affect creditors' priorities. These are covered in the subparagraphs below. In states that have adopted the amended Article 9 (1972 revision), some substantive law areas have changed. Therefore, local law should be consulted.

[¶3416.1]   Goods Covered by Documents

While goods are in the possession of the issuer of a negotiable document covering the goods, any security interest in the goods is subject to a security interest in the documents (UCC §9-304(2)).

[¶3416.2]   Proceeds

The secured party has a security interest in identifiable proceeds of collateral. But an interest in proceeds becomes unperfected 10 days after receipt by the debtor unless the filed financing statement also covers proceeds or the secured party gets possession within a 10-day period. In the event of the debtor's insolvency, the secured party's interest in the proceeds may extend under some conditions to cash and bank accounts of the debtor without regard to whether or not the funds are identifiable as cash proceeds of the collateral (UCC §9-306(2)-(4)).

[¶3416.3]   Repossessions

Goods that were subject to a security interest and then sold are resubjected to the prior security interest when the goods are returned to the seller. Although this interest is superior to the security interest of the assignee of the account created by the sale, a transferee of the chattel paper created by the sale may have a superior security interest (UCC §9-306(5) and §9-308).

[¶3416.4]   Buyers of Goods Protected

A buyer of inventory, other than farm products, in the ordinary course of business takes free of the security interest even if it is filed and he knows about it. In the case of consumer goods and farm equipment costing less than $2,500, a bona fide purchaser for value who has no knowledge of the security interest, buying for his own personal, family, or household use or his own farming operations takes free of an *unfiled* security interest (UCC §9-307).

[¶3416.5]   Purchaser of Chattel Paper or Nonnegotiable Instruments

A purchaser (including holder of security interest (§1-201(32), (33)) who gives new value and takes possession in the ordinary course of his business and without knowledge has priority over prior security interest perfected by filing or temporary perfection without filing. He also has priority over a security interest in chattel paper that is claimed merely as proceeds of inventory, even though he knows of prior interest (UCC §9-308).

[¶3416.6]   Purchasers of Instruments and Documents

A holder in due course of a negotiable instrument, a holder to whom a negotiable document of title has been duly negotiated, or a bona fide purchaser of a security takes priority over an earlier security interest even though it was perfected (UCC §9-309).

[¶3416.7]   Liens by Operation of Law

Common law or statutory liens for services or materials have priority, unless a statute provides otherwise (UCC §9-310).

[¶3416.8]   Crops

A party who gives new value within three months before planting, in order to enable the debtor to produce the crops, has priority over an earlier security interest in the crops that secures an obligation that is due more than six months before planting (UCC §9-312(12)).

[¶3416.9]   Purchase-Money Security Interests

A purchase-money security interest has priority over a conflicting security interest in collateral other than inventory, if it's perfected within 10 days after the debtor receives the collateral. If the collateral is inventory, it has priority over a conflicting security interest if it's filed and notice to other known or filed security interests is given before the debtor receives the collateral (UCC §9-312(3), (4)). Also, UCC §9-301(2) provides that if a purchase-money interest is filed within 10 days it takes priority over the rights of a transferee in bulk or of a lien creditor arising between the time the security interest attaches and is filed.

[¶3416.10]   Fixtures

A security interest *attaching to goods before they become fixtures* is superior to all prior claims in the real estate and also to all subsequent claims in the real estate, if it is filed before the later claims arise. A security interest in goods *attaching after they become fixtures* is superior only to subsequent interests in the real estate if filed before the later claims arise, or to prior claimants who have consented in writing to the security interest in the goods as fixtures (UCC §9-313). Both types of security interest, those attaching before and those attaching after the goods become fixtures, are subject to the interest of a prior real estate mortgage of record to the extent of subsequent advances contracted for without knowledge of the security interest and before it is filed (§9-313).

[¶3416.11] Goods Attached to Other Goods—Accessions

A security interest in goods attaching before the goods become accessions is superior to prior claims in the goods to which they are attached and is also superior to subsequent claims in the whole goods, if it is filed before the later claims arise. If the security interest attaches after the goods have become accessions, it is superior only to subsequent interests in the whole if it is filed before the subsequent interests arise. Both types of interest in accessions are subject to subsequent advances contracted for under a prior perfected security interest (UCC §9-314).

[¶3416.12] Commingled or Processed Goods

A perfected interest in goods that become part of a product or mass continues in the product or mass if (a) the goods lose their identity in processing, or (b) the financing statement covers the product. When more than one interest attaches to the mass or product, they rank equally in proportion to their contribution to the mass (UCC §9-315).

[¶3416.13] Unperfected Security Interests vs. Various Third Parties

An unperfected security interest is subordinate to the rights of:

(a) Persons entitled to priority under the special rules discussed above or the general rules of priority in UCC §9-312(5);

(b) A person who becomes a lien creditor without knowledge of the security interest;

(c) In the case of goods, instruments, documents, and chattel paper, a person who is not a secured party and who is a transferee in bulk or other buyer not in the ordinary course of business to the extent that he gives value and *receives* delivery of the collateral without knowledge of the security interest;

(d) In the case of accounts, contract rights, and general intangibles, a person who is not a secured party and who is a transferee to the extent that he gives value without knowledge of the security interest; and

(e) A buyer not in the ordinary course of business who, without knowledge and before the security agreement is perfected, makes a purchase.

These rules are subject to the rule that if the secured party files with respect to a purchase-money interest within 10 days after the collateral comes into possession of the debtor, he takes priority over the rights of a transferee in bulk or of a lien creditor arising between the time the purchase-money interest attached and was perfected (UCC §9-301).

[¶3417] SPECIAL RULES FOR SPECIAL TYPES OF COLLATERAL

While most of the provisions of Article 9 apply regardless of the type of collateral involved, some sections state special rules for particular types of collateral. The Official Comments following §9-102 set forth a complete index of these special rules for various types of collateral, more specifically, accounts and contract rights, chattel paper, documents and instruments, general intangibles, goods, consumer goods, equipment, farm products, and inventory.

[¶3418]   INSURANCE FOR CREDITORS

Insurance for creditors is sometimes deemed essential in a secured transaction, particularly when field warehousing is undertaken or when the creditor has possession of the debtor's goods. (See ¶2101 et seq. for additional information.)

[¶3419]   DEFAULT

When a debtor defaults under a security agreement, the proceedings are governed by Part B of Article 9 (UCC §9-501 et seq.). Under the UCC, the secured party may reduce his claim to judgment, foreclose, or enforce the security interest by any available judicial procedure. Unless otherwise agreed between the parties, a secured party has the right to take possession of the collateral when the debtor defaults. Normally, this may be done *without* judicial process, although there is some general feeling today that the security agreement should provide for this right to possession without breach of peace. Alternatively, the secured party is permitted to render equipment unusable in the event of default.

Following default, a secured party may sell, lease, or otherwise dispose of collateral. Proceeds must then be applied in the following order: To reasonable expenses for the retaking, holding, and selling of the collateral (plus reasonable attorney's fees—usually no more than 20%); satisfaction of the indebtedness secured by the security interest; satisfaction of indebtedness secured by any subordinate security agreement (junior debtors). Under all circumstances, the secured party must account to the debtor for any surplus above the amount that the agreement secures. The debtor is liable for any deficiency. (If the underlying secured transaction is the sale of a contract right or chattel paper or other "paper" sale, the debtor is not entitled to any surplus—and is not liable for any deficiency—unless the security agreement expressly provides for it.

Disposition of collateral may be done publicly or privately. Commercial reasonableness and notice to the debtor are the key ingredients (§9-504(c)(3)). Notice to the debtor is required unless a perishable commodity is involved or there is a recognized market on which it may be sold. This is designed to protect the debtor from a secured party's selling a particular item at an unusually low price and then holding the debtor liable for the difference. Purchasers of items sold by a secured party take free and clear of all rights and interests that the debtor may have had—even if the secured party fails to comply with the requirements of the UCC or any judicial proceedings.

[¶3420]   **CONSTITUTIONAL PROBLEMS**

Some very serious constitutional problems have resulted in the area of secured transactions as they relate to consumer-debtors. Principally, they relate to the ability of a secured creditor to seize collateral of the debtor without notice upon default—or when the secured creditor feels "insecure." This particular area of the law is in a state of flux, and the practitioner is well advised not only to consult local law, but also to keep abreast of pronouncements from the United States Supreme Court. To the extent possible, it is inevitably wiser for the practitioner to avail himself of judicial remedy than to exercise self-help—particularly when the latter course is likely to lead to a breach of peace. At least in the case of an individual, it is clear that consumers have rights beyond those spelled out in Article 9 of the UCC. Courts tend to look with a somewhat less critical eye on seeming violations of the rights of corporate debtors. In all instances, however, caution should be exercised to avoid any course under which fundamental fairness (or due process) might be deemed by a court to be lacking—unless there is a danger of a sudden dissipation of the original asset for which the secured party holds the agreement.

[¶3421]   **FOR FURTHER REFERENCE . . .**

Burke, W.M., "Secured Transactions," 33 Business Lawyer 1931-59 (April 1978).

Coogan, Hogan and Vagts, *Secured Transactions Under the UCC.*, Matthew Bender, New York, N.Y.

Coogan, P.F., "Article 9—an Agenda for the Next Decade," 87 Yale Law Journal 1012-55 (April 1978).

Denonn, *Secured Transactions Under the Laws of Code and Non-Code States,* Practising Law Institute, New York, N.Y.

Forms of Business Agreements (3 vol. looseleaf service), Institute for Business Planning, Inc., Englewood Cliffs, N.J.

Schmitt, M.A., and Johnson, D.B., "Poker Player's Guide to Uniform Commercial Code Secured Transactions," 10 Southwestern University Law Review 2089-113 (1978).

SECURITIES: THEIR OWNERSHIP AND TRANSFER

[¶3501] Registration, negotiability, and transfer of securities are governed by Article 8 of the UCC. However, as the Comment to §8-101 notes, "The Article is neither a Blue Sky law nor a corporation code." Where Article 8 has been adopted (in the District of Columbia and all states except Louisiana) it supplants both the Uniform Stock Transfer Act and the Uniform Negotiable Instruments Act. For many states, Article 8 also replaces the Uniform Act for Simplification of Fiduciary Security Transfers and the Model Fiduciaries Securities Transfer Act.

Definition: As used in Article 8 and defined in §8-102, a "security" is an instrument that:

(1) Is issued on bearer or registered form;

(2) Is a type commonly dealt in on securities exchanges or markets, or commonly recognized in any area in which it is issued, or dealt in as a medium for investment;

(3) Is either one of a class or series, or by its terms is divisible into a class or series of instruments; and

(4) Evidences a share, participation, or other interest in property or in an enterprise, or evidences an obligation of the issuer.

Article 8 is exclusive in its application to the extent that an instrument that falls within the "security" definition of §8-102 is to be governed solely by Article 8, even though it may also come within the scope of Article 3.

Statute of Frauds: UCC §8-319 is the Statute of Frauds for the transfer of securities. It provides that a contract for the sale of securities is not enforceable by way of action or defense unless:

(a) There is some writing signed by the party against whom enforcement is sought, or by his authorized agent or broker, sufficient to indicate that a contract has been made for sale of a stated quantity of described securities at a defined or stated price; or

(b) Delivery of the security has been accepted or payment has been made, but the contract is enforceable under this provision only to the extent of such delivery or payment; or

(c) Within a reasonable time a writing in confirmation of the sale or purchase and sufficient against the sender in paragraph (a) has been received by the party against whom enforcement is sought and he has failed to send written objection to its contents within 10 days after its receipt; or

(d) The party against whom enforcement is sought admits in his pleading, testimony, or otherwise in court that a contract was made for sale of a stated quantity of described securities at a defined or stated price.

Computerized Stock Transfer and Uncertified Securities: Increasing computerization of the stock transfer process has led to an unsettling revelation—Article 8 does not apply unless the security is *reified*—evidenced by a certificate or other instrument as defined by UCC §8-105 and 8-102. In order to resolve this problem, the American Law Institute (ALI) is currently considering a revision of UCC Article 8 that will deal with "uncertificated" securities.

[¶3502] DELIVERY REQUIREMENT FOR COMPLETION OF TRANSFER

A transfer is not effective between the parties until delivery takes place. When seller and buyer deal with each other directly, fulfilling the requirement of delivery is simple enough—the seller hands the certificate to the buyer. When dealing with a listed stock through a broker on a national or regional exchange, there might be a time lag of several days between the purchase and the purchaser's actual possession of the stock. Under the Uniform Stock Transfer Act (and the Negotiable Instruments Law in the case of bonds) transfer of possession of stock to the purchaser was the only method of delivery contemplated. However, the Uniform Commercial Code broadens the concept of delivery to conform to present-day conditions under which most stock transfers take place through brokers on organized exchanges. UCC §8-313 provides that delivery to the purchaser occurs when his broker gets possession of a security specially indorsed to or issued in the name of the purchaser, or his broker *sends* him confirmation of the purchase, or makes a book entry or otherwise identifies a specific security in his possession as belonging to the purchaser.

[¶3503] ISSUER'S DEFENSES AND RESPONSIBILITIES

The Article 8 definition of "issuer" is set forth at UCC §8-201.

An issuer may set forth the terms of the security on its face and may also incorporate additional terms by reference to "another instrument, indenture or document or to a constitution, statute, ordinance, rule, regulation, order or the like to the extent that the terms so referred to do not conflict with the stated terms" (§8-202). These terms apply even as against a purchaser for value and without notice.

Section 8-202(3) notes that an issuer may always assert the lack of genuineness of a security as a complete defense, even as against a purchaser for value and without notice. However, this is qualified somewhat by §8-205, which states that an *unauthorized* signature placed on a security prior to or in the course of issue is ineffective, except in favor of a purchaser for value and without notice of the lack of authority, if the signing has been done by (a) an authenticating trustee, registrar, transfer agent, or other person entrusted by the issuer with the signing of the security or of similar securities or their immediate preparation for signing, or (b) an employee of the issuer or of any of the foregoing entrusted with responsible handling of the security.

Section 8-202(4) makes clear that "all other defenses of the issuer including nondelivery and conditional delivery of the security are ineffective against a purchaser for value who has taken without notice the particular defense."

Alteration of Securities: Section 8-206 provides that any holder may now enforce the original terms of an altered security. In addition, when a security contains the signatures necessary to its issue or transfer but is incomplete in any other respect, any person may complete it by filling in the blanks as authorized,

369

and even though the blanks are incorrectly filled in, the security as completed is enforceable by a purchaser for value who took without notice of its incorrectness.

[¶3504]   PURCHASER FOR VALUE

Defenses of the issuer and those not available as against a "purchaser for value and without notice" are examined in the preceding paragraph. Article 8 defines "bona fide purchaser" in UCC §8-302 as a purchaser for value in good faith and without notice of any adverse claim who takes delivery of a security in bearer form, or of one in registered form issued to him, or endorsed to him, or in blank, or who takes delivery in a manner specified in §8-320. (UCC §1-201(19) defines "good faith" as "honesty in fact" on the conduct or the transaction concerned.)

[¶3505]   RECORDING TRANSFERS

The stock book, usually open to reasonable inspection by shareholders (and sometimes others), shows record ownership. Corporations are authorized by statute to rely on record ownership in determining to whom notices are to be sent, who may vote, receive dividends, etc. For these purposes a reasonable record date may be fixed, or the books may be closed to transfers. Bylaws may contain provisions regulating the transfer of stock. The recording of transfers, cancellation of the surrender certificates, and the issuance of new certificates in the name of the transferee may be carried out by an independent agent, e.g., the transfer agent, or by a department or employee of the corporation.

[¶3506]   LIABILITY FOR RECORDING TRANSFERS

The Uniform Commercial Code, §8-401 through 8-406, spells out the specific requirements in the recording of stock transfers and the duties and liabilities arising therefrom. The Official Comments to these Sections indicate that the UCC follows the "well-settled rules found in the case law as to duty to register and as to liability for improper registration of an unauthorized signature, or where the indorsement is not that of an appropriate person." In other areas, the potential liability for the issuer has been "substantially reduced."

Section 8-401 indicates that the issuer has a duty to record a transfer, provided that certain preconditions have been met:

(1) Appropriate indorsement (§8-308);

(2) Reasonable assurance as to genuineness of indorsements (§8-402);

(3) Compliance with applicable law regarding collection of taxes;

(4) Transfer made to bona fide purchaser, or transfer is otherwise rightful;

(5) Discharge of any duty to check into adverse claims (§8-403);

It should be noted that §8-401 is not absolute, in that the issuer can waive certain conditions, such as the assurances in (2) above, or the proof that the tax laws have been met.

If the issuer is presented with a security for transfer and registration, it may have a limited duty to inquire into adverse claims if it has received a written "stop transfer" notice from the owner of a lost or stolen security prior to a request for transfer, or if the issuer had any other reason to believe there were adverse claims.

Section 8-404 states the basic exonerative policy regarding an issuer's transfer of a security when there was no duty to inquire into adverse claims and when the security was properly indorsed. The Official Comment to this Section notes that the rightful owner of a wrongfully transferred security has the right to receive a new certificate, "except where an overissue would result [§8-104] and a similar security is not available for purchase."

[¶3507]   CHECKLIST FOR STOCK TRANSFER REQUIREMENTS

In addition to endorsement, delivery, and guarantee of signature, the requirements are these:

Registered Owner	Endorsement	Tax Waivers	Special Requirements
Individual(s)	Owner(s)	None	None
Individual	Agent or Attorney	None	Certified copy of power
Joint tenants	Surviving joint tenant	Usually from state of domicile of deceased—sometimes from state of incorporation. Affidavit of domicile may be called for.	Certified copy of death certificate of deceased joint tenant
Decedent	Executor or administrator	Usually from state of domicile of deceased—sometimes from state of incorporation. Affidavit of domicile may be called for.	Copy of letters testamentary or of administration certified within 60 days
Custodian for minor	Custodian	None	None
Minor or ward	Guardian	None	Copy of letters of guardianship certified within 60 days

Registered Owner	Endorsement	Tax Waivers	Special Requirements
Trustee, executor, administrator, or guardian	Registered owner	None	None
Corporation	Officer acting for corporation	None	Certified copy of resolutions or bylaws creating officer's authority for the transaction
Deceased or re-signed trustee	Endorsement by successor trustee	None	Certified copy of trust instrument showing succession

[¶3508]   NOTICE OF RESTRICTIONS ON TRANSFER

If the corporation or the transfer agent is notified that there is an adverse claim to stock affected by a proposed transfer or a restriction on transfer, the immunity from liability afforded by recent statutory enactments is withdrawn. This situation may exist in these circumstances:

(1) Corporations frequently file, and are sometimes required by the SEC to file, with the transfer agent a "stop transfer" notice if the shares have not been registered and if the transfer might require such registration—usually shares held by control stockholders. Such a "stop transfer" order usually requires that transfer may be made only with the submission of an opinion, usually by corporate or other designated counsel, that registration would not be required to make a particular transfer legal.

(2) Restrictions on transfer may be noted on the certificate, i.e., as is commonly done under an agreement for the restriction of transfers entered into by control stockholders.

(3) By formal written communication from a claimant of the shares that identifies him and the registered owner and the issue of which the security is a part (see UCC §8-402(1)(a)).

(4) The corporation or the transfer agent has demanded and received, in support of application for registration and for some purpose other than checking the endorsements, copies of the will, trust agreement, or other controlling instrument that indicates that the proposed transfer would not be proper.

[¶3509]   LOST, STOLEN, OR DESTROYED STOCK CERTIFICATES

If stock certificates are lost, stolen, or destroyed and the corporation replaces them with new certificates, it might incur a liability if the original certificate later appears in the hands of a bona fide purchaser. Corporate bylaws frequently provide for replacement conditioned upon the posting of an adequate bond to indemnify the corporation. The Uniform Stock Transfer Act provides for court procedure to compel replacement of a lost or destroyed certificate upon the posting of an adequate bond. Under UCC §8-405, the issuer is required to replace the lost certificate on the posting of a bond by the owner of the lost certificate, provided that the owner also satisfies any other requirements of the issuer.

If an owner of a security fails to inform the issuer in a timely and reasonable manner that the security has been lost, stolen, or destroyed, and the issuer subsequently registers a transfer of the security before such notification, the owner will not be able to sue the issuer for registering the security transfer, nor will the owner be able to sue for a replacement of the transferred security (§8-405(1)).

Once again, as in other UCC sections, the bona fide purchaser of the "original" security is protected even after the issuance of a new security and the owner of the replacement security may have to return it to the issuer (§8-405(3)).

[¶3510]   TRANSFER TAXES

New York and Florida require payment of a stock transfer tax.

New York's imposition of a stock transfer tax on out-of-state residents that differed substantially from a similar tax imposed on residents of New York State was declared unconstitutional by the U.S. Supreme Court (*Boston Stock Exchange v. State Tax Commission,* USSC No. 75-1019, 1/12/77). A unanimous Court found the 1968 law governing taxes on stock transferred in New York unconstitutional as an undue burden on interstate commerce. Regional stock exchanges in Boston, Detroit, Cincinnati, and the PBW group (Philadelphia, Baltimore, and Washington, D.C.) joined in the suit to have the differing tax rates declared unconstitutional. States in which these regional exchanges are located impose no stock transfer tax. In its opinion, the Court emphasized that its decision did "not prevent the states from structuring their tax systems to encourage the growth and development of intrastate commerce and industry." It did, however, rule out discriminatory tactics that tax products of one's own state less than those of another.

[¶3511]   SHOWING PAYMENT OF TAXES

The basic ways of showing payment of the taxes are: (1) with adhesive stamps, and (2) by a notation.

When stamps are used, the stamps are affixed to the certificate together with a bill of memorandum of sale showing the amount of shares, the corporate title of the stock, the price per share, and the net amount of the sale. Or a certificate to the effect that "these shares were sold by us at $_____ per share," signed by the seller and attached.

As an alternative to affixing the stamps, if the transaction is through a national securities exchange, the tax may be paid through the clearing house of the exchange and a member of the exchange may indicate payment, usually by rubber stamp.

[¶3512]   **TAX RATES**

State taxes vary both in amount and in the method of computation. The New York tax, for example, is exclusively based on selling price per share as follows: 1.25 cents on shares selling for less than $5; 2.5 cents on shares selling for more than $5 but less than $10; 3.75 cents on shares selling for more than $10 but less than $20; and 5 cents on shares selling for more than $20.

In Florida, the rate for shares with par value is .015 cents per $100 of par value. When shares have no-par value, the rate is .015 cents per share.

SURETIES, GUARANTORS, AND INDEMNIFICATION

[**¶3601**] Business people use various devices to assure that obligations owed to them will be fulfilled. One common method of protection is the use of a surety or guarantor. The law governing sureties and guarantors is somewhat specialized. Basically, it deals with the relationship of three individuals:

(1) The *obligee*: the person to be protected (the creditor);

(2) The *principal obligor*: the buyer, borrower, or contractor;

(3) The *surety or guarantor*: the person supplying the protection.

[¶3602] ## USE OF THE SURETY OR GUARANTOR

Sureties and guarantors are used most frequently when the obligee demands security because of the obligor's weak financial position. They can be used to secure an installment sale, for example, even though the seller retains a security interest in the property sold. Similarly, they may be used to back up a secured loan.

There are certain areas in which the functions of the surety and guarantor have special uses. One important area is in dealing with a newly formed corporation with thin capitalization. In such cases the stockholders will ordinarily be called on to act as sureties or guarantors for the corporation. In so doing they will aid both the creditor and the corporation. The creditor gets the personal liability of the stockholders; the corporation benefits to the degree that the stockholders, realizing their personal liability, will be less disposed to weaken the corporation's financial condition by making large withdrawals.

Sureties and guarantors are frequently required in building and construction contracts in order to guarantee performance. As a matter of fact, statutes may require the posting of surety bonds, especially when public contracts and, in some instances, private contracts are involved. Such surety contracts take on the appearance of insurance contracts and some states do look on them as such.

A third area of general use will involve the guarantee of a loan for a close relative who is starting a new venture. This arrangement might even be made without the principal obligor's knowledge, in order to place him on his own responsibility.

Businesses that have successfully operated for a while but have begun to falter may also be called on to furnish a surety or guarantor.

Forms of guarantee and indemnity agreements appear in *IBP Forms of Business Agreements and Resolutions*.

[¶3603] ## DISTINCTION BETWEEN SURETY AND GUARANTOR

Although some people tend to use the terms ''surety'' and ''guarantor'' interchangeably, there are some legal distinctions.

375

Both sureties and guarantors perform essentially the same commercial function. Both lend their names and credit standing to the principal obligor and agree to make good his shortcomings in the performance of his obligations to the obligee. But, according to many courts, there are differences:

☐ A surety is a co-promissor with the principal obligor and is equally liable with him on his obligation.

☐ A guarantor is a collateral promissor whose liability arises only after all attempts to make the principal obligor perform have failed.

On this basis, the guarantor must receive notice of the principal obligor's default before there can be any obligation on his part. However, the differences begin to break down when some of the same courts pronouncing these distinctions talk about sureties being guarantors of payment—a true guarantor, they say, is merely a guarantor of collection.

Other courts use the terms surety and guarantor interchangeably; the Uniform Commercial Code says the term surety includes guarantor (§1-201(40)).

In view of these problems, some states spell out specifically the obligation or liability of the third party to the deal. Generally, for him to guarantee payment it will not be enough to have him simply sign the instrument or contract to be guaranteed as a guarantor—he will have to endorse "payment guaranteed." On the other hand, if someone is asked to give a guarantee and all he wants to give is a guarantee of collection, he will have to spell that out—"collection guaranteed." This is important when dealing with an "instrument" within the reach of the Commercial Paper Article of the UCC, which says that use of words of guarantee, without more, operates to guarantee payment (UCC §3-416(3)).

[¶3604]   CAPACITY OF A PARTNERSHIP TO BECOME A SURETY OR GUARANTOR

Sureties and guarantors must have legal capacity to enter into a contract relationship. Age and mental capacity are usually not factors. However, a problem may arise when a partnership acts as a surety or guarantor. Ordinarily, a partner has no implied authority to enter into a contract of surety or guarantee in the firm name. Sometimes the required authority may be implied from the common course of business of the firm or from a previous course of dealing with the partnership. If the partner or partners do not have the express or implied authority to bind the firm, the obligee may only get the *individual* obligations of those purporting to act for the firm.

[¶3605]   CAPACITY OF A CORPORATION TO BECOME A SURETY OR GUARANTOR

A corporation's capacity to act as an uncompensated surety or guarantor is severely limited, as the following rules point out.

The first rule is that a corporation cannot become a surety or guarantor *solely* for the principal obligor's benefit, unless it is given such power by its charter or statute—as when it is in the business of being a surety. Within this prohibition are guarantees of loans to directors, officers, or stockholders. So far as the rule operates to protect stockholders, it can be circumvented by getting the consent of all of the stockholders. However, creditors of the corporation may claim that the obligation assumed was beyond the corporation's authority. Usually, such a claim would be made only in situations when the corporation is not meeting its obligations to its creditors and shouldn't present a grave problem if the corporation has a very good credit rating.

The second rule to bear in mind is that a corporation does not need *express* power to act as a surety or guarantor but has *implied* power to do so when such action will "directly" promote its business purpose. What kind of activity promotes business purpose? The following acts have been held to directly benefit the corporate business purpose:

(1) Guaranteeing a customer's loan when there is a potential benefit from increased sales.

(2) Protecting the corporation's own interest by guaranteeing a loan to a subsidiary.

(3) Guaranteeing a debt of one of the corporation's own debtors in order to keep him going and so increase its chances of being paid.

In order to rely on the corporation's obligation, a corporate resolution that directly relates the guarantee to the promotion of a business purpose must be passed. If a resolution cannot be legitimately formulated in these terms, two courses of action are then available: (1) unanimous stockholder consent, or (2) a guarantee by the stockholders or directors or some of them as individuals.

[¶3606] SELECTING A SURETY OR GUARANTOR

When dealing with a paid surety (one who is in the business of being a surety), ordinarily there will be no need to worry about the surety being able to make good on the principal's obligations. Since paid sureties are subject to state regulation, this gives some assurance of their financial condition. As for private sureties and guarantors their obligation is no better than their financial standing.

To rely on a nonprofessional guarantor or surety to back up the principal's obligation, run a credit check through an established agency and get character references and financial statements. The relationship of the surety or guarantor to the principal obligor is often an important consideration. The chances are that a surety acting for his son, for example, will be more apt to fulfill his obligations than if a stranger is involved.

[¶3607] THE SURETY OR GUARANTEE AGREEMENT—WRITING REQUIREMENT

The surety or guarantor's contract should be put in writing. Since these contracts are generally regarded as contracts to answer for the debt or default of another, under the Statute of Frauds they must be in writing. In addition, a written agreement helps avoid disputes as to the rights and obligations of the parties. What finally goes into the contract will depend on the skill and judgment of the parties and their relative bargaining position.

[¶3608]　　CHECKLIST FOR DRAFTING THE AGREEMENT

Here is a checklist for drafting for a suretyship or guarantee agreement.

☐　The obligation(s) secured—present, past, future.

☐　The nature of the guarantee or the suretyship.

(1)　Primary or secondary, payment or collection.

(2)　Conditions of liability.

(3)　Amount of liability.

　　(a)　Costs and expenses.

　　(b)　Attorney's fee.

　　(c)　Interest.

　　(d)　Limitation of liability to a specified maximum.

　　(e)　When there are two or more guarantors or sureties.

(4)　Duration of liability.

　　(a)　Revocation—when and how agreement can be revoked.

　　(b)　Effect of death, insolvency, etc., of co-sureties or co-guarantors.

(5)　Exceptions to liability—i.e., acts of God as excusing performance.

(6)　Persons protected and persons bound by the agreement.

☐　Notice to the guarantor or surety.

(1)　Principal's default.

(2)　Creation or amount of indebtedness.

(3)　Alterations or changes in contract.

(4)　Claims or liens against principal.

☐　The effect of alterations or changes in the principal's obligation.

(1)　Generally.

(2)　Compromise or settlement with principal debtor.

(3)　Time extensions to principal debtor.

☐　Indemnification of the surety or the guarantor.

☐　Subrogation to the rights of the principal or obligee.

☐　Waivers—necessity of having these in writing.

As stated above, these are the main points to watch for. Special situations may call for special provisions not suggested in this list.

Various forms of guarantee are found in *IBP Forms of Business Agreements and Resolutions*.

[¶3609]　　THE CONTINUING AND RESTRICTED GUARANTEE

A guarantee need not be restricted to a specific transaction. It can be a continuing one, contemplating future uses or a series of transactions.

The continuing guarantee can be a very dangerous and expensive instrument from the guarantor's point of view. Therefore, it is wise to set forth in detail the conditions of the guarantee. The most important thing is to limit the amount guaranteed, the period over which it will be effective, and the type of transaction for which it can be used. If this is not done, the guarantor may find himself guaranteeing some of the principal obligor's personal obligations.

[¶3610]   PRINCIPAL OBLIGOR'S SIGNATURE

Whether the principal obligor's signature must appear on the contract of the surety or guarantor is an issue that has given the courts considerable difficulty. While there are numerous decisions to the effect that the signature is not necessary, it is advisable to obtain the signature. In the rare instance when the principal is not to know that his obligation is being guaranteed, check applicable state law before entering into the contract.

[¶3611]   ACCEPTANCE, APPROVAL, AND FILING

A contract of suretyship, like any other contract, requires acceptance. When the obligation runs to a governmental body or agency, certain persons or officers will usually be entrusted with the duty of accepting and approving the bond or contract, and there may be special provisions for filing or recording the instrument after its approval.

[¶3612]   THE PRINCIPLE OF INDEMNITY

Once a surety or guarantor has paid the principal obligor's debt *or* performed his contract, he has a right to be reimbursed—indemnified—by the principal for the amount paid. There is no right of indemnity until the surety or guarantor has paid out money. Therefore, if he works out a compromise and settlement with the obligee for less than the full amount owing, he can enforce his right to indemnity only up to the compromised amount. A right of indemnity does not have to be spelled out in the contract—it will be implied. Nevertheless, it is best to put it in writing, specifying just how far indemnification goes (court costs, counsel fees, etc.) and how the surety or guarantor is to prove his payment before he has the right to indemnification.

[¶3613]   UNDERSTANDING THE CONCEPT OF EXONERATION

If the principal obligor's debt or performance becomes due, and the obligee fails to take action, statutes in many states allow the surety to bring a suit and compel the creditor (obligee) to sue the obligor and thus collect the debt. Some states even allow the surety to sue the principal to compel payment. In other words, the surety need not pay the obligee and then try to get reimbursed from the principal obligor—he can take the initiative in forcing the obligor to pay.

In the case of coguarantors, one guarantor may sue the other guarantors to compel payment of their share of the guarantee to the creditor, instead of paying the full amount due and then seeking contribution from the coguarantors (see ¶3615). Use of exoneration will prevent the coguarantor from having to pay more than his share of the guarantee, and will safeguard the creditor's rights. However, if the legal process of compelling such exoneration will be lengthy, many courts may be loath to require the creditor to wait so long for payment, and may require the guarantor to seek contribution from the other guarantors.

[¶3614]   SUBROGATION

The surety or guarantor can ''step into'' the obligee's shoes after he has paid the obligation. He is entitled to all the remedies that the obligee had against the principal and he can also have any collateral securities that the obligor pledged with the obligee. When the right of subrogation is coupled with indemnity, the surety may, in certain instances, acquire the preferred status of the obligee and thus be more likely to receive reimbursement. For example, suppose a person becomes a surety on a government contract and the principal obligor fails to perform. After the surety pays or performs for the government, he will be subrogated to the rights of the principal obligor and will then have the government's preferred status over other creditors.

[¶3615]   CONTRIBUTION

The issue of contribution only arises when there are two or more sureties or guarantors. Contribution means that a surety who pays the obligee can compel the other sureties to pay their shares in order to make all the shares equal. The only requisite for this right is that all concerned be sureties for the same principal and the same obligation. They may be bound on separate instruments and they may not have ever been aware of one another.

[¶3616]   DISCHARGE OF THE SURETY OR GUARANTOR

Some actions may automatically discharge the surety or guarantor's obligations, unless prior consent was obtained or subsequent approval by the surety or guarantor was given. Listed below are some of the main causes of automatic discharge:

(1) Material alteration of the principal obligor's contract.
(2) Extension of time for payment of the principal debt.

(3) Failure of obligee to comply with request or notice to sue the principal obligor where a statute gives the surety or guarantor that right.

(4) Release or loss of the security.

(5) Payment or performance by the principal obligor.

(6) Release or discharge of the principal obligor.

(7) Change of principals or obligees.

The following paragraph discusses some of the related problems regarding such a discharge.

[¶3617] ADDITIONAL COMPLICATIONS IN THE DISCHARGE OF THE SURETY OR GUARANTOR

A material alteration, even though it may be to the advantage of the principal, may cause a discharge in some states. Usually, a compensated surety will be less likely to be discharged than an unpaid one. The compensated surety will usually have to prove damages before release from the obligation.

Mere failure to pursue the principal when the debt falls due does not operate as an extension. The extension has to be the result of a positive act. Most states have an exception to the rule of discharge by extension—that there is no discharge if the obligee, in granting an extension, reserves his rights against the surety.

Release of the security held by the obligee will operate to release the surety *to the extent that the remaining security is not enough to cover the debt.* Similarly, negligence on the part of the obligee in dealing with the security in his hands, resulting in its loss, may release the surety. Failure to perfect or to record the security can also result in discharge. (See ¶3401 for perfecting and recording a security.)

A surety may be discharged in some states if the Statute of Limitations runs out on the principal debt. In other states this won't work a discharge. An obligee should not permit himself to be put in a position where the rule can be applied against him—go after the principal obligor as soon as he is in default.

Bankruptcy of the principal obligor, although it results in his discharge, won't discharge the surety. The surety in this situation can only claim reimbursement from the bankrupt's estate.

Changes in the personnel of a partnership, even though the partnership keeps the same name, can result in discharge, but a mere change in name of the principal obligor, whether a partnership or a corporation, will not have that effect.

[¶3618] ANTICIPATE AND PREVENT AUTOMATIC DISCHARGE

Try to anticipate the various causes for discharge when structuring the surety or guarantor relationship. Where necessary, insert in the agreement any limitations that give the surety or guarantor the protection he demands. If the requisite consent is not obtained initially, try to get it before anything occurs that can result in discharge. Consent to an extension of time, for example, may not be too hard to obtain if the surety can also see benefits for himself. If the consent is obtained, be sure to get it in writing.

In addition to "discharge" of the surety, there are other points for the obligee to remember if he is to hold the surety or guarantor to his contract. Although these things may not operate to "discharge," the effect will be the same. Included in this category are some matters already discussed, such as the capacity or authority of the surety or guarantor, and the necessity of a written agreement to hold someone responsible for the debt of another. Certain defects in the principal obligor's contract may discharge the surety's obligation, such as lack of consideration, illegality, usury, or impossibility of performance. The defect must be one that *voids* the contract, not one that makes it *voidable*. For example, if a principal has not reached the age at which he can enter into a legally binding contract, this fact will ordinarily operate to make his contract *voidable* and will not automatically relieve the surety of his obligation.

[¶3619]　　PROTECTING THE SURETY'S INTEREST IN OBLIGOR'S COLLATERAL

Sureties often require some type of security from the principal obligor. Usually it will be quite obvious that the security interest granted, if it's to be good against third persons, will have to be perfected in one of the ways discussed in the chapter on secured transactions (see ¶3401). But sometimes this won't be so obvious. For example, the surety on a contractor's bond demands and gets an assignment of the payments that become due under the contract in order to secure his rights against the principal. The surety will have to follow UCC procedures to perfect his interest and make it stand up against other creditors of the principal obligor or others claiming an interest in the payments through him.

If the assignment of payments under a contract covers payments due at the time of the assignment, a somewhat different approach may be required. A surety who requires tangible or intangible security from the obligor in order to protect himself must be alert to the possibility that he has a security interest that is not perfected against third persons unless he takes positive steps to this end.

[¶3620]　　SURETIES AND GUARANTORS ON COMMERCIAL PAPER

Accommodation parties on commercial paper, whether their names appear as makers, drawers, acceptors, or endorsers, are, in effect, sureties or guarantors, despite the lack of a separate contract or use of the term "surety" or "guarantor."

[¶3621]　　LIABILITY UNDER THE UCC

Under UCC §3-415(2), an accommodation party incurs contract liability on the instrument *in the capacity in which he signs*. Therefore, if he signs a note as a maker, he will have the liability of a maker; if he signs as an endorser, he will have the liability of an endorser. Payment by the accommodating party to the holder creates a cause of action in favor of the accommodating party based on the accommodated party's implied obligation to indemnify the accommodating party. Accommodation endorsers should include a waiver of suretyship defenses if that is the parties' intent. These various liabilities are discussed in detail beginning at ¶901. Here it is sufficient to point out that the obligee will be in a better position if the accommodation party can be induced to sign as maker. As maker, his liability will be primary and not conditioned on presentment of the note, as might be the case if he signs as endorser.

Under the UCC, the liability of an accommodation party will run to a holder for value, even though the holder knows of his accommodation nature. Under UCC §3-415(2), this is true only if the holder takes the instrument before it is due. And under this Section of the UCC, liability is imposed on an accommodation endorser even though the endorsement takes place after delivery to the holder.

Under the UCC, as against anyone taking the paper with knowledge of the accommodation character, or a holder who is not a holder in due course, the accommodation party can set up any of the defenses that an ordinary surety might set up to relieve himself of liability. For example, he can avoid liability by showing an extension of time for payment made without his consent, and without an effective reservation of rights against him (see UCC §3-606). He will also be discharged by a release of collateral. If the accommodation party consents to any action that might discharge him, he will be discharged. Therefore, consent in advance to certain actions, such as extension of time, is commonly incorporated in the instrument over the accommodation party's signature. If such consent is not obtained in advance, it can be given afterwards, and it will be binding even without consideration.

Normally, a holder in due course without actual notice of the accommodation need not be concerned about the defense of the accommodation party. However, an endorsement that is not in the chain of title—the irregular or anomalous endorsement—will be notice of the accommodation character (UCC §3-415(4)). Here's an example of such an endorsement: A note payable to Able or his order and made by Baker is endorsed by Charlie (the accommodation party) before Baker negotiates the note to a holder in due course.

The UCC makes it clear that both paid and gratuitous sureties may be accommodation parties.

[¶3622] UCC DISTINCTION BETWEEN GUARANTEEING PAYMENT AND COLLECTION

One who guarantees payment says in effect that he will pay the instrument when it becomes due, regardless of whether the holder has tried to collect from the party primarily liable. He waives presentment and any necessary notice of dishonor and protest and any demand the holder has against the maker or drawer. In short, he becomes a co-maker or co-drawer, jointly and separately liable.

On the other hand, one who guarantees collection says in effect that if the instrument is not paid when it becomes due, he will pay it, *if and only if* the holder first proceeds against the maker, drawer, or acceptor by suit and execution or shows that such action would be useless. However, he, in effect, also waives presentment and any necessary notice of dishonor or protest.

UCC §3-416 codifies these different meanings in accordance with commercial understanding and the accepted meaning of these terms under prior law.

When using these forms of guarantee consider:

(1) Limitation on the amount of the guarantee. It doesn't necessarily have to be for the full amount of the instrument.

(2) Consent to extension of time for payment or release of collateral.

(3) Payment of collection expenses, including attorneys' fees.

[¶3623] INDEMNITY AND HOLD HARMLESS AGREEMENTS

A business that can reduce its "cost of doing business" risks or shift these risks to others will be able to reduce costs and thus improve its competitive position. Indemnity and hold harmless agreements can be used to accomplish this.

Indemnity and hold harmless agreements are closely related. Whatever fine-spun distinctions there may be, the two forms of agreement can, for the most part, be considered identical and the terms are used interchangeably and refer to the parties in both types of agreements as indemnitor and indemnitee. These agreements may be used to:

(1) Assume the legal liability of others.

(2) Create an entirely new liability for the indemnitor.

(3) Create a contractual liability for the indemnitor in cases in which he is already liable in tort for the same risk.

Examples of these different uses appear in the following paragraphs. In connection with (3) above, there is the question of why anyone would want to add contractual liability to tort liability. Let's say a business person buys a heating plant and the seller agrees to install it. The seller will be liable in any case for negligence in installing it, but the buyer is in a better position if he has not only the seller's tort liability (negligence) but his contractual liability to hold the buyer harmless as well. There are a number of reasons for this, but the main ones are:

(1) In a contract action all the buyer will have to prove is the contract and the damages. He won't have to show negligence on the part of the seller and he won't have to worry about the defenses of contributory negligence or assumption of risk.

(2) The measure of damages can be spelled out in a contract action, and even without doing so, damages may be greater in a contract than in a tort action.

(3) The time to sue is usually longer for contract actions than for tort actions.

Various forms of indemnity agreements and clauses appear in *IBP Forms of Business Agreements and Resolutions.*

The indemnification of corporate directors, officers, and other employees is discussed in ¶1326 et seq.

[¶3624]   **LEGALITY OF A HOLD**
                        HARMLESS AGREEMENT

An indemnity agreement will not offer the indemnitee positive protection against his own wrongful or illegal acts if they are willful, grossly negligent, or contrary to strong public policy. The Restatement of Contracts §572 states that a bargain to indemnify another against the consequences of committing a tortious act is illegal, unless the performance of the tortious act is only an undesired possibility in the performance of the bargain and the bargain does not tend to induce the act. This leaves the door open for indemnification against acts of ordinary negligence and in this respect is in line with the law in most states. However, check state law.

Bear in mind that even though it is planned to insure the hold harmless agreement via contractual liability insurance, as discussed at ¶3627, the insurance cannot be any better than the agreement—if the agreement is void, the insurance will be useless.

[¶3625]   **CHECKLIST OF USE OF HOLD HARMLESS**
                AGREEMENTS IN COMMERCIAL
                        TRANSACTIONS

Indemnity or hold harmless agreements may be useful in the following situations:

☐ Protection of retailer or wholesaler against product liability.

☐ Protection of purchaser against claims, losses, or expenses growing out of delivery, installation, or use of equipment or merchandise.

☐ Protection of lessor of equipment against claims, losses, or expenses growing out of lessee's use of the equipment or failure to insure against liability or loss of the property leased.

☐ Protection of a secured creditor against failure of a debtor to insure his collateral.

☐ Protection of a guarantor.

☐ Protection of the endorser of commercial paper.

[¶3626]   **THE INDEMNITOR AS AN INSURER**

A hold harmless agreement, in effect, puts the indemnitor in the insurance business. But the usual indemnitor is not in the same class as a seasoned insurance carrier. Therefore, a hold harmless agreement will not be as good for the indemnitee as an insurance policy:

(1) If the hold harmless agreement is merely against loss, the indemnitee must pay the loss before seeking reimbursement from the insurer.

(2) The defense clause in an insurance policy is usually more favorable to the insured than such a clause is apt to be in a hold harmless agreement.

(3) Insurance carriers are likely to do a better job than the usual indemnitor in investigating and defending claims and suits.

(4) The financial worth of an insurance carrier and ability to make good on its obligation to the policyholder is apt to be better than that of the usual indemnitor.

[¶3627]   **INSURING THE HOLD
HARMLESS AGREEMENT**

Many indemnitees will not be satisfied with a simple hold harmless agreement—they will want it backed up by insurance. The indemnitor may also want to insure the hold harmless agreement since he probably lacks the ability to spread the risk assumed.

A special form of insurance known as *contractual liability insurance* can be used. This coverage is usually obtained by way of a special endorsement on the indemnitor's liability policy. (The usual liability policy won't cover assumed or contractual liability without a special endorsement because the standard form of exclusion in almost all forms of liability policies reads: "This policy does not apply to liability assumed by the insured under any contract or agreement.")

Contractual liability coverage will not automatically cover all contracts that the insured has undertaken or that he may undertake during the policy period. It will be tailored to the insured's particular situation and will cover only specific contracts or types of contracts, and will be subject to the exclusions set out below. The policy limits, in terms of amount, will normally be the same as those used in manufacturers' and contractors' liability policies. Rates will normally be fixed after submission of the specific contracts or types of contracts for rating.

[¶3628]   **ADDITIONAL INSURANCE COVERAGE
MAY BE REQUIRED**

The standard contractual liability endorsement has a number of exclusions (some of which may be deleted for an additional premium), such as:

☐ Liability for any warranty of goods or products. Products liability coverage is needed for this.

☐ Damages awarded in arbitration proceedings in which the insurer is not permitted to participate. Make sure, therefore, in drafting a hold harmless agreement, if it provides for arbitration, that the insurer is permitted to participate.

☐ Any obligation for which the insured may be held liable by a third-party beneficiary of a contract. This can be deleted for an additional premium.

☐ Defects in maps, plans, designs, or specifications of the insured. This can be deleted for an additional premium.

☐ War damages.

☐ Dram shop. Many states impose absolute liability on those selling or giving drinks to one already drunk for the damage the drunken person may do. This may be deleted for an additional premium.

☐ Workmen's compensation, unemployment compensation, or disability benefits laws. Contractual claims brought by an employee are not, however, excluded.

☐ Property owned, occupied, rented, or in the care, custody, or control of the indemnitor-insured if the hold harmless agreement includes claims for these types of property by the indemnitor-insured, he should obtain property damage insurance—inland marine or other.

☐ Goods, products, or work completed out of which the accident arises. This is the same exclusion found in products insurance and is used in contractual liability insurance for the same reason—to bar covering the insured's own business risk of replacing defective products or work out of which the accident arises.

☐ Water damage. This can be deleted for an additional premium.

☐ Nuclear energy. This hazard is covered by the nuclear energy pools.

A form to be used for insuring the hold harmless agreement appears in *IBP Forms of Business Agreements and Resolutions*.

[¶3629]   CHECKLIST FOR DRAFTING HOLD HARMLESS AGREEMENTS

Here are some main points to be covered in negotiating and drafting a hold harmless agreement:

☐ Names and addresses of indemnitors and indemnitees.

☐ Consideration for the agreement—if it is part of a sale or of a lease, a separate statement of consideration will not be necessary.

☐ Scope of the indemnity:

(1) Is the indemnity to be against *liability* or against *loss?* If against liability, the indemnitee's legal rights arise as soon as his liability becomes fixed. If against loss, his rights arise only after he has made payment or suffered an actual loss.

(2) Does it cover the costs and expenses of investigating or defending against liability or loss, including attorney's fees?

(3) Does it obligate the indemnitor to investigate and defend claims against the indemnitee?

(4) Is the indemnity agreement in limited, intermediate, or broad form? The limited form gives indemnification where the indemnitor is guilty of active negligence and the indemnitee's negligence, if any, is at most passive. The intermediate form indemnifies even though the indemnitee may be guilty of active negligence. The broad form gives third parties rights against the indemnitor irrespective of his or anyone else's fault. These forms correspond to the classes used for normal rating purposes when contractual liability insurance coverage is to be used. Insurance rates will vary considerably, depending on which form is adopted.

(5) Is interest to be included? If the parties intend indemnification for damages and interest, interest should be expressly mentioned because there have been decisions excluding interest unless it is expressly included.

(6) Maximum amount of liability of the indemnitor.

☐ Duration of the indemnity.

☐ Notice to the indemnitor:

(1) When necessary.

(2) Time, mode of service.

(3) Contents.

☐ Rule of strict construction against the indemnitee. Bear in mind that courts often manage to cut the heart out of indemnity agreements by adopting a rule of strict construction against the indemnitee—especially in the case of agreements in intermediate or broad form. If indemnification against the indemnitee's own acts of negligence is intended, say so expressly.

☐ Compromise of claims by the indemnitee.

☐ Evidence of liability or loss.

☐ Security for the performance of the indemnitor's obligations under the agreement:

(1) Insurance.

(2) Bond.

(3) Deposit.

Various forms of hold harmless agreements may be found in *IBP Forms of Business Agreements and Resolutions*.

[¶3630] TAX ASPECTS OF GUARANTEES AND INDEMNIFICATIONS

The different and not wholly consistent tax treatment given bad debts and losses under the tax law gives rise to the need for precision in the drafting of guarantee, surety, and indemnity agreements. If the deal goes sour, the party ultimately making good may have (1) the status of a creditor of the defaulting obligor (as in the case of a guarantor) and suffer a bad debt if he cannot collect, or (2) the legal status of an independent obligor himself (as in the case of an indemnitor) and simply be considered to have suffered a loss.

[¶3631] BAD DEBTS VS. LOSSES

The tax treatment of bad debts and losses as allowable deductions from taxable income revolves around four variables: Transactions by (1) individuals or (2) corporations that are (3) business or (4) nonbusiness. Corporations are generally deemed to be business entities, so their bad debts or losses are fully deductible. An individual is allowed a full deduction in a business transaction whether the obligation arises by way of bad debt or loss. Thus, in the case of corporations and individuals becoming obligated in *business* transactions, the distinction need not be so sharply drawn for tax purposes, unless the business nature of the transaction is itself in question. However, IRC §166(d) provides an individual with a limited deduction, equivalent to a short-term capital loss, for a nonbusiness bad debt, but allows no deduction at all for a loss sustained in a transaction not entered into for profit.

Note that IRC §166(d)(1)(B) provides that in the case of a taxpayer other than a corporation, if any nonbusiness debt becomes worthless within the taxable year, the loss resulting therefrom shall be considered a loss from the sale or exchange, during the taxable year, of a capital asset *held for not more than one year*. Nonbusiness bad debt is defined at IRC §166(d)(2).

[¶3632]   BUSINESS VS. NONBUSINESS BAD DEBTS

The development of judicial distinctions between transactions deemed to be business and those deemed nonbusiness has resulted in a confusing case law. The distinction between business bad debt and nonbusiness bad debt rests on whether the debt was incurred in connection with the trade or business of the taxpayer (covering debts becoming worthless after the taxpayer has gone out of business) or incurred in the taxpayer's business. If it was, it is business bad debt.

Of course, the IRC also provides for nonbusiness casualty losses at §165(c).

[¶3633]   STOCKHOLDER AS GUARANTOR OF CORPORATE DEBT

A stockholder's guarantee of his corporation's obligations is considered to be a nonbusiness transaction. If the stockholder is an individual and he has to make good, he is entitled to a short-term capital loss on a nonbusiness bad debt *(Putnam, 352 US 82, 1952)*. It is clear that this is the tax treatment even if the corporation is insolvent at the time of payment and it could be argued that a claim to reimbursement by subrogation to creditor's rights is worthless. Ordinary loss treatment is available to an officer or employee who had to make loans to hold onto his job *(Generes, 405 US 93, 1972)*.

[¶3634]   PARENT CORPORATION AS GUARANTOR OF SUBSIDIARY'S EXPENSES AND DIVIDENDS

Generally a parent corporation must capitalize payments made to pay a subsidiary's business expenses and dividends (when called upon to honor its guarantee) by adding the same to its basis for the stock of the subsidiary, unless a direct benefit to the parent can be shown—for example, when the subsidiary performs vital services for the parent. A bona fide loan by a parent to its subsidiary might be better, since at best a full business bad debt deduction could be taken and at worst it would be treated as a capital expenditure.

389

[¶3635]   PAYMENTS UNDER CERTAIN GUARANTEE AGREEMENTS NOT DEDUCTIBLE

Bad debt deductions are not allowed in the following situations:

(1) When the guarantee is given as a part of purchase price of a capital asset, as distinguished from guaranteeing a loan, the guarantor's payment to the creditor is treated as a capital expenditure when the debtor doesn't pay up.

(2) If a corporate guarantor pays off obligations of its stockholders—such payments are considered as dividends and are not deductible.

(3) Guarantee of the obligation of family member—this is closely scrutinized to determine whether there is a valid business purpose before the business bad debt deduction is allowed. If the guarantor never expected repayment from the debtor-relative, the transaction might be considered a gift.

(4) If debtor is not liable to guarantor at law or, at the time of making the guarantee, there was no reasonable expectation of repayment. Before the guarantor can get a bad debt deduction he must be able to show that (1) originally he had reason to expect repayment and (2) after he honors his guarantee, the debtor's obligation to him is worthless.

[¶3636]   TIMING OF LOSS BY CASH-BASIS TAXPAYER

To a large extent, given business justification, a cash-basis guarantor or indemnitor can choose the year in which his loss will occur, since the loss is sustained only when (1) the guarantor's claim against the original debtor is worthless due to the latter's insolvency, and (2) the guarantor actually makes out-of-pocket cash disbursements in satisfaction of his liability under the guarantee. If the guarantor gives the creditor a new note covering his liability under the guarantee such a note does not constitute a cash disbursement until payments are made on it. But the deduction can be lost if the guarantor does not exercise his legal rights—e.g., the Statute of Limitations runs against him.

[¶3637]   TIMING OF LOSS BY ACCRUAL-BASIS TAXPAYER

If an accrual-basis taxpayer is an indemnitor, he may be able to deduct an indemnity loss in advance of the actual payment, but if he is a guarantor, he will have to wait until the year of payment, since the debt between the guarantor and the debtor doesn't arise until then (which becomes bad if the debtor can't pay off guarantor).

[¶3638]   CAPITAL LOSS BY INDEMNITOR

Payment made under an indemnity agreement will be treated as a capital loss if the indemnity was given as a part of the consideration for the sale of a capital asset.

TAX DISPUTES

[¶3701] Tax disputes are seldom simple matters. Knowledge of IRS procedures is the basic ingredient for success. The person unfamiliar with the way IRS operates may use improper tactics or contact the wrong person in the course of the dispute, and IRS may end up with more than its due. The paragraphs below form a basic guide to successful negotiation of a tax dispute.

[¶3702]   PROCESSING OF RETURNS

When a tax return is filed, usually with a regional service center, it is first checked by IRS for form, execution, and mathematical accuracy. Math errors are corrected, and a notice of the error is sent to the taxpayer. Payment of any additional tax resulting from a math error is then demanded, or a refund of any overpayment is made.

Tax returns are classified for examination at the regional service center. Individual income tax returns with potentially unallowable items may be turned over to the Examination Division at the service center for correction by correspondence with the taxpayer. Otherwise, returns selected for their highest potential are turned over to the district Examination Divisions. Those most in need of review are selected for office or field examination by a Revenue Agent.

[¶3703]   DEALING WITH THE REVENUE AGENT

Original examination of a selected tax return falls to the examining officers in the Examination Division of each IRS district office, otherwise known as Revenue Agents. The Revenue Agent may examine a taxpayer's books, papers, records, or memoranda relating to items that should be included in his return. If, during the course of his examination, the Agent determines that there is a deficiency, the taxpayer may agree to pay the additional tax, which ends the dispute at that point. The Agent will require the signing of a formal settlement agreement (Form 870). The taxpayer can still sue for a refund, however, if he later changes his mind.

Of course, the first opportunity to settle the controversy is with the Revenue Agent. In dealing with the Revenue Agent, the taxpayer should remember that the Agent is trying to discharge his duty to the government and still dispose of the matter the best way he can. The most satisfactory results come from a climate within which the taxpayer and the Agent engage in a mutual endeavor to determine the proper tax liability.

[¶3703.1]   Limited Authority of Revenue Agent

The Revenue Agent is the principal fact-finder of IRS. He has the authority to determine what the facts are and apply them to the legal position taken by IRS.

A Revenue Agent, however, does not have discretion to dispose of an issue if:

(1) IRS has taken a position contrary to the Tax Court. He must follow the position taken by IRS.

(2) Regulations and rulings are available. He must follow these rules.

(3) The law on the subject is not clear.

Since the Revenue Agent has no authority to settle these issues, it's better not to argue them with him. No purpose is served. The best course for the taxpayer is to inform the Agent that he will not agree and give the Agent as much information on the issues as is pertinent.

[¶3703.2] Advantages of Settlement With the Revenue Agent

The advantages of a taxpayer's settling on the Revenue Agent's level are:

☐ He is required to show less evidence to establish a claim.

☐ He avoids the possibility of having other issues raised by other more experienced IRS agents.

☐ He avoids the expense and anxiety of further proceedings.

[¶3704]   OFFICE EXAMINATION PROCEDURE

There are two general types of audit, commonly called "office examinations" and "field examinations." An office examination may be conducted either through correspondence with the taxpayer or through an in-person interview at the district offices.

[¶3704.1] Adjustments by Examination Division at Regional Service Center

If a return is identified as containing a potentially unallowable item, it may be handled by the Examination Division of the Regional Service Center where the return was filed. Audits conducted from service centers involve correspondence only. If the taxpayer does not agree to proposed adjustments, then the regular IRS appeal procedures outlined in the following paragraphs will apply. If an interview becomes necessary, the case will be transferred to the IRS district office.

[¶3704.2] Examinations at the District Office

Individual income tax returns and some business returns are generally examined at district offices using the office examination technique. Office examinations conducted through a district office are conducted primarily by interview of the taxpayer. Examinations conducted by a district office are conducted by correspondence only when appropriate because of the nature of the questionable items on a return and the convenience and nature of the taxpayer.

If a return is subjected to an office examination by correspondence, the taxpayer will be asked to explain or send supporting evidence by mail. In an interview examination, the taxpayer is directed to go to the district office for an interview and to take certain records that will support the questionable items on his return.

During an interview examination, the taxpayer has the right to point out to the Agent any amounts included in the return that are not taxable, or any deductions that were not claimed. If it develops that a field examination is necessary, the Revenue Agent may conduct one.

[¶3705] FIELD EXAMINATION PROCEDURE

Certain returns are examined by field examination, which involves inspection of the taxpayer's books and records on the taxpayer's premises. If a return is subjected to a field examination, the Agent will check the entire return and will examine all pertinent books, papers, records, and memoranda dealing with anything that is required to be included.

If a return presents an engineering or appraisal problem, such as depreciation or depletion deductions, gains or losses from the sale of property, or abandonment losses, it may also be examined by an engineer agent. The engineer agent will make a separate report.

[¶3706] CONCLUDING THE OFFICE OR FIELD EXAMINATION

When the Revenue Agent concludes the examination of a return, the taxpayer will be asked to agree with his findings. If there is no agreement, the taxpayer has a right of appeal. These rights are discussed in the following paragraphs.

If the taxpayer agrees to the Agent's proposed changes, he'll be asked to sign Form 870. He'll also be asked to pay the additional tax plus any interest or penalties at this time.

[¶3707] TECHNICAL ADVICE

During the examination of a return, the district office may request technical advice from the National Office. Technical advice is usually made available if the disputed issue is either extremely complex or the disposition of similar cases has not been uniform among the district offices.

A taxpayer has the right to review the facts and issues presented to the National Office. If he disagrees with the district office's presentation, he can submit his own statement of facts.

[¶3707.1] Taxpayer's Request for Technical Advice

Taxpayers themselves can initiate the request for technical advice. Under the Freedom of Information Act and Tax Reform Act of 1976, IRS must make public its private letter rulings. Since a response to a request for technical advice is considered a ruling, it should be pointed out that information contained in a request *may* be made public. This may not be in a taxpayer's best interests, since confidential information may be revealed despite the law's requirement that private rulings be "sanitized" before release.

[¶3708] APPEALS OFFICE CONFERENCE

Failure to reach agreement with the Revenue Agent moves the tax dispute on to the next stage—the Appeals Office conference. The Appeals Office is a type of appellate tribunal within IRS. It is not a division of the district director's office; the district director has no jurisdiction over this department. The Appeals Office settlement authority is derived from the Regional Commissioners.

[¶3709] CONFERENCE PROCEDURE FOR OFFICE EXAMINATIONS

Conference procedures for office examinations are explained in the paragraphs that follow.

[¶3709.1] Correspondence Examination

In a correspondence office examination, the taxpayer is notified of the Agent's proposed findings by form letter. He can sign an agreement if he accepts the Agent's findings. If he disagrees, the form letter also instructs him on the course of appeal available to him.

If he disagrees with the Agent following a correspondence office examination, he is granted an Appeals Office conference on request. There is no need to submit a formal written protest.

[¶3709.2] Interview Examination

If the taxpayer disagrees with the Agent following an office interview examination, he is granted an immediate conference if possible, and if he so requests. If he does request an immediate conference, the examination report is mailed to him along with instructions for appeal. He will be granted a conference upon request, and he does not have to file a protest.

Note, however, that business returns examined in an office examination are handled in the same manner as returns examined in a field examination.

[¶3710] CONFERENCE PROCEDURE FOR FIELD EXAMINATIONS

Following a field examination of a return, a complete examination report is prepared that fully explains all proposed adjustments. This report and the overall case file is submitted to a District Review Staff for review. After the review, the taxpayer receives a copy of the examination report along with a 30-day letter outlining choices of action.

If the proposed adjustment does not exceed $2,500, a conference is granted upon request without the taxpayer having to file a protest.

If more than $2,500 is involved, a conference is granted only after the filing of a written protest, setting forth the facts, law, and the arguments on which the taxpayer relies.

[¶3711] AUTHORITY OF APPEALS OFFICE

The Appeals Office has broad authority to settle cases. It can evaluate and settle cases on the basis of IRS's and the taxpayer's respective strength and weakness and the risk of litigation. Issues of law and mixed issues of law and fact can be settled at this level. A settlement by the Appeals Office (by signing Form 870 AD) is considered by IRS to be a final disposition of the case.

[¶3712] APPEAL IN THE COURTS

If settlement is not reached in the Appeals Office, or the conference is waived, IRS then issues a statutory notice of deficiency setting forth its claim for additional tax. This notice is called the ''90-day letter.''

[¶3712.1] Taxpayer's Alternatives After Receiving ''90-Day Letter''

(1) Pay the tax and close the matter.

(2) Try a further settlement through a conference in the Appeals Office.

(3) Pay the tax demanded and file a suit for refund in the district court or in the United States Court of Claims.

(4) File a petition for redetermination in the Tax Court.

[¶3713] THE REFUND ROUTE

The taxpayer who takes this route has two courts in which to bring his suit: The United States District Court in the district where the tax was paid or the United States Court of Claims, which sits in Washington, D.C. Before a taxpayer is allowed to bring suit in one of these courts, he must pay the *entire* tax that is due (including interest and penalties). In these Courts he can only sue for refund of taxes paid.

The way to proceed is to first pay the tax and then file a claim for refund with IRS. Upon its rejection by IRS, or the expiration of six months, suit for refund is filed.

The taxpayer who takes this route cannot later bring suit in the Tax Court. In the first place, the 90-day period in all likelihood would have expired. Secondly, since the tax due is paid, there is no deficiency over which the Tax Court could take jurisdiction.

Taxpayers may not file petitions in the Tax Court and then pay the tax and sue for refund. Once the Tax Court has acquired jurisdiction it will not let go—even upon stipulation of counsel.

[¶3714]   SUIT FOR REFUND IN THE DISTRICT COURT

Suit in the district court is brought against the IRS District Director (personally) who collected the tax, or the United States Government. In either event, a jury trial is available. The availability of a jury is the major advantage of bringing the suit in the district court. Decisions in this court are appealable to the United States Circuit Court of Appeals.

[¶3715]   SUIT FOR REFUND IN COURT OF CLAIMS

The Court of Claims is a five-judge court that sits in Washington. Although there is no jury trial, this Court has been known to listen to the "equities" of a tax case. A decision by this Court is final, except for a reversal by the U.S. Supreme Court. Decisions are appealable only to the Supreme Court by grant of certiorari, which is not usually granted.

A taxpayer who elects to use this Court has to be mindful that he is giving up a valuable right to an appellate review of his case. But this may work to a taxpayer's benefit as well as to his detriment.

If the issue in dispute has been decided by this Court in the taxpayer's favor, he can be virtually assured of victory by paying the tax and then suing for refund in this Court.

[¶3716]   BURDEN OF PROOF

In either the district court or Court of Claims, the burden of proof is on the taxpayer to establish that he is entitled to the refund. But this is the same as in the Tax Court, except that there proof that the deficiency is wrong is required.

[¶3717]   TAX COURT ROUTE

The Tax Court's jurisdiction is invoked only after IRS has issued its "90-day letter," and the taxpayer has filed a *timely* petition to have its case heard. This petition must be filed within 90 days or the Tax Court will not get jurisdiction. There can be no extensions of time to file a petition.

One of the major advantages in filing a petition in the Tax Court is that the taxpayer can have the deficiency determined without paying any part of the tax that is due. Some taxpayers, after filing a petition, do pay the tax, but this is only to stop the running of interest. It is not necessary. In fact, if the tax is paid before the mailing of a statutory notice of deficiency, the Tax Court would not have jurisdiction over the dispute.

Decisions by the Tax Court are appealable to the United States Circuit Courts of Appeal. The circuit where taxpayer files a return is normally the place where an appeal will be taken. The Circuit Courts of Appeal have exclusive jurisdiction over decisions by the Tax Court and the district courts.

[¶3718]   TAX COURT SMALL CLAIMS PROCEDURE

The Tax Court has a small claims division that handles cases involving tax deficiencies or overpayments that do not exceed $5,000 ($1,500 before June, 1979). Both income and estate tax deficiencies are handled here. The decisions in these cases are based upon a brief summary opinion instead of formal findings of fact, and are not precedent for future cases. The procedure is optional with the taxpayer.

In addition to not serving as precedent for other cases, decisions rendered under the ''small tax case'' rules are final. Taxpayers electing this procedure give up any right to appeal the dispute to the Circuit Courts of Appeal.

[¶3719]   WHAT ARE THE TAXPAYER'S ODDS?

Appeals within IRS are settled by agreement about 70% of the time. A taxpayer's chances of securing at least partial relief in the Tax Court are approximately 45%. The following is a breakdown by court of taxpayers' 1977 ''win/loss'' record:

	Complete Victory	Partial Victory	Lost
Tax Court			
Small cases	10%	35%	55%
Regular tax cases	11	35	54
District Court	22	12	66
Court of Claims	27	5	68
Court of Appeals			
From District Court	29	7	64
From Tax Court	10	15	75

[¶3720]   FOR FURTHER REFERENCE . . .

Bertolini, A.L., ''Responding to the IRS' Eleven Questions Investigations: Where Practitioners Stand,'' 48 Journal of Taxation 16-20 (January 1978).

"Important Developments in Practice and Procedure Including 1976 TRA Changes: Symposium," 36 New York University Institute on Federal Taxation 1169-345 (1978).

Kapleau, P.H., "How to Choose an Effective Strategy When There Is Disagreement With an IRS Agent," 6 Taxation for Lawyers 100 (1977).

Nash, M.J., "Effective Internal Revenue Service Appellate Division Practice," 35 New York University Institute on Federal Taxation 325 (1977).

Piper, J.T., and Jerge, J.M., "Shifting the Burden of Proof in Tax Court," 31 Tax Lawyer 303-19 (Winter 1978).

Premis, M., "Audio Review Process," 11 Creighton Law Review 755-63 (March 1978).

Simon, H.P. and Burton, J.A., "How an Attorney Can Effectively Assist a Client Whose Return Is Being Examined," 6 Taxation for Lawyers 240 (1978).

TAX LIENS

[¶3801] Federal tax liens may accrue against any person who neglects or refuses to pay taxes. They apply to both real and personal property belonging to a taxpayer who is liable for the tax (IRC §6321). Liens in favor of the federal government arise at the time the assessment is made by IRS and continue until the lien is satisfied or expires through lapse of time. Priority over a federal tax lien accrues to any purchaser, the holder of a mechanic's lien, a judgment lien creditor, or the holder of a security interest who has established priority under the Uniform Commercial Code or other pertinent statutory device prior to the filing by IRS.

Even if notice of a lien imposed by IRS has been filed, it is ineffective with respect to a security interest that came into existence *after* filing of the tax lien by reason of a disbursement made prior to the 46th day after the date of filing. This exemption applies only to property covered by terms of a written agreement entered into prior to the filing of a tax lien that local law protects against judgment liens arising out of an unsecured obligation (IRC §6323(d)).

[¶3802] PLACE OF FILING FEDERAL TAX LIENS

The federal government may establish priority for federal tax lien purposes by filing (in the case of real property) in an office within the state, county, or other governmental subdivision designated by local law in which the property subject to the lien is situated (IRC §6323(f)(1)(A)).

[¶3803] LIENS AGAINST STOCKS AND SECURITIES

Any bond, debenture, note, or certificate of other indebtedness issued either by a corporation or a political subdivision of a government, interest coupons, shares of stock, warrants, negotiable instruments, or money may not be subject to a federal lien priority if the purchaser had no actual knowledge or notice of the existence of the lien and if the holder of the security interest in those items also had no bona fide actual knowledge or notice of existence of the lien (IRC §6323(b)(1)).

[¶3804] AUTOMOBILES AND FEDERAL TAX LIEN PRIORITY

A federal tax lien with respect to a motor vehicle (provided the auto is registered under the laws of any state or foreign country) is ineffective provided there was a bona fide purchase for value without notice or knowledge of the existence of the lien, and after the purchaser does obtain knowledge or notice of the lien there is no relinquishment of possession of the motor vehicle to the original seller or agent of the seller.

[¶3805]   "CASUAL SALES" AND FEDERAL TAX LIENS

Household goods, personal effects, or other tangible personal property purchased in a casual sale for less than $250 that are not intended for resale are taken
free of any federal tax lien, provided the purchaser has no actual knowledge of the
existence of the lien.

[¶3806]   MECHANIC'S LIENS ON REAL PROPERTY

Personal residences containing not more than four dwelling units on which a
mechanic's lien has been levied are subject to federal tax lien priorities if the
mechanic's lien for work performed is more than $1,000. If the contract with the
owner amounts to less than $1,000, the workman has a lien priority over the federal
government.

[¶3807]   ATTORNEY'S LIENS

An attorney is entitled to a lien priority to the extent of reasonable compensation for obtaining a judgment or procuring a settlement (IRC §6323(b)(8)).

[¶3808]   REPAIRMAN'S LIENS

Tangible personal property that has been repaired or improved and is in the
continuing possession of the repairman from the time the repair or improvement
was initiated is subject to priority over a federal tax lien (IRC §6323(b)(5)).

[¶3809]   CERTAIN LOANS

Passbook loans (provided the bank keeps the passbook in its possession until
the loan is paid) and insurance policy loans also have priority over a federal tax lien
(IRC §6323(d)(9)-(10)). A requisite element of this rule is that neither the insurance company nor the savings institution has actual notice or knowledge of the
existence of the lien.

[¶3810]   COMMERCIAL FINANCING AGREEMENTS

Loans to a taxpayer secured by commercial financing acquired in the ordinary
course of trade or business (resulting in the creation of commercial paper) are not
subject to a federal tax lien on the resulting security interest, provided there is a
written agreement entered into prior to the filing of the tax lien that constitutes a

commercial transaction financing agreement, or a real property construction or improvement financing agreement, or a disbursement agreement, provided that the underlying agreement under local law would be protected against a judgment lien arising out of an unsecured obligation (IRC §6323(c)).

[¶3811] EXTENSION OF PRIORITY FOR INTEREST AND OTHER EXPENSES

If the federal tax lien is not valid against other nongovernmental lien creditors or holders of securities interests, the priorities also extend to six years to the extent that under local law any of the items would have the same priority as the lien or security interest to which it relates. These include:

☐ Interest or carrying charges on the secured obligation;

☐ Reasonable charges and expenses of an indentured trustee holding the security interest;

☐ Reasonable expenses (including reasonable compensation for attorneys) incurred in the collection or enforcement of the secured obligation;

☐ Reasonable cost for insurance, preservation, or repair of the property to which the lien relates;

☐ Reasonable insurance costs;

☐ Amounts paid to satisfy any lien on the property to which the lien or security interest relates.

[¶3812]   FOR FURTHER REFERENCE . . .

Dowling, J.G., Jr., "Taxation of Contingent Interest in Executory Contract Is a Right to Property Which Federal Tax Lien Can Attach," 11 Suffolk University Law Review 1400-11 (Summer 1977).

"Internal Revenue Code §6323: The Treatment of Five Superpriorities," 11 Gonzaga Law Review 590-606 (1976).

J. McGregor and D. Davenport, "Collection of Delinquent Federal Taxes," 28 Southern California Tax Institute, 589-788 (1976).

"Priority Afforded Secured Parties Until Notice of Tax Lien Is Filed," 11 Gonzaga Law Review 550-570 (1976).

M. Saltzman, "IRS as a Creditor: Liens and Levies Preferences, Other Creditors, Tax Levy Authority, Discharge and Removal from Levy," 34 New York University Institute on Federal Taxation 433-462 (1976).

Schloss, R.H., "Federal Tax Liens Under the 1976 Tax Reform Act," 57 Michigan State Bar Journal 40 (1978).

"Superpriorities: An Analysis of Five Instances of Federal Tax Lien Subordination," 11 Gonzaga Law Review 571-589 (1976).

TAX PLANNING

[¶**3901**]   Many of the matters that the lawyer is called upon to deal with have income tax implications and present special opportunities for tax planning for the client. The areas in which tax planning can play a part range from the manner in which a new business is set up and the form it takes, through the operation of the business, the withdrawing of profits from the business, to the ultimate winding up of the business. It may touch on the type of investments in which a client is involved—real estate, securities, transactions to give tax-favored capital gains instead of highly taxed ordinary income. It can involve the personal relationships within the family and the desire to reduce the overall family tax bill (and preserve more capital for the family unit) by shifting income from high-bracket taxpayers to those in lower tax brackets. The attorney may be involved with trusts, family partnerships, and even alimony and other marital settlements.

The following paragraphs highlight the objectives and point out the techniques, and the pitfalls to avoid, in successful tax planning. Greater detail is available in *IBP Tax Planning*.

[¶3902]   **OBJECTIVES IN TAX PLANNING**
                              FOR THE BUSINESS

Tax planning usually has some combination of the following objectives:
  (1) To reduce unnecessary costs and increase net profit.
  (2) To increase the amount of cash at work in the business.
  (3) To secure business and competitive advantages through the desire of customers, suppliers, investors, and employees to minimize their own tax liability.

The main routes by which taxes can be saved are these:
  (1) Stabilizing income to keep out of peak brackets.
  (2) Spreading income over a long period of time to avoid peak rates and defer tax. The use of income averaging can reduce the tax on income bunched into one year.
  (3) Accelerating or postponing income and expenses as indicated by the tax rates, including the added tax on tax-preference income.
  (4) Dividing income among a number of taxpayers; i.e., spreading income among the members of a family partnership or the beneficiaries of a family trust.
  (5) Converting ordinary income into capital gain.
  (6) Building capital values by deductible expenditures; for example, promotion, research and development, and the 10% investment credit.
  (7) Utilizing the exemptions and deductions allowed under the law; for example, the depletion allowance or tax-exempt bonds.
  (8) Selecting a form of business appropriate for withdrawing income; for example, using a limited partnership, a proprietorship, or Subchapter S corporation to carry a venture through the period when anticipated losses can be charged against highly taxed personal income.

(9) Utilizing specific elections in the law, i.e., accounting elections, choices as to method of depreciation, class life election, etc.

(10) Creating business relationships between taxable entities that will make the most effective total use of applicable tax rates, earning power, actual and potential losses, depreciable assets (e.g., mergers, sale-leasebacks, other arm's-length contractual relationships).

[¶3903]   TAX CONSIDERATIONS IN SETTING
                              UP A BUSINESS

The form a business takes can make a world of difference in arriving at the bottom line for tax purposes, since the tax law treats different forms of business differently, recognizing some as separate entities and others as extensions of their owners. Under the tax law, there are three main forms of business—the sole proprietorship, the corporation, and the partnership. In addition, the tax law also recognizes some hybrids.

[¶3903.1]   **General Considerations in Choosing Form**

Different forms of business will be indicated at different times. The business owner and his advisor must determine what form should be adopted by studying the total economic situation surrounding the business. This includes the sources of outside income for each party involved in the business, the family composition, and tax status of each party.

The determination will be based on the following considerations:

☐   The form that provides the individual owners with the most after-tax business profits.

☐   Possibilities of greater tax savings by further subdividing corporations and partnerships into other entities.

☐   The tax cost of changing from one form to another form.

[¶3903.2]   **Particular Factors That Influence Choice of Business Form**

Apart from the general considerations, the particular aspects of the business venture play a large part in choosing the optimum vehicle for carrying on a business. Here are some examples of how particular circumstances influence the decision.

☐   *Is the Business Risky?* If the business venture is a risky one, a form of doing business should be adopted that allows the investors the maximum protection in the event the investment turns sour. For example, IRC §1244 stock allows a more favorable ordinary loss deduction if a corporate business goes awry.

☐   *Will There Be Tax-Preference Income?* If a substantial amount of tax-preference income (e.g., accelerated depreciation on real estate, capital gain, etc.) is likely, the corporate form may afford significant tax shelter.

☐   When the owners operate in corporate form and elect Subchapter S treatment, they should consider the effect of the passthrough of the corporation's tax preferences to their own individual taxes. The same precaution should be taken when a partnership or proprietorship is used. The tax preferences of these businesses are also passed through directly to the individual owners.

☐ *Are Personal Services Involved?* When the income from the business is mostly from personal services performed by the owners, a form that will make available the 50% rate ceiling on personal service income should be used. This will usually be an unincorporated form.

☐ *What Is the Spread Between Tax Rates?* When the business is one in which both personal services and capital are material income-producing factors, the corporate form may offer some tax shelter, at least temporarily, to the owners if there is a spread between their effective individual tax rates and that of the corporation.

☐ *Will Interest Deductions Be Lost?* When substantial sums of money have to be borrowed to acquire or carry an investment-type asset, the use of the corporate form avoids the limitation on the deduction for investment interest. If the corporate form is unsuitable for other reasons, the owners should consider converting the investment property to avoid the limitation. This can be done, for example, by turning a passive investment, such as land, into income-producing property.

☐ *Can Income Be Split Within the Family?* Taxes may be reduced by the use of family partnerships or family controlled corporations. Family members in lower tax brackets could receive some of the business income.

☐ *What About Retirement Benefits?* Owners, looking to build substantial retirement benefits, may decide to use the corporate form because of the substantial benefits that can be accumulated in a qualified pension or profit-sharing plan. They should avoid Subchapter S, however, since contributions on behalf of more-than-5% owners of Subchapter S corporations are limited to the lesser of 15% of earnings or $7,500. Excess amounts are currently taxable.

☐ *Will There Be Passive Income?* When the business will produce substantial passive income, the corporate form carries with it the danger of the imposition of the personal holding company penalty tax. If the corporate form is desirable for other reasons, increasing operating income or the number of shareholders may work to avoid the penalty.

☐ *Will There Be Start-Up Losses?* If it's anticipated that the business will incur operating losses during the initial years of operation, a form of business that allows the offset of business losses against the owner's other income should be used.

☐ *Will the Business Incur Debt?* Partnerships and Subchapter S corporations both allow a passthrough of losses to the owners, but only to the extent of their bases. If losses may be higher than the owners' capital contributions and loans to the business, the use of a partnership may be called for since the basis of a partner in the partnership includes the debts of the partnership, while the basis of Subchapter S stock does not include corporate debts.

☐ *Can the Business Be Divided?* Taxes may be reduced if the operations of a business are divided into different taxable entities. For example, using a partnership to operate the business and a corporation to own and hold the real estate that houses the business may produce some tax shelter for the owners.

[¶3904] TAX FEATURES OF SOLE PROPRIETORSHIP

The uncomplicated tax treatment of the sole proprietorship is one of the reasons behind the popularity of this form of business. Basically, the entire profits of the proprietorship are taxed to the individual owner as income in the year earned. The owner computes the business profits on Schedule C of Form 1040 by reporting the gross income of the business and deducting all his business expenses. The net figure is then added to his other income on his personal tax return.

The sole proprietorship qualifies for no special deductions and must meet the same rules of deductibility that any other business must meet. So in terms of income and deductions, there is nothing special about it.

The sole proprietorship is unique, however, in one particular situation. That is when the proprietor sells the business. Since the business is not recognized as a separate entity under the tax law, the proprietor is not allowed to engage in the fiction that he has sold a single asset—the business—but rather he is considered to have sold all the individual assets of the business and must allocate the purchase price to all the individual assets carried on the books, including goodwill. This means that he must recognize ordinary income on some of the assets, rather than report the whole gain as capital gain, which he could do if he sold all the stock in an incorporated business.

The obvious advantage of a sole proprietorship is that the business pays no tax at all—the income is taxed only to the proprietor. So unless the business produces a very large income, it is less costly for the owner to pick up the one tax himself, rather than pay two smaller taxes. When the income is so great that more than 50% is payable in individual taxes, it is often better to operate as a corporation.

[¶3905] TAX FEATURES OF PARTNERSHIP OPERATION

The tax treatment of the partnership lies somewhere between that of the sole proprietorship and that of the corporation. Like the corporation, the partnership is considered a separate entity under the tax law. However, like the proprietorship, it is not a taxable entity—rather, the earnings are taxed directly to the partners, whether distributed or not.

The partnership, however, is required to file a tax return, Form 1065, although it is merely an information return. The net income for the year shown on this return is deemed to be distributed to the partners ratably on the last day of the partnership year, and each partner must pick up his distributive share on his own income tax return. Each partner's share is normally computed in accordance with the partnership agreement.

A key difference between a corporation and a partnership is that losses to the partnership are passed directly through to the partners. This passthrough is not unlimited, but it can provide potential tax shelter. For this reason, many risky ventures are set up as partnerships, rather than some other form of business. Since joint ventures, syndicates, groups, or pools are taxed as partnerships, these forms are also used in such cases.

Under the tax law, and regardless of any state law to the contrary, a partnership is terminated only when no further business is carried on by any of the partners or there is a sale or exchange of 50% or more of the total interest in partnership capital and profits within 12 months. This allows the partnership to continue as a tax entity when one of the members dies or resigns, which would be a technical termination under the laws of many states. There are, however, special rules for mergers or divisions of partnerships.

Unlike the sole proprietorship, the partner's interest in his firm is nominally considered a capital asset. Thus, he will generally realize capital gain on the sale of it, or, if the partnership is liquidated and property distributed in kind to him, he will recognize no gain or loss until he disposes of the property. However, to the extent that the assets include "unrealized receivables" and "substantially appreciated inventory," the partner may realize ordinary income. These two categories also include IRC §1245 and §1250 recapture property.

[¶3905.1]　Checklist of Tax Advantages of Doing Business as a Partnership

Here are the basic tax advantages to be derived from doing business as a partnership:

☐　Earnings of a partnership are only subject to one tax. In a corporation, there is a double tax on profits when they are distributed as dividends.

☐　The tax rate on the individual partners may be less than the corporate tax rates.

☐　Partners are not taxed on exempt interest income or nontaxable amounts, like insurance proceeds, received from the firm—while dividends received from a corporation are taxable even if they are out of income that was not taxable to the corporation.

☐　Partnership losses can reduce a partner's other personal ordinary income. This may also result in a carryover that can reduce a partner's future taxes, or a carryback that will result in a return of a prior year's taxes.

☐　If capital gains are realized by the firm, the partners only have to pay one capital gain tax. Stockholders of a corporation realizing capital gain cannot ordinarily get this treatment (unless the corporation goes through a 12-month liquidation under IRC §337).

☐　A decision can be made as how to divide profits among the partners.

☐　Earnings already taxed increase the cost basis to the partner of his interest in his company. This is not true of the stockholder.

☐　If the owner of a corporate business is also employed by the corporation, he may have to draw a salary in loss years to justify its reasonableness in other years. Thus, he will have taxable income even though the business doesn't show a profit; not so in a partnership since distributions can be geared to the partnership's annual income.

☐　Capital losses of a partnership reduce capital gains of individual partners. This is not true for corporate shareholders.

☐　Partners (unlike stockholders) can deduct their share of partnership charitable contributions (up to their individual limits). Corporations are limited to 5%.

[¶3906]   **THE FAMILY PARTNERSHIP**

Family partnerships can achieve substantial tax savings in all three major federal tax areas:

☐   *Yearly income tax* can be reduced by splitting business income among family members. This divides the business income into lesser amounts taxable at lower rates.

☐   *Gift tax* liability can be minimized or eliminated by giving children ownership of business assets when values are low.

☐   *Estate tax* can be minimized. The increase in business assets, as well as accumulated income, will directly benefit children since it can free them of the burden of an estate tax that would be incurred if the assets had remained in a parent's estate.

Subject to certain requirements, a family partnership can save income taxes by dividing income among several family members. The federal income tax is a so-called progressive tax as it is applied to individuals. The higher the taxable income, the higher the rate at which that income is taxed. The rate for the lowest taxable income bracket is 14%. From this low, the taxable income brackets rise progressively until the highest taxable income bracket of 70% is reached.

However, there is a 50% ceiling on the rate of tax that may be imposed on an individual's personal service income (IRC § 1348(a)). Generally, personal service income is defined as net income received as the result of one's labor, e.g., wages, salaries, professional fees, and other personal service compensation.

This maximum limitation on tax may, in some cases, reduce the tax savings of shifting income. There are situations, however, in which the 50% rule would not apply, and the savings that may be achieved by a family partnership are quite substantial. Each situation, therefore, must be evaluated on the basis of its own circumstances. By no means should the use of a family partnership as a tax saver be automatically disregarded.

[¶3907]   **TAX FEATURES OF CORPORATIONS**

The tax treatment of corporations, in contrast to that of proprietorships and partnerships, is exceedingly complex. The main tax feature of the corporation is that it is treated as a separate entity under the tax law and pays tax at rates of from 17% to 46%, depending on how much income it makes. It is obvious that these rates are considerably lower than the highest individual tax rates, but there is a price for this—the corporation is not permitted to deduct dividends it pays to its shareholders, and they, in turn, must report the dividends as income. So, in most cases, corporate earnings are taxed twice before they bring any benefit to the shareholder—once as corporate income and again as dividends.

There are, however, other ways to get corporate earnings into the hands of shareholders besides paying dividends. To the extent that the double tax can be avoided, there is potential tax shelter in the corporate form.

Corporate deductions are also different from individual deductions and are generally more favorable. To the extent they are available, they also can provide potential tax shelter.

Finally, corporate ownership presents capital gain opportunities. Earnings accumulated in the corporation can be realized as capital gain by selling the stock. There are countless variations of this technique, involving not only sales, but liquidations, redemptions, reorganizations, and any number of other stock arrangements. The point is simply that since the stock is a capital asset whose value will depend on the earnings of the corporation, it presents many capital gain opportunities.

All these facts, plus the deduction for corporate salaries paid to shareholders, explain why the corporation can be a form of business with important tax advantages. Of course, there are many other advantages as well. These are summarized in the checklist below.

[¶3907.1]   Checklist of Tax Advantages of the Corporate Form

The following is a list of the main tax advantages that can result from operating a business in corporate form. Some may not apply in a particular case, but all can potentially result in tax savings.

☐ The corporate form may be used as a tax shelter.

☐ Corporations in foreign trade or in other ventures can get special tax exemptions.

☐ Members of a family may be stockholders without many of the burdens and restrictions of family partnerships.

☐ The corporate form makes it possible for owner-executives to realize better wealth-building advantages under a corporate pension or profit-sharing plan.

☐ Death benefits of up to $5,000 can be paid tax free to the beneficiaries of an employee.

☐ Incorporating avoids questions of the right to deduct losses. Individuals can deduct in full only casualty losses or losses incurred in a trade or business or in transactions entered into for profit (IRC §165(c)). Corporations are not so restricted. Losses are assumed to be incident to the business of the corporation.

☐ Deferred compensation and stock retirement plans can be utilized to achieve the financial planning purposes of the owner, his family, and his employees.

☐ Only 15% of dividend income is taxed to the corporation—100% is taxed to the partner or sole proprietor.

☐ The corporate form may facilitate saving income and estate taxes by gifts to children or to a family foundation.

☐ A new corporation is a new taxpayer. There may be a substantial advantage in choosing new tax elections.

☐ A corporation may be able to carry insurance on the lives of owner-executives at a reduced annual tax cost and then, without any further income tax burden, realize the proceeds and make them available to pay estate taxes. Working stockholders are eligible for $50,000 of tax-free group insurance coverage.

☐ Corporation stockholders can often control the dividend processes. Therefore, unlike partners or sole proprietors, they usually can dictate the year in which they will receive income, and can select the most favorable one. Control of dividends by corporate holders permits averaging of stockholders' income over a long period.

☐ Stockholders have a capital gain when the corporation is liquidated. This is not always so with partnerships. Stockholders may be able to liquidate in a year when they have losses to offset the gain from liquidation.

☐ A special provision allows withdrawal of accumulated corporate profits in an amount equal to death taxes and expenses on death of an owner-stockholder through a partial stock redemption.

☐ A corporation is allowed to accumulate earnings, free from penalty, for purposes of redeeming stock to pay death taxes of one or more of the owners.

☐ A corporation is also allowed, under certain circumstances, to accumulate earnings to redeem the stock held by a private foundation.

☐ Corporate owners are not likely to have ordinary income when their interest is sold and the business has substantially appreciated inventory. Noncorporate business property gives rise to full tax on the appreciation if the owner sells his interest or if he dies or retires.

☐ The working owners get the benefit of tax-free medical and hospital insurance, and the corporation is entitled to deduct its cost.

☐ The working owners may also receive tax-free salary continuation payments made on account of disability.

☐ Another incidental benefit concerns meals and lodging. Working stockholders may exclude from income the value of any meals or lodging furnished by the corporation for its convenience.

[¶3908]   **TAX FEATURES OF SUBCHAPTER S
CORPORATIONS**

There are many advantages to operating a business in corporate form, including limited liability and the ability to shift income to family members through gifts of stock. However, there is one major drawback: Income is taxed both to the corporation and later to the shareholder.

The double tax problem can be avoided by electing Subchapter S status. If the corporation qualifies, it is not subject to most corporate taxes; rather, it is treated as a mere conduit with all its income taxed directly to its shareholders. It is important to remember, though, that a Subchapter S corporation remains, in fact, a corporation. Thus, should the election be terminated, the corporation is subject to the full range of corporate taxes.

[¶3908.1]   **When to Elect Subchapter S**

Below is a checklist of situations in which a Subchapter S election can be beneficial.

☐ When the corporation has earnings that it wants to keep in the business and the stockholders are in a lower tax bracket than the corporation, a Subchapter S election causes the entire income to be taxed in the shareholder's bracket whether or not distributed.

☐ When the corporation has losses, a Subchapter S election allows the shareholders to use them to offset their other income.

☐ The undistributed taxable income of a Subchapter S corporation is taxed only to those who are shareholders at the end of the corporation's year. Thus, to shift an entire year's income yet retain control of it as long as possible, transfer stock prior to year's end.

☐ The major benefit of electing Subchapter S is the passthrough of most corporate income directly to the shareholders without any intervening corporate tax, in the same way as to partners in a partnership. The Subchapter S corporation, however, enjoys several advantages over a partnership.

☐ The corporation can choose a fiscal year that will permit it to defer some of the shareholders' taxes. This is of special importance to Subchapter S corporations since undistributed earnings are not taxed to the shareholder until the last day of the corporation's year. Thus, if a Subchapter S corporation has a fiscal year beginning February 1, 1978, and ending January 31, 1979, and does not distribute any income during the year, the shareholders will not have to pay taxes on the income until April 15, 1980.

☐ A Subchapter S corporation may offer such corporate benefits as qualified pension plans, medical reimbursement plans, health and accident insurance, and group term life insurance. All of these fringe benefits offer favorable tax consequences to the shareholders.

☐ The shareholder can give some of his stock to his children, who will probably be in a lower tax bracket.

[¶3909] SPECIAL CORPORATE TAX TRAPS

There are two possible penalty taxes that can be imposed upon a corporation. Tax planning for the incorporated business must be aimed at avoiding them. The penalty taxes are assessed for unreasonable accumulations of corporate income, and for the use of the corporation as a personal holding company. These penalty taxes are discussed in the following paragraphs.

[¶3909.1] Unreasonable Accumulations

When a corporation accumulates earnings and profits in excess of $150,000, it runs the risk of a penalty tax under IRC §531-537. The penalty applies to corporations formed or availed of for purposes of avoiding taxes by accumulating earnings instead of distributing them as dividends (IRC §532).

The tax is imposed on the current year's "accumulated taxable income" at the rate of 27½% on the first $100,000 and 38½% on any excess. This tax, like the personal holding company penalty surtax, is in addition to the regular corporate tax (IRC §532), but the current year's income must first be reduced by any amount of corporate tax paid (there are also other technical adjustments). If previous accumulations do not total $150,000, deduct from current income the amount required to bring the total up to $150,000. Then the excess current income (after the other adjustments) is subject to the penalty tax.

If the accumulation exceeds $150,000, the penalty tax can still be avoided by showing "reasonably anticipated needs of the business" as the purpose for the accumulation (IRC §537). It is not necessary to show that earnings and profits must be reinvested in the business immediately. It is enough to show that future needs of the business will require that these earnings and profits be plowed back (IRC §535(c)), but these future needs must be more than just vague or uncertain plans or ideas.

[¶3909.2] Personal Holding Companies

Prior to the enactment of the personal holding company tax provision (IRC §541), a tax loophole known as the "incorporated pocketbook" existed. High-bracket taxpayers, such as actors, would form a corporation to furnish an individual's services. The corporation would then accumulate part of the income and obtain the benefit of the lower corporate tax rates. This loophole was also commonly used by high-bracket investors.

The loophole was closed by imposing a 70% tax on all undistributed personal holding company income on top of the regular corporate taxes. However, the impact of the tax is not limited to the situations described above. Any corporation can fall prey if (1) 60% of its adjusted ordinary gross income is personal holding company income and (2) at any time during the last half of its taxable year more than 50% in the value of its outstanding stock is owned by not more than five individuals (IRC §542(a)). Note that intent is not a factor; if the conditions are met, the tax will be imposed—even if the shareholders were not seeking to avoid any tax.

The problem can often be avoided in one of these ways:

☐ Bring in additional operating income when the corporation will have large amounts of personal holding company income (i.e., dividends, royalties, rents, etc.).

☐ Pay out some of the corporation's income in bonuses and additional compensation to working stockholders. Any such distributions, however, must be made on the basis of the services performed by the stockholder-employees, not on the basis of their ownership interest in the corporation.

☐ Increase the number of stockholders. Only corporations with five or fewer stockholders are subject to the personal holding company tax.

☐ Have the corporation, and not the customers, designate who is to perform services under contracts with the corporation. The income from these contracts will not be treated as personal holding company income.

☐ If rental income is substantial, invest in property that will push rental income to over 50% of all corporate income. The corporation will then be considered an operating real estate company—not a personal holding company (IRC §543(a)(2)).

[¶3910] CUSHIONING PERSONAL AND BUSINESS LOSSES

The following checklist shows how the impact of a loss can be softened considerably through careful tax planning.

☐ Operating losses can be deducted against the investor's outside income by using a partnership or a Subchapter S corporation.

☐ Investment loss on stock can be deducted against ordinary income by issuing the stock under IRC §1244. Investors in small business corporations can get up to $50,000 in ordinary deductions ($100,000 on a joint return) per year for loss on common stock that is considered to be small business stock (§1244). This rule applies whether the loss was incurred on sale of the stock or on its becoming worthless. It can only be used by the original purchaser of the stock. Only the first $1,000,000 in stock qualifies for this special treatment.

☐ An investor can buy and own real estate or machinery and lend or lease to a corporate business. If there's a loss, he obtains a §1231 deduction. Also, he may trade current depreciation against ordinary income for capital gain by later sale to a corporation. This won't work with depreciation on personal property (IRC §1245) or the accelerated portion of depreciation on real property (IRC §1250). Capital gain treatment is also denied if he, his spouse, and his minor children and grandchildren own 80% or more of the outstanding stock (IRC §1239).

☐ Take debenture or preferred stock and give it to a foundation while it has original value. This gives cash back now as a tax deduction to the extent of the tax rate. For example, an investor in the 70% bracket donates preferred stock worth $5,000 directly to a foundation. In effect, this is an exchange of preferred stock for $3,500 cash.

☐ If an individual has a note that is a potential bad debt, he may find that by transferring it into a new corporation a greater tax saving can be obtained. The note will be picked up by the corporation at its value at the time of purchase or transfer to the corporation.

Thus, the deduction allowed will only be to the extent that the value of the debt at the time of purchase exceeds the amount received *(J.H. Hillman & Sons Co.,* TC Memo 1943). However, this deduction will be offset against ordinary income as a business bad debt deduction.

☐ Make an investment in a corporation, which has earning power sufficient to provide assurance against permanent loss, by putting money in this corporation for stock or debt, and then have the corporation make the loan to the new venture, provided the corporation has the power under its charter to make the loan.

[¶3911] ACCOUNTING METHODS AND TAXABLE YEARS

Having set up the business, consideration (from a tax viewpoint) is then focused on the accounting year and methods. While many of the accounting aspects of the business will naturally be the concern of the accountant, the lawyer has to be aware of the tax consequences of the selection of an accounting period and method so he can help his client with proper preparation.

Tax accounting in many respects differs from conventional business accounting. In other cases, it is the same, but elections of available choices must be made.

A good deal of tax planning may go into the choice of an accounting year. As for accounting method, in addition to the usual choice between a cash and accrual method (when that choice is available), special methods must be considered for special situations—i.e., deferring income on installment sales, treatment of long-term construction contracts.

Choice of methods also arises on valuing inventories—generally between the First-In-First-Out (FIFO) and the Last-In-First-Out (LIFO) methods.

[¶3912]   CASH METHOD OF ACCOUNTING

The cash receipts and disbursements method is used largely by individuals whose income is derived principally from salaries and wages; by retail merchants, shopkeepers, and professional men; and also by many large business enterprises in the service, financial, and real estate fields, when merchandise inventories are not a material income-producing factor.

[¶3912.1]   Basic Principles of Cash Method

Under this method, a taxpayer has income to the extent of cash or property actually or "constructively" (see below) received during the tax year; it makes no difference how much he actually earned during the year—it is the amount that he receives that is important under this method.

If payment is made in the form of property, there is income to the extent of the fair market value of the property. For example, if stock is given for services, income to the extent of its fair market value is received.

[¶3912.2]   Deductions Under Cash Method

Generally, deductions will be allowed in the year paid, even though they are incurred or relate to another year. Prepayment of supplies that are to be delivered the following year is deductible in the year of payment (*Ernst*, 32 TC 181, 1959).

If the prepayment results in the acquisition of a "capital asset," the deduction must be prorated over the related years. Thus, for example, commissions, legal fees, and other expenses incurred in negotiating a long-term lease or mortgage loan must be spread over the term of the lease or loan *(Spring City Foundry Co.*, 292 US 182, 1935). In addition, prepaid interest must be spread over the term of the loan.

[¶3912.3]   "Constructive Receipt"

Under this doctrine, a taxpayer is taxed on income even before it is actually received, if it is his for the asking. The most common examples are: Matured interest coupons on bonds that have not been cashed, declared dividends unqualifiedly subject to the stockholder's demand, and interest credited on savings bank deposits although not withdrawn.

[¶3912.4]   Who May Use the Cash Method?

It *may* be used by any taxpayer who does not use inventories to determine income or who does not keep books of account. Stockpiling of items used in a business can be construed to be an inventory. *Wilkinson-Bean, Inc.* (TC Memo 1969-79) involved a funeral director who kept a substantial supply of caskets because his supplier was far from his place of business. The Tax Court forced the funeral director to use the accrual method because it found that the income (about 14% of the gross income) from the sale of caskets was a significant income factor requiring the use of an inventory.

[¶3912.5]   Advantages of the Cash Method

☐   Taxes are not paid until the income is received.
☐   Receipts and disbursements for each year can be controlled so as to avoid higher tax rates on income piled up in a single year.
☐   Complicated records or books of account need not be maintained. In most cases, a checkbook or simple cashbook showing receipts and disbursements will suffice. There is no need for accruals.

[¶3912.6]   Disadvantages of the Cash Method

☐   The chief defect of the cash method is that it does not truly reflect annual net income. It produces "peaks" and "valleys."
☐   Income may pile up in a single year despite meticulous efforts to regulate income and outgo. For example, advance payments of rents, salaries, royalties, interest, etc.
☐   If the business is liquidated or sold, income may be "bunched" into one year and deductions forever lost. *Example:* When a cash-basis corporation liquidated and transferred its accounts receivable to its stockholders, the court held that the accounts receivable were taxable to the corporation as income realized prior to dissolution. The best way to avoid this tax trap is to continue the corporation in existence for a reasonable period until the outstanding accounts receivable are collected and the debts paid off. In any event, prepay all deductible items before dissolution.

[¶3913]   ACCRUAL METHOD OF ACCOUNTING

This method is used by businesses with numerous and complex transactions because it is a more scientific and accurate method for determining true income for any given period of time. It is used in practically all manufacturing, wholesale, or retail businesses, and service establishments when the production, purchase, or sale of merchandise is an "income-producing" factor.

[¶3913.1]   Basic Principles of Accrual Method

The accrual of income depends on the right to receive it, rather than actual receipt. There are three basic rules as to when the right to receive income becomes fixed and accruable. They are: (1) The taxpayer must have a valid, unconditional, and enforceable right to receive the income within the taxable year; (2) The amount due must be determinable or susceptible of reasonable estimate; (3) There must be a reasonable expectancy that the amount due will be paid and collected in due course.

The same rules apply to the deduction of expenses on the accrual basis. When all the events have occurred within the taxable year that fix the amount and the fact of the taxpayer's liability, such expenses are properly accruable and deductible for tax purposes, even though paid in a subsequent year. The amount accruing is the known liability at year end, without alteration for events and transactions of later years. This method may be used by any taxpayer who maintains records or books of account; it must be used by a taxpayer who uses inventories to determine income.

[¶3913.2]   Accrued Expenses in Family Business

In closely held corporations, or between members of a family, when the taxpayers use different accounting methods, care should be exercised in accruing expenses.

The deduction will be lost if:

(1) The expense (e.g., officer's year-end bonus) is not paid within two-and-a-half months after the close of the taxable year; and

(2) The method of accounting of the person to whom the payment is to be made does not require inclusion of the item in gross income unless paid. In other words, the payor is on the accrual basis, the payee on the cash basis; and

(3) Related taxpayers are involved. Related taxpayers include brothers, sisters, spouses, parents, grandparents, children, grandchildren, individuals and their more-than-50%-owned corporations, and two corporations in which more than 50% of the value is owned by the same individual.

[¶3913.3]   Adjustment of Accrued Liabilities

If the amount actually paid turns out to be more or less than the amount of expense accrued and deducted, it becomes necessary to reflect the difference in the tax return for the year of accrual or the year of payment.

When a dispute as to liability has been settled or finally adjudicated, you can deduct the amount determined to be due in the year of final determination, but you have to make the deduction in the year of actual payment if that occurs before the contest is settled.

[¶3914]   **HYBRID ACCOUNTING**

The Internal Revenue Code permits hybrid accounting when it is approved by the Regulations (see Reg. §1.446-1) as clearly reflecting income (§446(c)(4)). A hybrid method of accounting combines the principles of several recognized accounting methods. For example, many small retail stores use a combination of the cash and accrual methods. By this system, they are permitted to report gross income (gross receipts less cost of goods sold) on the accrual basis and deduct selling and administration expenses on the cash basis. This combination of accounting methods simply removes the bother of accruing small expenses and can be of substantial benefit in small business operations.

[¶3915]   **INSTALLMENT SALES**

If you're to be paid in installments, you're taxed pro rata as proceeds are received. Deferred and contingent sales are different in that they can postpone all tax until cost is fully recovered. The installment sale is available only to a dealer in personal property who regularly sells on the installment plan, a person who sells real property, or a person who makes a casual sale of personal property (other than merchandise) for a price exceeding $1,000.

For a sale of real property or a casual sale of personal property to qualify, payments in the year of sale can't be more than 30% of the purchase price.

Payments in the year of sale are called "initial payments." The term embraces not only cash payments but also payments with property, including the notes or other obligations of a third party. If there is no initial payment at all, the 30% requirement is of course met. However, the contract should provide for payment of fixed amounts at stated intervals.

[¶3916]   **DEFERRED PAYMENT SALES**

These are sales in which the value of the consideration given to the seller is unascertainable. Because the value is unascertainable the transaction is considered "open" and gain realized is not taxed until the seller has first recovered his costs. When the underlying asset is a capital asset, the amounts recovered that are received after the recovery of basis are taxed as capital gain so long as the transaction does not "close." Payments made after the transaction is closed are taxed as ordinary income.

[¶3917]   **LONG-TERM CONTRACTS**

Taxpayers engaged in heavy construction work meet special accounting problems. Usually building, installation, and construction projects require a considerable length of time to complete. Frequently, unforeseen difficulties are encountered before the contract is completed, for example, there may be price changes in materials used; losses and increased expenses due to strikes, weather conditions and work stoppages; penalties for delay; and unexpected difficulties in laying foundations.

These conditions make it impossible for a construction contractor, no matter how carefully he may estimate, to tell with any certainty whether he will make a profit or sustain a loss on a particular contract until it is completed.

Because of these problems, contractors are permitted to use two special methods of reporting their income from long-term contracts. The two special ways of accounting for long-term contracts are: the percentage of completion method and the completed contract method (Reg. §1.451-3).

[¶3918]　　WHEN SHOULD THE TAX YEAR START?

Picking the right taxable year for a business pays off in substantial tax savings as well as in other ways. The initial choice of an accounting period is generally within the control of the taxpayer and does not require the permission of IRS. However, many taxpayers forfeit this right of choice by giving the matter haphazard, last-minute consideration, with the result that they are forced to adopt an annual accounting period ill-suited to their business needs.

To be sure, it is possible to change your accounting period if the wrong one was selected in the first instance. However, that's not always easy to accomplish, because IRS's permission must be obtained and it won't be granted unless there is a valid business reason for making the change.

Four Possible Choices: The law requires that taxable income be computed on the basis of the taxpayer's taxable year. Generally, the taxable year covers a 12-month period. In certain exceptional instances, it may be a "short period" of less than 12 months. It may never be more than a full 12-month period, except in the case of a 52-53 week year.

Under the 1954 Code (IRC §441), only four types of taxable years are recognized. They are (Reg. §1.441-1):

(1) Calendar Year: A 12-month period ending on Dec. 31 (§441(d)).

(2) Fiscal Year: A 12-month period ending on the last day of any month other than December (§441(e)).

(3) 52-53 Week Year: A fiscal year, varying from 52 to 53 weeks in duration, which always ends on the same day of the week, which—
　　(a) occurs for the last time in a calendar month, or
　　(b) falls nearest the end of a calendar month (§441(f), Reg. §1.441-2).

(4) Short Period: A period of less than 12 months (allowed only in certain special situations such as initial return, final return, change in accounting period, and termination of taxable year by reason of jeopardy assessment) (§443(a)).

[¶3918.1]   Factors Determining Choice of Accounting Period

The conditions for each type of annual accounting period may be summarized as follows:

Taxable Year	*Conditions*
(1) Calendar Year *must* be used by a taxpayer, if . . .	(a) he keeps no books, (b) he has no annual accounting period, or (c) he has an accounting period (other than a calendar year) that does not qualify as a fiscal year.
(2) Fiscal Year *may* be used by a taxpayer, if . . .	(a) he keeps books, (b) he has definitely established such fiscal year as his accounting period before the close of his first fiscal year, and (c) his books are kept in accordance with such fiscal year.
(3) 52-53 Week Taxable Year *may* be used by a taxpayer, if . . .	(a) he keeps books, (b) he regularly computes his income on a 52-53 week basis, and (c) his books are kept on such 52-53 week basis.

[¶3919]   NATURAL BUSINESS YEAR

You won't find the term "natural business year" in the tax law. However, IRS looks upon it with favor and will readily grant permission to a taxpayer to change his established accounting period to conform with his natural business year.

What is the natural business year? It is an annual cycle of 12 consecutive months (or 52 to 53 weeks) that ends when the business activities of the enterprise are at their lowest point. At this point of the annual cycle, sales and production activities are at their lowest level, inventories and accounts receivable are at a minimum, and the cash or liquid position of the enterprise is at its highest level.

[¶3920]   PLANT AND EQUIPMENT

Once the business is ready to operate, a major expenditure will involve its plant and equipment. Tax considerations can have a decided influence on the methods of acquisition and maintenance of the property. Many of these factors will, of course, be taken into account by the lawyer in planning with the client the setting up of the business (in projecting capital needs, for example, the availability of tax credits and deductions can play a major role).

Many choices are available as to how necessary plant and equipment is acquired, maintained, and charged off. First, plant and equipment can be leased or purchased. If owned, it can be converted into working cash by a sale-leaseback.

In purchasing plant and equipment there are these tax opportunities:

(1) The 10% investment credit.

(2) The special 20% first-year depreciation allowance.

(3) The selection of a method of depreciation—200 or 150% (fastest rate on commercial real estate) declining balance, sum-of-the-year's-digits, or straight line.

(4) Selecting the class life system or establishing a useful life on a "facts and circumstances" basis.

(5) Deciding whether to sell all the equipment or trade it in.

(6) Deciding whether to build plant on leased or owned land.

By a proper maintenance policy, the value of plant and equipment can be kept up by deductible expenditures. It is necessary to know which costs can be expensed and which must be capitalized, and how the automatic percentage allowance under the class life system works.

[¶3921]   TAKING MONEY OUT OF THE CORPORATION

As early as the time a new corporation is set up, consider the tax cost of taking profits out of the business and getting them into the hands of the stockholders. Projecting ahead is an important tax planning requirement in determining the pros and cons of different business forms for a particular client.

Once the corporation is in operation, the owners can take money out as compensation subject to the maximum tax on personal service income to the extent of the reasonable value of the services they render to a corporation. Then they can declare dividends, which are usually fully taxable. They may be charged with the receipt of dividends if they have the corporation carry their expenses or assume other obligations, or even if they borrow from the corporation.

The owners may come out better in the long run if they accumulate earnings in the corporation and cash in by selling or redeeming stock or by selling or liquidating the entire business. There are, however, restrictions and penalties for accumulating earnings and failing to distribute the earnings of a personal holding company.

When money has been accumulated in the corporation, it may be withdrawn as capital gain by sales of stock, by liquidation, partial or complete, or by redemption of stock. At all times, however, the collapsible corporation rules must be kept in mind. These rules could convert capital gain into ordinary income.

[¶3922]   PLANNING FOR CAPITAL TRANSACTIONS

Special tax breaks are available for gains arising from capital transactions—deals involving sales other than in the ordinary course of business or income earned by investment property.

However, it is often possible, by casting a proposed course of action in a different mold, to convert what would otherwise be ordinary income into tax-favored capital gain. To do this, and to get the advantages of capital gain treatment in any event, it is necessary to know and follow the specific tax law requirements.

[¶3923]   ADVANTAGES OF CAPITAL GAIN TREATMENT

The advantage of capital gain treatment is the preferential tax rate. Basically, if an individual qualifies for capital gain treatment, only 40% of the gain is taxable. Corporations can have their capital gains taxed at ordinary corporate rates, or they can elect an alternative tax of 28%.

Since the corporate rates on the first $50,000 of income are less than 28%, elect to use the alternative tax only when corporate income exceeds $50,000.

To get capital gain treatment, two things are necessary: (1) Property that qualifies for capital gain treatment—capital assets, trade or business assets; (2) A sale or exchange—an actual sale or exchange or a transaction that by law is treated as if it were a sale or exchange. Otherwise, the gain is ordinary income, not capital gain.

Not all capital gains qualify for the preferred tax treatment; only long-term gains get that treatment. To have a long-term gain, a holding period for the property of more than one year is needed. The normal rule is that the holding period begins the day after purchase and ends on the day of sale.

[¶3924]   HOW TO CONVERT POTENTIAL ORDINARY INCOME TO CAPITAL GAIN

Proper planning can often convert what would otherwise have been ordinary income into tax-favored, long-term capital gain. The various techniques that may be applied are discussed below.

[¶3925]   COMPENSATION AND PROFESSIONAL FEES INTO CAPITAL GAIN

Salary or other compensation from the job can be turned into capital gain by:

☐ *Stock Warrants:* When a warrant is purchased from the employer, the ordinary income rate on any excess in value of the warrant at the time received over the purchase price is paid; increase in value of the stock is reflected in the value of the warrant, which can be sold after one year to produce capital gain.

☐ *Stock Purchase:* The employer finances or helps the employee finance the purchase of stock.

☐ *Profit-Sharing or Pension Plan:* Up to 15% of compensation can be paid tax free in the form of a contribution to a profit-sharing trust. If paid to the employee in a lump sum upon retirement, employer contributions are taxable under favorable special rates.

☐ *Restricted Property:* Restricted stock or other property given as compensation for services is taxable to the employee as though it were unrestricted. But if his right to the property is subject to a substantial risk of forfeiture, then it is not taxable to him until it becomes nonforfeitable, unless he elects to have it taxed to him on receipt. See IRC §83.

☐ *Stock With Low Value:* There is little or no tax upon the receipt of stock with low or only nominal value when received; if it has growth possibilities, the stock can be sold later, with the growth taxed as capital gain. Corporations sometimes organize new subsidiaries to undertake new projects. Selling stock at the beginning, when the value is low, to employees gives them the opportunity of cashing in at capital gain rates if the subsidiary is very successful.

☐ *Incorporating Your Talent:* This is done by actors and other professionals. The corporation should have some outside stockholders and engage in producing and other activities rather than merely representing the star. The star, in fact, might have no contract with his own corporation. Subsequent sale of the stock can give capital gain.

☐ *Sale of Properties in Related Fields:* Taking advantage of a talent to pick up properties in related fields can set up capital gain opportunities. For example, a motion picture producer was able to pick up some stories with movie possibilities and realize capital gain on selling them. This was not ordinary income because his business was producing pictures, not buying and selling stories.

☐ *Combine Salesmanship With a Distributorship:* Salesmanship can build up the value of a business. If the distributorship involves a capital investment in inventory, subsequent sale or cancellation of the distributorship will then produce capital gain.

☐ *Professional Fee in Stock of Company About to Go Public:* If an individual is willing to take a chance on a company's future, he should look for an opportunity to buy stock before it is offered to the public. At that time, the stock's future value is still uncertain (contingencies usually still have to be met before the public offering can be made). So a price can be paid based on what the company has at that time (i.e., its book value)—even if shortly after that the public is willing to pay more. Then later, when the stock is sold, there is capital gain for the increase over the price paid. Two cases have approved capital gains in this type of arrangement (*Berckmans,* TC Memo 1961-100; *McNatt,* CA-8, 321 F. 2d 143, 1963).

[¶3926]   **DIVIDENDS INTO CAPITAL GAIN**

Here are some ways dividends can be converted into capital gains:

☐ *Sale Before Stock Goes Ex-Dividend:* Selling after a big dividend has been declared, but before the record date determining eligibility, the dividend, reflected in the sale price, becomes taxable as capital gain instead of as ordinary income.

☐ *Sale After Stock Goes Ex-Dividend:* If a corporation buys stock before the date of dividend and sells the stock immediately after it goes ex-dividend, low capital gain rate is changed to even lower ordinary income rate. Dividend is reflected as a capital loss, to be offset against other capital gain. The 85% dividend deduction reduces the tax rate on the dividend to a maximum of 6.9%. But this method is now severely limited; corporation must hold the stock at least 16 days.

☐ *Sell Short Before Stock Goes Ex-Dividend:* Cover the sale after it goes ex-dividend. Assuming the stock drops by an amount equal to the dividend, this will convert a capital loss into an ordinary deduction by creating a capital gain.

Assuming a capital loss (not otherwise useful) before the deal, use that loss to offset the gain realized on covering the short sale. But since the stock paid a dividend, the amount of the dividend will have to be paid; and that is an ordinary deduction. *Note:* If a call is bought to assure that the stock can be purchased at pre-dividend date price less the dividend, the Tax Court says the short dividend is not deductible *(Main Line Distributors*, 37 TC 1090, 1962, *aff'd* CA-6, 321 F. 2d 562, 1963). So chances will have to be taken that the price will fall by about the amount of the dividend.

☐ **Mutual Funds:** Dividends are taxed as capital gains to the extent they arise from corporate capital gains. Note that mutual funds are allowed to pass through tax-exempt interest to shareholders.

☐ **Low-Dividend Stock:** A high-bracket taxpayer should buy into corporations with a policy of plowing back earnings rather than distributing them; increase in value will be capital gain when stock is sold.

☐ **Preferred Stock:** Unpaid preferred dividends included in the redemption price pay tax at the capital gain rate instead of the ordinary income rate.

☐ **Run Dividends Through Your Corporation:** A corporation gets an 85% credit for dividends received from another corporation; this isn't a capital gain angle, but taxable dividends can be cut 85% by having the corporation hold the stock—a better tax break than capital gains.

☐ **Dividends in Kind:** If property has appreciated in value, the corporate tax on the appreciation is avoided by distributing the property itself, rather than selling it and distributing the proceeds. But if property is depreciable, the corporation may realize gain under IRC §1245 or §1250.

☐ **Return of Capital Dividends:** Some corporations—including closed-end regulated investment companies—have large paper losses (on securities they've held since before the depression of the 1930s). Each year they sell enough of those loss securities to create a loss sufficient to wipe out their current earnings—for tax purposes. So any dividends they pay are tax free until basis is recovered; after that those dividends are taxed as capital gains.

[¶3927] CORPORATE PROFITS INTO STOCKHOLDERS' CAPITAL GAINS

Here are tested and approved methods of cashing in on a corporation's increased value via the capital gain route.

☐ **Sale to Outsiders:** This is the safest way to turn stock appreciation reflecting accumulated corporate profits into capital gain. Preferred stock can be sold without sacrificing voting control, provided it was original stock or stock issued for new capital.

☐ **Disproportionate Redemptions:** Capital gain can be produced by having the corporation redeem part of the stock. But, the stockholder must end up with less than 80% of the voting stock and the common stock interest held in the corporation before the stock was redeemed, as well as less than 50% of the corporation's voting stock.

☐ *Complete Redemption of One Stockholder's Interest:* Capital gain can be achieved if the stockholder's entire interest is redeemed and he is not deemed to be a stockholder because of others' holdings; he can continue on as a creditor.

☐ *Complete Liquidation of the Corporation:* This lets the stockholders pull out the corporation's accumulated earnings at capital gain rates. If they want to sell off the corporation's assets, that can be done via a 12-month liquidation without a double tax.

☐ *Partial Liquidation:* When there is a contraction of the business, stockholders can pull out part of the corporation's profits at capital gain rates via a partial liquidation.

☐ *Spin-offs, Split-offs, and Split-ups:* Dividing the corporate property into one or more additional corporations in a tax-free reorganization, with the original stockholders becoming stockholders in the new companies, sets up opportunities in the future to sell off some of the new companies at capital gain rates.

☐ *Selling the Operating Assets:* Continuing as an investment company after selling off the operating assets lets you avoid capital gain on liquidation of the non-operating (investment) assets.

[¶3928] INTEREST INTO CAPITAL GAIN

Opportunities to turn interest income into capital gains are very often overlooked. Here are two of them.

☐ *Redemption of Original Issue Discount Obligations Before Maturity:* Part of the discount can be converted into capital gain. But it must be demonstrated that there was no collusion between the stockholder and the issuing corporation to get early redemption. Original issue discount is required to be included in the holder's income on a ratable basis over the life of the bond (IRC §1232). As he includes the discount in income, his basis is correspondingly increased. When the bond is redeemed before maturity, he has capital gain based on his adjusted basis in the absence of collusion.

☐ *Mortgages, etc., Nearing Maturity:* By selling before maturity date, anything that would be taxable as ordinary income will become capital gain.

[¶3929] RENTS AND ROYALTIES INTO CAPITAL GAIN

Here's another area in which good opportunities are often overlooked:

☐ *Sublet Lease:* Rent from sublease of a leasehold is ordinary income. Sell the leasehold, and try for capital gain.

☐ *Saleback of Lease:* Business profits may be attributable in part to a low rent for a favorable location. If the landlord will pay to recover the property, gain on the saleback will be capital gain.

☐ *Sale vs. License of Patent:* Transfer of the right to make, use, and sell is a sale, taxed as capital gain. Transfer of anything less is a license, taxed as ordinary income.

423

☐ *Copyright:* Royalties from a copyrighted book, painting, composition, etc., are ordinary income. If transferred to a corporation, the profits can be turned into capital gain by liquidation of the corporation. But beware of the "collapsible" and personal holding company rules.

☐ *Improvements to Rented Property:* A landlord can turn ordinary income into capital gain by accepting lower rental in return for the tenant's agreeing to make improvements. Value of the latter becomes capital gain when the property is sold. Make sure that the tenant's improvements are not required as a substitute for additional rent; otherwise their value will be taxable as rent.

☐ *Inventions:* Professional or amateur inventors, or investors who finance inventions, can get capital gain treatment by transferring the rights to make, use, and sell. The same applies to the transfer of an undivided interest in an invention.

[¶3930] BUSINESS OPERATIONS GET CAPITAL GAIN

Capital gain opportunity isn't limited to salary and investment assets. Business operations can be used to produce capital gain through sales of:
(1) Operating equipment;
(2) Equipment used by salesmen, demonstrators, etc.;
(3) Assets leased to customers;
(4) Favorable contracts;
(5) Franchises, patents, trademarks, goodwill;
(6) Partnership interests.

[¶3931] INVESTMENT PLANNING

Many investments are particularly appealing because of the "tax shelter" or other tax advantage they may offer, subject to the possible effect of the added tax on tax preferences (IRC §56-58).

Some factors that give tax shelter to an investment are:
(1) The yield of tax-free income—e.g., tax-exempt bonds.
(2) A deduction from income that has no relationship to actual costs—e.g., the percentage depletion deduction allowed against income from oil, gas, and minerals.
(3) A return of capital tax free while investment yield is maintained and money value of the property may be maintained—e.g., income buildings, the cost of which is returned tax free via depreciation allowance, while inflation and deductible repairs may maintain—and even enhance—the value of the property.
(4) An assured buildup in value that can be realized tax free—e.g., life insurance proceeds.
(5) An assured buildup in value that can either be realized at capital gain rates or be used to produce income based on matured values—e.g., a timber tract, in which natural growth enhances value in such a way that higher values cannot be taxed until the property is sold.

(6) Definite buildup in value that cannot be taxed until realized and on which a substantial part of the realization can be indefinitely postponed—e.g., building up a cattle herd in which value is enhanced by both growth and propagation.

(7) Investments with a high degree of security against loss and also a potential of sizable capital gain—e.g., convertible bonds.

(8) Investment in which capital loss can be deducted against ordinary income over as many years as necessary at the rate of $3,000 a year, and in which the prospect of capital gain is high in relation to the impact of possible loss—e.g., common stock warrants.

(9) Investment yields having special protection—e.g., dividends received by a corporation.

(10) Income received at capital gain rates—e.g., sale of timber, mutual fund dividends.

(11) Income that can be taken or reported currently or postponed—e.g., interest on E bonds, forfeitable restricted property as compensation for services.

[¶3932]   INVESTMENTS IN REAL ESTATE

From the tax and financial standpoint, real estate is a highly flexible and versatile type of asset. Here are 19 tax features that can be used to bring about profitable real estate deals.

(1) Real estate can be purchased or rented, sold or leased, with different tax results. A piece of real estate can be divided into different types of fees, leasehold and mortgage investments, each tailored to the tax position of its owner.

(2) When sold at a loss, the loss may be fully deductible.

(3) When sold at a profit all or part of the gain may be qualified for favorable capital gain treatment.

(4) When leased, the cost of occupancy can be charged off fully.

(5) A properly arranged security deposit isn't taxed until the end of the lease.

(6) When owned, much of the cost of the investment can be recovered tax free by depreciation deductions. This reduces the size of the investment and steps up the yield that a real estate investment can show.

(7) Ownership can be financed in a way that gives the owner depreciation charges on the mortgagee's investment, increasing his equity with tax-free funds.

(8) The cost of land can be made tax deductible by a sale, followed by a leaseback for a long period. The investment in the building is recovered tax free through depreciation charges.

(9) The owner of real estate may be able to get his property improved tax free by having his tenant make the improvements.

(10) The owner can elect to deduct or capitalize interest and taxes paid to carry unimproved property.

(11) The owner of real estate can sometimes build up the value of his holdings by tax-deductible repair expenditures.

(12) The ownership of real estate can be held in whatever entity—partnership, corporation, trust, or personal ownership—will best protect the income from tax. When held in corporate ownership, income can accumulate at lower tax rates than might apply if personally owned. The tax savings can be applied to build up equity and future capital gain by improving the property and paying off mortgages.

(13) Tax on the sale of real estate may be postponed by electing the installment method of sale, a deferred payment sale, or by using option agreements, executory contracts, conditional contracts, leases with purchase options, escrow arrangements, and contingent price arrangements.

(14) Even after an installment sale, the gain can be taxed earlier, if that should prove to be desirable, by disposing of the installment obligations.

(15) On the sale of real estate, there are methods of getting cash in advance, yet deferring the taxability of gain.

(16) Real estate held for investment can be built up in value and traded tax free for other real estate to be held for investment.

(17) Leases can be canceled for money that is taxed as capital gain.

(18) Condemnation awards can be received without tax if reinvested in real estate.

(19) A residence can be sold with no or reduced tax if the proceeds are used to buy or build a new residence—or without reinvestment when sold by an individual over 55.

[¶3933]   SHIFTING INCOME IN THE FAMILY

Part of the answer to the problem of accumulating funds for education, retirement, etc., lies in shifting income into lower brackets. Here's a list of some methods that might be used:

☐ *Shifting income to relatives*—for example, to a child who has no income. Transferring $500 of annual income to a child so that it is taxable to him can save $250 a year for a parent-taxpayer in the 50% tax bracket. And the savings can be multiplied by the number of children involved. It doesn't matter how much income is shifted if the child is under 19 or if he is at school. The personal exemption for the child can be claimed by the parent as long as he remains the child's chief support. On the other hand, a man who is supporting a parent out of current income might save a good deal in income taxes if he could transfer income so that it is taxed to the parent. Each parent who is over 65 gets a double exemption. Besides, the IRC gives a person over 65 a credit for the elderly on up to $2,500 ($3,750 on a joint return, both 65 or over) a year.

The combination of the personal exemptions of $1,000 each, plus the $100 dividend exclusion, permits the tax-free transfer of $1,100 of investment income to a child or other member of the family who has no other income. If the child is under 19 or a full-time student even though he files a separate return and has income in excess of the amount of the personal exemption, the parent still may claim his child as a dependent provided he furnishes 50% or more of his support.

The child may utilize the zero bracket amount, but only to offset his or her own earned income.

□ *Passing up the income-splitting device normally used by the husband and wife*—letting each make a separate return—and letting each pay his or her own medical expenses or charitable contributions. The law limits the deduction for those items to percentage computations. Sometimes it is possible to gain considerably by having the husband and wife pay their own costs, or those of their direct dependents.

□ *Moving property and its income to lower bracket members of the family*—here you figure the graduated tax of a child, or a parent, against the taxpayer's. Then try to find the gift tax cost of what income-producing property can be given to them. In the end, there may be a lower tax in the assignments.

□ *Managing investments—shifting income within the family so one member fairly charges the other for the right to use the property*—this involves deductions charged the high-bracket taxpayer—and income assumed by the lower-bracket child, parent, or dependent.

□ *Incorporating family-owned property*—or family-owned business in order to get the advantages of stepped-up costs for assets (paying capital gain tax) and lots of other advantages that come with the incorporation of the family business. The corporation can be a tax shelter, but see that business policy and the character of investments afford protection from the penalty tax aimed at a tight dividend policy and the use of incorporated pocketbooks.

□ *Splitting a family business into a partnership*—or subdividing existing partnerships to get further income splitting can keep family business income in lower brackets. Limited partnerships can also be useful planning instruments. Great care must be exercised in drawing partnership agreements because they have so serious an impact on the tax result.

□ *Planning new ventures, new investments, new undertakings—so that the members of the family ratably take their share of income and losses*—for example, it is possible (without any gift tax) to take a couple of members of the family into a new business, and they might gain—without additional tax cost.

□ *Buying property through estates by entirety, or joint tenancies or tenancies in common*—each of these set-ups has its distinct tax pros and cons to consider with members of the family.

□ *Setting up family insurance in the most advantageous manner*—the net protection available may vary widely as ownership and premium paying responsibility falls on the insured, members of his family, a trust, a corporation.

□ *Setting up interfamily annuities—in which one member of a family transfers something for income from another*—these might produce considerable savings without gift taxes.

□ *Setting up family foundations* in which family income and capital can be conserved for educational, charitable, scientific, and religious work.

□ *Careful nursing of interfamily deals for interest, pay, rent, or anything else they may have between them*—penalty for sloppiness is usually loss of the deduction for the loss. There's a lot of ritual to watch here if the tax saving is to be made.

☐ *Making sure that alimony or separation payments allot the tax between the couple fairly*—there's a lot to be studied by the lawyer making these arrangements if he seeks the full deduction for the paying spouse.

[¶3934] **FOR FURTHER REFERENCE . . .**

"Accounting Treatment of Tax Items: Symposium," 36 New York University Institute on Federal Taxation 479 (1978).

Davis, P.M., and Crumbley, D.L., "Tax Benefits of Subchapter S Corporations Expanded by the Tax Reform Act of 1976," 6 Taxation for Lawyers 30 (1977).

Fink, P.R., "Selecting a Form of Business Predicated on Characterization of Income Flows," 56 Taxes 587 (October 1978).

Hauser, C.C., "Tax Reform Act Provisions Affecting an Individual's Business Activities; Subchapter S and Personal Holding Company Changes," 29 University of Southern California Institute on Federal Taxation 77 (1977).

Hess, R.P., Desk Book for Setting Up a Closely-Held Corporation, Institute for Business Planning, Inc., Englewood Cliffs, N.J. (1979).

Horwood, R.M., "Tax Considerations Involved in Deciding Whether a New Business Should Be Incorporated," 19 Taxation for Accountants 324 (1977).

Lehrman, A., *Tax Desk Book for the Closely-Held Corporation,* Institute for Business Planning, Inc., Englewood Cliffs, N.J. (1979).

Parkinson, J.L., "Choosing the Investment Vehicle: Corporations, Subchapter S Corporations, and Partnerships," 27 Tulane Tax Institute 20 (1977).

"Subchapter S Corporations: Modifications of the Tax Reform Act of 1976." 17 Washburn Law Journal 332 (Winter 1978).

Tax Planning (2 vol. looseleaf service) Institute for Business Planning, Inc., Englewood Cliffs, N.J.

Weary, D.C., "IRS Creation of Hybrid Methods: Prepayments and the Cash Method; Prepayments and the Accrual Method," 35 New York University Institute on Federal Taxation 59 (1977).

Wilson, G., "New Law Makes It Easier to Avoid Personal Holding Company Classification and Penalty Tax," 18 Taxation for Accountants 162 (1977).

TRUSTS

[¶4001]   When a trust is created, a fiduciary relationship arises between the trustee and beneficiaries. The trustee, who holds legal title to the trust property, must manage the assets prudently for the benefit of those named by the creator (settlor) of the trust. Trusts are created during the lifetime of the settlor (inter vivos trusts) or by will (testamentary trusts).

A trust is created when a settlor delivers trust property to a trustee, who is directed to manage the assets for the benefit of beneficiaries named by the settlor. The settlor must have intended to create the trust and may not form the trust for an unlawful purpose. Both settlor and trustee must be legally competent (i.e., of sound mind). Although failure to designate the trustee will not invalidate the trust, a settlor cannot name himself as sole beneficiary.

The trustee is deemed to have mere legal title to the property, while the beneficiaries hold the equitable interest in the trust assets. To be valid, the trust must also consist of property that is conveyable by the settlor. No formalities need be observed when the trust is created; however, a writing evidencing its creation may be necessary if an interest in real property is involved.

[¶4002]   **HOW TRUSTS ARE USED**

There are three broad reasons for the creation of a lifetime trust:

(1) To transfer the property beyond the control of the grantor to save estate taxes and to shift investment income produced by the trust property to the tax return of the trust or that of the trust beneficiaries. These purposes require an irrevocable trust.

(2) To shift income while retaining the privilege of using the trust property at a specified time in the future. This purpose requires a reversionary trust and its term must be at least 10 years.

(3) To transfer property to a trust for management during the life of the grantor and, if he doesn't revoke the trust before he dies, to have the trustee either continue to manage the property or make the testamentary distribution spelled out in the trust instrument. This is a revocable trust.

Apart from the tax savings, the practical purposes of a trust are to:

(1) Place the property beyond the reach of an inexperienced and possibly improvident member of the family or one who might be able to exercise an unfavorable influence over the beneficiary if the property were given to the beneficiary outright.

(2) Place the management of the trust property in the hands of an experienced and reliable trustee who can be given broad powers to manage the property to the best advantage, or whose investment activities can be restricted, controlled, and directed by the trust instrument.

(3) Create the authority and the capacity to apply the income and corpus of the trust to the problems of the beneficiaries as they develop in the future. This can

429

be done through discretionary powers to distribute, giving the beneficiary limited rights to a withdrawal, or creating powers of appointment over the corpus of the trust in persons who will be in a position to watch and understand the needs and problems of the family in the future.

(4) Obtain privacy and save probate expense at the death of the grantor who would, in the absence of the trust, own the property, and through whose estate it would have to pass.

[¶4003] TYPES OF TRUSTS

The following types of trusts are commonly employed:

(1) Revocable Trusts: Usually the settlor reserves the right to amend the trust terms, vary the amount of income to be paid out, alter the beneficiaries, or affect the disposition of the remainder interest.

(2) Pourover Trusts: Many states permit a testator to "pour over" his residuary estate into a preexisting inter vivos trust.

(3) Life Insurance Trusts: These trusts, whether testamentary or inter vivos, are funded by the proceeds of insurance on the settlor's life.

(4) Totten Trusts: This familiar transaction results when a settlor deposits funds into a bank in his own name, in trust for another. These trusts are revocable but become irrevocable at death, unless state law permits alteration of the trust in the settlor's will.

(5) Land Trusts: The land trust is basically a passive trust that consists of real estate. Often used as financing devices, land trusts permit convenient disposition of the beneficiaries' interests in the trust, without affecting title to the underlying property.

(6) Accumulation Trusts: Trusts that are directed to accumulate income are permissible for certain purposes (e.g., charitable); they cannot violate the rules against accumulations in the various states.

(7) Charitable Trusts: Trusts established for charitable purposes are governed by special rules but are generally favored among the state courts.

(8) Resulting Trusts: If a settlor fails to fully provide for the disposition of the trust assets, there arises a resulting trust in his favor.

(9) Constructive Trusts: These are not actually trusts, but are equitable devices used by the courts to rectify some sort of injustice. Thus, one who has wronged another will usually be deemed the constructive trustee of property for the benefit of the injured party. The "trust" serves as a mere conduit for passage of the property to the wronged party.

(10) Alimony Trusts: Trusts may be established to provide for the support of a separated or divorced spouse. They add a measure of security for the payee-spouse since trust assets cannot be attacked by the payor-spouse.

(11) Short-Term Trusts: Also known as Clifford trusts, these devices permit the settlor to shift income to low-bracket taxpayers for a specified period (at least 10 years) while retaining the reversionary interest in the trust assets.

(12) Spendthrift Trusts: The settlor can provide for improvident beneficiaries by prohibiting assignments of income in the trust instrument. In most jurisdictions such a provision must be expressly stated; some states automatically give this protection by statute.

[¶4004] TAXATION OF TRUSTS

The creation of a trust may result in the application of several taxes—income, estate, and gift. Many trusts are also affected by the generation-skipping tax, which was enacted by Congress in 1976.

[¶4005] INCOME TAXATION OF TRUSTS

The application of the income tax provisions of the Internal Revenue Code varies with the nature of the trust. Under these rules, the trust and its beneficiaries share the income tax burden on trust income. In general, income that is actually distributed or required to be distributed by the trust is taxable to its beneficiaries (this is the "conduit" concept). Income that is retained and accumulated by the trust is taxable to the trust.

The creation of a trust by lifetime transfer can save income taxes and accelerate the accumulation of capital in three basic ways, all of which can be combined with each other.

(1) Annual income tax savings can be achieved by the transfer of income-producing property to a trust in which the income is taxed either to the trust or to the trust beneficiary. This step will transfer income from the top brackets of the settlor to the lower bracket of a trust or beneficiary. Under IRC §677, income is taxed to the grantor if he retains any interest or power; §666 and 667 deal with the taxation of distributions of accumulated income.

(2) A trust arrangement may utilize the additional exemptions of the trust and the beneficiary to provide tax-free income.

(3) Income tax savings can be achieved by the so-called sprinkling trust, which gives the trustee discretion to distribute trust income among beneficiaries in varying proportions from year to year, depending on their needs. Trust income can be kept out of the higher income tax brackets by giving it to the beneficiaries in lower income brackets, who presumably need it more.

[¶4006] ESTATE AND GIFT TAXATION OF TRUSTS

Since the estate and gift tax laws have been consolidated into a unified system, the mere creation of an irrevocable trust does not serve to reduce the settlor's eventual estate. However, if these trusts are funded with amounts not in excess of the $3,000 annual gift tax exclusion, an estate tax saving may be realized. Any appreciation of these assets will also escape estate tax on the settlor's death. Otherwise gratuitous transfers to irrevocable trusts will incur gift tax if the value of the property transferred exceeds the settlor's available exclusion, deductions, and credits.

Trust property will be taxed in the grantor's (settlor's) estate if the grantor alone, or in conjunction with another, retains the power to alter, amend, or revoke the trust, or to designate who is to enjoy the trust income or corpus (IRC §2038). Retention of even the right to the income is sufficient to tax the grantor's estate. The grantor's estate is taxed also if the transfer to the trust isn't intended to take effect until his death (IRC §2037). Further, the trust property will be includible in the estate of the beneficiary if the beneficiary has too broad a power to withdraw or appoint the corpus as specified in IRC §2041.

[¶4007] GENERATION-SKIPPING TRUSTS

The typical long-term trust, which grants an income interest to a grantor's child and pays the remainder to the grantor's grandchild, can last as long as 100 years. No estate tax is imposed when the child dies, even if he or she has substantial powers with respect to the use, management, or disposition of trust assets, because the termination of an income interest is treated as a nontaxable event. This situation was partially rectified by the enactment of Chapter 13 of the IRC.

Generation-skipping trusts are defined as trusts (or their equivalents) that have beneficiaries in more than one generation younger than the grantor. In the trust described above, there are two generations younger than the grantor's—those of the grantor's child and grandchild. This is the most common generation-skipping trust.

[¶4008] INVASION OF TRUST PRINCIPAL

Trusts usually allow the beneficiary or trustee to invade trust principal in order to meet emergencies. If the invasion power is governed by a standard (e.g., support or maintenance of the beneficiary), the trustee can be compelled to make distributions from principal to satisfy the beneficiary's needs. If no power of invasion is specified in the trust, the courts can step in to authorize principal payments. Typical arrangements, along with their estate tax implications, are outlined below.

(1) Beneficiary has an unlimited right to withdraw all or any part of the trust corpus—The entire trust corpus would be included in the beneficiary's gross estate (IRC §2041(a)(2)).

(2) Beneficiary has a noncumulative right to withdraw up to 5% of the trust corpus or $5,000 annually, whichever is greater—This right will cause the

inclusion in the beneficiary's estate of only the amount of the unexercised withdrawal privilege in the year of the beneficiary's death (IRC §2041(b)(2)).

(3) Beneficiary has a right to withdraw such sums from trust corpus in his own discretion for health, support, and maintenance—No part of the trust corpus would be included in the beneficiary's gross estate solely due to this provision (IRC §2041(b)(1)(A)).

(4) Beneficiary is to receive a fixed amount of principal each year, these payments to cease upon the beneficiary's death—No part of the trust corpus would be included in the beneficiary's gross estate solely due to this provision.

(5) Beneficiary has no right of withdrawal, but trustee has the power to make payments of principal to the beneficiary for the beneficiary's support and maintenance, or for any reason—No part of the trust corpus should be included in the beneficiary's gross estate solely due to this provision. *(Note:* If a provision is made authorizing the trustee to invade principal for the income beneficiary's support and maintenance, sometimes a question arises as to whether the trustee should take the beneficiary's independent income and/or capital into account. It is wise to make a clear-cut provision covering this in the governing instrument so as to avoid a costly construction suit later on.)

[¶4009] TERMINATION OF THE TRUST

The disposition of trust assets remaining after the trust has been terminated may be specified in the trust instrument or by giving someone a lifetime or testamentary power of appointment over the assets.

If the power given is a *general power of appointment* so that the trust principal may be appointed to anybody at all including the holder, the principal will be included in the holder's gross estate whether or not the power is in fact exercised. (A beneficiary's absolute power to invade trust corpus for himself is the equivalent of a general power of appointment exercisable during lifetime.) A general power can be limited so that it can only be exercised by will.

If the right to appoint principal is limited to a certain class of beneficiaries, e.g., children, etc., then a *limited* or a *special power of appointment* results. Thus, if a power is given to a spouse as beneficiary to dispose of the trust corpus at his or her death only among the couple's issue, the trust corpus will not be included in the gross estate.

[¶4010] TRUST ADMINISTRATION

All jurisdictions impose certain duties on trustees. In general, these include fairness to all trust beneficiaries, restrictions on the types of investments that may be made, standards pertaining to the management of trust assets, and prohibitions against self-dealing. Many of the provisions may, however, be overridden by the settlor in the trust instruments.

(1) Powers and Duties: Trustees must exercise reasonable care and skill when handling trust assets. For example, they may invest in various kinds of enterprises (check local law), insure and repair trust property, and engage professional advice. They are usually required to make periodic accountings and to keep trust property separate from personal assets.

(2) Liabilities: If a trustee violates his fiduciary duties, he may be surcharged and made personally liable for any harm incurred by the beneficiaries. Many states prohibit clauses in trust instruments that excuse a trustee for breaching these duties. Trustees may also be personally liable in trust or contracts with third parties; however, then they may be entitled to indemnification by the trust (again depending on local law).

(3) Investments: Trustees may invest in those assets that a reasonable, prudent person would consider. While some estates restrict investments to "legals" (e.g., traded stocks), other jurisdictions merely apply the prudence standard.

(4) Allocation of Principal and Income: Proper application of the fairness standard requires trustees to allocate trust receipts and disbursements equitably between principal and income. Trustees must balance the interests of income beneficiaries (who would prefer investments in high-yield securities) and remaindermen (who would prefer growth property). Unless provided to the contrary in the trust instrument, statutory rules of allocation (e.g., the Uniform Principal and Income Act) govern. For example, interests and rates are allocated to income under the Uniform Act, while capital gains are attributed to principal.

[¶4011]   **FOR FURTHER REFERENCE . . .**

Casner, *Estate Planning* (2 vols.), Little Brown, Boston, Mass.

Cornfeld, D.L., "Accumulation Trusts," 12 Real Property, Probate and Trust Journal 419 (Fall 1977).

Covey, *Generation-Skipping Transfers in Trust,* American Bankers Association, Washington, D.C.

Estate Planning (2 vols.), Institute for Business Planning, Inc., Englewood Cliffs, N.J.

Institute on Estate Planning, Newkirk Associates, Inc., Latham, N.Y.

Lehrman, A., *Wills and Trusts Desk Book*, Institute for Business Planning, Inc., Englewood Cliffs, N.J. (1978).

Neumark, M.H., "How to Plan Trust Distributions in Light of the Elimination of the Exact Method," 48 Journal of Taxation 94-7 (February 1978).

Nossaman, *Trust Administration and Taxation,* Matthew Bender, New York, N.Y.

Restatement of Trusts, 2d, American Law Institute, St. Paul, Minn.

Scott, *Scott on Trusts,* Little Brown, Boston, Mass.

Verbit, G.P., "Annals of Tax Reform: the Generation-Skipping Transfer" 25 UCLA Law Review 700-37 (April 1978).

TRUTH-IN-LENDING

[¶**4101**] Truth-In-Lending (15 USC §1601 et seq.) is a basic generic term dealing with multiple types of federal consumer credit protection. Encompassing credit transactions, credit advertising, credit billing, and consumer leases, Truth-In-Lending is also supplemented by Regulation Z (12 CFR part 226) and Regulation B(12 CFR part 202), which are promulgated by the Board of Governors of the Federal Reserve System. Regulation Z covers definition and rules of construction, a listing of exempt transactions, rules for determination of finance charges, rules for determination of annual percentage rates in the granting of credit, general disclosure requirements, specific disclosure requirements on open-end credit accounts, disclosures required for credit that is not open ended, requirements for rescission of certain transactions, requirements for the statement of advertising credit terms, issuance and liability for credit card use, resolution procedures for billing errors, and consumer leasing. Regulation B covers the area of equal credit opportunity.

[¶4102] ## GOVERNMENT AGENCIES REGULATING TRUTH-IN-LENDING

The following federal agencies also regulate Truth-In-Lending transactions:

Agency	Function	Authority
Department of Agriculture	Regulated activity under the Packers and Stockyards Act of 1921	Truth-In-Lending Act §108
Civil Aeronautics Board	Airline advertising regulation Airline credit to passengers	14 CFR part 249 14 CFR part 374
Comptroller of the Currency	Disclosure compliance for institutions under its jurisdiction	Truth-In-Lending Act §108
Department of Defense	Regulation of personal commercial affairs of military and indebtedness of military personnel	32 CFR part 43 32 CFR part 43A
Farm Credit Administration	Disclosure compliance for Federal Land Banks, FLB associations, Federal Intermediate Credit Banks, and Production Credit Associations	Truth-In-Lending Act §108

Agency	Function	Authority
Farmers' Home Administration	Real estate loan disclosures—rescission rights in land transactions	7 CFR part 1808
Federal Aviation Administration	Aircraft registration, aircraft title records, aircraft truth-in-leasing	14 CFR part 47 14 CFR part 49 14 CFR part 91
Federal Deposit Insurance Corporation	Disclosure compliance for institutions under its jurisdiction	Truth-In-Lending Act §108
Federal Home Loan Bank Board	Disclosure compliance for institutions under its jurisdiction	Truth-In-Lending Act §108
Federal Trade Commission	Disclosure compliance for any person not under another agency's jurisdiction	Truth-In-Lending Act §108
National Credit Union Administration	Disclosure compliance for institutions under its jurisdiction	Truth-In-Lending Act §108
Department of Transportation	Odometer disclosure	49 CFR part 580

[¶4103]   EXEMPTION OF CERTAIN STATES

States that have "substantially similar" laws regulating consumer credit transactions are eligible for exemption by the Federal Reserve Board from certain requirements of the Truth-In-Lending Act. Only to the extent that the Federal Reserve Board grants exemption do local laws prevail over specific requirements of the Truth-In-Lending Act. The following states have been given partial exemptions under federal Truth-In-Lending: Maine, Oklahoma, Massachusetts, Connecticut, and Wyoming. It should be noted that some states that have adopted the Uniform Consumer Credit Code have been granted exemption under federal Truth-In-Lending. However, not all have been given exemption from Truth-In-Lending. It should also be noted that to the extent any state law is more stringent in its requirement than federal Truth-In-Lending, both the federal and state laws are applicable.

[¶4104]   THE ACT'S COVERAGE

Disclosure of certain basic information is the keystone to Truth-In-Lending. Before extending credit, every person granting consumer credit must disclose the credit charges in dollars and cents and as an annual percentage rate. Transactions specifically exempted from Truth-In-Lending coverage are found at ¶4107.

[¶4105]   **INSTALLMENT PAYMENTS**

Truth-In-Lending covers all consumer-related installment sales that involve four or more installment payments. Truth-In-Lending disclosure must be made even if the purchase price "on time" is identical to a one-time purchase price. In this case, regulations require that the creditor state: "Cost of credit is included in the purchase price."

[¶4106]   **LENDERS COVERED**

Under §103 of the Truth-In-Lending Act, the only individuals required to make disclosures are those who regularly extend credit to consumers, regularly arrange for the extension of credit to consumers, or regularly arrange for payments in which a finance charge is or may be required in connection with loans, sales of property, services, or otherwise. (The four-installment payment rule described above also applies—meaning that an individual who regularly extends credit in which payment can be made in three or fewer payments is not covered by Truth-In-Lending.)

[¶4107]   **EXEMPTIONS FROM FEDERAL**
                     TRUTH-IN-LENDING

The following transactions are exempt from the Act's provisions:
(1) Extensions of credit to:
    (a) Corporations;
    (b) Trusts;
    (c) Estates;
    (d) Partnerships;
    (e) Co-operatives;
    (f) Associations;
    (g) Government subdivisions or agencies.
(2) Extensions of credit for business or commercial purposes, other than agricultural.
(3) Transactions in securities or commodities accounts with a broker-dealer registered with the SEC.
(4) Nonreal property credit transactions in which the amount financed exceeds $25,000 or the express written commitment by the creditor to extend credit exceeds $25,000.
(5) Transactions involving services under public utility tariffs that are regulated by any governmental agency.
(6) Credit transactions primarily for agricultural purposes (including real property transactions) in which the amount financed exceeds $25,000.
(7) Lease transactions of personal property that are part of an overall lease of

437

real property that provide that the lessee has no liability for the value of property at the end of the lease (except for abnormal wear and tear) and where the lessee has no option to purchase the leased property (12 CFR §226.3(e),(f)).

[¶4108] WHO IS REQUIRED TO MAKE DISCLOSURES?

The following are various categories of individuals and businesses that generally are required to make disclosures: Automobile dealerships, bankers, dentists, doctors, credit unions, credit card issuers, retailers, savings and loan institutions, and even hospitals—provided they extend credit in the conventional sense or make special arrangements for payment of bills in which four or more installments are ordinarily involved—even if there is no finance charge.

[¶4109] TRUTH-IN-LENDING DISCLOSURE BY DOCTORS AND OTHER PROFESSIONALS

In a case where a patient is billed in full but unilaterally makes a partial payment that is accepted by the doctor, this does not constitute an "agreement" to accept more than four installments. Consequently, the professional is not subject to Regulation Z (Federal Reserve Board Letter No. 32, July 8, 1969). Additionally, if a patient decides on his own to pay a bill in installments "or whenever he can," Truth-In-Lending does not come into play (Federal Trade Commission Letter, July 1, 1969). However, if a finance charge is imposed, the transaction comes within the Act even though it is payable in fewer than four installments (Federal Reserve Board Letter, July 3, 1969). If a physician agrees with the patient that all obligations may be paid in more than four installments, the obligation becomes a consumer credit transaction and Regulation Z disclosures must be made even if no finance charge is assessed (Federal Reserve Board Letters, August 5, August 29, and October 15, 1969).

[¶4110] NONDISCLOSURE: OVERDUE TAXES

When a state and a taxpayer enter into an agreement for payment of delinquent taxes under a plan of regular monthly installments, this is not a credit transaction covered by Truth-In-Lending because, even if interest must be paid, the debt must be voluntarily entered into in order to fall within the Act's coverage—which is not the case with delinquent taxes (Federal Reserve Board Letter No. 166, October 20, 1969).

[¶4111] SPECIFIC AREAS IN WHICH DISCLOSURE IS REQUIRED

The following paragraphs discuss some of the specific areas when federal Truth-In-Lending disclosure is required.

[¶4111.1] Commitment Fees or Standby Fees From Real Estate Developer to Lender

Such fees are to be included in the finance charge as *prepaid finance charges*.

[¶4111.2] Compensating Balance

Disclosure must be made in credit transactions that require 20% deposit balances that will be taken out of the proceeds of a separate but simultaneous loan from the identical creditor. The 20% compensating balance could be provided from either a cash fund of the debtor, proceeds of a separate loan, or withholding from the proceeds of the loan being consummated.

For disclosure purposes in the first loan, the compensating balance must be deducted and disclosures made accordingly. But there is an exception for prior compensation balances that existed before the extension of credit and for those in which a bank has a security interest.

Observation: In order to provide the required compensating balance, sometimes a separate loan that would be subject to all the disclosure requirements of Regulation Z is granted. However, there is an exclusion provision concerning required deposit balances. The exception covers "a deposit balance or investment which was acquired or established from the proceeds of an extension of credit made for that purpose upon written request of the customer."

[¶4111.3] Note Renewals

When the original note is made, certain disclosures are required, but the original disclosures do not cover renewals. Renewals must be accompanied by full disclosure even though the interest remains unchanged and no "new" money is actually advanced.

[¶4111.4] Home Improvements

Real estate brokers who arrange financing for home improvements or remodeling as part of the sale of a house are also subject to the disclosure requirements.

[¶4111.5] Mortgage Transactions

Those who arrange for the extension of mortgage credit, as well as those fiduciary institutions (or individuals) who actually extend financing, must make full Truth-In-Lending disclosures. Failure to do so subjects the parties to federal penalties (including attorney's fees) and, in many instances, also subjects them to state penalties. In the paragraphs below, specific Regulation Z requirements for arranging credit, assumption of mortgages, refinancing mortgages, and issuing of second mortgages are examined.

Credit Arranger: Builders who prepare loan applications or initiate credit reports for a potential purchaser are not arrangers if they do not receive a fee for their work. If, however, the builder actually undertakes preparation of the note and mortgage or other contract documents, disclosure requirements must be met.

Assumption of Mortgages: If the purchaser of real estate will become personally liable for the debts of a primary mortgagee, Regulation Z provides that the mortgage has been assumed and the lender must give the purchaser of the real estate full and adequate disclosure. (If the mortgage lender does not participate in the assumption, no disclosure is required.)

Refinancing Mortgage: Each time a mortgage is materially altered, a new Truth-In-Lending transaction takes place, requiring additional disclosure.

Second Mortgages: Unlike first mortgages, in which the total dollar amount of the interest need not be given, full disclosure is required for all second mortgages.

Sole (Agricultural) Proprietor: Extensions of credit to a sole proprietorship for agricultural purposes are covered by Regulation Z (Federal Trade Commission Informal Staff Opinion, September 9, 1969).

[¶4111.6]   Corporate Sales of Stock

If a corporation distributes its own common stock and the purchaser may arrange to pay for it in more than four installments, the corporation cannot rely on being excluded from the definition of "creditor" simply because its primary business is other than selling stock or extending credit. Corporations are considered to be sophisticated parties fully capable of making the appropriate disclosures (Federal Reserve Board Letter No. 261, February 19, 1970).

[¶4111.7]   College Tuition Payment Plans

Deferred tuition payments with finance charges or that may be deferred into more than four parts are covered under Truth-In-Lending. The school's comptroller should subtract the total amount of the student's other financing from the amount owed, and make disclosures on the remaining balance (Federal Trade Commission Informal Staff Opinion, August 18, 1969).

[¶4112]   DEFINITIONS

Credit: "The right granted by a creditor to a customer to defer payment of debt . . . ." The Act contemplates a voluntary agreement between a debtor and creditor that gives rise to a debt.

Consumer Credit: Credit offered or extended to a natural person for personal, family, household, or agricultural purposes and for which either a finance charge is (or may be) imposed or that, by agreement, is or may be payable in more than four installments.

Creditor: Any person or business entity that in the ordinary course of business regularly extends or arranges for the extension of credit is a "creditor."

If a builder takes back a purchase-money second mortgage, that makes him a person who extends credit, and he must make disclosures. But a private party selling his own home who takes back a purchase-money mortgage is not one who extends credit under the law.

Advertisement: Any commercial message in any newspaper, magazine, or catalogue, or in a leaflet, flyer, direct-mail literature, or other printed material, or any broadcast medium such as radio, television, or even a public address system.

[¶4113] GENERAL DISCLOSURE REQUIREMENTS

Clear and conspicuous disclosure is required under the terms of Truth-In-Lending. All dollar amounts and percentages must be stated boldly and in numerical figures. The law also requires that annual percentage rates and finance charges be printed more conspicuously (in boldface type) than other terms. Guarantors, sureties, indorsers, and other individuals who are secondarily liable must also receive full disclosure. However, if two joint debtors (i.e., both primarily liable) are involved in a transaction, only one need be given a copy of federal disclosures.

[¶4114] CHECKLISTS OF SPECIFIC DISCLOSURE REQUIREMENTS

Federal Truth-In-Lending requires certain disclosure requirements. The Federal Reserve Board, through implementation of Regulation Z, has indicated that in connection with the sale of credit, as well as the sale of goods, certain items must be specifically listed. Checklists of these follow in the paragraphs below.

[¶4114.1] "Sale" of Credit (Extension of Credit Not in Connection With the Sale of Goods)

The following is a checklist of disclosure terms required for closed-end small loan transactions.

☐ Date of accrual of the finance charge (or date of transaction, if that is the date when accrual begins).

☐ Annual percentage rate of finance charge.

Note: If the finance charge is less than $5 and the amount financed does not exceed $75, no disclosure is required. If the total amount financed is more than $75 but the finance charge is less than $7.50, no disclosure is required.

☐ The number of scheduled payments.

☐ The dollar amount of scheduled payments.

☐ The due dates (or periods) of scheduled payments.

☐ The total amount (dollar value) of total payments.

☐   A statement of any "balloon" payment, and its amount.

☐   Means of computation of delinquency, default, or other charges resulting from late payment.

☐   Identification of any security interest retained by the creditor (UCC filings still required).

☐   Identification of the property to which the security interest attaches.

☐   Method of computation of any prepayment penalty that creditor may impose.

☐   Statement of the amount financed (the amount of credit excluding any prepaid finance charges that constitutes the amount of credit extended).

☐   Prepaid finance charges, if any.

☐   Amount of deposit, if any.

☐   Sum of any prepaid finance charges and deposits.

☐   Total amount of finance charge.

☐   Notes indicating rights of rescission by the consumer, if any.

[¶4114.2]   **Credit Sales**

For all regularly occurring credit sales transactions, the following Truth-In-Lending disclosures are applicable:

☐   Date on which the finance charge begins to accrue if different from date of transaction.

☐   The finance charge expressed as an annual percentage rate, using the term "annual percentage rate."

Exception: Disclosure of finance charge as an annual percentage rate is not required if (1) the finance charge does not exceed $5 and applies to an amount financed not exceeding $75, or (2) the finance charge does not exceed $7.50 and applies to an amount financed exceeding $75.

☐   Number, amount, and due dates or periods of scheduled payments and, with certain exceptions, the sum of such payments, using the term "total of payments." This does not apply to a loan secured by a first lien or equivalent security interest on a dwelling and made to finance the purchase of that dwelling, or in the case of a sale of that house.

☐   Identification of any "balloon" payment.

☐   Amount or method of computing amount of any default, delinquency, or similar charges payable in event of late payments.

☐   Description or identification of type of security interest held or to be retained or acquired by creditor, including statements concerning after-acquired property subject to the security interest or other or future indebtedness secured by any after-acquired property where appropriate.

☐   Identification of the property to which security interest relates.

☐   Description of any prepayment penalty that may be imposed by creditor or his assignee, with an explanation of the method of computation.

☐   Provisions concerning refund of unearned finance charges in the event of prepayment.

☐   Cash price of property or service purchased, using the term "cash price."

☐   Amount of buyer's down payment, itemized as applicable, using the term "cash down payment"; for property traded in, using the term "trade-in"; and the term "total down payment" for the sum of these.

☐   Difference between cash price and total down payment, using the term "unpaid balance of cash price."

☐   All charges, other than cash price, individually itemized, that are included in amount financed but that are not part of finance charge.

☐   The sum of unpaid balance of cash price and all other charges that are included in amount financed but that are not part of finance charge, using the term "unpaid balance."

☐   Amounts to be deducted for prepaid finance charge or required deposit balance. "Prepaid finance charge," "required deposit balance," and "total prepaid finance charge and required deposit balance" must be used where applicable.

☐   Difference between unpaid balance and prepaid finance charge or required deposit balance or total prepaid finance charge and required deposit balance, using the term "amount financed."

☐   Total amount of finance charge, with description of each amount included, using the term "finance charge."

Note: This is not required in most sales of dwellings, nor is the next item.

☐   Sum of the cash price, all other charges included in amount financed but that are not part of finance charge, and the finance charge, using the term "deferred payment price."

☐   Notice of customer's right of rescission, if applicable.

[¶4114.3]   Open-End Credit Transactions

Open-end credit transactions are agreements under which a consumer may, if he desires, keep on making new purchases under the original extension of credit and add the amount of these purchases to the outstanding balance, up to an agreed ceiling (i.e., revolving charge accounts). The consumer usually has the option of prepaying or of paying in stated installments. The creditor may impose a finance charge on the balance, and it is this total finance charge that is the subject of Truth-In-Lending's main thrust.

[¶4114.4]   New Accounts

Consumers seeking to open revolving credit accounts or credit card accounts from issuing authorities are entitled to certain basic information:

☐   *Conditions* under which a finance charge may be imposed, including an explanation of the time period, if any, within which any credit extended may be paid without incurring a finance charge.

☐   *Method of determining the balance* on which a finance charge may be imposed.

☐   *Method of determining the amount of the finance charge,* including the method of determining any minimum, fixed, check service, transaction, activity, or similar charge that may be imposed as a finance charge.

☐   *When one or more periodic rates* may be used to compute the finance charge, each such rate, the range of balances to which applicable, and the corresponding annual percentage rate determined by multiplying the periodic rate by the number of periods in a year.

☐   If the creditor so elects, the *Comparative Index of Credit Cost* in accordance with 12 CFR §226.11.

☐   *Conditions under which any other charges* may be imposed and method by which they will be determined.

☐   *Conditions under which creditor may retain or acquire any security interest* in any property to secure payment of any credit extended on the account, and description or identification of the type of interest or interests that may be so retained or acquired.

☐   *The minimum periodic payment required.*

[¶4114.5]   Periodic Billing

Creditors are required under federal Truth-In-Lending to make full disclosure of the following on each billing statement.

☐   *Outstanding balance* in the account at the beginning of the billing cycle, using the term "previous balance."

☐   *Amount and date of each extension of credit* or date such extension of credit is debited to the account during the billing cycle and, unless previously furnished, a brief identification of any goods or services purchased, or other extension of credit.

☐   *Amounts credited* to the account during the billing cycle for payments, using the term "payment," and for other credits including returns, rebates of finance charges, and adjustments, using the term "credits," and, unless previously furnished, a brief identification of each item included in such other credits. Separate itemizations are permitted if they do not appear on the face of the statement. They must, however, accompany the statement and identify each charge and/or credit.

☐   *Amount of any finance charge,* using the term "finance charge," debited to the account during the billing cycle, itemized and identified to show amounts, if any, due to the application of periodic rates and the amount of any other charge included in the finance charge, such as a minimum, fixed, check service, transaction, activity, or similar charge, using appropriate descriptive terminology.

Note, however, that this does *not* require the seller to state the portions of the finance charge due to application of two or more periodic rates separately. The periodic rates that apply to the account and the applicable range of the balances must be disclosed, but no further detailed breakdown is required.

Example: If the finance charge is 1½% per month for the first $500 of the balance and 1% per month for amounts exceeding $500, the total monthly charge on an outstanding balance of $600 would be $8.50, which must be stated. But the $7.50 and $1 components need not be spelled out.

☐   *Each periodic rate,* using the term "periodic rate" (or "rates"), that may be used to compute the finance charge, whether or not applied during the billing cycle, and the range of balances to which applicable.

☐ *Annual percentage rate or rates,* using the term "annual percentage rate" (or "rates"), and, if there is more than one rate, the amount of the balance to which each rate is applicable.

☐ If the creditor so elects, the *Comparative Index of Credit Cost* in accordance with 12 CFR §226.11.

☐ *Balance* on which the finance charge was computed, and a statement of how that balance was determined. If the balance was determined without first deducting all credits during the billing cycle, that fact and the amount of such credits must also be disclosed.

☐ *Closing date* of billing cycle and the outstanding balance in the account on that date, using the term "new balance," accompanied by the statement of the date by which, or the period, if any, within which, payment must be made to avoid additional finance charges.

[¶4114.6]   Finance Charges

Any charge that is imposed on the customer either directly or indirectly in order to obtain credit must be disclosed fully as a "finance charge." This classification includes, among others:

☐ Loan fees;
☐ Credit investigation fees;
☐ Finder's fees;
☐ Time-price differentials;
☐ Points in mortgages;
☐ Premiums for credit life or other credit insurance if required by the lender;
☐ Interest.

The following incidental charges are not deemed finance charges:

☐ Taxes;
☐ License fees;
☐ Registration fees;
☐ Certain title fees;
☐ Fees fixed by law and payable to public officials;
☐ Real estate appraisal fees.

Discounts for prompt payment are deemed finance charges but do not have to be disclosed on the original contract. Inclusion on the face of the regular statement rendered is sufficient for compliance.

Finance charges must be spelled out, both in total percentages and dollars and cents, to the closest quarter of 1% for most transactions. (Finance charges involving real estate may be rounded off to the nearest 1%.)

[¶4115]   CREDIT OTHER THAN OPEN-END

All required disclosures for transactions other than open-end credit agreements must be made together either (1) on the same side of the note or other instrument evidencing the obligation on the page and near the place for the customer's signature, or (2) on one side of a separate statement that identifies the transaction. The required disclosures must be made before the contractual relationship between the creditor and the customer is created, irrespective of the time of performance by either party, except in the case of orders by mail or telephone or a series of sales.

[¶4116]   **OPEN-END CREDIT**

Required disclosures for open-end credit accounts for which a billing cycle has been established must be made on the face of the periodic statement or on its reverse side or on an attached supplementary statement. A notice must direct the buyer to see the reverse side or accompanying statement(s) for important information.

The disclosures must not be separated in any manner that might confuse or mislead the customer or obscure or detract attention from the requisite information.

[¶4117]   **ANNUAL PERCENTAGE RATE**

The annual percentage rate is the actual true cost of the credit to a prospective customer. Actuarial tables are ordinarily used as a means of calculating this figure. To the extent that a loan is discounted, this method will show a higher rate of interest than that normally listed. For revolving charge accounts, the monthly rate is multiplied by the number of time periods used by the creditor in the course of the year (thus, a 1½% monthly charge on an unpaid balance has an annual percentage rate of 18%).

[¶4118]   **EXCEPTIONS TO DISCLOSURE**
                     REQUIREMENTS

Under the terms of Truth-In-Lending, any individual or business that regularly lends money or otherwise extends credit in which four or more installments may be used to pay back the amount (even if no actual "interest" is charged) is covered by the law. There are, however, certain specific exceptions to the disclosure requirements. These exceptions are discussed in the paragraphs that follow.

[¶4118.1]   **Homeowners**

Second mortgages taken back as part of the purchase price are not subject to Truth-In-Lending disclosure requirements; the seller is deemed not to be a creditor for Regulation Z purposes.

[¶4118.2] Farm Loans

Loans for agricultural purposes ordinarily are involved in the extensions of credit. Because it is often difficult to estimate the annual percentage rate, repayment schedules, or finance charges on seasonal loans, the Federal Reserve Board has made it easier for lenders to comply with the law. Thus, the lender is permitted merely to state those details that are known concerning a farm loan—giving details that are accurate to the extent possible—rather than estimate either the finance charge, the annual percentage rate, or other required information.

[¶4118.3] Periodic Statements by Mortgage Lenders

Mortgage loans are ordinarily classed as closed-end transactions, i.e., the lender doesn't have to make periodic statements. (Also, in the basic disclosure statement, the mortgage lender is not required to give the total amount financed.) If a mortgagor elects to send statements to the consumer, the disclosure of the annual percentage rate and dates by which payments must be made in order to avoid late charges must then be included.

[¶4118.4] Insurance Premiums

Direct financing of insurance premiums is an exempt transaction—even though insurance companies may levy a service charge on monthly installment payments by the insured. This opinion by the Federal Reserve Board specifically includes the situation where failure to make payments results in the cancellation of the policy. Generally, charges for property or liability insurance, as well as credit life, health, accident, or loss of income insurance written in connection with any credit transaction, must be included in the finance charge. The creditor may exclude insurance premiums from the finance charge only if insurance coverage is not required by the creditor, this fact is clearly and conspicuously disclosed in writing to the customer, and any customer desiring this type of insurance coverage gives a separately signed writing (specifically dated) indicating a desire to receive the insurance after having received a written disclosure of the cost of such insurance (12 CFR §226.4(a)(5)(i)(ii)).

[¶4118.5] Mail Order or Telephone Solicitation

Mail order and telephone solicitation based on a catalog that sets forth a deferred payment schedule (including finance charges) is specifically exempted from Truth-In-Lending disclosure requirements.

[¶4118.6] Add-on Sales

An add-on sale consists of a series of sales from the same buyer in which the deferred payment cost of the purchase price is added on to the outstanding balance contained in the consumer's account. Consumers must approve all terms in writing, and add-on sales are excluded from disclosure requirements only if the vendor takes no security interest in the property.

[¶4118.7] Student Loans

Prior to repayment, full disclosure must be made on the loan agreement. Disclosure need not be made, however, until final papers are prepared.

[¶4118.8] Purchase-Money Mortgages

When a mortgage is taken by an individual who ordinarily is not engaged in the business of extending credit, none of the Truth-In-Lending disclosure requirements is involved. If there is a first mortgage for the purchase of a home, it's ordinarily exempt from disclosure of the total dollar amount of the interest rate (though the percentage rate must always be clearly stated). The most common type of purchase-money mortgage involves two homeowners—one of whom is selling the home to the other for less cash than the actual purchase price. The balance is to be paid over a period of time by the purchaser at a specified credit rate. Ordinarily, this is not covered by federal Truth-In-Lending.

[¶4119] DISCLOSURES THAT ARE INCONSISTENT WITH LOCAL LAW

State law that differs in whole or in part from the requirements of Truth-In-Lending is not necessarily ineffective. To the extent that the state law does not expressly contradict Truth-In-Lending requirements, the two work in tandem. Except for a state that is specifically exempted from Regulation Z, its requirements can never overrule the federal law. Exemption has been granted to several states because their Regulations were deemed by the Federal Reserve Board to be "substantially similar," therefore making the preemptory Federal Regulation unnecessary. Only five states are currently exempt from Truth-In-Lending requirements: Maine, Oklahoma, Massachusetts, Connecticut, and Wyoming. Even in these states, certain aspects of Truth-In-Lending such as 12 CFR §226.12(c) have not been suspended. Some but not all of the states subscribing to the Uniform Consumer Credit Code (UCCC) have been granted exemption from federal Truth-In-Lending requirements.

[¶4120] RIGHT OF RESCISSION

Although the Truth-In-Lending law is primarily concerned with disclosures, it does confer an important substantive right on prospective borrowers: The right to rescind a contract within three days if the collateral is a "security interest" in the borrower's home. This does not include first mortgages or purchase-money mortgages but is aimed at situations in which an artisan's lien or mechanic's lien is retained as security. The right of rescission operates as follows:

A borrower has three days to rescind certain mortgage loans following the "date of consummation of the transaction." Under Regulation Z, that date occurs when a "contractual relationship" arises between the creditor and debtor.

A "security interest" is any interest in property that secures payment or performance of any obligation, including security interests under the Uniform Commercial Code; real property mortgages; deeds of trust; other liens whether or not recorded; mechanics', materialmen's, and artisans' liens; vendors' liens in both real and personal property; the interest of a seller in a contract for the sale of real property; any lien on property arising by operation of law; and any interest in a lease when used to secure payment or performance of an obligation.

A "residence" is any real property in which the customer resides or expects to reside and includes land on which the customer resides or expects to reside.

The creditor must furnish the customer with two copies of the required notice, printed in boldface type on one side of a separate statement that identifies the transaction to which it relates.

Unless the right of rescission does not apply or the customer has waived or modified his right to rescind until the three-day period has expired, the lender may not:

☐ Disburse any money other than in escrow;
☐ Make any physical changes in customer's property;
☐ Perform any work or service for customer; or
☐ Make any deliveries to the customer's residence.

[¶4120.1]   Timely Exercise

The right of rescission must be exercised by midnight of the third business day following consummation of the transaction or delivery of the required disclosures, whichever occurs later. Notice of rescission may be given by mail, telegram, or other writing. The creditor's notice of right to rescind can be used, if dated and signed by the customer, to rescind the transaction.

[¶4120.2]   Multiple Parties

The right of rescission may be exercised by any one of the joint owners who is a party to the transaction, and the effect of rescission will apply to all the owners.

[¶4120.3]   Handling Rescission From Lender's Viewpoint

Local law should be examined to ascertain whether confessions of judgment or cognovit clauses are permitted in transactions of the type governed by Truth-In-Lending. If they are still permitted in your jurisdiction, there is a strong possibility that their very inclusion in an agreement for a second mortgage or other lien on realty would trigger the borrower's exercise of the right of rescission. This would occur if the existence of such a clause results in a lien on the debtor's home without notice. The right of rescission may be sidestepped by setting up a commitment procedure with the object of creating a contract at the very outset.

449

[¶4120.4]   Waiver of Right of Rescission

The right to rescission must be printed in upper- and lower-case letters in not less than 12-point boldface type. If the notice appears on the reverse side of the evidence in the contract, the face of the statement must state: "See reverse side for important information about your right of rescission" (12 CFR §226.9(b)).

[¶4120.5]   Transactions to Which Right of Rescission Does Not Apply

Since the right of rescission was created primarily to avoid foreclosure on personal residences for liens not directly connected with homes, the law exempts the following transactions from the exercise of customer's right to rescind:

(a) Creation, retention, or assumption of a first lien or an equivalent security interest to finance acquisition of a dwelling in which a customer resides or expects to reside.

(b) A first lien retained or acquired by a creditor in connection with financing the initial construction of the customer's residence, or a loan committed prior to the completion of construction of the customer's residence to satisfy that construction loan and provide permanent financing.

(c) Any subordinated lien exempt from the right of rescission when originally created.

(d) Any advance for agricultural purposes made under an open-end real estate mortgage or similar lien provided the disclosure of the right to rescind was made when the security interest was acquired by the creditor or before the first advance was made.

(e) Any transaction in which an agency of a state is a creditor.

[¶4120.6]   Judgments

When a judgment is awarded by a court, the recipient is not a creditor, even if the person to whom the judgment is awarded permits satisfaction in more than four installments. Therefore, no Truth-In-Lending compliance is required—even if a charge is imposed for the deferral of the satisfaction (Federal Reserve Board Letter No. 161, October 17, 1969).

[¶4120.7]   Foreign Bank Transactions

Foreign branches of American banks do not have to comply with Truth-In-Lending requirements to Americans living or visiting abroad—unless the loan was consummated outside the United States for the express purpose of evading the requirements of Truth-In-Lending (Federal Reserve Board Letter No. 654, January 5, 1973).

[¶4120.8]   Medical Payments

Mere periodic payment for medical services as rendered (when there is no extension of credit) requires no disclosure. Even if services rendered outpace payments, Regulation Z is inapplicable unless more than four scheduled payments to repay the obligation are involved (Federal Reserve Board Letter No. 214, December 16, 1969; also see above).

[¶4120.9] Certain Loans

Loans payable in four or fewer installments that have no finance charge are exempt under the Truth-In-Lending Act.

[¶4121] SANCTIONS IMPOSED BY TRUTH-IN-LENDING

Civil damages for failure to make proper disclosures are pegged to the finance charges in the contract and may not exceed $1,000. In some instances, damages may be doubled. Erroneous disclosure may be corrected within 15 days of discovery to avoid these sanctions.

On the criminal side, however, fines of up to $5,000 and/or jail terms up to one year may be imposed for willful failure to comply with the law.

There is a one-year statute of limitations on civil suits. Creditors must keep records of compliance open for inspection for two years from the date on which disclosures were required to be made.

Even if a debtor recovers damages against a creditor who has violated the disclosure rules, he is still liable on the principal debt. Noncompliance by the lender does not operate as forgiveness of the debt.

Creditor's Defenses to Civil Suit: The creditor has the burden of proving that a violation was not willful. This means that he must show, by a preponderance of the evidence, that his violation was unintentional and that it was the result of an "honest" error.

[¶4122] ADVERTISING OF CONSUMER CREDIT

The federal Truth-In-Lending law also applies to advertising consumer credit. "Advertising" includes all types of publications, billboards, and radio and television commercials. The law prohibits stating that the advertiser will extend certain terms to buyers unless the advertiser usually and customarily arranges such terms for its customers.

In advertising open-end credit, if one single credit term is advertised, all other credit terms must be included. For example, the retailer cannot advertise "$20 down" for a dinette set and omit the rest of the terms, which might include details such as "balance to be paid in twelve monthly installments of $20 with carrying charges of. . . ."

Moreover, for closed-end credit transactions, the total sum due after adding down payment, installments, and all service charges must be stated, because it is definitely ascertainable beforehand.

Ads that contain no specific terms are still permissible. Thus, you can make one blanket statement, "easy credit terms," without any further amplification. However, if you do state any credit term, then you must include all terms—all or nothing at all.

Advertisers of residential real estate mortgages must comply, but advertisers of purchase-money first mortgages do not have to disclose either the deferred payment price or the sum of the payments.

Exceptions: As is true of other sections of the Truth-In-Lending law, the advertising requirements do not apply to commercial or business credit, securities transactions, transactions over $25,000, credit advanced to governmental units or organizations, or certain transactions involving public utility tariffs. However, transactions with securities salesmen who are not registered with the SEC *do* come within the purview of Truth-In-Lending.

The law specifically exempts media in which credit advertising appears from any liability for circulating false or misleading credit information contained in such advertisements.

[¶4123] RESTRICTIONS ON GARNISHMENT

Title III of the Truth-In-Lending law consists of federal restrictions on garnishment of wages. The amount that can be garnisheed in any single workweek is limited to the lesser of 25% of an employee's disposable income (gross pay minus all deductions required by law) or his disposable income less 30 times the federal minimum hourly wage. The law applies to any business directly or indirectly involved in interstate commerce and thus affects virtually every employer. The law also prevents employers from firing employees merely because their wages have been garnisheed.

When there is a conflict with existing state law, the more stringent of the two prevails. Thus, in a jurisdiction where garnishment is limited to an even lower percentage of wages, the state statute will control.

Creditors' Alternatives: For those creditors who fear an upsurge of uncollectible debt as a result of limitations on garnishment, utilization of confessions of judgment, or conventional wage assignments may be a more prudent course. Naturally, the credit rating of the debtor will determine the manner of assuring eventual repayment. An assignment of wages or salary is not the prudent way to deal with sales to highly paid executives or buyers who have substantial liquid or fixed assets.

[¶4124] ANTI-LOAN-SHARKING PROVISIONS

The Act makes it a federal crime to make "extortionate" loans (Title II). A loan transaction is deemed "extortionate" on its face if:

(1) It would be unenforceable at law; and

452

(2) The rate of interest is more than 45%; and

(3) The debtor knew, or had good reason to believe, at the time the credit was extended, that force or violence might be employed in collecting; and

(4) The debtor owes the creditor a total of more than $100.

Penalties for conviction are fines up to $10,000 and/or imprisonment for up to 20 years.

[¶4125]   UNIFORM CONSUMER CREDIT CODE (U3C)

The "states rights" answer to federal Truth-In-Lending is the Uniform Consumer Credit Code, often referred to in convenient shorthand as "U3C." The U3C aims to simplify, clarify, modernize, and codify laws governing retail installment sales, consumer credit, small loans, and usury—but with the following caveat: It only covers those sales (and credit) primarily for personal, family, or household use, or for agricultural purposes. Moreover, the U3C is applicable only if the consumer credit sale involving goods or services, or the consumer lease, or the consumer loan is less than $25,000. One of the more controversial features of the U3C is the elimination of usury ceilings, subject to certain exceptions (such as 18% for ordinary consumer loans, 36% on the first $300 of the unpaid balance for consumer credit sales other than revolving charge, and other variations).

Adoption of the U3C has been considered in 46 states, but in part because Truth-In-Lending is applied in tandem with the U3C unless the Federal Reserve Board grants specific exemption, the U3C is law in only nine states.

State	Effective Date	Citation
Colorado	10/1/71	Colo. Rev. Stat. §5-1-101 et seq.
Idaho	7/1/71	Code §28-31-101 et seq.
Indiana	10/1/71	Indiana Code 1971, title 24
Iowa	7/1/74	Iowa Laws of 1974 S.F. 1405
Kansas	7/1/74	Kan. Laws of 1973, ch. 85
Maine*	1/1/75	Rev. Stat. Maine, tit. 9A
Oklahoma*	7/1/69	14A Okla. Stat. 1970 Supp.
Utah	7/1/69	Utah Annot. Code §70B-1-101 et seq.
Wyoming*	7/1/71	Wyo. Stat. of 1957, title 40, §1-101 et seq.

---

*Asterisk denotes exemption from federal Truth-In-Lending requirements.

[¶4126]   **SIGNIFICANCE FOR THE PRACTITIONER**

Counsel for banks, retail merchants, small loan companies, medical groups, and artisans will have to review all installment agreements and scrutinize all advertising copy to insure full compliance. The paper work may seem astronomical at first, but there are many standard forms available.

As counsel on the other side of the fence—consumer advocate—naturally more questions about dubious practices and outright violations by lenders and sellers will arise. Remember that only the structure of the contract is covered by the federal law. Interest rates suspect as usury still are the province of local or state law. Be cognizant of consumers' civil remedies.

Other Statutory Considerations: When considering the total interest rate and all other finance charges, be certain to check local laws to guard against possible usury that would invalidate a transaction.

Also check to make sure a jurisdiction has not enacted its own version of the Uniform Consumer Credit Code or National Consumer Act that might affect the mode of making required disclosures under the federal act.

[¶4127]   **EQUAL CREDIT OPPORTUNITY**

Discrimination against applicants in credit transactions has been prohibited by the Equal Credit Opportunity Act (15 USC §1691), effective March 23, 1977. Under ECOA, creditors are prohibited from asking applicants certain questions or from even using what is termed "credit scoring" techniques. Under the law, creditors are prohibited from making oral or written statements in advertising or elsewhere that might have the effect of discouraging someone from applying for credit. Moreover, creditors are not permitted to use race, national origin, sex, marital status, or age for credit scoring purposes. Nor may a creditor discriminate against an applicant solely because his income derives from a public assistance program. Also, creditors may not inquire about marital status (except in community property states or where a "necessaries" doctrine is applicable). Inquiry concerning a spouse or former spouse is also prohibited conduct unless the spouse would be contractually liable (as in a jurisdiction where the husband is liable for his wife's necessaries), the applicant is relying upon a spouse's income, the spouse will be permitted to use the account, or the applicant relies on alimony or child support as the basis for repayment of the credit requested. Otherwise, a creditor may not inquire about alimony or child support payments unless the application states conspicuously that this information need not be revealed.

[¶4128]   **ACTION ON AN APPLICATION**

The Equal Credit Opportunity Act requires creditors to inform applicants of the action that has been taken on a credit application within 30 days after the creditor has received the completed application. If there has been adverse action, the creditor must either (a) state the reasons in writing, or (b) notify the applicant in writing of the adverse action, and state that the applicant has a right to know why, including the identity of the person or office that the applicant may contact to learn why the adverse action was taken.

The Act defines "adverse action" as: A denial or revocation of credit, a change in terms of an existing credit agreement, or a refusal to grant credit substantially in the same amount or on the same terms as requested in the application. Adverse action does not include a refusal to extend additional credit under an existing agreement to applicants who are delinquent, or if the additional credit would exceed a previously established limit.

[¶4129]   ENFORCEMENT AND LIABILITY

The federal agencies that administer the other sections of Truth-In-Lending also have responsibility for enforcing Equal Credit Opportunity Compliance. (See ¶4102 for a complete listing.)

Regulation B (12 CFR part 202), promulgated by the Federal Reserve Board, comprises Regulations to enforce the Act. Under Regulation B, model application forms have been issued. (These forms appear in *IBP Forms of Business Agreements and Resolutions, Vol. 3.)* However, use of these forms is not required, as long as the creditor does not request prohibited information. Also, a creditor is free to delete any information requests, or rearrange the format without modifying substance. Regulation B also makes it clear that a creditor does not have to use a written application form at all.

A creditor who violates any provisions of the Act or Regulation B may be subject to civil liability of up to $10,000 in punitive damages, plus any amount of actual damages. However, in a class action, liability may not exceed the lesser of $500,000 or 1% of the creditor's net worth.

[¶4130]   CONSUMER LEASES

Consumer Leasing Act came into effect on March 23, 1977, comprising § 181 through 186 of the Truth-In-Lending Act (Public Law 94-240, 15 USC § 1666k). This Act is designed to insure meaningful disclosure of personal property leases undertaken by consumers. Moreover, it is designed to limit the use of "balloon payments" in consumer leasing. Regulation Z Guidelines have been issued (12 CFR § 226.15 et seq.). The Consumer Leasing Act has five basic parts. First is a section requiring full disclosure of all material terms to a lease before the final lease agreement is signed. Second is a limitation on the consumer's liability following the expiration or termination of a lease. The content of advertisements relating to consumer lease transactions is regulated by a third section. A fourth section permits lawsuits by consumers who have been harmed by a failure to comply with the requirements of the Consumer Leasing Act. Finally, a fifth section is provided to indicate that new regulations do not either alter, annul, effect, or exempt any individual from complying with state law on consumer leases—except to the extent that the state law is inconsistent with federal law or regulation.

[¶4131] **PERSONAL PROPERTY LEASED FOR PERSONAL, FAMILY, OR HOUSEHOLD PURPOSES**

Personal property that is leased for personal, family, or household purposes is covered under the Consumer Leasing Act. Leases having a total contractual obligation of more than $25,000 or extending for a period of less than four months are not covered under the Act.

[¶4132] **DISCLOSURE PROVISIONS FOR CONSUMER LEASES**

Mandatory disclosures must be made in writing and given to a consumer covered by the Consumer Leasing Act before the lease transaction is consummated. Federal Trade Commission rules permit imprecise amounts or other information not known when the lease is signed to be estimated, provided that the leasing party informs the consumer of that fact in the disclosure statement.

A checklist of 11 key items is provided in §182 of Truth-In-Lending (Consumer Leases). This indicates the basic requirements for disclosure that must be included in every consumer leasing transaction covered by the Act. The Federal Reserve Board has summarized the major required disclosures as the following:

(1) A brief description of the leased property adequate to identify it to both parties to the lease.

(2) The total amount of any payment or payments the lessee is to pay at the consummation of the lease, such as a refundable security deposit, advance payment, or the like.

(3) The number, amount, and due dates of periodic payments and their total.

(4) The total amount of taxes, fees, and other charges involved.

(5) Identification of those responsible for maintaining or servicing the leased property.

(6) How any penalty or delinquency charge will be determined, and the amount.

(7) A statement of whether the lessee has an option to purchase the property at the end of the lease term, or earlier, and at what price.

(8) A statement of the conditions under which either party to the lease may terminate it, and how any penalty or other charge will be determined.

(9) A statement that the lessee is responsible for the difference between the estimated value of the property leased and its realized value at the end of the lease or upon earlier termination, if such liability exists.

456

(10) A statement that in an open-end lease the lessee may obtain a professional appraisal of the property by an independent third party at the end of the lease or on earlier termination, and that this appraisal will be binding.

(11) When the lessee's liability at the end of the lease term is based on the estimated value of the property: A statement of the value of the property at the consummation of the lease, the itemized total lease obligation at the end of the lease, and the difference between them.

[¶4133]   LIMITATIONS ON CONSUMER LIABILITY
ON A LEASE

When a consumer's lease for personal property is either terminated or expires and the terms of the lease make the consumer responsible for making a payment to the lessor based on the estimated residual value of the property, the liability of the consumer is limited by the Consumer Leasing Act. Penalty charges in the amount of the actual harm caused by a delinquency, default, or early termination are recoverable; however, all penalty charges are limited by amounts that are reasonable in light of the anticipated or actual harm caused by the consumer's action. The law creates a rebuttable presumption that the lessor's estimation of the residual value of goods leased by a consumer is unreasonable if the estimated residual value exceeds three times one monthly payment. Any amount in excess of that sum can only be recovered from the consumer if the lessor undertakes legal action.

[¶4134]   ATTORNEYS' FEES

If the lessor takes a consumer to court on a consumer leasing transaction, the lessor must pay the consumer's attorney's fees, unless the lessor can prove that excess liability resulted from unreasonable wear and tear or other major physical damage (Truth-In-Lending Act §183(a)).

[¶4135]   ADVERTISING CONSUMER LEASES

Full disclosure of all material parts of a lease transaction are required if an advertisement states the amount of any payment, the numbers of required payments, or that no down payment or any payment is required at the inception of the lease. The disclosures must include that the transaction advertised is in fact a lease; the amount of any down payments; number, amounts, due dates, or periods of scheduled payments; the total number of payments; the total amount of the payments; and an explanation of any liability that a consumer may have at the end of the term of the lease (Truth-In-Lending Act §184(a)). The employees or personnel of any medium in which an advertisement appears, or through which it is disseminated, have no liability under the Consumer Lease Advertising Section of the law (§184(b)).

[¶4136]   **EFFECTIVE STATE LAW**

By regulation, the Federal Reserve Board may exempt from requirements of the Consumer Leasing Act any class of lease transactions within any state if it determines that that class of transaction is subject to requirements that are "substantially similar" to those imposed by the Consumer Leasing Act. The law does not alter, annul, or otherwise affect state law, except to the extent of laws that are inconsistent with federal provisions.

The following states and commonwealths have no statutory provision governing false or deceptive advertising as to finance charges or interest rates: Arkansas, Louisiana, Puerto Rico, and West Virginia. The Uniform Consumer Credit Code (U3C) has separate provisions covering this.

[¶4137]   **FOR FURTHER REFERENCE . . .**

Acceleration and Prepayment Disclosures Under Truth-In-Lending: Nemesis of the Rule of 78's?'' 1978 Washington University Law Quarterly 141-66 (Winter 1978).

Clontz, Ralph C., Jr., *"Truth-In-Lending Manual,"* Revised Edition, 1970. The Banking Law Journal.

"Consumer Protection: Judicial Approaches to Rescission and Restoration Under the Truth-In-Lending Act," 53 Washington Law Review 301-17 (February 1978).

"Disclosure of Acceleration Clauses under Federal Truth-In-Lending," 26 Kansas Law Review 289-302 (Winter 1978).

"Equal Credit for All—An Analysis of the 1976 Amendments to the Equal Credit Opportunity Act," 22 St. Louis University Law Journal Review 326-65 (1978).

"Exercise of Consumer Rights Under the Equal Credit Opportunity and Fair Credit Billing Acts," 64 Federal Reserve Bulletin 363-6 (May 1978).

"Federal Truth-In-Lending Act," 5 *American Jurisprudence Legal Forms Anno.* §1285, Lawyers Co-operative Publishing Company, Rochester, N.Y.

Forms of Business Agreements (Vol. 3). Institute for Business Planning, Inc., Englewood Cliffs, N.J.

Jacobs, R.B., "Introduction to the Equal Credit Opportunity Act for the Commercial Creditor," 83 Commercial Law Journal 338-44 (August/September 1978).

Landers, J.M., "Truth-In-Lending: Closed End Credit," 24 Practical Lawyer 13-41 (June 1978).

Maltz, B.E.M., and Miller, F.H., "Equal Credit Opportunity Act and Regulation," 31 Oklahoma Law Review 1-62 (Winter 1978).

"Supplement VI to Regulation Z Truth-In-Lending," 64 Federal Reserve Bulletin 481-6 (June 1978).

"Truth-In-Lending Disclosure Requirements—Security Interest in After-Acquired Consumer Goods," 42 Missouri Law Review 675-81 (Fall 1977).

WILLS

[¶4201] Before actually drafting a will, it is essential to take the client through the estate planning process described in ¶1802 et seq. The following sections provide some guides to the procedure and mechanical steps in completing a will. See ¶4204 on the important marital deduction provisions. See ¶4001 for a discussion of trusts.

[¶4202]   WILL CHECKLIST

There is an infinite variety of detail that should be considered and discussed preliminary to the preparation of a will. Much of this detail comes out of the testator's own experience, his appraisal of his property and heirs, and his aspirations for them. There are some technical matters the testator should consider, so that he can discuss them properly with the estate planner.

The following checklist is designed to stimulate the estate owner's thinking prior to the preliminary conversation with his estate planner, and to help the planner make sure he has obtained all the necessary information.

☐ *Funeral Arrangements, Upkeep of Cemetery Plot, etc.:* Instructions can be spelled out in the will. Burial instructions in a will are useless if the provisions of the will remain secret until some date after death and after burial has already taken place. The matter can be left to the discretion of the family, or a special letter may be left addressed to the executor or to the family to acquaint them with the testator's wishes.

☐ *Personal Belongings:* If the disposition of clothing, jewelry, furniture, etc., are not provided for, such articles (unless state law provides otherwise) will go into the residue of the estate and possibly impose upon the executor the obligation to sell them. Tangible personal property should always be disposed of by separate will provisions, because under IRC §662 all amounts distributed to a beneficiary for the taxable year are included in the gross income of the beneficiary to the extent of the distributable net income of the estate. Under IRC §663, any amount that, under the terms of the will, is distributed as a gift of specific property all at once or in not more than three installments is excluded from the operation of IRC §662. Thus, if the tangible personal property is separately disposed of in the will and is distributed to the legatee all at once, its distribution will have no income tax consequences. However, if disposed of as part of the residue, its distribution might be taxable as income to the legatee. It may be wise to specify in the will the individuals who are to receive the most valuable personal possessions and leave the balance to someone in whom the testator has confidence, with instructions to divide them among those close to the testator.

☐ *Cash Bequests:* When a specific amount of money is left to an individual or to a charity, the executor is required to pay that amount in full before he makes any distribution to the beneficiaries who are to share the balance of the estate. If the estate should be smaller than expected, such a cash bequest could result in unintentionally making inadequate provision for other beneficiaries.

459

Guard against this contingency by providing that cash bequests be paid only if the total estate exceeds a specified minimum, or make bequests to individuals and charities in fractions or percentages of the estate, rather than in fixed dollar amounts.

☐ ***Real Estate:*** Is solely owned real estate to be left outright, in trust (possibly a residence trust where a spouse has the rights to the house), sold and the proceeds distributed, or to one beneficiary who has the right to use it for life with ownership going to the testator's children on his death? Under the law of some states, the testator's spouse may have dower or curtesy rights in the real estate.

☐ ***Income Interests:*** The testator may want to assure a regular income for his parents, dependent relatives, or others. This can be done through a trust established by will or by directing the executors to buy annuities for named beneficiaries. In the event that a trust is established, the testator can specify the individual to whom the trust property will go after it has produced the required income for a specified period of time.

☐ ***The Remainder:*** Decide who is to share in the bulk of the estate. Then divide the balance, after specific bequests, in fractions or percentages. By being overly exact in allocating particular assets to certain beneficiaries, or in specifying interest in dollar amounts, the testator can frustrate his own objectives in the event of important changes in the size or value of the estate. If the bulk of the estate is divided into fractions of a share, the testator won't be in the position of having to revise his will repeatedly because of changes in asset values. Be sure the will names alternate or contingent beneficiaries who are to receive the share of any beneficiary who does not survive the testator.

☐ ***Protection of Interests of Minor Beneficiaries:*** It is usually necessary to have a guardian appointed by the court to manage the child's property until he attains majority. The guardian must furnish bond, make periodic accountings, and secure court approval on many of the actions he will have to take. Guardianship is both burdensome and expensive. The will can simplify this matter by directing that the property be turned over to a trust to be held for the benefit of minors until majority. The trustee can be authorized to use the trust property to provide maintenance, support, and education for the minor.

☐ ***Trust Property:*** Subject to local law, the testator can determine whether the income of trust property is to be distributed or accumulated in order to build up future value. He can also determine how much of the income is to be distributed and how much of it is to go to each beneficiary, or authorize the trustee to distribute some of the trust principal if income is insufficient to maintain the beneficiaries' living standards or meet emergencies.

☐ ***Selection of Executor and Trustee:*** An executor and possibly a trustee must be designated to handle the settlement and management of the estate. This responsibility must be accepted; the details of settling an estate must be handled. The testator's property must be managed until it is turned over to his beneficiaries. These are tasks that call for a high degree of skill and experience. The choice of an executor and trustee may determine whether the testator's plans for his family and property succeed or fail.

☐ ***Survivor's Election Wills:*** The survivor's election will is the analog in community property states to the two-trust will often used in common-law jurisdictions. In the typical survivor's election will, one spouse disposes of the entire community by creating two trusts; one is to be funded by his community property interest and the other by the second spouse's share. The trust funded with the second spouse's share (the marital trust) normally pays income to that spouse for life, the remainder to the couple's children. An independent party is usually designated the trustee with power to invade this trust (subject to an ascertainable standard) for the second spouse's benefit. The other trust can be an accumulating trust, paying income to the second spouse only if the amount paid from the marital trust falls below a predetermined figure, or it can also pay income currently. Again, the remainder of the second trust is given to the children.

This arrangement requires the second spouse's consent to the disposition made in the will, since the second spouse has an indefeasible interest in his share of the community. The consent may be given in a document signed contemporaneously with the survivor's election will or may be made after his death. Once the consent is given, it is irrevocable. If no consent is given, the second spouse usually still receives an income interest in the first spouse's estate.

☐ ***Other Points to Consider:*** Whether or not the testator has a will, changes in the law and new developments in his affairs may have made his testamentary plans obsolete. For example,

(1) Does the will take full advantage of the marital deduction?

(2) Are insurance arrangements integrated with the will?

(3) Are inheritance taxes to be paid by each beneficiary or by the estate?

(4) Should the executor have authority to carry on the business or should he be directed to dispose of it?

(5) Have safeguards been established to minimize the possibility that the testator's property will be taxed twice—once when he dies and again when his spouse dies?

(6) Has provision been made for the possibility that the testator and his spouse may die under such circumstances that it is impossible to determine who died first?

(7) Does the executor have the right to borrow money, pledge estate assets, and renew existing obligations?

(8) Should the executor have the power to retain real estate or to sell, mortgage, or lease it?

(9) Should the executor have the right to retain assets owned by the testator at the time of his death, whether or not they constitute a legal investment for trust and estate funds?

(10) Does the trustee have broad discretion in the investment and reinvestment of trust funds? Should the trustee receive any specific instructions?

(11) Have income provisions for trust beneficiaries been protected against inflation?

(12) Does the trustee have the right to make special provision for beneficiaries in the event of emergencies?

(13) Will there by enough liquid funds to meet estate tax obligations and other cash requirements that will confront the executor and trustee?

(14) Has the future distribution of the estate been studied with a view to minimizing the tax drain on the income it will produce?

(15) Does the executor have the right to file a joint income tax return with the surviving spouse?

[¶4203]　　　WILL PROVISIONS CHECKLIST

Set out below is a checklist of will provisions, in approximately the order in which they might appear in wills.

☐ *Basic Introduction Identifying Testator*

☐ *Declaration of Domicile:* of governing law, of place and probate of property covered by this will (where other property is disposed of by another will)

☐ *Revocation of Prior Wills and Codicils*

☐ *Declaration of Marital Status:* possible preliminary naming of spouse and living children, together with birthdates, and obligations arising from divorce or prenuptial agreement

☐ *Disposition of Body:* better handled by supplementary instructions to members of immediate family

☐ *Funeral Directions:* same as Disposition of Body

☐ *Cemetery, Masses, Monument,* etc.

☐ *Debts and Funeral Expenses:* long-term debts, discharge, charge to general estate or specific property

☐ *Separate Distribution of Personalty:* avoiding income to beneficiaries under IRC §662, personal and household effects, disputes, insurance

☐ *Legacies:* general, specific, demonstrative, conditional

☐ *Percentage Limitation:* general legacy, residue

☐ *Charitable Bequest:* statutory limitation, tax exemption, ability to take, contingent on size of estate

☐ *Ademption*

☐ *Abatement*

☐ *Lapse*

☐ *Advancements*

☐ *Release of Indebtedness*

☐ *Family Support During Administration:* provision for

☐ *Real Estate:* encumbrances

☐ *Life Estate:* residence, waste, sale, maintenance costs

☐ *Residence Trust*

☐ *Surviving Spouse's Rights:* election against will, antenuptial agreement (reference to in will), abandonment

☐ *Marital Deduction Bequest:* formula (pecuniary or fractional), nonformula

☐ *Residue*

☐ *Children:* adopted, afterborn, step

☐ *Class Gifts:* per capita, per stirpes

☐ *Foreign Beneficiaries*

☐ *Infants, Incompetents:* guardianship, power in trust

☐ *Trusts:* pourover, spendthrift, sprinkling, marital deduction, power of appointment, discretionary, accumulation, perpetuities, invasion of corpus for or by beneficiary, persons to receive principal, declaration of purpose (e.g., charitable)

☐ *Power of Appointment in Testator:* separate provision exercising or refraining to exercise (otherwise will may operate or may not operate, depending on applicable state law, as an exercise of the power)

☐ *Appointment of Fiduciaries:* successors and alternates, bond, compensation, foreign fiduciaries, delegation among fiduciaries, majority rule or unanimous consent, resignation of fiduciary, appointment of substitute, exoneration, replacement

☐ *Annuities:* trust or purchase of policy, assignment

☐ *Insurance Policies:* owned by testator, payable to estate, marital deduction

☐ *Common Disaster:* simultaneous death, survival for period, etc.

☐ *Taxes:* provisions for, apportionment, allocation, nontestamentary property, compromise, authority to file joint returns, elections

☐ *Business Interest:* partnership, close corporation, proprietorship, lifetime agreements, employee interests

☐ *Administrative Powers of Fiduciaries:* investments, sales and exchanges, borrowing, voting

☐ *Disinheritance*

☐ *Clauses to Avoid Litigation*

☐ *Execution:* subscription at end, sign or initial each page, attestation clause for witnesses, residence of witnesses.

[¶4204]   **MARITAL DEDUCTION BEQUESTS**

For the individual who is married and wants his spouse to be a beneficiary of the estate, the easiest and most effective way of reducing estate taxes is to take advantage of the estate tax marital deduction. The greater of $250,000 or one-half the adjusted gross estate can pass to the surviving spouse tax free. The estate tax marital deduction must be reduced by the amount of the gift tax marital deduction allowed for lifetime gifts to a spouse in excess of 50% of the value of the gift. Of course, if the marital deduction property is not used up, it will be taxed in the survivor's estate. Special rules under IRC §2056 determine whether the type of interest passing to the surviving spouse qualifies for the marital deduction.

[¶4204.1]   **The Marital Deduction Trust**

In order to qualify a bequest in trust to the surviving spouse for the marital deduction, one requirement is that the survivor must be given ultimate control over the property.

The outline of one widely used form of the "marital deduction trust" method of property distribution is as follows:

(1) The testator directs by will that his estate should be divided into two equal parts.

(2) The first part (the maximum amount qualifying for the marital deduction)

is placed in a trust at his death for the benefit of the surviving spouse. The income from the property in the trust is paid to the spouse for life. The surviving spouse is given the power of appointment to direct in his will how and to whom the property should be distributed at his death. The testator's will also directs that the trust property pass to his children at the survivor's death in the event that the survivor failed to exercise the power of appointment.

(3) The will directs that all the taxes, charges, and expenses against the estate be paid out of the second part of the estate.

(4) The will directs that the balance remaining of the second part of his estate be transferred to a second trust. The income of this second trust is also paid to the surviving spouse for life. The property itself is distributed to the children at the survivor's death.

The above four-step outline sets forth the bare mechanics of IRC §2056. Provisions can be inserted to add to the trusts' flexibility. Forms to implement this outline and other marital deduction trust methods will be found in *IBP Estate Planning, Vol. II—Checklists/Forms*.

[¶4204.2]   Tax Formula Clauses

In planning for maximum overall estate tax savings, the objective is to come as close as possible to equalizing the taxable estates of the property owner and his spouse.

To obtain the maximum marital deduction, a formula marital deduction clause in the will is necessary. Without such a clause, the property owner can only estimate whether he is giving his spouse an amount equal to the maximum marital deduction. A subsequent increase or decrease in the first estate can cause either an underqualification or an overqualification. A tax formula clause, being based upon the value of the estate at the time of death (or alternative valuation date), assures that the surviving spouse will receive an amount exactly equal to the maximum marital deduction.

Although there are variations, the two main types of formula clauses are the pecuniary bequest and the fraction of the residue formula. The first provides for an amount equal to the greater of $250,000 or 50% of the adjusted gross estate to go to the surviving spouse; the second gives the surviving spouse that fraction of the residue that will equal the maximum marital deduction. In substance, they both aim at and achieve the same thing—the exact maximum marital deduction.

[¶4204.3]   The Nonmarital Deduction Trust

The nonmarital deduction property, if left outright, will be taxed both in the decedent's estate and again in the survivor's estate upon his subsequent death unless consumed or given away in the period between the two deaths. Thus, there is a good possibility that by the time the property reaches the children it will have been depleted by estate taxes in both parents' estates. By placing the property that qualifies for the deduction in a marital deduction trust and the remaining property in a second trust, the maximum marital deduction can be assured and a double estate tax on the nonmarital deduction property avoided.

The second trust, in a typical two-trust arrangement, is set up primarily for the protection of the surviving spouse during his life, but without giving him such control over the trust as to make its principal taxable on the survivor's subsequent death.

This kind of trust has the following objectives and possibilities:

(1) Income tax savings may be achieved by setting up a separate trust for each child beneficiary so that each trust will be considered a separate taxpayer. This accomplishes a division of the total income among several taxable entities, bringing lower annual income tax brackets into play.

(2) Provision may be made for the surviving spouse to receive the annual income from the trust property.

(3) It may not be desirable to direct the income to the surviving spouse if it will put him into an excessively high income tax bracket at a time when he will no longer enjoy the benefit of split income. In this case, provision may be made for the accumulation of trust income, state law permitting, or the distribution of trust income to the children, and protection for the survivor by giving the trustee discretion to apply the principal for the support and maintenance of the spouse and children if necessary.

(4) The trustee may be directed to "sprinkle" as much of the income of the nonmarital trust among the spouse, children, and the grandchildren of the testator as their maintenance and educational requirements dictate.

(5) The ultimate distribution of the corpus of the second trust must be specified. Provision may be made for the distribution of the corpus of each of the separate trusts when the child beneficiary attains a specified age, or portions of the corpus at various ages.

[¶4205]   **BEQUESTS TO ORPHANS**

Bequests to orphaned minor children are deductible for estate tax purposes. The orphans' deduction, similar to the marital deduction, is significant when the decedent's estate exceeds the exemption equivalent to the prevailing unified credit. The amount that may be deducted from the decedent's estate for each orphan cannot exceed an amount equal to $5,000 multiplied by the difference between the child's age at the decedent's death and 21. To illustrate, suppose a widower leaves three minor children surviving, aged 15, 6, and 3 years. The amount that may be deducted from the widower's estate is $5,000 multiplied by (21 − 15) plus (21 − 6) plus (21 − 3), or $5,000 times 39, which equals $195,000. If the widower dies after 1980, as much as $370,000 can be passed to his children tax free ($195,000 under the orphans' deductions and about $175,000 under the exemption equivalent to the unified credit after 1980). As this example demonstrates, the orphans' deduction provision can be a substantial benefit for estates of moderately wealthy testators with several young children.

Obviously, an outright bequest to a minor child qualifies for the deduction. However, it is more common for the testator to set up some sort of trust for the benefit of the children. When a trust is used, the terminable interest rules set forth under IRC §2056 must be observed if the orphans' deduction is to be preserved. Among the other factors the testator must consider when setting up the orphans' bequest are the size of his estate, the varying needs of the children, the tax need for such a bequest, the practicality of creating one or more trusts for the children, and whether each orphan should share equally in his estate.

[¶4205.1]   Qualified Minors' Trust

Under the 1976 Tax Reform Act, it was not possible to create a single trust for several orphaned children, unless the trust provided for separate shares for each child. The Revenue Act of 1978, however, permits an orphans' deduction for single ("pot") trusts if they meet certain qualifications (which relate to funding, beneficiary designations, distributions, and termination). Trustees of these "qualified minors' trusts" may accumulate income and make disproportionate distributions, provided that distributions are made under certain ascertainable standards and that each child will receive a pro rata portion of the trust upon its termination. The 1978 Act also extends the permissible duration of orphans' trusts until the youngest child reaches age 23.

[¶4206]   PREREQUISITES FOR VALID WILLS

A number of conditions must be satisfied before a document can be judicially accepted as a decedent's last will and testament.

☐ *Testamentary Capacity:* An individual of sound mind is considered competent to dispose of his property by will. As a corollary rule, minors are not deemed capable of making wills; the age requirement varies from state to state.

Therefore, if the testator understands what he is doing, generally knows the nature and extent of his property, knows who his next of kin are, and understands the provisions of his will, he is deemed capable of making and executing a will.

☐ *Intent to Make a Will:* The intent to make a will, manifested by a positive act (such as the naming of an executor), is also required.

☐ *Knowledge:* An understanding of the contents of one's will is another prerequisite.

☐ *Formal Requirements:* A will must comply with several statutory rules. In general, a will must be in writing and signed by the testator before several witnesses. Some jurisdictions require an individual to communicate to the witness that the document he is signing is, in fact, his will. Attestation—that is, an affirmance by witness that the will has been signed in accordance with statutory requirements—may also be required in some states.

☐ *Revocation:* A will may be revoked wholly or partially by operation of law, e.g., the death of a spouse, subsequent birth of a child, or by an act performed by the testator (or another at his direction). The basic requirement here is that the testator must intend to revoke the will. This can be accomplished by physical destruction or impliedly by the terms of a later will. (See Appendix.)

☐ **Special Wills:** Contracts to make wills are generally recognized. They do not have to comply with statutory provisions pertaining to wills but do, of course, have to be valid contracts.

Holographic wills (wills written entirely in an individual's own handwriting) and noncupative wills (oral wills) are valid in certain circumstances (e.g., if made by soldiers and sailors). Local law must be checked to determine the validity of these instruments.

☐ **Other Elements:** In addition to the conditions listed above, a will cannot be probated if it has been procured through undue influence, fraud, or mistake.

[¶4207] EXECUTION AND MAINTENANCE OF A WILL

The execution of a will should take place under the supervision of an attorney who is fully familiar with the requirements for the execution of wills. Only in exceptional cases should a will be executed without the presence of an attorney.

Strict observance of the statutory formalities governing the execution of wills is a must. To avoid invalidity or litigation, the attorney drafting the will must assume that the will may be offered for probate anywhere. In general, the validity of a will is judged by the law of the situs as to immovables and the law of the decedent's domicile at death as to movables. Every attorney should establish the exact procedure that will satisfy the laws of all states and follow it.

[¶4208] CHECKLIST FOR EXECUTING A WILL

The first step is to carefully check the statutory requirements of state law. The following checklist can help assure that the statutory requirements are observed.

☐ The will should be declared in an instrument in writing.

☐ The testator should sign it; if he can't do so, another person should sign for him in his presence and at his request.

☐ This signature of either the testator or the person who signs for him must follow the text of the will immediately, without leaving any intervening space.

☐ At least three witnesses should attest the testator's signature.

☐ None of the witnesses should be a beneficiary or person with a financial interest in the estate.

☐ The testator should expressly:

    (a) Declare the instrument to be his will; and

    (b) Ask the attesting witnesses to witness "the execution of his will."

☐ All the witnesses to the testator's signature should either:

    (a) See him sign; or

    (b) Hear him say that he acknowledges as his own a signature that is already on the instrument and that is pointed out to them and actually seen by all of them. If he can't write his signature, all of the witnesses should observe that:

    (1) The testator expressly requests the person who signs for him to sign; and

    (2) The person requested does sign in the presence of the testator.

☐ Each witness should sign his name and write his address in the testator's presence.

☐ All of the witnesses, the testator, and (if that is the case) the one who signs for the testator, should be present simultaneously throughout the entire process of execution. (Even if not required in some states, it is good practice to have witnesses and testator present throughout and see each other sign the will.)

☐ The will should be dated by fully and correctly stating the place and the day, month, and year it was executed.

☐ The typical attestation clause recites the formalities of execution in some detail. If none of the witnesses is available at the time of probate, the clause can be used to show that the statutory requirements were observed. It is not required by most states, but is used by most draftsmen.

The procedure of execution should follow precisely the statements that appear in the attestation clause. So where the clause recites ". . . this attestation clause having first been read aloud," the clause should be read out loud so all those present can hear what has been said. Such a reading seems more effective than merely having the witnesses sign below the attestation clause.

☐ Only the original of the will should be subscribed by the testator and the witnesses. If more than one copy of a will has been executed, all copies must be produced at the probate or their absence satisfactorily explained. For example, in most states, when an executed will or copy was known to be in the possession of the testator but it cannot be found at the time of probate, there is a presumption that the will was revoked by destruction by the testator.

To avoid the possibility that the testator might inadvertently sign a copy of his will at a later date, it may be a good idea to conform all copies at the time of execution.

☐ The original will should be placed in a safe place as soon as possible after execution. For convenience, the safe deposit box of either the drafter or the named executor would be suitable. If the testator's box is used, a court order to open the box must be obtained after the testator's death in most states before the will can be obtained. Also, if the original is in the possession of the testator, failure to produce it at the time of probate will bring into play the presumption of revocation by destruction by the testator. Some states provide for filing wills with the probate courts for safekeeping, but not much use is made of such provisions.

☐ Prior wills are, normally, revoked by later ones by specific language to that effect. But where nothing is said about prior wills, a will of prior date would be effective to dispose of property not covered by the later will. Also, where the testator has property in a number of states and foreign countries, it is not at all uncommon for him to have an "American Will," "French Will," etc., each disposing of property within the stated countries or places. In these instances, all pertinent wills would be probatable and should be treated as if they were the original and kept in the same place.

In other cases, a later will may be invalid for a number of reasons such as lack of testamentary capacity. In such cases, a prior last will, executed during a time when the testator did have testamentary capacity, may well be probatable.

WITNESSES

Although most states require only two witnesses, it is good practice to have three whenever possible. The will is then qualified for probate (at least as to the number of witnesses) in every state. Even though only two witnesses prove necessary, having a choice makes it easier to obtain two witnesses at probate.

Since the witnesses may be considered the most qualified persons to testify as to the testamentary capacity of the testator, if there are apt to be any questions on this score, they should be persons who know the testator well, can give favorable testimony, and are likely to be available when needed. The drafter should be a witness unless he is named as a beneficiary, since he is perhaps the best qualified to testify as to the testamentary capacity of the testator.

If the testator wishes a beneficiary to be a witness, he should be informed that should such beneficiary be necessary as a witness to probate the will, he may lose his bequest (at least to the extent it exceeds his intestate share).

[¶4210]   **MAINTAINING THE WILL**

To ensure that the will is kept intact and no pages or provisions are substituted, the following procedures are suggested:

(1) When a will is being typed, make it an invariable practice to use the same typewriter throughout. This may facilitate detection of forgery by typewriter.

(2) Avoid erasures (never allow corrections of figures or names). Use uniform margins at top, bottom, and sides of each page leaving as little room as possible for additional words to be filled in. Some drafters make it a practice to rule out all blank spaces at the end of sentences, etc.

(3) Tie the pages together with a ribbon and seal the ribbon on the last page, next to the testator's signature. Staples, brass fasteners, and the like may be removed and replaced without detection and don't give much protection.

(4) Have the testator sign or initial each page in the margin and refer to this fact in the attestation clause. A signature is harder to imitate than initials and so gives better protection.

[¶4211]   **FOR FURTHER REFERENCE . . .**

Becker, D.M., "Broad perspective in the Development of a Flexible Estate Plan," 63 Iowa Law Review 751-821 (April 1978).

Berall, "Drafting Wills and Trusts for Second Marriages: What Factors the Practitioner Must Consider," 4 Estate Planning 308 (1977).

Brody, "Benefits of Joint, Mutual, or Reciprocal Wills Are Often Outweighed by Their Tax Drawbacks," 5 Taxation for Lawyers 218 (1977).

Browder, O.L., "Giving or Leaving—What Is a Will" 75 Michigan Law Review 845-86 (April-May 1977).

Dukeminier and Johanson, *Family Wealth Transactions,* Little Brown and Co., Boston, Massachusetts.

Erdman, J., *Complete Guide to the Marital Deduction in Estate Planning,* Institute for Business Planning, Inc., Englewood Cliffs, N.J. (1978).

Gulliver, Clark, Lusky, and Murphy, *Gratuitous Transfers.* West Publishing Co., St. Paul, Minnesota.

Lehrman, A., *Complete Book of Wills and Trusts,* Institute for Business Planning, Inc., Englewood Cliffs, N.J. (1978).

APPENDIX

PRINCIPAL GOVERNMENT
REGULATORY AGENCIES

The Executive Office of the President and the Office of the Vice President are located at 1600 Pennsylvania Avenue, N.W., Washington, D.C. 20500.
Telephone number for President/Vice President is (202) 456-1414 (switchboard).

Name	*Address*	
Council on Environmental Quality	722 Jackson Place NW Washington, D.C. 20006	General Counsel: (202) 382-7965
Council on Wage and Price Stability	726 Jackson Place NW Washington, D.C. 20506	General Counsel: (202) 456-2653
Office of Management and Budget	726 Jackson Place NW Washington, D.C. 20503	Ass't to the Director of Public Affairs: (202) 395-4747
Office of the Special Representative for Trade Negotiations	1800 G St. NW Washington, D.C. 20506	General Counsel: (202) 395-5116
Department of Agriculture	Independence & 14th St. SW Washington, D.C. 20250	
International Affairs and Commodity Programs		Director of Foreign Marketing Information: (202) 447-3448 General Counsel: (202) 447-3351
Department of the Air Force	The Pentagon Washington, D.C. 20330	Ass't. General Counsel for Procurement: (202) 695-3928
Department of Commerce	14th St. & Constitution Ave. NW Washington, D.C. 20230	Assistant Secretary for Domestic and International Business: (202) 337-2867
Domestic and International Business Administration (Public Information)		General Counsel: (202) 337-4772 (202) 337-3808
Patent and Trade Mark Office		Director of the Office of Informational Services: (202) 557-3428

Name	Address	
Department of Defense	The Pentagon Washington, D.C. 20301	Office of General Counsel: (202) 695-3341
Department of Health, Education and Welfare	330 Independence Ave. SW Washington, D.C. 20201	Office of Consumer Affairs: (202) 245-6158 General Counsel: (202) 245-7780
Public Health Service: Center for Disease Control	1600 Clifton Rd. NE Atlanta, Ga. 30333	Information: (404) 633-3286
Social Security Administration	330 Independence Ave. SW Washington, D.C. 20201	Ass't General Counsel: (202) 594-2410
Department of Housing and Urban Development	451 Seventh St. SW Washington, D.C. 20410	General Counsel: (202) 755-7244 Ass't. Sec'y. for Fair Housing & Equal Opportunity: (202) 755-7252
Federal Insurance Administration		Administrator: (202) 755-6770
Department of the Interior	18th St. & C St. NW Washington, D.C. 20270	Bureau of Indian Affairs: (202) 343-5116 Solicitor: (202) 343-4722
Department of Justice	Constitution Ave & 9th St. NW Washington, D.C. 20530	Office of the Pardon Attorney: (202) 739-2894 U.S. Marshall's Service: (202) 739-5345 Immigration & Naturalization Service: (202) 376-8330 Anti-Trust Division Ass't. Attorney General: (202) 739-2401 Tax Division Ass't. Attorney General: (202) 739-2901 Board of Parole, Chairman: (202) 739-2871

Name	Address	
Department of Labor	200 Constitution Ave. NW Washington, D.C. 20210	Office of the Solicitor: (202) 523-7675 Occupational Safety & Health Administra- tion: (202) 523-6091 Employment Standards (Wage & Hour Division) Administrator: (202) 523-8305
Department of the Navy	The Pentagon Washington, D.C. 20350	Office of General Counsel: (202) 692-7328
Department of State	2201 C St. NW Washington, D.C. 20520	Office of the Legal Advisor: (202) 632-9598
Department of Transportation	400 7th St. SW Washington, D.C. 20590	Contract Appeals Board: (202) 426-4305 General Counsel: (202) 425-4972 Federal Aviation Administration Information Services: (202) 426-3883 Federal Highway Administration: (202) 426-0740 Urban Mass Transportation Administration (Counsel): (202) 426-4063
Department of Treasury	15th & Pennsylvania Ave. NW Washington, D.C. 20220	General Counsel: (202) 964-2093 Bureau of Alcohol Tobacco and Firearms (Counsel): (202) 961-7772 Comptroller of the Currency (Counsel): (202) 447-1896 U.S. Custom Service (Counsel): (202) 964-5476 Internal Revenue Service Chief Counsel: (202) 964-6364

INDEPENDENT AGENCIES

Name	*Address*	
Advisory Committee for Trade Negotiations	1800 G St. NW Washington, D.C. 20506	Executive Director: (202) 395-6131
Board of Governors of The Federal Reserve System	Federal Reserve Bldg. Constitution Ave. Washington, D.C. 20551	General Counsel: (202) 452-3293
Civil Aeronautics Board	1825 Connecticut Ave. NW Washington, D.C. 20428	General Counsel: (202) 382-7561
Commodity Futures Trading Commission	203 K St. NW Washington, D.C. 20581	General Counsel: (202) 254-8058
Consumer Product Safety Commission	1750 K St. NW Washington, D.C. 20207	General Counsel: (202) 634-7770
Environmental Protection Agency	401 M St. SW (waterside) Washington, D.C. 20460	General Counsel: (202) 755-0555
Equal Employment Opportunity Commission	2401 E St. NW Washington, D.C. 20506	General Counsel: (202) 634-6400
Federal Communications Commission	1919 M St. NW Washington, D.C. 20554	General Counsel: (202) 632-7020
Federal Election Commission	1325 K St. NW Washington, D.C. 20463	Informational Services: (202) 382-3192
Federal Trade Commission	Pennsylvania Ave. & 6th St. NW Washington, D.C. 20580	General Counsel: (202) 523-6313
General Services Administration	18th & F St. NW Washington, D.C., 20405	Director of Contract Compliance General Counsel: (202) 343-4284
Interstate Commerce Commission	12th & Constitution Ave. NW Washington, D.C. 20423	General Counsel: (202) 275-7312 Chief Administrative Law Judge: (202) 275-7408
National Labor Relations Board	1717 Pennsylvania Ave. NW Washington, D.C. 20570	General Counsel: (202) 254-5150
Occupational Safety and Health Review Commission	1825 K St. NW Washington, D.C. 20006	Information: (202) 634-7943
Overseas Private Investment Corporation	1129 20th St. NW Washington, D.C. 20527	General Counsel: (202) 632-1766

Independent Agencies *(continued)*

Name	*Address*	
Postal Rate Commission	2000 L St. NW Washington, D.C. 20268	Administrative Law Judge: (202) 254-3820 General Counsel: (202) 254-3824
Securities and Exchange Commission	500 N. Capital St. NW Washington, D.C. 20549	General Counsel: (202) 755-1108 Public Information: (202) 755-1712
Small Business Administration	1441 L St. NW Washington, D.C. 20416	General Counsel: (202) 382-5414
U.S. International Trade Commission	701 E St. NW Washington, D.C. 20436	General Counsel: (202) 523-0350
Veterans Administration	Vermont & H Sts. NW Washington, D.C. 20420	Dept. of Veterans Benefits Director: (202) 389-2455

475

FILING OF INCORPORATION PAPERS

In most jurisdictions, the charter and related papers must be filed with the secretary of state or other state officer. Except for two states, as indicated by asterisk, this state officer is also empowered to receive service of process against a corporation chartered in the state. Here is a list of the appropriate state officers:

State	Filing
Alabama	Secretary of State Montgomery, Alabama 36100
Alaska	Commissioner of Commerce Juneau, Alaska 99801
Arizona	Corporation Commission Phoenix, Arizona 85000
Arkansas	Secretary of State Little Rock, Arkansas 72200
California	Secretary of State Sacramento, California 95801
Colorado	Secretary of State Denver, Colorado 80200
Connecticut	Secretary of State Hartford, Connecticut 06100
Delaware	Secretary of State Dover, Delaware 19901
District of Columbia	Office of Supt. of Corporations Washington, D.C. 20001
Florida	Secretary of State Tallahassee, Florida 32301
Georgia	Secretary of State Atlanta, Georgia 30300
Hawaii	Director of Regulation Agencies P.O. Box 40 Honolulu, Hawaii 96810
Idaho*	Secretary of State Boise, Idaho 83700
Illinois	Secretary of State Springfield, Illinois 62700
Indiana	Secretary of State Indianapolis, Indiana 46200
Iowa	Secretary of State Des Moines, Iowa 50300
Kansas	Secretary of State Topeka, Kansas 66600

*Service of process is made upon the county auditor.

State	Filing
Kentucky	Secretary of State Frankfort, Kentucky 40601
Louisiana	Secretary of State Baton Rouge, Louisiana 70800
Maine	Secretary of State Augusta, Maine 04301
Maryland	State Dept. of Assessments and Taxation Baltimore, Maryland 21200
Massachusetts	Secretary of the Commonwealth Boston, Massachusetts 02100
Michigan	Department of Commerce Corporation Division P.O. Drawer C Lansing, Michigan 48904
Minnesota	Secretary of State St. Paul, Minnesota 55100
Mississippi	Secretary of State Jackson, Mississippi 39200
Missouri	Secretary of State Jefferson City, Missouri 65101
Montana	Secretary of State Helena, Montana 59601
Nebraska	Secretary of State Lincoln, Nebraska 68500
Nevada	Secretary of State Carson City, Nevada 89701
New Hampshire	Secretary of State Concord, New Hampshire 03300
New Jersey	Secretary of State Trenton, New Jersey 08600
New Mexico	State Corporation Commission Santa Fe, New Mexico 87501
New York	Secretary of State Albany, New York 12200
North Carolina	Secretary of State Raleigh, North Carolina 27600
North Dakota	Secretary of State Bismarck, North Dakota 58501
Ohio	Secretary of State Columbus, Ohio 43200
Oklahoma	Secretary of State Oklahoma City, Oklahoma 73100

State	Filing
Oregon	Corporation Commissioner Salem, Oregon 97301
Pennsylvania*	Department of State Harrisburg, Pennsylvania 17101
Puerto Rico	Secretary of State P.O. Box 3271 San Juan, Puerto Rico 00904
Rhode Island	Secretary of State Providence, Rhode Island 02900
South Carolina	Secretary of State Columbia, South Carolina 29200
South Dakota	Secretary of State Pierre, South Dakota 57501
Tennessee	Secretary of State Nashville, Tennessee 37200
Texas	Secretary of State Austin, Texas 78700
Utah	Secretary of State Salt Lake City, Utah 84100
Vermont	Secretary of State Montpelier, Vermont 05601
Virginia	State Corporation Commission Richmond, Virginia 23200
Washington	Secretary of State Olympia, Washington 98501
West Virginia	Secretary of State Charleston, West Virginia 25300
Wisconsin	Secretary of State Madison, Wisconsin 53700
Wyoming	Secretary of State Cheyenne, Wyoming 82001

*Service of process is made upon the Secretary of the Commonwealth, Harrisburg, Pa. 17101

INCORPORATING FEES (Principal Incorporating States)

The tables below are designed as a quick and ready reference to determine the costs incident to organizing corporations:

Alabama

☐ **Organization fee**—for filing and issuance of certificate of incorporation—$10, plus 15¢ per 100 words.

☐ **Charter tax**—$1 for every $1,000 of authorized stock, minimum of $5.

☐ No-par value stock is taken at actual value if value is shown, otherwise at $100 per share.

☐ **Paid-in capital requirement**—$1,000 and 20% of the subscribed capital.

Alaska

☐ **Organization fee**—based on authorized capital stock:

Authorized Capital Stock	Fee
$100,000 or less	$30
Over $100,000, but not over $1,000,000	$30, plus 20¢ for each $1,000 or fraction over $100,000
Over $1,000,000	$210, plus $15 for each $1,000,000 or fraction over $1,000,000

If no-par, stock valued at $10 per share.

☐ **Filing fee:** $30.

Arizona

☐ **Organization fee:**
Filing articles of incorporation .... $50.

Arkansas

☐ **Organization fee:**
(a) **Par Value Shares**

Up to $100,000 par value	$15
Over $100,000 and up to $1,000,000	$15 plus $1 for each $10,000 of value over $100,000
Over $1,000,000 and up to $10,000,000	$105 plus $1 for each $20,000 of value over $1,000,000
Over $10,000,000	$555 plus $1 for each $40,000 of value over $10,000,000

(b) **No-Par Value Shares**

Up to and including 2,000 shares	$15
Over 2,000 up to 10,000 shares	$15 plus $5 per 1,000 shares up to 10,000

Arkansas *(continued)*

Over 10,000 and up to 100,000 shares .... $55 plus $2.50 per 1,000 shares
up to 100,000

Over 100,000 shares .... $280 plus $1 per 1,000 shares
over 100,000

Minimum is $15. Fees are computed to the nearest $1.
If both par and no-par stock issued, fees computed separately for each class.

☐ **Paid-in capital requirement**—$300.

California

☐ **Organization fee**—a flat fee of $65 payable to Secretary of State. There is no fee based on authorized share structure.

☐ **Franchise tax**—prepayment of $200 minimum tax to franchise tax board, upon filing of articles of incorporation.

Colorado

☐ **Organization fee:**
Filing articles of incorporation .... $22.50, plus 2.25 for old age pen-
sion

Connecticut

☐ **Organization fee:** None.

☐ **Franchise tax:** 1¢ per share. Minimum franchise tax is $50.

☐ Filing certificate of incorporation .... $20.

☐ **Paid-in capital requirement**—$1,000.

Delaware

☐ **Organization fee** is based on authorized capital stock as follows:
(a) **Par Value Shares**
Up to $2,000,000 .... 1¢ per $100
$2,000,001 to $20,000,000 .... $200, plus ½¢ for each $100 over
$2,000,000
Over $20,000,000 .... $1,000, plus 1/5¢ for each $100
over $20,000,000

(b) **No-Par Value Shares**
Up to 20,000 shares .... ½¢ per share
20,001 shares to 2,000,000 shares .... $100, plus ¼¢ for each share over
20,000.
Over 2,000,000 shares .... $5,050, plus 1/5¢ for each share
over 2,000,000

Minimum tax is $10.

480

Delaware *(continued)*

☐ Fee for receiving, filing, and indexing certificate ..$25.

☐ Recording fee which varies according to county and amount of pages.

District of Columbia

☐ **Organization fee:**

Authorized Shares	Fee
Up to 10,000 shares	2¢ per share
The next 40,000 shares	1¢ per share
All shares over 50,000	½¢ per share

☐ **License fee—Minimum of $10.**

☐ Filing of articles of incorporation—$20.

☐ **Paid-in capital requirement—$1,000.**

Florida

☐ **Organization fee:**
(a) **Par Value Shares**

Up to $125,000	$4 per $1,000
$125,001 to $1,000,000	$500 plus $1 per $1,000 over $25,000
$1,000,001 to $2,000,000	$1,375 plus 50¢ per $1,000 over $1,000,000
Over $2,000,000	$1,875 plus 25¢ per $1,000 over $2,000,000

(b) **No Par Value Shares**

Up to 1,250 shares	50¢ per share
1,251 to 10,000 shares	$625 plus 10¢ per share over 1,250
10,001 to 20,000 shares	$1,500 plus 1/20¢ per share over 10,000
Over 20.000 shares	$1,505 plus 1/40¢ per share over 20,000

Minimum filing tax is $30.

☐ Filing certificate of designation of address of office for service of process and of resident agent, $3.

Georgia

☐ No incorporation fee.

☐ **County filing fee—$15, where Superior Court grants incorporation.**

481

Georgia *(continued)*

☐ **State filing fee**—$100 for Secretary of State granting charter.

☐ **Paid-in capital requirement**—$500.

Hawaii

☐ **Organization fees:** 20¢ per $1,000 on total amount of authorized capital. Minimum of $50. Maximum of $1,000.

☐ **Paid-in capital requirement**—$1,000 and 75% of subscribed capital stock.

Idaho

☐ **Organization fee:**

Authorized Capital Stock	Fee
When it does not exceed $25,000	$ 20
When it exceeds $25,000 and does not exceed $50,000	$ 40
When it exceeds $50,000 and does not exceed $100,000	$ 75
When it exceeds $100,000 and does not exceed $500,000	$100
When it exceeds $500,000 and does not exceed $1,000,000	$125
When it exceeds $1,000,000	$200

No-par stock is deemed to have a value of $100 per share.

☐ **Miscellaneous fees**—approximately $20.

Illinois

☐ **License tax**—based on value of entire consideration received for issued shares, at rate of 1/20 of 1%.

☐ No-par value stock is taken at consideration received therefore,
less: any part allocated to paid-in surplus, and
less: expenses of issuance.

☐ **Filing fee**—$75

☐ **Paid-in capital requirement**—$1,000.

Indiana

☐ **Organization fee**—par or no-par:

Authorized Shares	Fee
First 200,000 shares	2¢ per share
Next 800,000 shares	1¢ per share
All additional shares	2/10¢ per share

Minimum fee is $30 (1,000 shares or less).

☐ Fee of $4 for certificates of incorporation and $2 for each impression of seal.

☐ **Paid-in capital requirement**—$1,000.

Iowa

☐ **Organization fee** for filing articles of incorporation and issuance of the certificate of incorporation—$20.

☐ **Recording fee**—50¢ per page.

Kansas

☐ **Application and recordation fee**—$50.

☐ **Incidental fees**—approximately $30.

Kentucky

☐ **Organization fee:**

(a) **Par Value Shares**	Fee
1-20,000 shares	1¢ per share
Next 180,000 shares	1/2¢ per share
Balance over 200,000 shares	1/5¢ per share
(b) **No-Par Value Shares**	
1-20,000 shares	1/2¢ per share
Next 180,000 shares	1/4¢ per share
Balance over 200,000 shares	1/5¢ per share

Minimum fee is $10.

☐ **Filing fee**—$15; $5 for recording with County Clerk.

Louisiana

☐ **Organization fee:**

(a) **Par Value Shares**	Fee
Par value under $25,000	$10
Par value over $25,000	$50

483

Louisiana *(continued)*

(b) **No-Par Value Shares**

Under 10,000 shares $10

Over 10,000 shares $50

☐   **Paid-in capital**—only if there is a provision in the articles of incorporation.

Maine

☐   **Filing fee:** $5 plus $1 per page for filing articles plus $5 for each certificate.

☐   **Organization fee:**

(a) **Par Value Shares**   **Tax**

$2,000,000 or less	$10 for each $100,000
$2,000,001 to $20,000,000	$200 plus $50 for each $1,000,000 over $2,000,000
Over $20,000,000	$1,100 plus $20 for each $1,000,000 over $20,000,000

(b) **No-Par Shares**

20,000 shares or less	½¢ per share, but not less than $10
Over 20,000 to 2,000,000 shares	$100 plus ¼¢ per share
Over 2,000,000 shares	$5,050 plus 1/5¢ per share

Minimum tax is $10 ($20 if both par and no-par shares are used).

☐   Incidental and filing fees—$65.

☐   Articles of incorporation—$50.

Maryland

☐   **Organization fee:**

Authorized Capital Stock	Fee
Up to and including $100,000	$20
Over $100,000 up to and including $1,000,000	$20 plus $1 for each $5,000 or fraction in excess of $100,000
Over $1,000,000 up to and including $2,000,000 ...	$200 plus $10 for each $100,000 or fraction in excess of $1,000,000
Over $2,000,000 up to and incuding $5,000,000	$300 plus $15 for each $500,000 or fraction in excess of $2,000,000
Over $5,000,000	$390 plus $20 for each $1,000,000 or fraction in excess of $5,000,000

No-par value stock valued at $20 for tax purposes.

Minimum tax is $20.

Maryland *(continued)*

☐ **Recording fee**—$20 plus $2 for each page over 5.

Massachusetts

☐ **Organization fee**—1/20 of 1 per cent of total amount of authorized capital stock with par value and 1¢ per share for all no-par shares.

Minimum fee is $125 on original amount authorized.

☐ No additional filing fees.

Michigan

☐ **Organization fee**—½ mill per $1 of authorized capital stock. Fee on no-par shares is based on amounts proposed to be received for them.

Dollar value of no-par stock for computation of franchise fee is amount of consideration received for each share that shall be allocated to stated capital.

Minimum fee is $25.

Maximum fee for domestic regulated investment companies is $40.

Minnesota

☐ **Organization fee**—$62.50 for the first $25,000 or fraction thereof or par value of authorized capital stock. Add $1.25 for each $1,000 or fraction thereof over $25,000.

No-par stock is valued at $10 per share for computation of fees with certain exceptions.

Minimum stated capital for beginning business is $1,000.

☐ **Filing fee**—$12.50

☐ **Paid-in capital requirement**—$1,000.

Mississippi

☐ **Organization fee:**

Up to and including $5,000 in authorized capital stock	$25
Over $5,000 capital stock	$25 for first $5,000 plus $2 each $1,000 or fraction thereof over $5,000.

Minimum fee is $25; Maximum fee is $500.

Mississippi *(continued)*

Where there is no-par stock, fee calculated on sale price fixed by the charter of the corporation or, if articles fail to fix sale price, maximum fee, less sums previously paid, must be deposited.

☐ **Paid-in capital requirement—$1,000.**

Missouri

☐ **Organization fee:**
$30,000 or less authorized capital stock	$50
Over $30,000	$50 plus $5 for each $10,000 over $30,000.

No-par stock is valued at the sale price; however, it cannot be issued for consideration of less than $1.

Montana

☐ **License fee**—based on number of taxable shares.
(a) Par value shares: Each $100 unit = 1 taxable share.
(b) No-par shares: Each authorized share is considered having $1 par value (every 100 shares = 1 taxable share).

Taxable Shares	Fee
1 through 1,000 shares	10¢ for each share
1,001 through 2,500 shares	8¢ for each additional share through 2,500 shares
2,501 through 5,000 shares	6¢ for each additional share through 5,000 shares
5,001 through 10,000 shares	4¢ for each additional share through 10,000 shares
All shares in excess of 10,000	2¢ for each additional share over 10,000 shares

Minimum license fee is $50.

Nebraska

☐ **Organization fee:**
Authorized Capital Stock	Fee
$10,000 or less	$20
Over $10,000 but not exceeding $25,000	$35
Over $25,000 but not exceeding $50,00	$50
Over $50,000 but not exceeding $75,000	$75
Over $75,000 but not exceeding $100,000 ...	$100 plus $1.00 for each $1,000 in excess of $100,000

Minimum fee is $20.

Nebraska *(continued)*

☐ **Filing fee:** $2 per page plus $5.00 for certificate with seal.

☐ **City Clerk:** $4 for first 200 words and 6¢ for each 10 words thereafter for articles filed in his office.

Nevada

☐ **Organization fee:**

Authorized Capital Stock	Fee
$25,000 or less	$50
$25,000.01-75,000	$75
$75,000.01-200,000	$115
$200,000.01-500,000	$175
$500,000.01-1,000,000	$250
Over $1,000,000	$250 for first $1,000,000 and $125 for each additional $500,000 or fraction thereof

No-par is considered to be $10 per share.

If both par and no-par stock is issued, the value of shares for fee purposes is the aggregate par value of shares with par value plus the product of the number of no-par shares multiplied by $10.

Minimum fee is $50.

New Hampshire

☐ **Organization fee:** (includes issuing of certificate of incorporation):

Authorized Capital Stock	Fee
$15,000 or less	$ 60
Over $15,000 up to $50,000	$ 100
Over $50,000 up to $150,000	$ 300
Over $150,000 up to $250,000	$ 400
Over $250,000 up to $500,000	$ 800
Over $500,000 up to $1,000,000	$1500
Each additional $100,000 above $1,000,000	$ 100

No-par value stock is valued at $50 per share for first 20,000 shares and $1 per share thereafter.

New Jersey

☐ **Organization fee**—Based upon number of shares of authorized capital stock.

Rate is 1¢ per share up to and including first 10,000 share and 1/10¢ per share in excess of 10,000 shares.

Minimum fee is $25; Maximum fee is $1,000.

☐ **Filing fee**—$35.

New Mexico

☐ **Organization fee**—$1 on each $1,000 of authorized capital stock.

☐ No-par value stock is valued at $1 per share.

☐ Minimum fee is $50.

☐ Recording with county clerk: $1.75 for first page and $1.00 for each additional page.

New York

☐ **Organization tax:**
Based on authorized capital stock .... 1/20 of 1% of par value (50¢ per $1,000) and 5¢ per share for no-par stock.

☐ Minimum tax is $10.

☐ **Filing fee**—$50; filing with county clerk of county in which corporation is or is to be located—$3 except in New York City counties where fee is $25.

North Carolina

☐ **Organization tax:** 40¢ per $1,000 of total authorized capital stock.
No-par value shares are deemed to have a value of $1 each.
Minimum fee is $40; Maximum fee is $1,000.

☐ **Filing fee**—$5.

North Dakota

☐ **Filing articles**—$20.

☐ **Paid-in capital requirement**—$1,000.

Ohio

☐ **Organization fee** (for filing and recording articles of incorporation, including designation of agent):

Authorized Capital Stock	Fee
Up to and including 1,000 shares	10¢ for each share
Over 1,000 shares up to and including 10,000 shares	$100 plus 5¢ for each share over 1,000
Over 10,000 shares up to and including 50,000 shares	$550 plus 2¢ for each share over 10,000

488

Ohio *(continued)*

Over 50,000 shares up to and including
100,000 shares .... $1,350 plus 1¢ for each share over 50,000

Over 100,000 shares up to and including
500,000 shares .... $1,850 plus ½¢ for each share over 100,000

Over 500,000 shares .... $3,850 plus ¼¢ for each share over 500,000

Minimum fee is $50.

☐ **Paid-in capital requirement—$500.**

Oklahoma

☐ **Organization fee**—for filing articles and issuing certificates of incorporation: 1/10 of 1% of authorized capital stock.

No-par stock is deemed to be valued at $50 per share.

However, the Oklahoma Attorney General doubts the constitutionality of authorization of no-par stock and recommends that the Secretary of State refuse to file articles of incorporation that contain issuance of no-par stock, unless Oklahoma Supreme Court so directs.

Minimum fee is $3.

☐ **Filing fee:** $8 plus $2 for each county in which a copy must be filed, plus additional incidental fees.

☐ **Paid-in capital requirement:** $500.

Oregon

☐ **Organization fee:**

When Authorized Capital Stock is in excess of	But does not exceed	The fee is
$ 0	$ 5,000	$ 10
$ 5,000	$ 10,000	$ 15
$ 10,000	$ 25,000	$ 20
$ 25,000	$ 50,000	$ 30
$ 50,000	$ 100,000	$ 50
$100,000	$ 250,000	$ 75
$250,000	$ 500,000	$100
$500,000	$1,000,000	$125
Over $1,000,000		$200

No-par value shares are deemed to have a par value of $10 each.
Minimum fee is $10.

Corporation filing articles of incorporation must also pay first annual license fee computed in same manner.

Pennsylvania

☐ **Filing fee—$75**

Rhode Island

☐ **Organization fees** (whether shares are of par value or no-par value):

Authorized Shares	Fee
Up to and including first 10,000 shares	1¢ per share
Over 10,000 shares but up to and including 100,000	$100 plus ½¢ per share in excess of 10,000
Over 100,000 shares	$550 plus 1/5¢ per share in excess of 100,000

Minimum fee is $80.

☐ **Certificate of incorporation fee**—$30.

South Carolina

☐ **Incorporation tax**—40¢ for each $1,000 of aggregated value of shares authorized. No-par value stock is deemed to be valued at $10 per share. Minimum is $40; Maximum is $1,000.

☐ **Paid-in capital requirements**—$1,000 consideration, of which $500 is cash.

South Dakota

☐ **Organization fee:**

Authorized Capital Stock	Fee
$25,000 or less	$ 40
Over $25,000 and not exceeding $100,000	$ 60
Over $100,000 and not exceeding $500,000	$ 80
Over $500,000 and not exceeding $1,000,000 ...	$100
Over $1,000,000 and not exceeding $1,500,000	$150
Over $1,500,000 and not exceeding $2,000,000	$200
Over $2,000,000 and not exceeding $2,500,000	$250
Over $2,500,000 and not exceeding $3,000,000	$300
Over $3,000,000 and not exceeding $3,500,000	$350
Over $3,500,000 and not exceeding $4,000,000	$400
Over $4,000,000 and not exceeding $4,500,000	$450
Over $4,500,000 and not exceeding $5,000,000	$500
Over $5,000,000	$500 plus $40 for each additional $500,000 over $5,000,000

No-par value stock is valued at $100 per share.

$5 for certificate and 50¢ per page for certified copies.

Tennessee

☐ **License fees**—Each $100 unit of capital stock = 1 taxable share
(a) **Par Value Shares**
Up to 20,000 shares .... 1¢ per share

Tennessee *(continued)*

Next 180,000 shares .... 1/2¢ per share
Balance over 200,000 shares .... 1/5¢ per share
(b) No-Par Value Shares
Up to 20,000 shares .... 1/2¢ per share
Next 1,980,000 shares .... 1/4¢ per share
Balance over 2,000,000 shares .... 1/5¢ per share

☐ **Filing fee**—$10 plus fees for forwarding to city clerk for recording. $1 plus $5 plus 50¢ for each page in excess of 5 pages.

Minimum fee is $10.

☐ **Paid-in capital requirement:** $1,000.

Texas

☐ **Organization fee**—$100 (flat fee).

☐ **Paid-in capital requirement:** $1,000.

Utah

☐ **Organization fee**—1/20 of 1% on value of the proportion of total authorized shares. No-par shares are valued at $1 each.
Minimum fee is $50. Maximum fee is $525.

☐ **Filing fee**—$25.

Vermont

☐ **Organization fee:**

If Authorized Capital Stock exceeds	But does not exceed	Fee
$ 0	$ 5,000	$ 20
$ 5,000	$ 10,000	$ 40
$ 10,000	$ 50,000	$ 80
$ 50,000	$ 200,000	$160
$ 200,000	$ 500,000	$320
$ 500,000	$ 1,000,000	$475
$ 1,000,000	$ 2,000,000	$800
$ 2,000,000		$800 plus $150 for each $1,000,000 or fraction thereof over $2,000,000

No-par value stock is seemed to have a value of $100 per share.

491

Vermont *(continued)*

Minimum tax is $20 (if no capital stock).

Virginia

☐ **Charter tax:**

Capital Stock	Tax
Not over $50,000	$20
Over $50,000 and less than $3,000,000	40¢ for each $1,000 or fraction thereof
$3,000,000 and over	$1,200

No-par stock valued at $100.

Washington

☐ **Filing fee:**

Authorized Capital Stock	Fee
First $50,000 or less	$50
Over $50,000 up to and including	$50 plus $1 for each $1,000 over
$1,000,000	$50 plus $1 for each $1,000 over $50,000 (1/10 of 1%)
Over $1,000,000 up to and including $4,000,000	$1,000 plus 1/25 of 1% over $1,000,000
Over $4,000,000	$2,200 plus 1/50 of 1% in excess of $4,000,000.

No-par shares have value of amount to be allocated to stated capital for consideration for issuance.

Minimum fee is $50; Maximum fee is $5,000. Building and loan associations exempt from filing fees.

Surtax of 25% on all filing fees.

☐ **Paid-in capital requirements**—$500.

West Virginia

☐ **Filing fee**—For certificate of incorporation, $10. (No incorporation tax, but in lieu thereof, charter license tax.)

☐ **Recording fees**—State, $3.00; County, $1.25 plus 50¢ per page in excess of 2.

Wisconsin

☐ **Filing Fee:**
  (a) **Par Value Stock** .... $1.25 per 1,000 or
                                                      fraction thereof authorized
                                                      par value

  (b) **No-Par Value Stock** .... 2½¢ per share

Minimum fee is $55.

Wyoming

☐ **Organization fee:**

Authorized Capital Stock	Fee
$50,000 or less	$27.50
Over $50,000 and not exceeding $100,000	$52.50
Over $100,000	$52.50 plus 30¢ for each $1,000 over $100,000

☐ No-par shares are valued at $1 per share.

ANNUAL CORPORATE TAXES AND FEES

The table below shows the annual costs, taxes, and fees incident to operation of a corporation in the various states. These taxes and fees are subject to frequent change, so applicable state laws should be checked for any "last minute" changes.

Alabama

☐ **Franchise Tax:** $3 on each $1,000 of capital stock paid in and subject to call. Minimum—$25.

☐ **Annual Permit—Domestic Corporations:** Fee from $10 to $100 according to capitalization.

$25,000 or less	$ 10
$25,000—50,000	$ 20
$50,000—100,000	$ 30
$100,000—150,000	$ 50
Over $150,000	$100

☐ **Stock Tax:** Assessed on 30% of the actual value of the stock less the assessed value of real and personal corporate property located in Alabama and other states, and less certain other assessments.

☐ **Income Tax:** 5% on the entire net income. Certain deductions are allowed.

Alaska

☐ **Annual Corporation Tax:** $50.
New industrial developments are tax exempt within certain limitations.

☐ **Business License** (Gross Receipts): $25 plus ½% of gross receipts over $20,000 but not over $100,000; $400 plus ¼% over $100,000.

Arizona

☐ **Net Income Tax:** Taxable income of $1,000 or less—2½%; $1,000—$25 + 4% over $1,000; $2,000—$65 + 5% over $2,000; $3,000—$115 + 6½% over $3,000; $4,000—$180 + 8% over $4,000; $5,000—$260 + 9% over $5,000; $6,000 or more—$350 + 10½% over $6,000

☐ **Annual Report Fee:** $30.

Arkansas

☐ **Franchise Tax:** 11/100 of 1% on proportion of capital stock outstanding preceding December 31, which is employed in Arkansas. Minimum: $11.

☐ **Income Tax:** First $3,000 of net income or part thereof—1%; next $3,000—2%; next $5,000—3%; next $14,000—5%; on all net income in excess of $25,000—6%.

California

☐ **Franchise Income Tax** (imposed on all corporations doing intrastate business): 9% of such net income with minimum annual tax of $200. Corporate income tax generally applies to corporation not subject to franchise tax. 9% of net income derived from intrastate sources.

Colorado

☐ **Income Tax:** 5% of net income derived from property located in Colorado and business transacted in Colorado, or ½ of 1% of gross receipts of Colorado sales if selling is only Colorado activity.

☐ **Annual Report Fee:** $45.

Connecticut

☐ **Business Tax:** 10% of net income allocable to the state plus added tax of any amount equal to the amount by which 31/100 mill per $1 corporate excess allocable to Connecticut exceeds the 10% tax.

Minimum tax payable by companies doing business in the state is $50.

☐ **Annual Report Fee:** $21.

Delaware

☐ **Franchise Tax:** (lesser of (1) or (2)).
(1) Based on authorized shares—up to 1,000 shares—$20; over 1,000 shares up to 3,000 shares—$24.20; over 3,000 shares up to 5,000 shares—$30.25; over 5,000 shares up to 10,000 shares—$60.50; over 10,000 shares—$60.50 plus $30.25 for each 10,000 shares, or fraction thereof in excess of 10,000 shares.
(2) Based on assumed capital of authorized shares—$121 for each $1,000,000 or fraction thereof; whenever assumed par value capital is less than $1,000,000, tax is an amount that bears same relation to $121 as assumed par value capital bears to $1,000,000. Minimum: $20; Maximum: $110,000.

Filing fee: $10.

☐ **Income Tax:** 7.2% of taxable income from business and property within Delaware.

District of Columbia

☐ **Franchise Tax:** 9% for taxable years on or after 1/1/76, surtax of 10% for taxable years on or after 1/1/76 but before 1/1/78, on taxable income derived from District of Columbia sources.
Minimum tax: $25.

Florida

☐ **Annual Report Fee:** $10.

495

Florida *(continued)*

☐ **Income Tax:** 5% of net taxable income. Based on adjusted federal income, with adjustments, allocable to Florida law.

☐ **Intangible Personal Property Tax:** One mill per dollar. Intangible personal property means property which is not in itself intrinsically valuable but which derives its chief value from that which it represents, including but not limited to money, certified checks, etc.

☐ **Stamp Tax:** On each original issue whether organization or reorganization of certificates of stock issued by any corporation, 15¢ on each $100 of face value, or fraction thereof; if without face value, 15¢ on each $100 of actual value or fraction thereof.

Georgia

☐ **License Tax:** Based on net worth including capital stock, paid in surplus and earned surplus:

☐ Net worth over	But not over	Tax
$ 0	$10,000	$10
10,000	25,000	20
25,000	40,000	40
40,000	60,000	60
60,000	80,000	75
80,000	100,000	100
100,000	150,000	125
150,000	200,000	150
200,000	300,000	200
300,000	500,000	250
500,000	750,000	300
750,000	1,000,000	500
1,000,000	2,000,000	750
2,000,000	4,000,000	1,000
4,000,000	6,000,000	1,250
6,000,000	8,000,000	1,500
8,000,000	10,000,000	1,750
10,000,000	12,000,000	2,000
12,000,000	14,000,000	2,500
14,000,000	16,000,000	3,000
16,000,000	18,000,000	3,500
18,000,000	20,000,000	4,000
20,000,000	22,000,000	4,500
22,000,000		5,000

☐ **Income Tax:** 6% of net income from property owned and/or business done in Georgia. Some adjustments may be made under Georgia law.

☐ **Stock Tax:** $1 per $1,000 fair market value of bonds and debentures of corporations.

Hawaii

☐ **Annual Exhibit Fee:** $10.

☐ **Income Tax:** 5.85% on first $25,000 net taxable income; 6.435% on excess of net taxable income over $25,000. Capital gain taxed at rate of 3.08% is entitled to alternative tax treatment under IRC.

☐ **Excise Tax:** Rates depend on class of business engaged in, highest rate is 4% and lowest is ¾%. The tax is measured by the application of rates against values, gross proceeds of sales, or gross income.

Idaho

☐ **License Tax:** Based upon entire authorized capital stock. If total authorized capital stock is not in excess of $5,000—$20; $5,001 to $10,000—$25; $10,001 to $25,000—$30; $25,001 to $50,000—$50; $50,001 to $100,000—$75; $100,001 to $250,000—$100; $250,001 to $500,000—$150; $500,001 to $1,000,000—$180; $1,000,001 to $2,000,000—$250; over $2,000,000—$300. No-par value shares to be considered valued at $100 each. Minimum: $20; Maximum: $300.

☐ **Income Tax:** 6.5% of income derived from exercising corporate franchise in Idaho.

Illinois

☐ **Franchise Tax:** Rates paid according to sum of its stated capital and paid-in surplus, not over $50,000—$10; $50,001 to $200,000—$15; $200,001 to $500,000—$20; $500,001 to $1,000,000—$50; $1,000,001 to $10,000,000—$200; over $10,000,001—$500. Minimum $10; Maximum $500.

☐ **Capital Stock Tax:** Based upon value of all corporate assets over valuation of real estate and tangible personalty.

☐ **Income Tax:** 4% of corporation's net income for taxable years based upon the corporation's federal taxable income allocated and apportioned to Illinois—$1,000 standard exemption allowed.

☐ **Annual Report Fee:** $15.

Indiana

☐ **Annual Report Fee:** $15.

☐ **Franchise Tax:** No franchise tax is imposed on foreign or domestic corporations.

☐ **Income Tax:** Corporations are subject to both gross income tax and adjusted gross income tax and pay whichever is higher.

☐ **Supplemental Corporate Net Income Tax:** 3%.

Iowa

☐ **Annual License Fee:** $5 for stated capital up to $20,000; $10 over $20,000 to $40,000; $15 over $40,000 to $60,000; $20 over $60,000 to $80,000; $25 over $80,000 to $100,000; $30 over $100,000 to $150,000; $35 over $150,000 to $200,000; $40 over $200,000 to $250,000; $45 over $250,000 to $300,000; $50 over $300,000 to $350,000; $55 over $350,000 to $400,000; $60 over $400,000 to $500,000; $70 over $500,000 to $600,000; $80 over $600,000 to $700,000; $90 over $700,000 to $800,000; $100 over $800,000 to $900,000; $110 over $900,000 to $1,000,000; $175 over $1,000,000 to $2,500,000; $250 over $2,500,000 to $5,000,000; $350 over $5,000,000 to $10,000,000; $800 over $10,000,000 to $50,000,000; $1,200 over $50,000,000 to $100,000,000; $1,600 over $100,000,000 to $200,000,000; $2,000 over $200,000,000 to $300,000,000; $2,500 over $300,000,000 to $500,000,000; $3,000 over $500,000,000.

☐ **Income Tax:** 6% on first $25,000 or part thereof; 8% for $25,000 to $100,000; 10% on $100,000 and above.

Kansas

☐ **Annual Franchise Tax:** $1 per $1,000 of shareholders' equity attributable to Kansas. Minimum: $20; Maximum: $2,500. Paid when filing annual report.

☐ **Income Tax:** Based upon doing business in or deriving income from within Kansas at rate of 4½% on Kansas taxable income. A surtax of 2¼% is added on Kansas taxable income over $25,000.

Kentucky

☐ **Stock Tax:** Stockholders do not pay tax provided the corporation pays taxes to Kentucky on at least 75% of its total property.

☐ **License Tax:** 70¢ on each $1,000 based on fair value of the capital stock represented by property owned and business done in the state. Minimum: $10.

☐ **Income Tax:** Tax levied on "taxable net income"; first $25,000—4%; amounts over $25,000—5.8%.

☐ **Annual Report Fee:** $5.

Louisiana

☐ **Franchise Tax:** Basis for computation is determined by taking arithmetical average of (1) ratio that net sales in Louisiana and other revenue attributable to Louisiana bears to total net sales in regular course of business and other revenue, and (2) ratio of value of property in Louisiana to value of all property.
All shares taken at book value. Rate: $1.50 per $1,000. Minimum: $10.

☐ **Income Tax:** 4% of net income from sources within the state.

Maine

☐ **Annual Filing Fee:** $30.

498

Maine *(continued)*

☐ **Franchise Tax:** None.

☐ **Income Tax:** 5% of Maine net income up to $25,000, or $1,250 plus 7½% of taxable income over $25,000.

Maryland

☐ **Annual Report Fee:** $40 (in lieu of franchise tax).

☐ **Income Tax:** 7% of portion of net income allocable to state.

Massachusetts

☐ **Excise Tax:** (1) $2.60 per $1,000 on specified and allocated tangible property (if 10% or more such total assets are not locally taxed) or net worth if untaxed local tangibles are less than 10%. (2) 9.5% of net income attributable to Massachusetts. Minimum tax plus a 14% surtax, $228.

☐ **Income Tax:** 5% on net income derived from in-state business of corporations engaged in interstate commerce but not subject to an excise tax.

Michigan

☐ **Single Business Tax:** 2.35% of "adjusted tax base" (federal taxable income allocable to Michigan less deductions and exemptions) of every person with business activity in state allocated or apportioned to state.

☐ **Annual Report Filing Fee:** $10.

☐ **Franchise Tax:** Repealed, effective May 14, 1977.

Minnesota

☐ **Income Tax:** 12% based on net income earned in or allocable to activities in Minnesota less allowable deductions. Minimum tax: $100.

Mississippi

☐ **Income Tax:** Based upon income attributable to Mississippi at the rate of 3% for the initial $5,000 and 4% for amount thereover.

☐ **Annual Report Fee:** $5.

☐ **Franchise Tax:** $2.50 per $1,000 or fraction of capital used, invested, or employed in Mississippi. Minimum: $10.

Missouri

☐ **Franchise Tax:** 1/20 or 1% of par value of outstanding stock and surplus, or portion thereof employed in state.

☐ **Income Tax:** 5% of net income allocable to Missouri.

499

Missouri *(continued)*

☐ **Annual Registration Fee:** If registration filed within 30 days of July 1, $10; otherwise, if during August—$15; September—$25; October—$30; November—$35; December—$40.

Montana

☐ **License Tax:** 6¾% based on total net income received from all sources within or allocable to Montana. Minimum: $50. Additional license taxes imposed on specific industries.

☐ **Annual Report Fee:** $5.

Nebraska

☐ **Occupational Tax:** Based on the amount of paid up capital stock according to the following table:

When paid-up capital stock exceeds	But does not exceed	Such annual tax shall be
$ 0	$ 10,000	$ 10
10,000	20,000	15
20,000	30,000	22.50
30,000	40,000	30
40,000	50,000	37.50
50,000	60,000	45
60,000	70,000	52.50
70,000	80,000	60
80,000	90,000	67.50
90,000	100,000	75
100,000	125,000	90
125,000	150,000	105
150,000	175,000	120
175,000	200,000	135
200,000	225,000	150
225,000	250,000	165
250,000	275,000	180
275,000	300,000	195
300,000	325,000	210
325,000	350,000	225
350,000	400,000	250
400,000	450,000	275
450,000	500,000	300
500,000	600,000	340
600,000	700,000	380
700,000	800,000	420
800,000	900,000	460
900,000	1,000,000	500

Nebraska *(continued)*

When paid-up capital stock exceeds	But does not exceed	Such annual tax shall be
1,000,000	10,000,000	$ 500 plus $300 for each million or fraction thereof over and above one million dollars.
10,000,000	15,000,000	4,500
15,000,000	20,000,000	5,500
20,000,000	25,000,000	6,500
25,000,000	50,000,000	7,750
50,000,000	100,000,000	8,000
100,000,000		8,250

Minimum: $10.

☐ **Income Tax:** Income or franchise tax applies to taxable income of corporations derived from sources within state. Tax is flat percent of adjusted federal income tax liability of corporation with respect to tax income for taxable year. Current rate: 18%.

Rate of tax for corporations whose income consists exclusively of foreign or interstate commerce is 25% of rate for individuals on first $25,000 of taxable income, and 27½% of such rate in excess of $25,000.

Nevada

☐ **Annual Report Fee:** $20.

☐ **Franchise Tax:** None.

☐ **Income Tax:** None.

New Hampshire

☐ **Income Tax:** Imposed on taxable business profits at a rate of 7%.

☐ **Franchise Tax:** Every domestic corporation must pay annually at time of making its annual return a fee equal to amount paid upon filing its original record of organization, plus an amount equal to any additional payments for increases in authorized capital. If authorized capital is reduced, annual fee is amount required for original fee of a corporation capitalized at reduced amount. Minimum: $60; Maximum: $2,000.

☐ **Annual Report Fee:** $60.

New Jersey

☐ **Report Filing Fee:** $15.

☐ **Franchise Tax:** 7½% of net income plus (1) tax on net worth at 2 mills per $1 on first $100,000,000, 4 mills on second $100,000,000, .3 mills on third $100,000,000, .2 mills over $300,000,000
OR

501

New Jersey *(continued)*

(2) greatest of
(a) tax on "allocated assets" at .5 mills per $1 of allocated assets on first $100,000,000, .2 mills over $100,000,000;
(b) lesser of
(1) an amount based on authorized capital stock of $25 up to 5,000 shares, $55 up to 10,000 shares, $55 plus $27.50 per added 10,000 shares over 10,000 shares,
(2) 11/100 mill per $1 on total assets,
(3) $100,000,
(c) $25.

New Mexico

☐ **Franchise Tax:** Based on book value of the portion of corporation's capital stock represented by property and business in New Mexico. Rate—55¢ per $1,000 of taxable capital stock. Minimum: $10. (Capital stock of no-par value deemed to be valued at $100 per share.)

☐ **Net Income Tax:** 5% of the corporation's entire net income or portion thereof from business done or property located in the state.

☐ **Annual Report Fee:** $10.

New York

☐ **Franchise Tax:** The larger of: (1) 10% of entire net income allocated to New York; (2) 10% of allocated part of 30% of entire net income, salaries to officers and/or stockholders controlling in excess of 5% of issued capital stock, less $15,000 and any net loss for the year; (3) 1.78 mills on each dollar of allocated business and investment capital; (4) $250 less 35% if imposed for period of more than 6 months but not more than 9 months, and less 50% if imposed for 6 months or less. In addition there is a tax of 9/10 of a mill on each dollar of allocated subsidiary capital.

North Carolina

☐ **Income Tax:** 6% of net income allocable to North Carolina.

☐ **Franchise Tax:** $1.50 for each $1,000 of proportion of total issued and outstanding capital stock, surplus and undivided profits allocable to business in North Carolina.

North Dakota

☐ **Income Tax:** Based on net income attributable to sources within the state at the following rates: First $3,000—3%; over $3,000, up to $8,000—4%; over $8,000, up to $15,000—5%; over $15,000—6%.

☐ **Annual Report Fee:** $10.

☐ **Franchise Tax:** No provision.

502

Ohio

☐ **Franchise Tax:** The higher of (1) 5 mills times value of capital, surplus, undivided profits, and reserves allocable to Ohio, (2) 4% on first $25,000 and 8% over $25,000 of net income during preceding year allocable to Ohio. Minimum: $50.

Oklahoma

☐ **Franchise Tax:** $1.25 for each $1,000 or fraction thereof of the corporate capital used, invested, or employed in Oklahoma.
Minimum fee: $10; Maximum fee: $20,000.

☐ **Income Tax:** 4% based on income derived from property owned and business transacted in the state, less applicable credits.

Oregon

☐ **License Fee:** Corporation must pay annual license fee computed in accordance with fee for filing articles of incorporation.

☐ **Income Tax:** Based on Oregon proportion of total net income at the rate of 7% (7½% after 12/31/77).

☐ **Corporate Excise Tax:** Business corporations doing business in state must pay excise tax on net income—7% until 1/1/78, thereafter 7½%. Minimum tax is $10.

Pennsylvania

☐ **Capital Stock Tax:** 10 mills per dollar of taxable portion of the actual value of the whole capital stock.

☐ **Corporate Net Income Tax:** 9½% of net income allocated to Pennsylvania.

☐ **Corporate Loans Tax:** Tax of 4 mills per dollar on corporate loans held by Pennsylvania residents, if interest is paid thereon. Tax is on the holders of corporate loans but must be withheld by the corporation from the interest when paid, and remitted to the Commonwealth.

☐ **Excise Tax:** Repealed; remains on books only for purpose of collecting amounts due.

Rhode Island

☐ **Business Corporation Tax:** 8% of net income *or* 40¢ for each $100 of net worth, whichever is greater.

☐ **Franchise Tax:** $2.50 per $10,000 based on authorized capital stock as of the close of the preceding taxable year. No-par shares valued at $100 each (Minimum: $50), but there is no franchise tax if business income tax paid is itself more than this amount.

☐ **Annual Report Fee:** $15.

South Carolina

☐ **License Tax:** One mill on each dollar paid to the corporation on account of capital stock and paid-in surplus. Minimum fee: $10.

South Carolina *(continued)*

☐ **Annual Report Fee:** $5.

☐ **Income Tax:** 6% of net income for corporations whose entire business is transacted or conducted in the state, or for net income allocable to state.

South Dakota

☐ **Annual Report Filing Fee:** $10.

☐ **Franchise Tax:** None.

☐ **Income Tax:** Not applicable to corporations.

Tennessee

☐ **Gross Receipts Tax:** The tax is computed by one of two methods at the option of the taxpayer.
(1) ½ of 1% of the gross amount of receipts from intrastate business. Minimum: $25.
(2) On the amount of issued and outstanding capital stock at the following rates: capital stock up to and including $25,000—$5; over $25,000 and up to and including $50,000—$10; over $50,000 and up to and including $100,000—$20; over $100,000 and up to $250,000—$30; over $250,000 up to $500,000—$50; over $500,000 and less than $1,000,000—$100; over $1,000,000—$150. Minimum: $5; Maximum: $150. Banks and banking corporations are exempt.

☐ **Excise Tax:** Based on net earnings arising from business done in the state at the rate of 6%.

☐ **Franchise Tax:** Based on worth of capital invested in the state—15¢ per $100 or major fraction thereof.

☐ **Income Tax:** None.

Texas

☐ **Franchise Tax:** Based on higher of (1) proportion of stated capital, surplus, and undivided profits, plus amount of outstanding bonds, notes, and debentures, other than those maturing in less than a year from date of issue (but including such indebtedness that has been outstanding more than one year), as its gross receipts from Texas business bear to total gross receipts from all sources; or (2) the assessed valuation for county ad valorem tax purposes, of corporation's property in state; or $55. The rate is $4.25 for each $1,000 or fraction thereof; or minimum $55.
Corporations are taxed like individuals, and numerous taxes on gross receipts and tangible assets are imposed on various classes of corporations.

Utah

☐ **Franchise Tax:** 6% based on income attributable to the state. Minimum: $25.

☐ **Income Tax:** 4% of net income derived from Utah sources, less franchise tax paid for same period.

Vermont

☐ **Income Tax:** 5% on Vermont net income of $10,000 or less; $500 plus 6% over $10,000 for $10,001—$25,000; $1,400 plus 7% over $25,000 for $25,001—$250,000; $17,150 plus 7½% over $250,000 for $250,001 and over. Minimum: $50.

☐ **Annual Report Fee:** $2.

Virginia

☐ **Income Tax:** 6% based on net income attributable to business within the state.

☐ **Franchise Tax:** Based upon maximum authorized capital stock. If the value of the maximum authorized capital stock is up to $25,000 the tax is $20; $25,001-$50,000 — $40; $50,000.01-$100,000—$80; $100,000.01-$300,000—$120; $300,000.01-$500,000— $200; $500,000.01-$1 million—$400; $1-$50 million — $400 + $20 per $100,000 or fraction over $1 million; $50-$10,200 + $150 each million or fraction over $50 million; over $100 million — $20,000.

☐ **Registration Fee:** Based upon maximum authorized capital stock as of January 1. If the authorized capital stock has a value of up to $15,000, the fee is $10; over $15,000 but not over $50,000—$20; over $50,000 but not over $100,000—$30; over $100,000 but not over $300,000—$40; over $300,000—$50. No-par value stock is to be valued at $100 per share.

Washington

☐ **Franchise Tax:** Based upon authorized capital stock and paid in advance for the period July 1 to June 30. If the value of the authorized capital stock is $50,000 or less, the rate is $30; over $50,000 to $1,000,000—$30 plus 50¢ for each $1,000 over $50,000; over $1,000,000 to $4,000,000—$505 plus 20¢ for each $1,000 over $1,000,000; over $4,000,000—$1,105 plus 10¢ for each $1,000 over $4,000,000. Minimum: $30; Maximum: $2,500. Surtax of 25% superimposed on this rate structure.

☐ **Annual Report Filing Fee:** $2.

☐ **Business and Occupation Tax:** Gross receipts tax imposed for act or privilege of engaging in business activities in state, unless business specifically exempted. Rates depend on nature of business activity.

West Virginia

☐ **License Tax:** Based on authorized capital stock. If the authorized capital stock is $5,000 or less—$20; over $5,000 to $10,000—$30; over $10,000 to $25,000—$40; over $25,000 to $50,000—$50; over $50,000 to $75,000—$80; over $75,000 to $100,000—$100; over $100,000 to $125,000—$110; over $125,000 to $150,000—$120; over $150,000 to $175,000—$140; over $175,000 to $200,000—$150; over $200,000 to $1,000,000—$180 plus 20¢ on each $1,000 or fraction thereof over $200,000; over $1,000,000 to $15,000,000—$340 plus 15¢ on each fraction thereof over $1,000,000; over $15,000,000—$2,500. No-par value stock is to be valued at $25 per share unless originally issued for a higher consideration.

West Virginia *(continued)*

☐ **Corporate Net Income Tax:** 6% applicable to a corporation's taxable income derived from activity in state.

☐ **Filing Report of Officers:** $1.

Wisconsin

☐ **Income Tax:** Based on net income derived from business transacted and property located in the state. On the initial $1,000—2.3%; the second $1,000—2.8%; the third $1,000—3.4%; the fourth $1,000—4.5%; the fifth $1,000—5.6%; the sixth $1,000—6.8% and on the balance—7.9%.

☐ **Annual Report Fee:** $8.

Wyoming

☐ **Franchise Tax:** Based on value of capital, property, and assets in state. If the value is $50,000 or less—$5; over $50,000 up to and including $100,000—$10; over $100,000 up to and including $500,000—$25; over $500,000 up to and including $1,000,000—$50; over $1,000,000—$50 for every million dollars or fraction thereof.

☐ **Income Tax:** None.

CORPORATE INDEMNIFICATION STATUTES

Alabama	Bus. Corp. Act A. 623, A. '69 (eff. Aug. 29, 1969)
Alaska	Bus. Corp. Act §10.05.010 (eff. Sept. 7, 1970)
Arizona	Gen. Corp. Law §10-005
Arkansas	Bus. Corp. Act §64-309 (as amended, eff. Feb. 13, 1973)
California	Gen. Corp. Law §830 (as amended, eff. Nov. 12, 1968)
Colorado	Colorado Revised Stat. §7-3-101(o) (eff. July 6, 1973)
Connecticut	Stock Corp. Act §33-320a (eff. May 20, 1975)
Delaware	Gen. Corp. L. §145
District of Columbia	D.C. Code §29-904(p)
Florida	Gen. Corp. Act §5
Georgia	Bus. Corp. Code §22-717
Hawaii	Gen. Corp. Law §172-23(p)
Idaho	Bus. Corp. Act §30-166
Illinois	Bus. Corp. Act §42.11 (Contribution only); §25a (emergencies)
Indiana	Code §23-1-2-2(b)(9)
Iowa	Bus. Corp. Act §469A. 4(19)
Kansas	Gen. Corp. Code §27
Kentucky	Bus. Corp. Act §5
Louisiana	Bus. Corp. Law §12:83
Maine	Bus. Corp. Act §719 (eff. Oct. 3, 1975)
Maryland	Gen. Corp. L. §2-418 (eff. July 1, 1976)
Massachusetts	Corp. Law CH. 156B, §67
Michigan	Bus. Corp. Act. §561-569
Minnesota	Bus. Corp. Act §301.095
Mississippi	Code §79-3-7(o)
Missouri	Gen. & Bus. Corp. Law §351.355
Montana	Bus. Corp. Act §15-2204(o)
Nebraska	Bus. Corp. Act §2-2004(15)
Nevada	Gen. Corp. Law §78.751
New Hampshire	Gen. Corp. Law §294:3(IX)
New Jersey	Bus. Corp. Act §14A:3-5
New Mexico	Bus. Corp. Act §51-24-4(0)
New York	Bus. Corp. Law §721-726
North Carolina	Bus. Corp. Act §55-19 to §55-21
North Dakota	Bus. Corp. Act §10-19-04(15)
Ohio	Gen. Corp. Law §1701.13(E)
Oklahoma	Bus. Corp. Act §1.43a
Oregon	Bus. Corp. Act §57.255, 57.260
Pennsylvania	Bus. Corp. Law §410, 516
Rhode Island	Bus. Corp. Act §7-1. 1-4.1
South Carolina	Bus. Corp. Act §12-18.18
South Dakota	Code §47-2-58(15)

Tennessee	Gen. Corp. Act. §48-406 - 48-411
Texas	Bus. Corp. Act Art. 2.02(16)
Utah	Bus. Corp. Act §16-10-4(o)
Vermont	Bus. Corp. Act §1852(15)
Virginia	Stock Corp. Act §13.1-3.1
Washington	Bus. Corp. Act §23A.08.025
West Virginia	Corp. Act §31-1-9
Wisconsin	Bus. Corp. Law §180.05
Wyoming	Bus. Corp. Law §4(o)

STATE BLUE SKY LAWS

Alabama: Securities Act of Alabama, ch. 32, Code of Alabama, 1975, as amended.

Alaska: Alaska Securities Act of 1959; §45.55.010 et seq., Alaska Statutes, 1962, as amended.

Arizona: Arizona Revised Statutes, tit. 44, ch. 12, as amended.

Arkansas: Arkansas Statutes of 1947, tit. 67, as amended.

California: Corporate Securities Law of 1968, tit. 4, div. 1, California Codes, as amended.

Colorado: Securities Act, §11-51-101 et seq., Colorado Revised Statutes, 1973, as amended.

Connecticut: Connecticut Uniform Securities Act, Public Act No. 482, General Statutes of Connecticut, as amended.

Delaware: Delaware Securities Act, tit. 6, ch. 73, Delaware Code Annotated, as amended.

District of Columbia: District of Columbia Code, 1967, tit. 2, ch. 24.

Florida: Sale of Securities Law, §517, Florida Statutes, 1975, as amended.

Georgia: Georgia Securities Act of 1973, Act, No. 686, as amended.

Hawaii: Hawaii Revised Statutes, 1968, tit. 26, as amended.

Idaho: Idaho Securities Act, §30,1401 et seq., Idaho Code of 1947, as amended.

Illinois: Illinois Securities Law of 1953, H.B. No. 146, Illinois Revised Statutes, ch. 121-½.

Indiana: Indiana Code of 1976, §23-2-1-1 et seq., as amended.

Iowa: Iowa Uniform Securities Act, §502.101 et seq., Code of Iowa, 1977, as amended.

Kansas: Kansas Statutes Annotated, §17-1252 et seq., as amended.

Kentucky: Kentucky Revised Statutes, §292.310, as amended.

Louisiana: Louisiana Revised Statutes of 1950, tit. 51, §701 et seq., as amended.

Maine: The Maine Securities Act, tit. 32, Maine Revised Statutes Annotated, as amended.

Maryland: Maryland Securities Act of 1975, tit. 11, Annotated Code of Maryland, 1957, as amended.

Massachusetts: Uniform Securities Act of 1972, ch. 110A, General Laws of Massachusetts, 1932, as amended.

Michigan: Michigan Compiled Laws, 1970, §451.501 et seq., as amended.

Minnesota: Minnesota Statutes, 1971, §80A.01 et seq., as amended.

Mississippi: Mississippi Securities Law §75-71-1 et seq., Mississippi Code, 1972, Annotated, as amended.

Missouri: Missouri Revised Statutes, 1969, §409.101 et seq., as amended.

Montana: Securities Act of Montana, §15-2001 et seq., Revised Codes of Montana, 1947, as amended.

Nebraska: Revised Statutes of Nebraska, 1943, §8-1101 et seq., as amended.

Nevada: Nevada Revised Statutes, §90.010 et seq., as amended.

New Hampshire: New Hampshire Revised Statutes Annotated, 1955, §421:1 et seq., as amended.

New Jersey: Uniform Securities Law, 1967, §49:3-47 et seq., Revised Statutes of New Jersey, as amended.

New Mexico: Securities Act of New Mexico, §48-18-16 et seq., New Mexico Statutes, 1953, Annotated, as amended.

New York: Martin Act, General Business Law, art. 23-A, Consolidated Laws, ch. 20.

North Carolina: North Carolina Securities Act, 1974, ch. 1380, §78A-1 et seq., General Statutes of North Carolina, as amended.

North Dakota: Securities Act of 1951, ch. 106, §10-04-01 et seq., North Dakota Century Code, as amended.

Ohio: Ohio Revised Code, §1707.01, as amended.

Oklahoma: Oklahoma Securities Act, tit. 71, Oklahoma Statutes 1971, as amended.

Oregon: Oregon Securities Law, §59.005 et seq., Oregon Revised Statutes, as amended.

Pennsylvania: Pennsylvania Securities Act of 1972, §101 et seq., Purdon's Pennsylvania Statutes Annotated, as amended.

Puerto Rico: Uniform Securities Act, tit. 10, ch. 37, Laws of Puerto Rico Annotated, as amended.

Rhode Island: General Laws of Rhode Island, 1956 (Reenactment of 1969), §7-11-1 et seq., as amended.

South Carolina: Uniform Securities Act, §35-1-10 et seq., Code of Laws of South Carolina, 1976, as amended.

South Dakota: South Dakota Codified Laws, §47-31-1 et seq., as amended.

Tennessee: The Securities Law of 1955, §48-1601, Tennessee Code Annotated, as amended.

Texas: The Securities Act of 1957, ch. 269, Vernon's Annotated Revised Civil Statutes, art. 581, as amended.

Utah: Utah Code Annotated, 1953, §61-1-1 et seq., as amended.

Vermont: Vermont Statutes Annotated, Revision of 1959, §9-4201 et seq., as amended.

Virginia: Code of Virginia, 1950, §13.1-501 et seq., as amended.

Washington: 1976 Revised Code of Washington, §21.20.005 et seq., as amended.

West Virginia: West Virginia Uniform Securities Act of 1974, ch. 32, Code of West Virginia, 1931, as amended.

Wisconsin: Wisconsin Uniform Securities Law, §551.01 et seq., Wisconsin Statutes, 1975, as amended.

Wyoming: Wyoming Statutes, 1977 Republished Edition, §17-4-101 et seq., as amended.

WHEN INFANTS ARE COMPETENT TO CONTRACT

State	Age	State	Age
Alabama	19 (1)	Montana	18
Alaska	19 (5)	Nebraska	19 (2)
Arizona	18	Nevada	18
Arkansas	18 (6)	New Hampshire	18
California	18 (2) (7)	New Jersey	18
Colorado	18 (5)	New Mexico	18 (2)
Connecticut	18	New York	18 (2)
Delaware	18	North Carolina	18 (2)
District of Columbia	18	North Dakota	18
Florida	18	Ohio	18
Georgia	18 (5) (8)	Oklahoma	18 (6)
Hawaii	18 (2)	Oregon	18 (2)
Idaho	18 (2)	Pennsylvania	18
Illinois	18	Puerto Rico	21 (2)
Indiana	18	Rhode Island	18
Iowa	18 (2)	South Carolina	18 (6)
Kansas	18 (6) (9)	South Dakota	18
Kentucky	18	Tennessee	18 (6)
Louisiana	18 (10)	Texas	18 (6)
Maine	18	Utah	18 (2)
Maryland	18 (4)	Vermont	18
Massachusetts	18	Virginia	18
Michigan	18 (2) (6) (11)	Washington	18 (12)
Minnesota	18	West Virginia	18
Mississippi	21 (3)	Wisconsin	18
Missouri	18 (4)	Wyoming	19

---

(1) All married persons, widows and widowers over 18.
(2) Marriage removes disability.
(3) Married persons 18 and over.
(4) Married person has limited rights if spouse is of age.
(5) Married woman upon marriage.
(6) Court may authorize minors to transact business.
(7) Active duty in the military or living apart from parent or guardian with consent or is managing own financial affairs.
(8) Minors engaged in business with consent from parent or guardian.
(9) Married persons 16 and over.
(10) Parents may declare emancipation of minor at age 15.
(11) Active duty in the military or parental conduct or document indicating release of parental rights.
(12) Married person if spouse is of age.

STATE GUIDE TO ATTACHMENTS

State	Can Attachment Be Made Prior to Judgment?	Amount of Bond Required
Alabama	Yes	Amount approved by clerk of court.
Alaska	Yes	Twice amount claimed.
Arizona	Yes	Twice amount claimed.
Arkansas	Yes	Plaintiff shall pay defendant all damages sustained by reason of the attachment.
California	Yes	Twice amount claimed.
Colorado	Yes	Amount set by court, not exceeding twice amount claimed.
Connecticut	Yes	Twice amount claimed.
Delaware	Yes	No bond required.
District of Columbia	Yes	Amount approved by clerk of court.
Florida	Yes	Twice amount claimed.
Georgia	Yes	Twice amount claimed.
Hawaii	Yes	Twice amount claimed.
Idaho	Yes	Twice amount claimed.
Illinois	Yes	Twice amount claimed.
Indiana	Yes	Amount claimed.
Iowa	Yes	Twice amount claimed.
Kansas	Yes	Twice amount claimed.
Kentucky	Yes	Twice amount claimed.
Louisiana	Yes	Amount set by court.
Maine	Yes	Twice amount claimed.
Maryland	Yes	Amount set by court.
Massachusetts	Yes	Twice amount claimed.
Michigan	Yes, for goods up to $300 plus additional damages up to $300.	Twice amount claimed, but not less than $100.
Minnesota	Yes	Twice amount claimed.
Mississippi	Yes	Twice amount claimed.
Missouri	Yes	Twice amount claimed.
Montana	Yes	Twice amount claimed.
Nebraska	Yes	Twice amount claimed.
Nevada	Yes	Twice amount claimed.
New Hampshire	Yes	Twice amount claimed.
New Jersey	Yes	Twice amount claimed.

State	Can Attachment Be Made Prior to Judgment?	Amount of Bond Required
New Mexico	Yes	Twice amount claimed.
New York	Yes	Twice amount claimed.
North Carolina	Yes	Twice amount claimed.
North Dakota	Yes	Twice amount claimed.
Ohio	Yes	Amount sufficient to satisfy sheriff that in the event that suit is decided against plaintiff, he will pay costs pursuant to court order and expenses for maintaining the property.
Oklahoma	Yes	Twice amount claimed.
Oregon	Yes	Twice amount claimed.
Pennsylvania	Yes	Twice amount claimed.
Rhode Island	Yes	Twice amount claimed.
South Carolina	Yes	Twice amount claimed.
South Dakota	Yes	Twice amount claimed.
Tennessee	Yes	Amount set by court, but not exceeding amount claimed.
Texas	Yes	Twice amount claimed.
Utah	Yes	Twice amount claimed.
Vermont	Yes	Amount set by court.
Virginia	Yes	Twice amount claimed.
Washington	Yes	Twice amount claimed.
West Virginia	Yes	Twice amount claimed.
Wisconsin	Yes	Twice amount claimed.
Wyoming	Yes	Twice amount claimed.

STATE GUIDE TO INTEREST RATES*

State	Maximum Legal Rate	Maximum Contract Rate	Maximum Judgment Rate	Penalty for Usury	Corporation's Defense of Usury
Alabama	6%	8%	6%	Forfeit all interest.	No defense over $100,000.
Alaska	8%	5% above FRB discount rate of 12th Dist.	8%, but in no event over 10%.	Borrower recovers double interest paid; lender forfeits all interest.	No defense.
Arizona	6%	12%	As set out in contract.	Forfeit all interest; borrower recovers interest payments or applies them against principal.	No provision.
Arkansas	6%	10%	6%	Contract void.	No provision.
California	7%	10%	7%	Forfeit all interest; borrower recovers triple interest paid over 10%; violation is felony.	Can defend.
Colorado	8%	As set out in contract limited by U3C.	8%	No provision.	No defense.

State	Maximum Legal Rate	Maximum Contract rate	Maximum Judgment Rate	Penalty for Usury	Corporation's Defense of Usury
Connecticut	6%	12%	6%	Fine up to $1,000 or imprisonment up to 6 months or both; loan void.	No provision.
Delaware	6%	4% over FRB discount to member banks; above $100,000; no ceiling.	6%	Borrower recovers excess paid; greater of $500 or three times excess paid after maturity.	No defense.
District of Columbia	6%	8%	6%, but can set rate to 8%.	Forfeit all interest. Borrower recovers interest or applies it against principal	No defense.
Florida	6%	10%; 15% over $500,000.	Lesse of 6% or rate agreed on.	Forfeit all interest. When rate 25% or more. forfeit principal and interest.	Usury, if rate over 15%.
Georgia	7%	9%, if more than $100,000, any rate; 10% if secured by real estate.	7% (or if in writing, current rate).	Forfeit all interest; borrower may set off excess interest paid against principal.	No defense on loan over $2,500; no limit on loans of $100,000 or more.

State	Maximum Legal Rate	Maximum Contract rate	Maximum Judgment Rate	Penalty for Usury	Corporation's Defense of Usury
Hawaii	6%	1% a month.	6%	Recover only principal less interest paid.	No defense on loan over $750,000.
Idaho	8%	10% except as limited by U3C; nonresident loans no limit.	6%	Court determines amount but it cannot be less than $100 or more than $1,000.	No defense if over 12% and $10,000.
Illinois	5%	2½% over Monthly Index Long-Term, U.S. Bond yields secured by residential real estate, prepayment penalty prohibited; no limit on loans of $5,000 or more.	6%	Forfeit all interest; borrower recovers double interest.	No defense.
Indiana	8%	8% or per U3C.	8%	Amount determined by court not exceeding the greater of either the amount of credit service or loan finance charge or 10 times the amount of the excess charge.	No provision.

State	Maximum Legal Rate	Maximum Contract rate	Maximum Judgment Rate	Penalty for Usury	Corporation's Defense of Usury
Iowa	5%	Set by Bank Supt. issued quarterly; will be 2% over monthly average 10-year constant maturity interest rate of U.S. bonds. Limit at note signing applies until repayment is completed.	7%	Forfeit all interest, plus 8% of principal unpaid at time of judgment; additional 8% to school fund.	No defense.
Kansas	6%	10% or per U3C.	8% but may contract up to 10%	Twice the amount of the finance charge; however, liability cannot be less than $100, nor more than $1,000.	No defense.
Kentucky	6%	8½% up to $15,000; no limit over $15,000.	6%	Forfeit interest; debtor can recover twice interest paid.	No defense unless principal asset is one- or two-family house.
Louisiana	7%	8%; 10% immovables.	7%	Forfeit all interest.	No defense.

State	Maximum Legal Rate	Maximum Contract Rate	Maximum Judgment Rate	Penalty for Usury	Corporation's Defense of Usury
Maine	6%	No maximum, if in writing.	10% (after judgment).	No provision.	No provision.
Maryland	6%	8%; 10% home mortgages; no limit on business loans over $5,000.	6%	Forfeit greater of 3 times excess interest and charges or $500.	No defense.
Massachusetts	6%	No maximum stated.	No provision.	Criminal penalties.	No provision.
Michigan	5%	7%; no limit on corporate or business loans, on interest charged to employee or beneficiary on pension and profit-sharing plans meeting requirements of IRC §401(a), or land contracts $100,000 or more (except	6%	Forfeit all interest and charges, plus attorney's fee and court cost. It's criminal usury to charge interest over 25% a year.	No defense. Can agree in writing to any rate of interest.

State	Maximum Legal Rate	Maximum Contract Rate	Maximum Judgment Rate	Penalty for Usury	Corporation's Defense of Usury
Michigan (continued)		single family residences); other mortgage lenders 11% finance charge (as defined by Reg. Z).			
Minnesota	6%	8% (no limit on loans of $100,000 or more).	6%	Contract void, borrower gets back all interest paid but one-half goes to school fund.	No defense.
Mississippi	6%	10%; no limit up to $2,500 for corporations; 15% over $2,500.	6%; may contract to 8%.	Forfeit all interest; both interest and principal if rate is over 20%.	If loan under $2,500 no defense.
Missouri	6%	10%	6%; no limit on corporate loans, $5,000 and over loans secured by stocks, etc., and realty loans other than residential.	Forfeit excess, pay costs of action.	No defense.

State	Maximum Legal Rate	Maximum Contract Rate	Maximum Judgment Rate	Penalty for Usury	Corporation's Defense of Usury
Montana	6%	10% to $150,000, 10% over $150,000-$300,000	6%	Double interest charged.	No provision.
Nebraska	6%	11%	8%	Forfeit all interest.	No defense.
Nevada	7%	12%	7%, but may contract to 12%.	Forfeit excess over 12%.	No provision.
New Hampshire	6%	No limit.	6%	No provision.	No provision.
New Jersey	6%	8% less than $50,000; 9% for 1-3 family units; between 6% and 9% as prescribed by Banking Commissioner; no limit $50,000 or more.	No provision.	Forfeit all interest and costs.	No defense.
New Mexico	6%	10%; 12% if no collateral.	8%, but may contract to 12%.	Forfeit all interest; borrower recovers double interest paid.	No defense.

State	Maximum Legal Rate	Maximum Contract Rate	Maximum Judgment Rate	Penalty for Usury	Corporation's Defense of Usury
New York	8½%	8½%; no limit on notes over $5,000, with U3C collateral security.	6% except where otherwise prescribed by statute.	Contract void. Exception: savings banks and savings and loan assns. which forfeit all interest.	No defense unless (1) interest exceeds 25%, or (2) corporation's principal asset is 1- or 2-family house and corporation was formed or control of it acquired within 6 months before loan and mortgage.
North Carolina	6%	No limit on loans over $300,000; 12% over $100,000-$300,000; 9% on $100,000 or less; 10% over $50,000-$100,000.	6%	Forfeit all interest; borrower recovers double interest.	Can defend.
North Dakota	6%	Greater of 3% above maximum interest payable on time deposits maturing in 80 months authorized by state banking board, or 7%.	6%	Forfeit all interest plus 25% of principal; borrower recovers double interest paid plus 25% of principal or set off double interest against principal debt.	No defense; no limit on business loans over $25,000.

State	Maximum Legal Rate	Maximum Contract Rate	Maximum Judgment Rate	Penalty for Usury	Corporation's Defense of Usury
Ohio	6%	8%. No limit on loans over $100,000.	6%, but may contract to 8%.	Apply excess interest paid against principal.	No defense.
Oklahoma	6%	No limit if not subject to U3C.	10%	Amount determined by court, not exceeding the greater of either the amount of credit service or loan finance charge or 10 times the amount of the excess charge.	No defense.
Oregon	6%	10% (no limit if more than $50,000).	6%, but may contract to 10%.	Forfeit entire interest.	No defense if more than $50,000, otherwise, 12%.
Pennsylvania	6%	6%, up to $35,000 and business loan up to $10,000.	6%	Forfeit excess over 6%; borrower recovers excess paid over 6%.	No defense.

State	Maximum Legal Rate	Maximum Contract Rate	Maximum Judgment Rate	Penalty for Usury	Corporation's Defense of Usury
Rhode Island	6%	21%	6%	Contract void; borrower recovers all payments.	No provision.
South Carolina	6%	8%, sliding scale to 12% on contracts more than $100,000; no limit if above $500,000.	6%	Forfeit all interest; borrower recovers double interest paid	No defense if capital stock of $40,000 or more has been issued.
South Dakota	6%	10%	10%	Forfeit all interest.	No defense.
Tennessee	6%	10%	8%	Forfeit excess interest.	Can plead.
Texas	6%	10%	9%, but may contract to 10%.	Forfeit twice amount of interest charged, forfeit both principal and interest if rate is double allowed.	Subject to corporate rate of 1½% a month on amounts of $5,000 or more.
Utah	6%	No limit if not subject to U3C.	8%, but may contract to 10%.	Amount determined by court not exceeding the greater of either the amount of credit service or loan finance charge or 10 times the amount of the excess charge.	No provision.

523

State	Maximum Legal Rate	Maximum Contract Rate	Maximum Judgment Rate	Penalty for Usury	Corporation's Defense of Usury
Vermont	8½%	8½%; no limit for business loans; rate for 1- or 2-family dwellings set monthly by Commissioner of Banking; absolute limit 9¼%.	No provision.	Lender forfeits all interest and half of principal; borrower recovers excess paid plus interest, costs and attorney's fees; willful violation $500 fine, 6 mos. jail or both.	No provision.
Virginia	6%	8%; 12% on agricultural loans.	8%	Borrower can recover twice interest paid if suit brought within 2 years.	No defense.
Washington	6% usury laws apply to out-of-state loans made to residents, same as if loans made in state.	12%, plus "set up charge" of lesser of 4% or $15 on loans from $100 to $500; minimum of $4 on ones under $100.	8%, in no case to exceed 10%.	Forfeit all interest; borrower may apply double interest paid against principal; or can collect costs and reasonable attorney's fees.	No defense.

State	Maximum Legal Rate	Maximum Contract Rate	Maximum Judgment Rate	Penalty for Usury	Corporation's Defense of Usury
West Virginia	6%	8%	No provision.	Forfeit all interest; borrower can recover greater of $100 or 4 times interest charged.	No defense.
Wisconsin	5%	12%	7%	Forfeit all interest and principal under $2,000; borrower recovers interest paid and $2,000 of principal.	No defense.
Wyoming	7%	36% up to $300; 21% between $301 and $1,000; 15% or over $1,000; 18% on unpaid balances.	No provision.	Amount determined by court, not exceeding the greater of either the amount of credit service or loan finance charge or 10 times the amount of the excess charge.	No provision.

*Reprinted courtesy of Prentice-Hall, Inc., from the multi-volume "Consumer and Commercial Credit-Installment Sales."

JUDGMENT NOTES AND ATTORNEYS' FEES

Following is a chart designed to give basic information concerning confessions of judgment, judgment notes, and attorneys' fees provisions with pertinent limitations. The material appears courtesy of Prentice-Hall, Inc., Installment Sales (looseleaf service).

ALABAMA (Code of 1958). *Judgment notes:* No statutory provision. *Confessions of judgment:* Invalid, if made before suit. In Jefferson County, small loan licensee may not use judgment note. *Attorneys' fees:* No statutory provision.

ALASKA (Statutes). *Judgment notes:* No statutory provision. *Confessions of judgment:* Valid, if made by debtor in person, or by debtor's attorney-in-fact under power of attorney. *Attorneys' fees:* Retail installment contract may provide for reasonable attorneys' fees.

ARIZONA (Revised Statutes). *Judgment notes:* No statutory provision. *Confessions of judgment:* Valid only if executed after note matures; cannot be made in connection with small loan. *Attorneys' fees:* Motor vehicle time sales contract may provide for reasonable fees.

ARKANSAS (Statutes). *Judgment notes:* No statutory provision. *Confessions of judgment:* Valid if personally made by debtor in court. *Attorneys' fees:* Enforceable, if don't exceed 10% of principal and accrued interest.

CALIFORNIA (Calif. Codes). *Judgment notes:* No statutory provision. *Confessions of judgment:* Valid, if taken for money due or to become due, or to secure contingent liability. But prohibited in time sales contract; also, in contracts of industrial loan company or property broker or small loan licensee. *Attorneys' fees:* May be awarded to prevailing party in any action on time sales contract or installment contract, or on motor vehicle time sales contract.

COLORADO (Revised Statutes, 1963). *Judgment notes:* No statutory provision. *Confessions of judgment:* Void in consumer credit transactions. *Attorneys' fees:* Not over 15% or as directed by court.

CONNECTICUT (General Statutes, 1958). *Judgment notes:* No statutory provision. *Confessions of judgment:* May be offered before trial in pending action. Not permitted in time sales contract or installment loan contract, or in small loan contracts. *Attorneys' fees:* Valid in note or other evidence of indebtedness, but court may modify amount. Also valid in installment contract or installment loan contract, if not more than 15% of balance due.

DELAWARE (Code Anno.). *Judgment notes:* Valid. *Confessions of judgment:* Permitted, if made by warrant of attorney. *Attorneys' fees:* In action on note, contract, or other written instrument, court may award reasonable fees (up to 5% of amount awarded for principal and interest), if instrument provides for payment of such fees.

FLORIDA (Statutes, 1963). *Judgment notes:* No statutory provision. *Confessions of judgment:* Void if executed before or without an action; not permitted in small loan contracts. *Attorneys' fees:* Valid in time sales contracts of motor vehicles, or of other goods.

GEORGIA (Code). *Judgment notes:* No statutory provision. *Confessions of judgment:* Permitted only in suit; invalid in small loan contracts. *Attorneys' fees:* Void, unless debtor given 10 days' notice before suit and fails to pay.

HAWAII (Revised Laws). *Judgment notes:* No statutory provision. *Confessions of judgment:* Not enforceable. Not permitted in small loan contracts. *Attorneys' fees:* Court will award in actions on notes or contracts, if fees specified therein or in separate agreement; but not more than 25%.

IDAHO (Code). *Judgment notes:* No statutory provision. *Confessions of judgment:* Valid, if for money due or to become due, or to secure against contingent liability. Void in consumer credit transactions. Not permitted in small loan contracts. *Attorneys' fees:* Reasonable.

ILLINOIS (Revised Statutes). *Judgment notes:* Valid. *Confessions of judgment:* Enforceable in time sales contracts after buyer's default; valid in small loan contracts. *Attorneys' fees:* Enforceable in time sales contracts, if fee reasonable.

INDIANA (Burns Statutes, Anno.). *Judgment notes:* Void. *Confessions of judgment:* Void. Use of same or judgment note is misdemeanor. Void in consumer credit transactions. *Attorneys' fees:* Reasonable.

IOWA (Code, 1962). *Judgment notes:* No statutory provision. *Confessions of judgment:* Valid, if for money due or to become due, or to secure against contingent liability. Void in consumer credit transactions unless executed after default. *Attorneys' fees:* If note or contract provides for payment of fees, court will allow 10% on first $200, 5% on excess through $500, 3% on excess through $1,000, and 1% on amounts over $1,000.

KANSAS (General Statutes, 1949). *Judgment notes:* No statutory provision. *Confessions of judgment:* Void in consumer credit transactions. *Attorneys' fees:* Unenforceable in consumer credit transactions.

KENTUCKY (Revised Statutes). *Judgment notes:* No statutory provision. *Confessions of judgment:* Void. May not be included in motor vehicle time sales contracts, or in small loan contracts. *Attorneys' fees:* Permitted in motor vehicle time sales contracts, but can't exceed 15% of balance due.

LOUISIANA (Revised Statutes). *Judgment notes:* No statutory provision. *Confessions of judgment:* May not be made before obligation matures, except for purpose of executory process. *Attorneys' fees:* Permitted in motor vehicle time sales contract, if not more than 25% of balance due, with $15 minimum. Consumer credit transaction up to 25% of unpaid debt.

MAINE (Revised Statutes). *Judgment notes:* No statutory provision. *Confessions of judgment:* Prohibited in home repair agreement, and in consumer credit transactions. *Attorneys' fees:* Permitted in home repair agreement and motor vehicle time sales contracts, if reasonable fee. Prohibited in consumer credit sale, lease, or supervised loan; in any other consumer credit transaction up to 15% of unpaid debt.

MARYLAND (Code, 1957). *Judgment notes:* No statutory provision. *Confessions of judgment:* Prohibited in all time sales contracts; also, in small loan contracts. *Attorneys' fees:* Permitted in time sales contracts, up to 15% of balance due, and in retail credit accounts, if reasonable.

MASSACHUSETTS (General Laws). *Judgment notes:* Prohibited. *Confessions of judgment:* Inclusion in note or contract void. Prohibited in time sales contracts of goods and motor vehicles. *Attorneys' fees:* No statutory provision.

MICHIGAN (Statutes, Anno.). *Judgment notes:* No statutory provision. *Confessions of judgment:* Valid, if made in separate instrument. Prohibited in time sales contracts or retail charge agreements; also, in small loan contracts. *Attorneys' fees:* Permitted in home repair installment contract, but not to exceed 20% of balance due. Also permitted in retail charge agreement, if fee reasonable.

MINNESOTA (Statutes, 1961). *Judgment notes:* No statutory provision. *Confessions of judgment:* Valid, if made in separate verified statement. Prohibited in consumer credit transactions. *Attorneys' fees:* Enforceable in motor vehicle time sales contracts up to 15% of balance due.

MISSISSIPPI (Code, 1942). *Judgment notes:* Void. *Confessions of judgment:* Void, including small loan contracts. *Attorneys' fees:* Enforceable in motor vehicle time sales contracts, up to 15% of balance due.

527

MISSOURI (Revised Statutes, 1959). *Judgment notes:* No statutory provision. *Confessions of judgment:* Valid, if taken for money due or to become due, or as security against contingent liability, and made in separate verified statements. *Attorneys' fees:* Enforceable in time sales contracts of goods, up to 15% of balance due; also, on same conditions, in motor vehicle time sales contracts.

MONTANA (Revised Code). *Judgment notes:* Void. *Confessions of judgment:* Valid, if made by separate verified statement. *Attorneys' fees:* Enforceable in time sales contracts up to 15% of balance due.

NEBRASKA (Revised Statutes). *Judgment notes:* No statutory provision. *Confessions of judgment:* May be made by debtor in person, with creditor's consent. Not valid in small loan contracts. *Attorneys' fees:* Court may grant reasonable fees in action for balance due on purchase of necessaries, up to $1,000, and debtor failed to pay after 90-days' notice.

NEVADA (Revised Statutes). *Judgment notes:* No statutory provision. *Confessions of judgment:* Valid, if for sums due or to become due, or to secure contingent liability. Invalid in small loan contracts. *Attorneys' fees:* Provision for reasonable fee in time sales contract valid. Also valid in small loan contracts, if provide fee to be fixed by court in event suit necessary to collect.

NEW HAMPSHIRE (Revised Statutes). *Judgment notes:* No statutory provision. *Confessions of judgment:* Prohibited in motor vehicle time sales contracts; also prohibited in small loan contracts. *Attorneys' fees:* Provision for reasonable fee in motor vehicle time sales contracts valid; not recognized as permissible delinquency charge under small loan laws.

NEW JERSEY (Revised Statutes, 1937). *Judgment notes:* Not permitted. *Confessions of judgment:* Invalid in time sales contracts, or in separate instrument relating thereto; also invalid in home repair contracts and small loan contracts. *Attorneys' fees:* Enforceable in time sales contracts, and retail charge accounts if not more than 20% of first $500 and 10% of excess; also, in home repair contracts, if "reasonable." If state credit union reduces loan to judgment or gives to attorney for collection after default, it may collect attorneys' fees not to exceed 20% (minimum fee $10). Case law holds 20% fee for federal credit unions was reasonable (*Alcoa Edgewater No. FCU v. Carroll,* 210 A.2d 68, 1965).

NEW MEXICO (Statutes, Anno.). *Judgment notes:* Void. *Confessions of judgment:* Void, if made before cause of action accrues on negotiable instrument or contract to pay money. Not permitted in time sales contracts or retail charge agreements. *Attorneys' fees:* Provisions for reasonable fees permitted in time sales contracts, retail charge agreements, or small loan agreements.

NEW YORK (Consolidated Laws). *Judgment notes:* No statutory provision. *Confessions of judgment:* May be made on debtor's affidavit; but judgment void if entered on affidavit made before debtor's default on installment purchases up to $1,500 of goods for nonbusiness or noncommercial use. Prohibited in time sales contracts, including motor vehicles; revolving credit agreements; small loan contracts. *Attorneys' fees:* Valid up to 20% of balance due on revolving credit agreements; up to 15% of balance due on motor vehicle time sales contracts; void on retail installment contracts. Credit unions may collect reasonable fees actually spent for necessary court process after debtor's default.

NORTH CAROLINA (General Statutes). *Judgment notes:* Not recognized *Confessions of judgment:* Enforceable, if made by signed, verified statement for money due or to become due, or to secure against a contingent liability. Prohibited in small loan contracts. *Attorneys' fees:* Enforceable up to 15% of outstanding balance.

NORTH DAKOTA (Century Code, Anno.). *Judgment notes:* No statutory provision. *Confessions of judgment:* Enforceable, if entered on debtor's signed, verified statement for a specific sum. Invalid in time sales contracts; also, small loan contracts. *Attorneys' fees:* Void as against public policy in notes and other evidences of debt.

OHIO (Revised Code). *Judgment notes:* Recognized. *Confessions of judgment:* Invalid if made in connection with consumer loans or consumer transactions. *Attorneys' fees:* Not permitted in time sales contracts.

OKLAHOMA (Statutes, 1961). *Judgment notes:* No statutory provision. *Confessions of judgment:* Enforceable, if entered under warrant of attorney acknowledged by debtor, and if debtor first files affidavit as to the facts. Void in consumer credit transactions. *Attorneys' fees:* Reasonable if amount financed exceeds $1,000.

OREGON (Revised Statutes). *Judgment notes:* No statutory provision. *Confessions of judgment:* Valid, if for money due or to become due or to secure contingent liability; may be entered, with creditor's consent, if acknowledged by debtor. Unenforceable in motor vehicle time sales contracts; invalid as to small loan contracts. *Attorneys' fees:* May provide for reasonable fees in time sales contracts of goods and revolving charge accounts; also, in motor vehicle time sales contracts. Prevailing party in suit on contract gets reasonable fee.

PENNSYLVANIA (Purdon's Statutes). *Judgment notes:* Recognized. *Confessions of judgment:* Invalid in small loan contracts. Invalid if debtor's annual income less than $10,000. *Attorneys' fees:* Fees up to 20% of balance due permitted in home improvement contracts. Credit unions may collect fees to public officials and reasonable fees of attorneys and outside collection agencies; but total of such fees can't exceed 20% of outstanding loan balance.

RHODE ISLAND (General Laws, 1956). *Judgment notes:* No statutory provision. *Confessions of judgment:* Prohibited in small loan contracts. *Attorneys' fees:* Reasonable attorney's fees allowed if suit is brought to realize on collateral used to secure loan.

SOUTH CAROLINA (Code of Laws, 1962). *Judgment notes:* No statutory provision. *Confessions of judgment:* Enforceable, if made by verified statement. Prohibited in small loan contracts. *Attorneys' fees:* May provide in small loan contracts for reasonable fee to be fixed by court.

SOUTH DAKOTA (Code of 1939). *Judgment notes:* No statutory provision. *Confessions of judgment:* Valid, if made by verified statement. *Attorneys' fees:* Void as against public policy.

TENNESSEE (Code. Anno.). *Judgment notes:* Invalid. *Confessions of judgment:* Invalid, if made before action started. *Attorneys' fees:* No statutory provision.

TEXAS (Vernon's Statutes). *Judgment notes:* Invalid. *Confessions of judgment:* Invalid, if made before action started. Prohibited in small loan contracts. *Attorneys' fees:* No statutory provision.

UTAH (Code Anno., 1953). *Judgment notes:* No statutory provision. *Confessions of judgment:* Valid, if made on debtor's verified statement for money due or to become due or to secure contingent liability. Prohibited in consumer credit transactions. *Attorneys' fees:* Not to exceed 15% of unpaid debt in sale; reasonable fee for loan contract.

VERMONT (Statutes, Anno.). *Judgment notes:* No statutory provision. *Confessions of judgment:* Valid, if made by debtor in writing, with creditor's consent; void in consumer contracts. Prohibited in small loan contracts. *Attorneys' fees:* Enforceable as to time sales contracts of goods, revolving charge accounts, and motor vehicle time sales contracts.

VIRGINIA (Code of 1950). *Judgment notes:* Valid; but warrant of attorney in note must name attorney and court in which judgment may be confessed. *Confessions of judgment:* May be entered in clerk's office at any time, but debtor has 21 days after notice of entry in which to move to have judgment set aside. Prohibited in small loan contracts. *Attorneys' fees:* No statutory provision.

WASHINGTON (Revised Code). *Judgment notes:* No statutory provision. *Confessions of judgment:* May be made on debtor's verified statement. Prohibited in small loan contracts. *Attorneys' fees:* May provide for reasonable fee in time sales contracts or revolving charge accounts.

WEST VIRGINIA (Code of 1961, Anno.). *Judgment notes:* No statutory provision. *Confessions of judgment:* May be made in action. Prohibited in small loan contracts. *Attorneys' fees:* No statutory provision.

WISCONSIN (Statutes 1971). *Judgment notes:* Void and unenforceable. *Confessions of judgment:* Void and unenforceable. Prohibited in consumer credit transactions.

WYOMING (Statutes, 1957). *Judgment notes:* Valid. *Confessions of judgment:* May be made by debtor in open court, with creditor's consent; but attorney confessing judgment must show warrant of attorney. Void in consumer credit transactions. *Attorneys' fees:* Reasonable.

GARNISHMENT GUIDE

Below is a chart of state garnishment laws that summarizes the limitations imposed in each jurisdiction on wages subject to garnishment. Specific types of wage earners (such as heads of households) sometimes have different garnishment rates than other individuals, and these are noted in the chart. The figures in brackets following each state name refer to the footnotes following the chart, which indicate the penalties that may result from failure to follow the state practice correctly.

Federal restrictions: Federal law exempts an employee's earnings during a workweek equal to 30 times federal minimum wage or 75% of employee's "disposable earnings," whichever is greater. "Disposable earnings" means earnings minus all deductions required by law. Exemption won't apply, however, to any court order for support of any person; court order of bankruptcy (under Ch. XIII, Bankruptcy Act); or any debt due for any state or federal tax. Union dues, initiation fees, employees' share of health and welfare premiums and repayment of credit union loans aren't considered deductions required by law in determining "disposable income," but amounts withheld for unemployment and workmen's compensation insurance pursuant to state law are considered such deductions.

Law also prohibits employer from firing an employee by reason of the fact his wages have been garnisheed for any one indebtedness (i.e., a single debt regardless of number of garnishment proceedings brought to collect it). Penalty for willful violation: up to $1,000 fine or one year's imprisonment, or both.

If federal and state laws do not agree, law that provides for lesser garnishment or greater restriction on firing will control.

The U.S. Secretary of Labor, acting through Wage-Hour Division, will enforce federal garnishment provisions.

The chart and related materials originally appeared in Prentice-Hall, Inc., Installment Sales (looseleaf service).

ALABAMA (Code). [2] [5] *Laborers and resident employees:* 75% of wages is exempt.

Judgments on consumer credit sale, lease, or loan: Greater of 80% of disposable weekly earnings or 50 times federal hourly minimum wage in effect when payable is exempt; disposable earnings doesn't include periodic payments pursuant to pension, retirement, or disability program. No garnishment can be made before judgment.

ALASKA (Statutes). [2] Maximum amount subject to garnishment is (a) 25% of weekly disposable income, or (b) amount by which disposable earnings each week exceed 30 times federal minimum hourly wage in effect when payable. Multiple weekly wage for semi-monthly period is 2-1/6, for monthly period—4-⅓. Doesn't apply to support orders for any person, orders of bankruptcy court, or for debts for state or federal taxes.

Discharge: Employee can't be discharged for garnishment for any one indebtedness.

ARIZONA (Revised Statutes). [3] [5] [8] Greater of 75% of disposable income or 30 times the federal minimum hourly wage in effect when payable is exempt. This exemption doesn't apply to court support orders where only 50% of disposable income is exempt; or to any bankruptcy orders or debts for state or federal taxes where there is no exemption.

Earnings of a minor child aren't subject to garnishment for parent's debt if the debt wasn't for the special benefit of the child.

ARKANSAS (Statutes). [2] *Laborers and mechanics:* Wages for 60 days are exempt if employee files affidavit with court stating that 60 days' wages together with other personal property he owns doesn't exceed state constitutional limitation ($200 for single resident not head of family, $500 for married resident or head of family). First $25 of "net wages" of all mechanics and laborers absolutely exempt without need for filing schedule of exemptions. "Net wages" means gross wages less following deductions actually withheld: Ark. income tax, fed. income tax, Social Security, group retirement, group hospitalization insurance premiums and group life insurance premiums.

Employees of railroads have exemption of $200 before judgment by creditor.

CALIFORNIA (Deering's Calif. Codes) [2a] 100% of earnings received for personal services rendered within 30 days before date of a withholding by employer pursuant to a levy of execution is exempt if necessary for support of employee or employee's family residing in state. This exemption doesn't apply if debt is for (1) necessaries, or (2) personal services rendered by employee of debtor.

Greater of federal exemption or 50% of earnings received for personal services performed within 30 days before date of a withholding by employer pursuant to a levy of execution is exempt without filing claim for exemption.

Employer may be required to attend court and be examined.

Discharge: Employee can't be discharged because garnishment has been threatened or because wages have been subjected to garnishment for one judgment or for any one indebtedness.

COLORADO (Revised Statutes, 1973). [2] [5] *Head of family:* 70% of earnings, proceeds of health, accident, or disability insurance, and pension or retirement benefits is exempt. *Single persons:* 35% of such earnings and proceeds is exempt.

No garnishment can be made before judgment.

Priorities: Employer can withhold claims that he would have had if not garnisheed.

Discharge: Employee can't be discharged because garnishment has been attempted or because his wages have been garnisheed.

Judgment on consumer credit sale, lease, or loan: Lesser of 25% of disposable weekly earnings or excess over 30 times federal minimum hourly wage is maximum subject to garnishment.

CONNECTICUT (General Statutes). [2] [5] Greater of: 75% of disposable income or 40 times the federal minimum wage in effect when payable, is exempt.

Priorities: Only one execution at a time can be satisfied. They're satisfied in the order they're presented to employer. Execution on wages for support of wife or minor child (children) takes priority over other executions and two or more can be levied at the same time provided total levy leaves $50 of earnings a week. Voluntary wage deduction authorization for payment of amounts due for support in public welfare and other cases has same priority as execution on wages for support. (Voluntary wage execution will not be allowed unless prior order of support has been filed in circuit court. No voluntary wage deduction authorization will be effective less than 14 days from date of signing of authorization).

Discharge: Employer can't discipline, suspend, or discharge employee because his wages have been garnisheed, unless more than 7 garnishments in calendar year. Employer who violates provision is liable to employee for all wages and employment benefits lost by employee from time of unlawful discipline, suspension, or discharge to time of reinstatement.

DELAWARE (Code Anno.) [5] 85% of wages is exempt for all residents; *but* if debt is for a fine or costs, or state taxes, limit doesn't apply.

Priorities: Only one attachment may be made per month.

Discharge: It is unlawful for employer to dismiss employee for garnishment.

DISTRICT OF COLUMBIA (Code, 1973). [2] Greater of: (1) 75% of disposable weekly wages or (2) 30 times federal minimum hourly wage in effect when payable, is exempt. (Doesn't apply to judgments for support; instead, 50% of employee's gross wages is exempt.) Wages of D.C. employees are subject to garnishment for child support, maintenance, or alimony. Employer can't withhold more than 10% of employee's gross wages until total amount paid employee for all pay periods in month exceeds $200; can't withhold more than 20% of wages over $200 until total amount paid employee equals $500.

Wages of nonresident (if major portion earned outside D.C.) are exempt to same extent provided by laws of state of his residence. Exemption applies only to contracts or transactions entered into outside D.C.

$200 of earnings (other than wages), insurance, annuities, or pension or retirement payments for 2 months preceding issuance of garnishment is exempt if person is resident or earns major portion of his livelihood in D.C. and is principal support of family before service of garnishment papers. If husband and wife live together, their total earnings determine exemption; $60 of earnings (other than wages), insurance, etc., for 2 months before service of garnishment papers is exempt if person doesn't support family.

No garnishment can be made before judgment.

Priorities: Only one attachment is satisfied at a time in order of priority of delivery to marshal. However, judgment for support may take priority (in discretion of court).

Discharge: Employee can't be discharged for garnishment or for attempted garnishment.

FLORIDA (Statutes). [4] [17] [25] *Head of family residing in Fla.* All wages are exempt.

Earnings of any person or public officer, state or county (whether head of family residing in Fla. or not) are subject to garnishment to enforce Florida court order for alimony, suit money, or support. Court, in its discretion, determines amount to be garnisheed. Court may issue continuing writ of garnishment for periodic payment of child support, alimony, or both.

GEORGIA (Code). [3] [5] [8] Greater of 75% of disposable weekly earnings or 30 times federal minimum wage, in effect when payable, is exempt. Doesn't apply to judgments of alimony or for support of dependents. $1,000 of wages due deceased employee of railroad company or other corporation is exempt. Wages due employee after he's been ordered involuntarily hospitalized for mental illness are exempt. Salaries of employees and officers of the state and its political subdivisions are subject to garnishment, except where liability for the garnishment is incurred as a result of responding to an emergency while engaged in the scope of their employment. Under these circumstances, the garnishment summons is served upon the appropriate person of the political entity for which the official or employee works.

Default judgment against employer for failure to answer can be modified on motion to 125% of amount due employee, less exemption, from time of service to last day on which timely answer could be made but not less than 15% of amount judgment against employer or $50, whichever is greater.

Discharge: Employee can't be discharged for garnishment for any one indebtedness. Violations are misdemeanors.

HAWAII (Revised Statutes). [5] Following wages are exempt from garnishment: 95% of first $100 per month, 90% of next $100, and 80% of all sums over $200; all compensation for personal services that were rendered during a 31-day period before the date of the garnishment proceedings.

Employer can withhold (liquidated) claims that he would have had if he hadn't been garnisheed.

Priorities: Garnishments are paid in order of service of process on employer. If 2 or more are served at same time, order of issuance from court determines priority.

Discharge: Employer can't suspend or discharge employee because he was summoned as garnishee in action where employee is debtor or because employee filed petition to pay debts under wage earner plan of Bankruptcy Act.

IDAHO (Code). [4] [5] Greater of 75% of disposable earnings or 30 times federal minimum hourly wage, in effect when payable, is exempt. Doesn't apply to support orders, bankruptcy orders, debt for state or federal tax.

Married woman's wages are exempt from execution for husband's debt.

Judgments on consumer credit sale, lease, or loan: Lesser of 25% of disposable earnings or excess over 40 times federal minimum hourly wage, in effect when payable, is maximum subject to garnishment. No prejudgment garnishment permitted. Employee can't be discharged for garnishment; employee discharged in violation of provision has 60 days to bring civil action to recover lost wages and for order requiring reinstatement.

ILLINOIS (Revised Statutes). [2] [22] Lesser of: 15% of gross maximum wages, salary, commissions, bonuses, and periodic payments under a retirement or pension plan paid for the week or the amount by which disposable earnings for the week exceed 30 times the federal minimum hourly wage in effect when paid. No payroll deductions required by law to be withheld may be taken from the nonexempt amount.

Employer is entitled to fee consisting of the greater of $8 or 2% of amount paid pursuant to deduction order or series of orders on same debt.

Priorities: First summons served has priority over subsequent garnishments, which are effective until paid or until end of payroll period immediately prior to 56 days after service in the order in which they are served. Employer can withhold claims he would have had if he hadn't been garnisheed. *Note:* Claims for the support of a spouse or dependent children have priority over all other claims for garnishment of property or other liens obtained on an employee's wages.

Discharge: Employee can't be discharged or suspended for garnishment for any one indebtedness; violations are misdemeanors.

INDIANA (Code, 1971). [4] [18]. Wages can't be garnisheed if employee and creditor are nonresidents and employer is doing business in Ind.

Judgments on consumer credit sale, lease, or loan: Maximum subject to garnishment is 25% of disposable weekly earnings in excess of 30 times federal minimum wage in effect when payable. Doesn't apply to court orders for support of any person or decrees awarding alimony or attorney's fees. No prejudgment garnishment permitted. Employees can't be discharged for such garnishment; employees discharged in violation of provision have 6 months to bring civil action to recover lost wages and for order requiring reinstatement.

Priorities: Court-ordered assignment for child support has priority over all other assignments, garnishments, and attachments.

IOWA (Code, 1975). [2] [5] [19] Greater of 75% of disposable earnings or 30 times federal minimum hourly wage, in effect when payable, is exempt. Maximum amount that can be garnisheed in one calendar year is $250 for each creditor (except under decrees for support of minors).

Exemptions don't apply to judgments for (1) alimony or (2) support of minors.

Wages earned outside Iowa by nonresident, payable outside state, are exempt from garnishment where creditor is nonresident and cause of action arose outside state.

Exemptions don't apply to orders of bankruptcy court.

Discharge: Employee can't be discharged for garnishment.

Judgment on consumer credit sale, lease, or loan: Lesser of 25% of disposable earnings for week or excess over 40 times federal hourly wage in effect when payable; no prejudgment garnishments are permitted; employee can't be discharged for garnishment arising from consumer credit transaction.

KANSAS (Annotated Statutes, 1974). [2] [5] [10] [13] Greater of 75% of disposable

534

weekly earnings or 30 times federal minimum hourly wage. Doesn't apply to court order for support, order of bankruptcy court, or debt for state or federal tax. Limitation on garnishment for support of any person is 50% of an individual's disposable earnings *unless person seeking the garnishment specifies a greater amount to be withheld;* then maximum disposable earnings in a workweek subject to garnishment can't exceed: (1) 60% (65% if there are arrearages over 12 weeks), or (2) 50% if worker is supporting a spouse or dependent child other than the ones in the court order (55% if there are arrearages over 12 weeks). Those grounds must be clearly stated on order of garnishment.

Order effective against nonexempt portion of earnings for entire normal pay period in which order is served.

Wages earned and payable outside state are exempt where cause of action arose outside state unless debtor is personally served with garnishment.

If employee has been out of work for more than 2 weeks because of sickness (or sickness of family member), evidenced by his affidavit, all wages are exempt until 2 months after recovery.

Wages can't be garnisheed by collector or collecting agency.

No prejudgment garnishment orders can be issued against wages.

Priorities: No one creditor can issue more than one garnishment against earnings of same debtor during any months.

Discharge: Employee can't be discharged for garnishment for three or fewer debts; violations are misdemeanors.

KENTUCKY (Revised Statutes). [3] [5] [11] Greater of 75% of disposable earnings or 30 times federal minimum hourly wage in effect when payable is exempt. Doesn't apply to support orders, bankruptcy court orders, debt for state or federal tax.

Where wages are earned and payable outside of state, that state's law concerning exemptions applies to Kentucky garnishment *unless* employee was personally served in Kentucky or was Kentucky resident when debt or cause of action arose.

Prejudgment garnishments can be obtained by making demand on defendant in writing, advising him of grounds of suit and his right to hearing.

Priorities: Orders have priority according to date of service on employer. Court-ordered assignment for support of minor child has priority unless otherwise ordered by the court.

Discharge: No discharge for garnishment for any one indebtedness.

LOUISIANA (Revised Statutes, 1950; 1962 Cum. Supp.). [2] [10] [14] 75% of disposable earnings for any week, but exemption can't be less than $70 a week of disposable earnings.

Exemption doesn't apply to court-ordered support payments for parents by children or grandchildren.

Wages earned and payable outside state are exempt where cause of action arose outside of state.

Priorities: Debt between employer and employee is treated as prior garnishment. However, garnishment of father's wages for child's support always takes priority over all garnishment orders.

MAINE (Revised Statutes). [2] Greater of 75% of disposable earnings or 30 times federal minimum hourly wage prescribed by 206(a)(1) of Title 29 U.S.C. is exempt. If garnishment order is issued without notice (because employee failed to make payments under earlier order), exemption can't be less than $100 a week.

Wages of minor children and wife aren't subject to garnishment for parent's or husband's debt.

Discharge: Employee can't be discharged because earnings have been subject to garnishment orders.

Judgments on consumer credit sale, lease, or loan: Greater of 75% of disposable weekly earnings or 40 times federal minimum hourly wage in effect when payable is exempt; no prejudgment garnishments are permitted; employee can't be discharged for garnishment arising from consumer credit transaction.

MARYLAND (Code). [2] [9] Greater of $120 times number of weeks wages due at date of attachment, when earned, or 75% of such wages due, is exempt. *Caroline, Worcester, Kent, and Queen Anne's Counties:* Greater of 75% of wages due or 30 times federal minimum hourly wage in effect when payable is exempt. Exemptions don't apply to garnishment for state income tax.

Court can order lien on earnings of defendant in paternity suit. Nonsupport court orders will be lien on notification by Probation Dept.

Discharge: Employee can't be discharged for garnishment on any one indebtedness in calendar year; violations are misdemeanors punishable by fines of up to $1,000 and/or a year's imprisonment.

MASSACHUSETTS (General Laws). [4] $125 a week of wages due is exempt. $100 a week of pensions payable to employee is exempt.

Wages due for personal services of defendant's (employee's) wife or minor child are exempt.

Seaman's wages can't be garnisheed (subject to attachment by trustee process), but fisherman's can.

Priorities: Employer can withhold (liquidated) claims that he would have had if he hadn't been garnisheed (summoned as trustee). Valid wage assignment held as security for a debt has priority over garnishment (trustee process).

MICHIGAN (Statutes Anno.). [3] [5] If first garnishment—*Householder having a family:* 60% of wages is exempt. If wages are for one week's labor (or less), the most that is exempt is $50 and least is $30. If wages are for more than one week's labor, maximum exemption is $90, minimum, $60. *Others:* 40% of wages is exempt. Most that is exempt is $50 and least is $20.

All other cases—*Householder having a family*—60% of wages is exempt. If wages are for one week or less, most exempt is $30 and least is $12. If wages are for more than one week but no more than 16 days most that is exempt is $60 and least is $24. If wages are for more than 16 days, maximum exemption is $60 and minimum $30. *Others:* 30% of wages is exempt. Most that can be exempt is $20 and least is $10.

Wages earned at time garnishment papers are served on employer, but not payable on next regular payday, are *not* subject to garnishment.

Amount paid under judgment for alimony or child support is exempt from garnishment.

Priorities: Employer can offset claims he has against employee, except for unliquidated damages for wrongs or injustices.

Discharge: No employer can use garnishment as sole cause of discharge.

MINNESOTA (Statutes, 1971). [2] [5] Greater of 75% of disposable earnings for a pay period or an amount of such wages equal to 40 times the federal minimum hourly wage in effect when payable, times the number of work weeks in such pay period, is exempt. All earnings for preceding 30 days, if needed for use of family supported wholly or partly by his labor, are exempt. If the employee was on relief or in a state correctional institution, all his wages for 6 months after return to work, and after all public assistance has ended, are exempt. Such exemption can be applied only once every 3 years. Exempt disposable earnings are exempt for 20 days after deposit in any financial institution, and for 60 days after deposit if the employee was on relief or an inmate in a correctional institution prior to employment. Assignment, sale, or transfer of any earned or unearned wages is invalid if made after service of a garnishment exemption notice and within 10 days before receipt of the first garnishment or execution on the debt.

Earnings of minor child can't be garnisheed for debt of parent unless debt was for special benefit of minor.

If amount garnisheed is less than $10, garnishment is ineffective and employer is relieved of liability. Employer is relieved of liability after the expiration of 270 days in a prejudgment summons, or 180 days in summons served after garnishment.

Priorities: Garnishments are paid in order of service of garnishee papers on employer. More than one garnishment can be paid at a time limited to total nonexempt disposable earnings.

Discharge: Employee can't be discharged for garnishment. Employee has 90 days from discharge to bring civil action for twice wages lost due to violation and for reinstatement order.

Support: If court orders deductions from employee's pay for support of child supported in whole or part by public agency, employee must notify employer, who must withhold money according to order and remit quarterly to Commissioner of Public Welfare, Attn: Accounting Dept., Administrative Services. Employee can't be discharged or penalized because employer must withhold.

State taxes: Commissioner of Revenue can require withholding from wages of employee delinquent in state taxes. Employer must withhold subject to garnishment exemptions; continue to withhold each pay period until total amount is paid. State claim has priority over any subsequent garnishments or wage assignments. Employer can't discharge employee because of filing for delinquent taxes.

MISSISSIPPI [2] [5] 75% of wages, salary, or other compensation due resident employees or laborers is exempt.

Proceeds of any trust created by employer as part of pension plan, disability or death benefit plan, or any trust created under retirement plan that is exempt from federal income tax aren't subject to garnishment.

Court orders or judgments for payment of alimony, separate maintenance or child support are exempt from garnishment.

MISSOURI (Revised Statutes, 1969). [4] [5] Greater of (a) 75% of disposable weekly earnings; (b) 30 times federal minimum hourly wage in effect when payable; or (c) if resident head of family, 90% of disposable earnings is exempt. Doesn't apply to support orders, orders of bankruptcy court, or for debt due for state or federal taxes. (This includes garnishment to collect attorney's fees granted to wife in matrimonial action, *Dych v. GM, Kans. City District.*, No. 28876, 8/8/77).

Where wages are earned and payable outside of state, employee is exempt from garnishment *unless* personally served.

Discharge: Employee can't be fired for garnishment for any one indebtedness.

MONTANA (Revised Codes). [2] [5] All earnings for personal services performed within 45 days before service of garnishment papers are exempt, if necessary for support of employee's family. If debts are incurred by employee, his wife or family for necessaries of life or gasoline, then 50% of earnings are exempt.

Unmarried employee, over 60, is entitled to same exemption as head of family.

All earnings for preceding 30 days are exempt in actions for $10 or less.

Priorities: Executed in order received by the sheriff.

Discharge: Employee can't be discharged for garnishment served on employer.

NEBRASKA (Revised Statutes). [2] [5] Lessor of (a) 25% of weekly disposable earnings (including pension or retirement program payments); (b) excess of 30 times federal minimum hourly wage in effect when payable; or (c) 15% of disposable earnings if employee head of household, is subject to garnishment. Doesn't apply to support orders of any person, orders of bankruptcy court, or for debt due for state or federal taxes.

No prejudgment action for garnishment may be filed in small claims court.

537

Discharge: Employees can't be discharged for garnishment for any one indebtedness.

Child support: Court order for child support can require employer to withhold fixed amount or percentage from employee's nonexempt disposable earnings to reduce arrears or to pay child support payments and any attorney's fees. (Nonexempt disposable earnings are excess for each workweek of 30 times federal minimum hourly wage in effect when payable.) Employer can deduct a court-fixed amount up to $5 a month for costs. Employee can't be dismissed or penalized for any orders. Orders to withhold have priority over any other garnishment or wage assignment, unless otherwise ordered by court.

NEVADA (Revised Statutes). [2] [5] [8] Lesser of 25% of disposable weekly earnings or excess over 30 times federal minimum hourly wage in effect when payable is subject to garnishment. Exemption doesn't apply to any court orders in bankruptcy, for support or debt due for state or federal taxes.

Employer can offset amounts due him from employee *and* creditor.

Creditor must pay employer $5 fee at time of service of the writ of garnishment.

NEW HAMPSHIRE (Revised Statutes). [2] [5] [10] All wages earned by employee after service of garnishment papers on employer are exempt.

All wages earned before service of garnishment papers are exempt, unless judgment on debt was issued by N.H. court. In such cases, exemption for each week is 50 times federal minimum wage as set by F.L.S.A.

Earnings of wife and minor children of employee are exempt.

$50 a week of wages earned by employee before service of garnishment papers is exempt if main action is based on small loan contract.

All wages of married woman are exempt if action is based on small loan contract to which her husband is, or was at any time, obligor.

Exemptions don't apply in action for taxes by Tax Collector.

Child support: 50% of disposable earnings of responsible parent is exempt from garnishment for court order for child support. Order remains in effect until entire support debt is paid. Employee can't be discharged for support lien served on employer.

NEW JERSEY (Statutes Anno.). [1] If employee earns $48 or more a week, 10% of his wages may be garnisheed; if he earns less than $48, no garnishment. If employee earns more than $7,500 a year, a Court may increase percentage to be garnisheed.

Wages of nonresident employee can't be attached by nonresident creditor or his assigns.

Support: Court can order execution against wages, debts, earnings, salary, trust fund income, or profits for failure to make support or maintenance payments that are more than 45 days overdue.

Employer can retain as compensation 5% of amount deducted pursuant to garnishment.

Priorities: Only one execution can be satisfied at a time in order in which they are served on employer. *Exceptions:* support orders for child or wife have priority over other executions served on same day.

Discharge: Employer can't discharge or take any other disciplinary action against employee because his earnings have been subject to garnishment for one or more indebtedness.

NEW MEXICO (Statutes, Anno.). [2] [5] Either 75% of disposable earnings each pay period or 40 times federal minimum hourly wage each week, whichever is greater, is exempt.

Priorities: Liens will be satisfied in order in which they are served on employer.

NEW YORK (Consolidated Laws). [2] [5] [7] *Income execution:* 90% of earnings for personal services rendered within 60 days before, and any time after, income execution is exempt, *but* employee may be garnisheed to the extent of 10% of his wages only when he's receiving or will receive more than $85 a week.

Earnings of recipients of public assistance are exempt.

538

Garnishment proceeding, court not of record: 10% of earnings can be garnisheed by court order if judgment has been recovered in a court not of record against an employee whose income is (1) $30 or more a week if he resides or works in a city of 250,000 or more, or (2) $25 a week in any other case. Only one garnishment can be satisfied at a time. If 2 or more are issued simultaneously, they are satisfied in the order they are served on the employer.

Priorities: Garnishments are paid in the order in which the executions were delivered to an officer authorized to levy in the county, town, or city in which the employee resides or, if the employee's a nonresident, the county, town, or city in which he's employed. Assignment or court order for support of minor child and/or spouse takes priority over other assignment or garnishment of wages, etc., except as to deductions made mandatory by law.

Discharge: No employee may be laid off or discharged because one or more executions have been served against his wages; employee has 90 days from discharge to bring civil action for damages for wages lost (not to exceed lost wages for 6 weeks); court may order reinstatement. (Not more than 10% of the damages recovered in such action may be subjected to claims, attachments, or executions.)

NORTH CAROLINA (General Statutes). [2] [10] *Head of family:* All earnings for 60 days before service of garnishment papers are exempt if necessary for support of employee's family.

Garnishment is limited to 10% of salary or wages paid in any one month in state tax collection proceedings; to 10% of wages in any one pay period in municipal and county property tax collection proceeding. Wages due officials or employees of N.C., its agencies, instrumentalities, and political subdivisions are subject to garnishment for delinquent taxes.

Priorities: Priority in the order attachments were levied.

Child support: Independent garnishment proceeding is available for enforcement of child support obligations.

NORTH DAKOTA (Century Code, Anno.). [4] [8] [16] Greater of 75% of disposable weekly earnings or 40 times federal minimum hourly wage in effect when payable is exempt. Doesn't apply to court orders for support of any person or of bankruptcy court or for debt for state or federal taxes.

Judge may order all of employee's earnings for personal services within 60 days of order exempted if affidavit shows they're necessary for support of employee's family.

OHIO (Revised Code). [2] [10] [12] Greater of the following owed employee for services rendered within 30 days before attachment, process, judgment, or order is exempt: (1) 75% of disposable earnings owed, or (2) 30 times current federal minimum hourly wage in effect at time earnings are payable if paid weekly; 60 times if paid bi-weekly; 65 times if paid semi-monthly; 130 times if paid monthly. There must be at least 30 days between garnishments.

Support orders have priority over all other garnishments and no part of wages is exempt from them. They are paid in order received. Employer may deduct up to 1% as service charge.

Judgments for taxes, except for real estate, aren't entitled to exemptions.

Resident and nonresident can apply to court in jurisdiction of place of employment for appointment of trustee to avoid garnishment of nonexempt earnings.

Priorities: County court issuing first order served determines priorities. Priorities may be determined by court order.

Discharge: Employee can't be discharged solely for attachment for no more than one action in garnishment in any 12-month period.

OKLAHOMA (Statutes 1971). [2] [3] [5] *Resident homeowner or head of family:* 75% of all wages for services performed within last 90 days is exempt.

Resident employee can apply to have *all* wages for services performed within 90 days before issuing of garnishment papers exempted if necessary for support of his family, but not if judgment is for child support or maintenance.

Resident not head of family: 75% of all wages for service is exempt.

Exemptions don't apply to nonresidents, or to debtor in the act of removing his family from the state or who has absconded, taking with him his family.

Wages of any clerk, mechanic, laborer, or servant aren't entitled to exemption.

Prejudgment garnishment: Beginning 10/1/78, prejudgment garnishment of wages can be made for support payments provided in a divorce proceeding interlocutory order; 75% of earnings for personal services earned during last 90 days are exempt *except* for child support obligations; child support payments can be provided up to 33⅓% of parent's earnings, less income taxes withheld, if child needs such amount and employee's needs permit such payments.

Priorities: Priorities may be determined by court order.

Judgments on consumer credit sale, lease, or loan: Lesser of 25% of disposable earnings or excess over 30 times federal minimum hourly wage in effect when payable is maximum subject to garnishment. Employee's wages can't be garnisheed before judgment in an action. Employee can't be discharged unless employer garnisheed for 1 or more judgments on more than 2 occasions in 1 year.

OREGON (Revised Statutes, 1973). [3] [4] [5] Greater of 75% of disposable weekly earnings or 40 times federal minimum hourly wage in effect 3/31/75 is exempt. Doesn't apply to support orders (including awards of attorneys' fees or costs), bankruptcy orders, debt for state or federal tax. Protection of law can't be waived.

Any legal process served must indicate whether it is subject to garnishment restrictions.

Discharge: No employer can discharge any person for garnishment.

PENNSYLVANIA (Statutes, Anno.). [2] [26] All wages are exempt.

Exceptions: Wages are subject to garnishment for 4 weeks' board and lodging.

Husband's wages can be garnisheed to pay support for wife and children. Under Civil Procedural Support Law, wages may be attached to enforce support ordered by court; employer is authorized to deduct 2% of amount paid under order from employee's wages for clerical work and expense of complying.

Wages can be garnisheed for judgment in fornication and bastardy case.

On tax collector's written notice and demand, employer must deduct from employee's wages, commissions, or earnings then owing (or that become due within 60 days thereafter), or from any unpaid commissions or earnings in his possession (or that come into his possession within 60 days thereafter), a sum sufficient to pay employee's or his wife's delinquent *per capita, poll, occupation, occupational privilege, local earned income taxes,* and costs, and must pay this sum to tax collector within 60 days after receipt of notice. No more than 10% of wages, commissions, or earnings of delinquent taxpayer or husband can be deducted at one time. Employer may keep up to 2% of money collected for extra book-keeping expenses.

RHODE ISLAND (General Laws). [2] $50 a week of earnings is exempt; all earnings of wife and minor child of employee are exempt; all wages of seamen are exempt. If employee was on relief, all his wages for one year are exempt.

Priorities: Priority in order attachments were procured.

SOUTH CAROLINA (Code of Laws). [10] All earnings for personal services are exempt.

Judgments on consumer credit sale, lease, or loan: Creditor can't attach unpaid earnings of debtor by garnishment or like proceedings. Employee can't be discharged because of such garnishment.

SOUTH DAKOTA (Compiled Laws, Anno.). [2] [5] All earnings for personal services performed within 60 days before garnishment order are exempt if necessary for the use of a family supported wholly or partly by employee's labor.

Payments for foster care of children under programs of the division of child welfare of the department of public welfare aren't subject to garnishment, except for necessaries furnished for the subsistence and maintenance of such children.

Garnishment of earnings is prohibited before final judgment. ("Earnings" include periodic payments under pension or retirement programs.)

TENNESSEE (Code, Anno.). [2] [5] [23] Lesser of 25% of disposable earnings for the week, or excess over 30 times the federal minimum hourly wage in effect when earnings payable is subject to garnishment. Additional $2.50 a week for each dependent child under 16 is exempt. Judgment is a lien on wages due at time of service of execution and on subsequent earnings until judgment is satisfied or until expiration of payroll period immediately prior to 3 calendar months after service, whichever is first.

Exemptions don't apply if judgment against employee is for alimony or child support.

Above exemptions don't apply to taxes; or to fines and costs for voting out of district or ward where voter lives, carrying deadly or concealed weapons, or giving away or selling intoxicating liquors on election days.

Where wages are earned and payable outside of state, employee is exempt from garnishment *unless* actually served with process.

Priorities: Priorities are determined in order served.

TEXAS (West's Texas Statutes and Codes). All current wages for personal services are exempt.

UTAH (Code Anno.). [2] [5] [10] [21] *Head of family or married man:* 50% of earnings for personal services performed within 30 days before service of garnishment papers is exempt if necessary for support of family. Minimum exemption, $50.

Earnings of a minor child aren't subject to garnishment for parent's debt if debt wasn't for special benefit of child.

Employer can withhold claims that he would have had if he weren't garnisheed.

Discharge: Employee can't be discharged for garnishment for any one indebtedness.

Judgments on consumer credit sale, lease, or loan: Greater of 75% of disposable weekly earnings or 40 times federal minimum hourly wage in effect when payable is exempt. No prejudgment garnishment is permitted.

Child support: Maximum disposable earnings for any work pay period that can be garnisheed to enforce judgment arising out of failure to support dependent children can't exceed 50% of disposable earnings. Employer can deduct $3 for each payment. Employee can't be discharged because of such garnishment.

VERMONT (Statutes, Anno.). [2] [5] Where employee's weekly disposable earnings are $64 or less, only earnings in excess of $48 may be attached; if weekly disposable earnings exceed $64, no more than 25% may be attached. (Limits for pay periods other than weekly are those the U.S. Secretary of Labor prescribes by regulation.) "Earnings" includes periodic payments pursuant to a pension or retirement program.

Wages owed employee can't be garnisheed (subject to trustee process) until claim has been reduced to judgment.

Wages due minor child can't be garnisheed in action against parent; wages due married woman can't be garnisheed in action against husband.

Wages earned outside state by nonresident employee of a corporation are exempt if his state of residence also exempts them.

Employer can withhold claims (based on express or implied contract) that he would have had if he hadn't been garnisheed.

Weekly disposable earnings due in excess of 30 times federal minimum hourly wage in effect when payable are subject to a lien for delinquent poll tax or old age assistance tax at rate of $4 a week, regardless of any assignment of earnings.

Discharge: It is unlawful for employer to discharge employee because employee's compensation has been garnisheed unless employer has been previously garnisheed for that employee on 5 or more separate occasions arising from separate actions, or unless employer

541

establishes there were other substantial causes contributing to the discharge. Employer who wrongfully discharges employee is liable for up to one month's compensation, plus reasonable costs.

VIRGINIA (Code). [1] [5] [6] [11] Greater of 75% of disposable weekly earnings or 30 times federal minimum hourly wage in effect when payable is exempt. Doesn't apply to court-ordered support, bankruptcy order, or debt for state or federal taxes. Limitations on garnishment for support of any person: (1) 60% of disposable earnings for workweek (65% if arrearages of over 12 weeks); or (2) 50% of disposable earnings if supporting a spouse or dependent child other than person provided for in garnishment order (55% if arrearages of over 12 weeks). (Exemption doesn't extend to collection of local taxes.) "Earnings" includes periodic payments under pension or retirement program.

Every householder or head of a family residing in the state, in addition to the above exemption, is entitled to a $5,000 exemption. Veterans with a service-related disability of 40% or more also get another $2,000 exemption.

Wages of minors are exempt from garnishment for debts of parents.

Discharge: Employee can't be discharged for garnishment for any one indebtedness.

WASHINGTON (Revised Code, 1974). [3] [5] Greater of 40 times state minimum hourly wage or 75% of disposable weekly earnings is exempt. Deductions as contributions toward pension or retirement plan established pursuant to collective bargaining agreement aren't part of disposable earnings. Exemption doesn't apply to garnishment for child support if (a) based on judgment, court order, or order issued by Dept. of Social and Health Services, (b) amount doesn't exceed 2 months support payments, and (c) writ contains specific statutory language. Continuing lien on wages can be obtained.

"Earnings" includes periodic payments received pursuant to a pension or retirement program.

No garnishment action can be brought to recover the price or value of spirituous, malt, ardent, or intoxicating liquors sold at retail.

Priorities: Garnishment has priority over assignment by public employee filed with employer subsequent to service of the garnishee summons.

Discharge: Employer can't discharge employee because his earnings have been garnisheed for any one indebtedness. Willful violation may result in fine of up to $1,000 and/or imprisonment for up to one year.

Judgments on consumer credit transactions: Exemption is the greater of (1) 75% of disposable earnings, or (2) $15 per week per dependent (other than employee) claimed for federal income tax withholding purposes, plus 40 times federal minimum hourly wage in effect when payable. Employee can't be discharged for such garnishment; violations result in recovery of back wages and reinstatement if employee files action within 90 days.

WEST VIRGINIA (Code, Anno.). [2] [5] [20] 80% of earnings in a week is exempt; wages payable to employee can't be less than $20 a week.

Priorities: Only one garnishment is satisfied at a time. However, where 2 or more have been served and first garnishment has been satisfied, non-exempt wages remaining are applied toward satisfaction of junior garnishments in order of their priority. Garnishment has priority over assignment filed subsequent to notice of garnishment.

Judgments on consumer credit sale or loan: Greater of 80% of disposable weekly earnings or 30 times federal minimum hourly wage in effect when payable is exempt. No prejudgment garnishment is permitted. Employee can't be discharged because of such garnishment.

WISCONSIN (Statutes, 1973). [2] [5] [15] *Worker with no dependents:* Basic exemption—60% of income of employee for each 30-day period before service of process in proceeding to collect debt. Exemption cannot be less than $75 nor more than $100. Employee can elect to have exemption computed on 90-day basis.

Worker with dependents: Basic exemption—On income of employee for each 30-day period before service of process in proceeding to collect debt, $120 plus $20 for each dependent. However, total exemption cannot exceed 75% of total income. Employee can elect to have exemption computed on 90-day basis.

"Income" means gross receipts less federal and state withholding and Social Security taxes. A person's interest in any employee benefit plan, retirement, pension, disability, death benefit, stock bonus, or profit-sharing plan is not subject to garnishment.

Subsistence allowance: When earnings are subjected to garnishment, employer pays, on date earnings are payable, subsistence allowance to employee of greater of 75% of disposable weekly earnings or 30 times federal minimum hourly wage. Doesn't apply to support orders, bankruptcy orders, debt for state or federal tax, or orders in voluntary proceedings by wage earners. Garnishment action against earnings can't be started before judgment.

"Earnings" include periodic payments received pursuant to a pension or retirement program.

No garnishment action can be brought to recover the price or value of spirituous, malt, ardent or intoxicating liquors sold at retail.

Priorities: Garnishment has priority over assignment by public employee filed with employer subsequent to service of the garnishee summons.

Discharge: Employer can't discharge employee because his earnings have been garnisheed for any one indebtedness. Willful violation may result in fine of up to $1,000 and/or imprisonment for up to one year.

Judgments on consumer credit transactions: Exemption is the greater of (1) 75% of disposable earnings, or (2) $15 per week per dependent (other than employee) claimed for federal income tax withholding purposes, plus 40 times federal minimum hourly wage in effect when payable. Employee can't be discharged for such garnishment; violations result in recovery of back wages and reinstatement if employee files action within 90 days.

WYOMING (Statutes). [1] [5] *Head of resident family:* 50% of earnings for personal services performed within 60 days before service of garnishment papers is exempt, if necessary for support of family.

Priorities: Priorities may be determined by court order.

Judgments on consumer credit sale, lease, or loan: Lesser of 25% of disposable earnings or excess over 30 times federal minimum hourly wage in effect when payable is maximum subject to garnishment. No prejudgment garnishment permitted. Employee can't be discharged for such garnishment; employee wrongfully discharged has 45 days to bring civil action to recover lost wages and for order requiring reinstatement (damages recoverable can't exceed lost wages for 6 weeks).

Footnotes

[1] If employer doesn't follow garnishment procedure, he may be subject to civil action by his employee's creditor.

[2] If employer doesn't follow garnishment procedure, he may be liable for all or part of claim that creditor has against his employee.

[3] If employer doesn't follow garnishment procedure, he may be subject to contempt proceedings; in *Mich.*, he may be committed to jail.

[4] If employer doesn't follow garnishment procedure, judgment may be taken against him.

[5] Salaries of employees of state and/or its subdivisions may be subject to garnishment. In *Tenn.*, includes members of General Assembly.

[6] Employer is governed by return date of summons but after service or knowledge of issuance of summons, employer can only pay employee exempt wages (*Va.*).

Footnotes *(continued)*

[7] $85 a week floor on garnishable earnings applies to all income executions in effect on or after 9/1/70 even if previously filed; applies to gross income *(N.Y.)*.

[8] Based on decision in *Sniadach* case, laws in following states allowing prejudgment garnishments were ruled invalid: *Ariz. (Termplan, Inc., v. Superior Ct. of Maricopa Cty.,* 463 P. 2d 68, 1969); *Nev.; N. Dak.).*

[9] Under both state and federal law, exemption applies to employee's disposable earnings or net take-home pay after all lawful deductions or withholdings *(Md.)*.

[10] Application denied for exemption from federal restriction, *Ill.*, 12/10/70; *Kansas*, 10/30/70; *La.*, 5/25/71; *N.H.*, 8/10/70; *N.C.*, 12/3/70; *Ohio*, 11/25/70; *S.C.*, 12/3/70; *Utah* 2/5/71.

[11] States exempt from federal wage garnishment restrictions: *Ky.*, 12/5/70; *Va.*, 1/12/71. U.S. Labor Dept. retains enforcement responsibility for discharge provisions.

[12] One-garnishment-a-month provision stands *(Hodgson v. Cleveland Municipal Court,* 3/19/71; *Hodgson v. Hamilton Municipal Court,* 9/23/71; 7/31/72).

[13] When a person is employed out of state by employer doing "substantial" business in state, particularly when employer has resident agent in state, garnishment for unpaid state income tax can be used and taxpayer needn't be personally served with any papers. The exemption applies to court-ordered alimony payments but after a hearing, court can order that exemption does not apply unless

[14] State law on garnishment applies to teachers *(La.)*.

[15] **Judgment on consumer credit transactions:** When pay period is one calendar week or less, amount of wages exempt under provision exempting $15 per week per dependent plus 40 times federal minimum hourly wage is determined on calendar-week basis regardless of number of hours worked; when pay period is multiple of whole calendar weeks, exemption is weekly rate under exemption formula times number of calendar weeks in such pay period; when pay period is greater than one calendar week and not a multiple of whole calendar weeks, exemption is sum of exemption for each calendar week plus 1/7th of weekly rate of each additional day in pay period *(Wisc.)*.

[16] N. Dak. Code violates federal restrictions by allowing employer to pay entire amount of employee's paycheck to sheriff or clerk of court. Employee could be deprived of all accrued earnings pending court determination *(Hodgson v. Christopher et al.,* NE Div., No. 4693, 11/6/73) *(N. Dak.)*.

[17] Federal maximum amount of earnings allowed to be garnisheed preempts Fla. garnishment provision. Preemption doesn't invalidate entire Fla. garnishment statute *(Phillips v. General Finance Corp. of Fla., et al.,* Fla. Sup., Ct., No. 44, 212, 5/15/74) *(Fla.)*.

[18] Debtor who satisfies resident-householder garnishment exemption requirements and whose indebtedness comes from breach of contract will have protection of either this or the consumer credit exemption, whichever results in lesser amount of garnisheed income *(Mims v. Commercial Credit Corp.,* Ind. Sup. Ct., No. 374557, 3/13/74 *(Ind.))*.

[19] $250 maximum amount of earnings that can be garnisheed includes any costs of garnishment proceedings *(Iowa)*.

[20] For purposes of judgments on *consumer credit sale or lease,* to determine number of weeks in pay period, month equals 4-⅓ weeks; half-month 2-1/6 weeks *(W. Va.))*.

[21] Judgment for delinquent taxes obtained under garnishment procedures is subject to the 25% Utah ceiling *(State Tax Commission of the State of Utah v. Meier,* Utah Sup. Ct., No. 14315, 3/24/76).

[22] Municipal corporation isn't exempt from garnishment provisions *(Henderson v. Foster,* Ill. Sup. Ct., No. 46398, 11/27/74) *(Ill.)*.

[23] Costs of all garnishments are to be deducted from funds paid into court and not from funds exempt from garnishment *(Tenn.)*.

[24] Florida's garnishment was found to be constitutional by Fifth Circuit even though it permitted post-judgment garnishment of wages without prior notice of or an opportunity for a hearing *(Brown v. Liberty Loan Corp. of Duval,* CA-5, No. 75-1460, 10/6/76).

[25] Prejudgment garnishment procedure providing for no notice to debtor, and under which writ of garnishment may be issued on unsworn testimony of creditor or his attorney, violates due process *(Bunton v. First Nat. Bank of Tampa,* MD. Fla., 1975, 394 F. Supp. 793) *(Fla)*.

[26] Wages earned in Pa. may be attached for judgment entered in another state for debt incurred in that state *(Pa.)*.

[27] 80% of disposable monthly earnings is exempt from garnishment for child support obligations *(N.C.)*.

FEDERAL ESTATE AND GIFT TAX RATES

The uniform rate table, which is to be used to calculate both estate and gift taxes, is as follows:

If the amount with respect to which the tentative tax to be computed is:	The tentative tax is:
Not over $10,000	18 percent of such amount.
Over $10,000 but not over $20,000	$1,800, plus 20 percent of the excess of such amount over $10,000.
Over $20,000 but not over $40,000	$3,800, plus 22 percent of the excess of such amount over $20,000.
Over $40,000 but not over $60,000	$8,200, plus 24 percent of the excess of such amount over $40,000.
Over $60,000 but not over $80,000	$13,000, plus 26 percent of the excess of such amount over $60,000.
Over $80,000 but not over $100,000	$18,200, plus 28 percent of the excess of such amount over $80,000.
Over $100,000 but not over $150,000	$23,800, plus 30 percent of the excess of such amount over $100,000.
Over $150,000 but not over $250,000	$38,800, plus 32 percent of the excess of such amount over $150,000.
Over $250,000 but not over $500,000	$70,800, plus 34 percent of the excess of such amount over $250,000.
Over $500,000 but not over $750,000	$155,800, plus 37 percent of the excess of such amount over $500,000
Over $750,000 but not over $1,000,000	$248,300, plus 39 percent of the excess of such amount over $750,000.
Over $1,000,000 but not over $1,250,000	$345,800, plus 41 percent of the excess of such amount over $1,000,000.
Over $1,250,000 but not over $1,500,000	$488,300, plus 43 percent of the excess of such amount over $1,250,000.
Over $1,500,000 but not over $2,000,000	$555,800, plus 45 percent of the excess of such amount over $1,500,000.
Over $2,000,000 but not over $2,500,000	$780,800, plus 49 percent of the excess of such amount over $2,000,000.
Over $2,500,000 but not over $3,000,000	$1,025,800, plus 53 percent of the excess of such amount over $2,500,000.
Over $3,000,000 but not over $3,500,000	$1,290,800, plus 57 percent of the excess of such amount over $3,000,000.
Over $3,500,000 but not over $4,000,000	$1,575,800, plus 61 percent of the excess of such amount over $3,500,000.
Over $4,000,000 but not over $4,500,000	$1,880,800, plus 65 percent of the excess of such amount over $4,000,000.
Over $4,500,000 but not over $5,000,000	$2,205,800, plus 69 percent of the excess of such amount over $4,500,000.
Over $5,000,000	$2,550,800, plus 70 percent of the excess of such amount over $5,000,000.

Nonresident Aliens: A special rate schedule is provided for computing the estate tax on transfers of property situated in the U.S. by nonresident alien decedents. The rates range from 6% on the first $100,000 in taxable transfers to 30% on taxable transfers over $2 million. The special rate schedule is also used to determine the tax on taxable gifts made after December 31, 1976, for the purpose of computing the estate tax under the unified tax procedure.

STATE GIFT TAXES

Alabama

No gift tax.

Alaska

No gift tax.

Arizona

No gift tax.

Arkansas

No gift tax.

California

Exemptions:

Class A: Spouse: $60,000
Minor child: $12,000.
Lineal ancestor of donor, lineal issue of donor, mutually acknowledged child, and lineal issue of acknowledged child: $5,000.

Class B: Siblings and their descendants, wife or widow of son, or husband or widower of daughter: $2,000.

Class C: All others: $300.

Annual exclusion: $3,000.

*Range of rates (*value up to and in excess of $400,000).

Class A: 3%-14%.

Class B: 6%-20%.

Class C: 10%-24%.

Statute: Revenue and Taxation Code, Division 2, Part 9.

Colorado

Exemptions:

Class A: Parents, spouse, children, step-children, adopted children, any

Colorado (cont.)

lineal descendant.
Spouse: $20,000.
All others: $10,000.

Class B: Wife or widow of son, husband or widower of daughter, grandparents, siblings, or mutually acknowledged children: $2,000.

Class C: Uncles, aunts, nieces, nephews or any lineal descendant of same: $500.

Class D: All others: $500.

Annual exclusion:

Class A: $3,000.

Class B: $1,500.

Class C: $1,000.

Class D: $1,000.

Range of rates:

Class A: 2% - 8% (value up to and in excess of $500,000).

Class B: 3% - 10%- (value up to and in excess of $200,000).

Class C: 4% - 14% (value up to and in excess of $500,000).

Class D: 7% - 16% (value up to and in excess of $500,000).

Statute: Colorado Revised Statutes of 1973, Title 39, Article 25.

Connecticut

No gift tax.

Delaware

Exemptions: None

Annual exclusion: $3,000.

546

Delaware *(cont.)*

Range of rates (value up to and in excess of $200,000): 1%-6%.

Statute: Delaware Code of 1953, Title 30, Chapter 14. Applicable for last calendar quarter of 1971 and each calendar quarter thereafter.

District of Columbia

No gift tax.

Florida

No gift tax.

Georgia

No gift tax.

Hawaii

No gift tax.

Idaho

No gift tax.

Indiana

No gift tax.

Illinois

No gift tax.

Iowa

No gift tax.

Kansas

No gift tax.

Kentucky

No gift tax.

Louisiana

Exemptions:

No personal.

Louisiana *(cont.)*

Specific lifetime: $30,000

Annual exclusion: $3,000.

Range of rates (value up to and in excess of $15,000): 2%-3%.

Statute: Louisiana Revised Statutes of 1950, Title 47, Sub-Title II, Chapter 14.

Maine

No gift tax.

Maryland

No gift tax.

Massachusetts

No gift tax.

Michigan

No gift tax.

Minnesota

Exemptions:

Class A: Wife, minor or dependent child: $10,000.

Class B: Husband, adult child, other lineal descendant, stepchild, mutually acknowledged child or lineal descendants of such adopted or mutually acknowledged children; $5,000.
Lineal ancestor of the donor: $3,000.

Class C: Brother or sister and their descendants, wife or widow of a son, husband of a daughter: $1,000.

Class D: All others: $250.

Annual exclusion: $3,000.

Range of rates (value up to and in excess of $1,000,000):

Minnesota *(cont.)*

Class A: 1½% - 10%.

Class B: 2% - 10%.

Class C: 6% - 25%.

Class D: 8% - 30%.

Statute: Minnesota Statutes of 1971, Chapter 292.

Mississippi

No gift tax.

Missouri

No gift tax.

Montana

No gift tax.

Nebraska

No gift tax.

Nevada

No gift tax.

New Hampshire

No gift tax.

New Jersey

No gift tax.

New Mexico

No gift tax.

New York

Exemptions: None.

Annual exclusion: $3,000.

Range of rates (value up to and in excess of $10,100,000): 1.5%-15.75%.

Statute: Consolidated Laws, Chapter 60, Art. 26-A.

North Carolina

Exemptions:

Class A: Lineal issue, lineal ancestors, spouse, adopted child or step-child, $30,000.

Class B: Siblings or their descendants, uncles or aunts, by blood of the donor, no exemption.

Class C: All others, no exemption.

Annual exclusion: $3,000.

Range of rates:

Class A: 1% - 12% (value up to and in excess of $3,000,000).

Class B: 4% - 16% (value up to and in excess of $3,000,000).

Class C: 8% - 17% (value up to and in excess of $2,500,000).

North Dakota

No gift tax.

Ohio

No gift tax.

Oklahoma

Exemptions:

No personal.

Annual exclusion: $3,000.

Range of rates (value up to and in excess of $10,000,000): 1%-10%.

Statute: Oklahoma Statutes of 1971, Title 68, Article IX.

Oregon

Exemptions:

No personal.

Oregon *(cont.)*

Specific: $50,000 (1979-1980, $70,000; 1981-1982, $100,000; 1983-1984, $200,000; 1985-1986, $500,000).

Annual exclusion: $3,000.

Range of rates: Flat 12% (1987 and thereafter, 0)

Statute: Oregon Revised Statutes, Title 12, Chapter 119.

Pennsylvania

No gift tax.

Puerto Rico

Exemptions:

No personal.

Specific: $30,000 (plus a yearly exemption of $1,000 to each one of donor's children who are declared permanently mentally or physically disabled by the court).

Annual exclusion: $500.

Range of rates (value up to and in excess of $6,000,000): 2.25% - 52.5%

Statute: Laws of 1968, Chapter 3, Act 167.

Rhode Island

Exemptions:

No personal.

Specific: $25,000.

Annual exclusion: $3,000.

Range of rates (value up to and in excess of $1,000,000): 2% - 9%.

Statute: Rhode Island General Laws of 1956, Title 44, Chapter 24.

South Carolina

Exemptions:

No personal.

Specific: $60,000.

Annual exclusion: $3,000.

Range of rates (value up to and in excess of $100,000): 5%-7%.

Statute: South Carolina Code, Title 12, Chapter 17.

South Dakota

No gift tax.

Tennessee

Exemptions:

Class A: Spouse, children, lineal ancestor, lineal descendant, or legally adopted person, $10,000.

Class B: All others $5,000.

Annual exclusion: None.

Range of rates:

Class A: 1.4% - 9.5% (value up to and in excess of $500,000).

Class B: 6.5% - 20% (value up to and in excess of $250,000).

Statute: Tennessee Code Annotated of 1955, Title 67, Chapter 25.

Texas

No gift tax.

Utah

No gift tax.

Vermont

Exemptions:

No personal.

Specific: $30,000.

Annual exclusion: $3,000.

Range of rates: Measured by 30% of the federal gift tax liability assessed against Vermont gifts (for gifts made after 12/31/76, but before 1/1/79, the tax is reduced by the percentage which $60,000 is of the amount of the federal taxable gifts, but not reduced by more than 100%; after 12/31/78 it is reduced by the percentage which $120,000 is of the federal taxable gifts, but not reduced by more than 100%).

Statute: Vermont Statutes Annotated, Title 32, Chapter 190.

Virginia

Exemptions:

Class A: Spouse, parents, grandparents, children by blood or by legal adoption, stepchildren and all other lineal ancestors and lineal descendants, $5,000.

Class B: Siblings, nephews, nieces: $3,000.

Class C: All others: $3,000.

Annual exclusion: None

Range of rates:

Class A: 1% - 5% (value up to and in excess of $1,000,000).

Class B: 2% - 10% (value up to and in excess of $500,000).

Virginia *(cont.)*

Class C: 5% - 15% (value up to and in excess of $500,000).

Statute: Code of Virginia of 1950, Chapter 6 Secs. 213-238.

Washington

Exemptions:

Class A: Lineal ancestor, lineal descendant, husband, wife, stepchild or lineal descendant of a stepchild, adopted child or lineal descendant of an adopted child, adopted child of the lineal descendant of the donor, son-in-law or daughter-in-law, $10,000.

Class B: Brothers and sisters, $1,000.

Class C: All others, no specific exemption.

Annual exclusion: $3,000.

Range of rates:

Class A: 1% - 10% (value up to and in excess of $500,000).

Class B: 3% - 20% (value up to and in excess of $100,000).

Class C: 10% - 25% (value up to and in excess of $50,000).

Statute: Washington Revised Code of 1961, Chapter 8356, Title 38.

West Virginia

No gift tax.

Wisconsin

Exemptions:

Class A: Spouse, $100,000.
Lineal issue, lineal ancestor, wife or widow of a son, husband or widower of a daughter, or a mutu-

Wisconsin *(cont.)*

ally acknowledged child including his spouse and issue, $4,000.

Class B: Siblings or a descendant, no exemption.

Class C: Aunt or uncle or a descendant, no exemption.

Class D: All others, no exemption.

Annual exclusion: $3,000.

Range of rates:

Class A: Spouse, 1.25% - 6.25%

Wisconsin *(cont.)*

Lineal issue, 2.5% - 12.5% (value up to and in excess of $500,000).

Class B: 5% - 25% (value up to and in excess of $500,000).

Class C: 7.5% - 30% (value up to and in excess of $100,000).

Class D: 10% - 30% (value up to and in excess of $500,000).

Statute: Wisconsin Statutes, Title X, Chapter 72.

Wyoming

No gift tax.

STATE DEATH TAXES

The following chart provides a capsule description of each state's statutory scheme. Where the type of tax is listed as "credit estate tax" the tax levied is the maximum federal credit for state death taxes allowed under Code §2011. Where the tax is an inheritance tax, the exemptions and tax rates listed are the maximum and minimum amounts (e.g., in California, a spouse receives a $60,000 exemption and the tax rate is 6% to 14% depending on the size of the distribution; a nonrelative receives a $300 exemption and the tax is between 10% and 24%). Where both an inheritance or estate tax and a credit estate tax is listed, the credit estate tax is payable only if the tax under the basic state death tax is less than the maximum federal credit. "Payment due" indicates the time after death when the state tax is due (unless an extension is granted and payable without penalty). "Assessed on" indicates whether the tax is payable from the residuary estate or is paid proportionately by the beneficiaries (unless the will provides otherwise).

Caution: Local law should always be checked for recent changes enacted by state legislatures.

Alabama

Type: Credit estate tax
Payment due: 15 months
Assessed on: Residuary estate

Alaska

Type: Credit estate tax
Payment due: 15 months
Assessed on: Pro rata

Arizona

Type: Estate tax and credit estate tax
Exemptions: $100,000
Rates: 0.8% - 16%
Payment due: 9 months
Assessed on: Residuary estate

Arkansas

Type: Credit estate tax
Payment due: 9 months
Assessed on: Pro rata

California

Type: Inheritance tax and credit estate tax
Exemptions:

Class A: Spouse: $60,000
Minor child: $12,000
Lineal ancestors: $5,000

California *(cont.)*

Class B: Sibling: $2,000

Class C: Others: $300

Rates:

Class A: Spouse: 6% - 14%
Minor child, lineal ancestor:
3% - 14%

Class B: 6% - 20%

Class C: 10% - 24%

Payment due: 9 months
Assessed on: Pro rata

Colorado

Type: Inheritance tax and credit estate tax
Exemptions:

Class A: Spouse: $75,000
Minor child: $37,500
Parent and others: $25,000

Class B: Siblings, grandparents: $3,000

Class C: Aunt, uncle, nephew, niece: $500

Class D: Others: $500

Colorado *(cont.)*

Rates:

Class A: 3% - 9%

Class B: 4% - 11%

Class C: 7% - 17%

Class D: 11% - 20%

Payment due: 9 months
Assessed on: Pro rata

Connecticut

Type: Inheritance tax and credit estate tax
Exemptions:

Class AA: Spouse: $100,000

Class A: Parent, child, grandparent: $20,000

Class B: Sibling: $6,000

Class C: Others: $1,000

Rates:

Class AA: 3% - 8%

Class A: 2% - 8%

Class B: 4% - 10%

Class C: 8% - 14%

Payment due: 9 months
Assessed on: Pro rata

Delaware

Type: Inheritance tax and credit estate tax
Exemptions:

Class A: Spouse: $70,000

Class B: Child, parent, grandparent: $3,000

Class C: Sibling: $1,000

Class D: Others: none

Delaware *(cont.)*

Rates:

Class A: 2% - 4%

Class B: 1% - 6%

Class C: 5% - 10%

Class D: 10% - 16%

Payment due: 9 months
Assessed on: Pro rata

District of Columbia

Type: Inheritance tax and credit estate tax
Exemptions:

Class A: Spouse, parent, child, lineal descendant: $5,000

Class B: Repealed 12/15/71

Class C: Others: $1,000

Rates:

Class A: 1% - 8%

Class C: 5% - 23%

Payment due: 18 months
Assessed on: Pro rata

Florida

Type: Credit estate tax
Payment due: 9 months
Assessed on: Residuary estate

Georgia

Type: Credit estate tax
Payment due: On or before date of filing of the duplicate federal estate tax return.
Assessed on: Residuary estate

Hawaii

Type: Inheritance tax and credit estate tax
Exemptions:

Class A: Spouse: $100,000

553

Hawaii *(cont.)*

Class B: Parent, child: $50,000

Class C: Others: $5,000

Rates:

Class A: 2% - 7%

Class B: 3% - 8%

Class C: 3% - 10%

Payment due: 18 months
Assessed on: Pro rata

Idaho

Type: Inheritance tax and credit estate tax
Exemptions:

Class 1: Spouse, child: $30,000
Others: $15,000

Class 2: Sibling: $10,000

Class 3: Aunt, uncle: $10,000

Class 4: Others: $10,000

Rates:

Class 1: 2% - 15%

Class 2: 4% - 20%

Class 3: 6% - 25%

Class 4: 8% - 30%

Payment due: 9 months
Assessed on: Pro rata

Illinois

Type: Inheritance tax and credit estate tax
Exemptions:

Class A: Spouse, child $20,000 plus the lesser of: $20,000 or the sum which, deducted from the gross value of the transfers, reduces the tax by $1,200

Parent, lineal ancestor: $20,000
Sibling: $10,000

Illinois *(cont.)*

Class B: Uncle, aunt, niece, nephew: $500

Class C: Others: $100

Rates:

Class A: 2% - 14%

Class B: 6% - 16%

Class C: 10% - 30%

Payment due: At death of decedent or, if assessed or appraised by order, 10 months to pay.
Assessed on: Pro rata

Indiana

Type: Inheritance tax and credit estate tax
Exemptions:

Class A: Spouse: $60,000
Minor child: $5,000
Others: $2,000

Class B: Sibling: $500

Class C: Others: $100

Rates:

Class A: 1% - 10%

Class B: 7% - 15%

Class C: 10% - 20%

Payment due: 18 months
Assessed on: Pro rata

Iowa

Type: Inheritance tax and credit estate tax
Exemptions:

Class A: Spouse: $80,000
Child: $30,000
Parent, other lineal descendant: $10,000

Class B: Sibling: none

Class C: Others: none

554

Iowa *(cont.)*

Class D: Societies, institutions, or associations organized under law, for charitable, educational, or religious purposes: none

Class E: Firm, or corporation for profit: none

Rates:

Class A: 1% - 8%

Class B: 5% - 10%

Class C: 10% - 15%

Class D: Flat 10%

Class E: Flat 15%

Payment due: 12 months
Assessed on: Pro rata

Kansas

Type: Inheritance tax and credit estate tax
Exemptions:

Class A: Spouse: $250,000
Lineal descendants and ancestors: $30,000

Class B: Sibling: $5,000

Class C: Others: none (unless the share is less than $200, in which case the entire amount is exempt)

Rates:

Class A: Spouse: 0.5% - 2.5%
Lineal descendants and ancestors: 1% - 5%

Class B: 3% - 12.5%

Class C: 10% - 15%

Payment due: 9 months
Assessed on: Pro rata

Kentucky

Type: Inheritance tax and credit estate tax
Exemptions:

Kentucky *(cont.)*

Class A: Spouse: $50,000
Minor child: $20,000
Parent, grandchild: $5,000

Class B: Sibling, aunt, uncle, niece, nephew: $1,000

Class C: Others: $500

Rates:

Class A: 2% - 10%

Class B: 4% - 16%

Class C: 6% - 16%

Payment due: 18 months
Assessed on: Pro rata

Louisiana

Type: Inheritance tax and credit estate tax
Exemptions:

Class A: Spouse, direct descendant: $5,000

Class B: Sibling: $1,000

Class C: Others: $500

Rates:

Class A: 2% - 3%

Class B: 5% - 7%

Class C: 5% - 10%

Payment due: 9 months
Assessed on: Pro rata

Maine

Type: Inheritance tax and credit estate tax
Exemptions:

Class A: Spouse: $50,000
Parent, child, grandchild: $25,000 (if more than one grandchild, the total exemption is $25,000).
Grandparents: $2,000

Class B: Sibling: $1,000

555

Maine (*cont.*)

Class C: Others: $1,000

Rates:

Class A: 5% - 10%

Class B: 8% - 14%

Class C: 14% - 18%

Payment due: 12 months
Assessed on: Pro rata

Maryland

Type: Inheritance tax and credit estate tax
Exemptions:

Class A: Spouse, parent, children, lineal descendant or any joint savings account of less than an aggregate of $2,000 of any spouse of a lineal descendant of decedent: $150 Surviving spouse: additional $1,000
Unmarried child (under age 18): $500

Class B: Others: $150

Rates:

Class A: Flat 1%

Class B: Flat 10%

Payment due: Within 30 days after the time of the accounting for its distribution
Assessed on: Pro rata

Massachusetts

Type: Estate tax and credit estate tax
Exemptions: $30,000 unless the Massachusetts net estate is $60,000 or less, in which case the exemption is equal to the Massachusetts net estate.

Rates: 5% - 16%
Payment due: 9 months
Assessed on: Pro rata

Michigan

Type: Inheritance tax and credit estate tax
Exemptions:

Class A: Spouse: $65,000 (additional $5,000 exemption for each minor child to whom no property is transferred) Parent, child, sibling, grandchildren: $10,000

Class B: Others: none

Rates:

Class A: 2% - 10%

Class B: 10% - 17%

Payment due: 9 months
Assessed on: Pro rata

Minnesota

Type: Inheritance tax and credit estate tax
Exemptions:

Class 1: Spouse: $60,000
Minor child: $30,000

Class 2: Adult child or lineal descendant: $6,000

Class 3: Sibling or descendant of sibling: $1,500

Class 4: Others: $500

Rates:

Class 1: 1.5% - 10%

Class 2: 2% - 10%

Class 3: 6% - 25%

Class 4: 8% - 30%
(In lieu of the inheritance tax rates, there is the marital exemption tax, which can be used if it is less than the inheritance tax rates on prop-

Minnesota *(cont.)*

erty passing to the surviving spouse. The marital exemption is 50%, but not more than $250,000, of the net taxable value passing to the surviving spouse.)

Payment due: 12 months
Assessed on: Pro rata

Mississippi

Type: Estate tax
Exemptions: The value of the taxable estate is determined by deducting the following sums from the gross estate:
1978-$120,666; 1979-$134,000; 1980-$147,333; 1981-$161,563; 1982-or thereafter, $175,625.

Nebraska

Type: Inheritance tax and credit estate tax
Exemptions:

Class A: Spouse, parent, child, sibling, lineal descendant: $10,000

Class B: Uncle, aunt, niece, nephew: $2,000

Class C: Others: $500

Rates:

Class A: Flat 1%

Class B: 6% - 9%

Class C: 6% - 18%

Payment due: 10 months
Assessed on: Pro rata

Nevada

No state death tax.

New Hampshire

Type: Inheritance tax and credit estate tax
Exemptions: No tax on spouse, children, and parents.

New Hampshire *(cont.)*

Rates: All (except spouse, children, and parents) are taxed at a flat 15%.

Payment due: 12 months
Assessed on: Pro rata

New Jersey

Type: Inheritance tax and credit estate tax
Exemptions:

Class A: Spouse, parent, grandparent, child: $15,000

Class B: Repealed 7/1/63

Class C: Sibling: if share is less than $500, there is no tax; otherwise there is no exemption.

Class D: Others, same as Class C

Rates:

Class A: 2% - 16%

Class C: 11% - 16%

Class D: 15% - 16%

Payment due: 8 months
Assessed on: Pro rata

New Mexico

Type: Credit estate tax
Payment due: 9 months
Assessed on: Pro rata

New York

Type: Estate tax and credit estate tax

Credits: If tax is $2,750 or less: full amount of tax. If tax is between $2,750 and $5,000: difference between tax and $5,500.
If tax is more than $5,000: $500. Other credits: see statute.

Rates: 2% - 21%

New York *(cont.)*

Payment due: At time of decedent's death, but interest does not accrue until 6 months after death.
Assessed on: Pro rata

North Carolina

Type: Inheritance tax and credit estate tax
Exemptions:

Class A: Spouse $20,000
Minor child, or child over age of 18 who is physically or mentally disabled $5,000
Other beneficiaries listed in the statute $2,000

Class B: Sibling, aunt, uncle: none

Class C: Others: none

Rates:

Class A: 1% - 12%

Class B: 4% - 16%

Class C: 8% - 17%

Payment due: At decedent's death, but no interest is charged if the tax is paid within 9 months of the death.
Assessed on: Pro rata

North Dakota

Type: Estate tax
Exemptions: $200,000

Rates: 4% - 18%

Payment due: At decedent's death, but no interest is charged if the tax is paid within 15 months after death.
Assessed on: Pro rata

Ohio

Type: Estate tax and credit estate tax
Exemptions: $50,000 (but $30,000 for spouse, $7,000 for child

Ohio *(cont.)*

under 18, and $3,000 for child over 18).

Rates: 2% - 7%

Payment due: 9 months
Assessed on: Pro rata

Oklahoma

Type: Estate tax and credit estate tax
Exemptions:

Class 1: Parent, child, and lineal descendant: aggregate of $60,000 (there is a complete exemption for spouse except for calculating credit estate tax)

Class 2: Others: none

Rates:

Class 1: 1% - 10%

Class 2: 2% - 15%

Payment due: 9 months
Assessed on: Pro rata

Oregon

Type: Inheritance tax and credit estate tax
Exemptions: $50,000 (various credits allowed depending on the class of beneficiaries)

Rates: Flat 12%

Payment due: 9 months
Assessed on: Pro rata

Pennsylvania

Type: Inheritance tax and credit estate tax
Exemptions:

Class A: Spouse, parents, grandparents, child, lineal descendants: none (except, there is a $2,000 family exemption).

Class B: Others: none

Pennsylvania *(cont.)*

Rates:

Class A: Flat 6%

Class B: Flat 15%

Payment due: 9 months
Assessed on: Pro rata

Puerto Rico

Type: Estate tax
Exemption: $60,000

Rates: 3% - 70%

Payment due: 270 days
Assessed on: Pro rata

Rhode Island

Type: Estate tax, inheritance tax, and credit estate tax

Exemptions:

Estate tax: $10,000 (plus a marital deduction of $40,000)

Inheritance tax:

Class A: $50,000

Class B: Parents, children, grandparents: $10,000

Class C: Stepchildren, stepparents, siblings: $5,000

Class D: Nieces, nephews: $3,000

Class E: Others: $1,000

Rates:

Estate tax: Flat 1%

Inheritance tax:

Class A: 4% - 9%

Class B: 2% - 9%

Class C: 3% - 10%

Rhode Island *(cont.)*

Class D: 4% - 11%

Class E: 8% - 15%

Payment due: 6 months
Assessed on: Pro rata

South Carolina

Type: Estate tax and credit estate tax
Exemptions: $60,000

Rates: 4% - 6%

Payment due: 9 months
Assessed on: Pro rata

South Dakota

Type: Inheritance tax
Exemptions:

Class 1: Spouse: $80,000 (effective 7/1/79, $100,000) Lineal issue: $30,0000

Class 2: Lineal ancestor: $3,000

Class 3: Sibling: $500

Class 4: Aunt, uncle: $200

Class 5: Others: $100

Rates:

Class 1: 1.5% - 6%

Class 2: 3% - 12%

Class 3: 4% - 16%

Class 4: 5% - 20%

Class 5: 6% - 24%

Payment due: As soon as the amount is determined, but no interest is charged if the tax is paid within 12 months of decedent's death.
Assessed on: Pro rata

Tennessee

Type: Inheritance tax and credit estate tax
Exemptions:

Class A: Spouse, child, lineal ancestor
$120,000

Class B: Others $10,000

Rates:

Class A: 5.5% - 9.5%

Class B: 6.5% - 16%

Payment due: 9 months
Assessed on: Pro rata

Texas

Type: Inheritance tax and credit estate tax
Exemptions:

Class A: Spouse, direct lineal descendant,
children: $200,000 (effective
9/1/78 to 8/31/82); $250,000
(9/1/82 to 8/31/85); $300,000
(thereafter). (Exemption is divided proportionately if the value
passing to the beneficiaries exceeds the amount of the exemption.
However, no Class A beneficiary
will receive an exemption of less
than $25,000.)

Class B: United States to be used in the
state: $25,000

Class C: Sibling: $10,000

Class D: Aunt, uncle: $1,000

Class E: Others: $500

Rates:

Class A: 1% - 6%

Class B: 1% - 6%

Class C: 3% - 10%

Class D: 4% - 15%

Texas (cont.)

Class E: 5% - 20%

Payment due: 9 months
Assessed on: Pro rata

Utah

Type: Credit estate tax

Payment due: On or before the date the
federal estate tax return is
due.

Assessed on: Pro rata

Vermont

Type: Estate tax and credit estate tax
Exemptions: $60,000

Rates: 30% of federal estate tax (For decedents dying in 1977 and 1978, the amount of
the tax is to be reduced by the percentage
which $120,000 is of the amount of the
federal taxable estate, but is not to be reduced by more than 100%. For decedents
dying in 1979 and thereafter, the amount of
tax imposed shall be reduced by the percentage which $240,000 is of the amount of the
federal taxable estate, but is not to be reduced by more than $100.)

Payment due: 15 months.
Assessed on: Residuary estate

Virginia

Type: Inheritance tax and credit estate tax
Exemptions:

Class A: Spouse, child, parent, grandparent, lineal ancestors: $5,000

Class B: Siblings, nieces, nephews: $2,000

Class C: Grandnephews, grandnieces,
others: $1,000

Rates:

Class A: 1% - 5%

Class B: 2% - 10%

Virginia (cont.)

Class C: 5% - 15%

Payment due: 9 months
Assessed on: Pro rata

Washington

Type: Inheritance tax and credit estate tax
Exemptions:

Class A: Spouse, lineal ancestor or descendant: $5,000; additional $5,000 for surviving spouse and $5,000 for each child; if none survive, an overall exemption of $10,000 is allowed.

Class B: Sibling: $1,000

Class C: Others: none

Rates:

Class A: 1% - 10%

Class B: 3% - 20%

Class C: 10% - 25%

Payment due: 9 months
Assessed on: Pro rata

West Virginia

Type: Inheritance tax and credit estate tax
Exemptions:

Class A: Spouse: $30,000
Child, parent: $10,000
Grandchild: $5,000

Class B: Sibling: none (but if decedent dies unmarried, $10,000 exemption)

Class C: Persons further removed than sibling: none

Class D: Others: none

Rates:

Class A: 3% - 13%

West Virginia *(cont.)*

Class B: 4% - 18%

Class C: 7% - 25%

Class D: 10% - 30%

Payment due: 11 months
Assessed on: Pro rata

Wisconsin

Type: Inheritance tax and credit estate tax
Exemptions:

Class A: Spouse: $50,000
Lineal issue: $4,000

Class B: Sibling: $1,000

Class C: Aunt, uncle: $1,000

Class D: Others: $500

Rates:

Class A: Spouse: 1.25% - 6.25%
Lineal issue: 2.25% - 12.5%

Class B: 5% - 25%

Class C: 7.5% - 30%

Class D: 10% - 30%

Payment due: At time of decedent's death, but no interest is charged if tax is paid within 12 months of death.
Assessed on: Pro rata

Wyoming

Type: Inheritance tax and credit estate tax
Exemptions:

Class A: Spouse: $60,000
Child, parent, sibling: $10,000

Class B: Grandparent, grandchild: $5,000

Class C: Others: none

Wyoming (cont.)

Rates:

Class A: Flat 2%

Class B: Flat 4%

Wyoming *(cont.)*

Class C: Flat 6%

Payment due: 10 months
Assessed on: Pro rata

COMPUTATION OF MAXIMUM CREDIT FOR STATE DEATH TAXES

Taxable estate (1)	Taxable estate (2)	Credit on amount in column (1) (3)	Rate of credit on excess over amount in column (1) (4)
(Dollars)	(Dollars)	(Dollars)	(Percent)
100,000	130,000	....	.08
150,000	200,000	400	1.6
200,000	300,000	1,200	2.4
300,000	500,000	3,600	3.2
500,000	700,000	10,000	4.0
700,000	900,000	18,000	4.8
900,000	1,100,000	27,600	5.6
1,100,000	1,600,000	38,800	6.4
1,600,000	2,100,000	70,800	7.2
2,100,000	2,600,000	106,800	8.0
2,600,000	3,100,000	146,800	8.8
3,100,000	3,600,000	190,800	9.6
3,600,000	4,100,000	238,800	10.4
4,100,000	5,100,000	290,800	11.2
5,100,000	6,100,000	402,800	12.0
6,100,000	7,100,000	522,800	12.8
7,100,000	8,100,000	650,800	13.6
8,100,000	9,100,000	786,800	14.4
9,100,000	10,100,000	930,800	15.2
10,100,000	....	1,082,800	16.0

COMPARISON OF INSTALLMENT
PAYMENTS UNDER §6166A AND §6166

Qualifying Aspects	§6166A	§6166
Threshold qualification (necessary interest in closely held business)	(1) 35% of the value of the gross estate, or (2) 50% of the value of the taxable estate.	65% of the value of the adjusted gross estate.
Limitation on tax that can be deferred	Same percentage as ratio of closely held business amount to gross estate.	Same percentage as ratio of closely held business amount to adjusted gross estate.
Installments	Up to 10 annual installments after normal due date.	First principal payment 5 years after normal due date, 10 additional years for balance.
Eligible interests in a closely held business	(1) Proprietorship; (2) Partnership; if: (a) 20% capital interest included in gross estate, or (b) 10 or fewer partners; (3) Corporation, if: (a) 20% of the value of its voting stock in gross estate, or (b) 10 or fewer shareholders.	(1) Proprietorship; (2) Partnership, if: (a) 20% capital interest included in gross estate, or (b) 15 or fewer partners (immediate family members counted as one, according to 1978 Revenue Act); (3) Corporation, if: (a) 20% of the value of its voting stock in gross estate, or (b) 15 or fewer shareholders (immediate family members counted as one, according to 1978 Revenue Act).
Joint interest	No provision.	Community and jointly or commonly owned property: husband and wife treated as one shareholder or partner.
Attribution	No provision.	Shareholders, partners, and beneficiaries deemed to own property owned by corporations, partnerships, trusts, and estates in proportion to their interest in the entity.

Qualifying Aspects	§ 6166A	§ 6166
Multiple business interests	More than 50% of each included in gross estate: treat as one business interest.	More than 20% of each included in gross estate: treat as one business interest.
Acceleration of payments	(1) Undistributed net income in estate after 4 years; (2) Installment missed; (3) Disposition of 50% or more in value of qualified interest; (4) Withdrawal of 50% of the value of the business.	(1) Undistributed income in estate after 4 years; (2) Installment missed; (3) Disposition of ⅓ or more in value of qualified interest; (4) Withdrawal of 33⅓% of the value of the business.

TAX RETURN—FILING DATES, REQUIREMENTS

Type of Tax	Taxable Event	Person Liable	Due Date of Return and Tax	Threshold Amount	Requirements for Extension of Time to Pay Tax	Period of Extension	Interest on Deferred Tax
A. Income	(1) Income earned by decedent	Executor (or administrator) and/or surviving spouse (if joint return is filed)	April 15 for calendar-year taxpayers (Form 1040)	Gross income over $750 OR over $2,950 if decedent was not married	Undue hardship	Up to 6 months (longer if taxpayer is abroad)	6% interest on unpaid tax (as of Feb. 1978)
	(2) Income earned by estate	Executor or administrator	15th day of 4th month following close of fiscal year (Form 1041)	Gross income in taxable year over $600 OR $0 if any beneficiary is a nonresident alien	Undue hardship OR Tax may be paid in four equal, quarterly installments, beginning with the due date of the tax (Code §6152)	Up to 6 months (longer if taxpayer is abroad)	6% interest on unpaid tax (as of Feb. 1978)
B. Estate	(3) Death of U.S. citizen	Executor or administrator	9 months after date of death (Form 706)	Date of Death: / Gross Estate Over: / 1977 $120,000 / 1978 134,000 / 1979 147,000	Reasonable cause (Code §6161) OR	Up to 12 months or 10 years	6% interest on unpaid tax (as of

566

	Who files	When due (Form)	Filing requirement	Extension grounds	Extension period	Interest
or resident			1980 161,000 1981 and 175,000 after	Closely held interest represents at least 65% of adjusted gross estate (Code §6166) OR Closely held interest represents at least 35% of gross estate or 50% of taxable estate (Code §6166A)	Tax deferred 5 years; 10 more years for payment of balance 10 years	Feb. 1978) 4% interest on first $345,800 of tax less unified credit attributable thereto; 6% on balance 6% interest on unpaid tax (as of Feb. 1, 1978)
(4) Death of non-resident alien	Executor or administrator	9 months after date of death (Form 706NA)	Gross estate of U.S. property over $60,000	Reasonable cause	Up to 12 months	6% interest on unpaid tax (as of Feb. 1978)
C. Gift (5) Lifetime transfer to donees other than qualified charities	Donor	One month and 15 days after quarter in which gift is made. But no return due until cumulative gifts during year reach $25,000. In any case, return is due on February 15 for gifts made ...ing preceding year (Form 709)	$3,000 ($6,000 for split gifts under Code §2513)	Undue hardship (Reg. §25.6161-1(b))	Up to 6 months (longer if donor is abroad)	6% interest on unpaid tax (as of Feb. 1978)

567

Type of Tax	Taxable Event	Person Liable	Due Date of Return and Tax	Threshold Amount	Requirements for Extension of Time to Pay Tax	Period of Extension	Interest on Deferred Tax
C. Gift (cont.)	(6) Lifetime transfer to a qualified charity (Code §2522)	Donor	Same as for gifts to non-charities if, in fact, latter have been made. If not return is due Feb. 15 for gifts made during preceding year (Form 709)	No tax payable on these transfers	Not applicable	Not applicable	Not applicable
	(7) Creation or termination of tenancy by the entirety by spouses	Donor	If donor elects to have creation treated as a gift, one month and 15 days after tenancy is created (except for certain pre-1977 tenancies); otherwise, same as (5)	$0 if creation is treated as gift; for gifts, on termination, same rules as in (5)	Undue hardship	Up to 6 months (longer if taxpayer is abroad)	6% interest on unpaid tax (as of Feb. 1978)

Type of Tax	Taxable Event	Person Liable	Due Date of Return and Tax	Threshold Amount	Requirements for Extension of Time to Pay Tax	Period of Extension	Interest on Deferred Tax
D. Generation-Skipping	(8) Generation-skipping transfers	Trustee in case of a taxable termination; distributees in case of a taxable distribution	90th day after the close of the taxable year of the trust if the transfer occurred before the death of the deemed transferor.	Same as (3)	Undue hardship	Up to 6 months (longer if taxpayer is abroad)	6% interest on unpaid tax (as of Feb. 1978)
			90th day after the last day an estate tax return is due (including extensions) for the estate of a deemed transferor who has died on or before transfer OR, if later, 9 months after date of transfer	Same as (1)	Reasonable cause	Up to 12 months or 10 years	6% interest on unpaid tax (as of Feb. 1978)

EXECUTORS' COMMISSIONS

Most states have a statutory schedule of fees for executors. Some merely call for reasonable fees, the reasonableness to be determined by the courts. In a number of states, fees for testamentary trusts are the same as those allowed to executors. Some states provide for a distinct statutory fee for trusts, others provide for reasonable fees to be determined by the court, more often than not based in large measure upon trust receipts—with 5% annually being a fairly reasonable national average. In the case of both executors and testamentary trustees, additional reasonable fees may be charged for extraordinary services (these states are denoted by an asterisk).

The basis on which commissions are calculated also varies among the states. While many allow the fiduciary a percentage of all probate property, others exclude the value of unsold real property.

Alabama*

Not more than 2½% of receipts and disbursements. Additional 2½% allowed if land is sold for division (but limited to $100 unless otherwise specified in will).

Alaska

Reasonable compensation allowed.

Arizona

Reasonable compensation allowed.

Arkansas

First $1,000—Not more than 10%
Next $4,000—5%
Above $5,000—3%
Additional compensation allowed for substantial duties pertaining to real property.

California*

First $15,000—4%
Next $85,000—3%
Next $900,000—2%
Above $1,000,000—1%

Colorado

Reasonable compensation allowed.

Connecticut

Reasonable compensation allowed.

Delaware

Reasonable compensation allowed (usually 10% of estate).

District of Columbia

Not under 1% nor more than 10% of inventory.

Florida

Reasonable compensation allowed.

Georgia*

Flat 2½%.

Hawaii

Reasonable compensation allowed (effective 7/1/77).

Idaho

Reasonable compensation allowed.

Illinois

Reasonable compensation allowed.

Indiana

Reasonable compensation allowed.

Iowa

First $1,000—not more than 6%
Next $4,000—4%
All above $5,000—2%

Kansas

Reasonable compensation allowed.

Kentucky*

Not more than 5% of income and 5% of personal estate.

Louisiana

Fee is 2½% of the inventory of the estate—it may be increased by the court upon showing that usual commission is inadequate.

Maine

Up to 5% of personal estate; reduced for larger estates.

Maryland

For personal property:
First $20,000—up to 10%
Above $20,000—$2,000, plus 4% of the excess over $20,000.
For real property, up to 10% if sold.
If a will provides a stated compensation for the personal representative, additional compensation is allowed if the provision is insufficient in the judgment of the court.

Massachusetts

Reasonable compensation allowed.

Michigan

First $5,000 —5%
Next $20,000—4%
Next $50,000—3%
Above $75,000—2%

Minnesota

Reasonable compensation allowed.

Mississippi

Not less than 1% nor more than 7% on amount of estate administered.

Missouri

First	$ 5,000—5%	
Next	$ 20,000—4%	
Next	$ 75,000—3%	
Next	$300,000—2¾%	
Next	$600,000—2½%	
All above $1,000,000—2%		

Montana

First	$40,000—3%
Above	$40,000—2%

Nebraska

Reasonable compensation allowed.

Nevada

First	$1,000—6%
Next	$4,000—4%
Above	$5,000—2%

New Hampshire

Reasonable compensation allowed.

New Jersey

On income, 6%. On corpus not exceeding $100,000—5%.
On excess over $100,000, the percentage, not in excess of 5%, in discretion of the court.
Usual rates—5% of first $100,000 and 5% of excess.

New Mexico

First $3,000—10%
    All above $3,000—5%. For cash, U.S. Savings Bonds, or life insurance proceeds, the compensation is 5% on the first $5,000 and 1% on everything above that figure.

New York

First	$ 25,000—4%
Next	$125,000—3½%
Next	$150,000—3%
Above	$300,000—2%

North Carolina

Not more than 5% of receipts and disbursements. (If the gross value of the estate is $2,000 or less, the commission is at the discretion of the clerk of the Superior Court.)

North Dakota

Reasonable compensation allowed.

Ohio

First $1,000—6%
Next $4,000—4%
Above $5,000—2%

1% additional for unsold real property and nonprobate property subject to state estate tax.

Oklahoma

First $1,000—5%
Next $4,000—4%
Above $5,000—2½%

Oregon

First $ 1,000—7%
Next $ 9,000—4%
Next $40,000—3%
Above $50,000—2%

1% additional for nonprobate property (excluding insurance) that is subject to estate tax.

Pennsylvania

Reasonable compensation allowed (usually 5% for small estates and 3% for large estates).

Rhode Island

Reasonable compensation allowed.

South Carolina*

Not more than 2½% of receipts and disbursements.

South Dakota

First $1,000—5%
Next $4,000—4%
All above $5,000—2½%

Tennessee

Reasonable compensation allowed.

Texas

Not more than 5% of the value of the administered estate. If compensation unreasonably low, court may allow reasonable compensation.

Utah

First $ 1,000—5%
Next $ 4,000—4%
Next $ 5,000—3%
Next $40,000—2%
Next $50,000—1½%
All above $100,000—1%

Vermont*

Statute provides $4 for each day's attendance on business.

Virginia

Reasonable compensation allowed.

Washington

Reasonable compensation allowed.

West Virginia

Reasonable compensation allowed.

Wisconsin*

2% of estate.

Wyoming*

First	$ 1,000—10%
Next	$ 4,000—5%
Next	$15,000—3%
Above	$20,000—2%

Note that the general rule is that there is nothing to prevent the testator from specifying the executor's commission in the will (or even directing that there shall be no commissions). Then it is up to the executor to accept or refuse appointment.

REVOCATION OF WILLS
by Marriage, Divorce, or Birth of Child

All states recognize that wills are revocable. Revocation may occur by operation of law, by some physical act performed upon the will with intent to revoke, or expressly or impliedly by a subsequent instrument meeting the statutory requirements. The tables that follow outline the grounds that may cause revocation by operation of law: marriage, divorce, or birth of a child. Hence, they serve as a working guide to the situations in which a will should be revised to avoid revocation or modification.

Effect of Marriage

Alabama

Revokes will only if *woman* marries.

Alaska

Modifies will to give intestate share.

Arizona

Modifies will to give intestate share.

Arkansas

No effect.

California

The will is revoked as to the spouse, unless provision has been made for the spouse by marriage contract.

Colorado

Modifies will to give intestate share.

Connecticut

Completely revokes will.

Delaware

Modifies will to give intestate share.

District of Columbia

No effect.

Florida

Modifies will to give intestate share.

Georgia

Completely revokes will.

Hawaii

Modifies will to give intestate share.

Idaho

Modifies will to give intestate share.

Illinois

No effect.

Indiana

No effect.

Iowa

No effect.

Kansas

No effect, except it is revoked if the testator marries and has a child after he made the will.

Kentucky

Completely revokes will.

Effect of Marriage *(cont.)*

Louisiana

No effect.

Maine

No effect.

Maryland

No effect unless marriage is followed by birth of child after will was made; then the will is revoked.

Massachusetts

Completely revokes will.

Michigan

No effect.

Minnesota

No effect.

Mississippi

No effect.

Missouri

No effect.

Montana

Modifies will to give intestate share.

Nebraska

Modifies will to give intestate share.

Nevada

Will is revoked only as to the spouse.

New Hampshire

No effect.

New Jersey

No effect.

New Mexico

Modifies will to give inte.. ..te share.

New York

Modifies will to give intestate share.

North Carolina

No effect, except surviving spouse may dissent from will as though will were made subsequent to marriage.

North Dakota

Modifies will to give intestate share.

Oklahoma

No effect, except if testator marries and has a child after his will was executed. It is then revoked.

Oregon

Will is completely revoked.

Pennsylvania

Modifies will to give intestate share.

Puerto Rico

No effect.

Rhode Island

Will is completely revoked.

South Carolina

Revokes will completely.

South Dakota

Revokes will completely.

Tennessee

No effect, except if will is made before both marriage *and* birth of child.

Effect of Marriage *(cont.)*

Texas

No effect.

Utah

Will is completely revoked.

Vermont

No effect.

Virginia

No effect.

Washington

Completely revokes will.

West Virginia

Completely revokes will.

Wisconsin

Completely revokes will.

Wyoming

No effect.

Effect of Divorce

Alabama

Revokes part of will making provision for spouse.

Alaska

Revokes part of will making provision for spouse.

Arizona

Revokes part of will making provision for spouse.

Arkansas

Revokes part of will making provision for spouse.

California

No effect.

Colorado

Revokes part of will making provision for spouse.

Connecticut

Completely revoked.

Delaware

Revokes part of will making provision for spouse.

District of Columbia

No effect *except* the common-law rule that a divorce with property settlement may revoke husband's will by implication of law.

Florida

Revokes part of will making provision for spouse.

Georgia

Will is completely revoked unless it contains provision in contemplation of such event.

Hawaii

Revokes part of will making provision for spouse.

Idaho

Revokes part of will making provision for spouse.

Illinois

Revokes part of will making provision for spouse.

Indiana

Revokes part of will making provision for spouse.

577

Effect of Divorce *(cont.)*

Iowa

Revokes part of will making provision for spouse.

Kansas

Revokes part of will making provision for spouse.

Kentucky

Revokes entire will.

Louisiana

No effect.

Maine

No effect.

Maryland

Revokes part of will making provision for spouse.

Massachusetts

Revokes part of will making provision for spouse. Effective only with respect to decedents dying on or after 1/1/78.

Michigan

Implied revocation.

Minnesota

Revokes part of will making provision for spouse.

Mississippi

No effect.

Missouri

Revokes part of will making provision for spouse.

Montana

Revokes part of will making provision for spouse.

Nebraska

Revokes part of will making provision for spouse.

Nevada

Revokes part of will making provision for spouse.

New Hampshire

No effect.

New Jersey

Revokes part of will making provision for spouse.

New Mexico

Revokes part of will making provision for spouse.

New York

Revokes part of will making provision for spouse.

North Carolina

Revokes part of will making provision for spouse.

Ohio

Revokes part of will making provision for spouse.

Oklahoma

Revokes part of will making provision for spouse.

Oregon

Revokes part of will making provision for spouse.

Pennsylvania

Revokes part of will making provision for spouse.

Effect of Divorce *(cont.)*

Rhode Island

No effect.

South Carolina

Revokes part of will making provision for spouse.

South Dakota

No effect.

Tennessee

Divorce and property settlement agreement give rise to a conclusive presumption of revocation (*Remkin v. McDearmon,* 270 S.W. 2d 660, 1953).

Texas

Revokes part of will making provision for spouse.

Utah

No effect.

Vermont

No effect.

Virginia

Revokes part of will making provision for spouse.

Virgin Islands

No effect.

Washington

Revokes part of will making provision for spouse.

West Virginia

Revokes entire will.

Wisconsin

Revokes part of will making provision for spouse.

Wyoming

No effect except will leaving husband's entire estate to his first wife was impliedly revoked when his marriage was revoked, with property settlement, and he remarried (*Johnson v. Laird,* 52 P. 2d 1219, 1935).

Effect of Birth of Child

Alabama

Partially revokes will to give child intestate share.

Alaska

Modifies will to give child intestate share.

Arizona

Modifies will to give child intestate share.

Arkansas

Modifies will to give child intestate share.

California

Modifies will to give child intestate share.

Colorado

Modifies will to give child intestate share.

Connecticut

Completely revokes will.

Delaware

Modifies will to give child intestate share.

District of Columbia

No effect except there is a common-law rule that marriage and the birth of a child capable of inheriting revoke a prior will, if both occurred after its execution.

Effect of Birth of Child *(cont.)*

Florida	**Montana**
Modifies will to give child intestate share.	Modifies will to give child intestate share.
Georgia	**Nebraska**
Will is completely revoked.	Modifies will to give child intestate share.
Hawaii	**Nevada**
Modifies will to give child intestate share.	Modifies will to give child intestate share.
Idaho	**New Hampshire**
Modifies will to give child intestate share.	Modifies will to give child intestate share.
Illinois	**New Jersey**
Modifies will to give child intestate share.	Modifies will to give child intestate share.
Indiana	**New Mexico**
Modifies will to give child intestate share.	Modifies will to give child intestate share.
Iowa	**New York**
Modifies will to give child intestate share.	Modifies will to give child intestate share.
Kentucky	**North Carolina**
Modifies will to give child intestate share.	Modifies will to give child intestate share.
Louisiana	**North Dakota**
Completely revokes will.	Modifies will to give child intestate share.
Maine	**Ohio**
Modifies will to give child intestate share.	Modifies will to give child intestate share.
Maryland	**Oklahoma**
Modifies will to give child intestate share.	Modifies will to give child intestate share.
Massachusetts	**Oregon**
Modifies will to give child intestate share.	Modifies will to give child intestate share.
Mississippi	**Pennsylvania**
Modifies will to give child intestate share.	Modifies will to give child intestate share.
Missouri	**Rhode Island**
Modifies will to give child intestate share.	Modifies will to give child intestate share.

Effect of Birth of Child *(cont.)*

South Carolina	Virgin Islands
Modifies will to give child intestate share.	Modifies will to give child intestate share.
South Dakota	**Virginia**
Modifies will to give child intestate share.	Modifies will to give child intestate share.
Tennessee	**Washington**
Modifies will to give child intestate share.	Modifies will to give child intestate share.
Texas	**West Virginia**
Modifies will to give child intestate share.	Modifies will to give child intestate share.
Utah	**Wisconsin**
Modifies will to give child intestate share.	Modifies will to give child intestate share.
Vermont	**Wyoming**
Modifies will to give child intestate share.	Modifies will to give child intestate share.

STATUTORY RULES FOR ALLOCATION
OF PRINCIPAL AND INCOME

The National Conference of Commissioners on Uniform State Laws approved the Uniform Principal and Income Act in 1931. The Act has been adopted in whole or in part, often with textual variations, in the following states:

Alabama	Kentucky	Tennessee
Arizona	Montana	Texas
California	New Mexico	Utah
Colorado	North Carolina	Vermont
Connecticut	Oklahoma	Virginia
Florida	Oregon	West Virginia
Illinois	Pennsylvania	Wisconsin

Maine and New Jersey have adopted parts of the Uniform Act or similar statutes. In 1962, the National Conference of Commissioners on Uniform State Laws approved the Revised Uniform Principal and Income Act. It has been adopted in these states:

Arkansas	Maryland	North Carolina
California	Michigan	North Dakota
Florida	Minnesota	Oregon
Hawaii	Mississippi	South Carolina
Idaho	Nevada	Washington
Indiana	New Mexico	Wyoming
Kansas	New York	

Louisiana law contains provisions similar to the Revised Act.

SIMPLE INTEREST TABLE

Example of use of this table:
Find amount of $500 in 8 years at 6% simple interest.

From table at 8 yrs. and 6% for $1. .... 1.48

Value in 8 yrs. for $500 (500 × 1.48) $740

Number of Years	Interest Rate							
	3%	4%	5%	6%	7%	8%	9%	10%
1	1.03	1.04	1.05	1.06	1.07	1.08	1.09	1.10
2	1.06	1.08	1.10	1.12	1.14	1.16	1.18	1.20
3	1.09	1.12	1.15	1.18	1.21	1.24	1.27	1.30
4	1.12	1.16	1.20	1.24	1.28	1.32	1.36	1.40
5	1.15	1.20	1.25	1.30	1.35	1.40	1.45	1.50
6	1.18	1.24	1.30	1.36	1.42	1.48	1.54	1.60
7	1.21	1.28	1.35	1.42	1.49	1.56	1.63	1.70
8	1.24	1.32	1.40	1.48	1.56	1.64	1.72	1.80
9	1.27	1.36	1.45	1.54	1.63	1.72	1.81	1.90
10	1.30	1.40	1.50	1.60	1.70	1.80	1.90	2.00
11	1.33	1.44	1.55	1.66	1.77	1.88	1.99	2.10
12	1.36	1.48	1.60	1.72	1.84	1.96	2.08	2.20
13	1.39	1.52	1.65	1.78	1.91	2.04	2.17	2.30
14	1.42	1.56	1.70	1.84	1.98	2.12	2.26	2.40
15	1.45	1.60	1.75	1.90	2.05	2.20	2.35	2.50
16	1.48	1.64	1.80	1.96	2.12	2.28	2.44	2.60
17	1.51	1.68	1.85	2.02	2.19	2.36	2.53	2.70
18	1.54	1.72	1.90	2.08	2.26	2.44	2.62	2.80
19	1.57	1.76	1.95	2.14	2.33	2.52	2.71	2.90
20	1.60	1.80	2.00	2.20	2.40	2.60	2.80	3.00
21	1.63	1.84	2.05	2.26	2.47	2.68	2.89	3.10
22	1.66	1.88	2.10	2.32	2.54	2.76	2.98	3.20
23	1.69	1.92	2.15	2.38	2.61	2.84	3.07	3.30
24	1.72	1.96	2.20	2.44	2.68	2.92	3.16	3.40
25	1.75	2.00	2.25	2.50	2.75	3.00	3.25	3.50
26	1.78	2.04	2.30	2.56	2.82	3.08	3.34	3.60
27	1.81	2.08	2.35	2.62	2.89	3.16	3.43	3.70
28	1.84	2.12	2.40	2.68	2.96	3.24	3.52	3.80
29	1.87	2.16	2.45	2.74	3.03	3.32	3.61	3.90
30	1.90	2.20	2.50	2.80	3.10	3.40	3.70	4.00
31	1.93	2.24	2.55	2.86	3.17	3.48	3.79	4.10
32	1.96	2.28	2.60	2.92	3.24	3.56	3.88	4.20
33	1.99	2.32	2.65	2.98	3.31	3.64	3.97	4.30
34	2.02	2.36	2.70	3.04	3.38	3.72	4.06	4.40
35	2.05	2.40	2.75	3.10	3.45	3.80	4.15	4.50
36	2.08	2.44	2.80	3.16	3.52	3.88	4.24	4.60
37	2.11	2.48	2.85	3.22	3.59	3.96	4.33	4.70
38	2.14	2.52	2.90	3.28	3.66	4.04	4.42	4.80
39	2.17	2.56	2.95	3.34	3.73	4.12	4.51	4.90
40	2.20	2.60	3.00	3.40	3.80	4.20	4.60	5.00

COMPOUND INTEREST TABLE

Example of use of this table:

Find how much $1,000 now in bank will grow to in 14 years at 4% interest.

From table 14 years at 4% 1.7317

Value in 14 years of $1,000 . . . .$1731.70

Number of Years	Interest Rate							
	3-1/2%	4%	4-1/2%	5%	5-1/2%	6%	6-1/2%	7%
1	1.0350	1.0400	1.0450	1.0500	1.0550	1.0600	1.0650	1.0700
2	1.0712	1.0816	1.0920	1.1025	1.1130	1.1236	1.1342	1.1449
3	1.1087	1.1249	1.1412	1.1576	1.1742	1.1910	1.2079	1.2250
4	1.1475	1.1699	1.1925	1.2155	1.2388	1.2624	1.2864	1.3107
5	1.1877	1.2167	1.2462	1.2763	1.3069	1.3382	1.3700	1.4025
6	1.2293	1.2653	1.3023	1.3401	1.3788	1.4185	1.4591	1.5007
7	1.2723	1.3159	1.3609	1.4071	1.4546	1.5036	1.5539	1.6057
8	1.3168	1.3686	1.4221	1.4775	1.5346	1.5938	1.6549	1.7181
9	1.3629	1.4233	1.4861	1.5513	1.6190	1.6894	1.7625	1.8384
10	1.4106	1.4802	1.5530	1.6289	1.7081	1.7908	1.8771	1.9671
11	1.4600	1.5395	1.6229	1.7103	1.8020	1.8982	1.9991	2.1048
12	1.5111	1.6010	1.6959	1.7959	1.9012	2.0121	2.1290	2.2521
13	1.5640	1.6651	1.7722	1.8856	2.0057	2.1329	2.2674	2.4098
14	1.6187	1.7317	1.8519	1.9799	2.1160	2.2609	2.4148	2.5785
15	1.6753	1.8009	1.9353	2.0789	2.2324	2.3965	2.5718	2.7590
16	1.7340	1.8730	2.0224	2.1829	2.3552	2.5403	2.7390	2.9521
17	1.7947	1.9479	2.1134	2.2920	2.4848	2.6927	2.9170	3.1588
18	1.8575	2.0258	2.2085	2.4066	2.6214	2.8543	3.1066	3.3799
19	1.9225	2.1068	2.3079	2.5270	2.7656	3.0256	3.3085	3.6165
20	1.9898	2.1911	2.4117	2.6533	2.9177	3.2071	3.5236	3.8696
21	2.0594	2.2788	2.5202	2.7860	3.0782	3.3995	3.7526	4.1405
22	2.1315	2.3699	2.6337	2.9253	3.2475	3.6035	3.9966	4.4304
23	2.2061	2.4647	2.7522	3.0715	3.4261	3.8197	4.2563	4.7405
24	2.2833	2.5633	2.8760	3.2251	3.6145	4.0489	4.5330	5.0723
25	2.3632	2.6658	3.0054	3.3864	3.8133	4.2918	4.8276	5.4274
26	2.4460	2.7725	3.1407	3.5557	4.0231	4.5493	5.1415	5.8073
27	2.5316	2.8834	3.2820	3.7335	4.2444	4.8223	5.4756	6.2138
28	2.6202	2.9987	3.4297	3.9201	4.4778	5.1116	5.8316	6.6488
29	2.7119	3.1187	3.5840	4.1161	4.7241	5.4183	6.2106	7.1142
30	2.8068	3.2434	3.7453	4.3219	4.9839	5.7434	6.6143	7.6122
31	2.9050	3.3731	3.9139	4.5380	5.2580	6.0881	7.0443	8.1451
32	3.0067	3.5081	4.0900	4.7649	5.5472	6.4533	7.5021	8.7152
33	3.1119	3.6484	4.2740	5.0032	5.8523	6.8405	7.9898	9.3253
34	3.2209	3.7943	4.4664	5.2533	6.1742	7.2510	8.5091	9.9781
35	3.3336	3.9461	4.6673	5.5160	6.5138	7.6860	9.0622	10.6765
36	3.4503	4.1039	4.8774	5.7918	6.8720	8.1472	9.6513	11.4239
37	3.5710	4.2681	5.0969	6.0814	7.2500	8.6360	10.2786	12.2236
38	3.6960	4.4388	5.3262	6.3855	7.6488	9.1542	10.9467	13.0792
39	3.8254	4.6164	5.5659	6.7048	8.0694	9.7035	11.6582	13.9948
40	3.9593	4.8010	5.8164	7.0400	8.5133	10.2857	12.4160	14.9744

HOW MUCH $1 A YEAR WILL EQUAL

Example of use of this table:

How much is $1,000 a year invested at 5% worth in 20 years to a taxpayer in the 50% tax bracket.

The 50% tax bracket cuts the effective interest rate to 2½%.

At 2½% for 20 years, the figure is 26.183
For $1,000 a year, the amount is ....$ 26.183

Number of Years	1-1/2%	2%	2-1/2%	3%	3-1/2%	4%	4-1/2%	5%
1	1.015	1.020	1.025	1.030	1.035	1.040	1.045	1.050
2	2.045	2.060	2.076	2.091	2.106	2.122	2.137	2.153
3	3.091	3.122	3.153	3.184	3.215	3.246	3.278	3.310
4	4.152	4.204	4.256	4.309	4.362	4.416	4.471	4.526
5	5.230	5.308	5.388	5.468	5.550	5.633	5.717	5.802
6	6.323	6.434	6.547	6.662	6.779	6.898	7.019	7.142
7	7.433	7.583	7.736	7.892	8.052	8.214	8.380	8.549
8	8.559	8.755	8.955	9.159	9.368	9.583	9.802	10.027
9	9.703	9.950	10.203	10.464	10.731	11.006	11.288	11.578
10	10.863	11.169	11.483	11.808	12.142	12.486	12.841	13.207
11	12.041	12.412	12.796	13.192	13.602	14.026	14.464	14.917
12	13.237	13.680	14.140	14.618	15.113	15.627	16.160	16.713
13	14.450	14.974	15.519	16.086	16.677	17.292	17.932	18.599
14	15.682	16.293	16.932	17.599	18.296	19.024	19.784	20.579
15	16.932	17.639	18.380	19.157	19.971	20.825	21.719	22.657
16	18.201	19.012	19.865	20.762	21.705	22.698	23.742	24.840
17	19.489	20.412	21.386	22.414	23.500	24.645	25.855	27.132
18	20.797	21.841	22.946	24.117	25.357	26.671	28.064	29.539
19	22.124	23.297	24.545	25.870	27.280	28.778	30.371	32.066
20	23.471	24.783	26.183	27.676	29.269	30.969	32.783	34.719
21	24.838	26.299	27.863	29.537	31.329	33.248	35.303	37.505
22	26.225	27.845	29.584	31.453	33.460	35.618	37.937	40.430
23	27.634	29.422	31.349	33.426	35.667	38.083	40.689	43.502
24	29.063	31.030	33.158	35.459	37.950	40.646	43.565	46.727
25	30.514	32.671	35.012	37.553	40.313	43.312	46.571	50.113
26	31.987	34.344	36.912	39.710	42.759	46.084	49.711	53.669
27	33.481	36.051	38.860	41.931	45.291	48.968	52.993	57.403
28	34.999	37.792	40.856	44.219	47.911	51.966	56.423	61.323
29	36.539	39.568	42.903	46.575	50.623	55.085	60.007	65.439
30	38.102	41.379	45.000	49.003	53.429	58.328	63.752	69.761
31	39.688	43.227	47.150	51.503	56.335	61.701	67.666	74.299
32	41.299	45.112	49.354	54.078	59.341	65.210	71.756	79.064
33	42.933	47.034	51.613	56.730	62.453	68.858	76.030	84.067
34	44.592	48.994	53.928	59.462	65.674	72.652	80.497	89.320
35	46.276	50.994	56.301	62.276	69.008	76.598	85.164	94.336
36	47.985	53.034	58.734	65.174	72.458	80.702	90.041	100.628
37	49.720	55.115	61.227	68.159	76.029	84.970	95.138	106.710
38	51.481	57.237	63.783	71.234	79.725	89.409	100.464	113.095
39	53.268	59.402	66.403	74.401	83.550	94.026	106.030	119.800
40	55.082	61.610	69.088	77.663	87.510	98.827	111.847	126.840

DOLLAR BUYING POWER

Example of use of this table:

If I put $1,000 in the bank, how much can I take out each year for 5 years to use up the entire sum if the interest rate is 4%.

From the table at 5 years 0.2246

For $1,000 (1000 × 0.2184) $224.60

Number of Years	Interest Rate							
	1-1/2%	2%	2-1/2%	3%	3-1/2%	4%	4-1/2%	5%
1	1.0150	1.0200	1.0250	1.0300	1.0350	1.0400	1.0450	1.0500
2	0.5113	0.5150	0.5188	0.5226	0.5264	0.5302	0.5340	0.5378
3	0.3434	0.3468	0.3501	0.3535	0.3569	0.3603	0.3638	0.3672
4	0.2594	0.2626	0.2658	0.2690	0.2723	0.2755	0.2787	0.2820
5	0.2091	0.2122	0.2152	0.2184	0.2215	0.2246	0.2278	0.2310
6	0.1755	0.1785	0.1816	0.1846	0.1877	0.1908	0.1939	0.1970
7	0.1516	0.1545	0.1575	0.1605	0.1635	0.1666	0.1697	0.1728
8	0.1336	0.1365	0.1395	0.1425	0.1455	0.1485	0.1516	0.1547
9	0.1196	0.1225	0.1255	0.1284	0.1314	0.1345	0.1376	0.1407
10	0.1084	0.1113	0.1143	0.1172	0.1202	0.1233	0.1264	0.1295
11	0.0993	0.1022	0.1051	0.1081	0.1111	0.1141	0.1172	0.1204
12	0.0917	0.0946	0.0975	0.1005	0.1035	0.1066	0.1097	0.1128
13	0.0852	0.0881	0.0910	0.0940	0.0971	0.1001	0.1033	0.1065
14	0.0797	0.0826	0.0855	0.0885	0.0916	0.0947	0.0978	0.1010
15	0.0749	0.0778	0.0808	0.0838	0.0868	0.0899	0.0931	0.0963
16	0.0708	0.0737	0.0766	0.0796	0.0827	0.0858	0.0890	0.0923
17	0.0671	0.0700	0.0729	0.0760	0.0790	0.0822	0.0854	0.0887
18	0.0638	0.0667	0.0697	0.0727	0.0758	0.0790	0.0822	0.0855
19	0.0609	0.0638	0.0668	0.0698	0.0729	0.0761	0.0794	0.0827
20	0.0582	0.0612	0.0641	0.0672	0.0704	0.0736	0.0769	0.0802
21	0.0559	0.0588	0.0618	0.0649	0.0680	0.0713	0.0746	0.0780
22	0.0537	0.0566	0.0596	0.0627	0.0659	0.0692	0.0725	0.0760
23	0.0517	0.0547	0.0577	0.0608	0.0640	0.0673	0.0707	0.0741
24	0.0499	0.0529	0.0559	0.0590	0.0623	0.0656	0.0690	0.0725
25	0.0483	0.0512	0.0543	0.0574	0.0607	0.0640	0.0674	0.0710
26	0.0467	0.0497	0.0528	0.0559	0.0592	0.0626	0.0660	0.0696
27	0.0453	0.0483	0.0514	0.0546	0.0579	0.0612	0.0647	0.0683
28	0.0440	0.0470	0.0501	0.0533	0.0566	0.0600	0.0635	0.0671
29	0.0428	0.0458	0.0489	0.0521	0.0554	0.0589	0.0624	0.0660
30	0.0416	0.0446	0.0478	0.0510	0.0544	0.0578	0.0614	0.0651
31	0.0406	0.0436	0.0467	0.0500	0.0534	0.0569	0.0604	0.0641
32	0.0396	0.0426	0.0458	0.0490	0.0524	0.0559	0.0596	0.0633
33	0.0386	0.0417	0.0449	0.0482	0.0516	0.0551	0.0587	0.0605
34	0.0378	0.0408	0.0440	0.0473	0.0508	0.0543	0.0580	0.0618
35	0.0369	0.0400	0.0432	0.0465	0.0500	0.0536	0.0573	0.0611
36	0.0362	0.0392	0.0425	0.0458	0.0493	0.0529	0.0566	0.0604
37	0.0354	0.0385	0.0417	0.0451	0.0486	0.0522	0.0560	0.0598
38	0.0347	0.0378	0.0411	0.0445	0.0480	0.0516	0.0554	0.0593
39	0.0341	0.0372	0.0404	0.0438	0.0474	0.0511	0.0549	0.0588
40	0.0334	0.0366	0.0398	0.0433	0.0468	0.0505	0.0543	0.0583

DOLLAR SAVING POWER

Example of use of this table:

A 20-year endowment costs $46 per $1,000. How much would $1,000 in 20 years cost, on a regular investment schedule yielding 4% to a 50% bracket taxpayer?

Effective investment rate .50 × 4% 2%

From table under 20 years at 2% .... .0404

Cost per $1,000 ....$40.40

Number of Years	Interest Rate							
	1-1/2%	2%	2-1/2%	3%	3-1/2%	4%	4-1/2%	5%
1	.9852	.9804	.9756	.9709	.9662	.9615	.9569	.9524
2	.4889	.4853	.4818	.4783	.4748	.4713	.4679	.4646
3	.3235	.3204	.3172	.3141	.3111	.3080	.3051	.3021
4	.2408	.2379	.2349	.2321	.2292	.2264	.2237	.2210
5	.1912	.1884	.1856	.1829	.1802	.1775	.1749	.1724
6	.1582	.1554	.1527	.1501	.1475	.1450	.1425	.1400
7	.1345	.1319	.1293	.1267	.1242	.1217	.1193	.1170
8	.1168	.1142	.1117	.1092	.1067	.1044	.1020	.0997
9	.1031	.1005	.0980	.0956	.0932	.0909	.0886	.0864
10	.0921	.0895	.0871	.0847	.0824	.0801	.0779	.0757
11	.0831	.0806	.0782	.0758	.0735	.0713	.0691	.0670
12	.0756	.0731	.0707	.0684	.0662	.0640	.0619	.0598
13	.0692	.0668	.0644	.0622	.0600	.0578	.0558	.0538
14	.0638	.0614	.0591	.0568	.0547	.0526	.0506	.0486
15	.0591	.0567	.0544	.0522	.0501	.0480	.0460	.0441
16	.0549	.0526	.0503	.0482	.0461	.0441	.0421	.0403
17	.0513	.0490	.0468	.0446	.0426	.0406	.0387	.0369
18	.0481	.0458	.0436	.0415	.0394	.0375	.0356	.0339
19	.0452	.0429	.0407	.0387	.0367	.0348	.0329	.0312
20	.0426	.0404	.0382	.0361	.0342	.0323	.0305	.0288
21	.0403	.0380	.0359	.0339	.0319	.0301	.0283	.0267
22	.0381	.0359	.0338	.0318	.0299	.0281	.0264	.0247
23	.0362	.0340	.0319	.0299	.0280	.0263	.0246	.0230
24	.0344	.0322	.0302	.0282	.0264	.0246	.0230	.0214
25	.0328	.0306	.0286	.0266	.0248	.0231	.0215	.0200
26	.0313	.0291	.0271	.0252	.0234	.0217	.0201	.0186
27	.0299	.0277	.0257	.0239	.0221	.0204	.0189	.0174
28	.0286	.0265	.0245	.0226	.0209	.0192	.0177	.0163
29	.0274	.0253	.0233	.0215	.0198	.0182	.0167	.0153
30	.0263	.0242	.0222	.0204	.0187	.0171	.0157	.0143
31	.0252	.0231	.0212	.0194	.0178	.0162	.0148	.0135
32	.0242	.0222	.0203	.0185	.0169	.0153	.0139	.0127
33	.0233	.0213	.0194	.0176	.0160	.0145	.0132	.0119
34	.0224	.0204	.0185	.0168	.0152	.0138	.0124	.0112
35	.0216	.0196	.0178	.0161	.0145	.0131	.0117	.0105
36	.0208	.0189	.0170	.0153	.0138	.0124	.0111	.0099
37	.0201	.0181	.0163	.0147	.0132	.0118	.0105	.0094
38	.0194	.0175	.0157	.0140	.0125	.0112	.0100	.0088
39	.0188	.0168	.0151	.0134	.0120	.0106	.0094	.0084
40	.0182	.0162	.0145	.0129	.0114	.0101	.0089	.0079

587

HOW MUCH $1 A YEAR IS WORTH NOW

Example of use of this table:

Find discount payment for 5 years annual $600 premiums at 2½%.

From table at 2½% for 5 years 4.762

For $600 premiums (600 × 4.762) $2857.20

Number of Years	Interest Rate							
	1-1/2%	2%	2-1/2%	3%	3-1/2%	4%	4-1/2%	5%
1	1.000	1.000	1.000	1.000	1.000	1.000	1.000	1.000
2	1.985	1.980	1.976	1.971	1.966	1.962	1.957	1.952
3	2.956	2.942	2.927	2.913	2.900	2.886	2.873	2.859
4	3.912	3.884	3.856	3.829	3.802	3.775	3.749	3.723
5	4.854	4.808	4.762	4.717	4.673	4.630	4.588	4.546
6	5.783	5.713	5.646	5.580	5.515	5.452	5.390	5.329
7	6.697	6.601	6.508	6.417	6.329	6.242	6.158	6.076
8	7.598	7.472	7.349	7.230	7.115	7.002	6.893	6.786
9	8.486	8.325	8.170	8.020	7.874	7.733	7.596	7.463
10	9.361	9.162	8.971	8.786	8.608	8.435	8.269	8.108
11	10.222	9.983	9.752	9.530	9.317	9.111	8.913	8.722
12	11.071	10.787	10.514	10.253	10.002	9.760	9.529	9.306
13	11.908	11.575	11.258	10.954	10.663	10.385	10.119	9.863
14	12.732	12.348	11.983	11.635	11.303	10.986	10.683	10.394
15	13.543	13.106	12.691	12.296	11.921	11.563	11.223	10.899
16	14.343	13.849	13.381	12.938	12.517	12.118	11.740	11.380
17	15.131	14.578	14.055	13.561	13.094	12.652	12.234	11.838
18	15.908	15.292	14.712	14.166	13.651	13.166	12.707	12.274
19	16.673	15.992	15.353	14.754	14.190	13.659	13.160	12.690
20	17.426	16.678	15.979	15.324	14.710	14.134	13.593	13.085
21	18.169	17.351	16.589	15.877	15.212	14.590	14.008	13.462
22	18.900	18.011	17.185	16.415	15.698	15.029	14.405	13.821
23	19.621	18.658	17.765	16.937	16.167	15.451	14.784	14.163
24	20.331	19.292	18.332	17.444	16.620	15.857	15.148	14.489
25	21.030	19.914	18.885	17.936	17.058	16.247	15.495	14.799
26	21.720	20.523	19.424	18.413	17.482	16.622	15.828	15.094
27	22.399	21.121	19.951	18.877	17.890	16.983	16.147	15.375
28	23.068	21.707	20.464	19.327	18.285	17.330	16.451	15.643
29	23.727	22.281	20.965	19.764	18.667	17.663	16.743	15.898
30	24.376	22.844	21.454	20.188	19.036	17.984	17.022	16.141
31	25.016	23.396	21.930	20.600	19.392	18.292	17.289	16.372
32	25.646	23.938	22.395	21.000	19.736	18.588	17.544	16.593
33	26.267	24.468	22.849	21.389	20.069	18.874	17.789	16.803
34	26.879	24.989	23.292	21.766	20.390	19.148	18.023	17.003
35	27.482	25.499	23.724	22.132	20.701	19.411	18.247	17.193
36	28.076	25.999	24.145	22.487	21.001	19.665	18.461	17.374
37	28.661	26.489	24.556	22.832	21.290	19.908	18.666	17.547
38	29.237	26.969	24.957	23.167	21.571	20.143	18.862	17.711
39	29.805	27.441	25.349	23.492	21.841	20.368	19.050	17.686
40	30.365	27.903	25.730	23.808	22.102	20.524	19.230	18.017

COMPOUND DISCOUNT TABLE

Example of use of this table:

Find how much must be put at interest now to equal $10,000 in 12 years at a net rate of 4%

From table for 12 years at 4% .... .6246
Invest now for $10,000 (10,000 × .6246) .... $ 6246

Number of Years	Interest Rate				
	1-1/2%	2%	2-1/2%	3%	3-1/2%
1	0.9852	0.9804	0.9756	0.9709	0.9662
2	0.9707	0.9612	0.9518	0.9426	0.9335
3	0.9563	0.9423	0.9286	0.9151	0.9019
4	0.9422	0.9238	0.9060	0.8885	0.8714
5	0.9283	0.9057	0.8839	0.8626	0.8420
6	0.9145	0.8880	0.8623	0.8375	0.8135
7	0.9010	0.8706	0.8413	0.8131	0.7860
8	0.8877	0.8535	0.8207	0.7894	0.7594
9	0.8746	0.8368	0.8007	0.7664	0.7337
10	0.8617	0.8203	0.7812	0.7441	0.7089
11	0.8489	0.8043	0.7621	0.7224	0.6849
12	0.8364	0.7885	0.7436	0.7014	0.6618
13	0.8240	0.7730	0.7254	0.6810	0.6394
14	0.8118	0.7579	0.7077	0.6611	0.6178
15	0.7999	0.7430	0.6905	0.6419	0.5969
16	0.7880	0.7284	0.6736	0.6232	0.5767
17	0.7764	0.7142	0.6572	0.6050	0.5572
18	0.7649	0.7002	0.6412	0.5874	0.5384
19	0.7536	0.6864	0.6255	0.5703	0.5202
20	0.7425	0.6730	0.6103	0.5537	0.5026
21	0.7315	0.6598	0.5954	0.5375	0.4856
22	0.7207	0.6468	0.5809	0.5219	0.4692
23	0.7100	0.6342	0.5667	0.5067	0.4533
24	0.6995	0.6217	0.5529	0.4919	0.4380
25	0.6892	0.6095	0.5394	0.4776	0.4231
26	0.6790	0.5976	0.5262	0.4637	0.4088
27	0.6690	0.5859	0.5134	0.4502	0.3950
28	0.6591	0.5744	0.5009	0.4371	0.3817
29	0.6494	0.5631	0.4887	0.4243	0.3687
30	0.6398	0.5521	0.4767	0.4120	0.3563
31	0.6303	0.5412	0.4651	0.4000	0.3442
32	0.6210	0.5306	0.4538	0.3883	0.3326
33	0.6118	0.5202	0.4427	0.3770	0.3213
34	0.6028	0.5100	0.4319	0.3660	0.3105
35	0.5939	0.5000	0.4214	0.3554	0.3000
36	0.5851	0.4902	0.4111	0.3450	0.2898
37	0.5764	0.4806	0.4011	0.3350	0.2800
38	0.5679	0.4712	0.3913	0.3252	0.2706
39	0.5595	0.4619	0.3817	0.3158	0.2614
40	0.5513	0.4529	0.3724	0.3066	0.2526

PRESENT WORTH OF A SINGLE FUTURE PAYMENT

Example of use of this table:

Find how much must be put at interest now to equal $10,000 in 12 years at a net rate of 4%.

From table for 12 years at 4% .... .6246
Invest now for $10,000 (10,000 × .6246) .... $ 6246

Interest Rate

Number of Years	4%	4½%	5%	6%	7%	8%
1	0.9615	0.9569	0.9524	0.9434	0.9346	0.9259
2	0.9246	0.9157	0.9070	0.8900	0.8734	0.8573
3	0.8890	0.8763	0.8638	0.8396	0.8163	0.7938
4	0.8548	0.8386	0.8227	0.7921	0.7629	0.7350
5	0.8219	0.8025	0.7835	0.7473	0.7130	0.6806
6	0.7903	0.7679	0.7462	0.7050	0.6663	0.6302
7	0.7599	0.7348	0.7107	0.6651	0.6227	0.5835
8	0.7307	0.7032	0.6768	0.6274	0.5820	0.5403
9	0.7026	0.6729	0.6446	0.5919	0.5439	0.5002
10	0.6756	0.6439	0.6139	0.5584	0.5083	0.4632
11	0.6496	0.6162	0.5847	0.5268	0.4751	0.4289
12	0.6246	0.5897	0.5568	0.4970	0.4440	0.3971
13	0.6006	0.5643	0.5303	0.4688	0.4150	0.3677
14	0.5775	0.5400	0.5051	0.4423	0.3878	0.3405
15	0.5553	0.5167	0.4810	0.4173	0.3624	0.3152
16	0.5339	0.4945	0.4581	0.3936	0.3387	0.2919
17	0.5134	0.4732	0.4363	0.3714	0.3166	0.2703
18	0.4936	0.4528	0.4155	0.3503	0.2959	0.2502
19	0.4746	0.4333	0.3957	0.3305	0.2765	0.2317
20	0.4564	0.4146	0.3769	0.3118	0.2584	0.2145
21	0.4388	0.3968	0.3589	0.2942	0.2415	0.1987
22	0.4220	0.3797	0.3418	0.2775	0.2257	0.1839
23	0.4057	0.3634	0.3256	0.2618	0.2109	0.1703
24	0.3901	0.3477	0.3101	0.2470	0.1971	0.1577
25	0.3751	0.3327	0.2953	0.2330	0.1842	0.1460
26	0.3607	0.3184	0.2812	0.2198	0.1.22	0.1352
27	0.3468	0.3047	0.2678	0.2074	0.1609	0.1252
28	0.3335	0.2916	0.2551	0.1956	0.1504	0.1159
29	0.3207	0.2790	0.2429	0.1846	0.1406	0.1073
30	0.3083	0.2670	0.2314	0.1741	0.1314	0.0994
31	0.2965	0.2555	0.2204	0.1643	0.1228	0.0920
32	0.2851	0.2445	0.2099	0.1550	0.1147	0.0852
33	0.2741	0.2340	0.1999	0.1462	0.1072	0.0789
34	0.2636	0.2239	0.1904	0.1379	0.1002	0.0730
35	0.2534	0.2143	0.1813	0.1301	0.0937	0.0676
36	0.2437	0.2050	0.1727	0.1227	0.0875	0.0626
37	0.2343	0.1962	0.1644	0.1158	0.0818	0.0580
38	0.2253	0.1877	0.1566	0.1092	0.0765	0.0536
39	0.2166	0.1797	0.1491	0.1031	0.0715	0.0497
40	0.2083	0.1719	0.1420	0.0972	0.0668	0.0460

PRESENT WORTH OF PERIODIC FUTURE PAYMENTS

Example of use of this table:

To find the cost now of $1,000 of income per year for 20 years at 7%.

From table for 20 years at 7% 10.5940

Cost of $1,000 per year ($1,000 × 10.5940) $10,594

Interest Rate

Number of Years	3%	3½%	4%	4½%	5%	6%	7%	8%
1	0.9709	0.9662	0.9615	0.9569	0.9524	0.9434	0.9346	0.9259
2	1.9135	1.8997	1.8861	1.8727	1.8594	1.8334	1.8080	1.7833
3	2.8286	2.8016	2.7751	2.7490	2.7233	2.6730	2.6243	2.5771
4	3.7171	3.6731	3.6299	3.5875	3.5459	3.4651	3.3872	3.3121
5	4.5797	4.5151	4.4518	4.3900	4.3295	4.2124	4.1002	3.9927
6	5.4172	5.3286	5.2421	5.1579	5.0757	4.9173	4.7665	4.6229
7	6.2303	6.1145	6.0021	5.8927	5.7864	5.5824	5.3893	5.2064
8	7.0197	6.8740	6.7327	6.5959	6.4632	6.2098	5.9713	5.7466
9	7.7861	7.6077	7.4353	7.2688	7.1078	6.8017	6.5152	6.2469
10	8.5302	8.3166	8.1109	7.9127	7.7217	7.3601	7.0236	6.7101
11	9.2526	9.0016	8.7605	8.5289	8.3064	7.8869	7.4987	7.1390
12	9.9540	9.6633	9.3851	9.1186	8.8633	8.3838	7.9427	7.5361
13	10.6350	10.3027	9.9856	9.6829	9.3936	8.8527	8.3577	7.9038
14	11.2961	10.9205	10.5631	10.2228	9.8986	9.2950	8.7455	8.2442
15	11.9379	11.5174	11.1184	10.7395	10.3797	9.7122	9.1079	8.5595
16	12.5611	12.0941	11.6523	11.2340	10.8378	10.1059	9.4466	8.8514
17	13.1661	12.6513	12.1657	11.7072	11.2741	10.4773	9.7632	9.1216
18	13.7535	13.1897	12.6593	12.1600	11.6896	10.8276	10.0591	9.3719
19	14.3238	13.7098	13.1339	12.5933	12.0853	11.1581	10.3356	9.6036
20	14.8775	14.2124	13.5903	13.0079	12.4622	11.4699	10.5940	9.8181
21	15.4150	14.6980	14.0292	13.4047	12.8212	11.7641	10.8355	10.0168
22	15.9369	15.1671	14.4511	13.7844	13.1630	12.0416	11.0612	10.2007
23	16.4436	15.6204	14.8568	14.1478	13.4886	12.3034	11.2722	10.3711
24	16.9355	16.0584	15.2470	14.4955	13.7986	12.5504	11.4693	10.5288
25	17.4131	16.4815	15.6221	14.8282	14.0939	12.7834	11.6536	10.6748
26	17.8768	16.8904	15.9828	15.1466	14.3752	13.0032	11.8258	10.8100
27	18.3270	17.2854	16.3296	15.4513	14.6430	13.2105	11.9867	10.9352
28	18.7641	17.6670	16.6631	15.7429	14.8981	13.4062	12.1371	11.0511
29	19.1885	18.0358	16.9837	16.0219	15.1411	13.5907	12.2777	11.1584
30	19.6004	18.3920	17.2920	16.2889	15.3725	13.7648	12.4090	11.2578
31	20.0004	18.7363	17.5885	16.5444	15.5928	13.9291	12.5318	11.3498
32	20.3888	19.0689	17.8736	16.7889	15.8027	14.0840	12.6466	11.4350
33	20.7658	19.3902	18.1476	17.0229	16.0025	14.2302	12.7538	11.5139
34	21.1318	19.7007	18.4112	17.2468	16.1929	14.3681	12.8540	11.5869
35	21.4872	20.0007	18.6646	17.4610	16.3742	14.4982	12.9477	11.6546
36	21.8323	20.2905	18.9083	17.6660	16.5469	14.6210	13.0352	11.7172
37	22.1672	20.5705	19.1426	17.8622	16.7113	14.7368	13.1170	11.7752
38	22.4925	20.8411	19.3679	18.0500	16.8679	14.8460	13.1935	11.8289
39	22.8082	21.1025	19.5845	18.2297	17.0170	14.9491	13.2649	11.8786
40	23.1148	21.3551	19.7928	18.4016	17.1591	15.0463	13.3317	11.9246

HOW COMPOUNDING INTEREST BUILDS THE ESTATE

Compound interest in and of itself builds capital and prolongs the support which that capital can provide in retirement and to a surviving family. The following table shows how much can be accumulated by saving $1,200 a year for 15 years and how little the accumulated capital is reduced by withdrawing the same amount, $1,200 a year, regularly over the following 15 years.

Annual Savings and Withdrawals of $1,200

No. of Years	Savings of $1,200 Annually for 15 Years			No. of Years	Withdrawals of $1,200 Annually for 15 Years			
	Invested	4% Interest	Cumulative Total		With- drawals	4% Interest	Reduction of Principal	Remaining Principal
1	1,200	48	1,248	1	1,200	1,000	200	24,988
2	1,200	98	2,546	2	1,200	992	208	24,788
3	1,200	150	3,896	3	1,200	983	217	24,580
4	1,200	204	5,300	4	1,200	975	225	24,363
5	1,200	260	6,760	5	1,200	966	234	24,138
6	1,200	318	8,278	6	1,200	956	244	23,904
7	1,200	379	9,857	7	1,200	946	254	23,660
8	1,200	442	11,499	8	1,200	936	264	23,406
9	1,200	508	13,207	9	1,200	926	274	23,142
10	1,200	576	14,983	10	1,200	915	285	22,868
11	1,200	647	16,830	11	1,200	903	297	22,583
12	1,200	721	18,751	12	1,200	891	309	22,286
13	1,200	798	20,749	13	1,200	879	321	21,977
14	1,200	878	22,827	14	1,200	866	334	21,656
15	1,200	961	24,988	15	1,200	853	347	21,322
	18,000	6,988	24,988		18,000	13,987	4,013	20,975

These $100 a month payments could continue for an additional 30 years before the accumulated fund is exhausted. Thus, if a man of 25 lends his future $100 a month regularly until he is 40, he can pay himself back the same amount—regularly until he is 85.

Annual Savings of $1,200, Withdrawals of $1,800

If $100 a month is saved regularly for 20 years; $150 a month can be withdrawn for 20 years and there is still $27,822 left, as the following table indicates:

No. of Years	Savings of $1,200 Annually for 20 Years			No. of Years	Withdrawals of $1,800 Annually for 20 Years			
	Invested	4% Interest	Cumulative Total		With- drawals	4% Interest	Reduction of Principal	Remaining Principal
1	1,200	48	1,248	1	1,800	1,486	314	37,161
2	1,200	98	2,546	2	1,800	1,474	326	36,847
3	1,200	150	3,896	3	1,800	1,461	339	36,521
4	1,200	204	5,300	4	1,800	1,447	353	36,182
5	1,200	260	6,760	5	1,800	1,433	367	35,829
6	1,200	318	8,278	6	1,800	1,418	382	35,462
7	1,200	379	9,857	7	1,800	1,403	397	35,080
8	1,200	442	11,499	8	1,800	1,387	413	34,683
9	1,200	508	13,207	9	1,800	1,371	429	34,270
10	1,200	576	14,983	10	1,800	1,354	446	33,841
11	1,200	647	16,830	11	1,800	1,336	464	33,395
12	1,200	721	18,751	12	1,800	1,317	483	32,931
13	1,200	798	20,749	13	1,800	1,298	502	32,448

No. of Years	Savings of $1,200 Annually for 20 Years			No. of Years	Withdrawals of $1,800 Annually for 20 Years			
	Invested	4% Interest	Cumulative Total		With-drawals	4% Interest	Reduction of Principal	Remaining Principal
14	1,200	878	22,827	14	1,800	1,278	522	31,946
15	1,200	961	24,988	15	1,800	1,257	543	31,424
16	1,200	1,048	27,236	16	1,800	1,235	565	30,881
17	1,200	1,137	29,573	17	1,800	1,213	587	30,316
18	1,200	1,231	32,004	18	1,800	1,189	611	29,729
19	1,200	1,328	34,532	19	1,800	1,165	635	29,118
20	1,200	1,429	37,161	20	1,800	1,139	661	28,483
	24,000	13,161	37,161		36,000	26,661	9,339	27,822

Annual Savings of $1,200, Withdrawals of $2,400

If $100 a month is saved for 25 years, twice as much, $200 a month, for 25 years can be paid out and there will still be over $38,000 left, as the following table indicates:

No. of Years	Savings of $1,200 Annually for 25 Years			No. of Years	Withdrawals of $2,400 Annually for 25 Years			
	Invested	4% Interest	Cumulative Total		With-drawals	4% Interest	Reduction of Principal	Remaining Principal
1	1,200	48	1,248	1	2,400	2,079	321	51,972
2	1,200	98	2,546	2	2,400	2,066	334	51,651
3	1,200	150	3,896	3	2,400	2,053	347	51,317
4	1,200	204	5,300	4	2,400	2,039	361	50,970
5	1,200	260	6,760	5	2,400	2,024	376	50,609
6	1,200	318	8,278	6	2,400	2,009	391	50,233
7	1,200	379	9,857	7	2,400	1,994	406	49,842
8	1,200	442	11,499	8	2,400	1,977	423	49,436
9	1,200	508	13,207	9	2,400	1,961	439	49,013
10	1,200	576	14,983	10	2,400	1,943	457	48,574
11	1,200	647	16,830	11	2,400	1,925	475	48,117
12	1,200	721	18,751	12	2,400	1,906	494	47,642
13	1,200	798	20,749	13	2,400	1,886	514	47,148
14	1,200	878	22,827	14	2,400	1,865	535	46,634
15	1,200	961	24,988	15	2,400	1,844	556	46,099
16	1,200	1,048	27,236	16	2,400	1,822	578	45,543
17	1,200	1,137	29,573	17	2,400	1,799	601	44,965
18	1,200	1,231	32,004	18	2,400	1,775	625	44,364
19	1,200	1,328	34,532	19	2,400	1,750	650	43,739
20	1,200	1,429	37,161	20	2,400	1,724	676	43,089
21	1,200	1,534	39,895	21	2,400	1,697	703	42,413
22	1,200	1,644	42,739	22	2,400	1,668	732	41,710
23	1,200	1,758	45,697	23	2,400	1,639	761	40,978
24	1,200	1,876	48,773	24	2,400	1,609	791	40,217
25	1,200	1,999	51,972	25	2,400	1,577	823	39,426
	30,000	21,972	51,972		60,000	46,631	13,369	38,603

LIFE EXPECTANCY OF CAPITAL

The Life Expectancy of Capital table below will indicate how long a specified amount of capital will pay ½ of 1% of the principal sum monthly at a 5% rate of interest.

The table shows the life expectancy of capital earning interest at 5% as various amounts are withdrawn monthly. For example, $100 of monthly withdrawals on a starting amount of $20,000 can be expected for 33 years before the capital is completely destroyed.

Years of Withdrawal	$100 a Month Withdrawal	$200 a Month Withdrawal	$300 a Month Withdrawal	$400 a Month Withdrawal	$500 a Month Withdrawal
33	$20,000	$40,000	$60,000	$80,000	$100,000
32	19,767	39,534	59,301	79,068	98,836
31	19,522	39,045	58,567	78,090	97,612
30	19,265	38,531	57,331	77,062	96,323
29	18,995	37,991	56,986	75,981	94,977
28	18,712	37,423	56,135	74,846	93,553
27	18,414	36,827	55,241	73,654	92,068
26	18,100	36,201	54,301	72,401	90,502
25	17,771	35,543	53,314	71,085	88,856
24	17,426	34,851	52,277	69,702	87,128
23	17,062	34,125	51,187	68,249	85,312
22	16,681	33,362	50,042	66,723	83,404
21	16,280	32,560	48,840	65,119	81,399
20	15,859	31,717	47,576	63,435	79,293
19	15,416	30,832	46,248	61,665	77,081
18	14,951	29,902	44,854	59,805	74,756
17	14,463	28,925	43,388	57,851	72,314
16	13,950	27,899	41,849	55,798	69,748
15	13,410	26,821	40,231	53,641	67,052
14	12,844	25,688	38,532	51,376	64,219
13	12,249	24,497	36,746	48,995	61,244
12	11,623	23,247	34,870	46,494	58,117
11	10,967	21,933	32,900	43,866	54,833
10	10,276	20,554	30,829	41,105	51,382
9	9,551	19,102	28,654	38,205	47,756
8	8,789	17,579	26,368	35,157	43,947
7	7,989	15,978	23,967	31,956	39,945
6	7,148	14,296	21,444	28,592	35,740
5	6,264	12,529	18,793	25,058	31,322
4	5,336	10,672	16,009	21,345	26,681
3	4,361	8,722	13,083	17,444	21,805
2	3,336	6,673	10,009	13,346	16,682
1	2,260	4,520	6,780	9,040	11,300
11 months	1,129	2,258	3,387	4,516	5,645

594

UNIFORM ONE-YEAR TERM PREMIUM IN PENSION AND PROFIT-SHARING COVERAGE AND SPLIT-DOLLAR PLANS

When current life insurance protection is given to an employee as part of the employer contribution for retirement income or other form of insurance in a pension or profit-sharing plan, the cost of the so-called "pure insurance" factor of the coverage is taxable to the employee at the time of the employer's contribution. When an employee works out a split-dollar arrangement with his employer, the difference between what the employee contributes towards each year's premium and the one-year cost of the declining life insurance protection to which he is entitled from year to year is included in his gross income. The following Government table gives an acceptable-to-the-Government cost of one-year term insurance for these purposes:

Age	Cost per $1,000 of protection	Age	Cost per $1,000 of protection	Age	Cost per $1,000 of protection
15	$1.27	37	$3.63	60	$20.73
16	1.38	38	3.87	61	22.53
17	1.48	39	4.14	62	24.50
18	1.52			63	26.63
19	1.56	40	4.42	64	28.98
		41	4.73		
20	1.61	42	5.07	65	31.51
21	1.67	43	5.44	66	34.28
22	1.73	44	5.85	67	37.31
23	1.79			68	40.59
24	1.86	45	6.30	69	44.17
		46	6.78		
25	1.93	47	7.32	70	48.06
26	2.02	48	7.89	71	52.29
27	2.11	49	8.53	72	56.89
28	2.20			73	61.89
29	2.31	50	9.22	74	67.33
		51	9.97		
30	2.43	52	10.79	75	73.23
31	2.57	53	11.69	76	79.63
32	2.70	54	12.67	77	86.57
33	2.86			78	94.09
34	3.02	55	13.74	79	102.23
		56	14.91		
35	3.21	57	16.18	80	111.04
36	3.41	58	17.56	81	120.57
		59	19.08		

FAMILY INCOME RIDER

The family income rider provides a monthly income in the event of the death of the insured during the period selected. The period begins when the policy becomes effective. If, for example, the period selected is 20 years and the insured dies after the policy has been in effect 10 years, the beneficiary will receive payments for 10 years under the family income rider. After the 10-year period ends, the face amount of the policy will be paid. Each agreement may be written for any amount of monthly income from $10 to $50 for each $1,000 face amount of basic policy. This plan was designed primarily to provide (a) income during the school period, (b) a life income to the surviving spouse, and (c) funds to pay off a mortgage.

Tax Aspects of Family Income Rider: Regs. §1.101-3 and 1.101-4 say that a portion of each monthly payment under a family income rider represents interest on the proceeds of the basic policy retained by the insurance company until the end of the term period. To that extent, a surviving spouse is taxed each year on such interest. The monthly yield per $1,000 face amount depends upon the rate of interest guaranteed under the policy; at 2¼%, it would be $1.86; at 2½%, $2.06, etc.

The balance of each payment under the family income rider is attributable to both principal and interest payable in installments from the term rider. To the extent that such installment payment reflects interest, it is taxable. But the surviving spouse is entitled to exclude from gross income an amount up to $1,000 a year. The commuted value of the family income rider is income tax free as death proceeds.

As an example of how IRS taxes a surviving spouse as beneficiary of a policy with a family income rider, let's assume the insured (a married man) held a $100,000 ordinary life policy with a $1,000-a-month, 20-year rider. Suppose he died at the end of the seventeenth year, so that there are 36 monthly payments to be made to his widow under the family income rider. At the time of his death, the commuted value of the $36,000 total payments ($1,000 ×36) is $28,409.

Assuming an interest rate of 2¼%, here's how to figure the amount of each $1,000 monthly payment includible in the widow's gross income:

First: Compute the annual interest on the $100,000 basic policy which is retained by the insurance company for the duration of payments under the rider ($1,000 × 2¼% = $2,250). When reduced to 12 monthly installments with the necessary adjustments for monthly payments, this comes to $185. Thus, the widow will include in her gross income the $185 monthly payments under Code §101(c).

Second: Divide the commuted value of the family income rider by the number of monthly payments, $28,409 ÷ 36 = $789.14. So the $789.14 which represents distribution of principal under the rider is excluded under Code §101(d).

Third: The balance of each monthly installment, $25.86 ($1,000 minus $789.14 minus $185 = $25.86), represents interest on the proceeds of the family income rider. Since the sum of $25.86 is being distributed to the widow along with the principal, it qualifies for the annual exclusion. And since the annual total is less than $1,000 ($25.86 × 12 = $310.32), the entire amount is tax free.

Fourth: At the end of the monthly payments under the family income rider, the $100,000 proceeds of the basic ordinary life policy will then go to the widow tax free under Code §101(a).

SETTLEMENT OPTIONS

Optional modes of settlement provide that the whole or part of the net proceeds of a policy payable at death, or at maturity as an endowment, or of the cash value of a policy in force may be retained by the company for periodic disbursement in a number of ways.

To ascertain insurance requirements for income needs, it is necessary to determine what the settlement options will do in the way of income.

The following tables give the income payable, either for a specified number of years or for life under various insurance policy settlement options. The tables show how long various amounts of insurance will provide stipulated amounts of monthly income at various rates of interest and how much monthly life income will be available for periods certain for males and females. The tables are very conservative. Most insurance companies currently pay benefits computed at higher interest than the guaranteed rates.

Proceeds at Interest

The following table shows the monthly interest payable, at various guaranteed interest rates, when the proceeds are left with the insurance company to draw interest.

Interest Rate	Monthly Per $1,000 Proceeds
2% guaranteed	$1.65
2½% guaranteed	2.06
3% guaranteed	2.46

Proceeds Payable in Equal Monthly Payments for Fixed Period of Years

No. of Years Pay-able	When 3% Is Guaranteed			When 2½% Is Guaranteed			When 2% Is Guaranteed		
	Payments per $1,000 Proceeds	Proceeds Required for Payments of $25	$100	Payments per $1,000 Proceeds	Proceeds Required for Payments of $25	$100	Payments per $1,000 Proceeds	Proceeds Required for Payments of $25	$100
1	$84.47	$ 296	$ 1,184	$84.28	$ 297	$ 1,187	$84.09	$ 298	$ 1,190
2	42.86	584	2,334	42.66	587	2,345	42.46	589	2,356
3	28.99	863	3,450	28.79	869	3,474	28.59	875	3,498
4	22.06	1,134	4,534	21.86	1,144	4,575	21.65	1,155	4,619
5	17.91	1,396	5,584	17.70	1,413	5,650	17.49	1,430	5,718
6	15.14	1,652	6,606	14.93	1,675	6,698	14.72	1,699	6,794
7	13.16	1,900	7,599	12.95	1,931	7,723	12.74	1,963	7,850
8	11.68	2,141	8,562	11.47	2,180	8,719	11.25	2,223	8,889
9	10.53	2,375	9,497	10.32	2,423	9,690	10.10	2,476	9,901
10	9.61	2,602	10,406	9.39	2,663	10,650	9.18	2,724	10,894
11	8.86	2,822	11,287	8.64	2,894	11,575	8.42	2,970	11,877
12	8.24	3,034	12,136	8.02	3,118	12,469	7.80	3,206	12,821
13	7.71	3,243	12,971	7.49	3,338	13,352	7.26	3,444	13,775
14	7.26	3,444	13,775	7.03	3,557	14,225	6.81	3,672	14,685
15	6.87	3,640	14,557	6.64	3,766	15,061	6.42	3,895	15,577
16	6.53	3,829	15,314	6.30	3,969	15,874	6.07	4,119	16,475
17	6.23	4,013	16,052	6.00	4,167	16,667	5.77	4,333	17,332
18	5.96	4,195	16,779	5.73	4,364	17,453	5.50	4,546	18,182
19	5.73	4,364	17,453	5.49	4,554	18,215	5.26	4,753	19,012
20	5.51	4,538	18,149	5.27	4,744	18,976	5.04	4,961	19,842
21	5.32	4,700	18,797	5.08	4,922	19,686	4.85	5,155	20,619
22	5.15	4,855	19,418	4.90	5,103	20,409	4.67	5,354	21,414
23	4.99	5,011	20,041	4.74	5,275	21,098	4.51	5,544	22,173
24	4.84	5,166	20,662	4.60	5,435	21,740	4.36	5,734	22,936
25	4.71	5,308	21,232	4.46	5,606	22,422	4.22	5,925	23,697
26	4.59	5,447	21,787	4.34	5,761	23,042	4.10	6,098	24,391
27	4.47	5,593	22,372	4.22	5,925	23,697	3.98	6,282	25,126
28	4.37	5,721	22,884	4.12	6,068	24,272	3.87	6,460	25,840
29	4.27	5,855	23,420	4.02	6,219	24,876	3.77	6,632	26,526
30	4.18	5,981	23,924	3.93	6,362	25,446	3.68	6,794	27,174

HOW LONG INSURANCE PROCEEDS WILL LAST IF PAID OUT
MONTHLY UNTIL PRINCIPAL AND INTEREST ARE EXHAUSTED

% of proceeds Paid each year or	Dollars per Month per $1,000 of proceeds	Fund Will Last - When Guaranteed Rate of Interest Is:					
		2%		2-1/2%		3%	
		Yrs.	Mos.	Yrs.	Mos.	Yrs.	Mos.
5.0%	$ 4.17	25	5	27	6	30	2
5.4	4.50	23	0	24	8	26	9
5.5	4.58	22	6	24	1	26	0
6.0	5.00	20	2	21	5	22	11
6.5	5.42	18	3	19	3	20	5
6.6	5.50	17	11	18	11	20	0
7.0	5.83	16	9	17	7	18	6
7.2	6.00	16	2	16	11	17	10
7.5	6.25	15	5	16	1	16	11
7.8	6.50	14	9	15	4	16	1
8.0	6.67	14	4	14	11	15	7
8.4	7.00	13	6	14	0	14	7
8.5	7.08	13	4	13	10	14	5
9.0	7.50	12	6	12	11	13	5
9.5	7.92	11	9	12	2	12	7
10.0	8.33	11	1	11	5	11	10
10.2	8.50	10	10	11	2	11	6
10.5	8.75	10	6	10	10	11	2
10.8	9.00	10	2	10	6	10	9
11.0	9.17	10	0	10	3	10	6
11.4	9.50	9	7	9	10	10	1
12.0	10.00	9	1	9	3	9	6
12.5	10.42	8	8	8	10	9	1
13.0	10.83	8	4	8	6	8	8
13.5	11.25	8	0	8	2	8	4
14.0	11.67	7	8	7	10	8	0
15.0	12.50	7	1	7	3	7	5
16.0	13.33	6	7	6	9	6	10
17.0	14.17	6	2	6	4	6	5
18.0	15.00	5	10	5	11	6	0
19.0	15.83	5	6	5	7	5	8
20.0	16.67	5	3	5	3	5	4
21.0	17.50	4	11	5	0	5	1
22.0	18.33	4	9	4	9	4	10
23.0	19.17	4	6	4	7	4	7
24.0	20.00	4	4	4	4	4	5
25.0	20.83	4	1	4	2	4	3

MONTHLY LIFE INCOME PER $1000 OF PROCEEDS
AT VARIOUS AGES

(2½% Interest)

Male	Age Female	Life Income Only	5 Years Certain and Life	10 Years Certain and Life	15 Years Certain and Life	20 Years Certain and Life	Install- ment Re- fund
25	30	$3.08	$3.08	$3.08	$3.07	$3.05	$3.01
30	35	3.27	3.27	3.26	3.24	3.22	3.17
31	36	3.31	3.31	3.30	3.28	3.25	3.20
32	37	3.36	3.36	3.34	3.32	3.29	3.24
33	38	3.41	3.40	3.39	3.36	3.33	3.28
34	39	3.45	3.45	3.43	3.41	3.37	3.32
35	40	3.50	3.50	3.48	3.45	3.41	3.36
36	41	3.56	3.55	3.53	3.50	3.45	3.40
37	42	3.61	3.61	3.59	3.55	3.50	3.44
38	43	3.67	3.66	3.64	3.60	3.54	3.49
39	44	3.73	3.72	3.70	3.65	3.59	3.53
40	45	3.79	3.78	3.76	3.71	3.64	3.58
41	46	3.86	3.86	3.82	3.77	3.69	3.63
42	47	3.93	3.92	3.88	3.82	3.74	3.68
43	48	4.00	3.99	3.95	3.88	3.79	3.74
44	49	4.08	4.06	4.02	3.95	3.84	3.80
45	50	4.15	4.14	4.09	4.01	3.90	3.85
46	51	4.24	4.22	4.17	4.08	3.95	3.91
47	52	4.33	4.31	4.25	4.15	4.01	3.98
48	53	4.42	4.40	4.33	4.22	4.07	4.04
49	54	4.51	4.49	4.42	4.29	4.12	4.11
50	55	4.61	4.59	4.50	4.37	4.18	4.18
51	56	4.72	4.69	4.60	4.44	4.24	4.26
52	57	4.83	4.80	4.69	4.52	4.30	4.33
53	58	4.95	4.91	4.79	4.60	4.36	4.42
54	59	5.07	5.03	4.90	4.69	4.41	4.50
55	60	5.20	5.15	5.01	4.77	4.47	4.59
56	61	5.34	5.28	5.12	4.86	4.53	4.68
57	62	5.48	5.42	5.23	4.94	4.59	4.77
58	63	5.64	5.56	5.35	5.03	4.64	4.87
59	64	5.80	5.72	5.48	5.12	4.70	4.98
60	65	5.97	5.87	5.61	5.21	4.75	5.08
61	66	6.15	6.04	5.74	5.30	4.80	5.20
62	67	6.34	6.22	5.87	5.39	4.85	5.31
63	68	6.54	6.40	6.01	5.48	4.90	5.44
64	69	6.75	6.59	6.16	5.56	4.94	5.57
65	70	6.97	6.79	6.30	5.65	4.98	5.70
70	75	8.32	7.95	7.07	6.05	5.14	6.48

HOW MUCH OF ANNUITY INCOME IS TAXED?

Only part of each annuity payment received is taxed. The fraction formed by the cost of the annuity over the expected return determines the portion of each annuity payment that is tax free. The following tables are to be used in determining the expected return in various situations. These are tables issued by the Treasury.

Expected Return per $1 Annual Payment for
Single-Life Annuity (Government Table I)

Example of use of this table:

Find exempt portion of annuity of $100 per month for single male annuitant. Annuitant is 65. Contract cost $14,000.

$$\frac{\text{Cost of contract (\$14,000)}}{\text{Annual payments (\$1,200)} \times \text{multiple from table (15)}} = \frac{14}{18} \times \$100 = \$77.78$$

Ages		Expected Return Per $1 Annual Payment	Ages		Expected Return Per $1 Annual Payment	Ages		Expected Return Per $1 Annual Payment
Male	Female		Male	Female		Male	Female	
16	21	55.8	41	46	33.0	66	71	14.4
17	22	54.9	42	47	32.1	67	72	13.8
18	23	53.9	43	48	31.2	68	73	13.2
19	24	53.0	44	49	30.4	69	74	12.6
20	25	52.1	45	50	29.6	70	75	12.1
21	26	51.1	46	51	28.7	71	76	11.6
22	27	50.2	47	52	27.9	72	77	11.0
23	28	49.3	48	53	27.1	73	78	10.5
24	29	48.3	49	54	26.3	74	79	10.1
25	30	47.4	50	55	25.5	75	80	9.6
26	31	46.5	51	56	24.7	76	81	9.1
27	32	45.6	52	57	24.0	77	82	8.7
28	33	44.6	53	58	23.2	78	83	8.3
29	34	43.7	54	59	22.4	79	84	7.8
30	35	42.8	55	60	21.7	80	85	7.5
31	36	41.9	56	61	21.0	81	86	7.1
32	37	41.0	57	62	20.3	82	87	6.7
33	38	40.0	58	63	19.6	83	88	6.3
34	39	39.1	59	64	18.9	84	89	6.0
35	40	38.2	60	65	18.2	85	90	5.7
36	41	37.3	61	66	17.5	86	91	5.4
37	42	36.5	62	67	16.9	87	92	5.1
38	43	35.6	63	68	16.2	88	93	4.8
39	44	34.7	64	69	15.6	89	94	4.5
40	45	33.8	65	70	15.0	90	95	4.2

If annuity payments are other than monthly or if first annuity payment is earlier than regular period for payment thereafter, the figures in the table must be adjusted. Add or subtract as follows:

If the number of whole months from the annuity starting date to the first payment date is   0-1 2 3 4 5 6 7 8 9 10 11 12

And payments under the contract are to be made:	
Annually	+.5 +.4 +.3 +.2 +.1 0 - .1 - .2 -.3 -.4 -.5
Semiannually	+.2 +.1 0 0 -.1 -.2
Quarterly	+.1 0 -.1

600

Expected Return on Joint and Survivor Annuity—
Wife Younger—Uniform Payment
(Government Table II)

Example of use of this table:

Find exempt portion of annuity of $100 per month for a married couple. Husband is 67; wife is 62. Contract cost $21,000.

$$\frac{\text{Cost of contract (\$21,000)}}{\text{Annual payments (\$1,200} \times \text{ multiple from table (15))}} = \frac{210}{276} \times 100 = \$76.09$$

NOTE: See next page for use of Table II where variable annuity pays lesser amount to specified survivor. For adjustment for early or other monthly payments see Table I.

Age of Husband	Wife Younger by							
	1 yr.	2 yr.	3 yr.	4 yr.	5 yr.	6 yr.	7 yr.	8 yr.
45	39.9	40.5	41.1	41.7	42.3	--	---	---
46	38.9	39.5	40.1	40.7	41.4	42.0	---	---
47	38.0	38.6	39.2	39.8	40.4	41.1	41.8	---
48	37.1	37.7	38.3	38.9	39.5	40.2	40.8	41.5
49	36.2	36.8	37.3	38.0	38.6	39.2	39.9	40.6
50	35.3	35.8	36.4	37.0	37.7	38.3	39.0	39.6
51	34.4	34.9	35.5	36.1	36.7	37.4	38.0	38.7
52	33.5	34.0	34.6	35.2	35.8	36.5	37.1	37.8
53	32.6	33.1	33.7	34.3	34.9	35.6	36.2	36.9
54	31.7	32.2	32.8	33.4	34.0	34.7	35.3	36.0
55	30.8	31.4	31.9	32.5	33.1	33.8	34.4	35.1
56	29.9	30.5	31.1	31.6	32.2	32.9	32.5	34.2
57	29.1	29.6	30.2	30.8	31.4	32.0	32.6	33.3
58	28.2	28.8	29.3	29.9	30.5	31.1	31.7	32.4
59	27.4	27.9	28.5	29.0	29.6	30.2	30.9	31.5
60	26.5	27.1	27.6	28.2	28.8	29.4	30.0	30.6
61	25.7	26.2	26.8	27.3	27.9	28.5	29.1	29.8
62	24.9	25.4	25.9	26.5	27.1	27.7	28.3	28.9
63	24.1	24.6	25.1	25.7	26.2	26.8	27.4	28.1
64	23.3	23.8	24.3	24.9	25.4	26.0	26.6	27.2
65	22.5	23.0	23.5	24.1	24.6	25.2	25.8	26.4
66	21.7	22.2	22.7	23.3	23.8	24.4	25.0	25.6
67	21.0	21.4	21.9	22.5	23.0	23.6	24.1	24.7
68	20.2	20.7	21.2	21.7	22.2	22.8	23.4	23.9
69	19.5	19.9	20.4	20.9	21.5	22.0	22.6	23.2
70	18.7	19.2	19.7	20.2	20.7	21.2	21.8	22.4
71	18.0	18.5	19.0	19.5	20.0	20.5	21.0	21.6
72	17.3	17.8	18.2	18.7	19.2	19.8	20.3	20.9
73	16.7	17.1	17.5	18.0	18.5	19.0	19.6	20.1
74	16.0	16.4	16.9	17.3	17.8	18.3	18.8	19.4
75	15.3	15.7	16.2	16.6	17.1	17.6	18.1	18.7
76	14.7	15.1	15.5	16.0	16.4	16.9	17.4	18.0
77	14.1	14.5	14.9	15.3	15.8	16.3	16.7	17.3
78	13.5	13.8	14.3	14.7	15.1	15.6	16.1	16.6
79	12.9	13.2	13.6	14.1	14.5	15.0	15.4	15.9
80	12.3	12.7	13.0	13.5	13.9	14.3	14.8	15.3

Expected Return and Survivor Annuity—
Wife Younger—Different Amount After
First Death (Government Table IIA)

Example of use of this table:

Find exclusion ratio of joint and survivor contract of $100 per month as long as both husband and wife live and $50 per month after death of one. Husband is 70; wife is 67. Cost of contract is $13,500.

Multiple from Table II on page 587 for husband
70, wife 3 years younger 19.7
Multiple from Table below 9.3

Difference 10.4

Portion of expected return (reduced payment) 10.4 × $600 ....$ 6,240
Portion of expected return (full payment) 9.3 × $1,200 ....$ 11,160

Expected Return .... $ 17,400

$$\text{Exclusion Ratio} = \frac{13,500 \text{ (cost of contract)}}{17,400 \text{ (expected return)}}$$

Note: See Table I for early or other than monthly payment.

Age of Husband	Wife Younger by							
	1 yr.	2 yr.	3 yr.	4 yr.	5 yr.	6 yr.	7 yr.	8 yr.
45	24.4	24.7	25.0	25.2	25.5	---	---	---
46	23.6	23.9	24.2	24.4	24.7	24.9	---	---
47	22.9	23.1	23.4	23.7	23.9	24.2	24.4	---
48	22.1	22.4	22.7	22.9	23.2	23.4	23.6	23.8
49	21.4	21.6	21.9	22.2	22.4	22.6	22.9	23.1
50	20.6	20.9	21.2	21.4	21.7	21.9	22.1	22.3
51	19.9	20.2	20.5	20.7	20.9	21.2	21.4	21.6
52	19.2	19.5	19.8	20.0	20.2	20.4	20.7	20.9
53	18.5	18.8	19.1	19.3	19.5	19.7	19.9	20.1
54	17.9	18.1	18.4	18.6	18.8	19.0	19.2	19.4
55	17.2	17.5	17.7	17.9	18.1	18.4	18.6	18.7
56	16.6	16.8	17.0	17.3	17.5	17.7	17.9	18.1
57	15.9	16.2	16.4	16.6	16.8	17.0	17.2	17.4
58	15.3	15.5	15.8	16.0	16.2	16.4	16.6	16.7
59	14.7	14.9	15.1	15.3	15.5	15.7	15.9	16.1
60	14.1	14.3	14.5	14.7	14.9	15.1	15.3	15.5
61	13.5	13.7	13.9	14.1	14.3	14.5	14.7	14.9
62	12.9	13.2	13.4	13.6	13.7	13.9	14.1	14.3
63	12.4	12.6	12.8	13.0	13.2	13.3	13.5	13.7
64	11.8	12.0	12.2	12.4	12.6	12.8	12.9	13.1
65	11.3	11.5	11.7	11.9	12.1	12.2	12.4	12.5
66	10.8	11.0	11.2	11.4	11.5	11.7	11.9	12.0
67	10.3	10.5	10.7	10.9	11.0	11.2	11.3	11.5
68	9.8	10.0	10.2	10.4	10.5	10.7	10.8	11.0
69	9.4	9.6	9.7	9.0	10.0	10.2	10.3	10.5
70	8.9	9.1	9.3	9.4	9.6	9.7	9.8	10.0
71	8.5	8.7	8.8	9.0	9.1	9.3	9.4	9.5
72	8.1	8.2	8.4	8.5	8.7	8.8	8.9	9.1
73	7.7	7.8	8.0	8.1	8.2	8.4	8.5	8.6
74	7.3	7.4	7.6	7.7	7.8	8.0	8.1	8.2
75	6.9	7.0	7.2	7.3	7.4	7.6	7.7	7.8
76	6.5	6.7	6.8	6.9	7.1	7.2	7.3	7.4
77	6.2	6.3	6.4	6:6	6.7	6.8	6.9	7.0
78	5.9	6.0	6.1	6.2	6.3	6.4	6.5	6.6
79	5.5	5.7	5.8	5.9	6.0	6.1	6.2	6.3
80	5.2	5.3	5.5	5.6	5.7	5.8	5.9	6.0

Expected Return on Joint and Survivor Annuity—
Wife Older—Uniform Payment
(Government Table I)

Example of use of this table:

Find exempt portion of annuity of $100 per month for a married couple, husband is 62 and wife is 67. Contract cost $21,000.

$$\frac{\text{Cost of contract (\$21,000)}}{\text{Annual payment (\$1,200} \times \text{multiple from table (22.2)}} = \frac{210}{266.4} \times 100 = \$78.83$$

Age of Husband	Wife Same Age	1 yr.	2 yrs.	3 yrs.	Older by 4 yrs.	5 yrs.	6 yrs.	7 yrs.	8 yrs.
45	39.3	38.8	38.2	37.7	37.2	36.8	36.3	35.9	35.5
46	38.4	37.8	37.3	36.8	36.3	35.9	35.4	35.0	34.6
47	37.5	36.9	36.4	35.9	35.4	35.0	34.5	34.1	33.7
48	36.5	36.0	35.5	35.0	34.5	34.0	33.6	33.2	32.8
49	35.6	35.1	34.1	33.6	33.1	32.7	32.3	31.9	
50	34.7	34.2	33.7	33.2	32.7	32.3	31.8	31.4	31.0
51	33.8	33.3	32.8	32.3	31.8	31.4	30.9	30.5	30.1
52	32.9	32.4	31.9	31.4	30.9	30.5	30.1	29.7	29.3
53	32.0	31.5	31.0	30.5	30.1	29.6	29.2	28.8	28.4
54	31.2	30.6	30.1	29.7	29.2	28.8	28.3	27.9	27.6
55	30.3	29.8	29.3	28.8	28.3	27.9	27.5	27.1	26.7
56	29.4	28.9	28.4	27.9	27.5	27.1	26.7	26.3	25.9
57	28.6	28.1	27.6	27.1	26.7	26.2	25.8	25.4	25.1
58	27.7	27.2	26.7	26.3	25.8	25.4	25.0	24.6	24.3
59	26.9	26.4	25.9	25.4	25.0	24.6	24.2	23.8	23.5
60	26.0	25.5	25.1	24.6	24.2	23.8	23.4	23.0	22.7
61	25.2	24.7	24.3	23.8	23.4	23.0	22.6	22.2	21.9
62	24.4	23.9	23.5	23.0	22.6	22.2	21.8	21.5	21.1
63	23.6	23.1	22.7	22.2	21.8	21.4	21.1	20.7	20.4
64	22.8	22.3	21.9	21.5	21.1	20.7	20.3	20.0	19.6
65	22.0	21.6	21.1	20.7	20.3	19.9	19.6	19.2	18.9
66	21.3	20.8	20.4	20.0	19.6	19.2	18.8	18.5	18.2
67	20.5	20.1	19.6	19.2	18.8	18.5	18.1	17.8	17.5
68	19.8	19.3	18.9	18.5	18.1	17.8	17.4	17.1	16.8
69	19.0	18.6	18.2	17.8	17.4	17.1	16.7	16.4	16.1
70	18.3	17.9	17.5	17.1	16.7	16.4	16.1	15.8	15.5
71	17.6	17.2	16.8	16.4	16.1	15.7	15.4	15.1	14.8
72	16.9	16.5	16.1	15.8	15.4	15.1	14.8	14.5	14.2
73	16.2	15.8	15.5	15.1	14.8	14.4	14.1	13.8	13.6
74	15.6	15.2	14.8	14.5	14.1	13.8	13.5	13.2	13.0
75	14.9	14.5	14.2	13.8	13.5	13.2	12.9	12.6	12.4
76	14.3	13.9	13.6	13.2	12.9	12.6	12.3	12.1	11.8
77	13.7	13.3	13.0	12.6	12.3	12.1	11.8	11.5	11.3
78	13.1	12.7	12.4	12.1	11.8	11.5	11.2	11.0	10.7
79	12.5	12.2	11.8	11.5	11.2	11.0	10.7	10.5	10.2
80	11.9	11.6	11.3	11.0	10.7	10.4	10.2	10.0	9.7

**Expected Return on Joint and Survivor Annuity—
Wife Older—Different Amount
After First Death**

Example of use of this table:

Find the exclusion of joint and survivor contract which pays $100 per month while both husband and wife are living and $50 per month after the death of one. Husband is 67 and wife is 70. Cost of the contract is $13,500.

Multiple from Table 1 on page 605 for husband age 67, and for wife 3 years older	19.2
Multiple from Table below	9.5
Difference	9.7
Expected return for $100 payments 9.5 × $1,200	$11,400
Expected return for $50 payments 9.7 × $600	5,820
Total Expected Return	$17,220

Exclusion

$$\frac{\text{Costs of Contract (\$13,500)}}{\text{Expected Return (\$17,220)}} \times 100 = \$78.33$$

Age of Husband	Wife Same Age	1 yr.	2 yrs.	3 yrs.	Wife Older by 4 yrs.	5 yrs.	6 yrs.	7 yrs.	8 yrs.
45	24.1	23.8	23.4	23.1	22.7	22.4	22.0	21.6	21.2
46	23.3	23.0	22.7	22.3	22.0	21.6	21.2	20.9	20.5
47	22.6	22.2	21.9	21.6	21.2	20.9	20.5	20.1	19.8
48	21.8	21.5	21.2	20.9	20.5	20.2	19.8	19.4	19.1
49	21.1	20.8	20.5	20.1	19.8	19.5	19.1	18.8	18.4
50	20.4	20.1	19.8	19.4	19.1	18.8	18.4	18.1	17.7
51	19.7	19.4	19.1	18.8	18.4	18.1	17.8	17.4	17.0
52	19.0	18.7	18.4	18.1	17.8	17.4	17.1	16.8	16.4
53	18.3	18.0	17.7	17.4	17.1	16.8	16.4	16.1	15.8
54	17.6	17.3	17.0	16.8	16.4	16.1	15.8	15.5	15.1
55	16.9	16.7	16.4	16.1	15.8	15.5	15.2	14.9	14.5
56	16.3	16.0	15.8	15.5	15.2	14.9	14.6	14.3	13.9
57	15.7	15.4	15.1	14.9	14.6	14.3	14.0	13.7	13.4
58	15.1	14.8	14.5	14.3	14.0	13.7	13.4	13.1	12.8
59	14.4	14.2	13.9	13.7	13.4	13.1	12.8	12.6	12.3
60	13.9	13.6	13.4	13.1	12.8	12.6	12.3	12.0	11.7
61	13.3	13.0	12.8	12.6	12.3	12.0	11.8	11.5	11.2
62	12.7	12.5	12.3	12.0	11.8	11.5	11.2	11.0	10.7
63	12.2	11.9	11.7	11.5	11.2	11.0	10.7	10.5	10.2
64	11.6	11.4	11.0	10.7	10.5	10.2	10.0	9.7	

Age of Husband	Wife Same Age	1 yr.	2 yrs.	3 yrs.	Wife Older by 4 yrs.	5 yrs.	6 yrs.	7 yrs.	8 yrs.
65	11.1	10.9	10.7	10.5	10.2	10.0	9.8	9.5	9.3
66	10.6	10.4	10.2	10.0	9.8	9.5	9.3	9.1	8.8
67	10.1	9.9	9.7	9.5	9.3	9.1	8.9	8.6	8.4
68	9.7	9.5	9.3	9.1	8.9	8.6	8.4	8.2	8.0
69	9.2	9.0	8.8	8.6	8.4	8.2	8.0	7.8	7.6
70	8.8	8.6	8.4	8.2	8.0	7.8	7.6	7.4	7.2
71	8.3	8.1	8.0	7.8	7.6	7.4	7.2	7.0	6.8
72	7.9	7.7	7.6	7.4	7.2	7.0	6.8	6.6	6.4
73	7.5	7.3	7.2	7.0	6.8	6.7	6.5	6.3	6.1
74	7.1	7.0	6.8	6.6	6.5	6.3	6.1	6.0	5.8
75	6.8	6.6	6.4	6.3	6.1	6.0	5.8	5.6	5.5
76	6.4	6.3	6.1	6.0	5.8	5.6	5.5	5.3	5.2
77	6.1	5.9	5.8	5.6	5.5	5.3	5.2	5.0	4.9
78	5.7	5.6	5.5	5.3	5.2	5.0	4.9	4.7	4.6
79	5.4	5.3	5.2	5.0	4.9	4.7	4.6	4.5	4.3
80	5.1	5.0	4.9	4.7	4.6	4.5	4.3	4.2	4.1

COST OF CONTRACT WITH REFUND OR PAYMENT CERTAIN FEATURE (GOVERNMENT TABLE III)

Example of use of this table:

Find cost of contract of $100 per month to husband, age 65. Purchase price is $21,053 and refund of purchase price guaranteed.

Purchase price		$21,053
Annual payment	$ 1,200	
Years guaranteed ($21,053 refund ÷ $1,200		
annual payment)	17.5	
Rounded to nearest year	18	
% in table at age 65 for 18 years	30%	
Value of refund: 30% of	$21,053	6,316
Cost of Contract		$14,737

Note: See Table I for early or other than monthly payment.

Age		Years Guaranteed										
Male	Female	5	8	10	12	15	18	20	22	25	28	30	35
40	45	1%	2%	3%	3%	4%	6%	7%	8%	9%	11%	13%	17%
41	46	1	2	3	3	5	6	7	8	10	12	14	18
42	47	1	2	3	4	5	6	8	9	11	13	15	19
43	48	1	2	3	4	5	7	8	9	12	14	16	21
44	49	1	3	3	4	6	7	9	10	12	15	17	22
45	50	2	3	4	5	6	8	9	11	13	16	18	23
46	51	2	3	4	5	7	9	10	12	14	17	19	25
47	52	2	3	4	5	7	9	11	12	15	18	20	26
48	53	2	3	5	6	8	10	12	13	16	19	22	28
49	54	2	4	5	6	8	11	12	14	17	21	23	29
50	55	2	4	5	7	9	11	13	15	18	22	24	31
51	56	3	4	6	7	9	12	14	16	20	23	26	32
52	57	3	5	6	8	10	13	15	17	21	25	27	34
53	58	3	5	7	8	11	14	16	19	22	26	29	38
54	59	3	5	7	9	12	15	17	20	24	28	31	38
55	60	3	6	8	9	13	16	18	21	25	29	32	39
56	61	4	6	8	10	13	17	20	22	27	31	34	41
57	62	4	7	9	11	14	18	21	24	28	33	36	43
58	63	4	7	9	12	15	19	22	25	30	34	37	45
59	64	5	8	10	12	16	21	24	27	31	36	39	47
60	65	5	8	11	13	18	22	25	28	33	38	41	48
61	66	5	9	12	14	19	23	27	30	35	40	43	50
62	67	6	10	12	15	20	25	28	32	37	42	45	52
63	68	6	10	13	16	21	26	30	33	39	44	47	54
64	69	7	11	14	17	23	28	32	35	41	46	49	55
65	70	7	12	15	19	24	30	33	37	42	47	50	57
66	71	8	13	16	20	26	31	35	39	44	49	52	59
67	72	8	14	17	21	27	33	37	41	46	51	54	61
68	73	9	14	18	23	29	35	39	43	48	53	56	62
69	74	9	16	20	24	30	37	41	45	50	55	58	64
70	75	10	17	21	26	32	39	43	47	52	57	60	65
71	76	11	18	22	27	34	41	45	49	54	59	61	67
72	77	12	19	24	29	36	43	47	51	56	60	63	68
73	78	12	20	25	30	38	45	49	53	58	62	65	70
74	79	13	22	27	32	40	47	51	55	60	64	66	71
75	80	14	23	29	34	42	49	53	57	62	66	68	72

SELF-LIQUIDATING MORTGAGES—MONTHLY PAYMENTS

The following tables are useful planning tools that are to be used for quickly determining the constant monthly payments, annual interest, annual amortization payments, and remaining balance for mortgages at various interest rates, at different payout terms. In all cases the amounts shown are for $1,000 mortgages. Therefore, if you want to know the monthly payments on a $35,000 mortgage at 8½% interest to be liquidated over 25 years take the following steps:

(1) Turn to the table titled 25-YEAR TERM and locate the chart of 8½% interest, which shows a monthly payment of $8.05.

(2) Since $8.05 is the monthly payment on a $1,000 mortgage, multiply this by your mortgage amount to determine what your constant monthly payment will be (35 × $8.05 = $281.75).

5-YEAR TERM

Year	4% interest - $18.42 monthly payment			4-1/2% interest - $18.65 monthly payment			5% interest - $18.88 monthly payment		
	Interest	Amort.	Balance	Interest	Amort.	Balance	Interest	Amort.	Balance
1	36.63	184.41	815.59	41.26	182.54	817.46	45.91	180.65	819.35
2	29.14	191.90	623.69	32.88	190.92	626.54	36.64	189.92	629.43
3	21.31	199.73	423.96	24.11	199.69	426.85	26.92	199.64	429.79
4	13.19	207.85	216.11	14.94	208.86	217.99	16.74	209.82	219.97
5	4.67	216.11	0	5.34	217.99	0	5.99	219.97	0

Year	5-1/4% interest - $18.99 monthly payment			5-1/2% interest - $19.11 monthly payment			5-3/4% interest - $19.22 monthly payment		
	Interest	Amort.	Balance	Interest	Amort.	Balance	Interest	Amort.	Balance
1	48.23	179.65	820.35	50.53	178.79	821.21	52.85	177.79	822.21
2	38.55	189.33	631.02	40.44	188.88	632.33	42.37	188.27	633.94
3	28.37	199.51	431.51	29.79	199.53	432.80	31.26	199.38	434.56
4	17.65	210.23	221.28	18.58	210.74	222.06	19.47	211.17	223.39
5	6.33	221.28	0	6.63	222.06	0	7.00	223.39	0

Year	6% interest - $19.34 monthly payment			6-1/4% interest - $19.45 monthly payment			6-1/2% interest - $19.57 monthly payment		
	Interest	Amort.	Balance	Interest	Amort.	Balance	Interest	Amort.	Balance
1	55.19	176.89	823.11	57.51	175.89	824.11	59.85	174.99	825.01
2	44.29	187.79	635.32	46.18	187.22	636.89	48.13	186.71	638.30
3	32.70	199.38	435.94	34.16	199.24	437.65	35.63	199.21	439.09
4	20.39	211.68	224.26	21.35	212.05	225.60	22.30	212.54	226.55
5	7.33	224.26	0	7.72	225.60	0	8.04	226.55	0

Year	6-3/4% interest - $19.69 monthly payment			7% interest - $19.81 monthly payment			7-1/4% interest - $19.92 monthly payment		
	Interest	Amort.	Balance	Interest	Amort.	Balance	Interest	Amort.	Balance
1	62.20	174.08	825.92	64.51	173.21	826.79	66.85	172.19	827.81
2	50.07	186.21	639.71	52.01	185.71	641.08	53.95	185.09	642.72
3	37.10	199.18	440.53	38.57	199.15	441.93	40.06	198.98	443.74
4	23.23	213.05	227.48	24.18	213.54	228.39	25.17	213.87	229.87
5	8.41	227.48	0	8.75	228.39	0	9.13	229.87	0

Year	7-1/2% interest - $20.04 monthly payment			7-3/4% interest - $20.16 monthly payment			8% interest - $20.28 monthly payment		
	Interest	Amort.	Balance	Interest	Amort.	Balance	Interest	Amort.	Balance
1	69.18	171.30	828.70	71.54	170.38	829.62	73.87	169.49	830.51
2	55.89	184.59	644.11	57.83	184.09	645.53	59.81	183.55	646.96
3	41.58	198.90	445.21	43.08	198.84	446.69	44.56	198.80	448.16
4	26.12	214.36	230.85	27.08	214.84	231.85	28.06	215.30	232.86
5	9.45	230.85	0	9.85	231.85	0	10.21	232.86	0

Year	9% interest - $20.76 monthly payment			10% interest - $21.25 monthly payment		
	Interest	Amort.	Balance	Interest	Amort.	Balance
1	83.27	165.85	834.15	92.71	162.29	837.71
2	67.72	181.40	652.75	75.70	179.30	658.41
3	50.40	198.42	454.33	56.91	198.09	460.32
4	32.10	217.02	237.31	36.20	218.80	241.52
5	11.71	237.31	0	13.25	241.52	0

607

10-YEAR TERM

	4% interest - $10.13 monthly payment			4-1/2% interest - $10.37 monthly payment			5% interest - $10.61 monthly payment		
Year	Interest	Amort.	Balance	Interest	Amort.	Balance	Interest	Amort.	Balance
1	38.49	83.07	916.93	43.34	81.10	918.90	48.21	79.11	920.89
2	35.11	86.45	830.48	39.62	84.82	834.08	44.16	83.16	837.73
3	31.56	90.00	740.48	35.72	88.72	745.36	39.90	87.42	750.31
4	27.92	93.64	646.84	31.65	92.79	652.57	35.44	91.88	658.43
5	24.11	97.45	549.39	27.41	97.03	555.54	30.72	96.60	561.83
6	20.13	101.43	447.96	22.92	101.52	454.02	25.79	101.53	460.30
7	16.00	105.56	342.40	18.26	106.18	347.84	20.60	106.72	353.58
8	11.70	109.86	232.54	13.37	111.07	236.77	15.13	112.19	241.39
9	7.23	114.33	118.21	8.29	116.15	120.62	9.41	117.91	123.48
10	2.54	118.21	0	2.94	120.62	0	3.35	123.48	0

	5-1/4% interest - $10.73 monthly payment			5-1/2% interest - $10.86 monthly payment			5-3/4% interest - $10.98 monthly payment		
Year	Interest	Amort.	Balance	Interest	Amort.	Balance	Interest	Amort.	Balance
1	50.64	78.12	921.88	53.08	77.24	922.76	55.50	76.26	923.74
2	46.43	82.33	839.55	48.72	81.60	841.16	51.01	80.75	842.99
3	42.01	86.75	752.80	44.11	86.21	754.95	46.24	85.52	757.47
4	37.35	91.41	661.39	39.24	91.08	663.87	41.19	90.57	666.90
5	32.43	96.33	565.06	34.11	96.21	567.66	35.85	95.91	570.99
6	27.25	101.51	463.55	28.68	101.64	466.02	30.20	101.56	469.43
7	21.79	106.97	356.58	22.96	107.36	358.66	24.20	107.56	361.87
8	16.04	112.72	243.86	16.89	113.43	245.23	17.83	113.93	247.94
9	9.98	118.78	125.08	10.49	119.83	125.40	11.12	120.64	127.30
10	3.58	125.08	0	3.71	125.40	0	3.98	127.30	0

	6% interest - $11.11 monthly payment			6-1/4% interest - $11.23 monthly payment			6-1/2% interest - $11.36 monthly payment		
Year	Interest	Amort.	Balance	Interest	Amort.	Balance	Interest	Amort.	Balance
1	57.96	75.36	924.64	60.40	74.36	925.64	59.83	73.49	926.51
2	53.31	80.01	844.63	55.60	79.16	846.48	57.90	78.42	848.09
3	48.35	84.97	759.66	50.53	84.23	762.25	52.66	83.66	764.43
4	43.13	90.19	669.47	45.09	89.67	672.58	47.04	89.28	675.15
5	37.56	95.76	573.71	39.33	95.43	577.15	41.09	95.23	579.92
6	31.67	101.65	472.06	33.20	101.56	475.59	34.71	101.61	478.31
7	25.38	107.94	364.11	26.67	108.09	367.50	27.88	108.44	369.87
8	18.73	114.59	249.52	19.73	115.03	252.47	20.63	115.69	254.18
9	11.68	121.64	127.88	12.31	122.45	130.02	12.91	123.41	130.77
10	4.14	127.88	0	4.44	130.02	0	4.63	130.77	0

	6-3/4% interest - $11.49 monthly payment			7% interest - $11.62 monthly payment			7-1/4% interest - $11.75 monthly payment		
Year	Interest	Amort.	Balance	Interest	Amort.	Balance	Interest	Amort.	Balance
1	65.29	72.59	927.41	67.73	71.71	928.29	70.18	70.82	929.18
2	60.23	77.65	849.76	62.55	76.89	851.40	64.86	76.14	853.04
3	54.81	83.07	766.69	57.01	82.44	768.97	59.14	81.86	771.18
4	49.04	88.84	677.85	51.02	88.41	680.55	53.02	87.98	683.20
5	42.85	95.03	582.82	44.64	94.80	585.75	45.43	94.57	588.63
6	36.23	101.65	481.17	37.79	101.65	484.10	39.36	101.64	486.99
7	29.17	108.71	372.46	30.42	109.02	375.08	31.73	109.27	377.72
8	21.59	116.29	256.17	22.55	116.89	258.19	23.50	117.50	260.22
9	13.50	124.38	131.79	14.12	125.32	132.87	14.71	126.29	133.93
10	4.82	131.79	0	5.06	132.87	0	5.27	133.93	0

608

10-YEAR TERM (continued)

	7-1/2% interest - $11.88 monthly payment			7-3/4% interest - $12.01 monthly payment			8% interest - $12.14 monthly payment		
Year	Interest	Amort.	Balance	Interest	Amort.	Balance	Interest	Amort.	Balance
1	72.60	69.93	930.07	75.08	69.04	930.96	77.54	68.14	931.86
2	67.19	75.37	854.70	69.54	74.58	856.38	71.87	73.81	858.05
3	61.35	81.21	773.49	63.55	80.57	775.81	65.74	79.94	778.11
4	55.04	87.52	685.97	57.07	87.05	688.76	59.12	86.56	691.55
5	48.26	94.30	591.67	50.09	94.03	594.73	51.94	93.74	597.81
6	40.94	101.62	490.05	42.53	101.59	493.14	44.17	101.51	496.30
7	33.04	109.52	380.53	34.38	109.74	383.40	35.73	109.95	386.35
8	24.54	118.02	262.51	25.56	118.56	264.84	26.61	119.07	267.28
9	15.38	127.18	135.33	16.05	128.07	136.77	16.72	128.96	138.32
10	5.51	135.33	0	5.75	136.77	0	6.02	138.32	0

	8-1/2% interest - $12.40 monthly payment			8-3/4% interest - $12.53 monthly payment			9% interest - $12.67 monthly payment		
Year	Interest	Amort.	Balance	Interest	Amort.	Balance	Interest	Amort.	Balance
1	82.46	66.34	933.66	84.91	65.45	934.55	87.36	64.68	935.32
2	76.59	72.21	861.45	78.95	71.41	863.14	81.31	70.73	864.59
3	70.21	78.59	782.86	72.45	77.91	785.23	74.65	77.39	787.20
4	63.27	85.53	697.32	65.35	85.01	700.22	67.40	84.64	702.56
5	55.71	93.09	604.23	57.61	92.75	607.47	59.46	92.58	609.98
6	47.48	101.32	502.91	49.16	101.20	506.27	50.78	101.26	508.72
7	38.52	110.28	392.63	39.94	110.42	395.85	41.30	110.74	397.98
8	28.78	120.02	272.61	29.89	120.47	275.38	30.90	121.14	276.84
9	18.17	130.63	141.98	18.92	131.44	143.94	19.56	132.48	144.36
10	6.63	142.17	0.18	6.94	143.42	0.52	7.10	144.36	0

	9-1/4% interest - $12.80 monthly payment			9-1/2% interest - $12.94 monthly payment			9-3/4% interest - $13.08 monthly payment		
Year	Interest	Amort.	Balance	Interest	Amort.	Balance	Interest	Amort.	Balance
1	89.84	63.76	936.23	92.31	62.97	937.03	94.76	62.20	937.80
2	83.68	69.92	866.32	86.06	69.22	867.81	88.42	68.54	869.26
3	76.93	76.67	789.65	79.19	76.09	791.71	81.43	75.53	793.74
4	69.53	84.07	705.51	71.64	83.64	708.07	73.73	83.23	710.51
5	61.42	92.18	613.40	63.34	91.94	616.13	65.25	91.71	618.79
6	52.52	101.08	512.33	54.21	101.07	515.06	55.89	101.07	517.73
7	42.77	110.83	401.50	44.18	111.10	403.97	45.59	111.37	406.36
8	32.07	121.53	279.97	33.16	122.12	281.85	34.23	122.73	283.63
9	20.34	133.26	146.72	21.04	134.24	147.61	21.72	135.24	148.38
10	7.48	146.12	0.60	7.72	147.56	0.05	7.93	149.03	0.64

	10% interest - $13.22 monthly payment			10-1/4% interest - $13.35 monthly payment			10-1/2% interest - $13.49 monthly payment		
Year	Interest	Amort.	Balance	Interest	Amort.	Balance	Interest	Amort.	Balance
1	97.23	61.41	938.59	99.71	60.49	939.51	102.18	59.70	940.30
2	90.81	67.83	870.76	93.21	66.99	872.51	95.61	66.27	874.03
3	83.72	74.92	795.84	86.01	74.19	798.32	88.30	73.58	800.45
4	75.86	82.78	713.06	78.04	82.16	716.16	80.19	81.69	718.77
5	67.19	91.45	621.61	69.21	90.99	625.17	71.19	90.69	628.08
6	57.62	101.02	520.59	59.44	100.76	524.41	61.20	100.68	527.40
7	47.03	111.61	408.98	48.61	111.59	412.82	50.10	111.78	415.62
8	35.35	123.29	285.69	36.62	123.58	289.24	37.79	124.09	291.53
9	22.44	136.20	149.49	23.34	136.86	152.38	24.11	137.77	153.76
10	8.17	149.49	0	8.64	151.56	0.82	8.93	152.95	0.81

10-YEAR TERM (continued)

	10-3/4% interest - $13.63 monthly payment			11% interest - $13.77 monthly payment			11-1/4% interest - $13.92 monthly payment		
Year	Interest	Amort.	Balance	Interest	Amort.	Balance	Interest	Amort.	Balance
1	104.65	58.91	941.09	107.12	58.12	941.88	109.59	57.45	942.55
2	98.00	65.56	875.53	100.39	64.85	877.03	102.79	64.25	878.30
3	90.59	72.97	802.56	92.89	72.35	804.68	95.18	71.86	806.44
4	82.35	81.21	721.35	84.52	80.72	723.96	86.66	80.38	726.06
5	73.18	90.38	630.96	75.18	90.06	633.90	77.14	89.90	636.16
6	62.79	100.59	530.37	64.76	100.48	533.42	66.49	100.55	535.60
7	51.61	111.95	418.42	53.13	112.11	421.32	54.57	112.47	423.14
8	38.96	124.60	293.82	40.16	125.08	296.24	41.25	125.79	297.35
9	24.89	138.67	155.15	25.69	139.55	156.69	26.34	140.70	156.65
10	9.23	154.33	0.82	9.54	155.70	1.00	9.68	157.36	0.70

	11-1/2% interest - $14.06 monthly payment			11-3/4% interest - $14.20 monthly payment			12% interest - $14.35 monthly payment		
Year	Interest	Amort.	Balance	Interest	Amort.	Balance	Interest	Amort.	Balance
1	112.07	56.65	943.35	114.55	55.85	944.15	117.03	55.17	944.83
2	105.20	63.52	879.83	107.63	62.77	881.38	110.03	62.17	882.65
3	97.50	71.22	808.61	99.84	70.56	810.82	102.15	70.05	812.60
4	88.86	79.86	728.75	91.09	79.31	731.51	93.26	78.94	733.66
5	79.18	89.54	639.21	81.25	89.15	642.37	83.25	88.95	644.71
6	68.33	100.39	538.82	70.20	100.20	542.16	71.97	100.23	544.49
7	56.15	112.57	426.25	57.77	112.63	429.53	59.26	112.94	431.55
8	42.50	126.22	300.03	43.80	126.60	302.93	44.94	127.26	304.29
9	27.20	141.52	158.51	28.10	142.30	160.63	28.80	143.40	160.90
10	10.04	158.68	-0.15	10.45	159.95	0.67	10.62	161.58	-0.67

15-YEAR TERM

Year	4% interest - $7.40 monthly payment			4-1/2% interest - $7.65 monthly payment			5% interest - $7.91 monthly payment		
	Interest	Amort.	Balance	Interest	Amort.	Balance	Interest	Amort.	Balance
1	39.10	49.70	950.30	44.04	47.76	952.24	48.96	45.96	954.04
2	37.06	51.74	898.56	41.83	49.97	902.27	46.62	48.30	905.74
3	34.99	53.81	844.75	39.53	52.27	850.00	44.13	50.79	854.95
4	32.77	56.03	788.72	37.12	54.68	795.32	41.54	53.38	801.57
5	30.49	58.31	730.41	34.62	57.18	738.14	38.80	56.12	745.45
6	28.10	60.70	669.71	31.99	59.81	678.33	35.94	58.98	686.47
7	25.65	63.15	606.56	29.26	62.54	615.79	32.92	62.00	624.47
8	23.07	65.73	540.83	26.39	65.41	550.38	29.74	65.18	559.29
9	20.38	68.42	472.41	23.36	68.44	481.94	26.41	68.50	490.79
10	17.63	71.17	401.24	20.22	71.58	410.36	22.91	72.01	418.78
11	14.71	74.09	327.15	16.94	74.86	335.50	19.22	75.70	343.08
12	11.69	77.11	250.04	13.49	78.31	257.19	15.35	79.57	263.51
13	8.54	80.26	169.78	9.89	81.91	175.28	11.28	83.64	179.87
14	5.27	83.53	86.25	6.14	85.66	89.62	7.02	87.90	91.97
15	1.86	86.25	0	2.20	89.62	0	2.50	91.97	0

Year	5-1/4% interest - $8.04 monthly payment			5-1/2% interest - $8.18 monthly payment			5-3/4% interest - $8.31 monthly payment		
	Interest	Amort.	Balance	Interest	Amort.	Balance	Interest	Amort.	Balance
1	51.42	45.06	954.94	53.90	44.26	955.74	56.36	43.36	956.64
2	49.00	47.48	907.46	51.39	46.77	908.97	53.81	45.91	910.73
3	46.46	50.02	857.44	48.77	49.39	859.58	51.10	48.62	862.11
4	43.76	52.72	804.72	45.96	52.20	807.38	48.24	51.48	810.63
5	40.92	55.56	749.16	43.03	55.13	752.25	45.19	54.53	756.10
6	37.94	58.54	690.62	39.92	58.24	694.01	41.97	57.75	698.35
7	34.79	61.69	628.93	36.63	61.53	632.48	38.56	61.16	637.19
8	31.47	65.01	563.92	33.17	64.99	567.49	34.95	64.77	572.42
9	27.96	68.52	495.40	29.20	68.66	498.83	31.13	68.59	503.83
10	24.30	72.18	423.22	25.62	72.54	426.29	26.97	72.65	431.18
11	20.41	76.07	347.15	21.53	76.63	349.66	22.80	76.92	354.26
12	16.32	80.16	266.99	17.20	80.96	268.70	18.25	81.47	272.79
13	12.01	84.47	182.52	12.65	85.51	183.19	13.43	86.29	186.50
14	7.48	89.00	93.52	7.84	90.32	92.87	8.34	91.38	95.12
15	2.66	93.52	0	2.73	92.87	0	2.94	95.12	0

Year	6% interest - $8.44 monthly payment			6-1/4% interest - $8.58 monthly payment			6-1/2% interest - $8.72 monthly payment		
	Interest	Amort.	Balance	Interest	Amort.	Balance	Interest	Amort.	Balance
1	58.85	42.43	957.57	61.33	41.63	958.37	63.79	40.85	959.15
2	56.23	45.05	912.52	58.65	44.31	914.06	61.08	43.56	915.59
3	53.40	47.88	864.64	55.80	47.16	866.90	58.15	46.49	869.10
4	50.49	50.79	813.85	52.76	50.20	816.70	55.03	49.61	819.49
5	47.37	53.91	759.94	49.53	53.43	763.27	51.72	52.92	766.57
6	44.04	57.24	702.70	46.08	56.88	706.39	48.16	56.48	710.09
7	40.50	60.78	641.92	42.43	60.53	645.86	44.39	60.25	649.84
8	36.75	64.53	577.39	38.54	64.42	581.44	40.34	64.30	585.54
9	32.78	68.50	508.89	34.38	68.58	512.86	36.04	68.60	516.94
10	28.58	72.72	436.17	29.99	72.97	439.89	31.46	73.18	443.76
11	24.07	77.21	358.96	25.30	77.66	362.23	26.55	78.09	365.67
12	19.29	81.99	276.97	20.30	82.66	279.57	21.31	83.33	282.34
13	14.24	87.04	189.93	14.99	87.97	191.60	15.72	88.92	193.42
14	8.89	92.39	97.54	9.35	93.61	97.99	9.79	94.85	98.57
15	3.19	97.54	0	3.29	97.99	0	3.41	98.57	0

611

15-YEAR TERM (continued)

	6-3/4% interest - $8.85 monthly payment			7% interest - $8.99 monthly payment			7-1/4% interest - $9.13 monthly payment		
Year	Interest	Amort.	Balance	Interest	Amort.	Balance	Interest	Amort.	Balance
1	66.29	39.91	960.09	68.74	39.14	960.86	71.25	38.31	961.69
2	63.48	42.72	917.37	65.94	41.94	918.92	68.38	41.18	920.51
3	60.54	45.66	871.71	62.90	44.98	873.94	65.29	44.27	876.24
4	57.35	48.85	822.86	.59.65	48.23	825.71	61.98	47.58	828.66
5	53.93	52.27	770.59	56.16	51.72	773.99	58.39	51.17	777.49
6	50.30	55.90	714.69	52.42	55.46	718.53	54.55	55.01	722.48
7	46.41	59.79	654.90	48.39	59.49	659.04	50.45	59.11	663.37
8	42.28	63.92	590.98	44.10	63.78	595.26	46.02	63.54	599.83
9	37.80	68.40	522.58	39.56	68.32	526.89	41.25	68.31	531.52
10	33.04	73.16	449.42	34.55	73.33	453.56	36.13	73.43	458.09
11	27.94	78.26	371.16	29.26	78.62	374.94	30.60	78.96	379.13
12	22.51	83.69	287.47	23.59	84.29	290.65	24.71	84.85	294.28
13	16.68	89.52	197.95	17.48	90.40	200.25	18.33	91.23	203.05
14	10.42	95.78	102.17	10.96	96.92	103.33	11.52	98.04	105.01
15	3.76	102.17	0	3.94	103.33	0	4.16	105.01	0

	7-1/2% interest - $9.28 monthly payment			7-3/4% interest - $9.42 monthly payment			8% interest - $9.56 monthly payment		
Year	Interest	Amort.	Balance	Interest	Amort.	Balance	Interest	Amort.	Balance
1	73.73	37.63	962.37	76.20	36.84	963.16	78.72	36.00	964.00
2	70.77	40.59	921.78	73.26	39.78	923.38	75.71	39.01	924.99
3	67.64	43.72	878.06	70.05	42.99	880.39	72.48	42.24	882.75
4	64.25	47.11	830.95	66.59	46.45	833.94	68.98	45.74	837.01
5	60.59	50.77	780.18	62.89	50.15	783.79	65.17	49.55	787.46
6	56.66	54.70	725.48	58.84	54.20	729.59	61.02	53.70	733.76
7	52.38	58.98	666.50	54.49	58.55	671.04	56.60	58.12	675.64
8	47.83	63.53	602.97	49.78	63.26	607.78	51.77	62.95	612.69
9	42.89	68.47	534.50	44.71	68.33	539.45	46.55	68.17	544.52
10	37.59	73.77	460.73	39.23	73.81	465.64	40.89	73.83	470.69
11	31.87	79.49	381.24	33.29	79.75	385.89	34.78	79.94	390.75
12	25.68	85.68	295.56	26.89	86.15	299.74	28.15	86.57	304.18
13	19.04	92.32	203.24	19.98	93.06	206.68	20.96	93.76	210.42
14	11.88	99.48	103.76	12.49	100.55	106.13	13.16	101.56	108.86
15	4.15	103.76	0	4.41	106.13	0	4.76	108.86	0

	8-1/4% interest - $9.70 monthly payment			8-1/2% interest - $9.85 monthly payment			8-3/4% interest - $9.99 monthly payment		
Year	Interest	Amort.	Balance	Interest	Amort.	Balance	Interest	Amort.	Balance
1	81.19	35.22	964.79	83.68	34.53	965.48	86.17	33.72	966.29
2	78.18	38.23	926.56	80.63	37.58	927.90	83.10	36.79	929.51
3	74.90	41.51	885.06	77.31	40.90	887.01	79.75	40.14	889.38
4	71.34	45.07	840.00	73.69	44.52	842.49	76.10	43.79	845.59
5	67.48	48.93	791.07	69.76	48.45	794.05	72.11	47.78	797.82
6	63.29	53.12	737.96	65.48	52.73	741.32	67.76	52.13	745.69
7	58.74	57.67	680.29	60.82	57.39	683.93	63.01	56.88	688.81
8	53.80	62.61	617.68	55.74	62.47	621.47	57.83	62.06	626.75
9	48.43	67.98	549.71	50.22	67.99	553.48	52.17	67.72	559.04
10	42.61	73.80	475.91	44.21	74.00	479.49	46.00	73.89	485.15
11	36.28	80.13	395.79	37.67	80.54	398.96	39.27	80.62	404.54
12	29.42	86.99	308.80	30.55	87.66	311.30	31.93	87.96	316.59
13	21.96	94.45	214.36	22.81	95.40	215.90	23.92	95.97	220.62
14	13.87	102.54	111.82	14.37	103.84	112.07	15.18	104.71	115.91
15	5.08	111.33	0.50	5.20	113.01	0.94	5.65	114.25	1.66

612

15-YEAR TERM (continued)

Year	9% interest - $10.15 monthly payment			9-1/4% interest - $10.29 monthly payment			9-1/2% interest - $10.44 monthly payment		
	Interest	Amort.	Balance	Interest	Amort.	Balance	Interest	Amort.	Balance
1	88.66	33.14	966.86	91.16	32.33	967.68	93.65	31.64	968.37
2	85.55	36.25	930.61	88.04	35.45	932.23	90.51	34.78	933.60
3	82.14	39.66	890.95	84.62	38.87	893.36	87.06	38.23	895.37
4	78.43	43.37	847.58	40.86	42.63	850.74	83.27	42.02	853.35
5	74.34	47.46	800.12	76.75	46.74	804.00	79.10	46.19	807.17
6	69.92	51.88	748.24	72.24	51.25	752.76	74.51	50.78	756.39
7	65.03	56.77	691.97	67.29	56.20	696.56	69.47	55.82	700.58
8	59.72	62.08	629.39	61.87	61.62	634.94	63.93	61.36	639.23
9	53.90	67.90	561.49	55.92	67.57	567.38	57.85	67.44	571.79
10	47.53	74.27	487.22	49.40	74.09	493.29	51.15	74.14	497.66
11	40.57	81.23	405.99	42.25	81.24	412.06	43.79	81.50	416.17
12	32.92	88.88	317.11	34.41	89.08	322.98	35.71	89.58	326.59
13	24.59	97.21	219.90	25.81	97.68	225.30	26.82	98.47	228.12
14	15.50	106.30	113.60	16.38	107.11	118.19	17.04	108.25	119.88
15	5.51	113.60	0	6.04	117.45	0.75	6.30	118.99	0.89

Year	9-3/4% interest - $10.59 monthly payment			10% interest - $10.75 monthly payment			10-1/4% interest - $10.90 monthly payment		
	Interest	Amort.	Balance	Interest	Amort.	Balance	Interest	Amort.	Balance
1	96.15	30.94	969.07	98.62	30.38	969.62	101.14	29.67	970.34
2	92.99	34.10	934.97	95.46	33.54	936.08	97.95	32.86	937.48
3	89.51	37.58	897.40	91.95	37.05	899.03	94.42	36.39	901.09
4	85.68	41.41	856.00	88.06	40.94	858.09	90.51	40.30	860.80
5	81.46	45.63	810.38	83.78	45.22	812.87	86.18	44.63	816.17
6	76.81	50.28	760.10	79.04	49.96	762.91	81.38	49.43	766.75
7	71.68	55.41	704.70	73.81	55.19	707.72	76.07	54.74	712.02
8	66.03	61.06	643.65	68.03	60.97	646.75	70.19	60.62	651.40
9	59.81	67.28	576.37	61.64	67.36	579.39	63.68	67.13	584.28
10	52.95	74.14	502.23	54.30	74.40	504.99	56.46	74.35	509.93
11	45.38	81.71	420.53	46.79	82.21	422.78	48.48	82.33	427.61
12	37.05	90.04	330.50	38.18	90.82	331.96	39.63	91.18	336.43
13	27.87	99.22	231.28	28.70	100.30	231.66	29.83	100.98	235.46
14	17.75	109.34	121.95	18.20	110.80	120.86	18.98	111.83	123.64
15	6.61	120.48	1.47	6.57	120.86	0	6.97	123.84	.20

Year	10-1/2% interest - $11.05 monthly payment			10-3/4% interest - $11.21 monthly payment			11% interest - $11.37 monthly payment		
	Interest	Amort.	Balance	Interest	Amort.	Balance	Interest	Amort.	Balance
1	103.64	28.97	971.04	106.13	28.40	971.61	108.63	27.82	972.19
2	100.44	32.17	938.88	102.93	31.60	940.01	105.41	31.04	941.16
3	96.90	35.71	903.17	99.36	35.17	904.85	101.82	34.63	906.53
4	92.97	39.64	863.53	95.38	39.15	865.71	97.81	38.64	867.90
5	88.60	44.01	819.53	90.96	43.57	822.14	93.34	43.11	824.80
6	83.75	48.86	770.67	86.04	48.49	773.66	88.36	48.09	776.71
7	78.36	54.25	716.43	80.57	53.96	719.70	82.79	53.66	723.06
8	72.39	60.22	656.21	74.47	60.06	659.65	76.58	59.87	663.19
9	65.75	66.86	589.35	67.69	66.84	592.81	69.66	66.79	596.40
10	58.38	74.23	515.13	60.14	74.39	518.42	61.93	74.52	521.89
11	50.20	82.41	432.73	51.73	82.80	435.63	53.30	83.15	438.74
12	41.12	91.49	341.24	42.38	92.15	343.49	43.68	92.77	345.98
13	31.04	101.57	239.68	31.97	102.56	240.94	32.95	103.50	242.48
14	19.85	112.76	126.92	20.39	114.14	126.80	20.97	115.48	127.01
15	7.42	125.19	1.74	7.50	127.03	0.23	7.61	128.84	1.83

613

15-YEAR TERM (continued)

Year	11-1/4% interest - $11.52 monthly payment			11-1/2% interest - $11.68 monthly payment			11-3/4% interest - $11.84 monthly payment		
	Interest	Amort.	Balance	Interest	Amort.	Balance	Interest	Amort.	Balance
1	111.14	27.11	972.90	113.64	26.53	973.48	116.14	25.95	974.06
2	107.92	30.33	942.57	110.42	29.75	943.73	112.92	29.17	944.89
3	104.33	33.92	908.66	106.81	33.36	910.38	109.30	32.79	912.11
4	100.31	37.94	870.73	102.77	37.40	872.98	105.23	36.86	875.26
5	95.82	42.43	828.30	98.23	41.94	831.05	100.66	41.43	833.83
6	90.79	47.46	780.85	93.15	47.02	784.03	95.53	46.56	787.27
7	85.17	53.08	727.77	87.45	52.72	731.31	89.75	52.34	734.94
8	78.88	59.37	668.40	81.05	59.12	672.20	83.26	58.83	676.11
9	71.85	66.40	602.00	73.89	66.28	605.92	75.96	66.13	609.99
10	63.98	74.27	527.74	65.85	74.32	531.60	67.76	74.33	535.67
11	55.18	83.07	444.67	56.84	83.33	448.28	58.54	83.55	452.12
12	45.34	92.91	351.76	46.73	93.44	354.84	48.18	93.91	358.21
13	34.33	103.92	247.84	35.40	104.77	250.08	36.53	105.56	252.66
14	22.01	116.24	131.61	22.70	117.47	132.62	23.44	118.65	134.01
15	8.24	130.01	1.61	8.46	131.71	0.91	8.72	133.37	0.65

12% interest - $12.00
monthly payment

Year	Interest	Amort.	Balance
1	118.64	25.37	974.64
2	115.42	28.59	946.06
3	111.80	32.21	913.85
4	107.71	36.30	877.56
5	103.11	40.90	836.67
6	97.92	46.09	790.59
7	92.08	51.93	738.66
8	85.49	58.52	680.15
9	78.07	65.94	614.22
10	69.71	74.30	539.93
11	60.29	83.72	456.21
12	49.67	94.34	361.88
13	37.71	106.30	255.59
14	24.23	119.78	135.81
15	9.04	134.97	0.84

614

20-YEAR TERM

	4% interest - $6.06 monthly payment			4-1/2% interest - $6.33 monthly payment			5% interest - $6.60 monthly payment		
Year	Interest	Amort.	Balance	Interest	Amort.	Balance	Interest	Amort.	Balance
1	39.49	33.32	966.68	44.34	31.62	968.38	49.33	29.87	970.13
2	38.03	34.69	931.99	42.90	33.06	935.32	47.79	31.41	938.72
3	36.66	36.06	895.93	41.38	34.58	900.74	46.19	33.01	905.71
4	35.15	37.57	858.36	39.80	36.16	864.58	44.50	34.70	871.01
5	33.62	39.10	819.26	38.12	37.84	826.74	42.71	36.49	834.52
6	32.04	40.68	778.58	36.40	39.56	787.18	40.83	38.37	796.15
7	30.38	42.34	736.24	34.58	41.38	745.80	38.90	40.30	755.85
8	28.64	44.08	692.16	32.68	43.28	702.52	36.84	42.36	713.49
9	26.85	45.87	646.29	30.68	45.28	657.24	34.66	44.54	668.95
10	24.99	47.73	598.56	28.61	47.35	609.89	32.39	46.81	622.14
11	23.05	49.67	548.89	26.44	49.52	560.37	29.99	49.21	572.93
12	21.01	51.71	497.18	24.16	51.80	508.57	27.47	51.73	521.20
13	18.90	53.82	443.36	21.78	54.18	454.39	24.80	54.40	466.80
14	16.72	56.00	387.36	19.29	56.67	397.72	22.09	57.11	409.69
15	14.43	58.29	329.07	16.70	59.26	338.46	19.13	60.07	349.62
16	12.06	60.66	268.41	13.95	62.01	276.45	16.05	63.15	286.47
17	9.59	63.13	205.28	11.14	64.82	211.63	12.81	66.39	220.08
18	7.01	65.71	139.57	8.13	67.83	143.80	9.42	69.78	150.30
19	4.36	68.36	71.21	5.02	70.94	72.86	5.85	73.35	76.95
20	1.56	71.21	0	1.76	72.86	0	2.10	76.95	0

	5-1/4% interest - $6.74 monthly payment			5-1/2% interest - $6.88 monthly payment			5-3/4% interest - $7.03 monthly payment		
Year	Interest	Amort.	Balance	Interest	Amort.	Balance	Interest	Amort.	Balance
1	51.79	29.09	970.91	54.29	28.27	971.73	56.78	27.58	972.42
2	50.25	30.63	940.28	52.69	29.87	941.86	55.16	29.20	943.22
3	48.60	32.28	908.00	51.02	31.54	910.32	53.43	30.93	912.29
4	46.86	34.02	873.98	49.23	33.33	876.99	51.60	32.76	879.53
5	45.02	35.86	838.12	47.36	35.20	841.79	49.66	34.70	844.83
6	43.11	37.77	800.35	45.37	37.19	804.60	47.93	36.43	808.10
7	41.07	39.81	760.54	43.26	39.30	765.30	45.45	38.91	769.19
8	38.94	41.94	718.60	41.06	41.50	723.80	43.16	41.20	727.99
9	36.67	44.21	674.39	38.70	43.86	679.94	40.72	43.64	684.35
10	34.29	46.59	627.80	36.25	46.31	633.63	38.14	46.22	638.13
11	31.78	49.10	578.70	33.63	48.93	584.70	35.41	48.95	589.18
12	29.14	51.74	526.96	30.84	51.72	532.98	32.51	51.85	537.33
13	26.40	54.48	472.48	27.96	54.60	478.38	29.46	54.90	482.43
14	23.45	57.43	415.05	24.86	57.70	420.68	26.21	58.15	424.28
15	20.34	60.54	354.51	21.62	60.94	359.74	22.80	61.56	362.72
16	17.10	63.78	290.73	18.16	64.40	295.34	19.16	65.20	297.52
17	13.66	67.22	223.51	14.56	68.00	227.34	15.30	69.06	228.46
18	10.04	70.84	152.67	10.71	71.85	155.49	11.20	73.16	155.30
19	6.22	74.66	78.01	6.65	75.91	79.58	6.90	77.46	77.84
20	2.22	78.01	0	2.34	79.58	0	2.33	77.84	0

20-YEAR TERM (continued)

Year	6% interest - $7.17 monthly payment			6-1/4% interest - $7.31 monthly payment			6-1/2% interest - $7.46 monthly payment		
	Interest	Amort.	Balance	Interest	Amort.	Balance	Interest	Amort.	Balance
1	59.28	26.76	973.24	61.77	25.95	974.05	64.25	25.27	974.73
2	57.62	28.42	944.82	60.09	27.63	946.42	62.58	26.94	947.78
3	55.86	30.18	914.64	58.31	29.41	917.01	60.75	28.77	919.01
4	54.01	32.03	882.61	56.44	31.28	885.73	58.83	30.69	888.32
5	52.03	34.01	848.60	54.42	33.30	852.43	56.76	32.76	855.56
6	49.92	36.12	812.48	52.25	35.47	816.96	54.57	34.95	820.61
7	47.72	38.32	774.16	50.00	37.72	779.24	52.25	37.27	783.34
8	45.32	40.72	733.44	47.58	40.14	739.10	49.76	39.76	743.58
9	42.83	43.21	690.23	44.97	42.75	696.35	47.09	42.43	701.15
10	40.16	45.88	644.35	42.25	45.47	650.88	44.26	45.26	655.89
11	37.33	48.71	595.64	39.30	48.42	602.46	41.21	48.31	607.58
12	34.34	51.70	543.94	36.19	51.53	550.93	37.99	51.53	556.05
13	31.14	54.90	489.04	32.90	54.82	496.11	34.52	55.00	501.05
14	27.77	58.27	430.77	29.35	58.37	437.74	30.82	58.70	442.35
15	24.16	61.88	368.89	25.58	62.14	375.60	26.91	62.61	379.74
16	20.35	65.69	303.20	21.62	66.10	309.50	22.74	66.78	312.96
17	16.30	69.74	233.46	17.33	70.39	239.11	18.25	71.27	241.69
18	12.01	74.03	159.43	12.82	74.90	164.21	13.47	76.05	165.64
19	7.44	78.60	80.83	8.03	79.69	84.52	8.39	81.13	84.51
20	2.54	80.83	0	2.88	84.52	0	2.95	84.51	0

Year	6-3/4% interest - $7.61 monthly payment			7% interest - $7.76 monthly payment			7-1/4% interest - $7.91 monthly payment		
	Interest	Amort.	Balance	Interest	Amort.	Balance	Interest	Amort.	Balance
1	66.75	24.57	975.43	69.24	23.88	976.12	71.74	23.18	976.82
2	65.03	26.29	949.14	67.52	25.60	950.52	70.01	24.91	951.91
3	63.20	28.12	921.02	65.67	27.45	923.07	68.13	26.79	925.12
4	61.25	30.07	890.95	63.68	29.44	893.63	66.13	28.79	896.33
5	59.16	32.16	858.79	61.54	31.58	862.05	63.96	30.96	865.37
6	56.92	34.40	824.39	59.28	33.84	828.21	61.65	33.27	832.10
7	54.52	36.80	787.59	56.83	36.29	791.92	59.16	35.76	796.34
8	51.97	39.35	748.24	54.19	38.93	752.99	56.47	38.45	757.89
9	49.20	42.12	706.12	51.37	41.75	711.24	53.61	41.31	716.58
10	46.28	45.04	661.08	48.38	44.74	666.50	50.50	44.42	672.16
11	43.15	48.17	612.91	45.12	48.00	618.50	47.17	47.75	624.41
12	39.81	51.51	561.40	41.67	51.45	567.05	43.59	51.33	573.08
13	36.20	55.12	506.28	37.95	55.17	511.88	39.74	55.18	517.90
14	32.36	58.96	447.32	33.97	59.15	452.73	35.58	59.34	458.56
15	28.26	63.06	384.26	29.68	63.44	389.29	31.16	63.76	394.80
16	23.87	67.45	316.81	25.10	68.02	321.27	26.37	68.55	326.25
17	19.18	72.14	244.67	20.19	72.93	248.34	21.25	73.67	252.58
18	14.15	77.17	167.50	14.90	78.22	170.12	15.72	79.20	173.38
19	8.80	82.52	84.98	9.25	83.87	86.25	9.79	85.13	88.25
20	3.05	84.98	0	3.19	86.25	0	3.40	88.25	0

616

20-YEAR TERM (continued)

	7-1/2% interest - $8.06 monthly payment			7-3/4% interest - $8.21 monthly payment			8% interest - $8.37 monthly payment		
Year	Interest	Amort.	Balance	Interest	Amort.	Balance	Interest	Amort.	Balance
1	74.24	22.48	977.52	76.74	21.78	978.22	79.24	21.20	978.80
2	72.49	24.23	953.29	75.00	23.52	954.70	77.47	22.97	955.83
3	70.63	26.09	927.20	73.10	25.42	929.28	75.58	24.86	930.97
4	68.58	28.14	899.06	71.05	27.47	901.81	73.49	26.95	904.02
5	66.40	30.32	868.74	68.84	29.68	872.13	71.29	29.15	874.87
6	64.04	32.68	836.06	66.47	32.05	840.08	68.85	31.59	843.28
7	61.51	35.21	800.85	63.89	34.63	805.45	66.21	34.23	809.05
8	58.81	37.91	762.94	61.09	37.43	768.02	63.37	37.07	771.98
9	55.83	40.89	722.05	58.11	40.41	727.61	60.32	40.12	731.86
10	52.66	44.06	677.99	54.86	43.66	683.95	56.99	43.45	688.41
11	49.25	47.47	630.52	51.35	47.17	636.78	53.36	47.08	641.33
12	45.56	51.16	579.36	47.56	50.96	585.82	49.46	50.98	590.35
13	41.58	55.14	524.22	43.49	55.03	530.79	45.26	55.18	535.17
14	37.32	59.40	464.82	39.05	59.47	471.32	40.67	59.77	475.40
15	32.69	64.03	400.79	34.28	64.24	407.08	35.67	64.77	410.63
16	27.73	68.99	331.80	29.12	69.40	337.68	30.31	70.13	340.50
17	22.37	74.35	257.45	23.52	75.00	262.68	24.51	75.93	264.57
18	16.61	80.11	177.34	17.53	80.99	181.69	18.20	82.24	182.33
19	10.37	86.35	90.99	11.01	87.51	94.18	11.33	89.11	93.22
20	3.67	90.99	0	3.99	94.18	0	3.97	93.22	0

	8-1/4% interest - $8.52 monthly payment			8-1/2% interest - $8.68 monthly payment			8-3/4% interest - $8.84 monthly payment		
Year	Interest	Amort.	Balance	Interest	Amort.	Balance	Interest	Amort.	Balance
1	81.74	20.51	979.50	84.24	19.93	980.08	86.74	19.35	980.66
2	79.98	22.27	957.24	82.48	21.69	958.40	84.98	21.11	959.56
3	78.08	24.17	933.07	80.56	23.61	934.79	83.06	23.03	936.53
4	76.01	26.24	906.83	78.48	25.69	909.10	80.96	25.13	911.40
5	73.76	28.49	878.34	76.21	27.96	881.15	78.67	27.42	883.99
6	71.32	30.93	847.42	73.73	30.44	850.71	76.17	29.92	854.07
7	68.67	33.58	813.84	71.04	33.13	817.59	73.45	32.64	821.44
8	65.79	36.46	777.38	68.12	36.05	781.55	70.47	35.62	785.83
9	62.66	39.59	737.80	64.93	39.24	742.31	67.23	38.86	746.97
10	59.27	42.98	694.83	61.46	42.71	699.61	63.69	42.40	704.58
11	55.59	46.66	648.17	57.69	46.48	653.13	59.83	46.26	658.32
12	51.59	50.66	597.52	53.58	50.59	602.55	55.62	50.47	607.85
13	47.25	55.00	542.52	49.11	55.06	547.49	51.02	55.07	552.79
14	42.54	59.71	482.82	44.24	59.93	487.57	46.00	60.09	492.70
15	37.42	64.83	417.99	38.95	65.22	422.35	40.53	65.56	427.15
16	31.87	70.38	347.62	33.18	70.99	351.37	34.56	71.53	355.62
17	25.84	76.41	271.21	26.91	77.26	274.11	28.04	78.05	277.57
18	19.29	82.96	188.25	20.08	84.09	190.02	20.93	85.16	192.42
19	12.18	90.07	98.19	12.65	91.52	98.51	13.17	92.92	99.51
20	4.46	97.79	.40	4.56	99.61	1.10	4.71	101.38	1.87

617

20-YEAR TERM (continued)

Year	9% interest - $9.00 monthly payment			9-1/4% interest - $9.16 monthly payment			9-1/2% interest - $9.32 monthly payment		
	Interest	Amort.	Balance	Interest	Amort.	Balance	Interest	Amort.	Balance
1	89.24	18.76	981.24	91.75	18.18	981.83	94.25	17.60	982.41
2	87.47	20.53	960.71	89.99	19.94	961.89	92.51	19.34	963.07
3	85.56	22.44	938.27	88.07	21.86	940.04	90.59	21.26	941.81
4	83.45	24.55	913.72	85.96	23.97	916.07	88.48	23.37	918.45
5	81.14	26.86	886.86	83.65	26.28	889.79	86.16	25.69	892.76
6	78.64	29.36	857.50	81.11	28.82	860.98	83.61	28.24	864.52
7	75.83	32.17	825.33	78.33	31.60	829.38	80.81	31.04	833.48
8	72.85	35.15	790.18	75.28	34.65	794.73	77.73	34.12	799.36
9	69.56	38.44	751.74	71.93	38.00	756.74	74.34	37.51	761.86
10	65.96	42.04	709.70	68.27	41.66	715.08	70.62	41.23	720.63
11	62.01	45.99	663.71	64.25	45.68	669.40	66.52	45.33	675.31
12	57.70	50.30	613.41	59.84	50.09	619.31	62.03	49.82	625.49
13	52.97	55.03	558.38	55.00	54.93	564.39	57.08	54.77	570.73
14	47.80	60.20	498.18	49.70	60.23	504.16	51.65	60.20	510.53
15	42.19	65.81	432.37	43.89	66.04	438.13	45.67	66.18	444.36
16	35.99	72.01	360.36	37.51	72.42	365.71	39.11	72.74	371.62
17	29.20	78.80	281.56	30.52	79.41	286.31	31.89	79.96	291.66
18	21.86	86.14	195.42	22.86	87.07	199.24	23.95	87.90	203.76
19	13.76	94.24	101.18	14.45	95.48	103.77	15.23	96.62	107.15
20	4.93	101.18	0	5.24	104.69	0.91	5.64	106.21	0.94

Year	9-3/4% interest - $9.49 monthly payment			10% interest - $9.66 monthly payment			10-1/4% interest - $9.82 monthly payment		
	Interest	Amort.	Balance	Interest	Amort.	Balance	Interest	Amort.	Balance
1	96.75	17.14	982.87	99.25	16.67	983.33	101.76	16.09	983.92
2	95.01	18.88	963.99	97.49	18.43	964.90	100.04	17.81	966.11
3	93.08	20.81	943.19	95.59	20.33	944.57	98.12	19.73	946.39
4	90.96	22.93	920.26	93.44	22.48	922.09	96.00	21.85	924.55
5	88.62	25.27	895.00	91.09	24.83	897.26	93.66	24.19	900.36
6	86.04	27.85	867.16	88.51	27.41	869.85	91.06	26.79	873.57
7	83.21	30.68	836.48	85.62	30.30	839.55	88.18	29.67	843.90
8	80.08	33.81	802.67	82.45	33.47	806.08	84.99	32.86	811.05
9	76.63	37.26	765.42	78.94	36.98	769.10	81.46	36.39	774.66
10	72.83	41.06	724.36	75.08	40.84	728.26	77.55	40.30	734.36
11	68.64	45.25	679.12	70.81	45.11	683.15	73.22	44.63	689.74
12	64.03	49.86	629.26	66.07	49.85	633.30	68.42	49.43	640.31
13	58.95	54.94	574.32	60.86	55.06	578.24	63.11	54.74	585.58
14	53.34	60.55	513.78	55.11	60.81	517.43	57.23	60.62	524.97
15	47.17	66.72	447.07	48.71	67.21	450.22	50.72	67.13	457.84
16	40.37	73.52	373.55	41.68	74.24	375.98	43.51	74.34	383.50
17	32.87	81.02	292.53	33.90	82.02	293.96	35.52	82.33	301.18
18	24.61	89.28	203.25	25.32	90.60	203.36	26.67	91.18	210.00
19	15.50	98.39	104.87	15.83	100.09	103.27	16.87	100.98	109.03
20	5.47	108.42	3.55	5.35	103.27	0	6.02	111.83	2.79

Year	10-1/2% interest - $9.98 monthly payment			10-3/4% interest - $10.15 monthly payment			11% interest - $10.32 monthly payment		
	Interest	Amort.	Balance	Interest	Amort.	Balance	Interest	Amort.	Balance
1	104.27	15.50	984.51	106.78	15.03	984.98	109.29	14.56	985.45
2	102.57	17.20	967.31	105.08	16.73	968.26	107.60	16.25	969.20
3	100.67	19.10	948.22	103.19	18.62	949.64	105.72	18.13	951.08
4	98.57	21.20	927.02	101.09	20.72	928.93	103.62	20.23	930.86
5	96.23	23.54	903.49	98.75	23.06	905.87	101.28	22.57	908.29
6	93.64	26.13	877.36	96.15	25.66	880.21	98.67	25.18	883.12
7	90.76	29.01	848.35	93.25	28.56	851.66	95.76	28.09	855.04
8	87.56	32.21	816.15	90.02	31.79	819.87	92.51	31.34	823.70
9	84.01	35.76	780.40	86.43	35.38	784.50	88.88	34.97	788.74
10	80.07	39.70	740.70	82.44	39.37	745.13	84.84	39.01	749.73

618

20-YEAR TERM (continued)

	10-1/2% interest - $9.98 monthly payment (cont.)			10-3/4% interest - $10.15 monthly payment (cont.)			11% interest - $10.32 monthly payment (cont.)		
Year	Interest	Amort.	Balance	Interest	Amort.	Balance	Interest	Amort.	Balance
11	75.70	44.07	696.64	77.99	43.82	701.32	80.32	43.53	706.21
12	70.84	48.93	647.71	73.04	48.77	652.55	75.29	48.56	657.66
13	65.45	54.32	593.40	67.53	54.28	598.28	69.67	54.18	603.48
14	59.46	60.31	533.09	61.40	60.41	537.87	63.40	60.45	543.04
15	52.82	66.95	466.15	54.58	67.23	470.65	56.41	67.44	475.60
16	45.44	74.33	391.82	46.98	74.83	395.82	48.60	75.25	400.35
17	37.25	82.52	309.31	38.53	83.28	312.55	39.89	83.96	316.40
18	28.16	91.61	217.70	29.13	92.68	219.87	30.18	93.67	222.74
19	18.06	101.71	116.00	18.66	103.15	116.72	19.34	104.51	118.23
20	6.85	112.92	3.08	7.01	114.80	1.92	7.25	116.60	1.64

	11-1/4% interest - $10.49 monthly payment			11-1/2% interest - $10.66 monthly payment			11-3/4% interest - $10.84 monthly payment		
Year	Interest	Amort.	Balance	Interest	Amort.	Balance	Interest	Amort.	Balance
1	111.79	14.10	985.91	114.30	13.63	986.38	116.80	13.29	986.72
2	110.12	15.77	970.15	112.65	15.28	971.11	115.16	14.93	971.80
3	108.26	17.63	952.52	110.80	17.13	953.98	113.31	16.78	955.02
4	106.17	19.72	932.80	108.72	19.21	934.77	111.22	18.87	936.16
5	103.83	22.06	910.75	106.39	21.54	913.24	108.89	21.20	914.96
6	101.22	24.67	886.08	103.78	24.15	889.10	106.26	23.83	891.13
7	98.29	27.60	858.49	100.85	27.08	862.03	103.30	26.79	864.34
8	95.03	30.86	827.63	97.57	30.36	831.67	99.98	30.11	834.24
9	91.37	34.52	793.12	93.89	34.04	797.64	96.24	33.85	800.40
10	87.28	38.61	754.51	89.76	38.17	759.47	92.05	38.04	762.36
11	82.71	43.18	711.33	85.14	42.79	716.68	87.33	42.76	719.60
12	77.59	48.30	663.04	79.95	47.98	668.71	82.02	48.07	671.54
13	71.87	54.02	609.02	74.13	53.80	614.91	76.06	54.03	617.51
14	65.47	60.42	548.60	67.61	60.32	554.59	69.36	60.73	556.79
15	58.31	67.58	481.03	60.29	67.64	486.96	61.83	68.26	488.53
16	50.30	75.59	405.44	52.09	75.84	411.12	53.36	76.73	411.81
17	41.35	84.54	320.90	42.89	85.04	326.09	43.85	86.24	325.57
18	31.33	94.56	226.35	32.58	95.35	230.75	33.15	96.94	228.64
19	20.13	105.76	120.59	21.02	106.91	123.85	21.13	108.96	119.68
20	7.59	118.30	2.30	8.06	119.87	3.98	7.61	122.48	2.80

	12% interest - $11.01 monthly payment		
Year	Interest	Amort.	Balance
1	119.32	12.81	987.20
2	117.69	14.44	972.76
3	115.86	16.27	956.50
4	113.80	18.33	938.17
5	111.47	20.66	917.52
6	108.85	23.28	894.25
7	105.90	26.23	868.03
8	102.58	29.55	838.48
9	98.83	33.30	805.18
10	94.61	37.52	767.67
11	89.85	42.28	725.39
12	84.49	47.64	677.75
13	78.45	53.68	624.07
14	71.64	60.49	563.59
15	63.97	68.16	495.43
16	55.32	76.81	418.63
17	45.58	86.55	332.08
18	34.61	97.52	234.57
19	22.24	109.89	124.68
20	8.30	123.83	.86

619

25-YEAR TERM

Year	4% interest - $5.28 monthly payment			4-1/2% interest - $5.56 monthly payment			5% interest - $5.85 monthly payment		
	Interest	Amort.	Balance	Interest	Amort.	Balance	Interest	Amort.	Balance
1	39.56	23.80	976.20	44.54	22.18	977.82	49.54	20.66	979.34
2	38.60	24.76	951.44	43.54	23.18	954.64	48.48	21.72	957.62
3	37.57	25.79	925.65	42.44	24.28	930.36	47.36	22.84	934.78
4	36.55	26.81	898.84	41.35	25.37	904.99	46.19	24.01	910.77
5	35.45	27.91	870.93	40.18	26.54	878.45	44.98	25.22	885.55
6	34.31	29.05	841.88	38.97	27.75	850.70	43.67	26.53	859.02
7	33.13	30.23	811.65	37.70	29.02	821.68	42.30	27.90	831.12
8	31.89	31.47	780.18	36.34	30.38	791.30	40.87	29.33	801.79
9	30.61	32.75	747.43	34.98	31.74	759.56	39.39	30.81	770.98
10	29.28	34.08	713.35	33.53	33.19	726.37	37.81	32.39	738.59
11	27.91	35.45	677.90	31.96	34.76	691.61	36.16	34.04	704.55
12	26.45	36.91	640.99	30.38	36.34	655.27	34.41	35.79	668.76
13	24.94	38.42	602.57	28.71	38.01	617.26	32.59	37.61	631.15
14	23.38	39.98	562.59	26.96	39.76	577.50	30.66	39.54	591.61
15	21.75	41.61	520.98	25.14	41.58	535.92	28.65	41.55	550.06
16	20.05	43.31	477.67	23.22	43.50	492.42	26.52	43.68	506.38
17	18.29	45.07	432.60	21.23	45.49	446.93	24.27	45.93	460.45
18	16.46	46.90	385.70	19.14	47.58	399.35	21.93	48.27	412.18
19	14.54	48.82	336.88	16.97	49.75	349.60	19.46	50.74	361.44
20	12.55	50.81	286.07	14.66	52.06	297.54	16.86	53.34	308.10
21	10.49	52.87	233.20	12.28	54.44	243.10	14.15	56.05	252.05
22	8.32	55.04	178.16	9.77	56.95	186.15	11.57	58.93	193.12
23	6.10	57.26	120.90	7.15	59.57	126.58	8.24	61.96	131.16
24	3.73	59.63	61.27	4.44	62.28	64.30	5.07	65.13	66.03
25	1.31	61.27	0	1.56	64.30	0	1.75	66.03	0

Year	5-1/4% interest - $6.00 monthly payment			5-1/2% interest - $6.15 monthly payment			5-3/4% interest - $6.30 monthly payment		
	Interest	Amort.	Balance	Interest	Amort.	Balance	Interest	Amort.	Balance
1	52.03	19.97	980.03	54.51	19.29	980.71	57.02	18.58	981.42
2	50.96	21.04	958.99	53.44	20.36	960.35	55.90	19.70	961.72
3	49.82	22.18	936.81	52.27	21.53	938.82	54.77	20.83	940.89
4	48.63	23.37	913.44	51.07	22.73	916.09	53.52	22.08	918.82
5	47.38	24.62	888.82	49.79	24.01	892.08	52.23	23.37	895.44
6	46.01	25.99	862.83	48.42	25.38	866.70	50.82	24.78	870.66
7	44.70	27.30	835.53	46.98	26.82	839.88	49.39	26.21	844.45
8	43.16	28.84	806.69	45.50	28.30	811.58	47.83	27.77	816.68
9	41.63	30.37	776.32	43.88	29.92	781.66	46.18	29.42	787.26
10	40.00	32.00	744.32	42.20	31.60	750.06	44.48	31.12	756.14
11	38.27	33.73	710.59	40.42	33.38	716.68	42.61	32.99	723.15
12	36.47	35.53	675.06	38.55	35.25	681.43	40.67	34.93	688.22
13	34.55	37.45	637.61	36.55	37.25	644.18	38.62	36.98	651.24
14	32.54	39.46	598.15	34.44	39.36	604.82	36.41	39.18	612.06
15	30.42	41.58	556.57	32.22	41.58	563.24	34.11	41.49	570.57
16	28.16	43.84	512.73	29.90	43.90	519.34	31.65	43.95	526.62
17	25.82	46.18	466.55	27.41	46.39	472.95	29.07	46.53	480.09
18	23.34	48.66	417.89	24.79	49.01	423.94	26.27	49.33	430.76
19	20.71	51.29	366.60	22.04	51.76	372.18	23.41	52.19	378.57
20	17.98	54.02	312.58	19.12	54.68	317.50	20.33	55.27	323.30
21	15.06	56.94	255.64	16.01	57.79	259.71	17.05	58.55	264.75
22	11.99	60.01	195.63	12.76	61.04	198.67	13.61	61.99	202.76
23	8.76	63.24	132.39	9.32	64.48	134.19	9.94	65.66	137.10
24	5.36	66.64	65.75	5.70	68.10	66.09	6.07	69.53	67.57
25	1.78	65.75	0	1.83	66.09	0	1.97	67.57	0

620

25-YEAR TERM (continued)

	6% interest - $6.45 monthly payment			6-1/4% interest - $6.60 monthly payment			6-1/2% interest - $6.76 monthly payment		
Year	Interest	Amort.	Balance	Interest	Amort.	Balance	Interest	Amort.	Balance
1	59.52	17.88	982.12	62.01	17.19	982.81	64.50	16.62	983.38
2	58.41	18.99	963.13	60.91	18.29	964.52	63.41	17.71	965.67
3	57.24	20.16	942.97	59.73	19.47	945.05	62.21	18.91	946.76
4	55.99	21.41	921.56	58.48	20.72	924.33	60.95	20.17	926.59
5	54.66	22.74	898.82	57.17	22.03	902.30	59.58	21.54	905.05
6	53.23	24.17	874.65	55.73	23.47	878.83	58.14	22.98	882.07
7	51.78	25.62	849.03	54.22	24.98	853.85	56.62	24.50	857.57
8	50.20	27.20	821.83	52.61	26.59	827.26	54.97	26.15	831.42
9	48.53	28.87	792.96	50.89	28.31	798.95	53.23	27.89	803.53
10	46.74	30.66	762.30	49.09	30.11	768.84	51.37	29.75	773.78
11	44.84	32.56	729.74	47.14	32.06	736.78	49.34	31.78	742.00
12	42.84	34.56	695.18	45.08	34.12	702.66	47.22	33.90	708.10
13	40.72	36.68	658.50	42.88	36.32	666.34	44.98	36.14	671.96
14	38.44	38.96	619.54	40.54	38.66	627.68	42.54	38.58	633.38
15	36.05	41.35	578.19	38.06	41.14	586.54	39.95	41.17	592.21
16	33.50	43.90	534.29	35.42	43.78	542.76	37.21	43.91	548.30
17	30.80	46.60	487.69	32.64	46.56	496.20	34.26	46.86	501.44
18	27.93	49.47	438.22	29.60	49.60	446.60	31.12	50.00	451.44
19	24.87	52.53	385.69	26.40	52.80	393.80	27.17	53.34	398.10
20	21.62	55.78	329.91	23.03	56.17	337.63	24.19	56.93	341.17
21	18.18	59.22	270.69	19.41	59.79	277.84	20.40	60.72	280.45
22	14.53	62.87	207.82	15.56	63.64	214.20	16.32	64.80	215.65
23	10.64	66.76	141.06	11.46	67.74	146.46	12.00	69.12	146.53
24	6.53	70.87	70.19	7.10	72.10	74.36	7.34	73.78	72.75
25	2.17	70.19	0	2.48	74.36	0	2.40	72.75	0

	6-3/4% interest - $6.91 monthly payment			7% interest - $7.07 monthly payment			7-1/4% interest - $7.23 monthly payment		
Year	Interest	Amort.	Balance	Interest	Amort.	Balance	Interest	Amort.	Balance
1	67.02	15.90	984.10	69.51	15.33	984.67	72.02	14.74	985.26
2	65.92	17.00	967.10	68.40	16.44	968.23	70.91	15.85	969.41
3	64.72	18.20	948.90	67.20	17.64	950.59	69.72	17.04	952.37
4	63.45	19.47	929.43	65.94	18.90	931.69	68.44	18.32	934.05
5	62.10	20.82	908.61	64.62	20.22	911.47	67.01	19.75	914.30
6	60.66	22.26	886.35	63.12	21.72	889.75	65.58	21.18	893.12
7	59.09	23.83	862.52	61.55	23.29	866.46	64.01	22.75	870.37
8	57.44	25.48	837.04	59.85	24.99	841.47	62.30	24.46	845.91
9	55.68	27.24	809.80	58.06	26.78	814.69	60.47	26.29	819.62
10	53.77	29.15	780.65	56.12	28.72	785.97	58.49	28.27	791.35
11	51.74	31.18	749.47	54.05	30.79	755.18	56.39	30.37	760.98
12	49.57	33.35	716.12	51.81	33.03	722.15	54.10	32.66	728.32
13	47.24	35.68	680.44	49.44	35.40	686.75	51.66	35.10	693.22
14	44.78	38.14	642.30	46.87	37.97	648.78	49.02	37.74	655.48
15	42.10	40.82	601.48	44.14	40.70	608.08	46.20	40.56	614.92
16	39.24	43.68	557.80	41.20	43.64	564.44	43.15	43.61	571.31
17	36.22	46.70	511.10	38.03	46.81	517.63	39.89	46.87	524.44
18	32.98	49.94	461.16	34.65	50.19	467.44	36.35	50.41	474.03
19	29.51	53.41	407.75	31.02	53.82	413.62	32.59	54.17	419.86
20	25.79	57.13	350.62	27.12	57.72	355.90	28.53	58.23	361.63
21	21.79	61.13	289.49	22.99	61.85	294.05	24.15	62.61	299.02
22	17.56	65.36	224.13	18.48	66.36	227.69	19.47	67.29	231.73
23	12.99	69.93	154.20	13.67	71.17	156.52	14.43	72.33	159.40
24	8.11	74.81	79.39	8.52	76.32	80.20	8.98	77.78	81.62
25	2.92	79.39	0	3.01	80.20	0	3.17	81.62	0

621.

25-YEAR TERM (continued)

Year	7-1/2% interest - $7.39 monthly payment			7-3/4% interest - $7.56 monthly payment			8% interest - $7.72 monthly payment		
	Interest	Amort.	Balance	Interest	Amort.	Balance	Interest	Amort.	Balance
1	74.52	14.16	985.84	77.02	13.70	986.30	79.53	13.11	986.89
2	73.42	15.26	970.58	75.92	14.80	971.50	78.43	14.21	972.68
3	72.23	16.45	954.13	74.72	16.00	955.50	77.26	15.38	957.30
4	70.96	17.72	936.41	73.45	17.27	938.23	75.99	16.65	940.65
5	69.54	19.14	917.27	72.06	18.66	919.57	74.58	18.06	922.59
6	68.11	20.57	896.70	70.57	20.15	899.42	73.10	19.54	903.05
7	66.48	22.20	874.50	68.95	21.77	877.65	71.49	21.15	881.90
8	64.77	23.91	850.59	67.19	23.53	854.12	69.72	22.92	858.98
9	62.92	25.76	824.83	65.30	25.42	828.70	67.83	24.81	834.17
10	60.93	27.75	797.08	63.28	27.44	801.26	65.76	26.88	807.29
11	58.78	29.90	767.18	61.05	29.67	771.59	63.52	29.12	778.17
12	56.44	32.24	734.94	58.67	32.05	739.54	61.11	31.53	746.64
13	53.94	34.74	700.20	56.10	34.62	704.92	58.50	34.14	712.50
14	51.23	37.45	662.75	53.29	37.43	667.49	55.67	36.97	675.53
15	48.33	40.35	622.40	50.31	40.41	627.08	52.59	40.05	635.48
16	45.21	43.47	578.98	47.06	43.66	583.42	49.26	43.38	592.10
17	41.83	46.85	532.08	43.57	47.15	536.27	45.68	46.96	545.14
18	38.20	50.48	481.60	39.77	50.95	485.32	41.76	50.88	494.26
19	34.28	54.40	427.20	35.69	55.03	430.29	37.57	55.07	439.19
20	30.05	58.63	368.57	31.26	59.46	370.83	32.98	59.66	379.53
21	25.51	63.17	305.40	26.51	64.21	306.62	28.03	64.61	314.92
22	20.59	68.09	237.31	21.33	69.39	237.23	22.65	69.99	244.93
23	15.30	73.38	163.93	15.72	75.00	162.23	16.85	75.79	169.14
24	9.59	79.09	84.84	9.74	80.98	81.25	10.53	82.11	87.03
25	3.47	84.84	0	3.22	81.25	0	3.74	87.03	0

Year	8-1/4% interest - $7.88 monthly payment			8-1/2% interest - $8.05 monthly payment			8-3/4% interest - $8.22 monthly payment		
	Interest	Amort.	Balance	Interest	Amort.	Balance	Interest	Amort.	Balance
1	82.04	12.53	987.48	84.54	12.07	987.94	87.05	11.60	988.41
2	80.96	13.61	973.88	83.48	13.13	974.81	85.99	12.66	975.75
3	79.80	14.77	959.11	82.32	14.29	960.52	84.84	13.81	961.95
4	78.53	16.04	943.08	81.05	15.56	944.97	83.58	15.07	946.88
5	77.16	17.41	925.68	79.68	16.93	928.04	82.21	16.44	930.44
6	75.67	18.90	906.78	78.18	18.43	909.62	80.71	17.94	912.51
7	74.05	20.52	886.27	76.55	20.06	889.57	79.08	19.57	892.94
8	72.29	22.28	863.99	74.78	21.83	867.74	77.29	21.36	871.59
9	70.38	24.19	839.81	72.85	23.76	843.99	75.35	23.30	848.29
10	68.31	26.26	813.56	70.75	25.86	818.14	73.23	25.42	822.88
11	66.06	28.51	785.05	68.47	28.14	790.00	70.91	27.74	795.14
12	63.62	30.95	754.11	65.98	30.63	759.37	68.39	30.26	764.88
13	60.97	33.60	720.51	63.27	33.34	726.04	65.63	33.02	731.87
14	58.09	36.48	684.03	60.33	36.28	689.76	62.62	36.03	695.84
15	54.96	39.61	644.43	57.12	39.49	650.28	59.34	39.31	656.54
16	51.57	43.00	601.43	53.63	42.98	607.30	55.76	42.89	613.65
17	47.88	46.69	554.75	49.83	46.78	560.53	51.85	46.80	566.86
18	43.88	50.69	504.07	45.70	50.91	509.62	47.59	51.06	515.80
19	39.54	55.03	449.05	41.20	55.41	454.21	42.94	55.71	460.09
20	34.83	59.74	389.31	36.30	60.31	393.91	37.86	60.79	399.31
21	29.71	64.86	324.45	30.97	65.64	328.27	32.33	66.32	332.99
22	24.15	70.42	254.03	25.17	71.44	256.83	26.29	72.36	260.64
23	18.11	76.46	177.58	18.85	77.76	179.08	19.69	78.96	181.68
24	11.56	83.01	94.58	11.98	84.63	94.45	12.50	86.15	95.54
25	4.45	90.12	4.46	4.50	92.11	2.35	4.65	94.00	1.55

25-YEAR TERM (continued)

Year	9% interest - $8.40 monthly payment			9-1/4% interest - $8.56 monthly payment			9-1/2% interest - $8.74 monthly payment		
	Interest	Amort.	Balance	Interest	Amort.	Balance	Interest	Amort.	Balance
1	89.54	11.26	988.74	92.06	10.67	989.34	94.56	10.33	989.68
2	88.49	12.31	976.43	91.03	11.70	977.65	93.54	11.35	978.34
3	87.34	13.46	962.97	89.90	12.83	964.82	92.41	12.48	965.86
4	86.07	14.73	948.24	88.66	14.07	950.76	91.17	13.72	952.15
5	84.66	16.14	932.10	87.31	15.42	935.35	89.81	15.08	937.08
6	83.18	17.62	914.48	85.82	16.91	918.44	88.32	16.57	920.52
7	81.52	19.28	895.20	84.19	18.54	899.90	86.67	18.22	902.31
8	79.72	21.08	874.12	82.40	20.33	879.58	84.87	20.02	882.29
9	77.73	23.07	851.05	80.44	22.29	857.29	82.88	22.01	860.28
10	75.58	25.22	825.83	78.28	24.45	832.85	80.70	24.19	836.10
11	74.10	27.60	798.23	75.93	26.80	806.05	78.30	26.59	809.51
12	70.62	30.18	768.05	73.34	29.39	776.66	75.66	29.23	780.28
13	67.79	33.01	735.04	70.50	32.23	744.44	72.76	32.13	748.15
14	64.69	36.11	698.93	67.39	35.34	709.10	69.57	35.32	712.83
15	61.29	39.51	659.42	63.98	38.75	670.36	66.06	38.83	674.01
16	57.60	43.20	616.22	60.24	42.49	627.88	62.21	42.68	631.33
17	53.56	47.24	568.98	56.14	46.59	581.29	57.97	46.92	584.42
18	49.12	51.68	517.30	51.64	51.09	530.21	53.32	51.57	532.85
19	44.27	56.53	460.77	46.71	56.02	474.20	48.20	56.69	476.17
20	38.96	61.84	398.93	41.31	61.42	412.78	42.57	62.32	413.85
21	33.17	67.63	331.30	35.38	67.35	345.44	36.39	68.50	345.36
22	26.81	73.99	257.31	28.88	73.85	271.59	29.59	75.30	270.07
23	19.86	80.94	176.37	21.75	80.98	190.62	22.12	82.77	187.30
24	12.27	88.53	87.84	13.94	88.79	101.83	13.90	90.99	96.32
25	3.96	87.84	0	5.36	97.37	4.47	4.87	100.02	3.69

Year	9-3/4% interest - $8.91 monthly payment			10% interest - $9.09 monthly payment			10-1/4% interest - $9.26 monthly payment		
	Interest	Amort.	Balance	Interest	Amort.	Balance	Interest	Amort.	Balance
1	97.07	9.86	990.15	99.56	9.52	990.48	102.09	9.04	990.97
2	96.07	10.86	979.30	98.57	10.51	979.97	101.12	10.01	980.96
3	94.96	11.97	967.33	97.48	11.60	968.37	100.04	11.09	969.88
4	93.74	13.19	954.15	96.25	12.83	955.54	98.85	12.28	957.60
5	92.40	14.53	939.62	94.93	14.15	941.39	97.53	13.60	944.01
6	90.91	16.02	923.61	93.44	15.64	925.75	96.07	15.06	928.96
7	89.28	17.65	905.96	91.78	17.30	908.45	94.45	16.68	912.29
8	87.48	19.45	886.52	90.01	19.07	889.38	92.66	18.47	893.82
9	85.50	21.43	865.09	87.99	21.09	868.29	90.68	20.45	873.38
10	83.31	23.62	841.48	85.78	23.30	844.99	88.48	22.65	850.73
11	80.91	26.02	815.47	83.33	25.75	819.24	86.05	25.08	825.66
12	78.25	28.68	786.79	80.63	28.45	790.79	83.35	27.78	797.88
13	75.33	31.60	755.20	77.68	31.40	759.39	80.37	30.76	767.13
14	72.11	34.82	720.38	74.39	34.69	724.70	77.06	34.07	733.07
15	68.56	38.37	682.01	70.74	38.34	686.36	73.40	37.73	695.35
16	64.64	42.29	639.73	66.74	42.34	644.02	69.35	41.78	653.57
17	60.33	46.60	593.14	62.29	46.79	597.23	64.86	46.27	607.31
18	55.58	51.35	541.80	57.39	51.69	545.54	59.89	51.24	556.08
19	50.35	56.58	485.22	51.96	57.12	488.42	54.39	56.74	499.34
20	44.58	62.35	422.87	46.01	63.07	425.35	48.29	62.84	436.50
21	38.22	68.71	354.16	39.37	69.71	355.64	41.54	69.59	366.92
22	31.21	75.72	278.45	32.09	76.99	278.65	34.06	77.07	289.85
23	23.49	83.44	195.02	24.06	85.02	193.63	25.78	85.35	204.50
24	14.98	91.95	103.07	15.13	93.95	99.68	16.61	94.52	109.99
25	5.61	101.32	1.75	5.29	99.68	0	6.45	104.68	5.31

623

25-YEAR TERM (continued)

	10-1/2% interest - $9.44 monthly payment			10-3/4% interest - $9.62 monthly payment			11% interest - $9.80 monthly payment		
Year	Interest	Amort.	Balance	Interest	Amort.	Balance	Interest	Amort.	Balance
1	104.59	8.70	991.31	107.10	8.35	991.66	109.61	8.00	992.01
2	103.64	9.65	981.67	106.16	9.29	982.38	108.68	8.93	983.09
3	102.57	10.72	970.96	105.11	10.34	972.04	107.65	9.96	973.14
4	101.39	11.90	959.06	103.94	11.51	960.54	106.50	11.11	962.03
5	100.08	13.21	945.86	102.64	12.81	947.74	105.22	12.39	949.64
6	98.63	14.66	931.20	101.20	14.25	933.49	103.78	13.83	935.82
7	97.01	16.28	914.93	99.59	15.86	917.64	102.18	15.43	920.40
8	95.22	18.07	896.87	97.80	17.65	899.99	100.40	17.21	903.19
9	93.23	20.06	876.81	95.80	19.65	880.35	98.41	19.20	883.99
10	91.02	22.27	854.54	93.59	21.86	858.49	96.19	21.42	862.57
11	88.56	24.73	829.82	91.12	24.33	834.16	93.71	23.90	838.67
12	85.84	27.45	802.38	88.37	27.08	807.08	90.94	26.67	812.01
13	82.82	30.47	771.91	85.31	30.14	776.95	87.86	29.75	782.26
14	79.46	33.83	738.08	81.91	33.54	743.41	84.41	33.20	749.07
15	75.73	37.56	700.52	78.12	37.33	706.08	80.57	37.04	712.03
16	71.59	41.70	658.83	73.90	41.55	664.54	76.29	41.32	670.72
17	67.00	46.29	612.54	69.21	46.24	618.30	71.50	46.11	624.62
18	61.89	51.40	561.15	63.99	51.46	566.84	66.17	51.44	573.18
19	56.23	57.06	504.10	58.17	57.28	509.57	60.22	57.39	515.79
20	49.94	63.35	440.76	51.70	63.75	445.82	53.58	64.03	451.77
21	42.96	70.33	370.44	44.50	70.95	374.88	46.17	71.44	380.33
22	35.21	78.08	292.36	36.49	78.96	295.93	37.90	79.71	300.63
23	26.61	86.68	205.69	27.57	87.88	208.05	28.68	88.93	211.70
24	17.06	96.23	109.46	17.64	97.81	110.25	18.39	99.22	112.49
25	6.45	106.84	2.63	6.60	108.85	1.40	6.91	110.70	1.79

	11-1/4% interest - $9.98 monthly payment			11-1/2% interest - $10.16 monthly payment			11-3/4% interest - $10.35 monthly payment		
Year	Interest	Amort.	Balance	Interest	Amort.	Balance	Interest	Amort.	Balance
1	112.12	7.65	992.36	114.63	7.30	992.71	117.13	7.08	992.93
2	111.21	8.56	983.81	113.74	8.19	984.53	116.25	7.96	984.98
3	110.20	9.57	974.24	112.75	9.18	975.35	115.27	8.94	976.05
4	109.07	10.70	963.54	111.64	10.29	965.07	114.16	10.05	966.00
5	107.80	11.97	951.58	110.39	11.54	953.53	112.91	11.30	954.71
6	106.38	13.39	938.19	108.99	12.94	940.60	111.51	12.70	942.02
7	104.79	14.98	923.22	107.43	14.50	926.10	109.94	14.27	927.75
8	103.02	16.75	906.48	105.67	16.26	909.85	108.17	16.04	911.72
9	101.04	18.73	887.75	103.70	18.23	891.62	106.18	18.03	893.69
10	98.82	20.95	866.80	101.49	20.44	871.18	103.95	20.26	873.44
11	96.34	23.43	843.37	99.01	22.92	848.26	101.43	22.78	850.66
12	93.56	26.21	817.17	96.23	25.70	822.56	98.61	25.60	825.07
13	90.45	29.32	787.86	93.11	28.82	793.75	95.43	28.78	796.29
14	86.98	32.79	755.07	89.62	32.31	761.44	91.86	32.35	763.95
15	83.10	36.67	718.41	85.70	36.23	725.21	87.85	36.36	727.60
16	78.75	41.02	677.39	81.31	40.62	684.60	83.34	40.87	686.74
17	73.89	45.88	631.52	76.38	45.55	639.05	78.27	45.94	640.81
18	68.46	51.31	580.22	70.86	51.07	587.99	72.58	51.63	589.18
19	62.38	57.39	522.83	64.67	57.26	530.73	66.17	58.04	531.15
20	55.58	64.19	458.65	57.72	64.21	466.53	58.98	65.23	465.92
21	47.98	71.79	386.86	49.94	71.99	394.54	50.88	73.33	392.60
22	39.47	80.30	306.56	41.21	80.72	313.83	41.79	82.42	310.19
23	29.96	89.81	216.75	31.42	90.51	223.33	31.57	92.64	217.55
24	19.31	100.46	116.30	20.45	101.48	121.85	20.08	104.13	113.42
25	7.41	112.36	3.95	8.14	113.79	8.07	7.16	117.05	3.62

25-YEAR TERM (continued)

12% interest - $10.35
monthly payment

Year	Interest	Amort.	Balance
1	119.64	6.73	993.28
2	118.79	7.58	985.71
3	117.83	8.54	977.17
4	116.75	9.62	967.56
5	115.53	10.84	956.72
6	114.15	12.22	944.51
7	112.60	13.77	930.75
8	110.86	15.51	915.24
9	108.89	17.48	897.77
10	106.68	19.69	878.08
11	104.18	22.19	855.90
12	101.37	25.00	830.90
13	98.20	28.17	802.73
14	94.62	31.75	770.99
15	90.60	35.77	735.23
16	86.06	40.31	694.93
17	80.95	45.42	649.51
18	75.19	51.18	598.34
19	68.70	57.67	540.68
20	61.39	64.98	475.70
21	53.15	73.22	402.48
22	43.86	82.51	319.98
23	33.40	92.97	227.01
24	21.61	104.76	122.26
25	8.32	118.05	4.22

30-YEAR TERM

Year	4% interest - $4.77 monthly payment			4-1/4% interest - $4.92 monthly payment			4-1/2% interest - $5.07 monthly payment		
	Interest	Amort.	Balance	Interest	Amort.	Balance	Interest	Amort.	Balance
1	39.69	17.56	982.45	42.18	16.87	983.14	44.67	16.18	983.83
2	38.97	18.28	964.17	41.45	17.60	965.54	43.93	16.92	966.92
3	38.23	19.02	945.15	40.69	18.36	947.18	43.15	17.70	949.23
4	37.45	19.80	925.36	39.89	19.16	928.03	42.34	18.51	930.73
5	36.64	20.61	904.76	39.06	19.99	908.04	41.49	19.36	911.37
6	35.80	21.45	883.32	38.19	20.86	887.19	40.60	20.25	891.13
7	34.93	22.32	861.00	37.29	21.76	865.44	39.67	21.18	869.96
8	34.02	23.23	837.78	36.35	22.70	842.74	38.70	22.15	847.81
9	33.08	24.17	813.61	35.36	23.69	819.06	37.68	23.17	824.65
10	32.09	25.16	788.46	34.34	24.71	794.35	36.62	24.23	800.42
11	31.07	26.18	762.28	33.27	25.78	768.57	35.51	25.34	775.08
12	30.00	27.25	735.03	32.15	26.90	741.67	34.34	26.51	748.58
13	28.89	28.36	706.68	30.98	28.07	713.61	33.12	27.73	720.86
14	27.73	29.52	677.17	29.77	29.28	684.33	31.85	29.00	691.86
15	26.53	30.72	646.45	28.50	30.55	653.79	30.52	30.33	661.54
16	25.28	31.97	614.49	27.17	31.88	621.92	29.13	31.72	629.82
17	23.98	33.27	581.23	25.79	33.26	588.67	27.67	33.18	596.64
18	22.62	34.63	546.60	24.35	34.70	553.97	26.14	34.71	561.94
19	21.21	36.04	510.57	22.85	36.20	517.78	24.55	36.30	525.64
20	19.75	37.50	473.07	21.28	37.77	480.01	22.88	37.97	487.68
21	18.22	39.03	434.04	19.64	39.41	440.61	21.14	39.71	447.97
22	16.63	40.62	393.43	17.94	41.11	399.50	19.31	41.54	406.44
23	14.97	42.28	351.15	16.15	42.90	356.61	17.41	43.44	363.00
24	13.25	44.00	307.16	14.30	44.75	311.86	15.41	45.44	317.57
25	11.46	45.79	261.37	12.36	46.69	265.17	13.32	47.53	270.05
26	9.59	47.66	213.72	10.33	48.72	216.46	11.14	49.71	220.34
27	7.65	49.60	164.13	8.22	50.83	165.64	8.86	51.99	168.35
28	5.63	51.62	112.51	6.02	53.03	112.61.	6.47	54.38	113.98
29	3.53	53.72	58.79	3.72	55.33	57.29	3.97	56.88	57.10
30	1.34	55.91	2.89	1.32	57.73	.43	1.36	59.49	2.38

Year	4-3/4% interest - $5.22 monthly payment			5% interest - $5.37 monthly payment			5-1/4% interest - $5.52 monthly payment		
	Interest	Amort.	Balance	Interest	Amort.	Balance	Interest	Amort.	Balance
1	47.17	15.48	984.53	49.67	14.78	985.23	52.17	14.08	985.93
2	46.42	16.23	968.31	48.91	15.54	969.70	51.41	14.84	971.10
3	45.63	17.02	951.29	48.12	16.33	953.37	50.61	15.64	955.47
4	44.81	17.84	933.45	47.28	17.17	936.21	49.77	16.48	939.00
5	43.94	18.71	914.75	46.41	18.04	918.17	48.89	17.36	921.64
6	43.03	19.62	895.14	45.48	18.97	899.21	47.95	18.30	903.35
7	42.08	20.57	874.57	44.51	19.94	879.28	46.97	19.28	884.08
8	41.08	21.57	853.01	43.49	20.96	858.32	45.93	20.32	863.76
9	40.03	22.62	830.40	42.42	22.03	836.30	44.84	21.41	842.36
10	38.94	23.71	806.69	41.29	23.16	813.15	43.69	22.56	819.81
11	37.79	24.86	781.83	40.11	24.34	788.81	42.48	23.77	796.04
12	36.58	26.07	755.76	38.86	25.59	763.23	41.20	25.05	771.00
13	35.31	27.34	728.43	37.56	26.89	736.34	39.85	26.40	744.60
14	33.99	28.66	699.77	36.18	28.27	708.08	38.43	27.82	716.79
15	32.60	30.05	669.72	34.73	29.72	678.37	36.94	29.31	687.49
16	31.14	31.51	638.22	33.21	31.24	647.14	35.36	30.89	656.60
17	29.61	33.04	605.18	31.62	32.83	614.31	33.70	32.55	624.06
18	28.00	34.65	570.54	29.94	34.51	579.80	31.95	34.30	589.76
19	26.32	36.33	534.21	28.17	36.28	543.52	30.11	36.14	553.62
20	24.56	38.09	496.12	26.32	38.13	505.39	28.16	38.09	515.54
21	22.71	39.94	456.19	24.36	40.09	465.31	26.11	40.14	475.41
22	20.77	41.88	414.31	22.31	42.14	423.18	23.96	42.29	433.12
23	18.74	43.91	370.41	20.16	44.29	378.90	21.68	44.57	388.56
24	16.61	46.04	324.37	17.89	46.56	332.34	19.28	46.97	341.60
25	14.37	48.28	276.09	15.51	48.94	283.41	16.76	49.49	292.11
26	12.03	50.62	225.47	13.01	51.44	231.97	14.10	52.15	239.97
27	9.57	53.08	172.40	10.38	54.07	177.90	11.29	54.96	185.01
28	6.99	55.66	116.74	7.61	56.84	121.06	8.34	57.91	127.11
29	4.29	58.36	58.39	4.70	59.75	61.32	5.22	61.03	66.08
30	1.46	61.19	2.80	1.64	62.81	1.48	1.94	64.31	1.78

626

30-YEAR TERM (continued)

Year	5-1/2% interest - $5.68 monthly payment			5-3/4% interest - $5.84 monthly payment			6% interest - $6.00 monthly payment		
	Interest	Amort.	Balance	Interest	Amort.	Balance	Interest	Amort.	Balance
1	54.67	13.50	986.51	57.17	12.92	987.09	59.67	12.34	987.67
2	53.91	14.26	972.25	56.41	13.68	973.41	58.91	13.10	974.57
3	53.10	15.07	957.19	55.60	14.49	958.92	58.10	13.91	960.67
4	52.25	15.92	941.28	54.74	15.35	943.58	57.24	14.77	945.91
5	51.36	16.81	924.47	53.84	16.25	927.33	56.33	15.68	930.23
6	50.41	17.76	906.71	52.88	17.21	910.12	55.37	16.64	913.60
7	49.41	18.76	887.95	51.86	18.23	891.90	54.34	17.67	895.93
8	48.35	19.82	868.13	50.79	19.30	872.60	53.25	18.76	877.18
9	47.23	20.94	847.19	49.65	20.44	852.16	52.09	19.92	857.27
10	46.05	22.12	825.08	48.44	21.65	830.52	50.87	21.14	836.13
11	44.80	23.37	801.71	47.16	22.93	807.59	49.56	22.45	813.68
12	43.48	24.69	777.03	45.81	24.28	783.32	48.18	23.83	789.85
13	42.09	26.08	750.96	44.37	25.72	757.61	46.71	25.30	764.56
14	40.62	27.55	723.41	42.86	27.23	730.38	45.15	26.86	737.70
15	39.07	29.10	694.31	41.25	28.84	701.54	43.49	28.52	709.19
16	37.42	30.75	663.57	39.55	30.54	671.00	41.73	30.28	678.91
17	35.69	32.48	631.10	37.74	32.35	638.66	39.87	32.14	646.77
18	33.86	34.31	596.79	35.83	34.26	604.41	37.88	34.13	612.65
19	31.92	36.25	560.55	33.81	36.28	568.14	35.78	36.23	576.43
20	29.88	38.29	522.27	31.67	38.42	529.72	33.54	38.47	537.96
21	27.72	40.45	481.82	29.40	40.69	489.04	31.17	40.84	497.13
22	25.44	42.73	439.10	27.00	43.09	445.96	28.65	43.36	453.78
23	23.03	45.14	393.96	24.46	45.63	400.33	25.98	46.03	407.75
24	20.48	47.69	346.28	21.76	48.33	352.01	23.14	48.87	358.89
25	17.79	50.38	295.90	18.91	51.18	300.84	20.13	51.88	307.01
26	14.95	53.22	242.69	15.89	54.20	246.64	16.93	55.08	251.93
27	11.95	56.22	186.47	12.69	57.40	189.24	13.53	58.48	193.46
28	8.78	59.39	127.09	9.30	60.79	128.46	9.92	62.09	131.38
29	5.43	62.74	64.35	5.71	64.38	64.09	6.09	65.92	65.47
30	1.89	66.28	1.92	1.91	68.18	4.09	2.03	69.98	4.51

Year	6-1/4% interest - $6.16 monthly payment			6-1/2% interest - $6.32 monthly payment			6-3/4% interest - $6.49 monthly payment		
	Interest	Amort.	Balance	Interest	Amort.	Balance	Interest	Amort.	Balance
1	62.17	11.76	988.25	64.68	11.17	988.84	67.18	10.71	989.30
2	61.42	12.51	975.74	63.93	11.92	976.92	66.43	11.46	977.85
3	60.61	13.32	962.43	63.13	12.72	964.20	65.63	12.26	965.59
4	59.76	14.17	948.26	62.28	13.57	950.64	64.78	13.11	952.49
5	58.84	15.09	933.18	61.37	14.48	936.16	63.87	14.02	938.48
6	57.87	16.06	917.13	60.40	15.45	920.72	62.89	15.00	923.48
7	56.84	17.09	900.04	59.37	16.48	904.24	61.85	16.04	907.45
8	55.74	18.19	881.86	58.26	17.59	886.66	60.73	17.16	890.30
9	54.57	19.36	862.51	57.09	18.76	867.90	59.54	18.35	871.95
10	53.33	20.60	841.91	55.83	20.02	847.88	58.26	19.63	852.33
11	52.00	21.93	819.99	54.49	21.36	826.52	56.90	20.99	831.34
12	50.59	23.34	796.66	53.06	22.79	803.74	55.43	22.46	808.89
13	49.09	24.84	771.83	51.53	24.32	779.42	53.87	24.02	784.87
14	47.50	26.43	745.40	49.90	25.95	753.48	52.20	25.69	759.19
15	45.80	28.13	717.27	48.17	27.68	725.80	50.41	27.48	731.71
16	43.99	29.94	687.33	46.31	29.54	696.27	48.50	29.39	702.32
17	42.06	31.87	655.46	44.33	31.52	664.76	46.45	31.44	670.89
18	40.01	33.92	621.55	42.22	33.63	631.14	44.26	33.63	637.27
19	37.83	36.10	585.45	39.97	35.88	595.27	41.92	35.97	601.30
20	35.51	38.42	547.04	37.57	38.28	556.99	39.42	38.47	562.84
21	33.04	40.89	506.15	35.01	40.84	516.15	36.74	41.15	521.69
22	30.41	43.52	462.63	32.27	43.58	472.58	33.87	44.02	477.68
23	27.61	46.32	416.31	29.35	46.50	426.09	30.81	47.08	430.60
24	24.63	49.30	367.01	26.24	49.61	376.48	27.53	50.36	380.25
25	21.46	52.47	314.54	22.92	52.93	323.56	24.03	53.86	326.39
26	18.08	55.85	258.70	19.37	56.48	267.08	20.28	57.61	268.78
27	14.49	59.44	199.27	15.59	60.26	206.83	16.26	61.63	207.16
28	10.67	63.26	136.01	11.56	64.29	142.54	11.97	65.92	141.25
29	6.60	67.33	68.68	7.25	68.60	73.95	7.38	70.51	70.75
30	2.27	71.66	2.98	2.66	73.19	.76	2.48	75.41	4.66

627

30-YEAR TERM (continued)

	7% interest - $6.65 monthly payment			7-1/4% interest - $6.82 monthly payment			7-1/2% interest - $6.99 monthly payment		
Year	Interest	Amort.	Balance	Interest	Amort.	Balance	Interest	Amort.	Balance
1	69.68	10.13	989.88	72.19	9.66	990.35	74.69	9.20	990.81
2	68.95	10.86	979.03	71.46	10.39	979.97	73.98	9.91	980.91
3	68.17	11.64	967.40	70.69	11.16	968.81	73.21	10.68	970.23
4	67.33	12.48	954.92	69.85	12.00	956.81	72.38	11.51	958.73
5	66.43	13.38	941.54	68.95	12.90	943.92	71.49	12.40	946.33
6	65.46	14.35	927.19	67.98	13.87	930.06	70.53	13.36	932.98
7	64.42	15.39	911.81	66.95	14.90	915.16	69.49	14.40	918.58
8	63.31	16.50	895.31	65.83	16.02	899.14	68.37	15.52	903.07
9	62.12	17.69	877.62	64.63	17.22	881.93	67.17	16.72	886.35
10	60.84	18.97	858.65	63.34	18.51	863.42	65.87	18.02	868.34
11	59.47	20.34	838.31	61.95	19.90	843.52	64.47	19.42	848.92
12	58.00	21.81	816.50	60.46	21.39	822.14	62.96	20.93	828.00
13	56.42	23.39	793.12	58.86	22.99	799.15	61.34	22.55	805.46
14	54.73	25.08	768.04	57.13	24.72	774.43	59.59	24.30	781.16
15	52.92	26.89	741.15	55.28	26.57	747.87	57.70	26.19	754.98
16	50.97	28.84	712.32	53.29	28.56	719.31	55.67	28.22	726.77
17	48.89	30.92	681.40	51.15	30.70	688.62	53.48	30.41	696.36
18	46.65	33.16	648.25	48.85	33.00	655.62	51.12	32.77	663.60
19	44.26	35.55	612.70	46.37	35.48	620.15	48.58	35.31	628.29
20	41.69	38.12	574.58	43.71	38.14	582.02	45.84	38.05	590.24
21	38.93	40.88	533.71	40.86	40.99	541.03	42.88	41.01	549.24
22	35.98	43.83	489.88	37.78	44.07	496.97	39.70	44.19	505.06
23	32.81	47.00	442.88	34.48	47.37	449.60	36.27	47.62	457.44
24	29.41	50.40	392.48	30.93	50.92	398.69	32.57	51.32	406.13
25	25.77	54.04	338.45	27.11	54.74	343.96	28.59	55.30	350.83
26	21.86	57.95	280.50	23.01	58.84	285.13	24.30	59.59	291.24
27	17.67	62.14	218.37	18.60	63.25	221.88	19.67	64.22	227.03
28	13.18	66.63	151.74	13.86	67.99	153.90	14.69	69.20	157.83
29	8.36	71.45	80.30	8.77	73.08	80.82	9.31	74.58	83.26
30	3.20	76.61	3.70	3.29	78.56	2.26	3.52	80.37	2.90

	7-3/4% interest - $7.16 monthly payment			8% interest - $7.34 monthly payment			8-1/4% interest - $7.51 monthly payment		
Year	Interest	Amort.	Balance	Interest	Amort.	Balance	Interest	Amort.	Balance
1	77.20	8.73	991.28	79.70	8.39	991.62	82.21	7.92	992.09
2	76.50	9.43	981.85	79.01	9.08	982.54	81.53	8.60	983.50
3	75.74	10.19	971.67	78.25	9.84	972.71	80.80	9.33	974.17
4	74.92	11.01	960.67	77.44	10.65	962.06	80.00	10.13	964.04
5	74.04	11.89	948.78	76.55	11.54	950.53	79.13	11.00	953.04
6	73.09	12.84	935.94	75.60	12.49	938.04	78.19	11.94	941.10
7	72.05	13.88	922.07	74.56	13.53	924.52	77.16	12.97	928.14
8	70.94	14.99	907.09	73.44	14.65	909.87	76.05	14.08	914.07
9	69.74	16.19	890.90	72.22	15.87	894.00	74.85	15.28	898.79
10	68.44	17.49	873.41	70.90	17.19	876.82	73.54	16.59	882.20
11	67.03	18.90	854.52	69.48	18.61	858.21	72.12	18.01	864.19
12	65.52	20.41	834.11	67.93	20.16	838.06	70.57	19.56	844.64
13	63.88	22.05	812.06	66.26	21.83	816.24	68.90	21.23	823.41
14	62.11	23.82	788.24	64.45	23.64	792.60	67.08	23.05	800.36
15	60.19	25.74	762.51	62.49	25.60	767.01	65.10	25.03	775.34
16	58.13	27.80	734.71	60.36	27.73	739.28	62.96	27.17	748.17
17	55.89	30.04	704.68	58.06	30.03	709.26	60.63	29.50	718.68
18	53.48	32.45	672.23	55.57	32.52	676.75	58.10	32.03	686.65
19	50.87	35.06	637.18	52.87	35.22	641.53	55.36	34.77	651.89
20	48.06	37.87	599.32	49.95	38.14	603.40	52.38	37.75	614.14
21	45.02	40.91	558.41	46.78	41.31	562.10	49.14	40.99	573.16
22	41.73	44.20	514.22	43.36	44.73	517.37	45.63	44.50	528.67
23	38.18	47.75	466.48	39.64	48.45	468.93	41.82	48.31	480.36
24	34.35	51.58	414.90	35.62	52.47	416.46	37.68	52.45	427.92
25	30.21	55.72	359.19	31.27	56.82	359.65	33.19	56.94	370.98
26	25.73	60.20	299.00	26.55	61.54	298.11	28.31	61.82	309.16
27	20.90	65.03	233.97	21.45	66.64	231.48	23.01	67.12	242.05
28	15.68	70.25	163.72	15.91	72.18	159.30	17.26	72.87	169.18
29	10.03	75.90	87.83	9.92	78.17	81.14	11.02	79.11	90.07
30	3.94	81.99	5.85	3.44	84.65	-3.50	4.24	85.89	4.19

628

30-YEAR TERM (continued)

	8-1/2% interest - $7.69 monthly payment			8-3/4% interest - $7.87 monthly payment			9% interest - $8.05 monthly payment		
Year	Interest	Amort.	Balance	Interest	Amort.	Balance	Interest	Amort.	Balance
1	84.71	7.58	992.43	87.22	7.23	992.78	89.73	6.88	993.13
2	84.05	8.24	984.20	86.56	7.89	984.90	89.08	7.53	985.60
3	83.32	8.97	975.23	85.84	8.61	976.29	88.37	8.24	977.37
4	82.52	9.77	965.47	85.06	9.39	966.91	87.60	9.01	968.37
5	81.66	10.63	954.84	84.20	10.25	956.67	86.76	9.85	958.52
6	80.72	11.57	943.28	83.27	11.18	945.50	85.83	10.78	947.75
7	79.70	12.59	930.70	82.25	12.20	933.31	84.82	11.79	935.97
8	78.59	13.70	917.00	81.14	13.31	920.01	83.72	12.89	923.08
9	77.38	14.91	902.09	79.93	14.52	905.49	82.51	14.10	908.99
10	76.06	16.23	885.87	78.61	15.84	889.66	81.19	15.42	893.57
11	74.63	17.66	868.21	77.17	17.28	872.38	79.74	16.87	876.71
12	73.06	19.23	848.99	75.59	18.86	853.53	78.16	18.45	858.26
13	71.37	20.92	828.07	73.88	20.57	832.96	76.43	20.18	838.09
14	69.52	22.77	805.30	72.00	22.45	810.52	74.54	22.07	816.02
15	67.50	24.79	780.52	69.96	24.49	786.03	72.47	24.14	791.88
16	65.31	26.98	753.55	67.73	26.72	759.31	70.20	26.41	765.48
17	62.93	29.36	724.20	65.29	29.16	730.16	67.73	28.88	736.60
18	60.34	31.95	692.25	62.64	31.81	698.36	65.02	31.59	705.01
19	57.51	34.78	657.47	59.74	34.71	663.65	62.05	34.56	670.46
20	54.44	37.85	619.63	56.58	37.87	625.79	58.81	37.80	632.67
21	51.09	41.20	578.43	53.13	41.32	584.47	55.27	41.34	591.33
22	47.45	44.84	533.60	49.37	45.08	539.39	51.39	45.22	546.11
23	43.49	48.80	484.80	45.26	49.19	490.21	47.15	49.46	496.66
24	39.18	53.11	431.69	40.78	53.67	436.54	42.51	54.10	442.56
25	34.48	57.81	373.89	35.89	58.56	377.99	37.43	59.18	383.39
26	29.37	62.92	310.98	30.56	63.89	314.10	31.88	64.73	318.67
27	23.81	68.48	242.50	24.74	69.71	244.39	25.81	70.80	247.87
28	17.76	74.53	167.98	18.39	76.06	168.33	19.17	77.44	170.44
29	11.17	81.12	86.86	11.46	82.99	85.34	11.91	84.70	85.74
30	4.00	88.29	1.42	3.90	90.55	5.20	3.96	92.65	6.90

	9-1/4% interest - $8.23 monthly payment			9-1/2% interest - $8.41 monthly payment			9-3/4% interest - $8.59 monthly payment		
Year	Interest	Amort.	Balance	Interest	Amort.	Balance	Interest	Amort.	Balance
1	92.23	6.54	993.47	94.74	6.19	993.82	97.25	5.84	994.17
2	91.60	7.17	986.31	94.13	6.80	987.02	96.65	6.44	987.74
3	90.91	7.86	978.46	93.45	7.48	979.55	96.00	7.09	980.65
4	90.15	8.62	969.84	92.71	8.22	971.33	95.28	7.81	972.84
5	89.32	9.45	960.40	91.89	9.04	962.30	94.48	8.61	964.23
6	88.41	10.36	950.04	91.00	9.93	952.38	93.60	9.49	954.75
7	87.41	11.36	938.69	90.01	10.92	941.47	92.63	10.46	944.30
8	86.31	12.46	926.24	88.93	12.00	929.47	91.57	11.52	932.78
9	85.11	13.66	912.59	87.74	13.19	916.29	90.39	12.70	920.09
10	83.79	14.98	897.62	86.43	14.50	901.79	89.10	13.99	906.10
11	82.35	16.42	881.20	84.99	15.94	885.86	87.67	15.42	890.69
12	80.77	18.00	863.20	83.41	17.52	868.35	86.10	16.99	873.71
13	79.03	19.74	843.46	81.67	19.26	849.09	84.37	18.72	854.99
14	77.12	21.65	821.82	79.76	21.17	827.93	82.46	20.63	834.37
15	75.03	23.74	798.09	77.66	23.27	804.67	80.36	22.73	811.04
16	72.74	26.03	772.07	75.35	25.58	779.10	78.04	25.05	786.60
17	70.23	28.54	743.53	72.82	28.11	750.99	75.49	27.60	759.00
18	67.48	31.29	712.25	70.03	30.90	720.09	72.67	30.42	728.58
19	64.46	34.31	677.94	66.96	33.97	686.13	69.57	33.52	695.07
20	61.15	37.62	640.32	63.59	37.34	648.79	66.15	36.94	658.14
21	57.51	41.26	599.07	59.88	41.05	607.75	62.39	40.70	617.44
22	53.53	45.24	553.83	55.81	45.12	562.63	58.24	44.85	572.59
23	49.17	49.60	504.24	51.33	49.60	513.04	53.66	49.43	523.16
24	44.38	54.39	449.85	46.41	54.52	458.52	48.62	54.47	468.70
25	39.13	59.64	390.21	41.00	59.93	398.60	43.07	60.02	408.68
26	33.37	65.40	324.82	35.05	65.88	332.73	36.95	66.14	342.55
27	27.06	71.71	253.12	28.51	72.42	260.32	30.20	72.89	269.66
28	20.14	78.63	174.49	21.33	79.60	180.72	22.77	80.32	189.35
29	12.55	86.22	88.28	13.43	87.50	93.22	14.58	88.51	100.84
30	4.23	94.54	6.26	4.74	96.19	2.96	5.55	97.54	3.31

629

30-YEAR TERM (continued)

	10% interest - $8.78 monthly payment			10-1/4% interest - $8.96 monthly payment			10-1/2% interest - $9.15 monthly payment		
Year	Interest	Amort.	Balance	Interest	Amort.	Balance	Interest	Amort.	Balance
1	99.75	5.62	994.39	102.26	5.27	994.74	104.77	5.04	994.97
2	99.16	6.21	988.19	101.70	5.83	988.91	104.21	5.60	989.37
3	98.52	6.85	981.34	101.07	6.46	982.46	103.60	6.21	983.16
4	97.80	7.57	973.78	100.38	7.15	975.31	102.91	6.90	976.27
5	97.01	8.36	965.42	99.61	7.92	967.40	102.15	7.66	968.62
6	96.13	9.24	956.18	98.76	8.77	958.63	101.31	8.50	960.12
7	95.16	10.21	945.98	97.82	9.71	948.92	100.37	9.44	950.69
8	94.10	11.27	934.71	96.77	10.76	938.17	99.33	10.48	940.21
9	92.92	12.45	922.26	95.62	11.91	926.26	98.18	11.63	928.59
10	91.61	13.76	908.51	94.34	13.19	913.07	96.90	12.91	915.68
11	90.17	15.20	893.31	92.92	14.61	898.47	95.47	14.34	901.35
12	88.58	16.79	876.53	91.35	16.18	882.30	93.89	15.92	885.44
13	86.82	18.55	857.99	89.61	17.92	864.39	92.14	17.67	867.77
14	84.88	20.49	837.50	87.69	19.84	844.55	90.19	19.62	848.16
15	82.74	22.63	814.87	85.56	21.97	822.58	88.03	21.78	826.39
16	80.37	25.00	789.88	83.20	24.33	798.26	85.63	24.18	802.22
17	77.75	27.62	762.26	80.58	26.95	771.31	82.97	26.84	775.39
18	74.86	30.51	731.75	77.69	29.84	741.48	80.01	29.80	745.60
19	71.66	33.71	698.05	74.48	33.05	708.43	76.73	33.08	712.52
20	68.13	37.24	660.82	70.93	36.60	671.84	73.09	36.72	675.80
21	64.24	41.13	619.69	67.00	40.53	631.31	69.04	40.77	635.04
22	59.93	45.44	574.25	62.64	44.89	586.43	64.55	45.26	589.78
23	55.17	50.20	524.06	57.82	49.71	536.73	59.56	50.25	539.53
24	49.91	55.46	468.61	52.48	55.05	481.69	54.02	55.79	483.75
25	44.11	61.26	407.35	46.57	60.96	420.73	47.87	61.94	421.82
26	37.69	67.68	339.68	40.02	67.51	353.22	41.05	68.76	353.06
27	30.61	74.76	264.92	32.76	74.77	278.46	33.47	76.34	276.73
28	22.78	82.59	182.34	24.73	82.80	195.66	25.06	84.75	191.98
29	14.13	91.24	91.11	15.83	91.70	103.97	15.72	94.09	97.90
30	4.58	100.79	9.68	5.98	101.55	2.42	5.35	104.46	6.56

	10-3/4% interest - $9.33 monthly payment			11% interest - $9.52 monthly payment			11-1/4% interest - $9.71 monthly payment		
Year	Interest	Amort.	Balance	Interest	Amort.	Balance	Interest	Amort.	Balance
1	107.28	4.69	995.32	109.78	4.47	995.54	112.29	4.24	995.77
2	106.75	5.22	990.10	109.27	4.98	990.57	111.79	4.74	991.04
3	106.16	5.81	984.30	108.69	5.56	985.02	111.23	5.30	985.74
4	105.50	6.47	977.84	108.05	6.20	978.82	110.60	5.93	979.81
5	104.77	7.20	970.65	107.33	6.92	971.91	109.90	6.63	973.19
6	103.96	8.01	962.64	106.53	7.72	964.20	109.11	7.42	965.78
7	103.06	8.91	953.74	105.64	8.61	955.59	108.24	8.29	957.49
8	102.05	9.92	943.82	104.65	9.60	945.99	107.25	9.28	948.22
9	100.93	11.04	932.79	103.53	10.72	935.28	106.15	10.38	937.85
10	99.69	12.28	920.51	102.29	11.96	923.33	104.93	11.60	926.25
11	98.30	13.67	906.85	100.91	13.34	910.00	103.55	12.98	913.27
12	96.76	15.21	891.64	99.37	14.88	895.12	102.01	14.52	898.76
13	95.04	16.93	874.71	97.65	16.60	878.53	100.30	16.23	882.53
14	93.13	18.84	855.87	95.73	18.52	860.01	98.37	18.16	864.38
15	91.00	20.97	834.90	93.58	20.67	839.35	96.22	20.31	844.08
16	88.63	23.34	811.57	91.19	23.06	816.30	93.82	22.71	821.37
17	85.99	25.98	785.60	88.53	25.72	790.58	91.13	25.40	795.97
18	83.06	28.91	756.69	85.55	28.70	761.88	88.12	28.41	767.56
19	79.79	32.18	724.52	82.23	32.02	729.87	84.75	31.78	735.79
20	76.16	35.81	688.71	78.52	35.73	694.15	80.98	35.55	700.24
21	72.12	39.85	648.87	74.39	39.86	654.29	76.77	39.76	660.49
22	67.61	44.36	604.52	69.78	44.47	609.83	72.06	44.47	616.03
23	62.60	49.37	555.16	64.63	49.62	560.21	66.80	49.73	566.30
24	57.03	54.94	500.22	58.89	55.36	504.86	60.90	55.63	510.68
25	50.82	61.15	439.08	52.49	61.76	443.10	54.31	62.22	448.47
26	43.92	68.05	371.03	45.34	68.91	374.20	46.94	69.59	378.89
27	36.23	75.74	295.30	37.37	76.88	297.32	38.70	77.83	301.06
28	27.68	84.29	211.01	28.47	85.78	211.55	29.48	87.05	214.01
29	18.15	93.82	117.20	18.55	95.70	115.85	19.16	97.37	116.65
30	7.56	104.41	12.79	7.47	106.78	9.07	7.63	108.90	7.75

30-YEAR TERM (continued)

	11-1/2% interest - $9.90 monthly payment			11-3/4% interest - $10.09 monthly payment			12% interest - $10.29 monthly payment		
Year	Interest	Amort.	Balance	Interest	Amort.	Balance	Interest	Amort.	Balance
1	114.80	4.01	996.00	117.31	3.78	996.23	119.81	3.68	996.33
2	114.31	4.50	991.51	116.84	4.25	991.98	119.34	4.15	992.18
3	113.77	5.04	986.47	116.31	4.78	987.20	118.82	4.67	987.51
4	113.16	5.65	980.82	115.72	5.37	981.84	118.22	5.27	982.25
5	112.47	6.34	974.49	115.05	6.04	975.80	117.56	5.93	976.32
6	111.70	7.11	967.39	114.30	6.79	969.02	116.80	6.69	969.64
7	110.84	7.97	959.42	113.46	7.63	961.40	115.96	7.53	962.11
8	109.88	8.93	950.50	112.52	8.57	952.83	115.00	8.49	953.63
9	108.79	10.02	940.48	111.45	9.64	943.20	113.93	9.56	944.07
10	107.58	11.23	929.26	110.26	10.83	932.38	112.71	10.78	933.29
11	106.22	12.59	916.68	108.92	12.17	920.21	111.35	12.14	921.16
12	104.69	14.12	902.56	107.41	13.68	906.53	109.81	13.68	907.48
13	102.98	15.83	886.74	105.71	15.38	891.16	108.07	15.42	892.06
14	101.06	17.75	869.00	103.80	17.29	873.88	106.12	17.37	874.70
15	98.91	19.90	849.11	101.66	19.43	854.45	103.91	19.58	855.13
16	96.50	22.31	826.80	99.25	21.84	832.62	101.43	22.06	833.07
17	93.80	25.01	801.79	96.54	24.55	808.08	98.64	24.85	808.23
18	90.76	28.05	773.75	93.50	27.59	780.49	95.48	28.01	780.23
19	87.36	31.45	742.31	90.08	31.01	749.48	91.93	31.56	748.67
20	83.55	35.26	707.06	86.23	34.86	714.63	87.93	35.56	713.12
21	79.28	39.53	667.53	81.91	39.18	675.45	83.42	40.07	673.06
22	74.48	44.33	623.20	77.05	44.04	631.42	78.34	45.15	627.92
23	69.11	49.70	573.51	71.59	49.50	581.92	72.62	50.87	577.05
24	63.08	55.73	517.78	65.45	55.64	526.28	66.17	57.32	519.73
25	56.32	62.49	455.30	58.55	62.54	463.74	58.90	64.59	455.14
26	48.75	70.06	385.24	50.79	70.30	393.44	50.70	72.79	382.36
27	40.25	78.56	306.69	42.07	79.02	314.42	41.47	82.02	300.35
28	30.73	88.08	218.61	32.27	88.82	225.61	31.07	92.42	207.94
29	20.05	98.76	119.86	21.25	99.84	125.77	19.35	104.14	103.80
30	8.07	110.74	9.12	8.87	112.22	13.55	6.15	117.34	-13.53

631

INDEX

References are to Paragraph [¶] Numbers

—A—

References are to Paragraph [¶] Numbers

Partnerships (continued):
.tax (continued):
..consequences..2808
..features..3905
..savings, for family partnerships..3906
.term of..2809.4
.treated as corporation..2809.21
Patents..2202
.antitrust laws..216-219
.applying for..2204, 2205, 2207
.assignment vs. licensing..2211
.computing claims..2208
.duration of..2214
.employees'..2206
.infringement, suit for..2213
.inventions, *see* Inventions
.legal fees..2411
.misuse of privilege..2212
.preliminary search..2209
.protection, availability of..2203
Pension plans..1004
.profit-sharing plan compared..1005
.simplified employee pension..1007
Percentage rentals..2305, 2305.1
Personal holding companies..3909.2
Photocopies, copyright..1108
Plant and equipment, accounting method..3920
Post-mortem planning..1713
.checklist..1714
Pourover trusts..4003
Premium waiver rider, life insurance..2505.1
Presentment..928
Price-fixing..207
.interseller price verification..208
.seller-buyer vertical restraints..214
Principals (*see also* Agents)..101
Private annuities..1806
Proceeds from insurance, *see* Life insurance
Product liability insurance..2106
Professional license, deducting legal fees to defend..2408
Profit-sharing plans..1004
.cash vs. deferred..1006
.pension plan compared..1005
Profits:
.corporate, converting to capital gain..3927
.partnerships:
..allocating..2809.9
..tax treatment..2809.10
Promissory notes..904
.negotiability..905
.unconditional promise..906

Property (*see also* Real estate):
.community..1808
.insurance against loss..2107
.recovery of..3210
Proprietorship, sole, tax features..3904
Publications, government, copyright law..1110
Purchase-money mortgages..2911

—Q—

Quo warranto..3226

—R—

Real estate..2901
.assessments, *see* Assessments, real estate
.consumer protection..3001
.contingencies..2905
.contracts:
..drafting, checklist..2914
..pre-contract checklists..2913
.deposits..2903
.escrow closing..2921
..agreement contents, checklist..2922
.foreclosures, *see* Foreclosures
.investments in..3932
.leases (*see also* Leases)..2907
.mortgages (*see also* Mortgages)..2701
.performance time..2909
.personal property..2912
.pre-contract checklists..2913
.settlement process, *see* Real Estate Settlement Procedures Act
.surveys..2906
.title, *see* Title
.use limitations..2908
.zoning..2909
Real Estate Settlement Procedures Act (RESPA)..3001, 3005
.coverage..3006
.escrow account limitation..3013
.federally related mortgages..3007
.good-faith estimates..3009
.information booklets..3008
.kickbacks..3011
.settlement statement..3010
.state law, relation to..3014
.title insurance..3012
.unearned fees..3011
Reasonable compensation, *see* Compensation
Recordings, copyright..1109
Records, partnership..2809.14
Redemption, stock, *see* Stock · redemption

—S—